COMMERCIAL CONTRACTING: SALES, LEASES, AND COMPUTER INFORMATION SECOND EDITION

COMMERCIAL CONTRACTING: SALES, LEASES, AND COMPUTER INFORMATION

SECOND EDITION

FRANCIS J. MOOTZ III
William S. Boyd Professor of Law
University of Nevada, Las Vegas
William S. Boyd School of Law

DAVID FRISCH
Professor of Law
The University of Richmond
T.C. Williams School of Law

PETER A. ALCES
Rita Anne Rollins Professor of Law
College of William and Mary
Marshall-Wythe School of Law

ISBN: 978-1-4224-2387-5

> ## NOTE TO USERS
>
> To ensure that you are using the latest materials available in this area, please be sure to periodically check the LexisNexis Law School web site for downloadable updates and supplements at www.lexisnexis.com/lawschool.

Editorial Offices
744 Broad Street, Newark, NJ 07102 (973) 820-2000
201 Mission St., San Francisco, CA 94105-1831 (415) 908-3200
www.lexisnexis.com

MATTHEW BENDER

(2008–Pub.3156)

DEDICATION

For Lois and Pete Mootz who probably never guessed
that their troublesome kid would wind up being a law professor.
— FJM

To my daughters: Alexandria and Julianna.
— DF

Still for Eileen.
— PAA

PREFACE TO THE SECOND EDITION

We largely have retained the approach of the first edition, but have updated the materials. You should find that the text provides a succinct overview of each section, and then the cases and problems will support class discussion that takes the analysis to the next level. We have added a number of new cases and streamlined the book. Most important, we have eliminated references to Amended Article 2, which was adopted and submitted to the states by the National Conference of Commissioners on Uniform State Laws in 2003. As you will find in the introductory chapter, there was a long, drawn-out and politically-charged battle to update and revise Article 2. It now appears that even the "compromise" amendments will not be adopted. Your professor may choose to use the amended language for teaching purposes, but we no longer believe that it makes sense to burden the text with these references. We have adopted the same strategy with the Uniform Computer Information Transactions Act ("UCITA"), which was adopted in two states but now appears moribund.

We again owe many debts in connection with this book. Professor Mootz would like to thank Jennifer Stull ('08) for her superb research assistance, and especially for finding the Posner opinion regarding the aquarium set that came equipped with plastic piranhas and "fake blood." Jessica Vanderkam ('08) and Matt Hoover ('08) both did excellent work in proof-reading the entire text and making extremely helpful suggestions, and Jessica then provided careful review of the page proofs of the entire text. Professor Frisch wishes to express gratitude to Trevor Reid ('08) for his help in research and editing. Professor Alces would like to recognize the research assistance of Christine R. Tartamella ('07) and Marcus T. Massey ('07).

All three authors benefitted from the excellent and dedicated work of Felicia Burton, Director of the Office of Faculty and Academic Support at The College of William and Mary School of Law. Ms. Burton caught a number of errors and she produced a wonderfully clean text. It was a pleasure to work with her.

Finally, many of the changes to this edition reflect the feedback that we have received from students. We strive to present excellent teaching materials and look forward to hearing from you if we can improve this text in any way.

Francis J. Mootz III
Las Vegas, NV

David Frisch
Richmond, VA

Peter A. Alces
Williamsburg, VA

July 1, 2008

PREFACE TO THE FIRST EDITION

This casebook emphasizes that Uniform Commercial Code methodology contemplates more than "the skill of working out language puzzles." Professor Karl Llewellyn was primarily responsible for the drafting and adoption of Article 2—Sales. His unique vision as a legal scholar animates Article 2. These underlying jurisprudential and doctrinal principles provide a level of coherence and cohesiveness that is rarely found in statutory schemes. Our goal in this casebook is to expose these consistent threads of Article 2 to serve as a guide for learning the skill of statutory problem-solving.

Although the casebook emphasizes Article 2, we also refer to related law. These other laws include Article 2A—Leases (dealing with commercial leasing of goods), the Uniform Computer Information Transactions Act (dealing with the licensing of computer information), and the United Nations Convention on the International Sales of Goods (dealing with certain international sales). Perhaps most important, we constantly refer to the recently completed Amended Article 2, which is likely to be presented to the states for adoption in the near future. Although there is quite a bit of material in this course, you will find that by focusing on the underlying principles and policies of Article 2 and using these other sources of law for comparison purposes, it will be manageable. This is not a course about memorizing the rules; this is a course about learning how to use statutory law to anticipate and prevent, or (if that fails) to solve, your client's problems.

We have created a casebook that can be adapted to different teaching and learning styles. We have chosen a number of recent cases that provide a good introduction to current controversies, while still relating back to the underlying principles of Article 2. We have provided text that attempts to organize the material and to provide a description of the law that is as concise and clear as possible. Finally, we have provided a number of problems that require you to apply the text and cases to new scenarios. This casebook is suitable for courses that are taught exclusively by the case method, courses that are taught exclusively by the problem method, and courses that combine both approaches.

We do not believe that there is any purpose served by "hiding the ball." Our goal in this book is to establish the legal and business background through text and well-chosen cases, and then ask you to apply this knowledge to new or difficult scenarios raised in the cases and the problems. To help you to develop a sophisticated commercial perspective, we have included excerpts from thoughtful commentaries that clarify the caselaw or challenge the prevailing interpretations offered by courts. We begin with the assumption that neither the Code nor any line of cases can hope to be perfect, and we offer these scholarly excerpts to provide models of how you can adopt a critical perspective on the law. We are grateful to the scholars who have granted us permission to reproduce portions of their work.

This casebook would not have been completed without the assistance of many people. Professor Mootz was assisted by a number of students over a period of several years in putting together these materials, locating source material, and proofreading the text. He thanks Carrie A. Leslie ('02), Andrew T. Tillapaugh ('02), Thadeus M. Creech ('04), Aaron C. Jackson ('05), Elizabeth A. Johnson ('05), and Peter J. O'Mara ('05). He is particularly grateful for the two years of excellent research work provided by Melissa S. Hill ('03) and Samantha A. Wilcox ('03). Professor Frisch wishes to thank Ronna Kinsella ('05). Professor Alces extends his grateful appreciation to Brian C. Hayes ('05); Chasity N. Simpson ('05); Sarah C. Black ('05); Adam M. Nebeker ('05); Nicholas H. Grainger ('06); and Samuel M. Gross ('06), all JD, The College of William and Mary School of Law.

Finally, we extend our thanks to Della W. Harris, the Director of the Faculty Support Center at The College of William and Mary School of Law. She performed flawlessly, as usual, and the authors remain in her debt.

Professors Frisch and Mootz were pleased and honored to be invited to join Professor Alces on this new edition of the book, and all three authors acknowledge the continuing contribution of Professor Nathaniel Hansford that carries forward from the first edition.

Francis J. Mootz III
Carlisle, PA

David Frisch
Richmond, VA

Peter A. Alces
Williamsburg, VA

July 2004

TABLE OF CONTENTS

TABLE OF CONTENTS

TABLE OF CONTENTS

TABLE OF CONTENTS

TABLE OF CONTENTS

TABLE OF CONTENTS

TABLE OF CONTENTS

TABLE OF CONTENTS

TABLE OF CONTENTS

TABLE OF CONTENTS

TABLE OF CONTENTS

Chapter 1
THE JURISPRUDENCE OF ARTICLE 2

You might think that the law governing commercial contracting is going to be a rather boring collection of complex, technical, and mind-numbingly dry rules. However, Article 2 of the Uniform Commercial Code, which forms the core of this course, is anything but a list of rules. The readings in this chapter provide you with insight into the innovative jurisprudence (and underlying legal philosophy) of Article 2, and explain how this jurisprudential perspective has carried forward into other codifications that govern commercial contracting. The goal of this chapter is to provide you with a sense of the history and purpose behind the Uniform Commercial Code project, and to explore how Article 2 was drafted to free commercial parties from legalistic restraints that hindered commerce while still reinforcing norms of good business practice and fair dealing.

A. STATUTORY LAW GOVERNING SALES, LEASES AND COMPUTER INFORMATION

We begin with a brief overview of the bodies of law that we will consider in this course. The Uniform Commercial Code's Article 2 governs transactions in "goods," the buying and selling of things, as opposed to transactions in real estate, service contracts, or intangibles. Article 2 has been adopted by all states except Louisiana, which already had a code governing contract law, and it provides the basic rules for parties contracting for commercial sales. This casebook will refer to the 2001 Official Text of Article 2. Because Article 1 provides important general rules and definitions for the entire Uniform Commercial Code, it is an indispensable part of the law of sales. This casebook will refer to the 2001 Official Text of Article 1, which is now the law in a majority of states and is likely to be widely adopted by the time you graduate.

Take time to look at the index to the Uniform Commercial Code and understand how the law of sales fits within a much broader coverage of commercial law. The Uniform Commercial Code regulates payment mechanisms used by commercial parties (Articles 3, 4, 4A, and 5), regulates ownership of goods and bailment obligations (Articles 6 and 7), regulates the ownership of securities (debt and equity) in business entities (Article 8), and regulates security agreements that protect lenders to businesses and sellers who deliver goods without receiving full payment at the time of the sale (Article 9).

During the past decade, there have been a variety of efforts to revise or amend Article 2 to better deal with modern commercial contracting. The two sponsors of the Uniform Commercial Code project — the Uniform Law Commission (ULC) [formerly known as the National Conference of Commissioners on Uniform State Laws (NCCUSL)] and the American Law Institute (ALI) — have presented an Amended Article 2 to the states for adoption. Amended Article 2 primarily clarifies ambiguities in the text that have been resolved by courts, and is far less controversial than earlier, more far-reaching proposed revisions to Article 2. Nevertheless, no state has yet adopted Amended Article 2 and it now appears that the controversial sequence of events leading to its promulgation has precluded its success with state legislatures.

In 1987, the Permanent Editorial Board of the Uniform Commercial Code presented "Article 2A: Leases" for adoption, which was eventually adopted by the forty-nine states that have adopted Article 2. For a variety of reasons, commercial parties increasingly contract to lease goods rather than to buy them outright. For example, many firms find that there is a tax advantage to deducting lease expenses as they are paid rather than capitalizing the purchase price and depreciating its cost basis over time. Additionally, they find that leasing provides them with more flexibility to upgrade equipment in areas where technological innovation is rapid. As leasing became a more important feature of the economy, courts recognized that Article 2 was not perfectly suited to these transactions. Courts typically viewed leases as involving features of both a sale (governed by Article 2) and a secured transaction (governed by Article 9). Consequently, Article 2A borrowed from both Article 2 and Article 9 to codify the law of leasing. You will see frequent reference to Article 2A in this text.

In 1988, an important multilateral treaty became effective for governing certain contracts involving the international sale of goods. The United Nations Convention on Contracts for the International Sale of Goods was finalized for adoption at a Diplomatic Conference in Vienna in 1980. The Convention is referred to as the "Vienna Convention," or the "Convention for International Sale of Goods," and commonly is known by the acronym "CISG." The United States ratified the Convention, and is one of the Contracting States bound by the CISG. The text will refer to the CISG frequently for comparison purposes and to remind you of the significance of this multilateral treaty when the contracting parties are principally located in Contracting States which have ratified the CISG.

The special circumstances surrounding the software sales and licensing model presents a challenge to the UCC vision of contract law. Generally, software publishers do not want to sell consumers software, they want to sell consumers the permission to use their software (licenses). Article 2 of the UCC should and does cover the physical medium and documentation that may accompany a software product, but the value is in the intellectual property of the software rather than in the packaging or physical medium of distribution. In 1999, NCCUSL promulgated the Uniform Computer Information Transaction Act (UCITA) which would apply to all "computer information transactions." UNIFORM COMPUTER INFORMATION TRANSACTIONS ACT § 103(a) (1999). Forms of the Act were quickly passed in Maryland and Virginia, but failed in every other state where bills were proposed. VA. CODE ANN. § 59.1-501.1 (2001); MD. CODE ANN., COM. LAW § 22-101 (LexisNexis 2000). In fact, at least four states have passed "bomb-shelter" laws, designed to invalidate the choice of law provisions of contracts that name the laws of a UCITA state as the governing law of the contract. IOWA CODE § 554d.125 (2004); N.C. GEN. STAT. § 66-329 (2001); W. VA. CODE § 55-8-15 (2001); VT. STAT. ANN. tit. 9 § 2463a (2004); *see also* American Library Association, *UCITA & Related Legislation in Your State* (Oct. 11, 2006), http://www.ala.org/ala/washoff/woissues/copyrightb/ucita/states.cfm (last visited June 26, 2007) (UCITA related legislative histories of each state).

Originally, NCCUSL and ALI proposed an addition to the UCC to address computer information transactions. When ALI did not ratify the proposed Article 2B, NCCUSL struck out on its own and drafted UCITA rather than attempt to fashion a compromise acceptable to consumer protection groups. The implications of UCITA for traditional contract law are profound. To focus primarily on contract doctrine, under UCITA: A contract can be made non-cancelable, even in the event of material breach; support provisions and other material terms can be changed without the consumer's consent; the burden is placed on customers to find defects in a timely matter, otherwise they may be barred from rejecting the product as defective; publishers can hide the terms of the contract until after the customer has committed to the sale and paid for it; the implied warranty of merchantability is severely limited; perfect tender rule does not apply; publishers can make customers waive incidental damages even for defects that were known at the time of sale; failure of actual receipt allows for double charging; and publishers can limit customers in the support they can seek from third party software maintainers. Cem Kaner, *Software Engineering and UCITA*, 18 J. MARSHALL J. COMPUTER & INFO. L. 435, 444-48 (1999). UCITA also arguably implicates other areas of law, such as freedom of speech (software publishers can ban publication of negative reviews) and intellectual property (restricts fair use doctrine; eliminates first sale doctrine; allows terms of use that strip a software user of the IP right to work created using the software). *Id.* at 500-11.

ALI has also forged ahead on its own. ALI prepares the Restatements, and it is currently working on a Restatement-like Principles of the Law of Software Contracts. The purpose of the document is to synthesize the case law that judges are making, extract the common principles, identify the disparate ones, and propose recommenda-tions. PRINCIPLES OF THE LAW OF SOFTWARE CONTRACTS 2-3 (Discussion Draft Mar. 30, 2007). For example, with respect to clickwrap or browsewrap licensing, the PRINCIPLES "opt for creating additional incentives and opportunities for transferees to read terms." *Id.* at 134. The PRINCIPLES also provide comments and illustrations to help clarify different issues and make constant references to UCITA and its apparent and perceived shortcomings.

Finally, NCCUSL promulgated a much less controversial uniform law to address the explosion in the use of electronic communications to form contracts. The Uniform Electronic Transaction Act (UETA) validates electronic contracting and eliminates much of the need for paper-based records. For example, two contracting parties communicating solely by e-mail might be surprised to find that there is a potential question as to whether the statute of frauds has been satisfied. Amended Article 2 addresses these issues as well, replacing the requirement of a "writing" in various provisions with a requirement of a "record." These changes are designed to ensure that the law does not favor one medium of communication over another, and to foster the burgeoning field of electronic contracting by eliminating various requirements of paper writings.

B.   THE PHILOSOPHY OF ARTICLE 2

The readings in this chapter will address several major topics. First, we will explore the innovative jurisprudence of Article 2 as a response to the failures of previous statutory enactments. Although Article 2 is a codification of sales law, it is a "code" that invites a common law methodology to ensure that legal rules do not interfere with the natural growth and development of commerce. Second, we will cover in greater detail the expansion of commercial contracting law beyond Article 2 to Amended Article 2 and other statutory enactments. Finally, we will cover the scope of Article 2 and the continuing relevance of the common law of contracts to the extent that it is not displaced by Article 2. You will find that determining which cases fall within the scope of Article 2 provides you with your first exposure to the "common law" methodology of Article 2.

Karl Llewellyn, law professor at Columbia and Chicago law schools, was the principal author of Article 2 of the UCC. He set out to create a flexible statutory scheme that courts could adapt to fit a wide range of situations involving the sale of goods. He was inspired by earlier case law that demonstrated the usefulness of just such a scheme. For a pre-Code example of adaptability in action, recall the familiar case of *MacPherson v. Buick Motor Company*, 111 N.E. 1050 (N.Y. 1916), from your first year torts class.

In *MacPherson*, the New York Court of Appeals dealt with the aftermath of an automobile accident. The plaintiff purchased a car from a retail dealer, who had himself purchased it from the defendant (the manufacturer). One of the car's wheels was defective and collapsed, throwing the plaintiff from the car and injuring him. Citing a restrictive interpretation of *Thomas v. Winchester*,[1] the defense argued that since there was no privity of contract between the two parties, and since a car is not an "inherently dangerous" item (which would negate the need for privity), it did not owe any duty to the plaintiff.

Justice Cardozo's majority opinion in *MacPherson* illustrates the style of legal reasoning that Llewellyn admired and attempted to accommodate in Article 2. Rather than strictly applying the *Thomas* rule, Cardozo took a broader approach. First, citing *Devlin v. Smith*,[2] he determined that an automobile, while not "inherently dangerous"

---

[1] 6 N.Y. 397 (holding that a manufacturer of inherently dangerous items is liable for any harm caused by those items).

[2] 89 N.Y. 470 (holding that a scaffold was dangerous if improperly constructed, so the manufacturer had a duty to build it with care).

in the same way as an improperly labeled poison, still posed a potential for harm by its very nature. Since the car was designed to travel as fast as 50 miles per hour, negligence in its construction could result in serious injury.

Second, Cardozo dismissed the argument regarding lack of privity by pointing out that the car had more than one seat, which meant that the manufacturer clearly intended more than one person to use the car and could foresee injuries to persons not in privity. While Buick claimed it had privity only with the dealer, the dealer was the one person in the world that Buick could be reasonably certain would not be driving the car. Again citing *Devlin*, Cardozo held that since Buick clearly intended the car for use by someone other than the dealer, a lack of privity did not negate its duty to build the car with care.

Finally, Cardozo found that Buick could not escape liability simply because it did not manufacture the wheels but instead bought them from a third-party supplier. As a manufacturer, Buick owed a duty to ensure that components used in its cars were adequate for use. Buick's duty to the plaintiff as a the future purchaser of the car included inspecting the wheels that were to be installed on the car.

Justice Bartlett's dissent neatly demonstrates the "formal" style of legal reasoning that Cardozo, Llewellyn, and other legal realists were attempting to dispatch. Citing a lengthy list of cases, including *Winterbottom v. Wright*, *Thomas v. Winchester*, and *Statler v. Ray Manufacturing*, Bartlett argued that the requirement for contractual privity was inviolable. He attempted to distinguish *MacPherson* from *Devlin* on the theory that the *Devlin* scaffold was built specifically for a known group of painters rather than an anonymous consumer to be named later. Under his reasoning, there was no room for a variation of the decided law allowing the plaintiff to recover.

MacPherson is typically taught in a tort or product liability context, but Cardozo's opinion incorporates many contract themes that will recur throughout this course. For more insight on how this decision influenced Llewellyn and the U.C.C., consider the following excerpt in which Llewellyn comments on the case and then the excerpt from an article by Professor Alces.

Karl Llewellyn, The Common Law Tradition: Deciding Appeals
430-36 (1960)[3]

The sharp difference between a deliberate attack on a wide situation presented, and effort primarily at fair disposition on the case in hand, could hardly be better presented than in the familiar *MacPherson v. Buick*. Indeed, especially when the illuminating dissent of Willard Bartlett is studied along with the Cardozo opinion, that case lights up half a dozen of the points of theory raised by the present study, and provides as well a classic example of how a troubling sequence of cases can be handled in argument. Thus the case will again illustrate how the outcome, both on rule-for-future-guidance and on case-in-hand, may well differ according to the shift in lighting produced by inquiry addressed first to the type of situation with its equities and immanent sense, or, on the other hand, addressed first to the particular narrow facts and the individual equities. The case further illustrates again how a solution for the situation-type can (four times out of five, it does) carry with it a satisfying solution on the immediate "equities of the case" — partly because those equities themselves tend to line up more significantly and more incisively, when viewed against the larger situation. The case illustrates, yet again, the drive which an attack on the situation can bring forth a reformulation of a rule or principle of law which frees it of the accidental or historical sequence of prior language, and freshly tailors the words to what has now come to be perceived as the true sense in life of the situation-type. This malleability of language, we recall, is a major by-value of our manner of case law rule, notwithstanding all the "technical

---

[3] Copyright 1960 by Little, Brown & Co. Reprinted with permission.

deficiency" which, for a more tight-minded lawyer of the Continental type, appears to characterize our rules.

Equally important *MacPherson v. Buick* shows the "style of reason" at its best, in full recrudescence, indeed in full recapture, both in the deciding and in the opinion writing, and more than two generations ago. It displays, in addition, an identifiable manner and technique of opinion-writing peculiarly adapted to the present-day task of getting back to the reasoned creative method of the early nineteenth century, while both capitalizing on and reckoning with the insight and authority embodied in the intervening cases — while also disposing of such of them as may prove too remote from life because either the Formal Style or some other aberration has in the interim lost contact with life-needs or even made conscious rapprochement therewith seem immaterial.

For the prevailing opinion in the *Buick* case is cast in a characteristic and wholly communicable Cardozo pattern, one of his best patterns. A situation of breadth and significance is diagnosed and sense in it and for it is discovered. This I suspect to be the first vital step. An authority, preferably from before the Formal period, is examined and a principle, or the germ of a principle, is extracted from it which fits and serves the needed current sense. That principle is then *re*formulated to fit the modern need, to solve the case in hand, and to guide the future, its reason being made as explicit as itself. The intervening authorities are then dealt with, practically all of them. They are dealt with in time-perspective, and as if they had been a series of efforts along the line which has been thus redrawn; they are in consequence re-examined, exploited, distinguished, recast, or discarded, and, above all, *cleaned up*. It will be observed that this pattern of opinion not only has as obvious goals an accounting to the given authorities and then the provision of a fresh and fertile start, behind which there is no need to go back; but a start which utilizes all the prior experience. The pattern presents also a *method* for utilizing such experience, for profiting by past insights, for discarding past blobs, and for the forward-pointing of the central reformulation.

Across Bartlett's path, and in Cardozo's favor, was that bottle of aerated water which had exploded and injured the purchaser's servant, where the opinion had allowed recovery "under the doctrine of *Thomas v. Winchester* (*supra*), and similar cases based upon the duty of the vendor of an article *dangerous in its nature, or likely to become so in the course of use to be contemplated* by the vendor" to give warning or to take reasonable care to prevent danger. (The italics are Bartlett's, at page 398.) "Reasonable care" might of course be found, in the *Buick* case, in the record of experience with those prior eighty thousand wheels; still, the language was bothersome. But Bartlett's phrasing, to hold that language down, is master advocacy:

> The character *of the exception* to the general rule limiting liability for negligence to the original parties to the contract of sale, *was still more clearly stated by Judge Hiscock*, writing for the court . . . [three volumes later, in allowing recovery for injury from an exploding coffee urn] where he said that in the case of an article *of an inherently dangerous nature*, a manufacturer may become liable for a negligent construction which, when *added* to the *inherent character of* the appliance, makes it *imminently* dangerous. . . .

(*Ibid.* 398–399; all above italics mine). Hiscock, thus flatteringly quoted (thus, therefore, to be pinned to his own language?) was also sitting in *Buick*.

How anyone argues that Bartlett is not here presenting "good law," I do not see. It is not only technically sound; it is closer to the "feel" of both the authorities and the case in hand than is its opposite. Nor can I doubt the immediate fairness of protecting the Buick Company, if reasonable ways of doing business and reliance on real and long experience are to safeguard any outfit against liability. And "fifty miles an hour" is not before the court.

What, then, is wrong with this "correct" opinion by Willard Bartlett? Nothing, if the appellate court's function in our polity is to leave all work of legal readjustment to the legislature, and is merely to decide individual cases on the authorities as they happen to read, allowing nothing for differential wisdom, treating them as if they had all been decided on a single day, with no history, no growth, no errors, no insights better one time than another, and attending within that frame only to such immediate justice as may prove feasible without the ruffling of a hair. Nothing, either, if closely holding the "exception" down fits our modern need. Nothing, again, if "inherently" or "imminently" dangerous, covering a scaffold and a bottle of aerated water and a coffee urn, but excluding a defective automobile, lets any future court or lawyer know where he is at. Bartlett's opinion is solid on law and fact, and is both shrewd and stirring argument. The only thing wrong is that it would leave the meaning of this phase of law, in life, hopelessly tangled; that looks, in first instance, to the future. And that his opinion is out of line with needs which recurrent cases in his court and elsewhere have been forcing to attention; that looks again, in first instance, to the future.

Cardozo, as indicated, sees the case as presenting the purposed use of the car. In the context of precedent, this raises the question of "dangerous instruments" in modern conditions. The original "landmark" of *Thomas v. Winchester,* 6 N.Y. 397 (1852) — belladonna, mislabeled — Cardozo pins, by quotation: "The defendant's negligence put human life in imminent danger" (p. 385; watch here the immense covert expansion from "drugs" to "things"). That ruling is then explained: "Because the danger is to be foreseen, there is a duty to avoid the injury."

Now the point of method begins to develop. When precedents are to be straightened out, and some are to be avoided in favor of others, and language which has gotten too tangled to guide is to be recast, the appropriate common law tool is *principle*. That is one point. The second is, that if *principle* is to be *sound* principle with a life-basis, a sense-basis, and a solid guidesomeness into emerging conditions, then it must have an explicit *reason* which both displays its wisdom and helps to clarify its application.

The opinion in *Thomas v. Winchester* itself had spoken freely of cases where its rule on drugs did *not* apply; and among the instances was that of the carriage-builder. To this, Cardozo: "Some of the illustrations might be rejected today. The *principle* of the distinction is for present purposes the important thing." (His italics.)

> "*Thomas v. Winchester* became quickly a landmark of the law. In the application of its principle there may at times have been uncertainty or even error. There has never in this state been doubt or disavowal of the principle itself." (p. 385.)

It will be remembered that what *Thomas v. Winchester* had in fact had to say is here in process of being radically extended. Its "principle" is not being found in its language, qualified by its other language: it is a something larger, to be newly phrased. The cases are then lined up on the time-dimension — an extremely serviceable means of spanning over any embarrassing work of the most Formal period, and a no less serviceable means for charting a *direction*. "These early cases suggest a narrow construction of the rule. Later cases, however, evince a more liberal spirit." (p. 386.) "It may be that *Devlin v. Smith* [defective scaffold] and *Statler v. Ray Mfg. Co.* [exploding coffee urn] have extended the rule of *Thomas v. Winchester*. If so, this court is committed to the extension." (p. 387.) (Note that the *Winchester* "principle" has thus been here all along. The "rule," as we go back and pick it up, *may* have been a little small for the foot, at first; that is all.)

Cardozo now approaches the embarrassing language from Hiscock, quoted against him so tellingly by the Chief Judge. An almost unnoticeable shift of phrasing, from "dangerous" to "destructive," coupled with a stressing of fact and situation, and of the language *not* of Hiscock in a prior authoritative opinion for the court, but of the *defendant's* misguided counsel in the case in hand, bridges into the new principle which the Court approves. "The *defendant* argues that things imminently dangerous to life are poison, explosives, deadly weapons — things whose normal function is to injure or destroy. But whatever the rule of *Thomas v. Winchester* may once have been, it has no longer that restricted meaning. A scaffold (*Devlin v. Smith, supra*) is not inherently a *destructive* instrument. It becomes destructive only if imperfectly constructed." (*Ibid.*) "*Subtle* distinctions are drawn *by the defendant* between things inherently dangerous and things imminently dangerous, but the case does not turn upon these verbal niceties" (p. 394; my italics; but Hiscock, reviewing *his own* past judicial decision, concurred).

With this, the course of handling the authorities becomes clear. What remains is to state the principle in its new form, cleanly for guidance, and with its life-reason clear. That statement, on pages 389 and 390, is too long to quote. I note merely its method:

> It runs wholly free of all prior language, with a "We hold, then, that . . . ." Even in its expansion, it is expressly confined within the field of discussion forced by the initial posing of the issue. Its limitations and conditions are pointed in terms which not only guide, but persuade. The prose reflects the clean line of the thought. The application which follows, moreover, is not formal. The application is indeed made to illuminate the future by being an elucidation of the full-running *reason* of that application. "It was as much a thing of danger as a defective engine for a railroad. The defendant knew the danger. It knew also that the car would be used by other persons than the buyer. This was apparent from its size; there were seats for three persons. It was apparent also from the fact that the buyer was a dealer in cars, who bought to resell. . . . The dealer was indeed the one person of whom it might be said with some approach to certainty that by him the car would not be used . . . ." (p. 391).

The law of the country, and legal analogues, are then explored. This tests, checks up, lines up, and rounds out — as Cowen did with lunatics and strays. In one type of schoolman's theory of dogmatic strictness, such portions can be regarded as strays in the opinion. But *given the mastery of the whole area*, this type of semiconsolidation breaks out discrepant and troubling thought-tight bulkheads, and makes for comfortable and efficient work and planning.

Peter A. Alces, *Toward a Jurisprudence of Bank-Customer Relations*
32 Wayne L. Rev. 1279, 1300–03 (1986)[4]

Because the U.C.C. is a code, it makes demands on attorneys not fully appreciated by those who perceive its provisions as a system of discrete answers to typical controversies. Rarely is a commercial court constrained to reach a particular result under the most Llewellynesque provisions of Article 2. Instead, the sections invite a reexamination of the equities attending the particular facts in issue. "Article II . . . operated as a means of dictating a method. That method was designed to prompt decision not according to the letter or the logic of a statute or a juristic concept but rather according to the 'situation-reason.' " Though Llewellyn's elaboration of situation-reason, or situation-sense, has not provided a model of clarity, his persistent emphasis on the immanent law of a fact pattern suggests that he considered situation-sense to be a venerable juristic concept. For the commercial transactor and his counsel, nice questions of immanent justice do little to establish the contours of a deal or to reveal the best litigation posture when the deal falls apart. In *The Common Law Tradition*, Llewellyn argued that situation-sense has meaning on that pragmatic level. He used Justice Benjamin Cardozo's *MacPherson v. Buick Motor Co.* opinion to describe his concept of situation-sense. Llewellyn concluded that Cardozo's method reflected the "Grand Style" of adjudication. What can be distilled from Llewellyn's *MacPherson* section of *The Common Law Tradition* formulates what Llewellyn endeavored to draft into Article 2 of the Code.

Cardozo impressed Llewellyn by separating the *principle* or *reason* for a rule from

---

the *precedential authority:* "That principle is then *re*formulated to fit the modern need, to solve the case in hand, and to guide the future, its reason being made as explicit as itself." Precedent is thereby "*cleaned up.*" If the statute or code is the only source of the law, the creative judge need not expend efforts "cleaning up" precedent, and the less skilled jurist will not be distracted by the need to distinguish troublesome precedent. The U.C.C., because it is a code, is consistent with what Llewellyn admired in *MacPherson.* In his important article concerning U.C.C. methodology, Chancellor Hawkland recognized that courts construing provisions of the Code should focus more on the language of the Act's provisions than on other courts' construction of those provisions.

Llewellyn praised Cardozo's ability to manipulate the scope of the liability principle to suit the facts of the case. Cardozo observed: "Precedents drawn from the days of travel by stagecoach do not fit the conditions of travel today," and Llewellyn remarked: "A question seen thus widens out; and, as is familiar, the resulting rule or principle must therefore also widen out, to fit the *now perceived sense* and need which only such a viewing of the question could have opened." Good commercial law, for Llewellyn, would be drafted "to permit the continued expansion of commercial practices through custom, usage and agreement of the parties." Central concepts would be fluid, not static, and principle would "be recurred to constantly, so as to correct and readjust precedent." Justice Cardozo's method is the type of analysis vindicated by Llewellyn's legal realism. The dynamic nature of commercial transactions mandates such a method just as it seems most acutely to defy static formulation and application: "To speak of an exclusively correct interpretation, one which would be the true meaning of the statute from the beginning to the end of its day, is altogether erroneous."

Insofar as legal realism provides a means to discover and effectuate the goals and policies common among commercial transactors, it facilitates code treatment of commercial transactions. A code is a "pre-emptive, systematic, and comprehensive enactment of a whole field of law." Before an area of law may be codified successfully, it must be delimited along functional lines: to be "comprehensive" an enactment must describe the rights and liabilities that the set of laws "be sufficiently inclusive and independent to enable it to be administered in accordance with its own *basic policies.*"

As the preceding materials suggest, Article 2 (and perhaps all) of the Uniform Commercial Code was and continues to be a jurisprudential experiment. There has been considerable difference of opinion among commercial attorneys and commentators regarding the success of this experiment. While you work through the materials in this coursebook, particularly the materials in this introductory chapter, be sensitive to these differences of opinion and to the ways in which those differences are manifested. Does the way in which Article 2 is written seem to afford too numerous opportunities for the type of factual analyses that necessitate litigation? Does the volume of litigation to which a statute gives rise lead you to particular conclusions about the overall efficacy of the statute? To what extent, given Llewellyn's predispositions formulated above, is litigation a necessary result of drafting a statute to accommodate the Grand Style of adjudication? Those are fair questions, and it is entirely appropriate to keep in mind the "big picture" as you learn commercial law.

Karl Llewellyn principally was concerned with reforming sales law, and he took an active part in criticizing the Uniform Sales Act and developing its successor, the Revised Uniform Sales Act. William Schnader has described the legislative and legal landscape that attended development of the uniform law of sales.

While to a large degree Article 2 can be seen as an iteration of Karl Llewellyn's theoretical vision, there were many compromises to that vision in the final version of the original Article 2. As Llewellyn, himself, said of his final product:

I am ashamed of [the UCC] in some ways; there are so many pieces that I could make a little better; there are so many beautiful ideas I tried to get in that would have been good for the law, but I was voted down. A wide body of opinion has worked the law into some sort of compromise after debate and after exhaustive work. However, when you compare it with anything that there is, it is an infinite improvement.

Karl Llewellyn, *Why a Commercial Code?*, 22 Tenn. L. Rev 779, 784 (1953).

C.   THE SCOPE OF ARTICLE 2 AND THE CONTINUING RELEVANCE OF THE COMMON LAW

The most important provision in any statutory body of law is the one specifying the scope of the statute. The scope of Article 2 is set forth in § 2-102, which provides that Article 2 "applies to transactions in goods," but not to a "security transaction" governed by Article 9. However, this rule is modified by language that is highly atypical of statutory provisions relating to scope, because § 2-102 prefaces the scope provision with the qualifier: unless "the context otherwise requires." Literally speaking, the statute declares that it applies to transactions in goods, unless the situation dictates that the statute not apply. This is a particularly Llewellyn-esque provision, because it declines to state a legal rule in favor of commanding courts to utilize their "situation sense" to determine if the "patent reason" of Article 2 makes sense in the particular context at hand.

Even if a transaction falls within the scope of Article 2, principles of equity and the common law of contracts might still provide the applicable rule if Article 2 otherwise is silent. Section 1-103(b) provides that courts may invoke supplementary "principles of law and equity" to the extent that they have not been "displaced" by Article 2. This has led to similar "common law" reasoning by courts struggling to determine whether Article 2 has displaced a rule of the common law of contracts.

1.   Article 2 as a "Common Law Code"

The United States has followed the common law tradition of England, in which courts articulate the law through a series of decisions over a number of years. This approach stands in contrast to the European model of civil codes, the most famous of which is the Napoleonic Code. An important preliminary question in this course is whether Article 2 is a "code" in the European sense. Section 1-103 contains mixed signals. On one hand, § 1-103(a) makes clear that courts should liberally construe and apply the Uniform Commercial Code to promote its underlying purposes and policies, thereby suggesting that it is a self-contained code. On the other hand, § 1-103(b) makes clear that background principles of law and equity continue to apply to the extent that they are not displaced by the UCC, thereby suggesting that the code is a statutory overlay on the common law.

Perhaps the best way to understand the UCC is that it is both a genuine code and an invitation for courts to continue the common law tradition. As the following article makes clear, Llewellyn was steeped both in the European tradition of codes that provided general rules as well as the common law adjustment of rules to fit the case at hand. Understanding this background at the outset will assist you substantially in this course.

Shael Herman, *Llewellyn the Civilian: Speculations on the Contribution of Continental Experience to the Uniform Commercial Code*
56 TUL. L. REV. 1125, 1125–28, 1133–35, 1137, 1154, 1156–59,
1160–61, 1162–63, 1164–65, 1167 (1982)[5]

To a student of legislation drafted in the civilian tradition, the Uniform Commercial Code is an atypical, eccentric statute. Although it covers less ground than most civil and commercial codes, its voluminous editorial comments make it heftier and more talkative. The Uniform Commercial Code differs from Romanesque codes in both style and substance, but Llewellyn's task in drafting it was essentially like that of Portalis, chief drafter of the Code Napoleon: to divine essential features in the flux of daily conduct, and to embody in general propositions "principles . . . fertile in application" and free of "details of questions which may arise in particular instances."[6] Rooted in the view that history always outstrips the human imagination, Portalis' injunction to both himself and future drafters suggested that a workable code always had to be flexible for it could never be complete. Portalis' cardinal guide for action, one that he must have repeated often in hopes of saving his work from the fate of the overly particularistic Prussian code, was difficult to implement even in France where comprehensive legislation was the rule, not the exception. From Gény's *Méthode d'interpretation et sources in droit privé positif,* Llewellyn would have known Portalis' views, but their implementation in the United States might have seemed nearly impossible. In the United States, the codification movement had climaxed and then dissipated in the nineteenth century; Holmes' dictum from *Lochner v. New York* that "general propositions do not decide concrete cases"[7] had a powerful influence upon lawyers' minds. Often the sentiment Holmes expressed was translated into diatribes against codification. Llewellyn's campaign for the Uniform Commercial Code demonstrated that he did not subscribe to Holmes' dictum. He could not have ignored its power either, for it neatly summarized a powerful American preference for case law over organic legislation as a way to settle private disputes.

Llewellyn himself appreciated this American preference. He edited a superb casebook on sales,[8] and *The Common Law Tradition* was largely case analysis. In his view, the case method was an indispensable tool for bringing out the distinction between the actual decision and "passing dictum."[9] Yet for several reasons judicial lawmaking was inherently unsuited for the unification of commercial law. Judicial rulings, although they usually made "commonly good sense," were narrow. Even when judges innovated, their innovation was "confined regularly within rather narrow limits—partly by the practice of trying hard to square the new decision with old law; it [was] hard to keep daring innovations even verbally consistent with old rules."[10] Furthermore, innovation was "confined through conscious policy"; case law rules, even when they were new, were "applied *as if* they had always been the law."[11] This policy

---

[5] Shael Herman, *Llewellyn the Civilian: Speculations on the Contribution of Continental Experience to the Uniform Commercial Code,* originally published in 56 TULANE L. REV. 1125–70 (1982). Reprinted with the permission of the Tulane Law Review Association, which holds the copyright.

[6] [1] Portalis, Tronchet, Bigot-Préameneu & Maleville, *Discours Préliminaire,* in 1 J. Locré, La législation civile, commerciale et criminelle de la France 251, 255 (1827). A translation appears in Levasseur, *Code Napoleon or Code Portalis?,* 43 Tul. L. Rev. 762, 769 (1969). Llewellyn certainly knew of Portalis' role; he referred directly to Portalis in Llewellyn, *Case Law,* 3 Encyclopedia of the Social Sciences, 249, 250 (1930) [hereinafter cited as *Case Law*].

[7] [5] Lochner v. New York, 198 U.S. 45, 76 (1905) (Holmes, J., dissenting).

[8] [7] K. Llewellyn, Cases and Materials on the Law of Sales (1930).

[9] [8] Llewellyn, *Case Method,* 3 Encyclopedia of the Social Sciences 253 (1930) [hereinafter cited as *Case Method*].

[10] [9] K. Llewellyn, The Bramble Bush 78 (1960).

[11] [10] *Id.*

"derived from our convention that 'judges only declare and do not make the law.' "[12] Judges, because they could not tell how their retroactively effective rulings might upset human expectations, "moved very cautiously into new grounds."[13] For the unification of law, Llewellyn believed statutes were preferable to judicial decisions:

> Statutes are made relatively in the large, to cover wider sweeps, and looking forward. They apply only to events and transactions occurring *after* they have come into force; that element of caution disappears. They are . . . a recognized machinery for readjustment of the law. They represent not single disputes, but whole classes of disputes. They are political, not judicial in their nature, represent readjustments along the lines of balance of power, decide not single cases by a tiny shift of rule, but the rearrangement of a great mass of clashing interests. Statute-making . . . is confined within what in relation to society at large is a straitened margin of free movement. . . .[14]

Llewellyn's understanding of commercial law was profound. It was matched by his respect for the creative energy of commercial lawyers, a potential that could be tapped only if they could all be pointed in one direction. . . . Implicit in the articulation of general principles was a need to harness and channel the energies and even the biases of lawyers in a country where there had never been comprehensive codification. Underlying Llewellyn's explicit agenda—the articulation of first principles—lay the need to take account of context. This article examines drafting techniques Llewellyn used to assure that the Uniform Commercial Code would take hold and endure.

*   *   *

American statutes, unlike their continental counterparts, were not at the center of private law. American law was characterized by the supremacy the judiciary, so much so that a statute did not have meaning unless a judge construed it. As one commentator for the New York Law Revision Commission put it: "The political ideal of many lawyers and other conservatives was that case law, the traditional common law of England as adapted to American conditions, should be the type of law, and legislation should be an occasional intrusion."[15] Llewellyn realized that American lawyers and courts considered statutes "enemy invaders."[16] His task was to reverse this attitude.

Llewellyn used a host of techniques to make the code a "semi-permanent"[17] body of legislation, a centerpiece of commercial life, a *vade mecum* for commercial lawyers. He had stated fragments of a program for code drafting in many places, though sometimes his need to play to his audience with phrases like "dumbbell judges" kept him from developing his views systematically. About his cardinal drafting principles of "patent reason"[18] there was no doubt. "Every provision," he said, "should show its reason on its face. Every body of provisions should display on their face their organizing principle."[19] Second, the Uniform Commercial Code, while it adhered generally to the principle of freedom of contract, had to establish norms and confirm customs that could fill gaps in its provisions and parties' expressions of will. Third, the code had to be anchored in legal and commercial habits of mind. It was pointless to repeal doctrines embedded in legal

---

[12] [11] *Id.*

[13] [12] *Id.*

[14] [13] *Id.*

[15] [29] Patterson, [Codification of Commercial Law in Light of Jurisprudence, Rep. N.Y. L. Revision Commn.], at 41, 49 [(1955)].

[16] [30] Llewellyn, The Common Law Tradition, at 39.

[17] [31] U.C.C. § 1-102, comment 1.

[18] [32] Collection of Karl Llewellyn Papers, J, VI, I, e, at 5 (1944) (available in the University of Chicago Law School Library), *quoted in* Twining, [Karl Llewellyn and the Realist Movement], at 321-22 [(1973)].

[19] [33] *Id.*

consciousness only to have them return. Fourth, in accordance with the teaching of legal realism, criteria for action and decision had to be verifiable; rights and duties had to hinge on particular palpable events, not generalized invisible ideas. Fifth, a rigid doctrine of precedent needed to be replaced by a more supple one, actually rather close to the civilian *jurisprudence constante* that emphasized deriving a rule from a pattern or series of decisions, not an individual case.[20]

Purposive Interpretation

Llewellyn was dedicated to the proposition that rules are most effective and valuable when they are interpreted in light of their purposes and policies. To assure that the code was not sacrificed on an altar of literalism, section 1-102(2) provided that the underlying purposes of the Act are to simplify and modernize the law governing commercial transactions.[21]

Section 1-102 reflects the remedial nature of the Uniform Commercial Code drafted to avoid the complexities of "dissociated"[22] prior acts and judicial decisions that interpreted them. To assure that this statement of purpose was not treated merely as a preamble, the drafters directed: "This Act shall be liberally construed and applied to promote its underlying purposes and policies."[23] This injunction reflected Llewellyn's cardinal drafting "principle of the patent reason." Llewellyn elaborated on this principle in terms of demands of rationality and the aims of uniform and flexible commercial law:

> The rationale of this is that construction and application are intellectually impossible except with reference to some reason and theory of purpose and organization. Borderline, doubtful, or uncontemplated cases are inevitable. Reasonably uniform interpretation by judges of different schooling, learning and skill is tremendously furthered if the reason which guides application of the same language is the same reason in all cases. A patent reason, moreover, tremendously decreases the leeway open to the skillful advocate for persuasive distortion or misapplication of the language; it requires that any contention, to be successfully persuasive, must make some kind of sense in terms of the reason; it provides a real stimulus toward, though not an assurance of, corrective growth rather than straitjacketing of the Code by way of caselaw.[24]

* * *

Llewellyn consciously tried to root out judicial habits of statutory construction that allowed "any statute to remain as an undigested and indigestible lump in the middle of Our Law."[25] This indigestion resulted in an unnecessary literalism he associated with a formal period in judicial thinking when "statutes tended to be limited or even eviscerated by wooden and literal reading, in a sort of long-drawn battle between a balky, stiff-necked, wrongheaded court and a legislature which had only words with

---

[20] [34] The difference between *stare decisis* and *jurisprudence constante* "is of such importance that it may be said to furnish the fundamental distinction between the English and the Continental legal method." Goodhart, *Precedent in English and Continental Law*, 50 L.Q. Rev. 40, 42 (1934).

[21] [35] Underlying purposes and policies of the Act are

    (a) to simplify, clarify and modernize the law governing commercial transactions;

    (b) to permit the continued expansion of commercial practices through custom, usage and agreement of the parties;

    (c) to make uniform the law among the various jurisdictions. U.C.C. § 1-102(2).

[22] [36] [Llewellyn,] *Why a Commercial Code?*, [22 Tenn. L. Rev. 779], at 779 [(1953)].

[23] [37] U.C.C. § 1-102(1).

[24] [38] Twining, *supra* note 13, at 321–22.

[25] [44] Address by Karl Llewellyn, Conference of Chief Justices (Aug. 18-22, 1959), 9 U. Chi. L. Sch. Rec. 6 (1960), *quoted in* Common Law Tradition, supra note 3, at 378.

which to drive that court."[26] Although courts in the early 1800's had engaged in purposive statutory construction in the "grand style,"[27] formal style was of peculiar interest in the twentieth century because it established an orthodox ideology for modern thinking. As will be discussed later, the formalistic reasoning of "orthodox" scholars like Williston and Langdell also drew Llewellyn's fire.

* * *

Section 1-103—A Savings Clause?

At first blush, a broad savings clause, section 1-103, seems to frustrate purposive interpretation by saving pre-code cases unless they are displaced.[28]

In an excellent study, one writer has argued that this section may have preserved for the code method a reliance on precedent inconsistent with the policy oriented interpretation called for under section 1-102.[29] But section 1-103, read closely, saves *principles* of law and equity, not specific cases. In a sense, these principles are extra-codal imperative terms imposed on all agreements out of a fund of ideas that pre-existed the code. Llewellyn, having surveyed the evolution of the common law, realized that some doctrines could be abandoned and that others had become inevitable habits of mind, reflexes that no lawyer could abandon. Among dispensable doctrines was the election of remedy.[30] In contrast, the preference for substituted performance over performance in specie was embedded in lawyers' thinking and could not be inverted. Thus, section 2-716(1) preserved the common law antipathy to specific performance: "Specific performance may be decreed where the goods are unique or in other proper circumstances."

* * *

It must also be remembered that section 1-103 of the Uniform Commercial Code could not displace any remedies not sounding in contract. At first blush, this point seems trivial, but it is important in cases where a plaintiff injured by a defective item sues a supplier on the basis of strict liability as well as code warranties. Thus when section 2-607(3) requires the injured buyer to give a seller a notice of breach or "be barred from any remedy," the term "remedy" here must mean only "contractual remedy" or "remedy under the Uniform Commercial Code." It should not include tort remedies. . . .

A Gloss on the Comments

Commentaries in the civil law tradition have great influence. When law is made systematically and organically, its systematic exegesis is also thought to be necessary. At first, the effect of this exegesis is imperceptible because it affects mainly students. However, as Justinian and Napoleon realized, the students grow up; and when they eventually become judges and legislators, the scholar's exegesis can be profoundly

---

[26] [45] Common Law Tradition, *supra* note 11, at 374.

[27] [46] Id. at 38. The "Grand Style" and "Formal Style" are contrasted in Twining, *supra* note 15, 210–16 & 251–56.

[28] [113] U.C.C. § 1-103 provides: "Unless displaced by the particular provisions of this Act, the principles of law and equity, including the law merchant and the law relative to capacity to contract, principle and agent, estoppel, fraud, misrepresentation, duress, coercion, mistake, bankruptcy, or other validating or invalidating cause shall supplement its provisions."

[29] [114] Nickles, *Problems of Sources of Law Relationships Under the Uniform Commercial Code—Part I: The Methodological Problem and The Civil Law Approach*, 31 Ark. L. Rev. 1, 5–6 (1977).

[30] [115] According to U.C.C. § 2-703, comment 1, "[t]his Article rejects any doctrine of election of remedy as a fundamental policy and thus the remedies are essentially cumulative in nature and include all of the available remedies for breach."

influential. Furthermore, the thinking of scholars, because they do not belong to existing political structures, is not easily controlled or predicted. Their freewheeling speculation on the meaning of a text, rationalizing it by appeal to history and philosophy, can eventually corrode the imperative force of a rule. When commentary is authoritative, the potential for destruction of law is real.

The inclusion of editorial comments in the Uniform Commercial Code leads one to conclude that Llewellyn shared the convictions of Justinian and Napoleon as to the power of commentaries. Williston's treatise was a leading commentary on the Uniform Sales Act but it was also misleading. The courts had given it weight on the false assumption that it reflected the drafter's intent. Unlike Napoleon, Llewellyn realized that academic commentaries on the law were inevitable; nevertheless, their influence could be minimized. A semi-official exegesis of the code, if placed in proximity to the text itself, could effectively insulate the decisional process from academicians, leaving the judges in full control of legal evolution. Though the judges were not omnipotent, they were "interstitial legislators, whose duty (was) to adapt the legal system to existing needs."[31] Thus, in matters of interpretation of the Uniform Commercial Code, American academic writers, unlike their continental counter-parts, were not destined to occupy a quasi-political role as trustees of the law. According to Professor Hawkland, "much to the regret of some law review and treatise writers, the Uniform Commercial Code does not direct judges administering its provisions to seek aid in the 'discussion of informed men.' "[32] Professor Skilton has captured this sense of academic insulation from law creation in the title to his article, "Some Comments on the Comments to the Uniform Commercial Code."[33]

The editorial comments are nothing less than a primer for novices and a primary treatise for judges and lawyers. . . . They are instructive, even argumentative gap fillers. According to White and Summers, authors of a leading hornbook on the code, "the Official Comments . . . are by far the most useful aids to interpretation and construction. The courts take to the comments like ducks take to water even though the legislatures did not enact the Code comments."[34] Decisions that consciously deviate from the comments are distinguished by their rarity.

*   *   *

When a provision is inadequately or inartfully drafted, the comments can even save it from misconstruction. They direct attention to a kind of unprovided-for case that is within the thought construct of a rule though not literally in the rule itself. Thus, the text of section 2-615 literally concerns only cases where the seller fails to perform as agreed because such performance "has been made impracticable by the occurrence of a contingency the non-occurrence of which was a basic assumption on which the contract was made. . . ."[35] As Skilton has said, "The comment to section 2-615 recognizes that there is no comparable provision in Article 2 dealing with unforeseen circumstances which may excuse the buyer's performance. So it takes on the task."[36]

---

[31] [128] Präjudizienrecht [und Rechtssprechung in Amerika (1933)], at pt. 1, § 55, at 76-77, *translated in* Dawson, Comparative Law [(1951)].

[32] [129] Hawkland, *Uniform Commercial "Code" Methodology*, 1962 U. Ill. L. F. 291, at 302.

[33] [130] Skilton, *Some Comments on the Comments to the Uniform Commercial Code*, 1966 Wis. L. Rev. 597.

[34] [132] White & Summers, Uniform Commercial Code, at 12.

[35] [139] *Id.* § 2-615(a).

[36] [140] Skilton, *supra* note 28, at 615. The text of the comment to U.C.C. § 2-615 to which Skilton refers provides:

> Exemption of the buyer in the case of a "requirements" contract is covered by the" Output and Requirements" section both as to assumption and allocation of the relevant risks. But when a contract by a manufacturer to buy fuel or raw material makes no specific reference to a particular

Drafting Techniques: Fusion of Generalization with Palpable Events

*   *   *

Llewellyn's antipathy to conceptual jurisprudence is legendary. His campaign against the use of "heavenly concepts" to solve real problems is reminiscent of the struggle of the great German jurist, Rudolph von Jhering. As a young man, Jhering, under the influence of Pandectist learning, developed a highly refined conceptual jurisprudence. When he realized that the manipulation of his "juristic constructions" was akin to the work of alchemists, he discarded them in favor of a view that law was driven by purpose, not invisible concepts. Demonstration of Jhering's influence on legal realism is beyond the scope of this paper. Suffice it to say that Jhering, long before Holmes, pointed out that the life of the law was experience, not logic. Like Jhering and Holmes, Llewellyn maintained that law had to be functional. No one minded if the law was functional in heaven so long as it functioned on earth. A scientific view of law blinded many scholars to the need for functionalism. Even Landgell's case method became Llewellyn's target. According to Llewellyn, Langdell's scientific assumption that the case method would predict future outcomes as well as the "right" direction of the law "would not hold water."[37] To make the Uniform Commercial Code "hold water," Llewellyn, in reaction to arid conceptualism, made the merits of an issue depend on visible, palpable events, not general conceptual categories.

*   *   *

For Llewellyn, the code's objective was to state "legal consequences . . . as following directly from the contract and action taken under it without resorting to the idea of when property or title passed or was to pass as being the determining factor." . . .[38]

*   *   *

The Uniform Commercial Code would be more aesthetically pleasing if its style were more terse. Its detail is probably attributable to a real fear that lawyers, because they are unskilled in analogical interpretation of legislation, need the guidance of specific details. Even when it is verbose, however, it is workable because its solutions depend on palpable events. . . . [T]hese palpable events tend to make decisions turn on findings of fact, not questions of law. Thus, a focus on palpable events minimizes judicial elaboration of doctrine and the precedential value of cases.

2. Article 2's Scope: "Transaction in Goods"

Despite its brevity and seeming simplicity, the scope provision raises immediate questions. First, what is a "transaction" for purposes of § 2-102? Second, it is not clear whether Article 2 should apply to transactions that involve both goods and non-goods. If a nursery sells a tree to a homeowner and comes to the house to plant the tree, is this a sale of goods subject to Article 2, or is it a provision of landscaping services that falls

---

venture and no such reference may be drawn from the circumstances, commercial understanding views it as a general deal in the general market and not conditioned on any assumption of the continuing operation of the buyer's plant. Even when notice is given by the buyer that the supplies are needed to fill a specific contract of a normal commercial kind, commercial understanding does not see such a supply contract as conditioned on the continuance of the buyer's further contract for outlet. On the other hand, where the buyer's contract is in reasonable commercial understanding conditioned on a definite and specific venture or assumption as, for instance, a war procurement subcontract known to be based on a prime contract which is subject to termination, or a supply contract for a particular construction venture, the reason of the present section may well apply and entitle the buyer to the exemption.

U.C.C. § 2-615, comment 9.

[37] [148] *Case Law, supra* note 1, at 251–52.

[38] [156] U.C.C. § 2-101 Comment.

outside Article 2? The following cases address these and other questions. As you analyze the reasoning of the cases, determine whether the opinions embody Llewellyn's jurisprudential perspective.

SKELTON v. DRUID CITY HOSPITAL BOARD
Alabama Supreme Court
459 So. 2d 818 (1984)

EMBRY, JUSTICE.

This is an appeal occasioned by the grant of a partial summary judgment, made final pursuant to Rule 54(b), ARCP, in favor of Druid City Hospital Board (Druid City), a public hospital which serves the city and county of Tuscaloosa, Alabama. Druid City is one of five defendants named by Mr. and Mrs. M.C. Skelton in an action which arose from Mr. Skelton's alleged injury during a ventral hernia repair performed at the hospital. The Skeltons also claim damages for personal injuries against James H. Thomas, M.D., Anchor Manufacturing Company, Durr-Fillauer Medical, Inc., and Jimmy Thomas.

Count I of the Skeltons' complaint asserts that while M.C. Skelton was a patient at Druid City Hospital in Tuscaloosa, a surgical procedure was performed on Skelton by James H. Thomas, M.D. During the surgical procedure, a suturing needle being used by Dr. Thomas broke in Skelton's body, where part of it remains. Count I asserts negligence in the performance of their respective duties against all defendants.

Count II of the complaint claims damages for Mrs. Skelton as a result of her husband's injury.

Count III, the portion of the complaint that is the subject of summary judgment in favor of Druid City, asserts that Druid City Hospital Board, Anchor Manufacturing Company, Inc., Durr-Fillauer Medical, Inc., and Jimmy Thomas all impliedly warranted that the suturing needle which broke off in Skelton's body was fit for its intended purpose when sold or distributed to Skelton by such defendants. It further states the needle was not fit for its intended purpose and that as a direct result, Mr. Skelton was injured.

In response to the Skeltons' complaint, Druid City filed a motion to dismiss or, in the alternative, a motion for summary judgment. Summary judgment was granted by the trial court in Druid City's favor as to Count III.

The Facts

Prior to a full discussion of the issue presented, and in order to clarify the circumstances from which this case arose, it is necessary to set out a few relevant facts.

First, a clarification regarding the parties involved is in order. Anchor Manufacturing Company is claimed by the plaintiffs to be the manufacturer of the suturing needle which broke during Skelton's surgery. Durr-Fillauer is a distributor of surgical products. After obtaining needles from Anchor Manufacturing Company, Durr-Fillauer allegedly sold them to Druid City. Its salesperson, Jimmy Thomas, "called on" the hospital.

In opposition to Druid City's motion for summary judgment, plaintiffs presented the deposition of Mrs. Jane Sanders, the supervising nurse in Druid City's operating room. She testified regarding the care and use of suturing needles of the type involved in this case. Sanders stated she generally kept 12 dozen six packs of the suturing needles on hand (864 needles) for surgical procedures in the operating room. The needles were, she said, designed to be reusable and were sanitized between uses by nurses on the 3:00 to 11:00 P.M. shift. Those nurses were responsible for inspecting the needles and replacing those that had become bent or dull. Sanders approximated that each needle was used for six or eight operations, but stated that the hospital had no way of determining how many times a specific needle had been used because the needles were not stored in any particular order.

Simply put, Druid City contends no implied warranty arose from its transaction with Skelton for which liability can be asserted. It relies mainly on the language of § 7-2-315, Code 1975, which provides as follows:

> Where the seller at the time of contracting has reason to know any particular purpose for which the goods are required and that the buyer is relying on the seller's skill or judgment to select or furnish suitable goods, there is unless excluded or modified under the next section an implied warranty that the goods shall be fit for such purpose.

Druid City successfully argued to the trial court that the Skeltons could not prevail under Count III (alleging breach of implied warranty of fitness for particular purpose) because: (1) the hospital is in the business of providing a *service* to patients; it is not a "merchant" or a "seller" such that an implied warranty could arise from any transaction in goods between the institution and a patient; and (2) the suturing needle which broke off during Mr. Skelton's surgery was merely equipment used incident to providing a "service"; there was no "sale" of that needle to Skelton from which an implied warranty could arise.

The Skeltons argue on appeal to this court that Druid City did not meet its burden of proof as to the nonexistence of a genuine issue as to a material fact in support of the Skelton's implied warranty claims. Therefore, they contend, the trial Court erroneously determined summary judgment appropriate regarding their claim that Druid City is guilty of breach of an implied warranty of fitness for a particular purpose of the suturing needle used during Mr. Skelton's ventral hernia repair.

The Skeltons insist that the *Official Comments* to § 7-2-315, and various other provisions of the Commercial Code indicate that section is to be liberally construed and supplemented by common law. They contend that, under both the statute and common law, such a warranty has arisen. Two of the provisions they rely on are as follows:

> Although this section is limited in its scope and direct purposes to warranties made by the seller to the buyer as part of a contract for sale, *the warranty sections of this Article are not designed in any way to disturb those lines of case law growth which have recognized that warranties need not be confined to sales contracts* or to the direct parties to such a contract. . . . Beyond that, the matter is *left to the case law* with the *intention* that the *policies* of this Act may *offer useful guidance* in dealing with *further cases* as they arise.

(Emphasis added.) *Official Comment*, § 7-2-313, Code 1975.

> (1) This title shall be liberally construed and applied to promote its underlying purposes and policies.
>
> (2) Underlying purposes and policies of this title are:
>
> (a) To simplify, clarify and *modernize the law governing commercial transactions*; . . . .

(Emphasis added.) § 7-1-102, Code 1975.

For guidance in disposing of the issues presented by the factual circumstances of this case, we have considered the above and other provisions of the Commercial Code and cases which have arisen out of similar factual circumstances. For the reasons stated below, we reverse.

I

First, we consider the applicability of § 7-2-315 to the transaction between Mr. Skelton and Druid City. (We need not reach Skelton's contention that an implied warranty has arisen under the common law.)

Druid City attempts to define that transaction as wholly consisting of a "service" to Skelton. We do not agree with that characterization. It can make no serious contention that Skelton did not pay for the *use* of the suturing needle, or that patients generally do not buy supplies and pay charges for equipment used in the course of their treatment.

Because of the nature of the re-use of the suturing needle at issue here, we do agree with Druid City that there was no "sale" of the needle to Skelton. Rather, the instant transaction is more akin to a *lease or rental* of equipment than a sale. That does not, however, preclude an implied warranty of fitness for a particular purpose from arising from the transaction.

Article 2 of the Uniform Commercial Code applies, by its terms, to "transactions in goods." Section 7-2-102, Code 1975. That phrase is left undefined by the Code but a number of courts have held there is significance in the use of the term "transaction" rather than "sale." In light of the statement in the *Official Comment* to § 7-2-313, that the *warranty section of Article 2* "need not be confined to sales contracts," we opine our legislature intended that § 7-2-315 be broadly interpreted to include transactions in which there is no actual transfer of title, such as rental and lease transactions. Numerous courts have so held. [Citations omitted.]

Therefore, we conclude the transaction here involved is both a service transaction *and* a "transaction in goods." This court has previously addressed the issue whether implied warranties arise from "mixed" or "hybrid" agreements, those that involve both a sale of goods and a rendering of services. In *Caldwell v. Brown Service Funeral Home*, 345 So. 2d 1341 (Ala. 1977), the plaintiffs sought the service of a funeral home for the burial of their eight-year-old son. They signed a statement for the services and for a casket and vault in the aggregate sum of $860. Because the vault provided by the funeral home was too small for the casket, graveside services had to be conducted twice.

The plaintiffs sued on a theory of implied warranty of fitness and the trial court granted summary judgment in favor of the funeral home as to the implied warranty claims. The funeral home argued it had merely provided a "service" for the plaintiffs and, therefore, no warranty could have arisen. Reversing that court's judgment we stated:

> Here the funeral home knew that the Caldwells were purchasing a vault for the casket of their son, and that they were relying on the seller's judgment to furnish suitable goods. As a professional in this business, the seller could be expected to be aware of any size requirements for the vault to hold the casket which the seller also sold. This implied warranty of fitness was neither excluded nor modified in any way by the funeral home. Moreover, under § 2-715 of Title 7A, the Caldwells may be entitled to incidental and consequential damages resulting from the funeral home's breach.

345 So. 2d 1342.

The *Caldwell* case cannot be distinguished from the present case regarding the issue whether the provider of a service can be held liable under § 7-2-315. In both cases the plaintiffs went to the defendants seeking services and products necessary to those services; and in both cases the plaintiffs were submitted a total bill for the products and the services. In both cases the plaintiffs were injured by the products sold with the services, and in both cases the plaintiffs relied upon the skills and expertise of the defendants in selecting the involved products. This same approach to "hybrid" transactions has been adopted by other courts.

In *Newmark v. Gimbel's, Inc.*, 54 N.J. 585, 258 A.2d 697 (1969), the court found an implied warranty of fitness where a beauty parlor operator administered a permanent wave solution which injured a patron. It stated:

> A beauty parlor operator in soliciting patronage assures the public that he or

she possesses adequate knowledge and skill to do the things and to apply the solution necessary to produce the permanent wave in the hair of the customer. When a patron responds to the solicitation she does so confident that any product used in the shops has come from a reliable origin and can be trusted not to injure her. She places herself in the hands of the operator relying upon his or her expertise both in the selection of products to be used on her and in the method of using them. The administrations and the products employed on her are under the control and selection of the operator; the patron is a mere passive recipient.

258 A.2d at 701–702.

In *Berry v. G.D. Searle & Co.*, 56 Ill. 2d 54, 309 N.E.2d 550 (1974), the plaintiff suffered a stroke from birth control pills distributed by a Planned Parenthood Clinic. The Illinois Supreme Court rejected the conclusion that Planned Parenthood Association was merely performing an incidental service in distributing the drugs and was not engaged in selling these items. It subjected the clinic to implied warranty liability under the Uniform Commercial Code.

In *Mauran v. Mary Fletcher Hospital*, 318 F. Supp. 297 (D. Vt. 1970), implied warranty liability was imposed where a patient was injured when insulin was administered instead of preoperative medicine. That court stated: "[T]he fact that the sale of anesthesia here is a minimal element in the overall transaction does not mean that there cannot be a sale in the administration of anesthesia." *See also Shaffer v. Victoria Station*, 91 Wash. 2d 295, 588 P.2d 233 (1978); and *Providence Hospital v. Truly*, 30 U.C.C. Rep. Serv. 785, 611 S.W.2d 127 (Tex. Ct. Civ. App.1980).

Based on the above cited precedents regarding the application of U.C.C. § 2-315, and this court's prior construction of the language employed by the legislature in our § 7-2-315, we conclude Druid City is a "seller" of goods within its meaning.

*   *   *

III

Finally, we note that, were this court to exclude hospitals from the implied warranty provisions of the Code based on the arguments presented by Druid City, the effects would be far-reaching. The hospital's theory would, for example, create an exemption from § 7-2-315 for the *service* department of an automobile repair shop which installs defective brakes on a car. Assume that same business had a *parts* department which sold a consumer defective brakes to be installed by the consumer. Under Druid City's rationale, it would be liable under § 7-2-315.[39] We conclude the legislature adopted § 7-2-315 in anticipation of both situations.

That conclusion is further substantiated by the evidentiary problems which would arise from any other treatment of the hybrid sale/service transaction. For instance, release of the hospital from liability for breach of implied warranty would break the chain of the passage of the needle from the manufacturer to Skelton. The result would be that the manufacturer and the distributor of the needle could, at trial, attempt to "scapegoat" the hospital. In the instant case, the facts indicate the hospital claims to inspect the suturing needles before turning them over to surgeons for use. The hospital is, therefore, the only party defendant to the claim of breach of warranty that can rule out the possibility it has misused the needle. If this court were to release the hospital from responsibility on that count, it would make the burden of proof for the plaintiff onerous by creating an "empty chair" at the defense table.

---

[39] [1] To exclude the party that has provided *goods* plus a service for a *set price* from liability under § 7-2-315 is not logical because that party has an incentive — the maximization of profit — to use inferior goods.

For the above reasons, we hold the trial court erred in granting summary judgment in favor of Druid City Hospital Board on Count III of the plaintiffs' complaint alleging breach of an implied warranty. The judgment entered by that court is due to be, and is hereby, reversed, and this cause is remanded to that court for further proceedings in accordance with this opinion.

REVERSED AND REMANDED.

TORBERT, CHIEF JUSTICE (concurring specially).

The majority concludes that the agreement between Druid City Hospital Board (Druid City) and Skelton for the performance of a ventral hernia repair operation was a transaction involving "both a service transaction and a transaction in goods" and thereby giving rise to an implied warranty of fitness for a particular purpose under Code 1975, § 7-2-315.

The majority is correct in its holding that this court has previously addressed the issue of whether implied warranties arise from mixed or hybrid agreements. In *Caldwell v. Brown Service Funeral Home,* 345 So. 2d 1341 (Ala. 1977), the plaintiffs sought the services of a funeral home following the death of their son. They entered into an agreement with the funeral home for the rendering of graveside services and for the purchase of a casket and a vault. Following the graveside services, it was discovered that the vault was too small, and, as a result, the graveside services had to be conducted a second time the next day. The plaintiffs sued the funeral home on a theory of breach of implied warranty of fitness. The funeral home argued that it had merely provided the plaintiffs a service and therefore that no implied warranty had arisen. The trial court granted summary judgment in favor of the funeral home on the implied warranty claim. Reversing the summary judgment, we held that the funeral home knew the plaintiffs were relying on the funeral home's judgment to secure suitable goods, *i.e.,* a casket and vault, and that the funeral home could be expected to be aware of any difference in size between the vaults and the caskets which it sold. There was thus an implied warranty of fitness for the breach of which the plaintiffs might have been entitled to recover incidental and consequential damages. The determinative issue in this case, however, is not whether mixed or hybrid agreements give rise to the Uniform Commercial Code (U.C.C.) implied warranties, but rather how agreements involving both a transaction in goods and a rendering of services are to be classified so that it may *then* be determined whether the U.C.C. implied warranties apply.

In *Bonebrake v. Cox,* 499 F.2d 951 (8th Cir. 1974), the Eighth Circuit Court of Appeals, in an appeal from an adjudication on the merits following a bench trial, reached the conclusion that a contract to supply and install bowling equipment was predominantly a transaction in goods, even though the amount of services involved was substantial. Therefore, the U.C.C. was held to be applicable to the transaction.

The court, in making its determination, stated:

> The test for inclusion or exclusion [of agreements in, or from, the provisions of the U.C.C.] is not whether they are mixed, but, granting that they are mixed, whether their predominate factor, their thrust, their purpose, reasonably stated, is the rendition of service, with goods incidentally involved (*e.g.,* contract with artist for painting) or is a transaction of sale, with labor incidentally involved (*e.g.,* installation of a water heater in a bathroom).

499 F.2d at 960.

In *Coakley & Williams, Inc. v. Shatterproof Glass Corp.,* 706 F.2d 456 (4th Cir. 1983), the Fourth Circuit Court of Appeals reversed a district court's grant of a Rule 12(b)(6), Fed.R.Civ.P., motion dismissing the plaintiff builder's cause of action alleging breach of implied warranties of merchantability and fitness for a particular purpose. The Court of Appeals noted that the factfinder could have reasonably concluded that a contract between the builder and the company which installed windows predominantly concerned a sale of goods rather than services and, consequently, was governed by Maryland's enactment of the Uniform Commercial Code.

In *Pitler v. Michael Reese Hospital*, 92 Ill. App. 3d 739, 47 Ill. Dec. 942, 415 N.E.2d 1255 (1980), the plaintiff brought an action against the hospital, on a theory of breach of implied warranty, for personal injuries arising from radiation treatments. The Illinois Appellate Court rejected the plaintiff's argument that the U.C.C. governed the hospital's administration of medical care and held that Article 2 of the Code was inapplicable because the transaction predominantly involved the rendering of services, even though equipment was furnished in connection with those services.

The U.C.C. was also held not to apply to a mixed contract primarily for the rendering of services in *Ranger Construction Co. v. Dixie Floor Co.*, 433 F. Supp. 442 (D.S.C. 1977). There, the defendant agreed to provide all the labor and materials necessary to the installation of resilient flooring. The court, in holding the Code inapplicable, noted that the defendant was primarily a service oriented business and that the contract was basically one for the performance of services. Any sale of goods necessary to the performance of those services was merely incidental.

Whether a warranty of fitness for a particular purpose arises under Code 1975, § 7-2-315, is basically a question of fact to be determined by the circumstances. *Smith v. Crosrol, Inc.*, 498 F. Supp. 697 (M.D. Ala. 1980) (citing *Official Comment* to Code 1975, § 7-2-315). In the case at bar, the question as to whether or not the circumstances present give rise to an implied warranty of fitness can only be resolved by first determining whether the agreement between Druid City and Skelton was predominantly an agreement for services, in which case the U.C.C. would not be applicable, or for a transaction in goods, in which case the U.C.C. would be applicable.

For the foregoing reasons, I concur in the reversal of the summary judgment.

i.LAN SYSTEMS, INC. v. NETSCOUT SERVICE LEVEL CORP.
United States District Court, District of Massachusetts
183 F. Supp. 2d 328 (2002)

YOUNG, Chief Judge.

Has this happened to you? You plunk down a pretty penny for the latest and greatest software, speed back to your computer, tear open the box, shove the CD-ROM into the computer, click on "install" and, after scrolling past a license agreement which would take at least fifteen minutes to read, find yourself staring at the following dialog box: "I agree." Do you click on the box? You probably do not agree in your heart of hearts, but you click anyway, not about to let some pesky legalese delay the moment for which you've been waiting. Is that "clickwrap" license agreement enforceable? Yes, at least in the case described below.

I. INTRODUCTION

The plaintiff, i.LAN Systems, Inc. ("i.LAN"), helps companies monitor their computer networks. The defendant, NetScout Service Level Corp., formerly known as NextPoint Networks, Inc. ("NextPoint"), sells sophisticated software that monitors networks. In 1998, i.LAN and NextPoint signed a detailed Value Added Reseller ("VAR") agreement whereby i.LAN agreed to resell NextPoint's software to customers. This dispute concerns a transaction that took place in 1999.

i.LAN claims that for $85,231.42 it purchased the unlimited right to use NextPoint's software, replete with perpetual upgrades and support, whereby it effectively could rent, rather than sell, NextPoint's software to customers. In support of its argument, i.LAN points to the purchase order associated with the transaction. NextPoint, in response, points to the 1998 VAR agreement and the clickwrap license agreement contained in the software itself to reach a different conclusion.

The parties continued their relationship for several months without confronting their conflicting interpretations of the 1999 purchase order, but eventually the disagreement erupted into litigation. i.LAN filed a complaint that alleges, among other things, breach of contract and violation of Massachusetts General Laws Chapter 93A. The complaint properly invokes the Court's diversity jurisdiction, 28 U.S.C. § 1332(a)(1).

i.LAN quickly took the offensive and brought a motion for summary judgment, Fed.R.Civ.P. 56(a). i.LAN argued that it should be awarded specific performance — in particular, perpetual upgrades of NextPoint's software and unlimited support. Pl.'s Mot. at 2-3. The Court heard oral argument on i.LAN's motion and took the matter under advisement. Soon after, NextPoint brought a cross-motion for summary judgment, Fed.R.Civ.P. 56(b), the subject of this memorandum. NextPoint argued that even if i.LAN's allegations were true, the clickwrap license agreement limits NextPoint's liability to the price paid for the software, in this case $85,231.42. Def.'s Mot. at 2. The Court heard oral arguments on NextPoint's motion and soon after ruled in favor of NextPoint. This memorandum explains why.

II. DISCUSSION

Before turning to NextPoint's clickwrap license agreement, the stage must be set. First, the Court will identify the set of rules by which to judge this dispute. Next, the Court will examine what is at stake, in particular i.LAN's claim for specific performance and NextPoint's limitation-of-liability defense. Finally, the Court will address the enforceability of the clickwrap license agreement.

A. What Law Governs?

1. Precedence of the 1998, 1999, and Clickwrap Agreements

Three contracts might govern this dispute: the 1998 VAR agreement, the 1999 purchase order, and the clickwrap license agreement to which i.LAN necessarily agreed when it installed the software at issue. The key question for purposes of this memorandum is how the 1998 and 1999 agreements affect the clickwrap license agreement.

The clickwrap license agreement states that it does not affect existing or subsequent written agreements or purchase orders.[40] The language might be read to mean that the clickwrap license agreement is a nullity if a purchase order already exists, but that reading is not the natural one. The natural reading is that to the extent the 1998 VAR agreement and 1999 purchase order are silent, the clickwrap license agreement fills the void.

---

[40] [1] In particular, the clickwrap license agreement provides a limited exception to its integration clause:

This License Agreement does not affect any existing written agreement between Licensee and NEXTPOINT and may be superseded by a subsequent written agreement signed by both Licensee and NEXTPOINT. Except as indicated in the prior sentence, this License Agreement constitutes the entire agreement between NEXTPOINT and Licensee with respect to the use and license of the Licensed Products, and hereby supersedes and terminates any prior agreements or understandings relating to such subject matter, including but not limited to any evaluation or beta test licenses granted by NEXTPOINT to Licensee. No addendum, waiver, consent, modification, amendment or change of the terms of this Agreement shall bind either party unless in writing and signed by duly authorized officers of Licensee and NEXTPOINT. *Terms and conditions as set forth in any purchase order which differ from, conflict with, or are not included in this License Agreement, shall not become part of this License Agreement unless specifically accepted by NEXTPOINT in writing.*

Def.'s App. tab 8 (emphasis added).

2. Common Law vs. UCC

Two bodies of contract law might govern the clickwrap license agreement: Massachusetts common law and the Uniform Commercial Code ("UCC") as adopted by Massachusetts. Article 2 of the UCC applies to "transactions in goods," UCC § 2-102, Mass. Gen. Laws ch. 106, § 2-102, but "unless the context otherwise requires 'contract' and 'agreement' are limited to those relating to the present or future *sale* of goods," *id.* § 2-106(1) (emphasis added). Indeed, the title of Article 2 is "Sales" and the definition of "goods" assumes a sale: "goods" is defined as "all things (including specially manufactured goods) which are movable at the time of identification to the contract for sale . . . ." *Id.* § 2-105(1). The purchase of software might seem like an ordinary contract for the sale of goods, but in fact the purchaser merely obtains a *license* to use the software; never is there a "passing of title from the seller to the buyer for a price," *id.* § 2-106(1). So is the purchase of software a transaction in goods? Despite Article 2's requirement of a sale, courts in Massachusetts have assumed, without deciding, that Article 2 governs software *licenses. See Novacore Techs., Inc. v. GST Communications Corp.*, 20 F.Supp.2d 169, 183 (D.Mass.1998) (Saris, J.), *aff'd*, 229 F.3d 1133 (1st Cir.1999); *VMark Software, Inc. v. EMC Corp.*, 37 Mass.App.Ct. 610, 611 n.1, 642 N.E.2d 587 (1994); *USM Corp. v. Arthur D. Little Sys., Inc.*, 28 Mass.App.Ct. 108, 119, 546 N.E.2d 888 (1989). *See generally* Lorin Brennan, *Why Article 2 Cannot Apply to Software Transactions*, 38 Duq. L.Rev. 459, 545-77 (2000); Mark A. Lemley, *Intellectual Property and Shrinkwrap Licenses*, 68 S. Cal. L.Rev. 1239, 1244 n. 23 (1995).

Given the cases above, and others to the same effect, i.LAN argues that the UCC should govern the 1999 purchase order and clickwrap license agreement. NextPoint does not disagree with the idea that the UCC might apply to software purchases in general, but under NextPoint's theory of the case, the 1998 VAR agreement is most important to this dispute, and that agreement predominately concerns services, rather than the sale of goods. NextPoint, therefore, argues that the UCC should not govern any part of this dispute. *See, e.g., Cambridge Plating Co. v. Napco, Inc.*, 991 F.2d 21, 24 (1st Cir.1993) (considering "predominate factor, thrust, or purpose" of contract).

To the extent it matters — and given the facts of this case, it likely does not — the Court will examine the clickwrap license agreement through the lens of the UCC. Admittedly, the UCC technically does not govern software licenses, and very likely does not govern the 1998 VAR agreement, but with respect to the 1999 transaction, the UCC best fulfills the parties' reasonable expectations.

In Massachusetts and across most of the nation, software licenses exist in a legislative void. Legal scholars, among them the Uniform Commissioners on State Laws, have tried to fill that void, but their efforts have not kept pace with the world of business. Lawmakers began to draft a new Article 2B (licenses) for the UCC, which would have been the logical complement to Article 2 (sales) and Article 2A (leases), but after a few years of drafting, those lawmakers decided instead to draft an independent body of law for software licenses, which is now known as the Uniform Computer Information Transactions Act ("UCITA").[41] So far only Maryland and Virginia have adopted UCITA; Massachusetts has not. Accordingly, the Court will not spend its time considering UCITA. At the same time, the Court will not overlook Article 2 simply because its provisions are imperfect in today's world. Software licenses are entered into every day, and business persons reasonably expect that some law will govern them. For the time being, Article 2's familiar provisions — which are the inspiration for UCITA — better fulfill those expectations than would the common law. Article 2 technically does not, and certainly will not in the future, govern software licenses, but

---

[41] [2] As one would expect, drafts of UCC Revised Article 2, UCC Article 2B, and UCITA are available on the Internet. *See* http:// www.law.upenn.edu/bll/ulc/ulc_frame.htm.

for the time being, the Court will assume it does.

B. What Is at Stake?

[Ed. Note: The Court then analyzed Article 2's distinctive approaches to the issues in dispute: the availability of specific performance, the ability of a seller to limit its liability for breach through contract terms, and the validity of the "clickwrap" license agreement. We will consider how Article 2 addresses these substantive issues in later chapters.]

NOTES AND QUESTIONS

1. The *Skelton* court deemed the transaction in issue to be a hybrid or mixed agreement and relied upon authority concerning transactions in which both a service was rendered and goods were sold. Was that the case in *Skelton*? What, then, were the components of the hybrid? Was there any sale of goods in the case at all? If not, how could the court conclude that the hospital was a seller of goods?

2. What would provide a source of warranty or at least warranty-like liability if the *Skelton* court had determined the transaction was outside the scope of Article 2? When might it be appropriate to apply the Article 2 rules by analogy? Consider UCC § 1-103. Do you discern any similarities between the majority's opinion in *Skelton* and the Cardozo analysis in *MacPherson, supra*?

3. What criteria should courts use to determine the "predominant purpose" of the transaction? In *Kaitz v. Landscape Creations, Inc.*, 42 UCC Rep. Serv. 2d 691 (Mass. App. 2000), the court considered the predominant purpose of a landscaping contract:

> Several key factors point to this being a contract for landscape services in which goods were incidentally provided. First, the scope of the project was extensive, spanning several months to complete. Second, the project entailed the development or use of a landscape design, grading the soil, preparing and mulching plant beds, and then the purchase and planting of the trees, shrubs and plants. This made the project labor intensive rather than mere provision of goods. In addition, we note that the plaintiff's primary complaint stems from the landscaping services provided, not the plants and trees themselves. Specifically, the complaint alleges that the defendant failed to perform the work in a "workmanlike manner" and as a result certain trees and shrubs died. Another factor which supports a finding that this was predominantly a service contract is that the defendant is not a nursery that merely provides the materials, but is a landscaping company which has a full range of services available to a client.
>
> In a similar case, *Gallo Construction Company, Inc. v. Ghetti*, 1985 Mass. App. Ct. 189 (1985), the court found that the contract was predominantly one for the rendition of services, not the sale of goods. There, the landscaping contract was intended to prevent the erosion of a bank on the homeowner's property. The landscaping contractor had recommended that a landscape architect develop a plan to prevent the erosion. The homeowner rejected the recommendation and requested the landscaper to simply install loam and grass seed. The contractor performed the work and the homeowner refused to pay the remaining balance claiming the results were unsatisfactory. The contractor sued for the balance. In upholding the trial judges determination that the contract was for services, the Appeals Court stated, "[c]learly, the primary thrust or purpose was not the sale and delivery of loam, but the installation or grading of surface materials with a view toward thwarting or controlling erosion." *Id.* at 190.
>
> Similarly, the contract here had as its main thrust the design, layout, grading and beautification of the plaintiff's property. Incidental to this was the purchase of trees, shrubs and plants. The approximate time span of three months for the

completion of the landscaping project evidences more than the mere purchase of "goods." For these reasons, we decide that the predominant purpose of the contract was for the rendition of landscaping services. The trial judge erred in ruling otherwise.

See also, e.g., Morgan Publications, Inc. v. Squire Publishers, Inc., 26 S.W.3d 164 (Mo. 2000) (sale of an ongoing newspaper business and its assets was not predominantly a transaction in goods, given the extensive intangible assets involved and the significant value of these assets, despite the fact that the purchase agreement allocated slightly more than half of the purchase price to the goods involved (furniture and equipment)); *Colorado Carpet Installation, Inc. v. Palermo,* 668 P.2d 1384 (Col. 1983) (important criteria include (a) whether the agreement charges a single price or whether goods and nongoods are billed separately; (b) the ratio of the cost of goods to the overall contract price; and (c) the buyer's interest in and expectation of acquiring property interests in goods); *Micro-Managers, Inc. v. Gregory,* 434 N.W.2d 97, 100 (Wis. App. 1988) (court looked to the language of the home improvement contract, which spoke in terms of "man-days," "development," "time," and "design," and concluded that the parties primarily were engaged in a transaction of services); *Standard Structural Steel Co. v. Debron Corp.,* 515 F. Supp. 803 (D. Conn. 1980) (focus should be on the purpose of the agreement).

4. Several courts have developed an alternative to the predominant purpose test. In *Anthony Pools v. Sheehan,* 455 A.2d 434 (Md. App. 1983), the court found that a contract providing for the construction of an in-ground pool was primarily a services contract, since the majority of the contract price was allocated to construction, and the homeowners were interested primarily in having the pool constructed rather than in purchasing tile and cement. However, because the suit arose out of an allegedly defective diving board, the court held that the suit should be governed by Article 2. The court concluded that when the gravamen of the suit is a good, the rules of Article 2 provide the most appropriate guidance.

The *Anthony* court drew on several precedents. In *Worrell v. Barnes,* 484 P.2d 573 (Nev. 1971), the court determined that Article 2 applied to a home construction contract that primarily involved services. The homeowners alleged that a house fire was caused by a defective fitting installed by the contractor for connection to a propane appliance, and so the court deemed the case to involve the sale of goods. Similarly, in *Newmark v. Gimbel's Inc.,* 258 A.2d 697 (1969), the court held that a patron of a beauty shop who suffered personal injury during application of a permanent wave could sue for breach of warranty under Article 2, despite the fact that the transaction primarily was for services. The court reasoned:

> The transaction, in our judgment, is a hybrid partaking of incidents of a sale and a service. It is really partly the rendering of service, and partly the supplying of goods for a consideration. Accordingly, we agree with the Appellate Division that an implied warranty of fitness of the products used in giving the permanent wave exists with no less force than it would have in the case of a simple sale. Obviously in permanent wave operations the product is taken into consideration in fixing the price of the service. The no-separate-charge argument puts excessive emphasis on form and downgrades the overall substance of the transaction. If the beauty parlor operator bought and applied the permanent wave solution to her own hair and suffered injury thereby, her action in warranty or strict liability in tort against the manufacturer-seller of the product clearly would be maintainable because the basic transaction would have arisen from a conventional type of sale. It does not accord with logic to deny a similar right to a patron against the beauty parlor operator or the manufacturer when the purchase and sale were made in anticipation of and for the purpose of use of the product on the patron who would be charged for its use. Common sense demands that such patron be deemed a customer as to both manufacturer and

beauty parlor operator. [Citations omitted]

Newmark, 258 A.2d at 701.

5. Is the *i.LAN* court's answer to the applicability of Article 2 satisfactory? Is there a better justification for the court to apply Article 2 to this transaction?

6. Now that UCITA has foundered and is highly unlikely to be adopted by the majority of states, is it irrelevant? Could this court have looked to the rules embodied in UCITA even though Massachusetts has not adopted it?

7. Is the sale of an automobile obviously within Article 2? Does the goods portion of the transaction predominate even if the car incorporates numerous software programs? What if the jurisdiction uses the "gravamen test" to determine the applicability of Article 2, and the gravamen of the action involves the software? If an automobile is an easy case, what about VCRs, DVDs, television sets, Palm Pilots, digital cameras, video game machines and a host of kitchen appliances that rely on software? Does the method of delivering the computer information matter? For example, would disputes regarding the performance of software in an automobile still be within Article 2 if it were purchased separately and then downloaded into or electronically delivered to the automobile? What if factory-loaded software is updated regularly by the customer or service technicians? These are just some of the many questions that courts will continue to have to answer in common law fashion.

PROBLEM 1-1

You represent SoundPruf, Inc., a business that applies a dense coating to residential ceilings in apartment buildings. The coating suppresses noise, provides temperature insulation, and enhances the aesthetic appeal of the rooms in which it is applied. SoundPruf purchases the coating from a supplier, colors it as desired by customers, and then adjusts the consistency of the product so that the coating will adhere properly to the ceiling.

How would you prepare form contract documents for SoundPruf to, alternatively, (i) ensure that Article 2 would govern any disputes that arise, or (ii) ensure that Article 2 would not govern? Could you structure SoundPruf's contracts to ensure that Article 2 would govern its purchases of the coating from its supplier, but that the common law would govern its transactions with customers?

PROBLEM 1-2

Bravery Repaid is a non-profit corporation founded to provide funds and services to the families of police officers and firefighters killed in the line of duty. Bravery reached an agreement with Miles Sherman, an internationally known painter, to assist its fundraising efforts. Sherman agreed to appear on a two-hour television program and paint on camera, and then to donate the painting to Bravery for later auction. During the program, Bravery planned to encourage viewers to call a toll-free number and donate money. Additionally, Sherman estimated that his completed painting should auction for approximately $50,000. In return, Bravery agreed that Sherman could use video clips from the event to promote his career.

At the last minute, Sherman decided not to go through with the deal. Bravery sued, arguing that it had reserved air time and publicized the event, and that it lost the benefit of the expected donations and the value of the painting. Sherman moved for summary judgment, arguing that the statute of frauds under Article 2 was not satisfied, and therefore the contract was unenforceable. Bravery can prevail in the litigation if the common law of contracts governs the dispute. How should the parties argue the motion for summary judgment?

3. Supplementation by Common Law and Equitable Principles

The Uniform Commercial Code is not a "code" in the strictest sense. The answer to every problem is not necessarily to be found somewhere within the enacted provisions of one of the substantive articles. In addition to directing courts to be solicitous of the needs of commerce by using concepts like "commercial reasonableness," the UCC makes clear that courts may properly look to supplementary "principles of law and equity," unless such principles have been "displaced" by "particluar provisions" of the UCC § 1-103(b).

Section 1-103(b) provides a non-exhaustive list of supplementary principles, including "estoppel" and the familiar contract defenses of "fraud, misrepresentation, duress, coercion [and] mistake." The provision also expressly includes recourse to the "law merchant," a concept as time-proven and venerable as the commercial law itself. As we will see in Chapter 2, the "law merchant" provided for the continued expansion and elaboration of commercial principles in ways that accommodate the free and expeditious flow of commerce. The very existence of the principle recognizes the unique nature of the commercial community and the peculiar needs of commercial transactors. Given the generally phrased provisions of Article 2, and their express incorporation of considerations such as "commercial reasonableness," it is unlikely that many provisions of Article 2 will be deemed to have displaced the law merchant. Most generously read, then, one might conclude that when the needs of commerce are at odds with an accepted but general legal principle, the particular commercial interests should predominate under Article 2.

Comment 1 originally provided that supplementary sources of law have continuing applicability "except insofar as they are explicitly displaced" by the UCC. This obviously led courts to adopt a formalistic approach to displacement. When Article 1 was revised in 2001, Comment 1 was changed to emphasize the proper methodology for determining whether supplemental rules of law have been displaced. As Comment 1 now explains, Article 2 displaces "other law that is inconsistent with the purposes and policies of the Uniform Commercial Code, as well as with its text." § 1-103, Cmt. 2.

The following cases explore the reasons and limits for courts to refer to principles of law and equity that are not expressly stated in Article 2.

CITY DODGE, INC. v. GARDNER
Georgia Supreme Court
208 S.E.2d 794 (1974)

INGRAM, JUSTICE.

A suit in tort by a buyer against a seller for an alleged fraudulent misrepresentation of the seller's agent resulted in a jury verdict and judgment for the buyer and on appeal by the seller the Court of Appeals affirmed. *Certiorari* was granted to review this decision, and we have determined the judgment of the Court of Appeals should be affirmed.

In this case, the buyer contended that he purchased a used automobile with the understanding that the vehicle had never been wrecked. The seller denied that this representation was made by his agent (salesman) to the buyer. The buyer signed a sales agreement which contained the words, "no other agreement, promise, or understanding of any kind pertaining to this purchase will be recognized." In addition, the purchase agreement stated that the car is sold "as is." Subsequent to the purchase, the buyer discovered that the automobile had been wrecked, tendered the car to the seller, unilaterally rescinded the contract and brought the present action in tort for fraud and deceit.

The decisive issue we address is whether the language of the merger clause that "no other agreement, promise, or understanding of any kind pertaining to this purchase will be recognized," was legally effective to prevent the buyer from claiming that he relied on the seller's misrepresentation. It has been recognized that § 2-202 of the Uniform Commercial Code (Ga. Code Ann. § 109A-2-202) was intended to allow sellers to prevent buyers from making false claims of oral warranties in contract actions. *See* Note, 54 MINN. L. REV. 846, 849 (1970). Thus, in contract actions, the effect of merger and disclaimer clauses must be determined under the provisions of the Uniform Commercial Code.

However, under Georgia law, traditionally, two actions have been available to a buyer in which to sue a seller for alleged misrepresentation in the sale: the buyer could affirm the contract and sue in contract for breach or he could seek to rescind the contract and sue in tort for alleged fraud and deceit. *See Brown v. Ragsdale Motor Co.,* 65 Ga. App. 727, 16 S.E.2d 176, and *Eastern Motor Co. v. Lavender,* 69 Ga. App. 48, 24 S.E.2d 840. Our threshold question in this tort case is to determine whether the adoption of the Uniform Commercial Code (Ga. Code Ann. Title 109A) left available in Georgia a buyer's historic remedy in tort. The passage of the Uniform Commercial Code by the legislature evinced an intent to have that body of law control all commercial transactions. Ga. Code Ann. § 109A-1-102. However, while the Code is an attempt to make uniform the law among the various jurisdictions regarding commercial transactions, the draftsmen realized that it could not possibly anticipate all situations. Thus, § 1-103 (Ga. Code Ann. § 109A-1-103) states:

> Unless displaced by the particular provisions of this Act, the principles of law and equity, including the law merchant and the law relative to capacity to contract, principal and agent, estoppel, fraud, misrepresentation, duress, coercion, mistake, bankruptcy, or other validating or invalidating cause shall supplement its provisions.

In addition, Ga. Code Ann. § 109-A-2-721 provides that:

> Remedies for material misrepresentation or fraud include all remedies available under this Article for nonfraudulent breach. Neither rescission or a claim for a rescission of the contract for sale nor rejection or return of the goods shall bar or be deemed inconsistent with a claim for damages or other remedy.

The commentary by the drafters of the Uniform Commercial Code on this section states:

> Thus the remedies for fraud are extended by this section to coincide in scope with those for non-fraudulent breach. This section thus makes it clear that neither rescission of the contract for fraud nor rejection of the goods bars other remedies unless the circumstances of the case make the remedies incompatible:

See Official Comment, Uniform Commercial Code § 2-721.

We conclude from this language that neither the draftsmen nor the legislature intended to erase the tort remedy for fraud and deceit with the adoption of the Uniform Commercial Code in Georgia. In support of this conclusion, we find many Georgia cases subsequent to the adoption of the Uniform Commercial Code which recognize the tort remedy. (*E.g., Wade Form Inc. v. Perrin et al.,* 111 Ga. App. 794, 143 S.E.2d 420; *Rogers-Farmer Metro Chrysler-Plymouth, Inc. v. Barnett,* 125 Ga. App. 494, 188 S.E.2d 122.) No authority to the contrary has been cited to us, and we note that many of our sister states also provide a tort remedy. *See, e.g., Clements Auto Co. v. Service Bureau Corp.,* 444 F.2d 169 (8th Cir. 1971); *Sauerman v. Stan Moore Motors, Inc.,* 203 N.W.2d 191 (Iowa 1970); *Chester v. McDaniel,* 264 Or. 303, 504 P.2d 726 (1972). For additional supportive authority, see 3A *Bender's U.C.C. Services* § 14.10, and White & Summers, *Handbook of the Law under the Uniform Commercial Code* § 8-1, p. 248. The latter treatise notes that,

> [A]lthough their meaning is not crystal clear, it appears that the draftsmen contemplate a cause of action for fraud in which the buyer would have the right

to return the goods purchased and get his money back. Presumably, this right to return the goods and get his money back is a right to "rescission" which exists outside the Code.

White and Summers, *supra*, p. 248, n.9.

Having decided that a remedy in tort still exists in Georgia for actual fraud, we turn next to the seller's contention that the disclaimer language used here prevented any reliance by the buyer on the alleged fraudulent misrepresentation, and consequently the buyer's action must necessarily fail. The seller contends that there is no fraud on which the buyer relied that prevented him from knowing the contents of the contract, and, therefore, the buyer is bound by the terms of the contract. Some Georgia cases have held that a disclaimer clause in the contract prevents the buyer from asserting reliance, one of the requisite elements of fraud and deceit,[42] and have rejected a recovery in tort for fraud. (*E.g., Floyd v. Woods*, 110 Ga. 850, 36 S.E. 225; *Holbrook v. Capital Automobile Co.*, 111 Ga. App. 601, 142 S.E. 288.) Other Georgia cases have indicated that when the rescinded contract is found by the jury to be void because of antecedent fraud, the disclaimer therein is void and offers no protection to the seller. (*See Brown v. Ragsdale, supra; Eastern Motor Co. v. Lavender, supra*; and other cases noted in 36 A.L.R.3d 125, 151–172.)

We believe the better view is that the question of reliance on the alleged fraudulent misrepresentation in tort cases cannot be determined by the provisions of the contract sought to be rescinded but must be determined as a question of fact by the jury. It is inconsistent to apply a disclaimer provision of a contract in a tort action brought to determine whether the entire contract is invalid because of alleged prior fraud which induced the execution of the contract. If the contract is invalid because of the antecedent fraud, then the disclaimer provision therein is ineffectual since, in legal contemplation, there is no contract between the parties. In this case, parol evidence of the alleged misrepresentation was admissible on the question of fraud and deceit. As the antecedent fraud was proven to the satisfaction of the jury, it vitiated the contract. We hold, therefore, that the Uniform Commercial Code (Ga. Code Ann. Title 109A) does not preclude an action in tort based upon fraudulent misrepresentation inducing the sale where the plaintiff proves by a preponderance of the evidence the elements of fraud and deceit recognized under Georgia law, and that such a tort action cannot be controlled by the terms of the contract itself.

The judgment of the Court of Appeals will be affirmed.

QUESTIONS

1. At what point does a principle of law or equity displace rather than merely supplement a Code rule? Why was that point not reached in *City Dodge*? Upon what *statutory* evidence does the Georgia Supreme Court rely to conclude that fraud principles both generally and as applied to the facts of *City Dodge* were not displaced by Article 2?

2. Pay particular attention to the court's accommodation of contract and tort law. How do the two bodies of law interact? In what circumstances do they coalesce entirely? In what circumstances do they remain entirely distinct? As an attorney, when would you imagine you might prefer to prosecute a fraud action rather than an Article 2 action? Which theory would provide greater recovery? Which would provide the most obstacles to recovery?

3. The relationship between principles of fraud and misrepresentation and the

---

[42] [1] The five elements of fraud and deceit in Georgia are: (1) false representation made by the defendant; (2) scienter; (3) an intention to induce the plaintiff to act or refrain from acting in reliance by the plaintiff; (4) justifiable reliance by the plaintiff; (5) damage to the plaintiff. *See Eastern Motors Co. v. Lavender, supra*, 69 Ga. App. p. 52, 24 S.E.2d 840.

provisions of Article 2 has come under particular scrutiny in the computer software cases. *See* Mitchell-Lockyer, *Common Law Misrepresentation in Sales Cases — An Argument for Code Dominance*, 19 Forum 361 (1984). For a thorough treatment of fraud as it operates in the context of UCC § 2-721, see R. Hillman, J. McDonnell & S. Nickles, Common Law and Equity Under the Uniform Commercial Code § 9.06[2][a] (1985).

4. What rule in Article 2 might displace the fraud action in *City Dodge*? After determining that the plaintiff's fraud action was not displaced by Article 2 generally, the Court concludes that the existence of a merger clause in the agreement did not necessarily rebut the element of reliance for tort purposes. In light of this analysis, isn't there an argument that the parol evidence rule displaces this tort action? Although the parol evidence rule is probably only a vague and repressed memory from contracts class at this point, we will be covering the Article 2 parol evidence rule (§ 2-202) soon. For present purposes, recall that if the parties intend that a written memorial of their agreement serve as a complete statement of the terms of their agreement, a party is later prevented from seeking to introduce extrinsic evidence of terms not contained in the written memorial. Doesn't the parol evidence rule displace the plaintiff's attempt to prove that the car was warranted to be accident-free?

PALMER v. IDAHO PETERBILT, INC.
Idaho Court of Appeals
641 P.2d 346 (1982)

Burnett, Judge.

Richard L. Palmer sued Idaho Peterbilt, Inc. for breach of a contract to sell him a truck. The trial court awarded Palmer general damages but denied a claim for consequential damages. We affirm.

The buyer and seller in this case entered into a written contract for sale of a truck to be specially built by the manufacturer. The truck was stolen before it could be delivered to the buyer. The buyer and seller then entered into an oral contract for sale of another specially built truck. The buyer gave the seller a $500 cash deposit.

Numerous production delays ensued. The buyer became impatient, and the seller began to worry about the buyer's ability to pay for the truck. Finally, the seller's general manager sent a letter to the buyer, enclosing a refund of the deposit and stating that the relationship was terminated. The buyer accepted the money. However, several months later, he sued for damages.

I

The seller asserts that the buyer's acceptance of the refund should have been the end of the matter. The seller urges application of a host of general principles, including rescission, waiver, release, and accord and satisfaction. This case is governed by the Idaho Uniform Commercial Code ("Idaho U.C.C."). Idaho Code § 28-2-209 recognizes rescission and waiver. However, I.C. § 28-1-103 provides that existing general principles of law may only "supplement" the Idaho U.C.C. to the extent they are not displaced. General principles will not be applied where they conflict with particular provisions of the Code. *Cf. Prince v. LeVan*, 486 P.2d 959 (Alaska 1971).

By accepting the refund in this case, the buyer simply received so much of the price as he had paid. He was still entitled to his additional remedies under section 28-2-711. The general principles of rescission or waiver cannot work a contrary result.

The seller further asserts that the buyer's failure to object to the repudiation constituted rescission or waiver. We disagree for three reasons. First, comment four to I.C. § 28-2-610 states the following:

Inaction and silence by the aggrieved party may leave the matter open but it cannot be regarded as misleading the repudiating party [and] the aggrieved party is . . . free to proceed at any time with his options under this section . . . .

Second, as to rescission, I.C. § 28-2-720 provides that a rescission must be clearly intended, and that even the explicit use of the term "rescission" does not discharge a claim for damages unless there is such intent. The trial court made no finding of the requisite intent in this case. [Ed. Note: The third reason offered by the court is that there was no "waiver" of rights.] We conclude that the buyer was entitled to pursue his damage remedy under the Idaho U.C.C.

The judgment of the district court is affirmed. No costs or attorney fees on appeal.

QUESTIONS

1. Would understanding the legal realism that motivated Karl Llewellyn assist you in supporting the court's conclusions? Under baroque common law rules, parties often found that they had inadvertently waived rights or had elected remedies. Article 2 rejects such formalities generally, and the *Palmer* court taps into these currents of Article 2.

2. We will return to the question of supplementing Article 2 at various points during the course. Keep in mind that the statutory test — determining whether Article 2 has displaced the principles of law and equity on a particular point — must be informed by an understanding of the purpose of the Article 2 provision in question.

Chapter 2
CONTRACTING

A. FOUNDATIONAL TERMS AND PRINCIPLES

This book follows the organizational structure of Article 2, covering formation, terms, performance, breach and remedies. However, Article 2 employs several foundational terms and principles throughout the Code, and learning these basics up front will aid your study of the material that follows. In this section we will cover the definitions of the key terms "merchant," "unconscionability," and "good faith." You already have been introduced to the concepts of unconscionability and good faith in contract law, but the use of special rules when the transaction involves a "merchant" is new. We begin with this Article 2 concept that has deep roots in commercial practices.

1. Merchant Status

In the Middle Ages, traders from different kingdoms, states, and legal traditions created the principles of the Law Merchant to settle their differences. The Law Merchant regulated business based on the customs of the merchants themselves, as they had developed over centuries of trade, rather than according to parochial legal rules. Merchants regarded themselves as members of an emerging class that transcended national interests, and the certainty that the Law Merchant would apply regardless of the location of the deal was more beneficial to the merchants than seeking the protection of the laws of a particular country. The Law Merchant only applied to those who were merchants in their business dealings.

Karl Llewellyn viewed the Law Merchant as an important development in commercial law that should be recovered. In line with his legal realism, Llewellyn believed that commerce is best served if merchants operate in accordance with the norms of professionals in the trade, rather than in conformity with positive laws that might not be attentive to the needs of commerce. Although Llewellyn originally sought a much more prominent role for merchants in Article 2 — he even advocated the use of merchant juries to resolve disputes between merchants — the merchant rules of Article 2 represent a major development in the law. Essentially, a number of provisions in Article 2 set forth a "merchant rule" that holds merchants to different standards than nonmerchants.

Section 2-104 defines a merchant as "a person who deals in goods of the kind or otherwise by his occupation holds himself out as having knowledge or skill peculiar to the practices or goods involved in the transaction," or who employs an agent or intermediary having such knowledge or skill. Commentators generally have reorganized the language of the merchant definitions to provide clarity and to recognize that the law generally acknowledges two bases for recognizing that a party should be treated as a merchant.

Commentators use the term "goods merchant" to refer to a party who deals in goods of the kind, or by her occupation holds herself out as having knowledge or skill peculiar to the goods involved in the transaction. A person who regularly sells computers is a merchant with respect to computers, but is not a merchant with respect to bulldozers. On the other hand, some persons may have no special expertise with respect to the goods involved in the transaction, but nevertheless should be regarded as merchants with respect to the contracting practices involved. A "practices merchant" is one who by her occupation holds herself out as having particular knowledge or skill with respect to the practices involved. A person who owns a travel agency will not be a "goods merchant" with respect to office furniture that she is purchasing (because she does not deal in office furniture or have any particular knowledge or skill with respect to office furniture), but she may be deemed a "practices merchant" with respect to contracting practices in reaching an agreement for the purchase of office furniture.

Comment 2 to § 2-104 is an invaluable guide to understanding the definition of merchant. The Comment indicates that the merchant provisions in Article 2 are of three kinds: those that apply to "practices merchants," those that apply to "goods merchants," and those that apply to parties who are either goods merchants or practices merchants for the transaction. Read Comment 2 carefully to understand how these definitions must be further refined for purposes of application. The most important thing to understand is that people are not "merchants" for all purposes and all transactions: "merchant" is a functional designation, not an ontological characteristic. The definition of merchant is guided by the particular merchant provision at issue. For example, § 2-201(2) provides a special rule for satisfying the statute of frauds when the contract is "between merchants." Section 2-104, Comment 2 makes clear that a person need only be a "practices merchant" to trigger this rule, because the merchant rule rests "on normal business practices which are or ought to be typical of and familiar to any person in business." Moreover, the merchant rule would apply to a person only to the extent that she is acting in her "mercantile capacity; a lawyer or bank president buying fishing tackle for his own use is not a merchant." § 2-104, Comment 2.

Read the following case carefully, paying particular attention to the "merchant rule" involved, whether this merchant rule applies to a "goods merchant," a "practices merchant," or either type of merchant, and the corresponding language of Article 2 that articulates the applicable definition of merchant.

FERRAGAMO v. MASSACHUSETTS BAY TRANSPORTATION AUTHORITY
Massachusetts Supreme Judicial Court
481 N.E.2d 477 (1985)

Abrams, Justice.

On August 16, 1976, Michael Ferragamo died of respiratory failure after spending three weeks dismantling used trolley cars purchased by his brother, the plaintiff in this action, from the Massachusetts Bay Transportation Authority (MBTA). A jury found the defendant MBTA liable for negligence and breach of warranty resulting in the death of Michael Ferragamo. The judge granted the defendant's motion for judgment notwithstanding the verdict only with respect to those counts sounding in breach of warranty. Both parties appealed. We reverse the judgment notwithstanding the verdict on the breach of warranty claims, and affirm the judgment on the negligence claims.

The jury could have found the facts to be as follows. In June 1976, the defendant sent Paul Ferragamo an invitation to bid on eight trolley cars, no longer being used in the subway system.[1] Paul Ferragamo, as the successful bidder, signed a contract of sale which described the items purchased as "8-scrap P.C.C. Cars complete 'As is' 'Where is'." The contract further provided that "[a]ll property listed herein is offered for sale 'as is' and 'where is' and without recourse against the Authority. The Authority makes no guaranty, warranty, or representation, express or implied, as to the quantity, kind, character, quality, weight, size or description of any of the property. . . ." The purchaser was to be "solely responsible for all injuries to persons or damage to property occurring on account of, or in connection with" dismantling the cars and removing them from MBTA premises.

Car No. 3298, one of the eight cars purchased by Paul Ferragamo, had been "involved in [a] fire at the Kenmore Square M.B.T.A. station in July of 1975." The jury could have found that as a result of that fire, forty-five firemen, several passengers, and a number of MBTA employees had been treated for possible exposure to polyvinyl

---

[1] [2] The parties stipulated to the fact that "[t]he M.B.T.A. sells almost all of its M.B.T.A. trolley cars for scrap."

chloride (PVC) fumes;[2] that a chemist had determined that there was some "25.7 lbs. of PVC compound" in "the area of the fire"; and that Car No. 3298 was covered with drippings of melted plastic.

It was one year after the fire that Paul Ferragamo engaged his twenty year old brother, the decedent, to assist in dismantling the eight trolley cars at the defendant's Watertown yard. The decedent completed work on the first two cars without incident. The plaintiff and the decedent began to dismantle Car No. 3298 during the week of August 8, 1976. They first cleared the debris from the car and scraped off as much of the plastic drippings as possible, whereupon the decedent proceeded to cut through the remaining plastic with an acetylene torch. Wearing a dust mask only intermittently, the decedent cut the car from Monday through Friday in very hot weather. His voice became progressively more hoarse during the week and he experienced considerable shortness of breath and a sore throat. On the morning of August 16, 1976, the decedent was gasping for breath in his sleep. He was then taken by ambulance to the hospital where he died shortly thereafter "as a result of acute respiratory failure." On the day following his brother's death, Paul Ferragamo spoke with the MBTA foreman at the Watertown yard and told him about the death. Paul Ferragamo was then informed for the first time that "there was something wrong with that car, that there had been PVC near it or in it. . . ."

The plaintiff filed this action on July 11, 1978. The complaint embraced four counts. In Counts I and III, the plaintiff sought damages for the decedent's wrongful death and conscious suffering occurring as a result of the defendant's negligence. Counts II and IV sought damages on a theory of breach of warranty.[3] On May 6, 1983, a jury returned verdicts for the plaintiff on all four counts while finding the decedent contributorily negligent by thirty-five percent on the two negligence counts.

On May 16, 1983, the MBTA moved for judgment notwithstanding the verdicts. The judge allowed the motion as to Counts II and IV — the warranty counts — but denied the MBTA's motion as to Counts I and III — the negligence counts. He ruled "that on the facts in this case the defendant MBTA is not a 'Merchant' as the term is defined in M.G.L.A. Chap. 106, Sec. 2-104(1). Since the defendant is not a 'merchant' the provisions of M.G.L.A. Chap. 106, Sec. 2-314 do not apply and there was no implied warranty that the car in question was fit for the ordinary purpose for which it was sold." The judge further held that although "[t]he evidence on this question is slight," there was "enough to warrant a jury to find that PVC was present on or in the car; that this presence was known or should have been known to the defendant and imposed on the defendant a duty to warn of the danger involved in cutting up the car with an acetylene torch." Both parties then filed notices of appeal in the Appeals Court. We transferred the matter to this court on our own motion.

On appeal, the plaintiff argues that the MBTA is a merchant, for purposes of the implied warranty of merchantability set forth in G.L. c. 106, § 2-314(1) (1984 ed.),[4] and

---

[2] [3] According to one expert witness, polyvinyl chloride is "a material that is used widely in synthetic materials and specifically in plastics," and, which, on thermal degradation, releases hydrogen chloride gas. That gas "in high enough doses, in a high enough concentration, . . . will cause serious lung damage in practically everybody that inhales it."

[3] [4] The complaint alleged a breach of an implied warranty of merchantability and of an implied warranty of fitness for a particular purpose. The judge charged the jury on both types of warranty, but the special verdicts on Counts II and IV did not distinguish between the two. In this memorandum of decision on the defendant's motion for judgment notwithstanding the verdict, the judge stated that there was no "evidence on the part of the plaintiff that the buyer relied 'on the seller's skill or judgment to select or furnish suitable' cars." G.L. c. 106, § 2-315. The plaintiff does not challenge that ruling on this appeal.

[4] [6] General Laws c. 106, § 2-314(1), provides in relevant part: "Unless excluded or modified by section 2-316, a warranty that the goods shall be merchantable is implied in a contract for their sale if the seller is a merchant with respect to goods of that kind."

that the verdicts on the breach of warranty claims must thus be reinstated. The defendant contends that the trial court judge ruled correctly; that even if the MBTA were a merchant, the disclaimers in the contract of sale were effective; that the jury's special finding of comparative negligence ought either to bar the plaintiff's recovery for breach of warranty or to reduce that recovery by a factor proportionate to the decedent's negligence; and that, in any event, there was insufficient evidence for the jury to find that PVC was present on or in Car No. 3298 at the time Michael Ferragamo worked on it.

1. *The MBTA's status as a "merchant."* The parties do not dispute that the MBTA may not be held liable for breach of an implied warranty of merchantability under G.L. c. 106, § 2-314(1), unless the MBTA is a "merchant," within the meaning of the statute. The MBTA maintains, in essence, that because its sales of used trolley cars are "incidental" to its primary business as a matter of law, it cannot be viewed as a merchant of scrap trolley cars. We disagree.

The judge submitted the question whether "the M.B.T.A. was a merchant with respect to the sale of Car 3298" to the jury.[5] Only in his memorandum of decision on the motion for judgment notwithstanding the verdict did he rule that, as a matter of law, the MBTA was not a merchant. That ruling was incorrect.

The definition of "merchant" is set forth at G.L. c. 106, § 2-104(1) (1984 ed.):

> "Merchant" means a person who deals in goods of the kind or otherwise by his occupation holds himself out as having knowledge or skill peculiar to the practices or goods involved in the transaction or to whom such knowledge or skill may be attributed by his employment of an agent or broker or other intermediary who by his occupation holds himself out as having such knowledge or skill.

Further, a warranty of merchantability under G.L. c. 106, § 2-314, is implied only "if the seller is a merchant with respect to goods of that kind." "Obviously this qualification restricts the implied warranty to a much smaller group than everyone who is engaged in business and requires a professional status as to particular kinds of goods." G.L. c. 106, § 2-104 comment 2, at 190 (Law. Coop. 1984).

Thus, the dual requirements of G.L. c. 106, §§ 2-104(1) and 2-314, lead us to ask whether there was evidence that the MBTA "regularly deals in goods of the kind involved or otherwise has a professional status with regard to the goods involved such that [it] could be expected to have specialized knowledge or skill peculiar to those goods." *Cropper v. Rego Distribution Center, Inc.*, 542 F. Supp. 1142, 1154 (D. Del. 1982). Moreover, that inquiry "is of necessity highly dependent on the factual setting of the transaction in question. Consequently, whether a person is a merchant is to be determined according to the circumstances of each case." 1 R.A. Anderson, *Uniform Commercial Code* § 2-104:25 (3d ed. 1981). Particularly with respect to the seller of used equipment is such a determination contingent on the factual background. *See id.* at §§ 2-104:29 – 2-104:45. We conclude that the instant circumstances warranted the jury's determination that the MBTA is a merchant with respect to its sales of used trolley cars.

The jurors could have found the following facts: First, the MBTA stipulated that it "sells almost all of its old M.B.T.A. trolley cars for scrap." Second, the MBTA had solicited a bid from the plaintiff, among others, on the eight trolley cars to be sold. Third, the eight trolley cars were purchased by the MBTA in 1951 and were operated and repaired by MBTA employees for approximately twenty-five years. Fourth, MBTA

---

[5] [7] The judge approached the question of the MBTA's merchant status as a mixed question of law and fact, and we review the question on that basis. We leave open the possibility that, in other circumstances, the determination of merchant status might constitute solely an issue of law. *See, e.g.*, County of Milwaukee v. Northrop Data Sys., Inc., 602 F.2d 767, 771 (7th Cir. 1979); Cudahy Foods Co. v. Holloway, 55 N.C. App. 626, 629, 286 S.E.2d 606 (1982); Nelson v. Union Equity Coop. Exch., 548 S.W.2d 352, 354 (Tex. 1977). *See generally* 1 R.A. Anderson, *Uniform Commercial Code* § 2-104:12 (3d ed. 1981).

agents had originally designed the cars which were then built to their specifications.

This concatenation of facts and reasonable inferences drawn from them permitted the jury to find that the MBTA is a merchant with respect to used trolley cars. "The term 'merchant' . . . roots in the 'law merchant' concept of a professional in business. The professional status under the definition may be based upon specialized knowledge as to the goods. . . ." G.L. c. 106, § 2-104, comment 2, at 189 (Law. Coop. 1984). "Professionalism, special knowledge and commercial experience are to be used in determining whether a person in a particular situation is to be held to the standards of a merchant." *Decatur Coop. Ass'n v. Urban*, 219 Kan. 171, 176–77, 547 P.2d 323 (1976). "[T]he test is whether a person is so experienced and knowledgeable under the circumstances that he should be charged with the more substantial burden imposed upon a merchant" (citations omitted). *Sea Harvest, Inc. v. Rig & Crane Equip. Corp.*, 181 N.J. Super. 41, 48, 436 A.2d 553 (1981).

Here, the MBTA was highly "experienced and knowledgeable" with respect to the goods involved. The MBTA had, through its employees, a long-term and thorough acquaintance with the cars sold to the plaintiff: MBTA employees had contributed to the manufacture of the cars,[6] had operated, repaired, refurbished, and maintained them for twenty-five years.[7] The MBTA asserts that it cannot be a merchant because its principal business is solely the "operation of a mass transportation system" — not the sale of scrap. But while the MBTA may not be a merchant of scrap, there was sufficient evidence to conclude that it was a merchant of used trolley cars. Its supervision of a mass transit system implies professional expertise with respect to the medium of transit, namely trolley cars.[8] Indeed, by virtue of its very assertion that its business is the

---

[6] [8] One employee of the MBTA testified as follows:

Q: "And are you familiar with the cars known as Presidential Conference Committee Cars?"

A: "Somewhat."

Q: "And did you have an (sic) responsibility for the procurement, purchase, of those cars in the early fifties?"

A: "I was involved in the general design. We had a team at that time. We have a group, a team, and I was one of that group."

Q: "And did you prepare some sort of design drawings for the Presidential Conference Cars?"

A: "Yes."

Q: "Would you, for the jury's benefit, would you give them a bit of history of the M.B.T.A.'s acquisition of the PCC cars in the late forties and early fifties?"

A: "Well, the cars that we were operating were quite old, and we saw fit to make us update our system, and that's what we did. We prepared specifications, and we proceeded to have people build the cars."

[7] [9] Another employee of the MBTA testified as follows:

Q: "Can you tell me what your responsibilities have been over the last 15 or 20 years on the T?"

A: "I've been working on the old streetcars, what we call the PCC's for the past 20 years."

Q: "And can you give the jury an explanation of the kinds of things that were done to these — to this car, as well as the others in that series, over the period of time since they were bought by the T?"

A: "Well, one of the major overhauls began in 1961 after they were ten years old. They were taken to our Everette shops for overhauling, reconditioning. They painted the exterior and interior on them. Laid new tile, rubber tile flooring, wall to wall, and at a later date, they started installing the fiberglass seats in them. They overhauled the electrical and air components on those cars, installed new motors, new wheels, and then they were returned to our reservoir car house where I was inspector foreman."

[8] [10] The MBTA cites several cases for the proposition that incidental sales of used equipment do not place the seller in the position of a merchant under G.L. c. 106, § 2-314(1). *See, e.g.*, Bruce v. Martin-Marietta Corp., 544 F.2d 442 (10th Cir. 1976) (airline not a merchant in isolated sale of a used aircraft which it neither designed, manufactured, nor altered); Joyce v. Combank/Longwood, 405 So. 2d 1358 (Fla. Dist. Ct. App. 1981) (bank making occasional sales of repossessed automobiles not a merchant); Allen v. Nicole, Inc., 172 N.J.

"operation of a mass transportation system," the MBTA "by [its] occupation holds [itself] out as having knowledge or skill peculiar to the . . . goods involved in the transaction." G.L. c. 106, § 2-104(1). *See* 1 R.A. Anderson, *supra*, § 2-104:17.

The MBTA next maintains that "[t]he fact that [it] occasionally sells its old trolley cars for scrap does not render the MBTA a merchant of scrap goods." But "the fact that a person is not in the business of buying and selling a particular kind of goods does not mean that he is not a merchant with respect to such goods." 1 R.A. Anderson, *supra*, at § 2-104:14. The only apparent *sine qua non* of merchant status under G.L. c.106, § 2-314(1), is that the sale at issue not be "an isolated sale of goods." G.L. c. 106, § 2-314, comment 3, at 466 (Law. Coop. 1984). It appears from the record that the MBTA sold off its discarded cars; and, although the record does not reflect the number of occasions on which those cars were sold, the jurors could have inferred that the instant sale was not an isolated transaction. Thus, the sporadicity of sales does not vitiate the jurors' conclusion that the MBTA is a merchant. Because the MBTA possessed specialized knowledge of trolley cars, and because the transaction was not an isolated sale, we conclude that the jury could determine that the MBTA was a merchant with respect to used trolley cars.

* * *

QUESTIONS

1. Does the *Ferragamo* case properly apply the definition of merchant to the MBTA? Does the merchant provision in question (§ 2-314) call for a "goods merchant" or a "practices merchant"?

2. How does the court frame the test of merchant status it utilizes? *Ferragamo*'s analysis reinforces the flexible character of the definition of merchant. Is this approach to defining merchant too flexible? Does the concept of "professionalism" posited in the *Ferragamo* case provide some certainty in the application of the definition? Does the concept of "mercantile capacity"?

3. Note that CISG art. 35 includes warranty provisions similar to § 2-314, but the CISG does not distinguish between "merchants" and non-merchant parties. Does this mean that the scope of the CISG implied warranty of merchantability is broader than that of Article 2, that a definition of merchant is implied in the CISG, or that the drafters simply assumed that only merchants would be engaged in international sales?

PROBLEM 2-1

Sven Haanson cultivates extra-large and specialized strawberries on a small farm that has been in his family for 90 years. He sells his gourmet strawberries for premium prices through two produce wholesalers. Sven has worked on this farm for his entire life (he is now 68). He did not attend school past the eighth grade, and he has only rudimentary literacy skills. He has never signed the paperwork mailed to him by the wholesalers, but instead has relied on his oral agreements with them. He has never hired an attorney, although he does hire a local accountant to prepare his tax forms. Analyze the factual inquiry that you would undertake to determine if Sven should be considered a merchant under the following scenarios.

First Scenario: One of the wholesalers who purchases strawberries from Sven sues him, alleging that the most recent delivery of strawberries is unmerchantable under § 2-314, and cannot be resold.

Second Scenario: Sven is sued by one of the wholesalers when he allegedly breaches

---

Super. 442, 412 A.2d 824 (1980) (seller of amusement ride not a merchant where he lacked specialized knowledge or skill peculiar to goods involved). In each of these cases, the seller lacked the professional expertise with respect to the goods sold, which the MBTA possesses in the instant circumstances.

an agreement to sell strawberries in order to secure a higher price from the other wholesaler. Sven hires an attorney, who asserts the statute of frauds as a defense because Sven has not signed any paperwork relating to the alleged contract. In response, the wholesaler asserts the "confirmatory memorandum exception" to the statute of frauds provision in § 2-201(2), which only applies to agreements "between merchants."

Third Scenario: Sven decides to sell his farm because his children are not interested in the farming life. Sven sells all the assets of his farming business to Belinda, including the real estate, fixtures, and farming equipment. Seven months later, Belinda is severely injured when the tractor that she acquired as part of the asset sale flips over suddenly. Belinda sues Sven for breach of the warranty of merchantability under § 2-314.

2. Unconscionability

Section 2-302 is a rare "policing" provision in Article 2. It empowers courts to openly refuse to enforce "unconscionable" terms. Llewellyn believed that commercial interests would be served if a judge invalidated oppressive and unfairly secured terms directly and then honestly explained the basis for her decision. All too often at common law, Llewellyn believed, judges twisted doctrinal rules and massaged the facts of the case to reach a just result. The question is whether § 2-302 introduces uncertainty into Article 2, or whether it provides courts with a better means to effect results consistent with the expectations and needs of commerce. Reasonable legal scholars have differed in their assessment. The answer to this question probably depends on one's belief about the possibility of applying unconscionability analysis with consistency. What is unconscionability, and how can judges determine whether a term is unconscionable? The concept does not permit certain formulation, but does it provide sufficient guidance to permit consistent application? Comment 1 provides additional details for structuring an analysis of unconscionability; is this enough?

First, "outline" the elements of unconscionability as described in Comment 1, and then read the following cases. The first case involves the more typical application of the doctrine to a consumer sale. The second case and Problem 2-2 raise the more difficult question of when, if ever, courts should use unconscionability to police contracts between commercial parties.

TAYLOR v. BUTLER
Tennessee Supreme Court
142 S.W.3d 277 (2004)

Wᴉʟʟɪᴀᴍ M. Bᴀʀᴋᴇʀ, J.

We granted permission to appeal in this case to determine whether a claim for fraudulent inducement to a contract must be submitted to arbitration when the contract's arbitration clause covers "all claims, demands, disputes or controversies" and states that it is governed by the Federal Arbitration Act ("FAA"). We hold that parties may agree to arbitrate claims of fraudulent inducement despite prohibition of arbitration of such claims under Tennessee law, and because the parties in this case specifically agreed that the FAA governs the arbitration clause, they agreed to arbitrate the claim for fraudulent inducement of the contract. However, we also find that the arbitration clause in this case is unconscionable and therefore void because it reserves the right to a judicial forum for the defendants while requiring the plaintiff to submit all claims to arbitration. For these reasons, the trial court's dismissal of the complaint is overruled, and the decision of the Court of Appeals is affirmed.

FACTUAL BACKGROUND

On June 4, 1998, Sharon Taylor ("Taylor") purchased a car from City Auto Sales ("City Auto"). The parties signed a contract entitled "As Is Used Vehicle Retail Buyers Order" ("Buyers Order"). The Buyers Order provided that the total cost of the vehicle was $10,058.00. Taylor was to make a cash down payment to City Auto in the amount of $1,310.00 and finance the remainder. The Buyers Order contained an arbitration provision which stated that "all claims, demands, disputes or controversies of every kind or nature between [the parties] arising from the [sale of the vehicle] shall be settled by binding arbitration conducted pursuant to the provisions of the Federal Arbitration Act, 9 U.S.C. Section 12 et seq."

Taylor sold her car for $1,000.00 and used the proceeds therefrom as part of her down payment; she then signed a short-term promissory note agreeing to pay the remainder of the down payment over the following three months. City Auto delivered the vehicle to Taylor on the day the Buyers Order was signed. Taylor claims that City Auto told her at the time of delivery that her long-term financing had been approved. It is undisputed, however, that at the time of delivery, Taylor signed a separate "Spot Delivery Agreement." This agreement stated that City Auto was giving Taylor immediate possession of the car "pending the purchase of the installment sale agreement by a financing institution." The agreement also provided that, if proper financing could not be obtained within three days, City Auto would have the option to "immediately rescind the sale." Additionally, in the event that Taylor did not immediately return the vehicle, City Auto would "have the right to take immediate possession of the vehicle."

Approximately one week after the sale, City Auto notified Taylor that her application for financing had not been approved. When Taylor did not return the vehicle, City Auto repossessed the car along with personal items belonging to Taylor that were inside the vehicle at that time. City Auto retained possession of Taylor's personal belongings along with the $1,000.00 down payment.

Taylor filed suit against City Auto alleging a violation of the Tennessee Consumer Protection Act ("TCPA"), arguing that City Auto improperly obtained her $1,000.00 down payment and her personal property that was in the car by using deceptive tactics in violation of the TCPA. Taylor also alleged that she was told that the Spot Delivery Agreement was "simply a formality and did not change the fact that she had already been approved for financing" on the sale of the car. City Auto responded by filing a motion to dismiss.

The trial court granted City Auto's motion to dismiss the complaint, holding that Taylor was bound by the arbitration provision in the Buyers Order. The Court of Appeals reversed the trial court, holding that a plaintiff cannot be compelled to arbitrate a claim pursuant to an arbitration provision that was fraudulently induced.

We granted City Auto's application to appeal to determine whether parties can be bound to arbitrate a claim for fraudulent inducement when the arbitration clause specifically states that it is governed by the FAA. On appeal, Taylor also raises the issue of whether the arbitration agreement is unconscionable because it reserves for City Auto the right to pursue judicial remedies while limiting Taylor to arbitration.

ANALYSIS

I. Arbitration of Claim for Fraudulent Inducement

[Ed. note: The court held that Taylor was obligated under the FAA to arbitrate her claim that the contract was fraudulently induced.]

II. Was the Arbitration Provision Unconscionable?

Taylor also argues that the arbitration agreement is void because it is unconscionable. She maintains that even if the contract was not induced by fraud, the terms of the arbitration provision are unconscionable because the contract reserves for City Auto the right to litigate claims it may have against Taylor while requiring Taylor to submit any of her claims to arbitration.

A. Who Determines Whether the Arbitration Clause Is Unconscionable?

[Ed. note: The court held that the FAA provides that claims that specifically attack the formation of the arbitration provision of a contract are to be judicially determined.]

B. Is the Arbitration Provision in the Contract Unconscionable?

In her brief on appeal, Taylor focuses on the following provision contained in the arbitration agreement of the Buyers Order: "Dealer, however may pursue recovery of the vehicle under the Tennessee Uniform Commercial Code and Collection of Debt due by state court action." Taylor asserts that this provision renders the contract unconscionable because City Auto has retained for itself legal remedies beyond arbitration while restricting Taylor to those remedies available under the Federal Arbitration Act.

The question of whether a contract or provision thereof is unconscionable is a question of law. *See Lewis Refrigeration Co. v. Sawyer Fruit, Vegetable & Cold Storage Co.*, 709 F.2d 427, 435 n.12 (6th Cir. 1983).

If a contract or term thereof is unconscionable at the time the contract is made, a court may refuse to enforce the contract, or may enforce the remainder of the contract without the unconscionable term. *See Restatement (Second) of Contracts* § 208 (1981). "The determination that a contract or term is or is not unconscionable is made in the light of its setting, purpose and effect. Relevant factors include weaknesses in the contracting process like those involved in more specific rules as to contractual capacity, fraud, and other invalidating causes. . . ." *Restatement (Second) of Contract* § 208, cmt. a (1981).

Enforcement of a contract is generally refused on grounds of unconscionability where the "inequality of the bargain is so manifest as to shock the judgment of a person of common sense, and where the terms are so oppressive that no reasonable person would make them on the one hand, and no honest and fair person would accept them on the other." *Haun v. King*, 690 S.W.2d 869, 872 (Tenn. Ct. App. 1984) (quoting *In re Friedman*, 64 A.D.2d 70, 407 N.Y.S.2d 999 (1978)); *see also Aquascene, Inc. v. Noritsu Am. Corp.*, 831 F. Supp. 602 (M.D. Tenn. 1993). An unconscionable contract is one in which the provisions are so one-sided, in view of all the facts and circumstances, that the contracting party is denied any opportunity for meaningful choice. *Id.*

While Tennessee has yet to address the issue of whether an arbitration provision in a consumer contract which reserves a right to access to the courts only for the merchant and not the consumer is voidable on the basis of unconscionability, a number of other jurisdictions have addressed such one-sided arbitration provisions.

For example, the Supreme Court of West Virginia held that:

> [W]here an arbitration agreement entered into as part of a consumer loan transaction contains a substantial waiver of the borrower's rights, including access to the courts, while preserving the lender's right to a judicial forum, the agreement is unconscionable and, therefore, void and unenforceable as a matter of law.

Arnold v. United Cos. Lending Corp., 204 W. Va. 229, 511 S.E.2d 854, 862 (1998).

The Court in *Arnold* stated that "[a] determination of unconscionability must focus on the relative positions of the parties, the adequacy of the bargaining position, the meaningful alternatives available to the plaintiff, and 'the existence of unfair terms in the contract.' " *Id.* at 861 (quoting *Art's Flower Shop, Inc. v. Chesapeake & Potomac Tel. Co.*, 186 W. Va. 613, 413 S.E.2d 670 (1991)). Applying this test, the Court noted that "the relative positions of the parties, a national corporate lender on one side and elderly, unsophisticated consumers on the other, were 'grossly unequal.' " *Id.* (footnote omitted). Additionally, there was "no evidence that the loan broker made any other loan option available to the Arnolds." Finally, the Court found that "the terms of the agreement are 'unreasonably favorable' to United Lending." Based on these reasons, the Court found the arbitration agreement to be unconscionable.

Similarly, the Montana Supreme Court voided as unconscionable an arbitration provision contained in a contract for advertisement in a telephone directory that reserved the right to a judicial forum for the Publisher for collection of amounts due while limiting the consumer to arbitration of all claims. *Iwen v. United States West Direct*, 293 Mont. 512, 977 P.2d 989 (1999). The Montana Court held:

> [T]his case presents a clear example of an arbitration provision that lacks mutuality of obligation, is one-sided, and contains terms that are unreasonably favorable to the drafter. Because U.S. Direct presented this agreement on a take-it-or-leave-it basis, it is also a contract in which there was not meaningful choice on the part of the weaker bargaining party regarding acceptance of the provisions. . . . [D]isparities in the rights of the contracting parties must not be so one-sided and unreasonably favorable to the drafter, as they are in this case, that the agreement becomes unconscionable and oppressive.

Id. at 996; *see also Williams v. Aetna Fin. Co.*, 83 Ohio St. 3d 464, 700 N.E.2d 859 (1998), *cert. denied*, 526 U.S. 1051, 119 S. Ct. 1357, 143 L. Ed. 2d 518 (1999) (refusing to enforce an arbitration clause in a consumer loan contract which preserved for the finance company the judicial remedy of foreclosure on the debtor's mortgage but restricted the debtor's remedies solely to arbitration); *Lytle v. CitiFinancial Servs., Inc.*, 810 A.2d 643 (Pa. Super. Ct. 2002) (finding unenforceable an arbitration agreement that reserved access to the courts for CitiFinancial, absent "business realities" that would *compel* such a clause); *Showmethemoney Check Cashers, Inc. v. Williams*, 342 Ark. 112, 27 S.W.3d 361 (2000) (finding that the arbitration agreement lacked mutuality because it provided for a judicial forum for one party while restricting the other party to arbitration).[9]

The arbitration agreement in this case is comparable to those that were found to be unconscionable in the aforementioned cases. City Auto has a judicial forum for practically all claims that it could have against Taylor. Indeed, it is hard to imagine what other claims it would have against her other than one to recover the vehicle or collect a debt. At the same time, Taylor is required to arbitrate any claim that she might have against City Auto.

The contract signed between Taylor and City Auto is one of adhesion, in that it is a standardized contract form that was offered on essentially a "take it or leave it" basis without affording Taylor a realistic opportunity to bargain. *See* Black's Law Dictionary 40 (6th ed. 1990). We have previously determined that enforceability of contracts of adhesion generally depends upon whether the terms of the contract are beyond the reasonable expectations of an ordinary person, or oppressive or unconscionable. *See*

---

[9] [4] A minority of courts reach the opposite conclusion, holding that agreements to arbitrate which reserve certain judicial remedies to one party are not unconscionable. *See e.g.*, Stout v. J.D. Byrider, 228 F.3d 709 (6th Cir. 2000) (upholding an arbitration agreement which exempted from arbitration disputes regarding buyer's failure to pay because buyer failed to show the agreement to be one of adhesion or sufficiently one-sided as to be unconscionable); Conseco Fin. Serv. Corp. v. Wilder, 47 S.W.3d 335 (Ky. Ct. App. 2001) (holding that the arbitration agreement was not unconscionable even thought it allowed the lender to pursue judicial enforcement of the security agreement). We find the majority view to be more persuasive.

Buraczynski v. Eyring, 919 S.W.2d 314, 320 (Tenn. 1996). Courts will not enforce adhesion contracts which are oppressive to the weaker party or which serve to limit the obligations and liability of the stronger party. *Id.* Looking at the arbitration agreement in the present case, it is clear that it is unreasonably favorable to City Auto and oppressive to Taylor.

For these reasons, we find the arbitration clause in the Buyers Order to be invalid and unenforceable.

Generally, a void agreement to arbitrate, incorporated in a general contract, is treated as a separate contract. 4 Am. Jur. *Alternative Dispute Resolution* § 77 (Supp. 2002). If the agreement is not a part of the substance of the general contract, pertains to the remedy only, and is collateral to the contractual matters, it is severable from the main body of the contract. *Id.* In Tennessee, "[a]n agreement can be either an entire contract or a severable contract according to the intention of the parties, and the fact that divisible parts are included within the same document does not preclude them from being considered and enforced as separate contracts." *Penske Truck Leasing Co. v. Huddleston*, 795 S.W.2d 669, 671 (Tenn. 1990).

Because the arbitration provision in the Buyers Order only relates to remedy and is collateral to all other contract matters, we find that it is severable from the remaining portions of the contract.

CONCLUSION

In summary, we hold that a claim for fraudulent inducement was subject to arbitration in this case because the parties agreed in the Buyers Order to be governed by the FAA, and the FAA provides for arbitration of claims for fraud. However, we also find that the arbitration clause in the Buyers Order is unconscionable and therefore void because it reserves the right to a judicial forum for City Auto while requiring Taylor to submit all claims to arbitration. For these reasons, the decision of the Court of Appeals to overrule the trial court's dismissal of the complaint is affirmed, and the case is remanded to the trial court for further proceedings consistent with this opinion.

Costs of this appeal are assessed to City Auto Sales.

Janice M. Holder, J., concurring in part and dissenting in part.

I concur in the majority's holding that Taylor's claim for fraudulent inducement of the contract must be submitted to arbitration because the contract's arbitration provision covers "all claims, demands, disputes or controversies" and specifically states that it is governed by the Federal Arbitration Act. I write separately, however, because I disagree with the majority's decision to address the issue of unconscionability and with its conclusion that the arbitration provision in this case is unconscionable.

Unconscionability was not alleged in the pleadings, was not tried, and was not raised in the Court of Appeals. This line of argument appears for the first time in Taylor's brief to this Court. Therefore, I would hold that the issue was waived.

Moreover, even if the issue of unconscionability had not been waived, I disagree with the majority's conclusion that the arbitration provision in this case is unconscionable. The contract requires Taylor to arbitrate all of her claims against City Auto, while providing that: "Dealer, however may pursue recovery of the vehicle under the Tennessee Uniform Commercial Code and Collection of Debt due by state court action." The majority concludes that this arbitration agreement is unreasonably favorable to City Auto and oppressive to Taylor. I am not persuaded by the majority's analysis.

In my view, the mere fact that there are different forums available to the parties in this case does not make the arbitration provision unconscionable. Other jurisdictions have held that an arbitration provision granting one party the option to litigate its claims while binding the other party to arbitrate all of its claims is not unconscionable. *See, e.g., Harris v. Green Tree Fin. Corp.*, 183 F.3d 173, 183 (3d Cir. 1999); *Pate v. Melvin*

Williams Manufactured Homes, Inc. (In re Pate), 198 B.R. 841, 844 (Bankr. S.D. Ga. 1996); *Ex parte McNaughton*, 728 So. 2d 592, 599 (Ala. 1998); *Conseco Fin. Servicing Corp. v. Wilder*, 47 S.W.3d 335, 343–44 (Ky. Ct. App. 2001). A contract is unconscionable where the "inequality of the bargain is so manifest as to shock the judgment of a person of common sense, and where the terms are so oppressive that no reasonable person would make them on the one hand, and no honest and fair person would accept them on the other." *Haun v. King*, 690 S.W.2d 869, 872 (Tenn. Ct. App. 1984) (quoting *Brenner v. Little Red Sch. House, Ltd.*, 302 N.C. 207, 274 S.E.2d 206, 210 (1981)). Although the arbitration agreement requires Taylor to arbitrate all of her claims while providing a judicial forum to City Auto for certain claims, in my opinion this lack of symmetry does not rise to the level of being shocking or unfairly oppressive. Instead, it is not unreasonable for Taylor to agree to forego arbitration of a claim, such as the recovery of a vehicle, that can be decided expeditiously in a judicial forum. *See Conseco Fin. Servicing Corp.*, 47 S.W.3d at 343. Furthermore, there is no basis to presume that arbitration will not afford Taylor an adequate opportunity to present her claims. *See id.* at 344. I am of the opinion that the arbitration provision at issue should be enforced according to its terms. Therefore, I would affirm the trial court's dismissal of Taylor's complaint.

QUESTIONS

1. This case involved a contract for the sale of an automobile. Why didn't the court apply § 2-302, since the contract is within the scope of Article 2?

2. Generally speaking, the modern doctrine of unconscionability in the common law tracks § 2-302, as evidenced by the court's quotation from Restatement (Second) of Contracts § 208. If the court had applied § 2-302 to this case, would the result have been the same? Use the language of § 2-302 and the Official Comments to analyze the case.

BOSTON HELICOPTER CHARTER, INC. v. AGUSTA AVIATION CORPORATION
United States District Court, District of Massachusetts
767 F. Supp. 363 (1991)

MEMORANDUM

CAFFREY, Senior District Judge.

This action arises out of the sale, resale, and eventual crash of an Agusta A109 helicopter.

Defendant Costruzioni Aeronautiche Giovanni Agusta S.p.A. ("CAGA") is the Italian manufacturer of the helicopter, and defendant Agusta Aviation Corporation ("AAC") is its subsidiary responsible for marketing, distribution and support of CAGA products in North America. AAC sold the helicopter to co-defendant Hydroplanes, Inc., who in turn sold it to the plaintiff, Boston Helicopter Charter, Inc. ("Boston Helicopter"). Boston Helicopter and the individuals injured in the accident filed this action against all three defendants. . . .

I.

The following facts are undisputed, except where otherwise indicated. Defendant AAC sold the A109 helicopter to Hydroplanes on May 4, 1984 for $1,000,000.00. Hydroplanes did not take delivery of the helicopter until July 26, 1984. The purchase agreement between AAC and Hydroplanes contained the following warranty:

6. Warranty

a. New Equipment. The Equipment is purchased subject to Seller's standard warranty which is as follows: Seller hereby warrants to the original purchaser only each new helicopter and part thereof sold by Seller to be free from defects in material and workmanship under normal use and service, Seller's obligation under this warranty being limited to replacing or repairing such part at its designated place of business, with the charges payable by Purchaser for such repair or replacement to be prorated for hours of use against the established life of the part or 2,000 hours, whichever is the lesser (with no charges being payable to Purchaser in the event of repair or replacement within the first 500 hours of use), provided that such part shall have been returned to Seller's designated place of business, with transportation charges prepaid, within 1,000 hours of operation or one year, whichever shall first occur, after delivery of such part to the original purchaser, and provided further that Seller's examination shall disclose, to Seller's satisfaction, such part to have been defective. THIS WARRANTY IS GIVEN EXPRESSLY AND IN PLACE OF ALL OTHER EXPRESS OR IMPLIED WARRANTIES, INCLUDING MERCHANTABILITY AND FITNESS FOR A PARTICULAR PURPOSE, AND THIS WARRANTY IS THE ONLY WARRANTY MADE BY SELLER OR THE AGUSTA GROUP. The obligations of Seller under this warranty are limited to the repair of helicopter parts as provided herein and liability is excluded for incidental or consequential damages, including without limitation, damage to the helicopter or other property, and costs of expenses for commercial losses or lost profits due to loss of use of grounding of the helicopter or otherwise.

The 500 hour period for free replacement was substituted by the parties in lieu of a standard 200 hour provision. Moreover, the agreement between AAC and Hydroplanes provided that the warranty was transferrable.

More than one year later, on October 31, 1985, Hydroplanes entered into a purchase and sale agreement through which it agreed to sell the helicopter to the plaintiff, Boston Helicopter, for approximately $875,000.00. Paragraph 14I of the purchase and sale agreement between Hydroplanes and plaintiff provided for the transfer of the warranty to plaintiff.

*   *   *

The accident took place on January 13, 1987, when the helicopter had a total operation time of 566.8 hours. According to the factual report of the National Transportation Safety Board, the helicopter experienced a tail rotor blade failure shortly after liftoff from the helipad while hovering at twenty-five feet. The rotor blade that failed had a certified expected life of 1,400 hours. A certified expected life refers to the period of time that the certifying authorities permit the part to remain in use. (See Plaintiff's Exhibit L, Deposition of Paolo Ferreri at 115). The pilot attempted to set the helicopter down on the helipad, but made a hard landing. According to an estimate prepared by the defendants, it would cost $1,015,447.90 to repair the helicopter.

II.

[Ed. Note: The Court first ruled that the warranty expired at the earlier of 1,000 hours of operating time or one year after delivery to the original purchaser, and therefore that the warranty had expired prior to the crash. The plaintiff, Boston Helicopter Charter, Inc. then argued that the one year limitation was unconscionable and should not be enforced.]

The issue therefore is whether the durational limitation is unconscionable under Mass. Gen. L. Ann. ch. 106, § 2-302. *Hart Eng'g Co.*, 593 F. Supp. at 1480; *Clark*, 99 Idaho 326, 581 P.2d at 803. This question must be answered by the Court as a matter of law. *Zapatha v. Dairy Mart, Inc.*, 381 Mass. 284, 291, 408 N.E.2d 1370 (1980). Massachusetts has adopted a case by case approach to determining whether a given term is unconscionable. *Id.* at 292–93, 408 N.E.2d 1370. A court will declare a contract unconscionable in order to prevent oppression or unfair surprise. Mass. Gen. L. Ann. ch. 106, § 2-302 comment 1 (West 1990); *Zapatha*, 381 Mass. at 292, 408 N.E.2d 1370. The relevant consideration is the circumstances at the time the contract was made, and not the circumstances as they later developed. *Zapatha*, 381 Mass. at 291, 408 N.E.2d 1370. Significantly, however, the doctrine of unconscionability is not typically applied to commercial dealings between business entities, but has been invoked more often in consumer transactions. 2 W. Hawkland, *Uniform Commercial Code Series* § 2-302:06 (1984).

Against this background, it cannot be said that the durational limitation of the repair-or-replace warranty was unconscionable. First, the commercial, as opposed to consumer, setting is significant, as is the fact that Boston Helicopter, a business entity, was represented by counsel when it purchased the Agusta helicopter. (See Affidavit of Gary P. Lilienthal, Esq.). Likewise, plaintiff specifically negotiated the transfer of the warranty to it, suggesting that plaintiff was not the uninformed buyer that section 2-302 seeks to protect against unfair surprise. Second, plaintiff has not even argued that the limitation was unreasonable, or that the helicopter when originally sold had a latent defect; plaintiff has merely suggested that the fracture in the tail rotor blade began to develop within the warranty period. Certainly, one could find that most product failures secretly began within the warranty period. Third, it is significant that paragraph 6a, in disclaiming consequential and incidental damages, specifically mentioned "damage to helicopter" as not being recoverable. This explicit statement concerning the possibility that a defective part could damage the helicopter cuts against any argument that there has been any "unfair surprise." Similarly, defendants' warranty guide, in demonstrating how the proration formula would work, gives the following example: "Suppose that a tail rotor blade, whose cost is approximately $1,200.00 and retirement life is 1200 hours has failed after 400 hours of operation, the recognized credit would be. . . ." (Plaintiff's Exhibit Q, Guide to Commercial Warranty, para. 9). The possibility of a failure of the tail rotor blade was, therefore, not an "unfair surprise." Plaintiff would have this Court find such terms inapplicable and unconscionable due to plaintiff's failure to obtain a copy of the warranty. As will be discussed in more depth below, the fact that plaintiff did not obtain a copy of the warranty has no bearing on the applicability of its terms to plaintiff nor on the reasonableness of the limitation period.

There are other factors weighing against a finding of unconscionability. The period of 1,000 flight hours or one year, is ample, and typical of time limits upheld in other cases involving aircrafts. See, e.g., *Damin Aviation Corp. v. Sikorsky Aircraft, Div. of United Technologies Corp.*, 705 F. Supp. 170, 172 (S.D.N.Y.) (1,000 hours or 2 years), *aff'd*, 880 F.2d 1318 (2d Cir. 1989); Tokio Marine & Fire Ins., 617 F.2d at 941 (one year or 2,500 hours); *cf. Hart Eng'g Co.*, 593 F. Supp. at 1480 ("the durational restriction that Hart challenges does not span a mere matter of days."). Finally, this is not a case where "because of the seller's willful and dilatory disregard of its contractual obligations, fairly [cries] out for judicial intervention." Hart Eng'g Co., 593 F. Supp. at 1480. From all of the material presented to this Court, it appears that the defendants were forthright and prompt in fulfilling their warranty obligation, honoring more than thirty claims during the life of the warranty. The durational limitation is simply not unconscionable, but is a wise business practice of risk allocation.

NOTE

The Court emphasizes that "commercial" contracts, as opposed to "consumer" contracts, are unlikely to be found to have unconscionable terms. *See also, Citizens Ins. Co. v. Proctor & Schwartz, Inc.*, 802 F. Supp. 133, 145 (W.D. Mich. 1992) (unconscionability "is rarely found to exist in a commercial setting. Citizens has failed to show that this case presents the requisite extraordinary circumstances"). Judge Posner expressed this attitude by issuing (in dictum) a warning to corporations: "But for future reference we remind Northrup and companies like it that the defense of unconscionability was not invented to protect multi-billion dollar corporations against mistakes committed by their employees, and indeed has rarely succeeded outside the area of consumer contracts." *Northrup Corp. v. Litronic, Ltd.*, 29 F.3d 1173, 1179–80 (7th Cir. 1994) (Posner, J.). Does this judicial approach make sense? Should commercial parties ever be able to claim that they agreed to an unconscionable term?

<h3 style="text-align:center">PROBLEM 2-2</h3>

Best Look, Inc. is a multi-store clothing retailer headquartered in Grand Rapids, Michigan. Sure Sport, Ltd. is a manufacturer and distributor of women's clothing based in New York. On June 10, Best Look submitted a Purchase Order to Sure Sport, Ltd. for 5,000 items of women's holiday clothing to be delivered on October 10 for a price of $200,000. Sure Sport confirmed by telephone that it would manufacture the ordered garments and ship them on the indicated date, but there was no discussion of additional terms of their deal. Sure Spot signed and returned the Purchase Order. The Purchase Order contained the following clause printed on the back side of the form:

> Buyer reserves the right to terminate by notice to Seller all or any part of this Purchase Order with respect to Goods that have not actually been shipped by Seller or as to Goods which are not timely delivered for any reason whatsoever.

Best Look cancelled its order on September 28, without any prior warning. Best Look had been contacted by another manufacturer with excess inventory that was willing to sell holiday clothing at the manufacturing cost. Sure Sport protested vehemently, arguing that it was too late for Best Look to cancel the order because Sure Sport is unable to sell the garments for a reasonable price at this late date. Ultimately, Best Look agreed to purchase the clothes for $100,000.

Sure Sport is a small business; the seasonal order from Best Look comprised 25% of its business for the year. Additionally, Best Look has annual sales approximately twenty times the annual sales of Sure Sport. Sure Sport's president never read the clause in question, and would not have agreed to the terms if he understood that it could be cancelled unilaterally so late in the buying season. Sure Sport and Best Look have done business during the past five holiday seasons with no problems. In all cases, the Purchase Order submitted by Best Look included the clause in question.

Sure Sport comes to you and asks if the cancellation clause is enforceable under these circumstances. Can you use 2-302 to invalidate the clause and hold Best Look liable for breach of its obligation to purchase the clothing? Read Comment 1 carefully and determine the principles that inform the definition of "unconscionability," and decide what additional facts you would investigate.

3. Good Faith

The rules of the UCC are premised on commercial parties acting in accordance with accepted business practices. This accords with the expectations of contracting parties, who assume that their contracting partners will fulfill their obligations in good faith. In the common law of contracts, this commercial reality is handled by regarding every contract as including "an implied duty of good faith and fair dealing." The UCC renders this assumption explicit in 1-304, which provides that every "contract or duty within the [Uniform Commercial Code] imposes an obligation of good faith in its performance and enforcement." Comment 1 explains that this is a "basic principle running throughout" the Code, but also that there is no overarching duty of good faith that gives rise to an independent cause of action for breach. Instead, parties must meet their agreed obligations in good faith in order to fulfill them. It is tempting for students to characterize any seemingly sharp business practice as "bad faith," and then to assume that the other party has some recourse. However, it is necessary first to identify an obligation of the party under the agreement, and then to show that the obligation was not fulfilled in good faith.

Section 1-201(20) defines good faith as "honesty in fact" and "the observance of reasonable commercial standards of fair dealing." Prior to the 2001 Amendments to Article 1, good faith was defined only as "honesty in fact," and Article 2 added the additional requirement that merchants must observe "reasonable commercial standards of fair dealing in the trade." Now, the objective component of good faith applies to all parties, although it is obvious that courts will have to engage in something similar to a determination of merchant status in order to determine the applicable "reasonable commercial standard of fair dealing." The next case applies the old bifurcated definition of good faith to a merchant.

NEUMILLER FARMS, INC. v. CORNETT
Alabama Supreme Court
368 So. 2d 272 (1979)

SHORES, Justice.

Jonah D. Cornett and Ralph Moore, Sellers, were potato farmers in DeKalb County, Alabama. Neumiller Farms, Inc., Buyer, was a corporation engaged in brokering potatoes from the growers to the makers of potato chips. The controversy concerns Buyer's rejection of nine loads of potatoes out of a contract calling for twelve loads. A jury returned a verdict of $17,500 for Sellers based on a breach of contract. Buyer appealed. We affirm.

From the evidence, the jury could have found the following:

On March 3, 1976, the parties signed a written contract whereby Sellers agreed to deliver twelve loads of chipping potatoes to Buyer during July and August 1976, and Buyer agreed to pay $4.25 per hundredweight. The contract required that the potatoes be United States Grade No. 1 and "chipt [sic] to buyer satisfaction." As the term was used in this contract, a load of potatoes contains 430 hundredweight and is valued at $1,827.50.

Sellers' potato crop yielded twenty to twenty-four loads of potatoes and Buyer accepted three of these loads without objection. At that time, the market price of chipping potatoes was $4.25 per hundredweight. Shortly thereafter, the market price declined to $2.00 per hundredweight.

When Sellers tendered additional loads of potatoes, Buyer refused acceptance, saying the potatoes would not "chip" satisfactorily. Sellers responded by having samples of their crop tested by an expert from the Cooperative Extension Service of Jackson County, Alabama, who reported that the potatoes were suitable in all respects. After receiving a letter demanding performance of the contract, Buyer agreed to "try one more load." Sellers then tendered a load of potatoes which had been purchased from another grower, Roy Hartline. Although Buyer's agent had recently purchased potatoes from Hartline at $2.00 per hundredweight, he claimed dissatisfaction with potatoes from the same fields when tendered by Sellers at $4.25 per hundredweight. Apparently the jury believed this testimony outweighed statements by Buyer's agents that Sellers' potatoes were diseased and unfit for "chipping."

Subsequently, Sellers offered to purchase the remaining nine loads of potatoes from other growers in order to fulfil their contract. Buyer's agent refused this offer, saying " . . . 'I'm not going to accept any more of your potatoes. If you load any more I'll see that they're turned down.' . . . 'I can buy potatoes all day for $2.00'." No further efforts were made by Sellers to perform the contract.

At the time of Buyer's final refusal, Sellers had between seventeen and twenty-one loads of potatoes unharvested in their fields. Approximately four loads were sold in Chattanooga, Tennessee; Atlanta, Georgia; and local markets in DeKalb County. Sellers' efforts to sell their potato crop to other buyers were hampered by poor market conditions. Considering all of the evidence, the jury could properly have found that Sellers' efforts to sell the potatoes, after Buyer's final refusal to accept delivery, were reasonable and made in good faith.

This case presents three questions: 1) Was Buyer's refusal to accept delivery of Sellers' potatoes a breach of contract? 2) If so, what was the proper measure of Sellers' damages? and 3) Was the $17,500 jury verdict within the amount recoverable by Sellers under the proper measure of damages?

§ 7-2-703, Code of Alabama 1975 (U.C.C.), specifies an aggrieved seller may recover for a breach of contract "Where the buyer *wrongfully* rejects . . . goods. . . ." (Emphasis added.) We must determine whether there was evidence from which the jury could find that the Buyer acted wrongfully in rejecting delivery of Sellers' potatoes.

A buyer may reject delivery of goods if either the goods or the tender of delivery fails to conform to the contract. § 7-2-601, Code of Alabama 1975. In the instant case, Buyer did not claim the tender was inadequate. Rather, Buyer asserted the potatoes failed to conform to the requirements of the contract; *i.e.*, the potatoes would not chip to buyer satisfaction.

The law requires such a claim of dissatisfaction to be made in good faith, rather than in an effort to escape a bad bargain. *Shelton v. Shelton*, 238 Ala. 489, 192 So. 55 (1939); *Jones v. Lanier*, 198 Ala. 363, 73 So. 535 (1916); *Electric Lighting Co. v. Elder Bros.*, 115 Ala. 138, 21 So. 983 (1896).

Buyer, in the instant case, is a broker who deals in farm products as part of its occupation and, therefore, is a "merchant" with respect to its dealings in such goods. § 7-2-104, Code of Alabama 1975. In testing the good faith of a merchant, § 7-2-103, Code of Alabama 1975, requires " . . . honesty in fact and the observance of reasonable commercial standards of fair dealing in the trade." A claim of dissatisfaction by a merchant-buyer of fungible goods must be evaluated using an objective standard to determine whether the claim is made in good faith. Because there was evidence that the potatoes would "chip" satisfactorily, the jury was not required to accept Buyer's subjective claim to the contrary. A rejection of goods based on a claim of dissatisfaction, which is not made in good faith, is ineffectual and constitutes a breach of contract for which damages are recoverable.

QUESTIONS AND NOTES

1. Does the *Neumiller Farms* case rely on the subjective or objective component of bad faith? Do the facts support a finding of both subjective and objective bad faith? How do the factual inquiries differ between the two? Is there a practical, inevitable affinity between the two standards?

2. Why does the *Neumiller Farms* court refer to pre-Code law in its discussion of good faith? Does the court ultimately define good faith by reference to pre-Code case law?

3. Re-read Problem 2-2 and recall the difficulties that Best Look is likely to encounter if it argues that the termination clause is unconscionable. Does the duty of good faith provide better arguments? Does the existence of a general duty of good faith help to explain why unconscionability arguments will rarely succeed?

4. Article 7 of the CISG requires "the observance of good faith in international trade," but unlike the UCC does not explicitly define good faith. In an action governed by the CISG, the law of the forum nation would provide the substance of the definition of good faith, with attention to international commercial realities.

B. FORMATION IN GENERAL

1. Agreement as Bargain in Fact

Karl Llewellyn grounded the rules of Article 2 in commercial reality rather than in abstract legal principles. This is particularly evident in the provisions relating to formation of the sales agreement. The common law fixation on identifying a distinct offer, a distinct acceptance, and the existence of consideration led to many inequitable results that had to be corrected doctrinally in inelegant ways, such as by recognizing that an "implied" promise serves as the acceptance, or that promissory estoppel can serve as a substitute for consideration. In particular, Llewellyn took aim at the perceived need to sharply distinguish unilateral and bilateral contracts as symptomatic of the unrealistic and abstract approach of much contract doctrine. The following excerpts are vintage Llewellyn.

Llewellyn, *On Our Case-Law of Contract: Offer and Acceptance*
48 Yale L.J. 1, 1, 31–32 (Pt. 1, 1938), 48 Yale L.J. 779, 803–04 (Pt. 2, 1939)[10]

The thesis of this paper is that the cases, and indeed most that has been written *when the cases were immediately before the case-trained writer's eye*, contain a rather coherent and workable and moderately simple body of case-principle and even often of clean case-law about the formation of business agreements, at least in the matter of Offer and Acceptance. And the chief reason why this phase of the law of business agreement continues unnecessarily obscure, and troublesome, and more often unpredictable than Reason would allow, is that the sustained illumination of point after point after point has been presented with a certain almost desperate regularity as a series of minor qualifications of basic theories and of a basic analysis which have not for a century or so rested on either case-law or sense, and yet have not been re-examined in the light of their incessant and effective partial challenges. When the qualifications needed to make a supposedly simple basic structure of theory give accurate results in practice reach the point where the simplicity is overwhelmed by its own qualifications, and when the qualifications are not made to cohere in theory, though they do in meaning, then a fresh start becomes over-due.

* * *

Even case-law judges persist in an urge to shape results to the life-situation as they see it. Through open confusion and conflict runs their desire to find a doctrinal definition of any situation which is just to that situation in life. . . .

The great dichotomy in the orthodox doctrine of Offer and Acceptance is that between bilateral and unilateral contract. But there have been signs over thirty years or more of difficulty with it and its implications. Perhaps it is time to recanvass the *life-situation* with which it has to deal. And so to recanvass the cases which its office is to reflect and to guide.

This will not be easy doing. . . . For it was Offer and Acceptance which first led each of us out of laydom into The Law. Puzzled, befogged, adrift in the strange words and technique of cases, with only our sane feeling of what was decent for a compass, we felt the warm sun suddenly, we knew that we were arriving, we knew we too could "think like a lawyer": That was when we learned to down seasickness as A revoked when B was almost up the flag-pole. It is an area where we *want* no disturbance, and will brook none. It is the Rabbit-Hole down which we fell into the Law, and to him who has gone down it, no queer phenomenon is strange; he has been magicked; the logic of Wonderland we

---

[10] Copyright 1938. Reprinted by permission of The Yale Law Journal Company and William S. Hein Company from The Yale Law Journal, Vol. 48, pages 1–36 & 779–818.

then entered makes mere discrepant decision negligible.

*   *   *

What I think I see here is this: First, and most, a contagion of attitude from deals where there has been no attempt at early retraction, and where it is plain that the deal has been, shall I say, *lived* into, and where men's minds and courts' minds then naturally (though quite without necessity) date the closing as of the easiest time to see and think about: to wit, the time when agreement was expressed. When minds have really and unmistakably not only met but joined up, neither a precise process nor a precise instant has importance. But we pick a mile-stone. This sets a picture of non-inquiry into any "how much" or "whether" of demonstrable overt reliance; an inquiry which is administratively baffling, anyhow, and to be avoided if may be. Upon this plays the fact that, in life, expressed agreement does operate as a commitment. It just does.

Llewellyn incorporated the tenets of his legal realism in the formation provisions of Article 2. The basic rule of formation is that a "contract for sale of goods may be made in any manner sufficient to show agreement, including conduct by both parties which recognizes the existence of such a contract." § 2-204(1). Deviation from the conceptual model of offer and acceptance is emphasized in § 2-204(2), which recognizes a contract "even though the moment of its making is undetermined." In other words, there is no need to identify and match an "offer" and "acceptance" to have a sales contract. Nor is it necessary that the parties have agreed to all of the material terms. All that is necessary is that the parties have "intended to make a contract and there is a reasonably certain basis for giving an appropriate remedy." § 2-204(3).

Contract formation under Article 2 presents a straightforward question of fact: have the parties shown "agreement"? The fact-based approach of Article 2 is carried forward in the definition of agreement, which means "the bargain of the parties in fact, as found in their language or inferred from other circumstances, including course of performance, course of dealing, or usage of trade as provided in Section 1-303." Read § 1-303 and outline the elements of "agreement," and then work through the following problem to determine how you would investigate the existence of an "agreement" between the parties.

PROBLEM 2-3

Bosco Industries is a manufacturer in North Carolina. Sampson Mills is a steel mill in Ohio. Bosco has purchased cold rolled steel for use in its manufacturing process from Sampson for eight continuous years. Bosco faxed a rudimentary purchase order to Sampson on February 1 that called for six shipments of "36 inch cold rolled steel," and it accepted and paid for the first three shipments. However, Bosco rejected Sampson's tender of the fourth shipment and refused to pay for the steel, because the pieces of steel ranged in size from 35 inches to 37 inches. Bosco argued that the steel was nonconforming because the steel was not 36 inches wide, as clearly specified in the purchase order. Sampson argued that its performance was in accordance with their agreement, and demanded payment for the delivery.

Sampson comes to your office and seeks advice. Assume that the purchase order contains no other terms relating to the size of the steel being purchased. What facts will you investigate in order to determine whether Sampson has breached its agreement?

Read § 1-303(e) carefully. How will a court deal with a situation when the factual determinants of "agreement" do not mirror each other? Is it possible that Sampson can prevail if the written term of 36 inches is supported by evidence that the previous shipments during the past eight years were 36 inches, and the first three shipments under the current contract were 36 inches, but the usage of trade in the steel industry is that stated widths have a tolerance of plus or minus 1 inch?

As the problem made clear, the commercial attorney must be mindful of the Code's broad definition of agreement in her evaluation of a proposed sales transaction. First, she should ensure that the written contract includes all express terms of the parties' agreement. Second, the attorney should evaluate the effect that course of dealing and usage of trade will have on the interpretation and supplementation of these express terms. Past dealings and trade customs give meaning to all terms, unless it is clear that the parties intended those terms to have a meaning other than these factors would indicate. Finally, an attorney should recognize that once performance begins, the pattern of performance might provide a standard by which future performance is measured. A party must object seasonably to any unacceptable performance in order to protect its rights under the contract.

The drafters of Article 2A tracked the language of the Article 2 sections on formation of a sales contract and adhered to the same focus on commercial reality. The parties' intent controls lease formation, and these intentions are expressed in the terms of the written lease and, unless otherwise indicated, in the commercial setting of the agreement as shown by course of performance, course of dealing, and usage of trade. One important distinction between Articles 2 and 2A is that Article 2A does not contain gap-filler provisions (but consider § 2A-201(5) regarding duration of the lease term if none is stated in writing, for purposes of satisfying statute of frauds). If the agreement cannot be constructed from the express terms, conduct of the parties, and custom of the trade, Article 2A does not supply the terms. The omission of the gap-filler provisions may not have a major impact on lease formation, since § 2A-204 does provide that if a term is left open, the lease contract will not fail for indefiniteness, if the parties have intended to make a contract and there is a reasonably certain basis for giving an appropriate remedy. Market factors may often provide a reasonably appropriate basis for giving a remedy similar to the results reached through the Article 2 gap-filler sections.

2. The Common Law Concept of Consideration

Through the years, there have been challenges to the traditional doctrine of consideration. Consider the observations of Lord Mansfield at the dawn of the modern commercial era:

> I take it, that the ancient notion about the want of consideration was for the sake of evidence only: for when it is reduced into writing, as in covenants, specialties, bonds, etc., there was no objection to the want of consideration. And the Statute of Frauds proceeded upon the same principle.

> In commercial cases amongst merchants, the want of consideration is not an objection.

Pillans and Rose v. Van Mierop and Hopkins, 97 Eng. Rep. 1035 (1765). Of course, subsequent development of the common law of contracts in the United States proved Lord Mansfield wrong, as the exchange theory of consideration came to dominate the conceptual underpinnings of contract.

The doctrine of consideration has suffered severe stress not only in non-business settings (the classic examples are promises by family members or pledges to charitable institutions), but also in ordinary business situations. In response, judges have burdened legal doctrine with exceptions and qualifications that threaten to overwhelm the basic doctrine. Recall one of Justice Benjamin Cardozo's famous passages in which he finds that a contract is supported by consideration despite the lack of an express exchange between two business people:

> The agreement of employment is signed by both parties. It has a wealth of recitals. The defendant insists, however, that it lacks the elements of a contract. She says that the plaintiff does not bind himself to anything. It is true that he does not promise in so many words that he will use reasonable efforts to place

the defendant's indorsements and market her designs. We think, however, that such a promise is fairly to be implied. The law has outgrown its primitive stage of formalism when the precise word was the sovereign talisman, and every slip was fatal. It takes a broader view to-day. A promise may be lacking, and yet the whole writing may be "instinct with an obligation," imperfectly expressed. . . . If that is so, there is a contract.

Wood v. Lucy, Lady Duff-Gordon, 222 N.Y. 88, 90–91 (1917). Llewellyn echoed Cardozo's insight in his article on offer and acceptance: we recognize agreement as a lived experience that is only imperfectly captured in doctrinal formulations. Given the broad definition of agreement, and the absence of any requirement that there be promises exchanged by the parties, consideration plays a much less important role under Article 2 in line with the long-voiced criticisms of the doctrine. However, Article 2 does not appear to eliminate the requirement of consideration in cases where the "agreement" is founded on promises, inasmuch as § 2-205 provides that under certain circumstances, a firm offer can be binding *without* consideration.

3.   Formation in General

The fact-intensive approach to formation embodied in Article 2 does not prevent courts from filtering the facts through outmoded principles of contract law. The following case illustrates not only how courts can still revert to formalistic common law doctrinal rules when determining whether there is a "bargain in fact," but also how difficult it is to specify when there is a "bargain in fact."

KLEINSCHMIDT DIVISION OF SCM CORP. v. FUTURONICS, CORP.
New York Court of Appeals
363 N.E.2d 701 (1977)

[Ed. Note: This case is provided for its discussion of legal principles. The dissenting opinion provides a basic description of the facts, and the majority opinion's overly brief description has been eliminated to avoid confusion.]

Under the Uniform Commercial Code, if the parties have intended to contract, and if an appropriate remedy may be fashioned, a contract for sale does not fail for indefiniteness if terms, even important terms, are left open (§ 2-204, subd. (3)). It is no longer true that dispute over material terms inevitably prevents formation of a binding contract. What is true, and decisive in this case, is that when a dispute over material terms manifests a lack of intention to contract, no contract results.

The basic philosophy of the sales article of the Uniform Commercial Code is simple. Practical business people cannot be expected to govern their actions with reference to nice legal formalisms. Thus, when there is basic agreement, however manifested and whether or not the precise moment of agreement may be determined, failure to articulate that agreement in the precise language of a lawyer, with every difficulty and contingency considered and resolved, will not prevent formation of a contract (see Uniform Commercial Code, § 2-204). But, of equal importance, if there be no basic agreement, the code will not imply one. In this case, it was found as a fact by the trial court, a finding supportable by the evidence and affirmed by the Appellate Division, that there was no basic agreement.

Without agreement there can be no contract, and, of course, without a contract there can be no breach. This principle, basic as it is to contract law, finds explicit recognition in the Uniform Commercial Code (§ 1-201, subds. (3), (11); § 2-204, subds. (1), (2)). The principle should be dispositive of this case.

The court cannot subscribe to the concurring opinion for two reasons. First, that opinion engages in an extensive unwarranted evaluation of the facts, beyond mere description, an evaluation wholly inappropriate in light of the affirmed findings and this court's limited jurisdiction. Second, the opinion misconstrues the innovative liberalizing provision of the Uniform Commercial Code, which does not require agreement on all material terms as a prerequisite to formation of an enforceable commercial agreement (§ 2-204). There are other matters with which the court cannot agree, as for one example, the discussion of so-called "precatory conditions."

Accordingly, the order of the Appellate Division should be affirmed, with costs.

FUCHSBERG, JUDGE (concurring).

I respectfully suggest that the opinion of the majority represents too summary a disposition of this case. Here by our permission, both sides to this appeal have raised, and extensively briefed and argued to us, significant issues involving the construction and application of the Uniform Commercial Code to the factual findings made at Trial Term. In this great center of modern commerce, more business transactions undoubtedly are affected by the code than anywhere else in the world. When, therefore, leading authorities note that our State's nisi prius decisions in this area are in disarray (Duesenberg, *Sales, Bulk Transfers and Documents of Title*, 31 BUSINESS LAWYER 1533, 1543–1544), it seems to me that a fuller exposition of a legal rationale is very much in order.

I start by noting that the outcome of this appeal centers on whether the plaintiff, Kleinschmidt Division of SCM Corporation (hereinafter SCM), and the defendant, Futuronics Corporation (hereinafter Futuronics), entered into a binding agreement for the sale of 4,436 teletypewriters for a total price of over $4,700,000.

* * *

Principles of law are not to be applied in the abstract. Therefore, though bearing in mind that we are bound by the now affirmed findings of the trial court (N.Y. Const., art. VI, § 3, subd. a; *Rudman v. Cowles Communications*, 30 N.Y.2d 1, 10, 330 N.Y.S.2d 33, 39, 280 N.E.2d 867, 871; COHEN AND KARGER, POWERS OF THE NEW YORK COURT OF APPEALS, §§ 109, 119), we nevertheless must proceed to search the record for the pertinent proof upon which they had to depend for their support.

SCM and Futuronics were manufacturers of teletypewriters. On three occasions between 1968 and 1970 each bid to supply teletypewriter requirements of the United States Department of Defense. Futuronics was the successful bidder on each occasion; the defense contracts provided for a total price of some $5,400,000. During the course of prior contractual relationships with the Government, SCM had accumulated a substantial stock of completed teletypewriters and parts. Out of a desire to make use of that inventory and keep its labor force going, in the fall of 1970 the then newly appointed president of SCM's Kleinschmidt Division, Harry Gaples, informed Albert Blanck, the president of Futuronics, that it was interested in contracting to manufacture and sell to Futuronics the 4,436 teletypewriters needed to fill its three orders. That communication led to a meeting between Gaples and Blanck on October 6, 1970.

What transpired at that meeting was sharply disputed at trial. According to Blanck, there was a detailed discussion of the specifications of all the types of machines called for in Futuronics' three contracts, following which the parties then and there agreed upon all the terms of a contract for their manufacture. On the other hand, Gaples, who had joined SCM only about a month earlier, testified that he was not sufficiently familiar with the specifications to discuss them at that time, so that, though he had agreed on the quantity and price per unit of the teletypewriters to be supplied, on the fact that they were to be packed "commercially" rather than "militarily" and that SCM would credit Futuronics with the book value of the latter's work in progress "up to" $500,000, he had withheld any commitment on such patently vital matters, among others, as Futuronics' demands for prompt initial deliveries and whether SCM would be willing to depart from its insistence that it would undertake the manufacture of the machines only according to the specifications which it had followed in the past rather than as provided by Futuronics' military contracts.

Both agreed that though, at the conclusion of their meeting, Blanck prepared, signed and handed Gaples its "purchase order No. 6791," Gaples did not sign it at that time; nor does it appear that Blanck asked him to do so, despite the fact that the order form included a place for the seller's signature. The quantity of each of the kinds of teletypewriters required for each of the three lots and a uniform unit price of $1,076 did appear on the purchase order. But, under the heading "notes," it contained the following typewritten statement: "1. Delivery to be established by mutual agreement. 2. Payment schedule to be established by mutual agreement. 3. Specifications to be established. 4. Credit of $500,000 for work in progress, as is, to be given by Kleinschmidt to Futuronics Corporation."

Mr. Justice Helman, the Trial Judge, apparently crediting Gaples' version of the meeting over that of Blanck, rejected Futuronics' contention that the unilaterally signed purchase order was a confirmation of an oral agreement. In view of the language of the purchase order, he noted that "It is difficult to understand how sophisticated business people dealing with each other for the first time, in a transaction involving more than $5,000,000, could regard this document as a contract binding on each when so many important matters were left open." It is, of course, a basic rule of law that a contemplated contract will not have reached a legally enforceable stage while one or more of its material provisions is still in dispute (*Willmott v. Giarraputo*, 5 N.Y.2d 250, 253, 184 N.Y.S.2d 97, 98, 157 N.E.2d 282, 283 (Fuld, J.)), a general principle which survives the Uniform Commercial Code (*see, e.g.*, Uniform Commercial Code, § 1-103; *Olympic Jr. v. David Crystal, Inc.*, 3 Cir., 463 F.2d 1141; *ABC Trading Co. v. Westinghouse Elec. Supply Co.*, D.C., 382 F.Supp. 600, 603–604; *Viacom Int. v. Tandem Prods.*, D.C., 368 F.Supp. 1264; *Campbell v. WABC Towing Corp.*, 78 Misc.2d 671, 673, 356 N.Y.S.2d 455, 457).

For, under the Uniform Commercial Code itself, "[i]n spite of the validity of open terms permitting the other party to the transaction to specify various terms or aspects of performance, and of the liberal treatment given to new or additional terms in acceptance or confirmation, it is still necessary that there be an agreement of the parties, and when it is clear that they disagree as to material terms, there is, as under pre-Code authority, no sale or contract to sell" (1 ANDERSON, UNIFORM COMMERCIAL CODE (2d ed.), § 2-204.9, p. 316; *see also* WHITE & SUMMERS, UNIFORM COMMERCIAL CODE, p. 101).

* * *

Accordingly, the order of the Appellate Division must be affirmed.

QUESTIONS

1. Does the difference between the majority opinion and the concurring opinion seem like a tempest in a tea pot? Would the difference between the judges ever result in a different outcome?

2. Is it clear that the trial judge embraced the innovations of § 2-204 in assessing the facts? The majority defers to the trial judge's findings of fact, but how would the majority react in a case where the trial court found as a fact that the parties did not intend to be bound to a contract for sale, simply because the parties had not yet agreed to all of the material terms of the deal?

4.   Offer and Acceptance

Section 2-204 provides the basic rule of formation, which does not require a court to determine whether an offer was made and then subsequently accepted. Nevertheless, many commercial transactions do fit the pattern of the traditional model of offer and acceptance. Section 2-206 provides specific application of the general principles of § 2-

204 to settings involving an offer and acceptance. The next Problem covers some of the basic rules of § 2-206.

PROBLEM 2-4

Sandfill is a supplier of construction materials. On June 1, Brothers Construction sends an e-mail message to Sandfill that states: "Need 10,000 pounds Grade A sand for Tuesday delivery." Assess whether a contract for sale is formed in the following scenarios:

1. Sandfill replies with an e-mail message that states: "Will get the sand to you on Tuesday if possible. Are you willing to pay extra transport charges of.05 cents per pound?"

2. Sandfill arrives at Brothers' place of business on Tuesday, unloads 10,000 pounds of Grade B sand, and leaves.

3. Sandfill arrives at Brothers' place of business on Tuesday, presents Brothers with a Purchase Order providing that the 8,000 pounds of Grade A sand being delivered was the maximum that Sandfill could supply and was being offered to Brothers for its consideration and acceptance without any promise that additional sand could be delivered prior to Friday.

Modern commercial contracting does not always present such nice and neat problems involving an offer and acceptance. The following famous (for some, infamous) case introduces you to the complexities of contract formation in the modern economy.

HILL v. GATEWAY 2000, INC.
United States Court of Appeals, Seventh Circuit
105 F.3d 1147 (1997)

EASTERBROOK, Circuit Judge.

A customer picks up the phone, orders a computer, and gives a credit card number. Presently a box arrives, containing the computer and a list of terms, said to govern unless the customer returns the computer within 30 days. Are these terms effective as the parties' contract, or is the contract term-free because the order-taker did not read any terms over the phone and elicit the customer's assent?

One of the terms in the box containing a Gateway 2000 system was an arbitration clause. Rich and Enza Hill, the customers, kept the computer more than 30 days before complaining about its components and performance. They filed suit in federal court arguing, among other things, that the product's shortcomings make Gateway a racketeer (mail and wire fraud are said to be the predicate offenses), leading to treble damages under RICO for the Hills and a class of all other purchasers. Gateway asked the district court to enforce the arbitration clause; the judge refused, writing that "the present record is insufficient to support a finding of a valid arbitration agreement between the parties or that the plaintiffs were given adequate notice of the arbitration clause." Gateway took an immediate appeal, as is its right. 9 U.S.C. § 16(a)(1)(A).

The Hills say that the arbitration clause did not stand out: they concede noticing the statement of terms but deny reading it closely enough to discover the agreement to arbitrate, and they ask us to conclude that they therefore may go to court. Yet an agreement to arbitrate must be enforced "save upon such grounds as exist at law or in equity for the revocation of any contract." 9 U.S.C. § 2. *Doctor's Associates, Inc. v. Casarotto*, 134 L. Ed. 2d 902, 116 S. Ct. 1652 (1996), holds that this provision of the Federal Arbitration Act is inconsistent with any requirement that an arbitration clause be prominent. A contract need not be read to be effective; people who accept take the risk that the unread terms may in retrospect prove unwelcome. *Carr v. CIGNA Securities, Inc.*, 95 F.3d 544, 547 (7th Cir. 1996); *Chicago Pacific Corp. v. Canada Life*

Assurance Co., 850 F.2d 334 (7th Cir. 1988). Terms inside Gateway's box stand or fall together. If they constitute the parties' contract because the Hills had an opportunity to return the computer after reading them, then all must be enforced.

ProCD, Inc. v. Zeidenberg, 86 F.3d 1447 (7th Cir. 1996), holds that terms inside a box of software bind consumers who use the software after an opportunity to read the terms and to reject them by returning the product. Likewise, *Carnival Cruise Lines, Inc. v. Shute*, 499 U.S. 585, 113 L. Ed. 2d 622, 111 S. Ct. 1522 (1991), enforces a forum-selection clause that was included among three pages of terms attached to a cruise ship ticket. *ProCD* and *Carnival Cruise Lines* exemplify the many commercial transactions in which people pay for products with terms to follow; *ProCD* discusses others. 86 F.3d at 1451–52. The district court concluded in *ProCD* that the contract is formed when the consumer pays for the software; as a result, the court held, only terms known to the consumer at that moment are part of the contract, and provisos inside the box do not count. Although this is one way a contract could be formed, it is not the only way: "A vendor, as master of the offer, may invite acceptance by conduct, and may propose limitations on the kind of conduct that constitutes acceptance. A buyer may accept by performing the acts the vendor proposes to treat as acceptance." *Id.* at 1452. Gateway shipped computers with the same sort of accept-or-return offer ProCD made to users of its software. *ProCD* relied on the Uniform Commercial Code rather than any peculiarities of Wisconsin law; both Illinois and South Dakota, the two states whose law might govern relations between Gateway and the Hills, have adopted the UCC; neither side has pointed us to any atypical doctrines in those states that might be pertinent; *ProCD* therefore applies to this dispute.

Plaintiffs ask us to limit *ProCD* to software, but where's the sense in that? *ProCD* is about the law of contract, not the law of software. Payment preceding the revelation of full terms is common for air transportation, insurance, and many other endeavors. Practical considerations support allowing vendors to enclose the full legal terms with their products. Cashiers cannot be expected to read legal documents to customers before ringing up sales. If the staff at the other end of the phone for direct-sales operations such as Gateway's had to read the four-page statement of terms before taking the buyer's credit card number, the droning voice would anesthetize rather than enlighten many potential buyers. Others would hang up in a rage over the waste of their time. And oral recitation would not avoid customers' assertions (whether true or feigned) that the clerk did not read term X to them, or that they did not remember or understand it. Writing provides benefits for both sides of commercial transactions. Customers as a group are better off when vendors skip costly and ineffectual steps such as telephonic recitation, and use instead a simple approve-or-return device. Competent adults are bound by such documents, read or unread. For what little it is worth, we add that the box from Gateway was crammed with software. The computer came with an operating system, without which it was useful only as a boat anchor. *See Digital Equipment Corp. v. Uniq Digital Technologies, Inc.*, 73 F.3d 756, 761 (7th Cir. 1996). Gateway also included many application programs. So the Hills' effort to limit *ProCD* to software would not avail them factually, even if it were sound legally — which it is not.

For their second sally, the Hills contend that *ProCD* should be limited to executory contracts (to licenses in particular), and therefore does not apply because both parties' performance of this contract was complete when the box arrived at their home. This is legally and factually wrong: legally because the question at hand concerns the formation of the contract rather than its performance, and factually because both contracts were incompletely performed. *ProCD* did not depend on the fact that the seller characterized the transaction as a license rather than as a contract; we treated it as a contract for the sale of goods and reserved the question whether for other purposes a "license" characterization might be preferable. 86 F.3d at 1450. All debates about characterization to one side, the transaction in *ProCD* was no more executory than the one here: Zeidenberg paid for the software and walked out of the store with a box under his arm, so if arrival of the box with the product ends the time for revelation of contractual terms, then the time ended in *ProCD* before Zeidenberg opened the box. But of course ProCD had not completed performance with delivery of the box, and neither had Gateway. One element of the transaction was the warranty, which obliges sellers to fix defects in their products. The Hills have invoked Gateway's warranty and are not satisfied with its response, so they are not well positioned to say that Gateway's obligations were fulfilled when the motor carrier unloaded the box. What is more, both ProCD and Gateway promised to help customers to use their products. Long-term service and information obligations are common in the computer business, on both hardware and software sides. Gateway offers "lifetime service" and has a round-the-clock telephone hotline to fulfil this promise. Some vendors spend more money helping customers use their products than on developing and manufacturing them. The document in Gateway's box includes promises of future performance that some consumers value highly; these promises bind Gateway just as the arbitration clause binds the Hills.

Next the Hills insist that *ProCD* is irrelevant because Zeidenberg was a "merchant" and they are not. Section 2-207(2) of the UCC, the infamous battle-of-the-forms section, states that "additional terms [following acceptance of an offer] are to be construed as proposals for addition to a contract. Between merchants such terms become part of the contract unless. . . ." Plaintiffs tell us that *ProCD* came out as it did only because Zeidenberg was a "merchant" and the terms inside ProCD's box were not excluded by the "unless" clause. This argument pays scant attention to the opinion in *ProCD*, which concluded that, when there is only one form, "§ 2-207 is irrelevant." 86 F.3d at 1452. The question in *ProCD* was not whether terms were added to a contract after its formation, but how and when the contract was formed — in particular, whether a vendor may propose that a contract of sale be formed, not in the store (or over the phone) with the payment of money or a general "send me the product," but after the customer has had a chance to inspect both the item and the terms. *ProCD* answers "yes," for merchants and consumers alike. Yet again, for what little it is worth we observe that the Hills misunderstand the setting of *ProCD*. A "merchant" under the UCC "means a person who deals in goods of the kind or otherwise by his occupation holds himself out as having knowledge or skill peculiar to the practices or goods involved in the transaction," § 2-104(1). Zeidenberg bought the product at a retail store, an uncommon place for merchants to acquire inventory. His corporation put ProCD's database on the Internet for anyone to browse, which led to the litigation but did not make Zeidenberg a software merchant.

At oral argument the Hills propounded still another distinction: the box containing ProCD's software displayed a notice that additional terms were within, while the box containing Gateway's computer did not. The difference is functional, not legal. Consumers browsing the aisles of a store can look at the box, and if they are unwilling to deal with the prospect of additional terms can leave the box alone, avoiding the transactions costs of returning the package after reviewing its contents. Gateway's box, by contrast, is just a shipping carton; it is not on display anywhere. Its function is to protect the product during transit, and the information on its sides is for the use of handlers ("Fragile!" "This Side Up!") rather than would-be purchasers.

Perhaps the Hills would have had a better argument if they were first alerted to the bundling of hardware and legal-ware after opening the box and wanted to return the computer in order to avoid disagreeable terms, but were dissuaded by the expense of shipping. What the remedy would be in such a case — could it exceed the shipping charges? — is an interesting question, but one that need not detain us because the Hills knew before they ordered the computer that the carton would include *some* important terms, and they did not seek to discover these in advance. Gateway's ads state that their products come with limited warranties and lifetime support. How limited was the warranty — 30 days, with service contingent on shipping the computer back, or five years, with free onsite service? What sort of support was offered? Shoppers have three principal ways to discover these things. First, they can ask the vendor to send a copy before deciding whether to buy. The Magnuson-Moss Warranty Act requires firms to distribute their warranty terms on request, 15 U.S.C. § 2302(b)(1)(A); the Hills do not contend that Gateway would have refused to enclose the remaining terms too. Concealment would be bad for business, scaring some customers away and leading to excess returns from others. Second, shoppers can consult public sources (computer magazines, the Web sites of vendors) that may contain this information. Third, they may inspect the documents after the product's delivery. Like Zeidenberg, the Hills took the third option. By keeping the computer beyond 30 days, the Hills accepted Gateway's offer, including the arbitration clause.

The Hills' remaining arguments, including a contention that the arbitration clause is unenforceable as part of a scheme to defraud, do not require more than a citation to *Prima Paint Corp. v. Flood & Conklin Mfg. Co.*, 388 U.S. 395 (1967). Whatever may be said pro and con about the cost and efficacy of arbitration (which the Hills disparage) is for Congress and the contracting parties to consider. Claims based on RICO are no less arbitrable than those founded on the contract or the law of torts. *Shearson/American Express, Inc. v. McMahon*, 482 U.S. 220, 238–42. The decision of the district court is vacated, and this case is remanded with instructions to compel the Hills to submit their dispute to arbitration.

QUESTION

The court does not refer to the language of Article 2 (with the exception of § 2-207, which we will encounter next) to reach its holding that a contract that included an arbitration provision was formed between the parties. Use the language of §§ 2-204 and 2-206 to frame the arguments made by the Hills and Gateway. Is the court's holding justified?

5.   The Problems Presented by Form Contracts

In economies of mass production and distribution, certainty and efficiency may be more valuable than seeking agreement on the optimal terms for each particular transaction. Businesses often use forms when dealing with customers to ensure that their transactions are governed by the same terms every time and to avoid the time and expense of negotiating unique terms for every deal. But if both parties to the transaction seek certainty and efficiency by using standard forms, a significant problem arises. If a customer submits an order form with its "standard" terms, but a vendor responds by sending its own "standard" sales form, how can the parties determine whether they have an enforceable agreement and, perhaps even more importantly, how can they determine the terms of any resulting agreement? This so-called "Battle of the Forms" scenario provided the impetus for § 2-207.

Form contracts increasingly play a large role in modern contracting practices outside the realm of businesses exchanging forms which contain their own "standard terms and conditions." In the first subsection we work through the solution to the battle of the forms provided by § 2-207 (with substantial judicial assistance).

Though, as we have seen in *Hill*, many transactions concluded by phone or over the internet involve prepayment and then delivery of the goods with a manufacturer's standard terms enclosed with the goods. In this situation, there is no "battle" between two forms, but nevertheless, the terms of § 2-207 might productively be used in determining the extent to which the form enclosed with the goods governs the contract. Rather than a "Battle of the Forms," this situation might best be described as an "Attack of a Single Form." We consider the application of § 2-207 to this scenario.

Finally, electronic contracting has reached the point that electronic records may supplant paper forms altogether. Website owners argue that visitors to their websites are subject to terms of use posted on the site, and sellers present the terms of sale electronically as part of the ordering process and then require customers to click "I agree." In the final part of this section we consider how these new electronic contracting practices are assessed under Article 2.

a. The classic "battle of the forms"

Section 2-207(1) provides that a "definite and seasonable expression of acceptance" embodied in a form is effective as an acceptance, "even though it states terms additional to or different from those" in the offering form, "unless acceptance is expressly made conditional on assent to the additional or different terms." The goal of this provision is clear: it rejects the "mirror image rule" of the common law that required an acceptance to mirror the offer in all respects in order to be effective as an acceptance. The "mirror image rule" of formation had the pernicious effect of creating a "last shot rule" as to the terms of the contract when the parties exchanged form agreements. The party sending the second form (the "last shot") would be deemed to have made a counter-offer to the first form, which then was accepted by performance by both parties. Prior to performance, either party could walk away from the deal because the exchange of non-mirroring forms did not create a binding agreement. This formalistic legal approach contradicted the lived reality of the business people who believed that they had concluded a deal by exchanging their forms.

Article 2 clearly intended to change these results by providing that an exchange of forms that differ from each other nevertheless can create a binding agreement. But rejecting the "mirror image rule" is not easily accomplished. The analysis under § 2-207 requires a determination of when the second form should be regarded as a "definite and seasonable expression of acceptance," despite the inevitable differences between the two standard forms.

Subsection 2 recognizes that the "last shot rule" should not be transformed to an equally unsatisfactory "first shot rule." Therefore, it provides that, between merchants, additional terms in the "second" form become part of the contract between the merchants unless the second form expressly limits the contract to its own terms, materially alters the terms of the original form, or the party sending the first form objects to the additional terms within a reasonable time. The elaboration of what this rule means in actual cases has filled many a commercial law professor's tenure file and occupied numerous lawyers and judges over the past few decades.

The rule of § 2-207(2) regarding the terms of the agreement is triggered not only by an exchange of forms in the process of contract formation, but also by "a written confirmation which is sent within a reasonable time" of the formation of a contract (presumably by oral agreement). § 2-207(1) and Comment 1. In other words, if merchant parties orally agree to the key terms of their agreement, and then one or both parties confirm the agreement with forms that contain additional terms, the additional terms contained in the confirmatory form(s) can become part of their agreement by virtue of § 2-207(2).

The following cases provide some assistance in deciphering § 2-207 and the comments. In *Flender Corp.*, the court considers how to determine the terms of the agreement when two forms are deemed to show agreement even though they are not mirror images of each other. The court adopts the "knock-out rule" explained in Comment 6, although this Comment does not directly apply to the situation before the court. To understand the case, be sure that you understand the factual circumstances to which Comment 6 is addressed, and why the court follows the majority trend to apply the "knock out rule" of Comment 6 to the factual circumstances of the case. In *Posh Pooch*, the court tackles the problem of determining when an "additional term" in a form does not "materially alter" the agreement, and therefore becomes a term of the agreement between two merchants pursuant to § 2-207(2). After reading the case and outlining the various applications of § 2-207, work through the scenarios in the problem that follows.

FLENDER CORP. v. TIPPINS INTERNATIONAL, INC.
Pennsylvania Superior Court
830 A.2d 1279 (2003)

OPINION BY JOHNSON, J.

Tippins International, Inc., appeals the trial court's order denying its motion to compel arbitration under the terms of a commercial contract. The trial court determined that the arbitration clause on which Tippins relies was merely a part of its offer of purchase and never became a part of the parties' contract. The court determined, in addition, that the parties formed a contract through course of conduct pursuant to section 2207[(3)] of the Pennsylvania Commercial Code that did not include an arbitration provision. Upon review, we conclude that the trial court did not commit reversible error. Consequently, we affirm the court's order.

This matter arose out of a "battle of the forms" in which the two contracting parties attempted to impose differing terms on the purchase of goods. Tippins, a Pittsburgh company then engaged in the construction of a steel rolling mill in the Czech Republic, sought to purchase gear drive assemblies from Flender Corporation for installation at the new facility. In January 1998, Tippins mailed a purchase order to Flender specifying terms of sale. The order limited the form in which Flender could acknowledge and accept Tippins's offer and required that the parties' disputes under any resulting contract be submitted to arbitration. The order stated Tippins's terms as follows: "Tippins['s] purchase order is expressly limited to acceptance of 'Standard General Conditions Nova Hut Purchase Order' and special conditions of purchase, which take precedence over any terms and conditions written on the back of the purchase order." The "Standard General Conditions Nova Hut Purchase Order" included the arbitration clause at issue here, requiring that all claims or disputes arising out of the contract must be submitted to arbitration before the International Chamber of Commerce in Vienna, Austria, and would be governed by Austrian law. Moreover, the order limited the form of Flender's acceptance as follows: "AS PART OF THIS OFFER TO PURCHASE GOODS OR SERVICES THE ATTACHED ACKNOWLEDGMENT FORM OF THE PURCHASE ORDER "MUST" BE SIGNED AND RETURNED. . . . [NEITHER] TIPPINS NOR ANY OF ITS AFFILIATES RECOGNIZES ANY OTHER DOCUMENT AS AN ACKNOWLEDGMENT."

Flender did not sign the attached acknowledgment form or issue any other written acceptance of Tippins's offer, but instead manufactured and shipped the finished drive assemblies. Flender's invoice, which accompanied the drive assemblies, provided "Conditions of Sale and Delivery" that attached conditions to Flender's acceptance of Tippins's order. Flender's conditions provided as follows:

> These terms and conditions will govern all quotations covering purchase orders for and sales of Seller's products and are the sole terms and conditions on which the order of buyer will be accepted. Seller's acceptance of Buyer's order will not constitute an acceptance of printed provisions on Buyer's order form which are inconsistent with or additional to these terms and conditions unless specifically accepted in writing by the Seller. Buyer's agreement and Buyer's form containing inconsistent or material terms shall not be deemed a specific objection to any terms hereof.

The invoice did not, however, require that Tippins accept these additional terms in order for the parties to form a binding contract.

The invoice also provided a mechanism for dispute resolution. The dispute resolution clause required that "exclusive jurisdiction and venue of any dispute arising out of or with respect to this Agreement or otherwise relating to the commercial relationships of the parties shall be vested in the Federal and/or State Courts located in Chicago, Illinois. . . ." Tippins accepted and installed the gear drives but, subsequently, failed to pay the balance due on the shipment. Flender then commenced this action in the Court of Common Pleas of Allegheny County seeking to recover an amount outstanding of $238,663.15, plus $76,372.16 in service charges.

In the trial court, Tippins filed preliminary objections to Flender's complaint asserting, pursuant to Civil Rule 1028(a)(6), that the parties' contract of sale required that Flender submit its claim to arbitration in Vienna, Austria. The trial court, the Honorable Ronald W. Folino, denied Tippins's objections, reasoning that the arbitration clause on which Tippins relied had been "knocked out" because it was materially different from the dispute resolution clause in Flender's invoice. Trial Court Opinion, 9/9/02, at 4-5. The court concluded, in addition, that because both parties proceeded with the transaction as if they had a contract, although neither party had accepted the other's terms, the only contract they could be deemed to have was established by course of conduct under section 2207[(3)] of the Pennsylvania Commercial Code. Trial Court Opinion, 9/9/02, at 4. Because such an implied contract was, per force, silent on the issue of dispute resolution, it posed no impediment to litigation of Flender's complaint in the Court of Common Pleas. Tippins then filed this interlocutory appeal of right pursuant to 42 Pa.C.S. section 7320(a)(1) and Appellate Rule 311(a)(8).

* * *

All parties agree that Commercial Code section 2207 and cases applying it are dispositive of the issue before us. They disagree sharply, however, concerning which subsections apply and whether the difference in provisions governing dispute resolution apparent in the parties' respective forms served to "knock out" both provisions. Accordingly, we shall determine whether the trial court erred in interpreting section 2207 to conclude that Tippins's arbitration provision was, indeed, "knocked out" and that the contract the parties formed did not compel arbitration.

* * *

Tippins's argument poses a novel question in Pennsylvania, as neither our Supreme Court nor we have determined when a written contract may be formed based on differing terms in competing writings, the so-called "battle of the forms." Nor have our courts considered whether, as the trial court concluded, the "knockout rule" is properly applied to cancel conflicting terms in competing writings, thereby creating a contract out of the terms on which the parties actually agree. The text of Section 2207 and decisions of the federal courts predicting adoption of the "knockout" rule in Pennsylvania provide guidance on these questions.

* * *

Section 2207 provides a remedy for the shortcomings of common law contract theory, which required parties entering a contract to reach agreement on all material terms. *See Reilly Foam Corp. v. Rubbermaid Corp.*, 206 F. Supp. 2d 643, 652 (E.D. Pa. 2002) ("Under the common law, a document qualifying as an offer could only be 'accepted' by a second document expressing acceptance on terms identical to the offer."). In the absence of such "mirror-image" correspondence between the terms, the offeree's "acceptance" would be deemed a mere counter-offer subject to acceptance by the original offeror. *See Daitom, Inc. v. Pennwalt Corp.*, 741 F.2d 1569, 1578 (10th Cir. 1984) (interpreting Pennsylvania law). Because this "mirror-image rule" did not comport with the typical course of dealing in business transactions, the American Law Institute promulgated section 2207 as part of the Uniform Commercial Code (numbered 2-207) and recommended its adoption by the states. *See Reilly*, 206 F. Supp. 2d at 653 n.4. Pennsylvania has since adopted that provision.

Section 2207[(1)] provides that an expression of acceptance may operate to accept an offer even if it contains terms additional to or different from those stated in the offer. *See id.* (citing section 2207[(1)]). Thus, mere non-conformance between competing forms will not undermine the formation of a contract, so long as the parties demonstrate their mutual assent to essential terms. *See Daitom*, 741 F.2d at 1576. Under such circumstances, a written contract is deemed to exist consisting of the essential terms of the offer, to which the offeree's response has established its agreement. The formation of a written contract is defeated only where the offeree responds with different or additional terms and "explicitly communicate[s] his or her unwillingness to proceed with the transaction" unless the offeror accepts those terms. *See id.* (citing *Dorton v. Collins & Aikman Corp.*, 453 F.2d 1161 (6th Cir. 1972)).

In this case, Flender, through its course of conduct and subsequent invoice, accepted the essential terms of Tippins's offer. Although the invoice provided terms that did not appear in Tippins's offer, Flender did not communicate its unwillingness to proceed without them or condition the transaction on Tippins's acceptance of those terms. *See* 13 Pa.C.S. 2207[(1)]. Consequently, we agree with Tippins that the parties did form a written contract under section 2207[(1)]. However, the content of that contract, beyond essential terms, and whether it includes the arbitration clause on which Tippins relies, remain to be determined.

As noted, Flender, in its invoice, included terms that were either *additional to* or *different from* the terms of the offer embodied in Tippins's purchase order. The treatment of *additional* terms, i.e., those for which no comparable provisions appear in the offer, is addressed in section 2207[(2)]. Under that section "*additional* terms become part of the contract unless: (1) the offer expressly limits acceptance to the terms of the offer; (2) the inserted term materially alters the offer; or (3) notification of objection to the inserted terms has been given or is given within a reasonable time." *Reilly Foam*, 206 F. Supp. 2d at 652–53 (citing 13 Pa.C.S. 2207[(2)(a)–(c)]). If one of these circumstances occurs, the terms of the offer control and the additional terms will be treated merely as proposals for incorporation into the contract subject to the offeror's acceptance. *See Daitom*, 741 F.2d at 1578. If, however, none of those circumstances occurs, the offeree's acceptance controls and the additional terms become part of the parties' contract. *See id.*

Nevertheless, the fate of *different* terms, i.e., those for which a comparable provision does appear in the offer, is substantially less clear. Nowhere in its text does section 2207[(2)] address them; rather, it confines its discussion to *additional* terms. *See* 13 Pa.C.S. 2207 ("The additional terms are to be construed as proposals for addition to the contract. Between merchants such terms become a part of the contract. . . ."). *See also Daitom*, 741 F.2d at 1578 ("Section [2207(2)] is silent on the treatment of terms stated in the acceptance that are different[.]"); *Reilly Foam*, 206 F.Supp.2d at 653 ("Section 2207(2) does not directly address different terms in an acceptance [.]"). Thus, the language of the statute provides little guidance on the question of which set of terms controls when an offeree's acceptance proposes terms different from those included in the offer. *See Daitom*, 741 F.2d at 1578 ("It is unclear whether different terms in the acceptance are intended to be included under the aegis of additional terms in 2207(2) and, therefore, fail to become part of the agreement if they materially alter the contract.").

This question of whether different terms are to be treated as additional terms under section 2207[(2)] has divided Commercial Code scholars White and Summers and prompted courts to adopt competing majority and minority views. In *Reilly Foam*, The Honorable Berle Schiller, formerly a distinguished member of this Court, now a federal trial judge, cogently explained these competing schools of thought:

> The minority view permits the terms of the offer to control. Because there is no rational distinction between additional terms and different terms, both are handled under § 2207[(2)]. For support, advocates of this position point to Official Comment 3: "Whether or not *additional or different terms* will become part of the agreement depends upon the provisions of subsection (2)." Professor Summers, the leading advocate of the minority rule, reasons that offerors have more reason to expect that the terms of their offer will be enforced than the

recipient of an offer can hope that its inserted terms will be effective. *See* James J. White & Robert S. Summers, Uniform Commercial Code § 1-3 at 35 (5th ed. 2000). The offeree at least had the opportunity to review the offer and object to its contents; if the recipient of an offer objected to a term, it should not have proceeded with the contract. *See id.*

Reilly Foam, 206 F. Supp. 2d at 653 (internal citations and footnote omitted). This approach treats "different" terms as "additional" terms addressed in section 2207[(2)], *see Daitom*, 741 F.2d at 1579, and is the approach advocated by Tippins in this case, *see* Brief for Appellant at 16–21.

The alternate approach, recognized as preferable by the federal courts in both *Daitom* and *Reilly Foam*, is known as the "knockout" rule, so called because conflicting terms in the offer and acceptance cancel one another, i.e., are "knocked out." "Different" terms are not treated as "additional" terms for disposition under section 2207[(2)], and section 2207[(2)] is limited to its express language.

> Under this view the offeree's form is treated only as an acceptance of the terms in the offeror's form which did not conflict. The ultimate contract, then, includes those non-conflicting terms and any other terms supplied by the U.C.C., including terms incorporated by course of performance (§ 2-208), course of dealing (§ 1-205), usage of trade (§ 1-205), and other "gap fillers" or "off-the-rack" terms (e.g., implied warranty of fitness for particular purpose, § 2-315).

Daitom, 741 F.2d at 1579. In *Reilly Foam*, Judge Schiller explained the pragmatic basis for this approach:

> This approach recognizes the fundamental tenet behind U.C.C. § 2207: to repudiate the "mirror-image" rule of the common law. One should not be able to dictate the terms of the contract merely because one sent the offer. Indeed, the knockout rule recognizes that merchants are frequently willing to proceed with a transaction even though all terms have not been assented to. It would be inequitable to lend greater force to one party's preferred terms than the other's. As one court recently explained, "An approach other than the knock-out rule for conflicting terms would result in . . . [ ] any offeror . . . [ ] always prevailing on its terms solely because it sent the first form. That is not a desirable result, particularly when the parties have not negotiated for the challenged clause." *Richardson v. Union Carbide Indus. Gases, Inc.*, 347 N.J. Super. 524, 790 A.2d 962, 968 (N.J. Super. Ct. App. Div. 2002).

Reilly Foam, 206 F. Supp. 2d at 653–54. Professor White advocates this approach as the most fair and consistent with the purposes of section 2207. *See Daitom*, 741 F.2d at 1579 (citing James J. White & Robert S. Summers, Uniform Commercial Code, § 1-2 at 29 (2d ed. 1980)). It has now been adopted by a strong majority of U.S. jurisdictions that have considered the issue, and the federal courts have predicted its adoption in others. [Citations omitted.]

Flender urges us to apply the "knockout" rule in this case. Brief for Appellee at 11. Upon review of the substantial authority, supra, supporting application of the "knock-out" rule, coupled with the cogent discussions provided by the courts in *Daitom* and *Reilly Foam* predicting its adoption in Pennsylvania, we now join the majority of courts that have considered the issue in declaring that differing terms between a section 2207 offer and acceptance are properly subject to the "knockout" rule. This approach finds support in the pragmatic considerations observed in *Reilly Foam*, 206 F. Supp. 2d at 653–54, and in the plain language of section 2207.

As we have discussed, the language of section 2207[(2)], under the auspices of which adherents of the minority rule would provide the same treatment to both "different" and "additional" terms, does not address "different" terms. *See Daitom*, 741 F.2d at 1578 ("Section [2207(b)] is silent on the treatment of terms stated in the acceptance that are different[.]"). Because section 2207[(1)] makes express reference to "different" and "additional" terms, the reference in subsection [(2)] only to "additional" terms is significant. As our Supreme Court has recently observed, "although 'one is admonished to listen attentively to what a statute says[;] one must also listen attentively to what it does not say.'" *Kmonk-Sullivan v. State Farm Mut. Auto. Ins. Co.*, 567 Pa. 514, 788 A.2d 955, 962 (2001) (quoting Felix Frankfurter, *Some Reflections on the Reading of Statutes*, 47 COLUM. L. REV. 527, 536 (1947)). Thus, our courts have long recognized that "where [in a statute] certain things are specifically designated, all omissions should be understood as exclusions." *Strunack v. Ecker*, 283 Pa. Super. 585, 424 A.2d 1355, 1357 (1981) (*rev'd on other grounds*, 496 Pa. 290, 436 A.2d 1187 (1981)). We are, therefore, unable to insert language into a statute that the legislature, or in this case, the framers of the Uniform Commercial Code, failed to supply. *See Key Sav. & Loan Ass'n, v. Louis John, Inc.*, 379 Pa. Super. 226, 549 A.2d 988, 991 (1988). In this case, the minority approach and the position espoused by Tippins would effectively require that we do exactly that. Consequently, we find both untenable.

Applying the "knockout" rule espoused in the majority approach to the facts before us, it is apparent that the arbitration clause upon which Tippins relies is not part of the parties' contract. The dispute provision in Flender's acceptance, requiring resolution of the parties' disagreements in state or federal courts in Chicago, is clearly at odds with and quite "different" from the clause in Tippins's offer requiring arbitration of disputes before the International Chamber of Commerce in Vienna. By operation of the rule we adopt today, those provisions are both, quite clearly, "knocked out." Neither became a part of the parties' contract. Accordingly, the trial court did not err in refusing to compel arbitration in response to Tippins's preliminary objections.

For the foregoing reasons, we affirm the trial court's order.

POSH POOCH INC. v. ARGENTI
New York Supreme Court
815 N.Y.S.2d 495 (2006)

BERNARD J. FRIED, J.

Plaintiffs Posh Pooch Inc. and G Style Couture, Inc. brought this lawsuit against Defendant Nieri Argenti s.a.s., alleging conversion, misrepresentations, delays in delivery of goods, and failure to deliver goods, and seeking replevin of Plaintiffs' intellectual property and other property and damages. Defendant moved to dismiss the Complaint based on lack of personal jurisdiction and seeking enforcement of a forum selection clause on Defendant's invoices. For the reasons that follow, I deny Defendant's motion to dismiss in its entirety.

Plaintiffs Posh Pooch Inc., which designs couture pet carriers and accessories, and G Style Couture, Inc., which designs couture ladies' handbags and accessories, are both New York corporations located in New York. Ms. Giancci Genau is the president of both companies. Defendant Nieri Argenti s.a.s. is an Italian corporation located in Florence, Italy. Plaintiffs engaged Defendant to manufacture various fine leather and related goods. Plaintiff picked up some of the goods in Italy, but at least seven shipments were sent to Plaintiffs in New York. At the bottom of twelve invoice forms sent to Plaintiffs appears a seven-line paragraph written in tiny type in Italian, under the heading: "CONDIZIONI GENERALI DI VENDITA." The last sentence of this paragraph reads: "Per controversie competente il Foro di Firenze." Translated into English, this sentence reads: "The courts of Florence have jurisdiction over disputes." Other than this paragraph, most of the invoice is either written in English or translated into English. The parties do not dispute that Defendant can communicate in English, and that Ms. Genau, Plaintiffs' principal, does not speak or understand Italian.

There is no evidence that the parties otherwise discussed the forum for resolution of disputes. At oral argument, the parties seemed to presume the existence of a contract between them for the sale of goods, but apparently they did not sign any written purchase contract. The parties did enter into two written Confidentiality and Non-Disclosure Agreements in 2003 with respect to Plaintiffs' proprietary information. Both were written in English, and both provided that New York law and international law would govern the construction of those agreements.

* * *

Forum Selection Clause

Defendant also contends that I should dismiss this action based on the forum selection clause written in Italian in tiny type at the bottom of several invoices sent to Plaintiffs. I do not need to reach the question of whether a forum selection clause written in Italian is enforceable against a plaintiff that does not read or understand Italian, because I find that the forum selection clause is unenforceable under § 2-207(2)(b) of the New York Uniform Commercial Code Law, which governs disputes arising out of a contract for the sale of goods between merchants.

Section 2-207(2)(b) provides that additional terms to a contract for the sale of goods "are to be construed as proposals for addition to the contract" and do not become part of the contract between merchants if they "materially alter it," unless both parties explicitly agree to the alteration. *Marlene Indus. Corp. v. Carnac Textiles, Inc.*, 45 N.Y.2d 327, 333, 380 N.E.2d 239, 242, 408 N.Y.S.2d 410, 413 (N.Y. 1978).

In *Marlene Industries*, the New York Court of Appeals refused to enforce an arbitration provision contained in an "acknowledgment of order" form sent by a seller to a buyer. This form, which instructed the buyer to "sign and return one copy," had not been signed and returned. It had been sent to the buyer in response to a purchase order form sent by the buyer to the seller, which also was unsigned, did not contain an arbitration clause, and provided that its terms could not be "superceded by an unsigned contract notwithstanding retention." Both parties agreed that they had entered into a (presumably oral) contract for the sale of goods, but they disagreed as to whether their agreement included a provision for the arbitration of disputes arising from the contract.

The Court held that the arbitration clause contained in the seller's form: (1) was a proposed additional term to the parties' contract, which was a contract between merchants, (2) had materially altered the contract, and (3) was therefore unenforceable under § 2-207(2)(b), unless both parties "explicitly agreed to it." *Id.* at 333, 408 N.Y.S.2d 410, 380 N.E.2d 239. Moreover, *Marlene Industries* noted that § 2-207(2)(b) was intended to include at least two distinct situations: "one in which the parties have reached a prior oral contract and any writings serve only as confirmation of that contract; and one in which the prior dealings of the parties did not comprise actual formation of a contract, and the writings themselves serve as offer and acceptance." *Id.* at 333 n. 2, 408 N.Y.S.2d 410, 380 N.E.2d 239. The instant case falls within the purview of § 2-207(2)(b), because the parties presume the existence of a contract for the sale of goods, although they have not explained when or how or precisely on what terms it arose.

Following this reasoning, the forum selection clause in Defendant's invoices is unenforceable. A forum selection clause is indisputably a material term of a contract for the sale of goods between merchants. *See Hugo Boss Fashions, Inc. v. Sam's European Tailoring, Inc.*, 293 A.D.2d 296, 297, 742 N.Y.S.2d 1 (1st Dep't 2002) (forum selection clause in seller's confirmatory invoices materially altered parties' oral contract for sale of goods, where parties had not agreed upon the forum for the resolution of disputes at the time the contract was made); *Pacamor Bearings, Inc. v. Molon Motors & Coil, Inc.*, 102 A.D.2d 355, 477 N.Y.S.2d 856 (3d Dep't 1984) (buyer was not bound by forum selection clause in sales order sent by seller to confirm terms of sale in response to purchase order from buyer, where forum selection clause materially altered parties' agreement and was not consented to by defendant); *General Instrument Corp. v. Tie Mfg., Inc.*, 517 F. Supp. 1231, 1233–34 (S.D.N.Y. 1981) (buyer was not bound by forum selection clause in written acknowledgment form sent by seller, where there was "no evidence that the forum for resolution of disputes was discussed at the time the contract was made," applying New York law).

While Defendant points out that Plaintiffs never *disputed* the terms and conditions written on the invoices, *Marlene Industries* holds that a buyer must explicitly *agree* to them. Here there is no allegation or evidence that Plaintiffs signed and returned any of the invoices to indicate their assent to the forum selection clause or in any other way explicitly agreed to it. Consequently, under N.Y. U.C.C. Law § 2-207(2)(b) and *Marlene Industries*, the forum selection clause did not become part of the contract between the parties.[11] Therefore the issue of whether a forum selection clause in a fully executed contract is prima facie valid, *see M/S Bremen v. Zapata Off-Shore Co.*, 407 U.S. 1, 32 L. Ed. 2d 513, 92 S. Ct. 1907 (1972), does not even arise.

This case is also distinguishable from the decisions cited by Defendant, in which courts enforced a material alteration in a contract for the sale of goods, after the buyer had explicitly expressed agreement with it. *See, e.g., Ernest J. Michel & Co., Inc. v. Anabasis Trade, Inc.*, 50 N.Y.2d 951, 409 N.E.2d 933, 431 N.Y.S.2d 459 (N.Y. 1980) (enforcing arbitration clause contained in a confirmation of order form sent by the seller, where the form was signed by the buyer "with admitted knowledge that an arbitration clause was contained therein"); *ISPO, Inc. v. Clark-Schwebel Fiber Glass Corp.*, 140 A.D.2d 195, 197, 528 N.Y.S.2d 48, 50 (1st Dept. 1988) (enforcing arbitration clause contained in sales confirmation forms sent by the seller in response to its purchase orders, relying on fact that buyer had seven times explicitly expressed agreement with the terms by signing and returning the form).

Although there was no "battle of the forms" in this case, as there was in *Marlene Industries* and *ISPO*, the holdings in those decisions depended less on whether both parties had sent forms than on whether the buyer had explicitly expressed agreement with the additional, material term proposed by the seller in its sales confirmation form or invoice.[12]

Consequently, the forum selection clause in the invoices is unenforceable under § 2-207(2)(b). For the foregoing reasons, it is hereby: ORDERED that Defendant's motion to dismiss is denied in its entirety.

NOTES

1. The *Posh Pooch* court cites cases that held that an arbitration clause is a material alteration of the agreement for purposes of § 2-207(2)(b). Because the Federal Arbitration Act prevents states from discouraging or discriminating against contractual agreements to arbitrate as a method of dispute resolution, however, courts cannot adopt a per se rule that regards arbitration as a material alteration as a matter of law. *See, e.g., Aceros Prefabricados, S.A. v. TradeArbed, Inc.*, 282 F.3d 92, 100 (2d Cir. 2002).

2. As with most rules under Article 2, determining whether an additional term is a "material alteration" calls for a contextual, fact-intensive inquiry. As one court recently explained:

---

[11] [1] Although the two Confidentiality and Non-Disclosure Agreements provide that New York and international law govern any dispute arising out of those two agreements, they do not select a forum. Moreover, it is unclear that these choice of law provisions would control the choice of law in a dispute arising out of the parties' contract or contracts for the sale of goods.

[12] [2] *Brower v. Gateway 2000, Inc.*, 246 A.D.2d 246, 676 N.Y.S.2d 569 (1st Dept. 1998), cited by Defendant, does not govern this case because in *Brower*, the parties were not both merchants, and therefore § 2-207(2)(b) would not apply.

We find no Michigan case that has addressed whether an integration clause is considered a material alteration. The general rule for determining whether an additional term is a material alteration is whether the alteration " 'results in surprise or hardship if incorporated without the express awareness by the other party'." *American Ins. Co. v. El Paso Pipe & Supply Co.*, 978 F.2d 1185, 1189 (10th Cir. 1992), quoting Official Comment 4 to UCC 2-207. The majority of the courts reviewing whether an additional term is a material alteration hold that it depends on the unique facts of each particular case. *American Ins. Co., supra* at 1190.

The determination whether a term results in surprise or hardship requires a factual evaluation of the parties' position in each case. *Id.* Courts should determine whether a nonassenting party knew or should have known that such a term would be included. *Id.* at 1191. Courts should consider many factors in determining whether a party was unreasonably surprised by an additional term, such a prior course of dealing; the number of confirmations exchanged; absence of industry custom; whether the addition was clearly marked; and whether the addition is contained within the party's own standard contract. With regard to hardship, "the analysis of the existence of hardship focuses on whether the clause at issue 'would impose "substantial economic hardship" on the nonassenting party'." *Id.* (citations omitted).

Given the analysis required in assessing whether an additional term is a material alteration and the fact that the court failed to apply this analysis, we remand this case to the trial court to address this analysis in the first instance, which provides the parties opportunity for argument on this point.

Plastech Engineered Prods. v. Grand Haven Plastics, Inc., 56 UCC Rep. Serv. 2d 910 (Mich. App. 2005).

3. The CISG adopted a much stricter and more traditional approach to the "battle of the forms." Under the CISG, an acceptance that adds terms to the offer is considered a rejection of the offer, in effect adopting the American common law "mirror image" rule. However, Article 19(2) provides for an exception, stating that non-material alterations will not render an acceptance ineffective unless the offeror objects to the new terms within a reasonable time. Article 2 and the CISG thus have several important differences. First, while material alterations preclude contract formation under the CISG, this is not necessarily true under the UCC. Second, if the offeror objects to an immaterial alteration under the CISG, then the varied acceptance is a rejection. However, under § 2-207, an objection keeps the immaterial modification out of the contract, but does not prevent contract formation. The CISG's preference for uniformity and absolute clarity is reflected in Article 19(3), which indicates that nearly any alteration in the acceptance would be material, and would therefore preclude contract formation.

PROBLEM 2-5

Behemoth Heating Systems specializes in the installation of large heating systems in commercial facilities. Sanders Furnace, Inc. manufactures and sells commercial boilers. Behemoth obtained a contract to install a new heating system in a car manufacturing facility in Detroit, and solicited price quotes from Sanders for the boilers.

On March 27, Sanders issued a proposal for supplying four XR-7 boilers for the total price of $556,000, with an estimated delivery time of four weeks. The proposal stated, "the specified time of delivery is approximate, and is subject to adjustment." On April 18, Behemoth issued a purchase order for four XR-7 boilers for $540,000, subject to a number of conditions. On April 26, Behemoth wrote to Sanders and noted that the boilers need not include the burner units, requested an amended price quote that eliminated the burner units, and included the notation: "Date Required: 4 weeks." Sanders responded on May 1 with an amended price quotation for four XR-7 boilers, without burner units, for $540,000. However, instead of a four-week delivery schedule, it provided a shipping date of July 1. During April, Sanders had received a number of orders and could no longer provide a four-week shipment term.

First Scenario: Behemoth responded by submitting a revised purchase order on May 4 that contained the essential terms of Sanders's May 1 price quotation, but provided the following delivery term: "Delivery no later June 1 — Time is of the essence." On May 6, Sanders delivered shop drawings of the boilers in correspondence that referred to "our contract." On May 10, Behemoth paid 25% of the contract price, as provided in the May 1 price quotation. On June 1, Behemoth demands delivery, but Sanders advises that delivery will not be possible before July 1.

When is Sanders obligated to deliver the goods? Does the answer change under the Amended Code? Note that the delivery "gap-filler" in Article 2 provides that if the parties have not agreed to a time for delivery, the delivery term is a "reasonable time." See § 2-309(1).

Second Scenario: Behemoth responded by calling Sanders and insisting that it required a delivery no later than June 1. Sanders agreed to this delivery date, but only if the price was adjusted to $550,000. Behemoth agreed to the price adjustment. Behemoth then sent a letter to Sanders confirming the agreed price and delivery date. Behemoth's letter concluded by stating: "You must call at least four days prior to delivery to permit us to prepare to receive the goods."

On May 23, Sanders arrived at the automobile facility with the boilers, but without having called in advance. This disrupted Behemoth's construction schedule and caused it to lose time and money on the project. Behemoth deducted $5,000 from the purchase price, claiming that Sanders had breached its agreement to provide at least four days' notice prior to delivery. Sanders countered that it never agreed to provide such notice.

Is the notice provision a term of the contract between the parties?

Third Scenario: Behemoth submitted a new proposal that included the material terms but also stated in conspicuous print: "We reject your proposed delivery date and insist upon June 1 as the latest date. Confirm immediately." Sanders responded with a new price quotation that included all of the material terms, but stated in conspicuous print: "We cannot guarantee June 1 delivery and do not agree to that term. We will expedite the order and attempt to deliver by that date, but cannot promise to do so." There were no further communications between the parties.

On June 5, Sanders delivered the units. However, Behemoth deducted $5,000 from the purchase price due to delay penalties that it was obligated to pay to its purchaser. Was Sanders obligated to deliver by June 1?

b. The "attack" of a single form: The problem of "layered contracts" and "rolling contract formation"

You will recall that the court in *Hill* concluded that § 2-207 does not apply to a situation in which only one party presents a form agreement to the other. Does this conclusion comport with the language of § 2-207 and the Comments? The following cases consider whether courts should apply § 2-207 to situations in which one party presents the other with a form after they have initially agreed to some of the basic terms of the agreement.

Given the clear provision in § 2-204(2) that it is unimportant to determine the moment at which the contract is formed, some courts have found it helpful to view some transactions as involving an agreement reached over time rather than at a discrete moment. The view that the process of contracting can be "layered" or "rolling" arose out of the *Hill v. Gateway* line of cases. Consider how this approach to contract formation works in the following cases.

M.A. MORTENSON CO., INC. v. TIMBERLINE SOFTWARE CORP.
Washington Supreme Court
998 P.2d 305 (2000)

JOHNSON, J.

This case presents the issue of whether a limitation on consequential damages enclosed in a "shrinkwrap license" accompanying computer software is enforceable against the purchaser of the licensed software. Petitioner M.A. Mortenson Company, Inc. (Mortenson), a general construction contractor, purchased licensed computer software from Timberline Software Corporation (Timberline) through Softworks Data Systems, Inc. (Softworks), Timberline's local authorized dealer. After Mortenson used the program to prepare a construction bid and discovered the bid was $1.95 million less than it should have been, Mortenson sued Timberline for breach of warranties alleging the software was defective. The trial court granted Timberline's motion for summary judgment. The Court of Appeals affirmed the order of summary judgment, holding (1) the purchase order between the parties was not an integrated contract; (2) the licensing agreement set forth in the software packaging and instruction manuals was part of the contract between Mortenson and Timberline; and (3) the provision limiting Mortenson's damages to recovery of the purchase price was not unconscionable. *M.A. Mortenson Co. v. Timberline Software Corp.*, 93 Wn. App. 819, 826–37, 970 P.2d 803 (1999). We granted Mortenson's petition for review and affirm the Court of Appeals.

FACTS

Petitioner Mortenson is a nationwide construction contractor with its corporate headquarters in Minnesota and numerous regional offices, including a northwest regional office in Bellevue, Washington. Respondent Timberline is a software developer located in Beaverton, Oregon. Respondent Softworks, an authorized dealer for Timberline, is located in Kirkland, Washington and provides computer-related services to contractors such as Mortenson.

Since at least 1990, Mortenson has used Timberline's Bid Analysis software to assist with its preparation of bids. Mortenson had used Medallion, an earlier version of Bid Analysis, at its Minnesota headquarters and its regional offices. In early 1993, Mortenson installed a new computer network operating system at its Bellevue office and contacted Mark Reich (Reich), president of Softworks, to reinstall Medallion. Reich discovered, however, that the Medallion software was incompatible with Mortenson's new operating system. Reich informed Mortenson that Precision, a newer version of Bid Analysis, was compatible with its new operating system.

Mortenson wanted multiple copies of the new software for its offices, including copies for its corporate headquarters in Minnesota and its northwest regional office in Bellevue. Reich informed Mortenson he would place an order with Timberline and would deliver eight copies of the Precision software to the Bellevue office, after which Mortenson could distribute the copies among its offices.

After Reich provided Mortenson with a price quote, Mortenson issued a purchase order dated July 12, 1993, confirming the agreed upon purchase price, set up fee, delivery charges, and sales tax for eight copies of the software. . . . The purchase order did not contain an integration clause.

Reich signed the purchase order and ordered the requested software from Timberline. When Reich received the software, he opened the three large shipping boxes and checked the contents against the packing invoice. Contained inside the shipping boxes were several smaller boxes, containing program diskettes in plastic pouches, installation instructions, and user manuals. One of the larger boxes also contained the sealed protection devices for the software.

All Timberline software is distributed to its users under license. Both Medallion and Precision Bid Analysis are licensed Timberline products. In the case of the Mortenson shipment, the full text of Timberline's license agreement was set forth on the outside of each diskette pouch and the inside cover of the instruction manuals. The first screen that appears each time the program is used also references the license and states, "this software is licensed for exclusive use by: Timberline Use Only." Clerk's Papers at 302. Further, a license to use the protection device was wrapped around each of the devices shipped to Mortenson. The following warning preceded the terms of the license agreement:

> CAREFULLY READ THE FOLLOWING TERMS AND CONDITIONS BEFORE USING THE PROGRAMS. USE OF THE PROGRAMS INDI-CATES YOUR ACKNOWLEDGMENT THAT YOU HAVE READ THIS LICENSE, UNDERSTAND IT, AND AGREE TO BE BOUND BY ITS TERMS AND CONDITIONS. IF YOU DO NOT AGREE TO THESE TERMS AND CONDITIONS, PROMPTLY RETURN THE PROGRAMS AND USER MANUALS TO THE PLACE OF PURCHASE AND YOUR PURCHASE PRICE WILL BE REFUNDED. YOU AGREE THAT YOUR USE OF THE PROGRAM ACKNOWLEDGES THAT YOU HAVE READ THIS LICENSE, UNDERSTAND IT, AND AGREE TO BE BOUND BY ITS TERMS AND CONDITIONS.

Clerk's Papers at 305. Under a separate subheading, the license agreement limited Mortenson's remedies and provided:

> LIMITATION OF REMEDIES AND LIABILITY. NEITHER TIMBER-LINE NOR ANYONE ELSE WHO HAS BEEN INVOLVED IN THE CREATION, PRODUCTION OR DELIVERY OF THE PROGRAMS OR USER MANUALS SHALL BE LIABLE TO YOU FOR ANY DAMAGES OF ANY TYPE, INCLUDING BUT NOT LIMITED TO, ANY LOST PROFITS, LOST SAVINGS, LOSS OF ANTICIPATED BENEFITS, OR OTHER INCIDENTAL, OR CONSEQUENTIAL DAMAGES ARISING OUT OF THE USE OR INABILITY TO USE SUCH PROGRAMS, WHETHER ARISING OUT OF CONTRACT, NEGLIGENCE, STRICT TORT, OR UNDER ANY WARRANTY, OR OTHERWISE, EVEN IF TIMBERLINE HAS BEEN ADVISED OF THE POSSIBILITY OF SUCH DAMAGES OR FOR ANY OTHER CLAIM BY ANY OTHER PARTY. TIMBERLINE'S LIABILITY FOR DAMAGES IN NO EVENT SHALL EXCEED THE LICENSE FEE PAID FOR THE RIGHT TO USE THE PROGRAMS.

Clerk's Papers at 305.

Reich personally delivered the software to Mortenson's Bellevue office, and was asked to return at a later date for installation. The parties dispute what happened next. According to Neal Ruud (Ruud), Mortenson's chief estimator at its Bellevue office, when Reich arrived to install the software Reich personally opened the smaller product boxes contained within the large shipping boxes and also opened the diskette packaging. Reich inserted the diskettes into the computer, initiated the program, contacted Timberline to receive the activation codes, and wrote down the codes for Mortenson. Reich then started the programs and determined to the best of his knowledge they were operating properly. Ruud states that Mortenson never saw any of the licensing information described above, or any of the manuals that accompanied the software. Ruud adds that copies of the programs purchased for other Mortenson offices were forwarded to those offices.

Reich claims when he arrived at Mortenson's Bellevue office, he noticed the software had been opened and had been placed on a desk, along with a manual and a protection device. Reich states he told Mortenson he would install the program at a single workstation and "then they would do the rest." Clerk's Papers at 176. Reich proceeded to install the software, and a Mortenson employee attached the protection device. Reich claims he initiated and ran the program, and then observed as a Mortenson employee repeated the installation process on a second computer. An employee then told Reich that Mortenson would install the software at the remaining stations.

In December 1993, Mortenson utilized the Precision Bid Analysis software to prepare a bid for a project at Harborview Medical Center in Seattle. On the day of the bid, the software allegedly malfunctioned multiple times and gave the following message: "Abort: Cannot find alternate." Clerk's Papers at 60. Mortenson received this message 19 times that day. Nevertheless, Mortenson submitted a bid generated by the software. After Mortenson was awarded the Harborview Medical Center project, it learned its bid was approximately $1.95 million lower than intended.

Mortenson filed an action in King County Superior Court against Timberline and Softworks alleging breach of express and implied warranties. After the suit was filed, a Timberline internal memorandum surfaced, dated May 26, 1993. The memorandum stated, "[a] bug has been found [in the Precision software] . . . that results in two rather obscure problems," and explained, "[t]hese problems only happen if the following [four] conditions are met." Clerk's Papers at 224. The memorandum concluded, "given the unusual criteria for this problem, it does not appear to be a major problem." Clerk's Papers at 224. Apparently, other Timberline customers had encountered the same problem and a newer version of the software was sent to some of these customers. After an extensive investigation, Timberline's lead programmer for Precision Bid Analysis acknowledged if the four steps identified in the memo were "reproduced as accurately as possible," Mortenson's error message could be replicated. Clerk's Papers at 248.

Timberline moved for summary judgment of dismissal in July 1997, arguing the limitation on consequential damages in the licensing agreement barred Mortenson's recovery. Mortenson countered that its entire contract with Timberline consisted of the purchase order and it never saw or agreed to the provisions in the licensing agreement. The trial court granted Timberline's motion for summary judgment. The trial judge stated, "if this case had arisen in 1985 rather than 1997, I might have a different ruling" but "the facts in this case are such that even construing them against the moving party, the Court finds as a matter of law that the licensing agreements and limitations pertaining thereto were conspicuous and controlling and, accordingly, the remedies that are available to the plaintiff in this case are the remedies that were set forth in the licensing agreement. . . ." Report of Proceedings (Aug.15, 1997) at 49.

Mortenson appealed the summary judgment order to the Court of Appeals. The Court of Appeals affirmed the trial court and held (1) the purchase order was not an integrated contract; (2) the license terms were part of the contract; and (3) the limitation of remedies clause was not unconscionable and, therefore, enforceable. *M.A. Mortenson Co. v. Timberline Software Corp.*, 93 Wn. App. 819, 826–37, 970 P.2d 803 (1999). Mortenson petitioned this court for review, which we granted.

* * *

Applicable Law

Article 2 of the Uniform Commercial Code (U.C.C.), chapter 62A RCW, applies to transactions in goods. RCW 62A.2-102. The parties agree in their briefing that Article 2 applies to the licensing of software, and we accept this proposition. *See, e.g., Aubrey's R.V. Ctr., Inc. v. Tandy Corp.*, 46 Wn. App. 595, 600, 731 P.2d 1124 (1987) (accepting agreement of parties that U.C.C. Article 2 applied to transaction involving defective software); *Advent Sys. Ltd. v. Unisys Corp.*, 925 F.2d 670, 675–76 (3d Cir. 1991) (holding that computer software falls within definition of a "good" under U.C.C. Article 2).[13]

---

[13] [6] In 1999 the National Conference of Commissioners on Uniform State Laws promulgated the Uniform Computer Information Transactions Act (UCITA) to cover agreements to "create, modify, transfer, or license computer information or informational rights in computer information." UCITA sec. 102(a)(12), U.L.A. (2000); *see also* UCITA sec. 103, U.L.A. (2000). The UCITA, formerly known as proposed U.C.C. Article 2B, was

Integration of the Contract

[Ed. Note: The Court determined that the purchase order was not a "complete and exclusive statement of the agreement of the parties" under the parol evidence rule provision of Article 2, § 2-202.]

Terms of the Contract

Mortenson next argues even if the purchase order was not an integrated contract, Timberline's delivery of the license terms merely constituted a request to add additional or different terms, which were never agreed upon by the parties. Mortenson claims under RCW 62A.2-207 the additional terms did not become part of the contract because they were material alterations. Timberline responds that the terms of the license were not a request to add additional terms, but part of the contract between the parties. Timberline further argues that so-called "shrinkwrap" software licenses have been found enforceable by other courts, and that both trade usage and course of dealing support enforcement in the present case.

For its section 2-207 analysis, Mortenson relies on *Step-Saver Data Sys., Inc. v. Wyse Tech.*, 939 F.2d 91 (3d Cir. 1991). There, Step-Saver, a value added retailer,[14] placed telephone orders for software and confirmed with purchase orders. The manufacturer then forwarded an invoice back to Step-Saver.

The software later arrived with a license agreement printed on the packaging. *Step-Saver*, 939 F.2d at 95–96. Finding the license "should have been treated as a written confirmation containing additional terms," the Third Circuit applied U.C.C. section 2-207 and held the warranty disclaimer and limitation of remedies terms were not part of the parties' agreement because they were material alterations. *Step-Saver*, 939 F.2d at 105–06. Mortenson claims *Step-Saver* is controlling, as "virtually every element of the transaction in the present case is mirrored in *Step-Saver*." Br. of Appellant at 26. We disagree.

First, *Step-Saver* did not involve the enforceability of a standard license agreement against an *end user* of the software, but instead involved its applicability to a value added retailer who simply included the software in an integrated system sold to the end user. In fact, in *Step-Saver* the party contesting applicability of the licensing agreement had been assured the license did not apply to it at all. *Step-Saver*, 939 F.2d at 102. Such is not the case here, as Mortenson was the end user of the Bid Analysis software and was never told the license agreement did not apply.

Further, in *Step-Saver* the seller of the program twice asked the buyer to sign an agreement comparable to their disputed license agreement. Both times the buyer refused, but the seller continued to make the software available. *Step-Saver*, 939 F.2d at 102–03. In contrast, Mortenson and Timberline had utilized a license agreement throughout Mortenson's use of the Medallion and Precision Bid Analysis software. Given these distinctions, we find *Step-Saver* to be inapplicable to the present case. We conclude this is a case about contract formation, not contract alteration. As such, RCW 62A.2-204, and not RCW 62A.2-207, provides the proper framework for our analysis.

RCW 62A.2-204 states:

(1)   A contract for sale of goods may be made *in any manner sufficient to show*

---

approved and recommended for enactment by the states in July 1999.

[Ed. Note: Only Maryland and Virginia have adopted versions of UCITA, and a strong consumer-oriented campaign led NCCUSL to abandon efforts to secure enactment of UCITA by the states.]

[14] [8] A value added retailer evaluates the needs of a particular group of potential computer users, compares those needs with the available technology, and develops a package of hardware and software to satisfy those needs. *Step-Saver*, 939 F.2d at 93.

agreement, including conduct by both parties which recognizes the existence of such a contract.

(2) An agreement sufficient to constitute a contract for sale may be found *even though the moment of its making is undetermined.*

(3) Even though one or more terms are left open a contract for sale does not fail for indefiniteness if the parties have intended to make a contract and there is a reasonably certain basis for giving an appropriate remedy.

(Emphasis added.)

Although no Washington case specifically addresses the type of contract formation at issue in this case, a series of recent cases from other jurisdictions have analyzed shrinkwrap licenses under analogous statutes. *See Brower v. Gateway 2000, Inc.,* 246 A.D.2d 246, 250–51, 676 N.Y.S.2d 569 (1998); *Hill v. Gateway 2000, Inc.,* 105 F.3d 1147 (7th Cir.), *cert. denied,* 522 U.S. 808 (1997); *ProCD, Inc. v. Zeidenberg,* 86 F.3d 1447 (7th Cir. 1996).

In *ProCD,* which involved a retail purchase of software, the Seventh Circuit held software shrinkwrap license agreements are a valid form of contracting under Wisconsin's version of U.C.C. section 2-204, and such agreements are enforceable unless objectionable under general contract law such as the law of unconscionability. *ProCD,* 86 F.3d at 1449–52. The court stated, "notice on the outside, terms on the inside, and a right to return the software for a refund if the terms are unacceptable (a right that the license expressly extends), may be a means of doing business valuable to buyers and sellers alike." *ProCD,* 86 F.3d at 1451.

In *Hill,* the customer ordered a computer over the telephone and received the computer in the mail, accompanied by a list of terms to govern if the customer did not return the product within 30 days. *Hill,* 105 F.3d at 1148. Relying in part on *ProCD,* the court held the terms of the "accept-or-return" agreement were effective, stating, "competent adults are bound by such documents, *read or unread.*" *Hill,* 105 F.3d at 1149 (emphasis added). Elaborating on its holding in *ProCD,* the court continued:

> The question in *ProCD* was not whether terms were added to a contract after its formation, but how and when the contract was formed — in particular, whether a vendor may propose that a contract of sale be formed, not in the store (or over the phone) with the payment of money or a general "send me the product," but after the customer has had a chance to inspect both the item and the terms. *ProCD answers "yes," for merchants and consumers alike.*

Hill, 105 F.3d at 1150 (emphasis added).

Interpreting the same licensing agreement at issue in *Hill,* the New York Supreme Court, Appellate Division concluded shrinkwrap license terms delivered following a mail order purchase were not proposed additions to the contract, but part of the original agreement between the parties. *Brower,* 246 A.D.2d at 250–51. The court held U.C.C. section 2-207 did not apply because the contract was not formed until after the period to return the merchandise. *Brower,* 246 A.D.2d at 250.[15]

We find the approach of the *ProCD, Hill,* and *Brower* courts persuasive and adopt it to guide our analysis under RCW 62A.2-204. We conclude because RCW 62A.2-204 allows a contract to be formed "in any manner sufficient to show agreement . . . even though the moment of its making is undetermined," it allows the formation of "layered

---

[15] [10] The fact the approach utilized by the *ProCD, Hill,* and *Brower* courts represents the overwhelming majority view on this issue is further demonstrated by its adoption into the UCITA. *See* UCITA sec. 208 cmt. 3 (Approved Official Draft), U.L.A. (2000) (noting intent to adopt the rule in these cases). The UCITA embraces the theory of "layered contracting," which acknowledges while "some contracts are formed and their terms fully defined at a single point in time, many transactions involve a rolling or layered process. An agreement exists, but terms are clarified or created over time." UCITA sec. 208 cmt. 3 (Approved Official Draft).

contracts" similar to those envisioned by *ProCD, Hill,* and *Brower. See ProCD,* 86 F.3d at 1452–53 (holding shrinkwrap license agreement was a valid form of contracting under U.C.C. section 2-204). We, therefore, hold under RCW 62A.2-204 the terms of the license were part of the contract between Mortenson and Timberline, and Mortenson's use of the software constituted its assent to the agreement, including the license terms.

The terms of Timberline's license were either set forth explicitly or referenced in numerous locations. The terms were included within the shrinkwrap packaging of each copy of Precision Bid Analysis; they were present in the manuals accompanying the software; they were included with the protection devices for the software, without which the software could not be used. The fact the software was licensed was also noted on the introductory screen each time the software was used. Even accepting Mortenson's contention it never saw the terms of the license, as we must do on summary judgment, it was not necessary for Mortenson to actually read the agreement in order to be bound by it. *See Yakima County Fire Protection Dist. No. 12 v. City of Yakima,* 122 Wn. 2d 371, 389, 858 P.2d 245 (1993) (citing *Skagit State Bank v. Rasmussen,* 109 Wn. 2d 377, 381–84, 745 P.2d 37 (1987)); *Hill,* 105 F.3d at 1148; *Kaczmarek v. Microsoft Corp.,* 39 F. Supp. 2d 974, 977 (N.D. Ill. 1999).

Furthermore, the U.C.C. defines an "agreement" as "the bargain of the parties in fact as found in their language *or by implication from other circumstances including course of dealing or usage of trade* or course of performance. . . ." RCW 62A.1-201(3) (emphasis added). Mortenson and Timberline had a course of dealing; Mortenson had purchased licensed software from Timberline for years prior to its upgrade to Precision Bid Analysis. All Timberline software, including the prior version of Bid Analysis used by Mortenson since at least 1990, is distributed under license. Moreover, extensive testimony and exhibits before the trial court demonstrate an unquestioned use of such license agreements throughout the software industry. Although Mortenson questioned the relevance of this evidence, there is no evidence in the record to contradict it. While trade usage is a question of fact, *undisputed* evidence of trade usage may be considered on summary judgment. *Graaff v. Bakker Bros. of Idaho, Inc.,* 85 Wn. App. 814, 818, 934 P.2d 1228 (1997). As the license was part of the contract between Mortenson and Timberline, its terms are enforceable unless "objectionable on grounds applicable to contracts in general. . . ." *ProCD,* 86 F.3d at 1449.

* * *

CONCLUSION

Mortenson has failed to set forth any material issues of fact on the issue of contract formation. . . . We affirm the Court of Appeals, upholding the trial court's order of summary judgment of dismissal and denial of the motions to vacate and amend.

QUESTION

Does the express adoption of the "rolling" contract formation approach of UCITA, despite the fact that this statute has been adopted in only two states and is no longer supported by ALI and NCCUSL for adoption by the states, solve the problems raised in the *Hill* case?

KLOCEK v. GATEWAY, INC.
United States District Court, District of Kansas
104 F. Supp. 2d 1332 (2000)

KATHRYN H. VRATIL, UNITED STATES DISTRICT JUDGE.

MEMORANDUM AND ORDER

William S. Klocek brings suit against Gateway, Inc. and Hewlett-Packard, Inc. on claims arising from purchases of a Gateway computer and a Hewlett-Packard scanner. This matter comes before the Court on the Motion to Dismiss (Doc. # 6) which Gateway filed November 22, 1999 and Defendant Hewlett-Packard, Inc.'s Motion To Dismiss.

*   *   *

A. Gateway's Motion to Dismiss

Plaintiff brings individual and class action claims against Gateway, alleging that it induced him and other consumers to purchase computers and special support packages by making false promises of technical support. . . . Individually, plaintiff also claims breach of contract and breach of warranty, in that Gateway breached certain warranties that its computer would be compatible with standard peripherals and standard internet services. . . .

Gateway asserts that plaintiff must arbitrate his claims under Gateway's Standard Terms and Conditions Agreement ("Standard Terms"). Whenever it sells a computer, Gateway includes a copy of the Standard Terms in the box which contains the computer battery power cables and instruction manuals. At the top of the first page, the Standard Terms include the following notice:

NOTE TO THE CUSTOMER:

This document contains Gateway 2000's Standard Terms and Conditions. By keeping your Gateway 2000 computer system beyond five (5) days after the date of delivery, you accept these Terms and Conditions.

The notice is in emphasized type and is located inside a printed box which sets it apart from other provisions of the document. The Standard Terms are four pages long and contain 16 numbered paragraphs. Paragraph 10 provides the following arbitration clause:

DISPUTE RESOLUTION. Any dispute or controversy arising out of or relating to this Agreement or its interpretation shall be settled exclusively and finally by arbitration. The arbitration shall be conducted in accordance with the Rules of Conciliation and Arbitration of the International Chamber of Commerce. The arbitration shall be conducted in Chicago, Illinois, U.S.A. before a sole arbitrator. Any award rendered in any such arbitration proceeding shall be final and binding on each of the parties, and judgment may be entered thereon in a court of competent jurisdiction.[16]

Gateway urges the Court to dismiss plaintiff's claims under the Federal Arbitration

---

[16] [1] Gateway states that after it sold plaintiff's computer, it mailed all existing customers in the United States a copy of its quarterly magazine, which contained notice of a change in the arbitration policy set forth in the Standard Terms. The new arbitration policy afforded customers the option of arbitrating before the International Chamber of Commerce ("ICC"), the American Arbitration Association ("AAA"), or the National Arbitration Forum ("NAF") in Chicago, Illinois, or any other location agreed upon by the parties. Plaintiff denies receiving notice of the amended arbitration policy. Neither party explains why — if the arbitration agreement was an enforceable contract — Gateway was entitled to unilaterally amend it by sending a magazine to computer customers.

Act ("FAA"), 9 U.S.C. § 1 et seq. The FAA ensures that written arbitration agreements in maritime transactions and transactions involving interstate commerce are "valid, irrevocable, and enforceable." 9 U.S.C. § 2. Federal policy favors arbitration agreements and requires that we "rigorously enforce" them. . . .

Gateway bears an initial summary-judgment-like burden of establishing that it is entitled to arbitration. . . . In this case, Gateway fails to present evidence establishing the most basic facts regarding the transaction. The gaping holes in the evidentiary record preclude the Court from determining what state law controls the formation of the contract in this case and, consequently, prevent the Court from agreeing that Gateway's motion is well taken.

Before granting a stay or dismissing a case pending arbitration, the Court must determine that the parties have a written agreement to arbitrate. . . . When deciding whether the parties have agreed to arbitrate, the Court applies ordinary state law principles that govern the formation of contracts. . . . The existence of an arbitration agreement "is simply a matter of contract between the parties; [arbitration] is a way to resolve those disputes — but only those disputes — that the parties have agreed to submit to arbitration." . . . If the parties dispute making an arbitration agreement, a jury trial on the existence of an agreement is warranted if the record reveals genuine issues of material fact regarding the parties' agreement. . . .

Before evaluating whether the parties agreed to arbitrate, the Court must determine what state law controls the formation of the contract in this case. . . . In diversity actions, the Court applies the substantive law, including choice of law rules, that Kansas state courts would apply. . . . Kansas courts apply the doctrine of *lex loci contractus*, which requires that the Court interpret the contract according to the law of the state in which the parties performed the last act necessary to form the contract. . . .

The parties do not address the choice of law issue, and the record is unclear where they performed the last act necessary to complete the contract. Gateway presents affidavit testimony that it shipped a computer to plaintiff on or about August 31, 1997, . . . but it provides no details regarding the transaction. Plaintiff's complaint alleges that plaintiff lives in Missouri and, if Gateway shipped his computer, it presumably shipped it to Missouri. . . . In his response to Gateway's motion, however, plaintiff states that on August 27, 1997 he purchased the computer in person at the Gateway store in Overland Park, Kansas, and took it with him at that time. . . . Depending on which factual version is correct, it appears that the parties may have performed the last act necessary to form the contract in Kansas (with plaintiff purchasing the computer in Kansas), Missouri (with Gateway shipping the computer to plaintiff in Missouri), or some unidentified other states (with Gateway agreeing to ship plaintiff's catalog order and/or Gateway actually shipping the order).[17]

The Court discerns no material difference between the applicable substantive law in Kansas and Missouri and — as to those two states — it perhaps would not need to resolve the choice of law issue at this time.[18]

The Uniform Commercial Code ("UCC") governs the parties' transaction under both Kansas and Missouri law. . . . Regardless whether plaintiff purchased the computer in person or placed an order and received shipment of the computer, the parties agree that

---

[17] [4] While Gateway may have shipped the computer to plaintiff in Missouri, the record contains no evidence regarding how plaintiff communicated his order to Gateway, where Gateway received plaintiff's order or where the shipment originated.

[18] [5] Paragraph 9 of the Standard Terms provides that "this Agreement shall be governed by the laws of the State of South Dakota, without giving effect to the conflict of laws rules thereof." Both Kansas and Missouri recognize choice-of-law provisions, so long as the transaction at issue has a "reasonable relation" to the state whose law is selected. . . . At this time, because it must first determine whether the parties ever agreed to the Standard Terms, the Court does not decide whether Kansas or Missouri (or some other unidentified state) would recognize the choice of law provision contained in the Standard Terms.

plaintiff paid for and received a computer from Gateway. This conduct clearly demonstrates a contract for the sale of a computer. *See, e.g., Step-Saver Data Sys., Inc. v. Wyse Techn.*, 939 F.2d 91, 98 (3d Cir. 1991). Thus the issue is whether the contract of sale includes the Standard Terms as part of the agreement.

State courts in Kansas and Missouri apparently have not decided whether terms received with a product become part of the parties' agreement. Authority from other courts is split. *Compare Step-Saver*, 939 F.2d 91 (printed terms on computer software package not part of agreement); *Arizona Retail Sys., Inc. v. Software Link, Inc.*, 831 F. Supp. 759 (D. Ariz. 1993) (license agreement shipped with computer software not part of agreement); *and United States Surgical Corp. v. Orris, Inc.*, 5 F. Supp. 2d 1201 (D. Kan. 1998) (single use restriction on product package not binding agreement); *with Hill v. Gateway 2000, Inc.*, 105 F.3d 1147 (7th Cir.), *cert. denied*, 522 U.S. 808, 139 L. Ed. 2d 13, 118 S. Ct. 47 (1997) (arbitration provision shipped with computer binding on buyer); *ProCD, Inc. v. Zeidenberg*, 86 F.3d 1447 (7th Cir. 1996) (shrinkwrap license binding on buyer); *and M.A. Mortenson Co., Inc. v. Timberline Software Corp.*, 140 Wn. 2d 568, 998 P.2d 305 (Wash. 2000) (following *Hill* and *ProCD* on license agreement supplied with software).[19] It appears that at least in part, the cases turn on whether the court finds that the parties formed their contract before or after the vendor communicated its terms to the purchaser. *Compare Step-Saver*, 939 F.2d at 98 (parties' conduct in shipping, receiving and paying for product demonstrates existence of contract; box top license constitutes proposal for additional terms under § 2-207 which requires express agreement by purchaser); *Arizona Retail*, 831 F. Supp. at 765 (vendor entered into contract by agreeing to ship goods, or at latest by shipping goods to buyer; license agreement constitutes proposal to modify agreement under § 2-209 which requires express assent by buyer); *and Orris*, 5 F. Supp. 2d at 1206 (sales contract concluded when vendor received consumer orders; single-use language on product's label was proposed modification under § 2-209 which requires express assent by purchaser); *with ProCD*, 86 F.3d at 1452 (under § 2-204 vendor, as master of offer, may propose limitations on kind of conduct that constitutes acceptance; § 2-207 does not apply in case with only one form); *Hill*, 105 F.3d at 1148–49 (same); *and Mortenson*, 998 P.2d at 311–314 (where vendor and purchaser utilized license agreement in prior course of dealing, shrinkwrap license agreement constituted issue of contract formation under § 2-204, not contract alteration under § 2-207).

Gateway urges the Court to follow the Seventh Circuit decision in *Hill*. That case involved the shipment of a Gateway computer with terms similar to the Standard Terms in this case, except that Gateway gave the customer 30 days — instead of 5 days — to return the computer. In enforcing the arbitration clause, the Seventh Circuit relied on its decision in *ProCD*, where it enforced a software license which was contained inside a product box. *See Hill*, 105 F.3d at 1148–50. In *ProCD*, the Seventh Circuit noted that the exchange of money frequently precedes the communication of detailed terms in a commercial transaction. . . . Citing UCC § 2-204, the court reasoned that by including the license with the software, the vendor proposed a contract that the buyer could accept by using the software after having an opportunity to read the license.[20] . . . Specifically, the court stated:

---

[19] [7] The *Mortenson* court also found support for its holding in the proposed Uniform Computer Information Transactions Act ("UCITA") (formerly known as proposed UCC Article 2B) (text located at www.law.upenn.edu/library/ulc/ucita/UCITA99.htm), which the National Conference of Commissioners on Uniform State Laws approved and recommended for enactment by the states in July 1999. *See Mortenson*, 998 P.2d at 310 n.6, 313 n.10. The proposed UCITA, however, would not apply to the Court's analysis in this case. The UCITA applies to computer information transactions, which are defined as agreements "to create, modify, transfer, or license computer information or informational rights in computer information." UCITA, §§ 102(11) and 103. In transactions involving the sale of computers, such as our case, the UCITA applies only to the computer programs and copies, not to the sale of the computer itself. *See* UCITA § 103(c)(2).

[20] [8] Section 2-204 provides: "A contract for sale of goods may be made in any manner sufficient to show

A vendor, as master of the offer, may invite acceptance by conduct, and may propose limitations on the kind of conduct that constitutes acceptance. A buyer may accept by performing the acts the vendor proposes to treat as acceptance.

ProCD, 86 F.3d at 1452. The *Hill* court followed the *ProCD* analysis, noting that "practical considerations support allowing vendors to enclose the full legal terms with their products." *Hill*, 105 F.3d at 1149.[21]

The Court is not persuaded that Kansas or Missouri courts would follow the Seventh Circuit reasoning in *Hill* and *ProCD*. In each case the Seventh Circuit concluded without support that UCC § 2-207 was irrelevant because the cases involved only one written form. . . . This conclusion is not supported by the statute or by Kansas or Missouri law. Disputes under § 2-207 often arise in the context of a "battle of forms," . . . but nothing in its language precludes application in a case which involves only one form. The statute provides:

Additional terms in acceptance or confirmation.

(1) A definite and seasonable expression of acceptance or a written confirmation which is sent within a reasonable time operates as an acceptance even though it states terms additional to or different from those offered or agreed upon, unless acceptance is expressly made conditional on assent to the additional or different terms.

(2) The additional terms are to be construed as proposals for addition to the contract [if the contract is not between merchants]. . . .

By its terms, § 2-207 applies to an acceptance or written confirmation. It states nothing which requires another form before the provision becomes effective. In fact, the official comment to the section specifically provides that §§ 2-207(1) and (2) apply "where an agreement has been reached orally . . . and is followed by one or both of the parties sending formal memoranda embodying the terms so far agreed and adding terms not discussed." Official Comment 1 of UCC § 2-207. Kansas and Missouri courts have followed this analysis. *See Southwest Engineering Co. v. Martin Tractor Co.*, 205 Kan. 684, 695, 473 P.2d 18, 26 (1970) (stating in dicta that § 2-207 applies where open offer is accepted by expression of acceptance in writing or where oral agreement is later confirmed in writing);[22] *Central Bag Co. v. W. Scott and Co.*, 647 S.W.2d 828, 830 (Mo. App. 1983) (§§ 2-207(1) and (2) govern cases where one or both parties send written confirmation after oral contract). Thus, the Court concludes that Kansas and Missouri courts would apply § 2-207 to the facts in this case. *Accord Avedon* [*Engineering, Inc. v. Seatex*], 126 F.3d [1279] at 1283 [(10th Cir. 1997)] (parties agree that § 2-207 controls whether arbitration clause in sales confirmation is part of contract).

In addition, the Seventh Circuit provided no explanation for its conclusion that "the vendor is the master of the offer." *See ProCD*, 86 F.3d at 1452 (citing nothing in support of proposition); *Hill*, 105 F.3d at 1149 (citing *ProCD*). In typical consumer transactions,

---

agreement, including conduct by both parties which recognizes the existence of such contract." K.S.A. § 84-2-204; V.A.M.S. § 400.2-204.

[21] [9] Legal commentators have criticized the reasoning of the Seventh Circuit in this regard. [Citations omitted.]

[22] [10] In *Southwest Engineering*, the court was concerned with the existence of an enforceable contract under the UCC statute of frauds and it determined that the parties' notes satisfied the writing requirement. It found that a subsequent letter which contained additional material terms did not become part of the agreement under § 2-207, however, because the parties did not expressly agree to the change in terms. *See Southwest Engineering*, 205 Kan. at 693–94, 473 P.2d at 25. The court further found that § 2-207 did not apply to its analysis because at the time of the letter, the parties had already memorialized the agreement in writing and there was no outstanding offer to accept or oral agreement to confirm. *See Southwest Engineering*, 205 Kan. at 695, 473 P.2d at 26.

the purchaser is the offeror, and the vendor is the offeree. *See Brown Mach., Div. of John Brown, Inc. v. Hercules, Inc.*, 770 S.W.2d 416, 419 (Mo. App. 1989) (as general rule, orders are considered offers to purchase); *Rich Prods. Corp. v. Kemutec Inc.*, 66 F. Supp. 2d 937, 956 (E.D. Wis. 1999) (generally price quotation is invitation to make offer and purchase order is offer). While it is possible for the vendor to be the offeror, *see Brown Machine*, 770 S.W.2d at 419 (price quote can amount to offer if it reasonably appears from quote that assent to quote is all that is needed to ripen offer into contract), Gateway provides no factual evidence which would support such a finding in this case. The Court therefore assumes for purposes of the motion to dismiss that plaintiff offered to purchase the computer (either in person or through catalog order) and that Gateway accepted plaintiff's offer (either by completing the sales transaction in person or by agreeing to ship and/or shipping the computer to plaintiff).[23] . . .

Under § 2-207, the Standard Terms constitute either an expression of acceptance or written confirmation. As an expression of acceptance, the Standard Terms would constitute a counter-offer only if Gateway expressly made its acceptance conditional on plaintiff's assent to the additional or different terms. . . . "The conditional nature of the acceptance must be clearly expressed in a manner sufficient to notify the offeror that the offeree is unwilling to proceed with the transaction unless the additional or different terms are included in the contract." *Brown Machine*, 770 S.W.2d at 420.[24] Gateway provides no evidence that at the time of the sales transaction, it informed plaintiff that the transaction was conditioned on plaintiff's acceptance of the Standard Terms. Moreover, the mere fact that Gateway shipped the goods with the terms attached did not communicate to plaintiff any unwillingness to proceed without plaintiff's agreement to the Standard Terms. *See, e.g., Arizona Retail*, 831 F. Supp. at 765 (conditional acceptance analysis rarely appropriate where contract formed by performance but goods arrive with conditions attached); *Leighton Indus., Inc. v. Callier Steel Pipe & Tube, Inc.*, 1991 U.S. Dist. LEXIS 1749, 41 U.C.C. Rep. Serv. 2d (Callaghan) 1128 (N.D. Ill. Feb. 6, 1991) (applying Missouri law) (preprinted forms insufficient to notify offeror of conditional nature of acceptance, particularly where form arrives after delivery of goods).

---

[23] [11] UCC § 2-206(b) provides that "an order or other offer to buy goods for prompt or current shipment shall be construed as inviting acceptance either by a prompt promise to ship or by the prompt or current shipment . . . ." The official comment states that "either shipment or a prompt promise to ship is made a proper means of acceptance of an offer looking to current shipment." UCC § 2-206, Official Comment 2.

[24] [12] Courts are split on the standard for a conditional acceptance under § 2-207. *See Daitom [Inc. v. Pennwalt Corp.]*, 741 F.2d [1569] at 1576 [(10th Cir. 1984)] (finding that Pennsylvania would most likely adopt "better" view that offeree must explicitly communicate unwillingness to proceed with transaction unless additional terms in response are accepted by offeror). On one extreme of the spectrum, courts hold that the offeree's response stating a materially different term solely to the disadvantage of the offeror constitutes a conditional acceptance. *See Daitom*, 741 F.2d at 1569 (citing *Roto-Lith, Ltd. v. F.P. Bartlett & Co.*, 297 F.2d 497 (1st Cir. 1962)). At the other end of the spectrum courts hold that the conditional nature of the acceptance should be so clearly expressed in a manner sufficient to notify the offeror that the offeree is unwilling to proceed without the additional or different terms. *See Daitom*, 741 F.2d at 1569 (citing *Dorton v. Collins & Aikman Corp.*, 453 F.2d 1161 (6th Cir. 1972)). The middle approach requires that the response predicate acceptance on clarification, addition or modification. *See Daitom*, 741 F.2d at 1569 (citing *Construction Aggregates Corp. v. Hewitt-Robins, Inc.*, 404 F.2d 505 (7th Cir. 1968)). The First Circuit has since overruled its decision in *Roto-Lith, see Ionics, Inc. v. Elmwood Sensors, Inc.*, 110 F.3d 184, and the Court finds that neither Kansas nor Missouri would apply the standard set forth therein. *See Boese-Hilburn Co. v. Dean Machinery Co.*, 616 S.W.2d 520 (Mo. App. 1981) (rejecting *Roto-Lith* standard); *Owens-Corning Fiberglas Corp. v. Sonic Dev. Corp.*, 546 F. Supp. 533, 538 (D. Kan. 1982) (acceptance is not counteroffer under Kansas law unless it is made conditional on assent to additional or different terms (citing *Roto-Lith* as comparison)); *Daitom*, 741 F.2d at 1569 (finding that *Dorton* is "better" view). Because Gateway does not satisfy the standard for conditional acceptance under either of the remaining standards (*Dorton* or *Construction Aggregates*), the Court does not decide which of the remaining two standards would apply in Kansas and/or Missouri.

Because plaintiff is not a merchant, additional or different terms contained in the Standard Terms did not become part of the parties' agreement unless plaintiff expressly agreed to them. *See* K.S.A. § 84-2-207, Kansas Comment 2 (if either party is not a merchant, additional terms are proposals for addition to the contract that do not become part of the contract unless the original offeror expressly agrees).[25] Gateway argues that plaintiff demonstrated acceptance of the arbitration provision by keeping the computer more than five days after the date of delivery. Although the Standard Terms purport to work that result, Gateway has not presented evidence that plaintiff expressly agreed to those Standard Terms. Gateway states only that it enclosed the Standard Terms inside the computer box for plaintiff to read afterwards. It provides no evidence that it informed plaintiff of the five-day review-and-return period as a condition of the sales transaction, or that the parties contemplated additional terms to the agreement.[26] *See Step-Saver*, 939 F.2d at 99 (during negotiations leading to purchase, vendor never mentioned box-top license or obtained buyer's express assent thereto). The Court finds that the act of keeping the computer past five days was not sufficient to demonstrate that plaintiff expressly agreed to the Standard Terms. *Accord Brown Machine*, 770 S.W.2d at 421 (express assent cannot be presumed by silence or mere failure to object). Thus, because Gateway has not provided evidence sufficient to support a finding under Kansas or Missouri law that plaintiff agreed to the arbitration provision contained in Gateway's Standard Terms, the Court overrules Gateway's motion to dismiss.

The motion also must be overruled because Kansas and Missouri law may not apply. As noted above, the Court must interpret the contract according to the law of the state in which the parties performed the last act necessary to form the contract. Gateway's motion does not address the choice of law issue, and the record is woefully unclear where the parties performed the last act necessary to complete the contract. Gateway therefore has not established that its motion is meritorious. If Gateway contends that the issue of contract formation is governed by some law other than that of Kansas or Missouri, it shall file a supplemental motion which cites the factual and legal basis for its position. The Court will review that submission and decide whether to order a jury trial on the existence of an agreement to arbitrate. . . .

*   *   *

IT IS THEREFORE ORDERED that the Motion to Dismiss . . . which defendant Gateway filed November 22, 1999 be and hereby is OVERRULED.

c. Beyond the battle of the forms: Contracting in the electronic age

Advances in technology during the past twenty years have raised questions about the validity of electronic contracts and the efficacy of electronic signatures. Two important legislative efforts have addressed the basic formation questions: the Uniform Electronic Transactions Act (UETA) and the Electronic Signatures in Global and National Commerce Act (ESIGN). ESIGN is a federal statute that provides an exemption to preemption for states that enact UETA. The basic principles of these Acts are relatively straightforward. First, the medium of the memorial of the contract, the signatures to the contract, and the records used to show agreement are immaterial. As stated in the Prefatory Note to UETA, its purpose "is to remove barriers to electronic

---

[25] [13] The Court's decision would be the same if it considered the Standard Terms as a proposed modification under UCC § 2-209. *See, e.g., Orris*, 5 F. Supp. 2d at 1206 (express assent analysis is same under §§ 2-207 and 2-209).

[26] [14] The Court is mindful of the practical considerations which are involved in commercial transactions, but it is not unreasonable for a vendor to clearly communicate to a buyer — at the time of sale — either the complete terms of the sale or the fact that the vendor will propose additional terms as a condition of sale, if that be the case.

commerce by validating and effectuating electronic records and signatures." Moreover, UETA addresses details such as record retention obligations, requirements of notarization, and coordination with specific rules that appear in other laws.

There are now no barriers to using electronic means to contract, and companies have quickly sought to use the Internet for commercial advantage. Consumers using the Internet no longer receive terms in the box with the ordered product after placing an order by telephone. Instead, websites regularly present "standard terms and conditions" in a text box with a scroll bar, or as a hyperlink, followed by an "I agree" icon that must be clicked to conclude the transaction. Commercial parties increasingly have stopped exchanging standard form documents as their mode of contracting, choosing instead to place and receive orders through web applications that utilize the same "I agree" icon structure. This form of contracting, known as "click-wrap" contracting, is likely to overtake the "terms-later" contracting (often called "shrink-wrap" contracting) that was the subject of the *Mortenson* case.

Clickwrap contracting has readily been enforced by courts under traditional formation principles, since both parties appear to be manifesting their intention to be bound by a single set of "terms and conditions." *See, e.g., Feldman v. Google, Inc.*, 513 F. Supp. 2d 229, 2007 U.S. Dist. LEXIS 22996 *24 (E.D. Pa. Mar. 24, 2007) ("By clicking on 'Yes, I agree to the above terms and conditions' button, Plaintiff indicated assent to the terms. . . . Plaintiff's failure to read the Agreement, if that were the case, does not excuse him from being bound by his express agreement.") Consumers have been signing standard form agreements for decades, and courts have generally utilized the unconscionabilty doctrine and specially-enacted consumer protection laws to prevent overreaching by commercial parties. There is reason to believe that courts will similarly protect consumers from oppressive click-wrap agreements. *See, e.g., Brower v. Gateway*, 2000, 246 A.D.2d 246, 676 N.Y.S.2d 569 (1998) (arbitration provision requiring customers to arbitrate their disputes in Chicago pursuant to International Chamber of Commerce rules that required a non-refundable filing fee that exceeded most claims was unconscionable).

Commercial parties are embracing electronic contracting with enthusiasm. Manufacturers are developing increasingly sophisticated inventory control, production management and supply-chain integration, all of which require that they manage orders in a computerized fashion. The same dynamic holds true for buyers, who benefit by purchasing raw materials and component parts by means of highly sophisticated software that invites approved sellers to make offers on the buyer's website, thereby integrating their purchasing needs with nearly simultaneous offers that can be automatically accepted and confirmed. As commercial parties continue to transition to web-based inventory control and ordering, there no longer will be a battle of paper forms. Instead, the parties will be manifesting assent to a single set of terms and conditions that appear on a website. It remains to be seen whether courts will need to more closely police click-wrap agreements between commercial parties, since the protections afforded to both parties under § 2-207 will no longer be relevant.

C. THE WRITING REQUIREMENTS

The Code's formation provisions do not require sales agreements to be memorialized in writing. In fact, §§ 2-204(1) and 2-207(3) both recognize that an agreement might be reflected in the conduct of the parties and not reduced to terms expressed in language. However, Article 2 includes a statute of frauds provision that may be satisfied by a signed writing, and so there is motivation for the parties to reduce their agreements to writing. Additionally, § 2-205 permits a party to make an irrevocable, or "firm," offer without need for separate consideration, but only if the offer is set forth in a signed writing. As we consider these two specific writing requirements, keep in mind that there is no general requirement that a sales agreement be memorialized in writing.

1. The Statute of Frauds

In 1677, the English Parliament passed the Statute of Frauds for "prevention of many fraudulent practices." The Statute of Frauds required a written record in several contexts, including contracts for the sale of land, for suretyship contracts, for contracts which could not be performed within one year, and for sales of goods over a certain value. The writing requirement was intended to prevent fraud by a party who might falsely allege that a contract was formed orally, or that certain terms were orally agreed. Although the British Parliament concluded that the Statute of Frauds provided a technical defense that had the potential to cause injustice and therefore repealed all but two sections of the Statute of Frauds in 1954, every American state retains some variation on the original Statute of Frauds.

Over three hundred years of common law baggage burdens the Statute of Frauds. Different interpretations have been offered for each of its elements, and the exceptions to its rules are substantial and complex. Section 2-201 continues the policy of the original Statute of Frauds in Article 2, but, drawing from common law experience, it expressly recognizes a number of exceptions to the writing requirement. Moreover, Article 2 adopted a completely new orientation by viewing the purpose of the writing requirement as evidencing that a contract for sale has been made, rather than providing evidence of the terms of the contract.

Because § 2-201 has not been amended in over 40 years, the threshold for falling within the statute of frauds is quite low. Contracts for the sale of goods of $500 or more are within the statute, and therefore the formality of § 2-201 applies to vast numbers of agreements.

It is important to keep the Statute of Frauds distinct from questions of contract formation. Even if a party is able to satisfy the Statute of Frauds, that party may be unable to meet its burden of proving that it had an agreement with the other party. It is necessary to satisfy the Statute of Frauds to enforce an agreement, but satisfying the Statute of Frauds is not sufficient to prove the existence of a contract.

a. Satisfying the statute of frauds with a signed writing

At common law, courts interpreted the Statute of Frauds to require a writing signed by the party to be bound to the contract which set forth the material terms of the bargain. The two-fold purpose of the writing requirement was to establish the existence of the contract and also to provide evidence of the material terms to which the parties had agreed. Section 2-201(1) takes a markedly different approach by requiring only that the signed writing "indicate that a contract for sale has been made." The writing need not contain all of the material terms, and may even incorrectly state the agreed terms. However, the contract will not be enforced beyond the quantity shown in the signed writing. Consequently, a much broader range of writings will satisfy the writing requirement, eliminating the need felt at common law to link together disparate writings to provide evidence of all of the material terms.

PROBLEM 2-6

Barry agreed orally to purchase 30 bird feeders for his nature store from Sheena, at a cost of $20 each. Sheena subsequently received a better offer, and refused to sell the bird feeders to Barry. At the small claims trial, Barry produces a signed letter that he received from Sheena that reads: "Barry: I am truly sorry but I cannot go through with our deal. Perhaps we can do business next spring?" Can Barry satisfy the requirements of § 2-201(1)?

SIAM NUMHONG PRODUCTS CO. v. EASTIMPEX
United States District Court, Northern District of California
866 F. Supp. 445 (1994)

PATEL, Judge.

Plaintiff Siam Numhong Products, Co., Ltd. ("SNH") brought this action against defendant Eastimpex alleging breach of two written contracts and one oral contract for the manufacture and purchase of Thai bamboo shoots. Eastimpex filed related counterclaims. Now before the court is Eastimpex's motion for summary judgment on SNH's first and third claims for relief for breach of written contract and breach of oral contract.

*   *   *

BACKGROUND

Plaintiff SNH is a Thai company that processes and sells Thai agricultural products to foreign distributors. Defendant Eastimpex is a California corporation that, among other things, imports foreign foodstuffs for resale to restaurant suppliers.

[Ed. Note: The parties agreed to the sale of cultivated bamboo shoots in their first sales contract.]

Between August 1, 1991 and August 1, 1992 the market price for bamboo shoots declined. Between February 1992 and May 1993, SNH resold some of the SE-8917 product. By July 1992, SNH had resold at least 9,763 of the 30,000 cartons of bamboo shoots contracted for in the SE-8917 contract.

In June, 1991 Eastimpex opened a letter of credit in favor of SNH for a second agreement, this one involving wild bamboo shoots ("Wild Bamboo Shoot Contract"). No written purchase order was ever issued for this contract. Eastimpex refused to take up delivery of all of the wild bamboo shoot product it had ordered, claiming that there were problems with the product. On January 10, 1992 Eastimpex wrote that it would not extend the Wild Bamboo Shoot Contract letter of credit.

On October 19, 1993 SNH filed this action against Eastimpex alleging, inter alia, breach of . . . oral contract.

*   *   *

DISCUSSION

Eastimpex moves for summary judgment on SNH's first and third claims for relief. The court will discuss each claim in turn.

*   *   *

II. The Wild Bamboo Shoot Oral Contract

In its third claim for relief, SNH alleges that in July 1991 Eastimpex orally agreed to purchase 30,000 cartons of wild bamboo shoots from SNH for a certain price ("Wild Bamboo Shoot Agreement"), and that Eastimpex breached the agreement by taking delivery of only 22,500 of 30,000 cartons ordered.

Eastimpex argues that it is entitled to summary judgment on this claim for relief because the Wild Bamboo Shoot Agreement was oral and is therefore unenforceable under the statute of frauds. Eastimpex places a premium on SNH's admission and characterization of the Wild Bamboo Shoot Agreement as an oral rather than written contract. . . . In response, SNH contends that the irrevocable letter of credit issued at Eastimpex's direction constitutes a written contract. Neither party's contention is entirely persuasive.

It is undisputed that Eastimpex issued an irrevocable letter of credit in favor of SNH for the Wild Bamboo Shoot Contract. This letter of credit described the goods, sales price, date for delivery, identity of the parties and the bank's obligations. . . . California courts have held that such letters of credit satisfy the requirements of sections 2201(1) and (2) and are enforceable against the sender. *See Procyon Corp. v. Components Direct, Inc.*, 203 Cal. App. 3d 409, 411–13, 249 Cal. Rptr. 813 (1988). Like the letter of credit in *Procyon*, Eastimpex's letter of credit incorporated the terms of the oral contract and its very purpose was to guarantee payment and bind Eastimpex.

With respect to the requirement of a signature, the court in *Procyon* reasoned that the company that directed the bank to issue the letter and supplied the relevant terms "signed" it upon its issuance, since the bank "was acting as [the sender's] agent when it sent the letter." . . . Similarly, Eastimpex instructed the issuing bank as to the terms of the letter of credit and must be held responsible upon issuance.

Although the letter of credit did not constitute a written contract, as urged by SNH, it did sufficiently "indicate that a contract for sale has been made between the parties" within the meaning of 2201(1). Accordingly, because SNH has produced probative evidence that takes the Wild Bamboo Shoot Contract out from under the statute of frauds, Eastimpex's motion for summary judgment on this claim must be denied.

*   *   *

b. The "confirmatory memorandum" exception for agreements between merchants

One of the curious effects of the common law statute of frauds was that it permitted one party to speculate at the expense of the other party. If the buyer confirmed an oral agreement in a signed writing and delivered it to the seller, the buyer could no longer raise a statute of frauds defense to a claim for breach of contract. However, as long as the seller didn't sign a similar writing, it would still be able to assert a statute of frauds defense in the event that it decided not to perform. Section 2-201(2) mitigates this potential for unfair speculation for transactions between merchants. The "confirmatory memorandum" exception provides that if one merchant sends a written confirmation that is sufficient against the sender as a signed writing under § 2-201(1) to another merchant, and the receiving merchant has reason to know of its contents, the merchant receiving the confirmation should not be permitted to raise a statute of frauds defense if it has not objected in writing to the contents of the confirmation within ten days after the confirmation is received. The basic idea is one of "silent acceptance": if one merchant confirms that a contract for sale has been made, the failure by another merchant to object to this confirmation is strong indication that a contract for sale has been made, and therefore the purpose of § 2-201 has been met and the case should go to the trier of fact.

ST. ANSGAR MILLS, INC. v. STREIT
Iowa Supreme Court
613 N.W.2d 289 (2000)

*   *   *

III. Statute of Frauds.

*   *   *

One statutory exception or modification to the statute of frauds which has surfaced applies to merchants. *Id.* § 554.2201(2). Under section 554.2201(2), the writing requirements of section 554.2201(1) are considered to be satisfied if, within a reasonable time, a writing in confirmation of the contract which is sufficient against the sender is received and the merchant receiving it has reason to know of its contents, unless written notice of objection of its contents is given within ten days after receipt. *Id.* Thus, a writing is still required, but it does not need to be signed by the party against whom the contract is sought to be enforced. The purpose of this exception was to put professional buyers and sellers on equal footing by changing the former law under which a party who received a written confirmation of an oral agreement of sale, but who had not signed anything, could hold the other party to a contract without being bound. *See* WHITE & SUMMERS § 2-3, at 55; *Kimball County Grain Coop. v. Yung*, 200 Neb. 233, 263 N.W.2d 818, 820 (Neb. 1978). It also encourages the common, prudent business practice of sending memoranda to confirm oral agreements. WHITE & SUMMERS § 2-3, at 55.

While the written confirmation exception imposes a specific ten-day requirement for a merchant to object to a written confirmation, it employs a flexible standard of reasonableness to establish the time in which the confirmation must be received. Iowa Code § 554.2201(2). The Uniform Commercial Code specifically defines a reasonable time for taking action in relationship to "the nature, purpose and circumstances" of the action. *Id.* § 554.1204(2). Additionally, the declared purpose of the Uniform Commercial Code is to permit the expansion of commercial practices through the custom and practice of the parties. *See* Iowa Code Ann. § 554.1102 cmt. 2 (course of dealings, usage of trade or course of performance are material in determining a reasonable time). Furthermore, the Uniform Commercial Code relies upon course of dealings between the parties to help interpret their conduct. Iowa Code § 554.1205(1). Thus, all relevant circumstances, including custom and practice of the parties, must be considered in determining what constitutes a reasonable time under section 554.2201(2).

Generally, the determination of the reasonableness of particular conduct is a jury question. *See Pirelli-Armstrong Tire Co. v. Reynolds*, 562 N.W.2d 433, 436 (Iowa 1997); *see also Harvey v. Great Atl. & Pac. Tea Co.*, 388 F.2d 123, 125 (5th Cir. 1968) (passing judgment on the reasonableness of conduct of the parties must be accomplished in light of all the circumstances of the case and should rarely be disposed of by summary judgment). Thus, the reasonableness of time between an oral contract and a subsequent written confirmation is ordinarily a question of fact for the jury. *MortgageAmerica Corp. v. American Nat'l Bank*, 651 S.W.2d 851, 856 (Tex. Ct. App. 1983); *Schiavi Mobile Homes, Inc. v. Gagne*, 510 A.2d 236, 238 (Me. 1986) (reasonableness of parties' time for action is a question of fact). It is only in rare cases that a determination of the reasonableness of conduct should be decided by summary adjudication. *Harvey*, 388 F.2d at 125. Summary judgment is appropriate only when the evidence is so one-sided that a party must prevail at trial as a matter of law. *Ridgeway v. Union County Comm'rs*, 775 F. Supp. 1105, 1109 (S.D. Ohio 1991).

There are a host of cases from other jurisdictions which have considered the question of what constitutes a reasonable time under the written confirmation exception of the Uniform Commercial Code. *See Gestetner Corp. v. Case Equip. Co.*, 815 F.2d 806, 810 (1st Cir. 1987) (roughly five-month delay reasonable in light of merchants' relationship and parties' immediate action under contract following oral agreement); *Serna, Inc. v. Harman*, 742 F.2d 186, 189 (5th Cir. 1984) (three and one-half month delay reasonable in light of the parties' interaction in the interim, and non-fluctuating prices, thus no prejudice); *Cargill, Inc. v. Stafford*, 553 F.2d 1222, 1224 (10th Cir. 1977) (less than one-month delay unreasonable despite misdirection of confirmation due to mistaken addressing); *Starry Constr. Co. v. Murphy Oil USA, Inc.*, 785 F. Supp. 1356, 1362–63 (D. Minn. 1992) (six-month delay for confirmation of modification order for additional oil unreasonable as a matter of law in light of Persian Gulf War, thus increased prices and demand); *Rockland Indus., Inc. v. Frank Kasmir Assoc.*, 470 F. Supp. 1176, 1179 (N.D. Tex. 1979) (letter sent eight months after alleged oral agreement for two-year continuity agreement unreasonable in light of lack of evidence supporting reasonableness of delay); *Yung*, 263 N.W.2d at 820 (six-month delay in confirming oral agreement delivered one day prior to last possible day of delivery unreasonable); *Azevedo [v. Minister]*, 471 P.2d [661] at 666 [(Nev. 1971)] (ten-week delay reasonable in light of immediate performance by both parties following oral agreement); *Lish v. Compton*, 547 P.2d 223, 226–27 (Utah 1976) (twelve-day delay "outside the ambit which fair-minded persons could conclude to be reasonable" in light of volatile price market and lack of excuse for delay other than casual delay). Most of these cases, however, were decided after a trial on the merits and cannot be used to establish a standard or time period as a matter of law. Only a few courts have decided the question as a matter of law under the facts of the case. *Compare Starry*, 785 F. Supp. at 1362–63 (granting summary judgment), *and Lish*, 547 P.2d at 226–27 (removing claim from jury's consideration), *with Barron v. Edwards*, 45 Mich. App. 210, 206 N.W.2d 508, 511 (Mich. Ct. App. 1973) (remanding for further development of facts, summary judgment improper). However, these cases do not establish a strict principle to apply in this case. The resolution of each case depends upon the particular facts and circumstances.

In this case, the district court relied upon the large amount of the sale, volatile market conditions, and lack of an explanation by St. Ansgar Mills for failing to send the written confirmation to Duane in determining St. Ansgar Mills acted unreasonably as a matter of law in delaying delivery of the written confirmation until August 10, 1996. Volatile market conditions, combined with a large sale price, would normally narrow the window of reasonable time under section 554.2201(2). However, they are not the only factors to consider. Other relevant factors which must also be considered in this case reveal the parties had developed a custom or practice to delay delivery of the confirmation. The parties also maintained a long-time amicable business relationship and had engaged in many other similar business transactions without incident. There is also evidence to infer St. Ansgar Mills did not suspect John's failure to follow his customary practice in July of stopping by the business was a concern at the time. These factors reveal a genuine dispute over the reasonableness of the delay in delivering the written confirmation, and make the resolution of the issue appropriate for the jury. Moreover, conduct is not rendered unreasonable solely because the acting party had no particular explanation for not pursuing different conduct, or regretted not pursuing different conduct in retrospect. The reasonableness of conduct is determined by the facts and circumstances existing at the time.

Considering our principles governing summary adjudication and the need to resolve the legal issue by considering the particular facts and circumstances of each case, we conclude the trial court erred by granting summary judgment. We reverse and remand the case for further proceedings.

REVERSED AND REMANDED.

All justices concur except NEUMAN, J., who takes no part.

PROBLEM 2-7

On February 1, Bicycles Galore! orally agreed to purchase 10,000 bicycles for $100 each from Szerejko Distributors. On the following day, Szerejko mailed a confirmation of the agreement, which read as follows:

Acknowledgment

Date: February 2

Bicycles Galore! agrees to purchase 10,000 bicycles, Model PF-14, for the price of $100 each, including delivery charges and taxes. Delivery will be prior to April 30, delivered to Bicycles Galore!'s warehouse in Atlanta. Any and all disputes relating to this transaction will be settled by binding arbitration under the auspices of the National Arbitration Forum.

/s/ Szerejko Distribution

First Scenario: Bicycles Galore! responds to the acknowledgment by sending the following e-mail message on February 7:

> Received your February 2 Acknowledgment. Arbitration was never part of our deal, and we refuse to agree to arbitrate our disputes as a matter of policy. We do not consider this a binding agreement until you confirm the terms as originally agreed.

On February 9, Bicycles Galore! decides to purchase its bicycle needs from another supplier that coincidentally is offering the same units for $95 each. When Szerejko sues for breach of contract, Bicycles Galore! raises the statute of frauds defense. Will enforcement of the oral agreement be barred by the statute of frauds?

Second Scenario: Bicycles Galore! has an annual two-week corporate shut-down during the first two weeks in February, which this year falls on February 3–17. On February 20, Bicycles Galore! responds to the Acknowledgment by sending the following e-mail message:

> Received your February 2 Acknowledgment. We do not consider ourselves to have a deal. As you know, we have not yet settled on our purchasing strategies for the coming season, and so our discussions were intended to be only preliminary. Should we wish to proceed with this proposal, we will contact you.

Bicycles Galore! never contacted Szerejko. Szerejko subsequently brings suit for breach of contract, and Bicycles Galore! argues that the statute of frauds prevents enforcement of the alleged oral agreement. Will enforcement of the oral agreement be barred by the statute of frauds?

c. Additional exceptions to the writing requirement

Section 2-201(3) contains additional exceptions to the writing requirement. Each exception involves circumstances that provide independent confirmation that a contract for sale has been made, and therefore makes the existence of a signed writing moot.

WEBCOR PACKAGING CORP. v. AUTOZONE, INC.
United States Court of Appeals, Sixth Circuit
158 F.3d 354 (1998)

NATHANIEL R. JONES, Circuit Judge.

The parties in this case have framed the issue as one of first impression: whether the "ultimate purchaser" of unique goods may be considered as the buyer for purposes of the specially manufactured goods exception to the statute of frauds. We conclude that the district court was correct in its reliance upon the circumstances of manufacture. In doing so, we take this opportunity to refine and extend the analysis of the district court.

I.

We recite the undisputed facts of this case relying heavily upon the background summary provided by the district court.

Autozone, Inc. (Autozone), the defendant in this matter, retails aftermarket automotive parts and supplies under its own brand name in more than 1,000 stores throughout the United States. Autozone does business by purchasing "retail ready" aftermarket automotive parts from a constantly changing number of manufacturers and suppliers (the "Autozone venders"). When sold by the Autozone vendor to Autozone, a "retail ready" part is pre-packaged and ready to be placed on the shelf for consumer sale from Autozone's outlets.

Plaintiff, Webcor Packaging Corporation (Webcor), manufactures and sells commercial packaging. For several years it contracted with the Autozone vendors to manufacture packaging for parts retailed by Autozone under the trade name "Duralast." Autozone frequently directed its vendors to Webcor as a possible manufacturer of "Duralast" cartons; however, the referral implied no obligation to purchase from Webcor. The art work and other specifications for the "Duralast" brake parts packaging were provided to Webcor by Autozone.

Prior to 1991, Webcor maintained a 30-day supply of "Duralast" cartons to meet vendor demand. Although Autozone never directly contracted with Webcor for exclusive manufacture and sale of "Duralast" cartons, it occasionally purchased the packaging for its own use by purchase order.

By late 1990, Autozone had experienced tremendous growth as consumer demand for its products increased. During that same year, Webcor received unusually large requests for "Duralast" cartons from Autozone vendors, depleting Webcor's 30-day inventory. In November 1991, Joel Liggett, a Webcor sales representative, telephoned Autozone brake parts purchasing manager Joe Turman and explained that Webcor's inventory of "Duralast" packaging would have to be increased to a 60-day supply in order to satisfy vendor demand. Mr. Liggett claims that he requested and obtained assurances from Mr. Turman that Autozone would "cover" payment for the 60-day inventory in the event it became obsolete. However, there is no signed writing between the parties to such effect.

Mr. Turman's recollection directly contradicts that of Mr. Liggett. Mr. Turman recalls no telephone conversation with Mr. Liggett in which the parties agreed that Autozone would guarantee a 60-day inventory of "Duralast" cartons manufactured by Webcor. Mr. Turman further testified that he would have had no authority to enter into an agreement with Webcor as described.

In July 1993, David Wilhite, Turman's successor at Autozone, instructed Webcor to stop manufacturing "Duralast" packaging, as Autozone had decided to change to a new brand name and symbol. Subsequent to this instruction, Webcor managed to sell a portion of its remaining "Duralast" inventory. The remainder of the obsolete inventory, the interest on financing its manufacture, as well as the cost of warehousing it, comprise damages of $101,736.12 claimed by Webcor.

During the one day bench trial, held on March 12, 1996, John Maher, a vice-president of Webcor, testified that at a meeting on April 6, 1994, Mr. Wilhite "reaffirmed" the parties' November 1991 oral agreement by promising to cut a check for Webcor's outstanding "Duralast" inventory. Mr. Wilhite denied this allegation at trial, stating that he had no recollection of such an oral agreement, that he did not offer to make the alleged payment to Webcor and that he would not have had authority to do so.

The district court, in its findings of fact, concluded that the November 1991 phone conversation did take place and that Mr. Liggett did state "that a 60 day inventory would result in better service to the vendors." Further, the district court found that the "only writing memorializing this conversation was an in-house memo signed by Joel Liggett stating 'Per Joe Turman at Autozone, he will cover a 2-month inventory.'" Finding that no signed written agreement had been made, the district court engaged in what it termed a "straightforward" analysis of the specially manufactured goods exception to the statute of frauds, concluding that the exception "contemplates [that] there may be only a single buyer[.]" Thus, given the multiple purchasers involved, the district court concluded that the "Duralast" cartons were not specially made for Autozone and that the statute of frauds precluded enforcement of the alleged oral agreement.

Webcor filed this timely appeal.

II.

A.

The district court interpreted the Michigan specially manufactured goods exception under Michigan Compiled Laws § 440.2201(3)(a). We therefore review the district court judgment de novo. . . . Under the Michigan statute of frauds, a contract for the sale of goods priced over five hundred dollars must be in writing as a general matter. Mich. Comp. Laws § 440.2201(1). However, where a manufacturer produces special goods for a buyer, courts may permit evidence of the oral agreement at trial:

> If the goods are to be specially manufactured for the buyer and are not suitable for sale to others in the ordinary course of the seller's business and the seller, before notice of repudiation is received and under circumstances which reasonably indicate that the goods are for the buyer, has made either a substantial beginning of their manufacture or commitments for their procurement.

Mich. Comp. Laws § 440.2201(3)(a). The long-accepted justification for this statutory rule lies in the assurance that, by virtue of the unique nature of the goods, the manufacturer would not have produced such unique goods absent an agreement with the alleged buyer. "The modern justification for the exception often stresses the need to protect the special manufacturer against the peculiar vulnerability that attends his station. He is more seriously injured than other sellers when a buyer successfully reneges on an oral contract, because the special manufacturer is then left with goods that, by definition, are not readily resalable to others." WILLIAM D. HAWKLAND, UNIFORM COMMERCIAL CODE SERIES § 2-201:03 (1984). It is worth emphasizing that the statute of frauds is a rule of evidence. Thus, upon favorable judgment, a proponent-party — one seeking to invoke the exception — may attempt to prove the validity of the alleged oral agreement. . . .

B.

Courts generally use a four-part standard to determine whether the specially manufactured goods exception applies in a given case. Under that formulation, the circumstances of manufacture must manifest the following:

1) the goods must be specially made for the buyer;
2) the goods must be unsuitable for sale to others in the ordinary course of the seller's business;
3) the seller must have substantially begun to have manufactured the goods or to have a commitment for their procurement; and
4) the manufacture or commitment must have been commenced under circumstances reasonably indicating that the goods are for the buyer and prior to the seller's receipt of notification of contractual repudiation. . . .

In determining whether goods are specially manufactured, courts have traditionally looked to the goods themselves. "The term 'specially manufactured,' therefore, refers to the nature of the particular goods in question and not to whether the goods were made in an unusual, as opposed to the regular, business operation, or manufacturing process of the seller." . . . Thus, under circumstances where two parties dispute the existence of an oral agreement, the proponent must convince the court that the goods themselves have some feature that makes the product marketable only to the buyer. Where the goods have such unique traits, courts are allowed to permit parol evidence as to the existence of the alleged agreement. The district court in this case reached an impasse as it attempted to identify the buyer, "uncovering no case interpreting the phrase [for the buyer]." In the end, the district court based its decision on two independent grounds. First, it found that the specially manufactured goods exception "contemplates that there may be only a single buyer for the exception [ ] to apply." Second, the district court concluded, the fact that "Webcor sold 'Duralast' packaging to multiple buyers" made the exception inapplicable. Given the facts of this case, we conclude that the reliance of the district court upon the existence of multiple purchasers provided a sound basis for its decision. However, we take note of the significant wrinkle presented in this case — a series of three-layered transactions involving multiple parties — as it impacts the traditional "look to the goods" rule in determining the buyer.

The latent shortcoming of the traditional test, as evidenced by the present case, is that the first and second prong of the *Colorado Carpet [Installation, Inc. v. Palermo*, 668 P.2d 1384, 1389 (Colo. 1983),] test form a somewhat circular meaning in the case law. On the one hand, goods are deemed "specially manufactured" when no other buyer would reasonably purchase the goods. . . . On the other hand, the buyer is deemed the party for whom the otherwise unsalable goods have been produced. Specially manufactured goods are therefore necessarily goods unsuitable for sale to others in the ordinary course of the seller's business. . . . In addition, however, the exception requires the presence of "circumstances which reasonably indicate that the goods are for the buyer." HAWKLAND, *supra*; *Colorado Carpet Installation*, 668 P.2d at 1390 (Colo. 1983) ("The term 'specially manufactured' refers to the character of the goods as specially manufactured *for a particular buyer*, and not to whether they were 'specially made' in the usual course of the seller's business."). This plain but somewhat tautological construction of the phrase "specially manufactured for the buyer" persists in the case law. . . .

The leading specially manufactured goods case, *Impossible Electronics Techniques, Inc. v. Wackenhut Protective Systems, Inc.*, 669 F.2d 1026 (5th Cir. 1982), provides a classic example of the circular treatment of the exception in the case law. In that case, George Wackenhut, chairman of the Wackenhut Company, the parent company of Wackenhut Protective Systems, Inc. (WPS), the defendant in the case, purchased a new security system for his home through a local retailer and installer of security equipment, Jackson & Church Electronics, Inc.

. . . .

At trial, IET argued that Mr. Wackenhut had entered into an oral agreement during the initial meeting in which he selected the IET closed-circuit system. Wackenhut asserted that the Florida statute of frauds precluded enforcement of the alleged oral agreement. IET then sought to invoke the specially manufactured goods exception.

The district court granted summary judgment to the defendants, finding that the statute of frauds prevented the alleged oral agreement from being deemed admissible at trial. Reversing the district court decision, the Fifth Circuit provided some insight into the question before this court when it observed: "The crucial inquiry is whether the manufacturer could sell the goods in the ordinary course of his business to someone other than the original buyer. If with slight alterations the goods could be so sold, then they are not specially manufactured; if, however, essential changes are necessary to render the goods marketable by the seller to others, then the exception does apply." The *Impossible Electronic Techniques* court answered the inquiry by finding that the cameras at issue had been specially made for Wackenhut, because the cameras had been specially created to automatically adjust to the extreme nighttime darkness and daytime sunlight reflecting off the beach and sea near the Wackenhut home. Thus, the court found that the unique relationship between the goods and the alleged buyer was sufficient to permit evidence of an oral agreement.

In the present case, the application of the "look to the goods rule" presents the following problem. There is no question that the "Duralast" logo and coloring affixed to the cartons at issue conform to the packaging used by Autozone, the only retailer in the business of selling "Duralast" brake parts. Thus, in looking to the goods, this court might well have concluded that the rule favors Webcor.[27] However, it is also true that

---

[27] [2] Indeed, Hawkland suggests that the plaintiff need only demonstrate a minimal relationship between the goods and the alleged buyer to justify a finding in its favor:

> "The fact that the seller has on hand goods that are particularly suitable for the buyer (for example, goods on which the buyer's name has been engraved, or a machine that only the buyer's factory can use) does not necessarily prove that the buyer ordered them. Apparently, however, *any indication in the goods themselves that they are for the buyer and are not suitable for sale to others*

numerous purchasers — the Autozone vendors — had an interest in purchasing the "Duralast" cartons to fulfill their obligations to provide packaged brake parts to Autozone. Even though those Autozone vendors purchased the cartons with intentions to sell them to Autozone, their very presence complicates the question of whether Autozone can be implicated as the buyer in this case.

Were our consideration solely limited to identifying the buyer under the exception, we might address this conundrum in two distinct ways. First, we might conclude that, notwithstanding the intermediate purchasers, the "Duralast" cartons were made especially for Autozone under the "ultimate purchaser" theory advanced by Webcor. Under that theory, intermediate purchasers are incidental to the inquiry. If the court "looks to the goods" and can determine that the goods have been made for a single downstream purchaser, the argument goes, that single purchaser is vulnerable under the specially manufactured goods exception. If this court took such a position, Autozone might well be found to be the buyer for purposes of the exception.[28]

In the alternative, we might adopt the district court's "single buyer" theory, which places a premium on a direct and singular economic relationship between the parties. Under this view, a court limits the applicability of the exception to instances in which no other purchasers of the unique goods could reasonably be expected to purchase the goods absent major alterations. However, this theory carries the significant disadvantage of being overly rigid in a world of increasingly complex business transactions.[29]

Although we leave the debate about which approach would prevail in cases where the "look to the goods" rule fails to provide a ready answer for another day, we implore courts to maintain the simplicity of the traditional rule — look to the goods themselves and make a determination of fact and law. As the *Colorado Carpet* formulation makes clear, identifying the buyer is not the sole issue in deciding whether to apply the specially manufactured goods exception.

In plain truth, the specially manufactured goods exception demands that we also consider factors other than the identity of the buyer. Although the parties attempt to confine the issue of whether the exception applies in this case to the identity of the buyer, the district court opinion went further than that and noted an independent basis for non-application of the exception. Were we to assume, for the sake of argument, that the district court erred in its determination of the buyer, the court still found that "the manufacture [had not been] commenced under circumstances reasonably indicating that the goods are for the buyer," when it stated in clear fashion that, "because Webcor sold 'Duralast' packaging to multiple buyers, the 'specially manufactured' exception to the UCC's statute of frauds is not applicable to the facts before the court." This determination operates as a separate basis upon which to affirm.

In reviewing this determination, we adopt an analysis that looks to several factors: (1) the course of dealings between the parties; (2) the flow of the allegedly specially manufactured goods; (3) the essence of goods to be received by the alleged buyer; and

---

is enough to satisfy section 2-201(3)(a), even where the buyer denies making the contract." HAWKLAND, *supra* (italics added).

[28] [3] The effect of such finding, however, would not automatically trigger reversal of the disposition below, because, as will be seen, the district court made an apparent determination that the presence of multiple intermediate purchasers served as a basis for finding the specially manufactured goods exception inapplicable here.

[29] [4] It would seem that, had Webcor sued the intermediaries, the single buyer theory would have operated to exclude all Autozone vendors as well, since there were numerous such vendors. In most instances, the single buyer rule operates in a manner consistent with the policy reasons supporting the exception. However, the rule seems to fail where a class of purchasers interested in the same unique goods prevails upon a manufacturer to produce such goods. We are assured by virtue of the goods themselves that they were produced for the benefit of a single downstream buyer. We are mindful, however, that the goods could have been sold by Webcor to any number of parties. The facts of the present case split the policy of the exception.

(4) the duty to compensate the manufacturer undertaken by or the existence of any right of repudiation of the alleged buyer. . . .

C.

Applying those factors to the instant case, we find that the "Duralast" cartons were not specially manufactured for Autozone. The course of dealings between the parties indicates that Webcor had long engaged in transactions with Autozone vendors and only rarely sold "Duralast" cartons directly to Autozone itself. The ongoing communications between Webcor and Autozone took place to the mutual benefit of both parties. Autozone reduced the risk of error in the manufacture of its cartons by referring its vendors to Webcor, a manufacturer experienced in the production of the "Duralast" cartons, while Webcor satisfied its direct clientele. Moreover, the referrals by Autozone were communicated directly to its vendors and implied no obligation on the part of those vendors to purchase the cartons from Webcor. Thus, the course of dealings indicates that Webcor formed agreements with many intermediate vendors and its usual contacts with Autozone only supplemented those agreements. Further, the alleged oral contract in which Autozone is claimed to have agreed to cover the increased supply of the cartons is consistent with Webcor's desire to supply such goods to the intermediaries. Therefore, the course of dealings factor weighs in favor of Autozone.

With regard to the second factor, there is no question that the "Duralast" cartons at issue in this case were manufactured for sale to the Autozone vendors (for later sale to Autozone). Therefore the cartons at issue would have flowed from Webcor to the Autozone vendors and only then to Autozone. The passage of the cartons through sale to Autozone vendors diminishes our usual assurance that production of special goods can be linked to the alleged buyer.

The essential goods to be received by Autozone under the arrangements existing at the time of the alleged oral agreement were finished brake parts, not empty "Duralast" cartons. While the cartons were part of the finished product, they did not, as a matter of course, comprise the complete purchase.

Finally, there has been no suggestion that Autozone had any duty to compensate Webcor for its production of "Duralast" cartons or any right to preempt production of the cartons on its own. Although Autozone did contact Webcor directly to convey that it planned to discontinue the "Duralast" line, this communication does not itself prove that such a duty prevailed upon Autozone.

Given that the four factors weigh in favor of Autozone, we conclude that the circumstances of manufacture of the "Duralast" cartons were so attenuated that the specially manufactured goods exception should not apply.

III.

Although the parties present the ultimate question in this case as a matter identifying the buyer, we conclude that the circumstances of manufacture do not manifest that the "Duralast" cartons were produced for Autozone. Accordingly, we AFFIRM.

QUESTIONS

1. Did the court find that course of dealing can trump the express language of the statute? Does the express language of the statute recognize that course of dealing might alter the effect of its provisions?

2. Is the specially manufactured goods exception grounded in equitable

considerations? What are those considerations in the *Webcor* case?

PROBLEM 2-8

Binghamton Auto Supplies reaches an oral agreement with Singh Packaging to purchase 24,000 custom designed boxes over a two-year period. Singh agrees to ship 1,000 boxes on the 15th day of each month during the two-year period. Singh created the templates for the boxes and created the first 1,000 boxes, which it shipped to Binghamton. However, Binghamton wrongly refused to accept the boxes and disclaimed any contractual obligation. Singh sues for breach of an agreement to purchase 24,000 boxes. Will Singh be able to avoid summary judgment under § 2-201?

SIAM NUMHONG PRODUCTS CO. v. EASTIMPEX
United States District Court, Northern District of California
866 F. Supp. 445 (1994)

PATEL, Judge.

[Ed. Note: This excerpt is a continuation of the opinion that appears above.]

There is a further reason why Eastimpex is not entitled to summary judgment on this claim: the judicial admissions exception to the statute of frauds. Eastimpex has acknowledged the existence of a wild bamboo shoot contract in numerous pleadings and papers submitted to this court. . . .

California amended its statute of frauds in 1988, effective 1990, to provide a "judicial admissions" exception where "the party against whom enforcement is sought admits in his or her pleading, testimony, or otherwise in court that a contract for sale was made . . . ." Cal. Com. Code § 2201(3)(b). The adoption of the judicial admissions exception emphasizes the evidentiary purpose of the statute of frauds. The California Supreme Court previously recognized this purpose in *Seaman's Direct Buying Service, Inc. v. Standard Oil Co.*, 36 Cal. 3d 752, 764, 206 Cal. Rptr. 354, 686 P.2d 1158 (1984), noting that the statute of frauds' primary purpose is to bar fraud-induced enforcement of contracts never actually made by requiring reliable evidence of the existence and terms of the contract. The statute of frauds is meant to prevent courts from enforcing an alleged oral contract that never actually was entered into, not to prevent enforcement of *all* oral contracts. *See id.*; Cal. Com. Code § 2201 Comm. 9. Thus, the statute of frauds defense may be asserted only against a wrongful allegation that one is a party to a contract, not simply to prevent enforcement of an agreement that happened to be oral.

There is no California case-law defining "judicial admission" under section 2201(3)(b). However, authorities from other jurisdictions with a similar exception are instructive. The rationale for the exception is that a party charged with a contractual obligation should not be able to assert the defense where it has admitted the existence of the contract. Courts have recognized that the danger of perjury by the party seeking to enforce the contract is dispelled when the other party admits to the oral agreement. *See Anchorage-Hynning & Co. v. Moringiello*, 225 U.S. App. D.C. 114, 697 F.2d 356, 360–63 (D.C. Cir. 1983) (discussing the exception as a judicially-created one although the District of Columbia statute contains such an exception).

A judicial admission may be contained in a statement of undisputed facts, an answer, a bill of particulars or any other pleading, or it may be contained in testimony such as a deposition. . . . Furthermore, the admission need not contain all the terms of the contract; it is sufficient if it describes the "conduct or circumstances from which the trier of fact can infer a contract." *Gruen Indus., Inc. v. Biller*, 608 F.2d 274, 278 (7th Cir. 1979) (discussing the Wisconsin statutory exception, which is more restrictive than California's).

The court finds that Eastimpex's numerous "admissions" that an oral contract existed constitute a judicial admission within the meaning of section 2201(3)(b), and therefore defeat its reliance on the statute of frauds.

NOTE

The *Siam* case indicates that Eastimpex "acknowledged existence of a wild bamboo shoot contract in numerous pleadings and papers." There is no detail given as to whether the admissions include admission of specific terms of the agreement, admission of the agreement as stated by the opposing party, or merely an admission that some agreement did in fact exist with no reference to specific terms. The court indicates that it is not necessary for the admission to contain all of the terms of the contract and that the facts need only provide enough evidence that the finder of fact could infer that a contract has been made. It is important to remember that whether there is an agreement, and the terms of any such agreement, are not questions that can be resolved by the judicial admission provision of § 2-201(3)(b). If the statute of frauds is satisfied with a judicial admission as to the existence of a contract for the sale of goods, then the admission would be evidence that might also be used to prove the existence of an agreement under § 2-204 and the terms of that agreement.

B & W GLASS, INC. v. WEATHER SHIELD MFG., INC.
Wyoming Supreme Court
829 P.2d 809 (1992)

THOMAS, Justice.

The only question involved in this case is the one certified to this court by the United States Court of Appeals for the Tenth Circuit. In the Certification of Question of State Law, that court states the certified question to be:

> Under the law of the State of Wyoming, may an oral promise otherwise within the statute of frauds as pronounced in Wyo. Stat. § 34.1-2-201 [1991] and the Uniform Commercial Code, nevertheless be enforceable on the basis of promissory estoppel? *See* Restatement (Second) of Contracts § 90 (1981).

We hold that the doctrine of promissory estoppel can be applied under these circumstances to enforce an oral promise, and the certified question is answered in the affirmative.

An understanding of the application of the doctrine of promissory estoppel by the federal district court in this case requires a careful review of the business transaction which preceded this litigation. B & W Glass, Inc. (B & W) is a Wyoming corporation that sells and installs windows in both commercial and residential buildings. The principals in B & W are three brothers, Larry, Tom, and Doug Ludtke. Sometime during the first three months of 1987, Larry Ludtke learned of a General Services Administration (GSA) project that called for replacement of all the windows in the federal courthouse in Casper, Wyoming. After reviewing the GSA plans, Larry Ludtke prepared a list of specifications for the windows to be replaced, including dimensions, depth, and types of glazing required.

Doug Ludtke then contacted Weather Shield Mfg., Inc. (Weather Shield) which is a Wisconsin corporation engaged in the manufacture of both standard size and custom windows. The purpose of Doug Ludtke's contact was to obtain a price quotation. Robert Schwalbe (Schwalbe), an experienced salesman familiar with bidding practices and price quotation procedures, acted on behalf of Weather Shield. Using the list of specifications that Larry Ludtke had prepared, Doug Ludtke discussed the GSA project with Schwalbe in Denver, Colorado. In the course of the first meeting, Schwalbe indicated he thought Weather Shield could produce the windows required for the project, but he explained he needed to check with company officials in Wisconsin.

At a brief second meeting between Schwalbe and Doug Ludtke, Schwalbe presented an itemized, written quotation, dated March 24, 1987, for windows to be used on the project. There is a dispute between the parties with respect to the specific type of windows quoted. Weather Shield's claim is that the quotation was for windows that are mass produced and normally stocked or carried in the company's catalog. B & W's contention is that the quotation included custom windows as well as stock windows. Subsequently, Larry Ludtke reviewed the written quotation, and he telephoned Schwalbe advising him there were too many size discrepancies in the quotation and custom windows, designed to meet GSA specifications, would be required.

A third meeting was scheduled between Schwalbe and Doug Ludtke, in Denver, for the purpose of reviewing the complete GSA project plans and specifications. At trial, Doug Ludtke testified that, at this third meeting, he and Schwalbe went through the plans and specifications together. He said Schwalbe indicated using custom windows would increase the cost, but Weather Shield had no problem in making the custom windows. Doug Ludtke stated that, at the conclusion of this meeting, he gave Schwalbe a copy of the plans and specifications to use preparing a bid. Schwalbe testified, to the contrary, that he could not have been provided with plans and specifications since he spent only forty-five minutes preparing the new quotation.

It is uncontroverted that, following the third meeting with Doug Ludtke, and on or before April 14, 1987, Schwalbe telephoned Larry Ludtke to quote a price of $101,725 for the Weather Shield windows to be used on the project. B & W never received written confirmation of this oral price quotation.

On April 14, 1987, B & W, relying upon the Weather Shield price quotation, submitted its bid to the project's general contractor. The B & W bid was oral and was delivered by telephone around noon on the day that the general contractor's bid for the project was submitted. Two days later, Larry Ludtke was advised that B & W was the low bidder for supplying and installing the windows on the project. B & W also received a letter of intent, dated April 20, 1987, from the general contractor. Larry Ludtke then telephoned Schwalbe to advise him that B & W had received the letter of intent and that B & W would purchase Weather Shield windows for the project.

In either May or June, 1987, Larry Ludtke and Schwalbe met in Cheyenne to review the plans and specifications in detail. Schwalbe received another set of the plans and specifications to send to the Weather Shield plant so that "shop drawings" could be prepared for the construction of the windows. Schwalbe and Larry Ludtke exchanged numerous telephone calls during the balance of the summer in the course of which they discussed the progress of the shop drawings and delivery and production schedules.

After B & W signed a contract with the general contractor in August of 1987, Larry Ludtke arranged for "field measurements" on the existing windows at the Casper federal courthouse. Larry Ludtke, accompanied by an architect from the Cheyenne area, met with Schwalbe in Denver in September to discuss these measurements. During that meeting, Larry Ludtke delivered a letter to Schwalbe, dated September 21, 1987, requesting the shop drawings and providing another set of plans which contained the "field measurements" of the window sizes.

Following that meeting, from late September to December 3, 1987, Larry Ludtke telephoned Schwalbe on numerous occasions, each time requesting the shop drawings and other information. Finally, during the December 3 telephone call, Schwalbe committed to the completion of the shop drawings by December 14, 1987. This commitment was ineffectual, however, because Schwalbe's employment with Weather Shield was terminated in December, 1987. When Larry Ludtke failed to receive the shop drawings and was not able to contact Schwalbe, other Weather Shield employees were contacted. Ultimately, on December 30, 1987, Tom Ludtke spoke to a Weather Shield supervisor, Dan Emerich, who said that Weather Shield could not produce the windows.

After Weather Shield declined to produce the windows, B & W obtained custom windows from another manufacturer at a total cost of $226,579. Upon demand, Weather Shield refused to pay B & W the difference between Weather Shield's quoted price and the actual cost of the windows purchased from the other manufacturer.

B & W then filed suit in the District Court of the First Judicial District of the State of Wyoming in and for Laramie County. Weather Shield answered and successfully petitioned for removal of the case to the United States District Court for the District of Wyoming, pursuant to 28 U.S.C. § 1332 (1986). Extensive discovery followed, after which Weather Shield moved for summary judgment on the ground that no written contract existed between the parties and the purported oral contract was unenforceable under the Wyoming enactment of the Uniform Commercial Code (UCC) statute of frauds. At the same time, B & W moved to amend its complaint to add a claim of promissory estoppel. Weather Shield's motion for summary judgment was denied, and the B & W motion to amend was granted. The United States District Court ruled that Wyoming would allow the doctrine of promissory estoppel to remove an oral contract from the statute of frauds provision found in the UCC.

The case went to trial on three theories: breach of contract; breach of good faith and fair dealing; and promissory estoppel. The United States District Court granted a directed verdict in favor of Weather Shield on the breach of contract and good faith and fair dealing claims. The promissory estoppel theory was submitted to the jury. The jury found in favor of B & W, but it was deadlocked with respect to damages, and the United States District Court declared a mistrial. Weather Shield then moved for a directed verdict and to strike the jury and enter judgment in its favor. The United States District Court granted Weather Shield's motion to strike the jury, but it entered judgment in favor of B & W.

In an opinion order, the United States District Court found that Schwalbe was an authorized agent of Weather Shield and was aware of the plans and specifications for the courthouse project prior to making the oral bid. The court ruled that the bid quotation was made "without any exceptions," which, under usage of the trade, meant the quote was for products meeting the plans and specifications that had been provided. The United States District Court concluded that promissory estoppel had been established and the oral contract between the parties existed and was enforceable despite the statute of frauds provision in Wyoming's version of the UCC. Judgment was entered against Weather Shield for breach of contract in the amount of $100,214.48, with interest. Weather Shield took an appeal to the United States Court of Appeals for the Tenth Circuit, which certified the promissory estoppel question to this court.

The facts stated above essentially are contained in the Findings of Fact entered in the United States District Court and the Certification of Question of State Law from the United States Court of Appeals for the Tenth Circuit, both of which were made a part of the record before this court. Other than certain preliminary matters, the parties sharply contest the facts of this case. In its appeal to the United States Court of Appeals for the Tenth Circuit, Weather Shield has assigned error with respect to some of the district court findings. That dispute is not a part of the case before this court, however. The role of this court in answering certified questions does not include fact finding.

*   *   *

The answer to a pure question of law presented for our determination does not require certainty with respect to the facts.

*   *   *

The certified question presented by the United States Court of Appeals for the Tenth Circuit asks whether an equitable principle, promissory estoppel, will be applied to defeat the operation of a statute of frauds. The philosophical conflict embodied in this question implicates principles of statutory construction, fundamental fairness, and certainty in the law which have been the subject of legal debate in the English common law system since the Middle Ages. *See* HENRY L. McCLINTOCK, HANDBOOK OF THE PRINCIPLES OF EQUITY § 22 (2nd ed. 1948). The policy choice required by this certified question is one that demands a detailed review. The analysis pursued considers the specific section or sections of the UCC that are applicable in this controversy; the effect of that application; the authorization under the UCC to invoke equitable principles generally; whether the UCC displaced equitable principles with its statute of frauds; the role of promissory estoppel in Wyoming's jurisprudence apart from statutes; and, finally, the application of promissory estoppel in the context of the UCC statute of frauds. *See* Robert S. Summers, *General Equitable Principles Under Section 1-103 of the Uniform Commercial Code*, 72 Nw. U. L. REV. 906 (1978) [hereinafter General *Equitable Principles*].

Promissory estoppel is a doctrine incorporated in the law of contracts. Restatement (Second) Contracts § 90 (1981). Judge Posner has provided a considered and succinct description of the doctrine: "If an unambiguous promise is made in circumstances calculated to induce reliance, and it does so, the promisee if hurt as a result can recover damages." *Goldstick v. ICM Realty*, 788 F.2d 456, 462 (7th Cir. 1986). Promissory estoppel is recognized as both a sword and a shield — a cause of action and a defense. Equitable estoppel is a close relative, but it is a tort doctrine that requires proof of misrepresentation. *Goldstick*.

Neither party disputes the applicability of the UCC, as adopted in Wyoming, to the transaction that resulted in this litigation. At its most basic level, that transaction involved a sale of goods, windows, by a seller, Weather Shield, to a buyer, B & W. B & W contends an oral contract was formed between the parties upon which it relied, to its detriment. Weather Shield challenges the reliance upon an oral contract contending that, even if one existed, it was for goods priced at $500 or more and cannot be enforced under the UCC statute of frauds . . . .

In this case, there is no writing that satisfies the requirements of § 2-201(a) or (b). None of the three exceptions to the writing requirement, set forth in subsection (c) of the statute, apply to the facts as stated. Weather Shield contends that the exceptions found in subsections (b) and (c) are the exclusive exceptions to the statute of frauds recognized under the UCC. Weather Shield supports this argument by reference to the language: "Except as otherwise provided in this section . . . ." Wyo. Stat. § 34.1-2-201(a) (1991). Weather Shield asserts that this language demonstrates the legislative intent to limit the exceptions. Acceptance of this restrictive view espoused by Weather Shield would result in a conclusion that the effect of § 2-201 is to prevent enforcement of the oral agreement between the parties.

B & W argues that the UCC, read as a whole, incorporates a provision that supplements the language of § 2-201 with the principles of equity, including promissory estoppel. It points to the provisions of Wyo. Stat. § 34.1-1-103 (1991), previously codified as Wyo. Stat. § 34-21-103 (1977) (hereinafter § 1-103) . . . .

*   *   *

B & W's argument is that the language of § 2-201 does not specifically displace promissory estoppel as that doctrine supplements the provisions of the code pursuant to § 1-103. Acceptance of the liberal view espoused by B & W results in a conclusion that the effect of § 1-103 is to allow promissory estoppel to defeat the operation of the statutes of frauds.

. . . The majority position espouses the rule that principles of promissory estoppel under § 1-103 operate as an exception to the statute of frauds. The minority position is that estoppel does not constitute an exception to the requirements of § 2-201. Note, *Promissory Estoppel: Subcontractors' Liability in Construction Bidding Cases*, 63 N.C. L. REV. 387 (1985). B & W and Weather Shield vigorously urge the positions found in the authorities that support their respective views. We have identified appropriate points of departure for consideration in our review of this issue.

Two general themes can be identified in the authorities of those jurisdictions that approve a promissory estoppel exception to the UCC statute of frauds. If an estoppel exception has been generally recognized in that jurisdiction under other statutes of frauds, then the exception usually has been found in § 2-201. *See, e.g., R.S. Bennett &*

Co., Inc. v. Economy Mechanical Industries, Inc., 606 F.2d 182 (7th Cir. 1979) (applying Illinois law); *Ralston Purina Co. v. McCollum*, 271 Ark. 840, 611 S.W.2d 201 (Ark. Ct. App. 1981); *Warder & Lee Elevator, Inc. v. Britten*, 274 N.W.2d 339 (Iowa 1979); *Decatur Co-op Ass'n v. Urban*, 219 Kan. 171, 547 P.2d 323 (Kan. 1976); *Potter v. Hatter Farms, Inc.*, 56 Ore. App. 254, 641 P.2d 628 (Or. Ct. App. 1982). These courts in approving of the exception have held that § 1-103 allows the doctrine of promissory estoppel to supplement § 2-201. *Allen M. Campbell Co., General Contractors, Inc. v. Virginia Metal Industries, Inc.*, 708 F.2d 930 (4th Cir. 1983) (applying North Carolina law).

The *Allen M. Campbell* case, arising under factually similar surroundings to this case, provides a useful example of the analysis and rationale used by those courts approving the use of promissory estoppel. Allen M. Campbell Co. had prepared a bid on a Department of the Navy contract to construct housing. Only one-half hour before the bids were due, Virginia Metal Industries telephoned Allen M. Campbell Co. and quoted a price for hollow metal doors and frames that would meet the plans and specifications. Allen M. Campbell Co. based its bid on the quoted price and was awarded the contract. Virginia Metal Industries then backed out of the contract and Allen M. Campbell Co. covered by purchasing doors from another supplier at a higher cost. The United States Court of Appeals for the Fourth Circuit ruled that North Carolina recognized and applied the doctrine of promissory estoppel. *Allen M. Campbell.* The court stated that, pursuant to § 1-103, equitable principles were available to supplement § 2-201 and, after surveying relevant case law, the court concluded that North Carolina's approval of promissory estoppel provisions in the Restatement (Second) of Contracts §§ 90, 139 (1981) signaled its acceptance of the view that promissory estoppel avoids the statue of frauds.

In those jurisdictions that have espoused the rule that promissory estoppel is not available to avoid the statue of frauds under the UCC, consistent themes also are discernable. The fundamental distinction begins with the refusal to consider § 1-103 as supplementing the UCC with principles of equity, including estoppel. *See, e.g., C.R. Fedrick, Inc. v. Borg-Warner Corp.*, 552 F.2d 852 (9th Cir. 1977) (applying California law); *McDabco, Inc. v. Chet Adams Co.*, 548 F. Supp. 456 (D.S.C. 1982) (applying South Carolina Law); *Cox v. Cox*, 292 Ala. 106, 289 So. 2d 609 (Ala. 1974); *C.G. Campbell & Son, Inc. v. Comdeq Corp.*, 586 S.W.2d 40 (Ky. Ct. App. 1979); *Anderson Const. Co., Inc. v. Lyon Metal Products, Inc.*, 370 So. 2d 935 (Miss. 1979). Another reason those courts have chosen to deny the use of promissory estoppel as available to avoid § 2-201 is the refusal in those jurisdictions to permit the doctrines of estoppel to defeat general statutes of frauds . . . .

A leading decision that rejects the application of promissory estoppel to avoid the statute of frauds found in § 2-201 is *Lige Dickson [Co. v. Union Oil Co. of California]*, 96 Wash. 2d 291, 635 P.2d 103 [(Wash. 1981)]. The question presented in that case to the Supreme Court of Washington was whether an oral price protection agreement with a liquid asphalt supplier would be upheld. The buyer relied on the consistent selling price in submitting bids for construction contracts. The Washington court reviewed its previous position denying the invocation of promissory estoppel to overcome the general statute of frauds and noting the limiting language at the beginning of § 2-201, that court ruled promissory estoppel is not available to overcome the UCC's statute of frauds. The need for uniformity among different jurisdictions and decisions affecting commercial transactions was offered as another reason not to permit promissory estoppel to circumvent the statute of frauds in the UCC.

Conflicting decisions of state and federal courts in the same jurisdiction further magnify the divergence in precedent. *Compare, e.g., McDabco* (holding estoppel not available in South Carolina to defeat § 2-201), with *Atlantic Wholesale Co., Inc. v. Solondz*, 283 S.C. 36, 320 S.E.2d 720 (S.C. Ct. App. 1984) (holding a silver dealer would be allowed to recover for the buyer's breach of an oral contract because, in South

Carolina, estoppel prevented the buyer from asserting a defense of failure to comply with § 2-201); *see also Goldstick* (declining to rule on present status of Illinois law). Another example is found in California where the Ninth Circuit Court of Appeals applied state law and ruled the doctrine of estoppel could not be used to defeat the need for a writing under § 2-201. *C.R. Fedrick.* The California Court of Appeal, however, ruled in *Allied Grape Growers v. Bronco Wine Co.*, 203 Cal. App. 3d 432, 249 Cal. Rptr. 872 (Cal. Ct. App. 1988), that promissory estoppel constituted an exception to § 2-201. The *Allied Grape* court critically said the Ninth Circuit used inconsistent analysis, failed to consider the effect of § 1-103 and, in conclusional fashion, found the statute of frauds would be eviscerated if estoppel applied.

In our view, the better-reasoned approach is articulated by those courts that have approved the majority view that promissory estoppel avoids § 2-201. We do not accept, however, the argument that this question can be resolved by simply adopting the logic of one line of decisions. The divergent authorities offer an opportunity for choice without specific policy concerns. That approach leads away from a primary duty of this court which is the charge that we implement legislative policy found in the enactment of the UCC. We conclude that the analysis of the certified question becomes primarily a matter of statutory interpretation for which Wyoming has established standards.

Questions that reach to statutory interpretation require the court to endeavor to perceive the legislative intent. *Phillips v. Duro-Last Roofing, Inc.*, 806 P.2d 834 (Wyo. 1991). Legislative intent is to be ascertained, insofar as possible, from the language incorporated in the statute, which is viewed in light of its object and purpose. *Belle Fourche Pipeline Co. v. State*, 766 P.2d 537 (Wyo. 1988). Statutes that relate to the same subject matter should be harmonized whenever that is possible. *Stauffer Chemical Co. v. Curry*, 778 P.2d 1083 (Wyo. 1989). In pursuing this endeavor every subsection of a statute must be read in the context of all others to ascertain the meaning of the whole statute. *Gookin v. State Farm Fire and Casualty Ins.*, 826 P.2d 229 (Wyo. 1992); *Story v. State*, 755 P.2d 228 (Wyo. 1988).

In addition to these general rules of statutory construction, the UCC also has incorporated within it useful rules of construction and a statement of its purpose. The act is to be liberally construed and applied to promote its underlying purposes and policies. Wyo. Stat. § 34.1-1-102(a) (1991); *Century Ready-Mix Co. v. Lower & Co.*, 770 P.2d 692 (Wyo. 1989), *appeal after remand sub nom. Century Ready-Mix Co. v. Campbell County School Dist.*, 816 P.2d 795 (1991). According to the legislative pronouncement, the purposes of the UCC are to simplify, clarify, and modernize the law governing commercial transactions; to permit continued expansion of commercial practices through custom, usage, and agreement of the parties; and to make uniform the law among the various jurisdictions. Wyo. Stat. § 34.1-1-102(b) (1991). Professors White and Summers suggest a further purpose of the UCC is "that the law of commercial transactions be, so far as reasonable, liberal and nontechnical." 1 JAMES J. WHITE & ROBERT S. SUMMERS, UNIFORM COMMERCIAL CODE § 4 (3d ed. 1988) [hereinafter WHITE & SUMMERS]. The authors apparently disagree, however, on the application of the doctrine of estoppel to avoid the statute of frauds. WHITE & SUMMERS §§ 2-6, 2-8. The official comments attached to the UCC, while not controlling an interpretation of the scope and intent of the Code, are persuasive. *ABM Escrow Closing and Consulting, Inc. v. Matanuska Maid, Inc.*, 659 P.2d 1170 (Alaska 1983).

In Wyoming, rigid adherence to the UCC statute of frauds is contrary to the liberal construction philosophy surrounding the code. *Century Ready-Mix.* Professor Corbin, in urging the adoption of the UCC by the several states, noted: "The purpose of the statute of frauds is to prevent the enforcement of alleged promises that never were made; it is not, and never has been, to justify contractors in repudiating promises that were in fact made." Arthur L. Corbin, *The Uniform Commercial Code — Sales; Should It Be Enacted?*, 59 YALE L.J. 821, 829 (1950). Another commentator asserts that the statute of frauds is the weapon of the written law to prevent fraud; estoppel is the equitable means invoked to achieve this end. 3 WALTER H.E. JAEGER, WILLISTON ON CONTRACTS § 533A (3d ed. 1960).

In light of our approach to statutory construction, we are satisfied that, if promissory estoppel is to become an exception to § 2-201, it must be because of the provisions of § 1-103. Estoppel is specifically included in the listing of principles supplementing the UCC. Wyo. Stat. § 34.1-1-103 (1991). We previously have recognized the entree to general principles of law and equity found in § 1-103 to supplement the UCC. *Western Nat. Bank of Casper v. Harrison*, 577 P.2d 635 (Wyo. 1978) (allowing the law of waiver to supplement UCC provisions). Unless it is displaced, § 1-103 imposes a duty to interpret and construe the UCC by taking into account the equities of a particular case. *General Equitable Principles*, 72 Nw. U. L. REV. 906.

We adopt the suggestions of Professor Summers as a framework for our analysis of whether the equitable principle of promissory estoppel can apply despite the statute of frauds in the UCC. His proposition is that the supplementary principles of law and equity incorporated into the operation of the UCC by virtue of § 1-103 survive unless it can be established that: (1) the principle is explicitly displaced by name in the plain language of the statute; (2) the specific objectives of the section would be served only by displacement of the principles of law and equity; (3) the general objectives of the UCC are best furthered by displacement of those principles; and (4) the legislative history plainly indicates displacement. *General Equitable Principles*, 72 Nw. U. L. REV. 906. We will apply these criteria in our consideration of the question of whether § 2-201 displaces promissory estoppel.

Certainly, the UCC does require that supplemental bodies of law be "explicitly displaced" to void the effect of § 1-103. Wyo. Stat. § 34.1-1-103 (1991) (Official Comment 1). Neither the text of § 2-201 nor the comments following it specifically refer to estoppel. WHITE & SUMMERS § 2-7. This silence on the part of the legislature in the language of the statute can not be construed to constitute a displacement of estoppel principles. *Potter*, 641 P.2d 628. For this reason, we disagree with the conclusions of the court in *Futch v. James River-Norwalk, Inc.*, 722 F. Supp. 1395 (S.D. Miss.), *aff'd*, 887 F.2d 1085 (5th Cir. 1989), and *McDabco*, 548 F. Supp. 456, that the opening language of § 2-201 represents a displacement of the principles of promissory estoppel. As found in § 2-201, the phrase "except as otherwise provided in this section" is simply a clause modifying the first subsection. Wyo. Stat. § 34.1-2-201(a) (1991). The intention of the Wyoming legislature in beginning Subsection (a) with that clause, is apparent from a reading of the entire section. Subsection (a) is the general statement of the statute of frauds applicable to the sale of goods. WHITE & SUMMERS § 2-3. The effect of the initial limiting language in subsection (a) is to alert the reader that the remaining subsections are disjunctive, and it serves to advise the reader of the proposition that the statutory exceptions to the statute of frauds are contained in subsections (b) and (c). Furthermore, the statutory exceptions listed in § 2-201(c) are not exhaustive. *Warder & Lee Elevator*, 274 N.W.2d 339; WHITE & SUMMERS § 2-7. Neither the language of the statute of frauds nor any legislative history indicates that § 2-201 displaces promissory estoppel.

Secondly, we conclude the specific objectives of § 2-201 would not be served by displacing promissory estoppel. The long-stated purpose of the statute of frauds is to prevent fraud from perjured testimony about nonexistent oral agreements. However, the concepts of equity and the passage of years resulted in the creation of exceptions to the writing requirement as a necessity to prevent substantive fraud. The part performance doctrine is one such exception that is specifically stated in the UCC. Wyo. Stat. § 34.1-2-201(c)(iii) (1991). Still, the UCC was not dated to anticipate the equities of every possible transaction. The specific inclusion of § 1-103 permits the invocation of principles of both law and equity as necessary to the resolution of commercial disputes. An adherence to a strict policy of demanding a writing in all cases that are not specifically exempted by § 2-201(b) or (c) would allow unscrupulous contractors to perpetrate fraud after creating reliance. The courts should be vigilant to inhibit the defense of the statute of frauds when that defense becomes an instrument for perpetrating fraud. *Vogel v. Shaw,* 42 Wyo. 333, 294 P. 687 (1930).

The third factor to be considered is whether the general objectives of the UCC would be served by displacement of promissory estoppel. We conclude they would not. The *Lige Dickson* court argued that uniformity among the several jurisdictions was the reason not to allow promissory estoppel to avoid the statute of frauds. *Lige Dickson,* 96 Wash. 2d 291, 635 P.2d 103. That logic is not persuasive in view of the fact that the majority of jurisdictions allow promissory estoppel to avoid the provisions of § 2-201. *Drennan v. Star Paving Co.,* 51 Cal. 2d 409, 333 P.2d 757 (Cal. 1958), is a leading case allowing promissory estoppel to defeat a general statute of frauds. Writing for the Supreme Court of California, Justice Traynor clearly set forth the principle of fairness implicit in recognizing the doctrine of promissory estoppel:

> When [the general contractor] used [the subcontractor's] offer in computing his own bid, he bound himself to perform in reliance on [the subcontractor's] terms. Though [the subcontractor] did not bargain for this use of its bid neither did [the subcontractor] make it idly, indifferent to whether it would be used or not. On the contrary it is reasonable to suppose that [the subcontractor] submitted its bid to obtain the subcontract. It was bound to realize the substantial possibility that its bid would be the lowest, and that it would be included by [the general contractor] in his bid. It was to its own interest that the contractor be awarded the general contract; the lower the subcontract bid, the lower the general contractor's bid was likely to be and the greater its chance of acceptance and hence the greater [the subcontractor's] chance of getting the paving subcontract. [The subcontractor] had reason not only to expect [the general contractor] to rely on its bid but to want him to. Clearly [the subcontractor] had a stake in [the general contractor's] reliance on its bid. Given this interest and the fact that [the general contractor] is bound by his own bid, it is only fair that [the general contractor] should have at least an opportunity to accept [the subcontractor's bid] after the general contract has been awarded to him.

Drennan, 333 P.2d at 760.

The invocation of the doctrine of promissory estoppel to avoid § 2-201 is consistent with authority that permits promissory estoppel to avoid a general statute of frauds. *See* Robert A. Brazener, Annotation, *Comment Note — Promissory Estoppel as Basis for Avoidance Statute of Frauds,* 56 A.L.R.3d 1037 (1974 & Supp. 1991). The argument that application of promissory estoppel should change depending upon whether goods (UCC) or services (general statute) are involved simply begs the fundamental question of fairness. If the application of promissory estoppel is fair in one context, it must also be in the other. Reliance created by a subcontractor, who quotes a price for services, is the same as that which is created by another subcontractor, who quotes a price for goods. Therefore, in addition to the statutory exceptions found in § 2-201, the nonstatutory exception to the writing requirement, promissory estoppel, is also present through § 1-103. *Northwest Potato Sales, Inc. v. Beck,* 208 Mont. 310, 678 P.2d 1138 (Mont. 1984); WHITE & SUMMERS § 2-6.

A recognition that promissory estoppel avoids the UCC statute of frauds is consistent with our prior Wyoming cases. *See Inter-Mountain Threading, Inc. v. Baker Hughes Tubular Services, Inc.,* 812 P.2d 555 (Wyo. 1991), and the cases cited in that opinion. While some courts have expressed a reservation to the effect that recognizing nonstatutory exceptions to the statute of frauds may render it a nullity, *McDabco,* 548 F. Supp. 456, Wyoming has accepted a role of leadership in invoking equitable principles to avoid injustice. The need to enforce an implied promise to mortgage some cattle resulted in the first approval in Wyoming of the doctrine of promissory estoppel as stated in the Restatement of Contracts, § 90 (1932). *Hanna State & Savings Bank v. Matson,* 53 Wyo. 1, 77 P.2d 621 (1938). In *Tremblay v. Reid,* 700 P.2d 391 (Wyo. 1985),

Wyoming adopted the principles of promissory estoppel as they are stated in the Restatement (Second) Contracts § 90(1) (1981).

The drafters of the Restatement (Second) have taken an even more definite position on the availability of promissory estoppel to avoid the statute of frauds:

> (1) A promise which the promissor should reasonably expect to induce action or forbearance on the part of the promisee or a third person and which does induce the action or forbearance is enforceable notwithstanding the Statute of Frauds if injustice can be avoided only by enforcement of the promise. The remedy granted for breach is [to] be limited as justice requires.

Restatement (Second) Contracts § 139 (1981). The drafters of the Restatement (Second) use *Vogel*, 42 Wyo. 333, 294 P. 687, as an illustration of the section's application to avoid injustice. Restatement (Second) Contracts § 139 (Reporter's Note 1981). In *Remilong v. Crolla*, 576 P.2d 461 (Wyo. 1978), this court approved the use of promissory estoppel, as phrased in the Restatement (Second), to avoid the general statute of frauds in Wyoming. In that case, we ruled that buyers of land could enforce an oral promise from the seller that all trailers would be removed from adjacent lands.

Our most recent cases are demonstrative of the safeguards that are present in the application of the doctrine of promissory estoppel. The elements of promissory estoppel demand evidence that establishes: "(1) a clear and definite agreement; (2) proof that the party urging the doctrine acted to its detriment in reasonable reliance on the agreement; and (3) a finding that the equities support enforcement of the agreement." *Inter-Mountain Threading*, 812 P.2d at 559; *Provence v. Hilltop Nat. Bank*, 780 P.2d 990, 993 (Wyo. 1989). The party who is asserting promissory estoppel is assigned the burden of establishing all of the elements of the doctrine with a standard of strict proof. *Provence*. In both *Inter-Mountain Threading* and *Provence*, the party seeking relief by invoking promissory estoppel failed to establish the requisite elements. *Inter-Mountain Threading; Provence. See also Four Nines Gold, Inc. v. 71 Const., Inc.*, 809 P.2d 236 (Wyo. 1991).

We do not share the concern that was present in the English courts of the 17th Century to the effect that a writing is the sole method to avoid undetected perjured testimony. Our judicial system is capable of discerning perjury and reaching a determination in an instance in which a litigant establishes promissory estoppel by appropriately assuming his burden.

Consistently with the majority rule and the law in Wyoming relating to general statutes of frauds, we conclude that promissory estoppel can and does justify the enforcement of an oral promise otherwise within the statute of frauds in the UCC, as articulated in Wyo. Stat. § 34.1-2-201 (1991). Under the foregoing analysis, our answer to the certified question is "yes."

QUESTIONS

1. The *B & W Glass* court focused on the introductory clause of § 2-201(1): "[e]xcept as otherwise provided in this section . . . ." Jurisdictions are split over the precise meaning of this language. Most jurisdictions hold that the phrase does not limit the exceptions to the writing requirement to only those enumerated. However, a minority refuses to recognize any exceptions to the statue of frauds other than those provided in §§ 2-201(3)(b) and (c).

2. Refer back to the discussion of the "judicial admission" exception in *Siam v. Eastimpex*. Given the *B&W Glass* holding that promissory estoppel can serve as an exception to the statute of frauds writing requirement, could the court in *Siam* have reached the same result on a theory of estoppel rather than "judicial admission"?

2. The Enforceability of Firm Offers Not Supported by Consideration

Under ordinary principles of contract law, a promise to hold an offer open is considered an "option" contract, which must meet all the requirements for a contract, including consideration. However, option contracts are an ordinary feature of commercial life, and it would pose problems to enforce only those firm offers that were supported by bargained-for consideration. In § 2-205, Article 2 ensures that firm offers are enforceable if set forth in a signed writing, despite the absence of separate consideration, subject to certain limitations. Although this rule is intended to make it easier for parties to enforce firm offers made by merchants, the details of the rule introduce their own complexities.

The CISG provides a good contrast to § 2-205. The CISG provides a much more relaxed standard for enforceability. Under Article 16(2)(a), an offeror may make an offer irrevocable "by stating a fixed time for acceptance or otherwise." Unlike the UCC, which limits the period of an irrevocable offer to three months, the CISG imposes no limit.

COASTAL AVIATION, INC. v. COMMANDER AIRCRAFT CO.
United States District Court, Southern District of New York
937 F. Supp. 1051 (1996)

WILLIAM C. CONNER, Senior United States District Judge.

Plaintiff Coastal Aviation Incorporated ("Coastal") brings this action against defendant Commander Aircraft Company ("Commander"), seeking $5,319,424 in damages arising out of an alleged breach of a contract for Coastal's exclusive dealership rights to sell Commander airplanes. This court conducted a two-day bench trial on May 21–22, 1996. This opinion constitutes the court's findings of fact and conclusions of law pursuant to Fed. R. Civ. P. 52(a). For reasons discussed below, we enter judgment in favor of defendant on all claims.

*   *   *

CONCLUSIONS OF LAW

*   *   *

Plaintiff Coastal asserts two breach of contract claims: (1) breach of an option contract for the sale of aircraft for the New York Area and (2) breach of a contract for the sale of aircraft for the Southeast Territory. Coastal seeks damages in lost profits for these purported breaches. In addition, Coastal seeks reimbursement for out-of-pocket expenses incurred when its officers traveled to the roll-out in Bethany, Oklahoma. At trial, Coastal submitted letters that were transmitted between the parties during negotiations. In addition, officers of Coastal testified regarding oral and written communications and negotiations that had taken place between the parties. Finally, Coastal produced two experts (Zweifler and Lomas) who testified as to the amount of damages suffered as a result of the purported breaches. Defendant Commander cross-examined Coastal's witnesses, but produced no witnesses of its own. Commander maintains that Coastal has failed to prove that there was either an option contract for the New York Area or that there was a contract for the Southeast Territory. Commander also argues that, even assuming that Coastal has proved there was a contract for either or both of these areas, Coastal has failed to prove damages with the requisite level of certainty to recover under New York law.

I. CONTRACT FORMATION

To succeed in a breach of contract claim, four elements must be satisfied: the making of a contract, performance of the contract by the plaintiff, breach of the contract by the defendant, and damages suffered by the plaintiff. . . . Commander challenges the first and fourth elements in this action.

Basic principles of contract law and Article 2 of the Uniform Commercial Code ("UCC") as adopted by New York govern because the overall contract as alleged was predominantly for the sale and delivery of goods. . . .

A. THE NEW YORK AREA OPTION

We first address Coastal's claim that Commander granted it an option for the New York Area. Coastal rests this claim on Boettger's March 19, 1992 letter indicating that Boettger had requested Goodman to reserve the New York Area for Coastal during the pendency of their negotiations. ("I have requested [Goodman] to reserve New York and New Jersey for Coastal until we have finished our discussions.").

> An option contract is an agreement to hold an offer open; it confers upon the optionee, for consideration paid, the right to purchase at a later date. . . . Coastal has neither alleged nor argued that any consideration was paid for this purported option.

However, under New York law, a "firm offer" by a merchant can create an option contract enforceable against the merchant by the offeree, even in the absence of consideration:

> An offer by a merchant to buy or sell goods in a signed writing which by its terms gives assurance that it will be held open is not revocable, for lack of consideration, during the time stated or if no time is stated for a reasonable time, but in no event may such period of irrevocability exceed three months; but any such term of assurance on a form supplied by the offeree must be separately signed by the offeror.

N.Y. U.C.C. § 2-205 (McKinney 1993).[30] Based on this section, Coastal argues that Boettger's letter of March 19, 1992 creates a binding option contract under New York law in favor of Coastal. We disagree.

In order to establish an option under the merchant's firm offer rule, there must be an "offer by a merchant to buy or sell goods in a signed writing which by its terms *gives assurance that it will be held open.*" N.Y. U.C.C. § 2-205 (McKinney 1993) (emphasis added). Boettger's letter of March 19, 1992 is devoid of any offer within the meaning of section 2-205. Rather, Boettger relays a statement about a communication that occurred between him and Goodman. In so doing, Boettger merely expresses his willingness to reserve the New York Area for future discussions with Coastal in hopes of reaching an agreement for a dealership in that area. He conveys no assurance that the New York Area will be available, nor a commitment on the part of Commander to reserve the New York Area for Coastal. An enforceable legal right cannot arise in contract without the

---

[30] [3] New York General Obligations Law contains a similar provision for contracts falling outside section 2-205 of the New York Uniform Commercial Code:

> Except as provided in section 2-205 of the uniform commercial code with respect to an offer by a merchant to buy or sell goods, when an offer to enter into a contract is made in a writing signed by the offeror, or by his agent, which states that the offer is irrevocable during a period set forth or until a time fixed, the offer shall not be revocable during such period or until such time because of the absence of consideration for the assurance of irrevocability. When such a writing states that the offer is irrevocable but does not state any period or time of irrevocability, it shall be construed to state that the offer is irrevocable for a reasonable time . . . .

N.Y. GEN. OBLIG. LAW § 5-1109 (McKinney 1989).

expression of mutual consent to be bound. *Teachers Ins. and Annuity Assoc. of America v. Tribune Co.*, 670 F. Supp. 491, 497 (S.D.N.Y. 1987) (Leval, J.). We conclude that his statement does not evince an intent to be bound by a promise to hold the New York Area open for Coastal. Nor can Coastal argue that it reasonably relied on this statement to its detriment or suffered any damages as a result of Boettger's statement that he had asked Goodman to reserve the New York Area for negotiations with Coastal. As such, we conclude that the evidence fails to establish the existence of an option for the sale of aircraft for a New York Area dealership.

* * *

CONCLUSION

For the foregoing reasons, we find in favor of defendant on all claims. Each party shall bear its own costs.

SO ORDERED.

PROBLEM 2-9

Supplies, Inc., provides gravel and other construction supplies in bulk quantities to contractors. Big Time Construction, Inc., in preparation for submitting a bid to supply and pour concrete at a large construction project, sent the following form to all of its suppliers, including Supplies, Inc.

FIRM OFFER TO SELL

1. Big Time Construction, Inc. ("Buyer"), is preparing to bid for certain work on a construction project known as <u>Century Tower Office Complex</u>. For this project Buyer will need to purchase approximately <u>950–1100</u> tons of gravel.

2. <u>Supplies, Inc.</u> ("Seller"), hereby agrees to supply Buyer's requirements for the project at a unit cost of _____.

3. Seller also hereby agrees that THIS OFFER WILL BE HELD OPEN FOR 60 DAYS AFTER BUYER'S RECEIPT. Seller acknowledges that Buyer will rely on this price quote to bid on the project.

4. Seller agrees that the unit costs quoted above include all applicable taxes and are based on delivery to Buyer at Seller's principal place of business, located at _____

5. Buyer shall accept this offer by signing and returning it to Seller.

_____
Seller

Agreed and accepted _____
Buyer

The underlined portions of the form were typed in by Buyer's bidding agent. Seller received the form on September 1. Seller completed paragraph 2 by typing in a unit price of $200, completed paragraph 4 by typing in its address, signed the bottom of the form, and mailed the form to Buyer. Buyer received the form on September 3. Buyer used Seller's quoted price of $200 per ton to calculate and submit its bid on the Century Tower Project.

On October 15, Buyer was awarded the contract for Century Tower, signed a written agreement with the owner, and began to schedule its performance. On October 17, Seller sent an e-mail message to Buyer advising that, due to dramatic increases in labor costs under a new collective bargaining agreement, it was withdrawing its price of $200 per ton and substituting an offer of $230 per ton.

Buyer notes that the price increase will increase its cost of performance approximately $28,500–$33,000 and insists that it is entitled to purchase its gravel requirements from Seller at the cost of $200 per ton. Can Buyer accept Seller's written offer at this point? Regardless of Buyer's rights under Article 2, can Buyer enforce Seller's original offer on the basis of the principles of promissory estoppel? *Cf. Drennan v. Star Paving Co.*, 51 Cal. 2d 409, 333 P.2d 757 (1958) (famous opinion by Justice Robert Traynor) and Restatement (Second) Contracts § 87(2), especially comment e and illustration 6.

D. THE PAROL EVIDENCE RULE

Nearly every law student recalls his or her introduction in the first-year contracts class to the mystifying doctrine known as the parol evidence rule. If one had to pick a single common law doctrine that could benefit from simplification and the adoption of a realistic approach that would better serve the needs of modern commerce, many would choose the parol evidence rule. Karl Llewellyn attempted in § 2-202 to embrace the then-emerging modern view of the parol evidence rule, and his efforts helped to overcome many of the baroque qualities of the common law. However, as you will see, complexities remain in applying the somewhat poorly structured rules of § 2-202.

The purpose of the parol evidence rule is to respect the parties' freedom to clearly state (and thereby limit) their obligations to the terms set forth in a writing. In common law terminology, a "partially integrated" writing is one in which the parties have memorialized some of the terms of their agreement, but have not necessarily set forth all of the terms to which they have agreed. If a party seeks to introduce "parol" evidence (evidence of agreements reached prior to the adoption of a formal writing), it will be admissible only if it does not contradict the terms set forth in the partially integrated document. A "completely integrated" writing is one that contains all of the agreed terms, and therefore parol evidence of additional terms is inadmissible even if the additional term is consistent with the writing.

Early common law applications of the parol evidence rule placed great faith in the definitiveness of written documents. If a document appeared on its face (within the "four corners") to be a complete statement of the agreement of the parties, many courts presumed that the document was a "complete integration" of the agreement and refused to admit parol evidence of additional terms. The modern approach of contract law is to focus on the parties' intentions: if all of the relevant evidence, including parol evidence, establishes that the parties intended their writing to be a partial or complete integration, then the court applies the parol evidence rule accordingly.

Section 2-202 was a forerunner of the modern approach, but it has a broader scope. The "writing" for purposes of the parol evidence rule may be a writing that the parties intend "as a final expression of their agreement with respect to such terms as are included," or it may be confirmatory memoranda sent by each party, to the extent that the confirmatory memoranda include the same terms. Thus, the parol evidence rule is triggered even in the absence of a formal, written memorial of the parties' agreement. Section 2-202 also uses different terminology. The corollary to a "partial integration" is just the confirmatory memoranda or the writing described above. If the parties intend to adopt a writing as a "complete integration" of their agreement, § 2-202(b) characterizes the writing as "a complete and exclusive statement of the terms of the agreement."

Unfortunately, § 2-202 is constructed in an awkward manner, and it pays to begin by rephrasing the rule. First, if the parties adopt a writing (or send confirmations to each other that contain some of the same terms) that is intended to be a final expression of the terms in that writing, the terms in the writing may not be contradicted by evidence of a *prior agreement*, but may be explained or supplemented by evidence of their *agreement* (which includes evidence of course of performance, course of dealing and usage of trade) and also may be explained or supplemented by evidence of prior agreements that are consistent with the writing. However, if the writing is intended by the parties to be a complete and exclusive statement of the terms of the deal, evidence of a *prior agreement* (e.g., "you promised that you would provide free filters for the life of the machine") is not admissible even if the term is consistent with the writing, but the full range of evidence as to the *agreement in question* (including the writing, course of performance, course of dealing and trade usage) would be admissible to determine the parties' agreement.

The CISG makes no mention of the parol evidence rule. In fact, Article 8(3) of the CISG directs courts to examine "all relevant circumstances of the case including the negotiations . . . " to establish the intent of the parties. *MCC-Marble Ceramic Center, Inc. v. Ceramica Nuova D'Agostino, S.P.A.*, 144 F.3d 1384 (11th Cir. 1998), addressed the issue of parol evidence under the CISG and held that parol evidence of negotiations between the parties should be admitted and considered in order to determine the parties' subjective intent. According to one scholar, "Article 8(3) relieves tribunals from domestic rules that might bar them from 'considering' any evidence between the parties that is relevant. This added flexibility for interpretation is consistent with a growing body of opinion that the 'parol evidence rule' has been an embarrassment for the administration of modern transactions." JOHN O. HONNNOLD, UNIFORM LAW FOR INTERNATIONAL SALES 121 (3d ed. 1999). Unlike the United States, a large number of countries participating in the CISG reject the parol evidence rule under their domestic law.

1. A Writing Intended as a Final Expression of One or More Terms

The following materials concern the court's determination as to whether a writing adopted by the parties was intended by them to be a final expression of one or more of the terms of their agreement, and whether that writing was intended by the parties to be a complete and exclusive statement of the terms of their agreement. If there is at least a partial integration, consistent additional terms may be proved by parol evidence of an agreement prior to the adoption of the writing; if the writing is a complete and exclusive statement of the agreed terms, parol evidence of a prior agreement is inadmissible, even if it is consistent with the writing.

**ALASKA NORTHERN DEVELOPMENT, INC. v.
ALYESKA PIPELINE SERVICE CO.**
Alaska Supreme Court
666 P.2d 33 (1983)

COMPTON, Justice.

Alaska Northern Development, Inc. ("AND") appeals a judgment in favor of Alyeska Pipeline Service Co. ("Alyeska") in a dispute involving contract formation and interpretation. For the reasons stated below, we affirm.

I. FACTUAL AND PROCEDURAL BACKGROUND

In late October or early November 1976, David Reed, a shareholder and corporate president of AND, initiated discussion with Alyeska personnel in Fairbanks regarding the purchase of surplus parts. The Alyeska employees with whom Reed dealt were Juel Tyson, Clarence Terwilleger, and Donald Bruce.

After a series of discussions, Terwilleger indicated that Reed's proposal should be put in writing so it could be submitted to management. With the assistance of AND's legal counsel, Reed prepared a letter of intent dated December 10, 1976. In this letter, AND proposed to purchase "the entire Alyeska inventory of Caterpillar parts." The place for the purchase price was left blank.

Alyeska responded with its own letter of intent dated December 11, 1976. The letter was drafted by Bruce and Tyson in consultation with William Rickett, Alyeska's manager of Contracts and Material Management. Again, the price term was absent. The letter contained the following language, which is the focus of this lawsuit: "Please consider this as said letter of intent, *subject to the final approval of the owner committee.*" (Emphasis added.)

Reed was given an unsigned draft of the December 11 letter, which was reviewed by AND's legal counsel. Reed then met with Rickett, and they agreed on sixty-five percent of Alyeska's price as the price term to be filled in the blank on the December 11 letter. Rickett filled in the blank as agreed and signed the letter. In March 1977, the owner committee rejected the proposal embodied in the December 11 letter of intent.

AND contends that the parties understood the subject to approval language to mean that the Alyeska owner committee[31] would review the proposed agreement only to determine whether the price was fair and reasonable. Alyeska contends that Reed was never advised of any such limitation on the authority of the owner committee. In April 1977, AND filed a complaint alleging that there was a contract between AND and Alyeska, which Alyeska breached. The complaint was later amended to include counts for reformation and punitive damages.

Alyeska moved for summary judgment on the punitive damages and breach of contract counts. The superior court granted summary judgment in favor of Alyeska on the punitive damages count. The court initially denied Alyeska's motion for summary judgment on the breach of contract claim; however, based on a review of the case after discovery had closed, the court announced at a hearing on September 26, 1980, that it would reverse its earlier ruling and grant Alyeska's motion. The court confirmed this ruling at a hearing on November 5, 1980, after consideration of AND's Motion for Clarification.

The superior court explained its rationale for granting summary judgment against AND on the breach of contract claim as follows. The court recognized that AND predicated its breach of contract claim on the theory that Reed's letter of December 10th was an offer and that Rickett's letter of December 11th was an acceptance of that offer. Viewed in that light, the court addressed "four theoretical possibilities in analyzing the interplay between the December 11th letter and the December 10th letter." First, the writings could be construed as an offer with a responding promise to pass the offer on to the owner committee, which was responsible for making such determinations. Second, the letters could be construed as an offer and a counter-offer that AND rejected. Third, the letters could be considered as an offer with a responding counter-offer containing, among other things, the unlimited right of the owner committee to review and approve. The court ruled that if the letters were ultimately found to fall into one of these three categories, AND would not prevail, either because the offer embodied in the December 10 letter was never accepted, or because the owner committee never approved the proposal.

The only way in which AND might prevail was on the fourth possibility, i.e., the letters could be construed as an offer followed by a counter-offer limiting the authority of the owner committee to review only the contract price. The court ruled that AND could not establish a breach of contract claim under the fourth construction of the letters because the parol evidence rule barred the admission of extrinsic evidence that might limit the scope of the owner committee's approval power. The only recourse for AND, therefore, was to seek reformation of the December 11 letter that limited the owner committee approval clause.

The case proceeded to trial on the reformation claim. After a six-week trial, the superior court concluded that AND had failed to establish that a specific agreement was not properly reduced to writing and therefore rejected its request to reform the

---

[31] [1] The owner committee is composed of the owner oil companies of Alyeska, a joint venture.

December 11 letter. Attorney's fees were awarded to Alyeska.

On appeal, AND does not challenge the superior court's denial of reformation. Instead, it contends that the superior court erred in granting summary judgment on the breach of contract and punitive damages counts, erred in denying a trial by jury on the reformation count, erred in not permitting cross-examination for purposes of impeachment, and erred in awarding attorney's fees to Alyeska.

II. APPLICATION OF THE PAROL EVIDENCE RULE

The superior court held that the parol evidence rule of the Uniform Commercial Code, section 2-202, codified as AS 45.02.202, applied to the December 11 letter and therefore no extrinsic evidence could be presented to a jury which limited the owner committee's right of approval. AND contends that the court erred in applying the parol evidence rule. We disagree.

In order to exclude parol evidence concerning the inclusion of additional terms to a writing, a court must make the following determinations. First, the court must determine whether the writing under scrutiny was integrated, i.e., intended by the parties as a final expression of their agreement with respect to some or all of the terms included in the writing. Second, the court must determine whether evidence of a prior or contemporaneous agreement contradicts or is inconsistent with the integrated portion. If the evidence is contradictory or inconsistent, it is inadmissible. If it is consistent, it may nevertheless be excluded if the court concludes that the consistent term would necessarily have been included in the writing by the parties if they had intended it to be part of their agreement. AS 45.02.202; *Braund, Inc. v. White*, 486 P.2d 50, 56 (Alaska 1971); UCC § 2-202 comment 3 (1977).

A. *Was the December 11 Letter a Partial Integration?*

An integrated writing exists where the parties intend that the writing be a final expression of one or more terms of their agreement. *Kupka v. Morey*, 541 P.2d 740, 747 n.8 (Alaska 1975); Restatement (Second) of Contracts § 209(a) (1979). Whether a writing is integrated is a question of fact to be determined by the court in accordance with all relevant evidence. Restatement (Second) of Contracts § 209 comment c (1979).

In granting summary judgment on the breach of contract claim, the superior court stated that it had carefully considered all relevant evidence, including oral and written records of all facets of the business deal in question, to arrive at its finding that the agreement was partially integrated.[32] After the six-week trial on the reformation issue, the superior court reaffirmed this finding:

35. The plaintiff initially contends that the letter of December 11, 1976 (the letter) was not integrated or partially integrated and therefore the court was in error in granting summary judgment in favor of defendant on the contract counts of the plaintiff's complaint on September 26, 1980.

36. After considering the evidence submitted at trial, the court reaffirms its prior conclusion that the letter was integrated as to the Owners Committee's approval clause.

---

[32] [4] At the hearing on AND's Motion for Clarification, the superior court stated:

[I]t seems to me absolutely conclusive on this evidence, and I'm making this as a finding of fact, that this agreement is partially integrated, and I'm not making it by reference only to the four corners of the — of the writings but reference to all the extrinsic evidence that has been proffered to me, read everybody's deposition, considered in detail all the processes of negotiations, everything that was said and done by everybody as related by them up till the time that Rickett included the language in the letter and turned it over to Reed. So we're not here talking about the for [sic] corners or ambiguity or anything like that. We're talking about all the extrinsic evidence, meaning on balance to a conclusion more probable than not that this is a partially integrated agreement.

37. The parties intended to write down their discussions in a comprehensive form which allowed Reed to seek financing and allow the primary actors (Tyson, Bruce, Terwilleger, Rickett) to submit the concept embodied by the letter to higher management . . . .

38. There are three subjects upon which plaintiff seeks reformation. . . . As to the first, [limiting the Owner Committee to a consideration of price] which has been plaintiff's primary focus, the court finds that such reference was integrated such that the parole [sic] evidence rule would bar any inconsistent testimony. Testimony that the owners were limited to "price" in their review is inconsistent.

*   *   *

41. With respect to the Owners Committee's approval clause, according to the plaintiff's contention the owners were entitled to review the transaction, on whatever basis, only one time. This was testified to by both Mr. Reed and argued by plaintiff in closing . . . . It was also conceded in closing that the review by the owners, on whatever standard, would occur prior to any formal contract being negotiated and executed . . . . This is also consistent with the testimony of each of the participants.

42. In addition, Mr. Reed, in consultation with Ed Merdes and Henry Camarot, his attorneys, tendered the letter of March 4, 1977, as a document which could serve as "the contract" . . . . The March 4 letter contains no further reference to the Owners Committee's approval function . . . . Therefore, I find that as to the Owners Committee's approval . . . the letter of December 11 constitutes an integration or partial integration . . . . This having been established, the analysis outlined by the court on September 26, 1980, when granting defendant's motion for summary judgment on the contract claims is applicable. [Citations omitted.]

After reviewing the record, we cannot say that this finding of a partial integration was clearly erroneous.

*   *   *

B. *Does the Excluded Evidence Contradict the Integrated Terms?*

Having found a partial integration, the next determination is whether the excluded evidence contradicts the integrated portion of the writing. Comment b to section 215 of the Restatement (Second) of Contracts is helpful in resolving this issue. Comment b states:

> An earlier agreement may help the interpretation of a later one, but it may not contradict a binding later integrated agreement. Whether there is a contradiction depends . . . on whether the two are consistent or inconsistent. This is a question which often cannot be determined from the face of the writing; the writing must first be applied to its subject matter and placed in context. The question is then decided by the court as part of a question of interpretation. Where reasonable people could differ as to the credibility of the evidence offered and the evidence if believed could lead a reasonable person to interpret the writing as claimed by the proponent of the evidence, the question of credibility and the choice among reasonable inferences should be treated as questions of fact. But the asserted meaning must be one to which the language of the writing, read in context, is reasonably susceptible. If no other meaning is reasonable, the court should rule as a matter of law that the meaning is established.

According to comment b, therefore, a question of interpretation may arise before the contradiction issue can be resolved. If the evidence conflicts, the choice between competing inferences is for the trier of fact to resolve. *Alyeska Pipeline Service Co. v. O'Kelley*, 645 P.2d 767, 771 n.2 (Alaska 1982). The meaning is determined as a matter of law, however, if "the asserted meaning [is not] one to which the language of the writing, read in context, is reasonably susceptible." Restatement (Second) of Contracts § 215 comment b (1979). *See also* J. CALAMARI & J. PERILLO, THE LAW OF CONTRACTS §§ 3-12, 3-13 (2d ed. 1977).

AND contends that the superior court erred in granting summary judgment because the evidence conflicted as to the meaning of the owner committee approval clause. It concludes that under *Alyeska* it was entitled to a jury trial on the interpretation issue. Alyeska contends, and the superior court ruled, that a jury trial was inappropriate because, as a matter of law, AND's asserted meaning of the clause at issue was not reasonably susceptible to the language of the writing. The superior court stated:

> The Court is making the . . . ruling that the offer of evidence to show that Rickett's letter really meant to limit owner committee approval to the price term alone . . . is not reasonably susceptible — or the writing is not reasonably susceptible to that purpose. And therefore, that extrinsic evidence operates to contradict the writing, not specific words in the writing, but the words in the context of the totality of the writing and the totality of the extrinsic evidence.

We agree that the words used in the December 11 letter are not reasonably susceptible to the interpretation advanced by AND. Therefore, we find no merit to AND's contention that it was entitled to a jury trial on the interpretation issue.

After rejecting the extrinsic evidence for purposes of interpretation, the superior court found AND's offered testimony, that the owner committee's approval power was limited to approval of the price, to be inconsistent with and contradictory to the language used by the negotiators in the December 11 letter. AND contends that the offered testimony did not contradict, but rather explained or supplemented the writing with consistent additional terms. For this contention, AND relies on the standard articulated in *Hunt Foods & Industries, Inc. v. Doliner*, 26 A.D.2d 41, 270 N.Y.S.2d 937 (N.Y. App. 1966). In *Hunt Foods*, the defendant signed an option agreement under which he agreed to sell stock to Hunt Foods at a given price per share. When Hunt Foods attempted to exercise the option, the defendant contended that the option could only be exercised if the defendant had received offers from a third party. The court held that section 2-202 did not bar this evidence from being admitted because it held that the proposed oral condition to the option agreement was not "inconsistent" within the meaning of section 2-202; to be inconsistent, "the term must contradict or negate a term of the writing. A term or condition which has a lesser effect is provable." *Id.* 270 N.Y.S.2d at 940.

The narrow view of consistency expressed in *Hunt Foods* has been criticized. In *Snyder v. Herbert Greenbaum & Associates, Inc.*, 38 Md. App. 144, 380 A.2d 618 (Md. App. 1977), the court held that the parol evidence of a contractual right to unilateral rescission was inconsistent with a written agreement for the sale and installation of carpeting. The court defined "inconsistency" as used in section 2-202(b) as "the absence of reasonable harmony in terms of the language *and* respective obligations of the parties." *Id.* 380 A.2d at 623 (emphasis in original) (citing UCC § 1-205(4)). *Accord: Luria Brothers & Co. v. Pielet Brothers Scrap Iron & Metal, Inc.*, 600 F.2d 103, 111 (7th Cir. 1979); *Southern Concrete Services, Inc. v. Mableton Contractors, Inc.*, 407 F. Supp. 581 (N.D. Ga. 1975), *aff'd mem.*, 569 F.2d 1154 (5th Cir. 1978).

We agree with this view of inconsistency and reject the view expressed in *Hunt Foods*.[33] Under this definition of inconsistency, it is clear that the proffered parol evidence limiting the owner committee's right of final approval to price is inconsistent

---

[33] [6] *Hunt Foods* was implicitly rejected in *Johnson v. Curran*, 633 P.2d 994, 996–97 (Alaska 1981) (parol evidence concerning an early termination right based on nightclub owner's dissatisfaction with the band's performance was inconsistent with parties' written contract specifying definite time without mention of any right of early termination and thus inadmissible).

with the integrated term that unconditionally gives the committee the right to approval. Therefore, the superior court was correct in refusing to admit parol evidence on this issue.

*   *   *

For the foregoing reasons, the judgment of the superior court is AFFIRMED.

QUESTIONS

1. The *AND* court adopts the *Snyder* definition of the meaning of "consistent," but does not provide much basis for its decision. What policy arguments support this result? Keep this in mind when you read the *Nanakuli* case below.

2. Should courts defer entirely to a "merger clause" in the parties' agreement as evidence of a mutual intention that the written memorial be deemed final and complete? One court found as a general principle that a merger clause is "strong evidence" that the writing reflects the complete and exclusive statement of the terms of the agreement. *Betaco, Inc. v. Cessna Aircraft Co.*, 103 F.3d 1281 (7th Cir. 1996). Is this the appropriate standard?

In *AND*, the trial court determined only that the writing was final as to the approval clause in the writing, and did not find that the writing was a complete and exclusive statement of the terms of the agreement. Based on the facts reported by the appellate court, would the trial court have a factual basis for concluding that the writing was a complete and exclusive statement? In making this determination, courts look to the surrounding circumstances and seek to determine the parties' intentions. *Betaco, Inc. v. Cessna Aircraft Co.*, 103 F.3d 1281 (7th Cir. 1996), mentioned in the previous note, provides a good example of this inquiry.

In *Betaco*, the buyer sued to recover the deposit paid to the seller regarding the purchase of an airplane, alleging that the range of the airplane was less than the salesperson had represented. The court held the parol evidence rule barred introduction of evidence that the salesperson made any such representations, because the writing was a complete and exclusive statement of the terms of the agreement. In assessing the intent of the parties, the court weighed the following factors: (1) the inclusion of merger or integration clauses in the document under consideration; (2) the disclaimer of warranties; (3) whether the extrinsic term is one that the parties would certainly have included in the document had it been part of their agreement; (4) the sophistication of the parties; and (5) the nature and scope of both prior negotiations between the parties and any purported extrinsic terms. The court concluded that the parties intended the writing to be a complete and exclusive statement of the terms of their agreement because plain and clear language to this effect was included in the document, the buyer was an experienced businessman and pilot, the buyer understood the integration clause, the purchase agreement addressed the issue of the range of the airplane with specificity, and the writing specifically disclaimed any warranties not included in the writing.

2. The Interpretation Exception to the Parol Evidence Rule

The *AND* case also applies one of the most important exceptions to the parol evidence rule. Before analyzing whether the parol evidence was consistent, the court assessed whether the evidence should be admitted for the purpose of interpreting the writing. Even in the case of a writing that is a complete and exclusive statement of the terms of the agreement, parol evidence may be introduced to interpret the writing.

Allapattah Services, Inc. v. Exxon Corp., 61 F. Supp. 2d 1300 (S.D. Fla. 1999), illustrates the significance of this exception to the parol evidence rule. Exxon had sales agreements with various dealers that contained open price terms, permitting Exxon to adjust prices, higher or lower, in response to the commercial dynamics of particular markets. Article 2 imposes a duty of good faith in such situations. *See* § 2-305(2). The dealers sued Exxon for breach of its pricing obligations and sought to introduce evidence of prior statements, course of dealing, trade usage, and expert testimony to explain the requirements of good faith in the circumstances. Exxon sought to bar such evidence, arguing that the written agreement was a complete and exclusive statement of the terms of the agreement, but the court refused to limit the introduction of the evidence, concluding that it was offered to interpret the writing. The court reasoned:

> Extrinsic evidence which explains the agreement and Exxon's good faith obligations is admissible. "[T]he test of admissibility is not whether the contract appears on its face to be complete in every detail, but whether the proffered evidence of course of dealing[, course of performance,] and trade usage reasonably can be construed as consistent with the express terms of the agreement." *Nanakuli Paving & Rock Co.*, 664 F.2d at 796 (quoting source omitted).

> Cases cited by the parties indicate that extrinsic evidence also will be used to determine whether the good faith obligation had been breached. For example, in *Ervin* [*v. Amoco Oil Co.*, 885 P.2d 246 (Col. App. 1994),] the court considered evidence that Amoco had not been duplicating the charges to its dealers, but actually set its wholesale prices to offset the amount of the credit card processing charge. In *East Bay Running Store, Inc. v. Nike, Inc.*, 890 F.2d 996, 1000 (7th Cir. 1989), the court had to use extrinsic evidence to determine that "the implementation of [Nike's] policy does not appear to be an underhanded attempt on the part of Nike to drive any individual dealer out of business." Here, both of these allegations are at issue. Plaintiffs contend that Exxon was double charging them for the cost of credit card processing, and allege that Exxon's purpose was partly to drive unproductive dealers out of business, in violation of federal law. It is possible for a jury to conclude that, should these allegations be proven, Exxon breached its duty of good faith.

> Moreover, extrinsic evidence may be offered to show that the offset arrangement Exxon implemented with its dealers was common in the trade. Oil companies' DFCs [Discount for Cash programs] were the result of the enactment of the Cash Discount Act, passed by Congress on July 27, 1981. The Act prohibited retailers from placing a surcharge on credit sales, while permitting an unlimited discount to cash purchasers. Thus, commencing in 1982, several major U.S. oil companies implemented the DFC. Evidence as to whether these other companies charged twice for the recovery of credit card processing is relevant to ascertain the appropriate usage in the trade of the DFC offsetting mechanism.

> In sum, the UCC's rules governing admissibility of evidence "allows the jury to take into account consistent parol evidence when it attempts to discern the meaning of a written contract." *Sundlun v. Shoemaker*, 421 Pa. Super. 353, 617 A.2d 1330, 1334 (1992). "The law has nothing to do with the actual state of the parties' minds. In contract, as elsewhere, it must go by externals, and judge parties by their conduct." *MCC-Marble Ceramic Ctr., Inc.*, 144 F.3d at 1387 n.8 (quoting Oliver W. Holmes, *The Common Law* 242 (Howe ed., 1963)).

> In the instant action, Plaintiffs allege that oral statements were made and written representations were disseminated by Exxon in the course of dealing. Exxon even admits that it did, at least for a period of time, deduct the credit card processing fee from its wholesale prices to dealers, thus, establishing a course of performance. "Unless carefully negated by the written terms of the contract, the parties' course of dealing [and course of performance], including any inconsistent oral representations, become an element of the meaning of the words used." *Sundlun*, 617 A.2d at 1334. Additionally, Plaintiffs may explain the meaning and understanding of the agreement, regarding the open price term,

with evidence showing that a course of performance resulting in acquiescence, was meant to be incorporated into the written terms of the Sales Agreement. *See Nanakuli Paving & Rock Co.*, 664 F.2d at 795. "[T]he use of such evidence 'simply places the court in the position of the parties when they made the contract, and enables it to appreciate the force of the words they used in reducing it to writing'." *Id.* at 798 (quoting *Chase Manhattan Bank v. First Marion Bank*, 437 F.2d 1040, 1048 (5th Cir. 1971)).

Allapatah Services, 61 F. Supp. 2d at 1307–08. The interpretation exception to the parol evidence rule is well-established at common law, and § 2-202 Comment 1(b) strongly reinforces the fact-driven inquiry into the meaning of written terms by emphatically rejecting the "premise that the language used has the meaning attributable to such language by rules of construction existing in the law rather than the meaning which arises out of the commercial context in which it was used . . . ."

3. Distinguishing Evidence of Agreement from Evidence of "Prior Agreement"

Thus far, § 2-202 has mirrored the modern approach to the parol evidence rule. However, § 2-202 is awkwardly constructed to provide a cross-reference to the determination of the agreement of the parties under § 1-303 in the middle of setting forth the parol evidence rule. After stating that contradictory evidence is barred when the writing is final as to one or more terms, and before providing that even evidence of consistent additional terms is barred when the writing is a complete and exclusive statement of the terms of the agreement, § 2-202 provides that a writing "may be explained or supplemented (a) by course of performance, course of dealing, or usage of trade (Section 1-303)."

Many commentators refer to this language as the "false parol evidence rule," because the parol evidence rule is triggered only by evidence of a *prior* agreement, whereas the elements listed in § 1-303 are part of *the agreement in question* rather than prior agreements. If a party seeks to introduce evidence of course of performance, course of dealing, or usage of trade, the evidence should be admitted if it is competent evidence of the agreement of the parties, as determined under § 1-303(e), and should not be subject to the parol evidence rule. The following classic case explains this distinction.

NANAKULI PAVING & ROCK CO. v. SHELL OIL CO.
United States Court of Appeals, Ninth Circuit
664 F.2d 772 (1981)

[Ed. Note: Nanakuli, the second largest asphalt paving contractor in Hawaii, had purchased all of its asphalt requirements from Shell from 1963 to 1974 under two long-term contracts. Nanakuli sued Shell for breach, alleging that Shell was required to "price protect" its purchases, but nevertheless Shell raised prices in 1974 on 7200 tons of asphalt from $44 to $76 per ton. Nanakuli argued that Shell's agreement to "price protect" under the contract meant that Shell was obligated to maintain the price of the tonnage of asphalt for which Nanakuli had already committed to its buyers. Nanakuli offered evidence that it had agreed to supply 7200 tons of asphalt to its buyer at prices based on Shell's current price of $44 per ton. Nanakuli also offered expert testimony that "price protection" was a routine practice in the asphalt business at the time in question.

At trial, the jury found that Shell breached its contract with Nanakuli, but the district judge set aside the verdict. The Ninth Circuit resolved several issues on appeal. This excerpt considers the following two questions: 1. What are the limits of the applicable trade usage; and 2. Could the jury have construed an express written term of

"Shell's posted price at delivery" as being reasonably consistent with the trade usage of "price protection"?]

Scope of Trade Usage

*   *   *

We approach the first issue in this case mindful that an underlying purpose of the UCC as enacted in Hawaii is to allow for liberal interpretation of commercial usages. The Code provides, "This chapter shall be liberally construed and applied to promote its underlying purposes and policies." Haw. Rev. Stat. § 490:1-102(1). Only three purposes are listed, one of which is "[t]o permit the continued expansion of commercial practices through custom, usage and agreement of the parties; . . . ." *Id.* § 490:1-102(2)(b). The drafters of the Code explain:

> This Act is drawn to provide *flexibility* so that, since it is intended to be a semipermanent piece of legislation, it will provide its own machinery for *expansion of commercial practices*. It is intended to make it possible for the law embodied in this Act to be *developed* by the courts in the light of *unforeseen and new circumstances and practices* . . . .
>
> . . . The text of each section should be *read in the light of the purpose and policy* of the rule or principle in question, as also of the Act as a whole, and the application of the language should be *construed narrowly or broadly*, as the case may be, in *conformity with the purposes and policies* involved.
>
> . . . [T]he Code seeks to *avoid . . . interference with evolutionary growth* . . . .
>
> This principle of *freedom of contract is subject* to specific *exceptions* found elsewhere in the Act. . . . *In this connection,* Section 1-205 incorporating into the agreement *prior course of dealing and usages of trade is of particular importance.*

Id., Comments 1 & 2 (emphasis supplied). We read that to mean that courts should not stand in the way of new commercial practices and usages by insisting on maintaining the narrow and inflexible old rules of interpretation. We seek the definition of trade usage not only in the express language of the Code but also in its underlying purposes, defining it liberally to fit the facts of the particular commercial context here.

The Code defines usage of trade as "any practice or method of dealing having such regularity of observance in a *place, vocation or trade* as to justify an expectation that it will be observed with respect to the transaction in question." *Id.* § 490:1-205(2) (emphasis supplied). We understand the use of the word "or" to mean that parties can be bound by a usage common to the place they are in business, even if it is not the usage of their particular vocation or trade. That reading is borne out by the repetition of the disjunctive "or" in subsection 3, which provides that usages "in the vocation or trade in which they are engaged or of which they are or should be aware give particular meaning to and supplement or qualify terms of an agreement." *Id.* § 490:1-205(3). The drafters' Comments say that trade usage is to be used to reach the " . . . commercial meaning of the agreement . . . " by interpreting the language "as meaning what it may fairly be expected to mean to parties involved in the particular transaction *in a given locality or* in a given *vocation or trade." Id.,* Comment 4 (emphasis supplied). The inference of the two subsections and the Comment, read together, is that a usage need not necessarily be one practiced by members of the party's own trade or vocation to be binding *if* it is so commonly practiced in a locality that a party should be aware of it. Subsection 5 also shows the importance of the place where the usage is practiced: "An applicable usage of trade in the place where any part of performance is to occur shall be used in interpreting the agreement as to that part of the performance." The validity of this interpretation is additionally demonstrated by the Comment of the drafters: "Subsection (3), giving the prescribed effect to usages of which the parties 'are or should be aware', reinforces the provision of subsection (2) requiring not universality but only the described 'regularity of observance' of the practice or method. This subsection also reinforces the point of subsection (2) that such usages may be either *general to trade or particular to a special branch of trade." Id.*, Comment 7 (emphasis supplied). This language indicates that Shell would be bound not only by usages of sellers of asphalt but by more general usages on Oahu, as long as those usages were so regular in their observance that Shell should have been aware of them. This reading of the Code, in our opinion, achieves an equitable result. A party is always held to conduct generally observed by members of his chosen trade because the other party is justified in so assuming unless he indicates otherwise. He is held to more general business practices to the extent of his actual knowledge of those practices or to the degree his ignorance of those practices is not excusable: they were so generally practiced he should have been aware of them.

No UCC cases have been found on this point, but the court's reading of the Code language is similar to that of two of the best-known commentators on the UCC:

> Under pre-Code law, a trade usage was not operative against a party who *was not a member of the trade unless he actually knew of it or the other party could reasonably believe he knew of it.*

J. White & R. Summers, Uniform Commercial Code, § 12-6 at 371 (1972) (emphasis supplied) (citing 3 A. Corbin, Corbin on Contracts § 557 at 248 (1960)). *See also* Restatement of Contracts § 247, Comment b (1932); 5 S. Williston, Williston On Contracts § 661 at 113–18 (3d ed. 1961). White and Summers add (emphasis supplied):

> This view has been carried forward by 1-205(3), ... [U]sage of the trade is only binding on *members of the trade* involved *or persons who* know or *should know about it.* Persons who should be aware of the trade usage doubtless *include those who regularly deal with members of the relevant trade*, and also members of a second trade that commonly deals with members of a relevant trade (for example, farmers should know something of seed selling).

White & Summers, *supra*, § 12-6 at 371. Using that analogy, even if Shell did not "regularly deal" with aggregate supplies, it did deal constantly and almost exclusively on Oahu with one asphalt paver. It therefore should have been aware of the usage of Nanakuli and other asphaltic pavers to bid at fixed prices and therefore receive price protection from their materials suppliers due to the refusal by government agencies to accept escalation clauses. Therefore, we do not find the lower court abused its discretion or misread the Code as applied to the peculiar facts of this case in ruling that the applicable trade was the asphaltic paving trade in Hawaii. An asphalt seller should be held to the usages of trade in general as well as those of asphalt sellers and common usages of those to whom they sell. Certainly, under the unusual facts of this case it was not unreasonable for the judge to extend trade usages to include practices of other material suppliers toward Shell's primary and perhaps only customer on Oahu. He did exclude, on Shell's motion *in limine*, evidence of cement suppliers. He only held Shell to routine practices in Hawaii by the suppliers of the two major ingredients of asphaltic paving, that is, asphalt and aggregate. Those usages were only practiced towards two major pavers. It was not unreasonable to expect Shell to be knowledgeable about so small a market. In so ruling, the judge undoubtedly took into account Shell's half-million dollar investment in Oahu strictly because of a long-term commitment by Nanakuli, its actions as partner in promoting Nanakuli's expansion on Oahu, and the fact that its sales on Oahu were almost exclusively to Nanakuli for use in asphaltic paving. The wisdom of the pre-trial ruling was demonstrated by evidence at trial that Shell's agent in Hawaii stayed in close contact with Nanakuli and was knowledgeable about both the asphaltic paving market in general and Nanakuli's bidding procedures and economics in particular.

Shell argued not only that the definition of trade was too broad, but also that the practice itself was not sufficiently regular to reach the level of a usage and that Nanakuli failed to show with enough precision how the usage was carried out in order for a jury to calculate damages. The extent of a usage is ultimately a jury question. The Code provides, "The existence and scope of such a usage are to be proved as facts." Haw. Rev. Stat. § 490:1-205(2). The practice must have "such regularity of observance . . . as to justify an expectation that it will be observed . . . ." *Id.* The Comment explains:

> The ancient English tests for "custom" are abandoned in this connection. Therefore, it is not required that a usage of trade be "ancient or immemorial," "universal" or the like . . . . [Full] recognition is thus available for new usages and for usages currently observed by the great majority of decent dealers, even though dissidents ready to cut corners do not agree.

Id., Comment 5. The Comment's demand that "not universality but only the described 'regularity of observance' " is required reinforces the provision only giving "effect to usages of which the parties 'are or should be aware' . . . " *Id.*, Comment 7. A "regularly observed" practice of protection, of which Shell "should have been aware," was enough to constitute a usage that Nanakuli had reason to believe was incorporated into the agreement.

Nanakuli went beyond proof of a regular observance. It proved and offered to prove[34] that price protection was probably a universal practice by suppliers to the asphaltic paving trade in 1969.[35] It had been practiced by H.C. & D. since at least 1962, by P.C. & A. since well before 1960, and by Chevron routinely for years, with the last specific instance before the contract being March, 1969, as shown by documentary evidence. The only usage evidence missing was the behavior by Shell, the only other asphalt supplier in Hawaii, prior to 1969. That was because its only major customer was Nanakuli and the judge ruled prior course of dealings between Shell and Nanakuli inadmissible. Shell did not point in rebuttal to one instance of failure to price protect by any supplier to an asphalt paver in Hawaii before its own 1974 refusal to price protect Nanakuli. Thus, there clearly was enough proof for a jury to find that the practice of price protection in the asphaltic paving trade existed in Hawaii in 1969 and was regular enough in its observance to rise to the level of a usage that would be binding on Nanakuli and Shell.

Shell next argues that, even if such a usage existed, its outlines were not precise enough to determine whether Shell would have extended the old price for Nanakuli for several months or would have charged the old price on the volume of tonnage committed at that price. The jury awarded Nanakuli damages based on the specific tonnage committed before the price increase of 1974. Shell says the jury could not have ascertained with enough certainty how price protection was carried out to calculate such an award for Nanakuli. The argument is not persuasive. The Code provides, "The remedies provided by this chapter shall be liberally administered to the end that the aggrieved party may be put in as good a position as if the other party had fully performed . . . ." *Id.* § 490:1-106(1). The Comments list as one of three purposes of this section "to reject any doctrine that damages must be calculable with mathematical accuracy. Compensatory damages are often at best approximate: they have to be proved with whatever definiteness and accuracy the facts permit, but no more." *Id.*, Comment 1. Nanakuli got advance notices of each but the disputed increase by Shell, as well as an extension of several months at the old price in 1970, 1971, 1977, and 1978. Shell protests that in 1970 and 1971 Nanakuli's protected tonnage only amounted to 3,300 and 1,100

---

[34] [29] Nanakuli made an offer of proof, which the judge rejected as not sufficiently relevant to the asphaltic paving trade, that cement suppliers routinely price protected pavers for years.

[35] [30] All evidence was that trade usage continued to be universally practiced after 1969, even by Shell.

tons, respectively. Chevron's price protection of H.B. in 1969 however, is also part of the trade usage; H.B.'s protection amounted to 12,000 tons. The increase in Nanakuli's tonnage by 1974 is explained by its growth since the 1970 and 1971 increases.

In addition, the scope of protection offered by a particular usage is left to the jury:

> In cases of a well established line of usage varying from the general rules of this Act where the precise amount of the variation has not been worked out into a single standard, the party relying on the usage is entitled, in any event, to the minimum variation demonstrated. The whole is not to be disregarded because no particular line of detail has been established. In case a dominant pattern [of usage] has been fairly evidenced, the party relying on the usage is entitled . . . to go to the trier of fact on the question of whether such dominant pattern has been incorporated into the agreement.

Id. § 490:1-205, Comment 9. Summers and White write that a usage, under the language of 1-205(2), need not be "certain and precise" to fit within the definition of "any practice or method of dealing." WHITE & SUMMERS, *supra*, § 3-3 at 87. The manner in which the usage of price protection was carried out was presented with sufficient precision to allow the jury to calculate damages at $220,800.

*　*　*

Express Terms as Reasonably Consistent With Usage in Course of Performance

Perhaps one of the most fundamental departures of the Code from prior contract law is found in the parol evidence rule and the definition of an agreement between two parties. Under the UCC, an agreement goes beyond the written words on a piece of paper. " 'Agreement' means the bargain of the parties in fact as found in their language or by implication from other circumstances including course of dealing or usage of trade or course of performance as provided in this chapter (sections 490:1-205 and 490:2-208)." *Id.* § 490:1-201(3). Express terms, then, do not constitute the entire agreement, which must be sought also in evidence of usages, dealings, and performance of the contract itself. The purpose of evidence of usages, which are defined in the previous section, is to help to understand the entire agreement.

> [Usages are] a factor in reaching the commercial meaning of the agreement which the parties have made. The language used is to be interpreted as meaning what it may fairly be expected to mean to parties involved in the particular commercial transaction in a given locality or in a given vocation or trade . . . . Part of the agreement of the parties . . . is to be sought for in the usages of trade which furnish the background and give particular meaning to the language used, and are the framework of common understanding controlling any general rules of law which hold only when there is no such understanding.

Id. § 490:1-205, Comment 4. Course of dealings is more important than usages of the trade, being specific usages between the two parties to the contract. "[Course] of dealing controls usage of trade." *Id.* § 490:1-205(4). It "is a sequence of previous conduct between the parties to a particular transaction which is fairly to be regarded as establishing a common basis of understanding for interpreting their expressions and other conduct." *Id.* § 490:1-205(1). Much of the evidence of prior dealings between Shell and Nanakuli in negotiating the 1963 contract and in carrying out similar earlier contracts was excluded by the court.

A commercial agreement, then, is broader than the written paper and its meaning is to be determined not just by the language used by them in the written contract but "by their action, read and interpreted in the light of commercial practices and other surrounding circumstances. The measure and background for interpretation are set by the commercial context, which may explain and supplement even the language of a formal or final writing." *Id.*, Comment 1. Performance, usages, and prior dealings are important enough to be admitted always, even for a final and complete agreement; only if they cannot be reasonably reconciled with the express terms of the contract are they not binding on the parties. "The express terms of an agreement and an applicable course of dealing or usage of trade shall be construed wherever reasonable as consistent with each other; but when such construction is unreasonable express terms control both course of dealing and usage of trade and course of dealing controls usage of trade." *Id.* § 490:1-205(4).

Of these three, then, the most important evidence of the agreement of the parties is their actual performance of the contract. *Id.* The operative definition of course of performance is as follows: "Where the contract for sale involves repeated occasions for performance by either party with knowledge of the nature of the performance and opportunity for objection to it by the other, any course of performance accepted or acquiesced in without objection shall be relevant to determine the meaning of the agreement." *Id.* § 490:2-208(1). "Course of dealing . . . is restricted, literally, to a sequence of conduct between the parties previous to the agreement. However, the provisions of the Act on course of performance make it clear that a sequence of conduct after or under the agreement may have equivalent meaning (Section 2-208)." *Id.* § 490:1-205, Comment 2. The importance of evidence of course of performance is explained: "The parties themselves know best what they have meant by their words of agreement and their action under that agreement is the best indication of what that meaning was. This section thus rounds out the set of factors which determines the meaning of the 'agreement' . . . ." *Id.* § 490:2-208, Comment 1. "Under this section a course of performance is always relevant to determine the meaning of the agreement." *Id.*, Comment 2.

Our study of the Code provisions and Comments, then, form the first basis of our holding that a trade usage to price protect pavers at times of price increases for work committed on nonescalating contracts could reasonably be construed as consistent with an express term of seller's posted price at delivery. Since the agreement of the parties is broader than the express terms and includes usages, which may even add terms to the agreement, and since the commercial background provided by those usages is vital to an understanding of the agreement, we follow the Code's mandate to proceed on the assumption that the parties have included those usages unless they cannot reasonably be construed as consistent with the express terms.

Federal courts usually have been lenient in not ruling out consistent additional terms or trade usage for apparent inconsistency with express terms. The leading case on the subject is *Columbia Nitrogen Corp. v. Royster Co.*, 451 F.2d 3 (4th Cir. 1971). Columbia, the buyer, had in the past primarily produced and sold nitrogen to Royster. When Royster opened a new plant that produced more phosphate than it needed, the parties reversed roles and signed a sales contract for Royster to sell excess phosphate to Columbia. The contract terms set out the price that would be charged by Royster and the amount to be sold. It provided for the price to go up if certain events occurred but did not provide for price declines. When the price of nitrogen [sic: phosphate] fell precipitously, Columbia refused to accept the full amount of nitrogen [sic: phosphate] specified in the contract after Royster refused to renegotiate the contract price. The District Judge's exclusion of usage of the trade and course of dealing to explain the express quantity term in the contract was reversed. Columbia had offered to prove that the quantity set out in the contract was a mere projection to be adjusted according to market forces. Ambiguity was not necessary for the admission of evidence of usage and prior dealings.[36] Even though the lengthy contract was the result of long and careful

---

[36] [35] As discussed earlier, the District Judge here mistakenly equated ambiguity with admissibility. He said, "I think this is a close case. On the face of the contract it would seem to be unambiguous," although acknowledging that liberal commentators on the Code would let in evidence of usage and performance even

negotiations and apparently covered every contingency, the appellate court ruled that "the test of admissibility is not whether the contract appears on its face to be complete in every detail, but whether the proffered evidence of course of dealing and trade usage reasonably can be construed as consistent with the express terms of the agreement." *Id.* at 9. The express quantity term could be reasonably construed as consistent with a usage that such terms would be mere projections for several reasons:[37] (1) the contract did not expressly state that usage and dealings evidence would be excluded; (2) the contract was silent on the adjustment of price or quantities in a declining market; (3) the minimum tonnage was expressed in the contract as Products Supplied, not Products Purchased; (4) the default clause of the contract did not state a penalty for failure to take delivery; and (5) apparently most important in the court's view, the parties had deviated from similar express terms in earlier contracts in times of declining market. *Id.* at 9–10. As here, the contract's merger clause said that there were no oral agreements. The court explained that its ruling "reflects the reality of the marketplace and avoids the overly legalistic interpretations which the Code seeks to abolish." *Id.* at 10. The Code assigns dealing and usage evidence "unique and important roles" and therefore "overly simplistic and overly legalistic interpretation of a contract should be shunned." *Id.* at 11.

Usage and an oral understanding led to much the same interpretation of a quantity term specifying delivery of 500 tons of stainless-steel solids in *Michael Schiavone & Sons, Inc. v. Securalloy Co.*, 312 F. Supp. 801 ([D.] Conn. 1970). In denying summary judgment for plaintiff-buyer, the court ruled that defendant-seller could attempt to prove that the quantity term was modified by an oral understanding, in line with a trade usage, that seller would only supply as many tons as he could, with 500 tons the upper limit. The court reasoned that an additional term with a lesser effect than total contradiction or negation of a contract term can be a consistent term and "[evidence] that the quantity to be supplied by defendant was orally understood to be up to 500 tons cannot be said to be inconsistent with the terms of the written contract which specified the quantity as '500 Gross Ton'." *Id.* at 804.[38]

---

without ambiguity. He only let in usage evidence because Shell's answer to interrogatory 11 provided some ambiguity, saying "I think if these can be consistently used to explain the apparently unambiguous terms, they should be allowed in." In fact, this court has ruled that ambiguity is not necessary to admit usage evidence. *Board of Trade of San Francisco v. Swiss Credit Bank*, 597 F.2d 146, 148 (9th Cir. 1979).

[37] [36] State court cases have interpreted express quantity as mere projections in similar circumstances. *E.g.*, *Campbell v. Hostetter Farms, Inc.*, 251 Pa. Super. 232, 380 A.2d 463, 466–67 (1977) (express agreement to sell a specified number of bushels of corn, wheat, and soy beans was not, as a matter of law, inconsistent with a usage of the trade that amounts specified in contracts are only estimates of a seller-farmer's farms); *Loeb & Co. v. Martin*, 295 Ala. 262, 327 So. 2d 711, 714–15 (Ala. 1976) (it was a jury question whether, in light of trade usage, "all cotton produced on 400 acres" called for all cotton seller produced on 400 acres or for 400 acres of cotton.); *Heggblade-Marguleas-Tenneco, Inc. v. Sunshine Biscuit, Inc.*, 59 Cal. App. 3d 948, 131 Cal. Rptr. 183, 188–89 (1976) (usage in the potato-processing trade that the amount specified in the contract was merely an estimate of buyer's requirements was admissible); *Paymaster Oil Mill Co. v. Mitchell*, 319 So. 2d 652, 657–58 (Miss. 1975) (additional term that the seller was not obliged to deliver the full 4000 bushels of soy beans called for in the contract was admissible).

[38] [37] The Seventh Circuit in dicta has implied that a written contract calling for 36-inch wide steel could be modified by a usage in the steel industry that a 36-inch specification "includes by definition steel which actually measures 37 in width." *Decker Steel Co. v. Exchange National Bank*, 330 F.2d 82, 85 (7th Cir. 1964). That circuit has not been as generous in allowing modification of express terms by course of performance or additional terms. In *V-M Corp. v. Bernard Distributing Co.*, 447 F.2d 864 (7th Cir. 1971), when the manufacturer sued the distributor of electronic equipment for goods delivered, distributor Bernard counterclaimed for breach of warranty. The counterclaim was dismissed because the written contract expressly disclaimed all but an express warranty and limited liability by excluding consequential or special damages, even though the course of performance by V-M had been to accept return of a portion of the goods that were not defective under the express warranty. Where the course of performance cannot be harmonized with the express terms, the court held, the express controls. *Id.* at 867–68. Although the court did not say so, the result might well have been different had usage evidence been presented to reinforce the acts constituting course of performance. In *Luria Brothers & Co. v. Pielet Brothers Scrap Iron & Metal, Inc.*, 600 F.2d 103, 110 (7th Cir.

[Ed. Note: The Court then discussed several cases from other circuits where the courts upheld the UCC emphasis on admitting evidence of trade usage liberally.]

Numerous state courts have interpreted their own state's versions of the Code in line with the weight of federal authority on the UCC to admit freely evidence of additional terms, usages, and prior dealings and harmonize them in most instances with apparently contradictory express terms.

*   *   *

Probably the two leading cases that have rejected usage evidence as inconsistent with express terms are *Southern Concrete Services, Inc. v. Mableton Contractors, Inc.*, 407 F. Supp. 581 (N.D. Ga. 1975), *aff'd*, 569 F.2d 1154 (5th Cir. 1978) (unpublished opinion), and *Division of Triple T Service, Inc. v. Mobil Oil Corp.*, 60 Misc. 2d 720, 304 N.Y.S.2d 191 (Sup. Ct. 1969). In *Southern Concrete* the District Court, distinguishing its facts from those in *Columbia Nitrogen, supra*, held that evidence of a trade usage and an agreement to additional terms was not admissible. The usage allegedly was that contract quantity specifications were not mandatory on either buyer or seller. The court acknowledged that UCC § 2-202 "was meant to liberalize the common law parol evidence rule to allow evidence of agreements outside the contract, without a prerequisite finding that the contract was ambiguous" and "requires that contracts be interpreted in light of the commercial context in which they were written and not by the rules on legal construction." *Southern Concrete, supra*, at 582–83. Nevertheless, the court held, the express quantity term in the contract and the usage could not be construed as reasonably consistent. "A construction which negates the express terms of the contract by allowing unilateral abandonment of its specifications is patently unreasonable." *Id.* at 585. The court's attempt to differentiate its facts from those in *Columbia Nitrogen* was unsuccessful; the distinctions discussed were very minor. The difference between the two results should depend less on such subtle variations in contract language and more on the strength of the usage evidence and whether the parties are or should be aware of the usage and thus should be bound by it. The court in *Southern Concrete* acknowledged that *Columbia Nitrogen* is not the only case at odds with its holding that a usage that quantities are projections cannot modify a seemingly unambiguous quantity term. *Southern Concrete, supra*, at 585–86.

The other leading case cited by Shell is a New York case, *Triple T, supra*. Because the express term of the franchise agreement gave either party the right to terminate on 90-days' notice, the court refused to find as reasonably consistent with that term a usage of the trade that a gasoline franchisor could only terminate a dealer for "cause." "[T]he express terms of the contract cover the entire area of termination and negate plaintiff's argument that the custom or usage in the trade implicitly adds the words 'with cause' in the termination clause. The contract is unambiguous and no sufficient basis appears for a construction which would insert words to limit the effect of the termination clause." *Id.* at 203. The court then held that only consistent usages are admissible, which is an incorrect reading of the Code. Usage is always admissible, even though the express term controls in the event of inconsistency, which is a jury question.

Higher New York courts have not been as quick to reject evidence of additional terms for inconsistency as was the Supreme Court in *Triple T* in rejecting usage evidence.

*   *   *

Some guidelines can be offered as to how usage evidence can be allowed to modify a contract.[39] First, the court must allow a check on usage evidence by demanding that it

---

1979), the court upheld a jury verdict for plaintiff-buyer in a suit for nondelivery, affirming the exclusion of parol evidence of an additional term that seller's obligation to sell scrap metal was conditioned on its ability to obtain the metal from a particular supplier.

[39] [44] White and Summers write that usage and dealings evidence "may not only supplement or qualify

be sufficiently definite and widespread to prevent unilateral post-hoc revision of contract terms by one party. The Code's intent is to put usage evidence on an objective basis. J.H. Levie, *Trade Usage and Custom Under the Common Law and the Uniform Commercial Code*, 40 N.Y.U. L. REV. 1101 (1965), states:

> When trade usage adds new terms to cover matters on which the agreement is silent the court is really making a contract for the parties, even though it says it only consulted trade usage to find the parties' probable intent. There is nothing wrong or even unusual about this practice, which really is no different from reading constructive conditions into a contract. Nevertheless the court does create new obligations, and perhaps that is why the courts often say that usage . . . must be proved by clear and convincing evidence.

Id. at 1102. Although the Code abandoned the traditional common law test of nonconsensual custom and views usage as a way of determining the parties' probable intent, *id.* at 1106–07, thus abolishing the requirement that common law custom be universally practiced, trade usages still must be well settled, *id.* at 1113. *Columbia Nitrogen, supra,* has been criticized as allowing the introduction of evidence of a usage that was not proved to be sufficiently well-established and that was not clearly applicable to the particular facts of the detailed contract between Royster and Columbia Nitrogen. Kirst, *Usage of Trade and Course of Dealing: Subversion of the UCC Theory*, 1977 LAW FORUM, 811; Note, *Commercial Law — Course of Dealing and Usage of Trade Affect Express Terms*, 1973 WISC. L. REV. 934, 94–43.

Evidence of a trade usage does not need to be protected against perjury because, as one commentator has written, "an outside standard does exist to help judge the truth of the assertion that the parties intended the usage to control the particular dispute: the existence and scope of the usage can be determined from other members of the trade." Kirst, *supra*, at 839. Kirst sets out guards on jury determination of usage evidence:

> Questions of the parties' intentions concerning an asserted trade usage or course of dealing will not always require a jury determination. If the evidence fails to show a practice is regularly observed, the judge can exclude the evidence because it does not show a course of dealing or usage of trade as defined in the Code. If the members of the trade confirm an actual usage but do not support the assertion that the usage applies to the particular facts in litigation, the judge will exclude evidence of the usage as irrelevant. If the parties used new and different language to convey their agreed intention to abandon the past practice, the court will recognize that practice under the old language is irrelevant to the contract containing the new language and, consequently, will exclude the evidence.

---

express terms, but in appropriate circumstances may even override express terms." WHITE & SUMMERS, *supra*, § 3-3 at 84. "[T]he provision that express terms control inconsistent course of dealing and [usages and performance evidence] really cannot be taken at face value." *Id.* at 86. That reading, although at odds with the actual wording of the Code, is a realistic reading of what some of the cases allow. A better formulation of the Code's mandate is offered by R. W. Kirst, *Usage of Trade and Course of Dealing: Subversion of the U.C.C. Theory*, 1977 LAW FORUM 811:

> The need to determine whether the parties intended a usage . . . to be part of the contract does not end if the court finds that the commercial practice is inconsistent with or contradicts the express language of the writing. If an inconsistency exists, the intention of the parties remains unclear. The parties may have intended either to include or exclude the practice. Determining the intent of the parties requires that the court attempt to construe the written term consistently with the commercial practice, if that is reasonable. If consistent construction is unreasonable the Code directs that the written term be taken as expressing the parties' intent. Before concluding that a jury could not reasonably find a consistent construction, the judge must understand the commercial background of the dispute.

Id. at 824.

In *Columbia Nitrogen, supra,* the court should have examined the relationship of the usage to the facts of the case, for example, by determining whether any of the contracts that had been treated as only "fair estimates" in the past were the detailed result of long negotiations, as was the contract in *Columbia Nitrogen.* That contract

> was the result of extensive negotiations for the sale of part of Royster's output from a major new facility covering sales for three years. If contracts of similar detail, covering similar time periods, and negotiated with similar care were regarded as estimates by others in the trade, then the court should have admitted the asserted usage of trade. If the contracts treated as estimates, however, were always form contracts, or short term contracts, or otherwise substantially different, then the court should have excluded the evidence as irrelevant to the dispute.

Id. at 845. That formulation of relevance of the usage evidence seems a fair one to follow in this case. Here the evidence was overwhelming that all suppliers to the asphaltic paving trade price protected customers under the same types of circumstances. Chevron's contract with H.B. was a similar long-term supply contract between a buyer and seller with very close relations, on a form supplied by the seller, covering sales of asphalt, and setting the price at seller's posted price, with no mention of price protection. The same commentator offers a second guideline:

> Because the stock printed forms cannot always reflect the changing methods of business, members of the trade may do business with a standard clause in the forms that they ignore in practice. If the trade consistently ignores obsolete clauses at variance with actual trade practices, a litigant can maintain that it is reasonable that the courts also ignore the clauses. Similarly, members of a trade may handle a particular subset of commercial transactions in a manner consistent with written terms because the writing cannot provide for all variations or contingencies. Thus, if the trade regards an express term and a trade usage as consistent because the usage is not a complete contradiction but only an occasional but definite exception to a written term, the courts should interpret the contract according to the usage.

Kirst, *supra,* at 824. Levie, *supra,* at 1112, writes, "Astonishing as it will seem to most practicing attorneys, under the Code it will be possible in some cases to use custom to contradict the written agreement . . . . Therefore usage may be used to 'qualify' the agreement, which presumably means to 'cut down' express terms although not to negate them entirely." Here, the express price term was "Shell's Posted Price at time of delivery." A total negation of that term would be that the buyer was to set the price. It is a less than complete negation of the term that an unstated exception exists at times of price increases, at which times the old price is to be charged, for a certain period or for a specified tonnage, on work already committed at the lower price on nonescalating contracts. Such a usage forms a broad and important exception to the express term, but does not swallow it entirely. Therefore, we hold that, under these particular facts, a reasonable jury could have found that price protection was incorporated into the 1969 agreement between Nanakuli and Shell and that price protection was reasonably consistent with the express term of seller's posted price at delivery.

* * *

QUESTION

The *Nanakuli* court finds that the evidence of trade usage should be admitted unless it totally negates the term in the writing. This amounts to adopting the "*Hunt Foods* test" for "consistency" that the *AND* case specifically rejected. Are *Nanakuli* and *AND* at odds, or is there a basis for distinguishing the two cases?

PROBLEM 2-10

Block Construction, Inc. is a contractor, and Supplies Unlimited is a wholesale supplier of concrete blocks. Block agrees to purchase its requirements for concrete blocks from Supplies for the coming year. The parties sign a written document that includes the following price term: "Block will pay Supplies' posted price at the time of delivery." Determine the admissibility of the following proffered evidence:

1. Block attempts to testify that before the contract was signed, Supplies promised that it would hold its prices for the duration of a particular construction project, to the extent that Block was contractually committed to provide concrete blocks for that particular construction project. The parties agree that this practice is known as "price protection";

2. Block seeks to introduce expert testimony that concrete block suppliers regularly price protect for their "favored" customers;

3. Block seeks to introduce expert testimony that concrete suppliers consistently price protect their customers, but Supplies responds by pointing to a clause of the contract which reads: "The terms and meaning of this contract are to be determined from the words used herein. Evidence of trade usage and course of dealing shall not be admissible for purposes of determining the terms and meaning of this contract"; and

4. Block seeks to introduce evidence that for 14 years it has had similarly worded contracts with Supplies, and that Supplies has always price protected Block until this contract.

E.   MODIFICATION AND WAIVER

Things don't always go as planned, and so even the most carefully conceived agreement might not serve the parties' interests when the time for performance arrives. The broad principle of freedom of contract has always permitted parties to modify their agreements to deal with circumstances unforeseen at the time of contracting, including the changing needs and desires of the parties. The common law regarded modifications as substitute contracts, and imposed the full requirements of formation (mutual assent and consideration) to validate modifications. This orientation gave rise to the "pre-existing duty rule," which provided that modifications are unenforceable for lack of (additional) consideration if only one party's contractual obligations are adjusted by the modification. Unfortunately, this rule conflicts with the commonplace practice of commercial parties to make unilateral concessions in the interest of strengthening their long-term relationship. Under the pre-existing duty rule, if one party agreed to modify the contract by making a concession (lowering the price, for example), the modification would be unenforceable in court because the other party failed to give a new promise as consideration for the concession.

Section 2-209(1) addresses the problem of the "pre-existing duty rule" by eliminating it. The parties are free to modify their agreements without consideration, but modifications are subject to the general obligation of good faith, as explained in Comment 2. This is revealing, because the duty of good faith applies only to the performance and enforcement of rights under a contract, and not to contract formation. Thus, it is clear that Article 2 reconceptualizes contract modifications to be part of the ongoing performance of the parties, rather than as the formation of a new contract.

1. The Requirement of Good Faith

You have discovered that assessing a party's "good faith" requires a fact-intensive analysis that is sensitive to the business context in which the parties operate. The *Duffy Tool & Stamping* case is a classic example of one party using economic duress to secure a purported modification.

DUFFY TOOL & STAMPING, INC. v. BOSCH AUTOMOTIVE MOTOR SYSTEMS CORP.

Tennessee Court of Appeals
2000 Tenn. App. LEXIS 63 (2000)

OPINION

Koch

This appeal involves a contract dispute between a manufacturer of automobile parts and one of its suppliers. After the manufacturer complained repeatedly about the quality of its parts, the supplier informed the manufacturer that it would no longer supply the parts even though two years remained on its contract. The manufacturer rejected a portion of the supplier's last shipment of parts and contracted with another supplier to take over the manufacturing of the parts. The original supplier then filed suit against the manufacturer in the Chancery Court for Sumner County for the balance due on its last shipment, and the manufacturer counterclaimed for breach of the supply contract. The trial court heard the case without a jury and determined that the supplier had breached the supply contract but was also entitled to a set-off based on its last delivery of parts. Accordingly, the trial court awarded the manufacturer a $133,542.66 judgment against the supplier. On this appeal, the supplier takes issue with the judgment on three grounds: that the parties modified their original contract; that the manufacturer waived its breach of contract claim; and that the trial court did not employ the proper measure of damages. We have determined that the evidence supports the trial court's conclusion that the supplier breached the contract but that the trial court incorrectly calculated the damages. Accordingly, we reduce the manufacturer's judgment against the supplier to $18,953.

I.

Bosch Automotive Motor Systems Corporation ("Bosch") is the American subsidiary of a German corporation that is one of the world's largest independent manufacturers of automobile parts. It operates a plant in Hendersonville, Tennessee where it manufactures air conditioner blower motors, most of which it sells to Ford Motor Company for use in the Windstar van and the Taurus and Lincoln Continental automobiles.

In July 1993, Bosch entered into a three-year contract with Duffy Tool & Stamping, Inc. ("Duffy Tool"), an Indiana corporation, to supply mounting plates for the air conditioner motors being sold to Ford. The contract required the mounting plates to be manufactured to Bosch's specifications and also required Bosch to pay Duffy Tool $140,000 up front to enable Duffy Tool to design and install the special tooling needed to produce mounting plates consistent with Bosch's specifications.

Difficulties arose almost as soon as Duffy Tool began delivering mounting plates to Bosch. The parties had a running dispute over the scratching, bending, and rusting of the plates being delivered to Bosch in Tennessee. This dispute over the quality of the mounting plates proved to be an unresolvable sore spot between the parties. Duffy Tool began losing even more money under the contract following an increase in the cost of the steel used to make the mounting plates. In June 1994, with two years still remaining on an already unprofitable contract, Duffy Tool gave Bosch six weeks notice of its decision to stop supplying mounting plates under the contract.

Duffy Tool's abrupt decision to walk away from the contract imperiled Bosch's ability to perform its contract with Ford because Bosch could not supply air conditioners without mounting plates. In turn, Bosch's inability to perform would affect Ford's production of its motor vehicles. Accordingly, Bosch sought to meet with Duffy Tool to discuss how to continue receiving mounting plates until a new supplier could be found. At a meeting on July 8, 1994, Duffy Tool informed Bosch that it would continue to supply mounting plates for a limited time, but only if Bosch would agree to a ten percent price increase, as well as a $3,000 daily tooling set-up charge.

In an August 30, 1994 letter, Duffy Tool set out specifically its terms to "wind down the pre-existing agreement between our companies." The letter proposed (1) that Duffy Tool would continue to supply mounting plates through January 1995; (2) that part prices would be increased retroactively by ten percent from July 11, 1994; and (3) that Duffy Tool would be held harmless "on the tooling issue and all other claims related to the transition." In his September 2, 1994 response, Bosch's president replied that Bosch would not sue Duffy Tool "relative to the transactions involved on the tooling issue and in making a transition." He also alluded to other, otherwise unidentified, telephone conversations in which "certain agreements were reconfirmed between Duffy Tool and [Bosch] relative to our July 8 meeting."

In the latter half of 1994, Bosch contracted with Pax Machine Works, Inc., ("Pax Machine") of Celina, Ohio to take over the manufacturing of the mounting plates. This new contract required Bosch to pay a higher price for the mounting plates than it had originally agreed to pay Duffy Tool and to pay Pax Machine an additional $134,850 for the new tooling required to produce the mounting plates.

Duffy Tool delivered its last shipment of mounting plates to Bosch in December 1994 along with an invoice for $58,752.21. Bosch notified Duffy Tool in February 1995 that some of the mounting plates were defective. In response, Duffy Tool instructed Bosch to inspect all the plates and promised to make an adjustment if a significant number of the plates were damaged. Bosch sorted out the damaged mounting plates and scrapped them, but the parties could never agree on an adjustment. Accordingly, Bosch did not pay Duffy Tool's last invoice.

Duffy Tool sued Bosch in the Chancery Court for Sumner County to collect for the last shipment of mounting plates, and Bosch counterclaimed for breach of the supply contract. The trial court heard the case without a jury and found in favor of both parties. First, it determined that Duffy Tool had breached the supply contract and awarded Bosch a judgment for $182,522.93. The trial court also determined that Bosch owed Duffy Tool $48,980.27 for its last delivery of parts. Accordingly, the trial court set off Duffy Tool's judgment against Bosch's judgment and awarded Bosch $133,542.66. Duffy Tool has appealed from this judgment.

*   *   *

[Ed. note: The court first held that Bosch had not expressly waived its breach of contract claim, nor had it failed to give proper notice of the breach as required by 2-607(3).]

*   *   *

III.

Modification of the Original Contract

Duffy Tool also asserts that it cannot be liable for breach of the original contract because the parties agreed to modify that contract in mid-1994 to allow Duffy Tool to substitute reduced performance. The trial court rejected this argument on grounds that

Bosch was under economic duress in July 1994 when it consented to accept a reduced performance. Duffy Tool now challenges that conclusion. For the purposes of this appeal, we will review the trial court's understanding and application of the legal doctrine of economic duress de novo, *see Rice v. Sabir*, 979 S.W.2d 305, 308 (Tenn. 1998), but we will presume that the trial court's underlying factual determinations on this issue are correct unless the evidence preponderates otherwise. *See* Tenn. R. App. P. 13(d); *Branum v. Akins*, 978 S.W.2d 554, 557 (Tenn. Ct. App. 1998).

A.

Commercial parties are undoubtedly free to modify their contracts consensually. *See* Tenn. Code Ann. § 47-2-209 (1996). Modifications of contracts governed by the Uniform Commercial Code are subject to the general obligation of good faith, which the Code defines as "honesty in fact and the observance of reasonable commercial standards of fair dealing in the trade." Tenn. Code Ann. § 47-2-103(1)(b) (1996). Thus, a modification of a contract for the sale of goods procured under circumstances of economic duress is voidable by the victim. *See Cumberland & Ohio Co. of Tex., Inc. v. First Am. Nat'l Bank*, 936 F.2d 846, 850 (6th Cir. 1991); *Exum v. Washington Fire & Marine Ins. Co.*, 41 Tenn. App. 610, 620, 297 S.W.2d 805, 809 (1955).

The sort of economic duress that will render a contract voidable is the "imposition, oppression . . . or taking of undue advantage of the business or financial stress or extreme necessities . . . of another . . . [so] that the party profiting thereby has received money, property or other advantage [that in equity the party] ought not be permitted to retain." *Johnson v. Ford*, 147 Tenn. 63, 92–93, 245 S.W. 531, 539 (1922). Tenn. Code Ann. § 47-1-103 (1996) preserves the applicability of economic duress as a defense in dealings between commercial actors. As a general matter, economic duress will make an agreement voidable by the strapped party when that party's assent has been induced by an "improper threat by the other party that [has left] the victim no reasonable alternative." Restatement (Second) Contracts § 175(1) (1981).[40]

In this case, Duffy Tool's conduct was more than a mere threat to refuse to deliver plates. In June 1994, Duffy Tool unilaterally informed Bosch that it would discontinue supplying mounting plates in six weeks even though approximately two years remained on its contract.[41] At trial, Duffy Tool's president endeavored to downplay Duffy Tool's notification as a mere "request" to be released from the contract. Far from being a request, however, it was a renouncement of the contract. The weight of the evidence makes plain that when Bosch subsequently demanded that Duffy Tool perform the contract without modification, Duffy Tool rebuffed Bosch with "[t]hat decision has already been made."

Bosch's vice president of engineering described quite succinctly the predicament Bosch found itself in at the July 8, 1994 meeting with Duffy Tool. He explained that "without those mounting plates we could not have delivered the product. . . . The alternatives were to continue getting mounting plates from Duffy Tool or to stop the

---

[40]   [4] One of the examples used by the American Law Institute to illustrate the use of economic duress to induce an increase in the price of goods is strikingly similar to the facts of this case:

> A, who has contracted to sell goods to B, makes an improper threat to refuse to deliver the goods to B unless B modifies the contract to increase the price. B attempts to buy substitute goods elsewhere but is unable to do so. Being in urgent need of the goods, he makes the modification. B has no reasonable alternative. A's threat amounts to duress, and the modification is voidable by B.

Restatement (Second) Contracts, § 175, illustration 5.

[41]   [5] Duffy Tool's lengthy argument that there could be no economic duress because Duffy Tool sought a contract modification in good faith does not fit this case's facts. In June 1994 Duffy Tool did more than merely request a contract modification. It flatly informed Bosch, "Duffy Tool & Stamping will be able to provide mounting flange[s] . . . for six more weeks. As a result, the confirmation of a new vendor must be done as soon as possible." Duffy Tool's statement amounted to an anticipatory repudiation of the parties' contract.

supply of [air conditioner] motors to Ford if we would not have gotten the mounting plates from Duffy Tool." He continued that "[i]f we would have stopped the production of motors with this mounting plate to Ford, we would have stopped a Ford assembly plant because we were the only or the sole supplier for that motor to Ford, so the cars would not have been produced." Noting that failing to supply in the automotive industry is the "biggest sin you can commit," he explained that "I was in a position where I felt I was against the wall or had a gun to my head and had to agree to a compromise to be able to continue getting mounting plates."

Having reviewed the record and considered both sides' arguments, we hold that the trial court correctly determined that the doctrine of economic duress applied to the facts of this case. We also hold that the evidence does not preponderate against the trial court's conclusion that Bosch was acting under economic duress when it consented to a reduced performance by Duffy Tool at the July 8, 1994 meeting.

B.

Duffy Tool argues that even if economic duress forced Bosch to agree to modify the original contract, Bosch later waived its economic duress defense or, in the alternative, that Bosch ratified the modified agreement after the duress had ceased. We reject these arguments because the record shows that Bosch acted timely in asserting its economic duress defense once Duffy Tool commenced litigation.

Duffy Tool's complaint does not allege that its last shipment of mounting plates was delivered under a modified agreement. Instead, Duffy Tool expressly sued for an unpaid balance "on an open purchase account as evidenced by Invoices." The parties only settled into opposing legal theories of contract modification and economic duress as the litigation progressed. Once Duffy Tool attempted to blunt Bosch's countersuit by asserting consensual modification, Bosch promptly responded by asserting economic duress. We find no waiver.

We reach the same conclusion with regard to Duffy Tool's ratification theory. A party may, without question, ratify a voidable contract. See *Brandon v. Wright*, 838 S.W.2d 532, 534 (Tenn. Ct. App. 1992); *Valley Fidelity Bank & Trust Co. v. Cain Partnership Ltd.*, 738 S.W.2d 638, 639 (Tenn. Ct. App. 1987). Thus, a victim of economic duress who, over a significant time, accepts the benefits flowing from a voidable contract may be deemed to have ratified the contract. See *Carlile v. Snap-on Tools*, 648 N.E.2d 317, 324 (Ill. App. Ct. 1995); *Niosi v. Niosi*, 641 N.Y.S.2d 93, 94–95 (App. Div. 1996). However, a finding of ratification hinges on proof of the party's intent to operate under the voidable arrangement, manifested once the party is free from duress. See *United States v. McBride*, 571 F. Supp. 596, 613 (S.D. Tex. 1983).

We should keep in mind that when great pressure exists and when the time for performance is short, it is neither uncommon nor unreasonable for commercial actors to wait until the pressure has passed before asserting a breach of contract claim. See, e.g., *Garcia v. Kastner Farms, Inc.*, 789 S.W.2d 656, 659–60 (Tex. App. 1990) (finding no ratification of an alleged modification). Additionally, before reading an intent to ratify into a party's conduct, we should be sure that the conduct is not ambiguous. Ordinarily, conduct evidencing ratification should be inconsistent with anything other than approval of the contract. See *Page v. Woodson*, 200 S.W.2d 768, 771 (Ark. 1947); *Kennedy v. Roberts*, 75 N.W. 363, 366 (Iowa 1898).

We find *Hassett v. Dixie Furniture Co.*, 425 S.E.2d 683 (N.C. 1993) instructively similar to this case on this issue. In that case, a furniture designer entered a four-year contract to provide exclusive design services to a furniture manufacturer. The manufacturer later decided that the designer was not living up to the contract and sent the designer a termination agreement providing that the manufacturer would pay the designer for a limited future period in lieu of paying the designer for the rest of the contract's term. The designer refused to sign the termination agreement because it contained terms he had not agreed to. Thereafter, the manufacturer paid the designer for the limited period defined in the termination agreement and then hired other designers. When the designer sued for breach of the original four-year contract, the manufacturer contended that he had ratified the termination agreement by accepting payments under it. The designer countered that he was entitled to those same payments under the original contract and that he had accepted them under that contract which was still in its time of performance. He argued that he should not be required to refuse a performance otherwise contractually due him at the risk of being held to have agreed to a modification. The North Carolina Supreme Court agreed with the designer and held that for a party to merely accept benefits already due was conduct too ambiguous to support ratification of a subsequent contract modification. *See Hassett v. Dixie Furniture Co.*, 425 S.E.2d at 687.

In this case, Duffy Tool asserts that Bosch ratified a modification of the parties' contract by accepting its continued performance after the July 1994 meeting. We disagree. From July 1994 through December 1994, Bosch got from Duffy Tool just what Duffy Tool was originally obligated by contract to supply-air conditioner motor mounting plates. Bosch took what plates it could get for as long as it could get them. When Duffy Tool stopped supplying plates, Bosch considered Duffy Tool in breach, and after Pax Machine was in place as a supplier and the duress removed, Bosch asserted breach. We agree with the analysis in *Hassett v. Dixie Furniture Co.* and find Bosch's conduct in accepting mounting plates from July to December 1994 entirely too ambiguous to support a finding of ratification.

* * *

TODD, P.J., M.S., and CANTRELL, J., concur.

QUESTIONS

1. Did Duffy act in bad faith by seeking price concessions, or by the manner in which it sought the concessions? Can a party ever act in bad faith simply by asking for a modification?

2. If Duffy had sought a modification in good faith, would Bosch have been obligated to agree to the requested price concessions? If Bosch had agreed to price increases and winding down the relationship in response to such a request, would the modification have been enforceable?

2. Modifications and the Statute of Frauds

Section 2-209(3) succinctly and clearly provides that the "requirements of the statute of frauds section of this Article (Section 2-201) must be satisfied if the contract as modified is within its provisions." However, the meaning of this rule is less than clear. Some courts have concluded that § 2-209(3) means that all modifications must themselves satisfy the requirements of the statute of frauds in order to be enforceable. Comment 3 suggests that this is the appropriate interpretation of the rule, but the language of § 2-209(3) does not compel this interpretation. Read the following case and work through the problem with the goal of identifying persuasive arguments that § 2-209(3) should not be interpreted in this fashion.

CLOUD CORP. v. HASBRO, INC.
United States Court of Appeals, Seventh Circuit
314 F.3d 289 (2002)

POSNER, Circuit Judge.

"Wonder World Aquarium" is a toy that Hasbro, Inc., the well-known designer and marketer of toys, sold for a brief period in the mid-1990s. The toy comes as a package that contains (we simplify slightly) the aquarium itself, some plastic fish, and, depending on the size of the aquarium (for this varies), large or small packets of a powder that when dissolved in distilled water forms a transparent gelatinous filling for the aquarium. The gel simulates water, and the plastic fish can be inserted into it with tweezers to create the illusion of a real fish tank with living, though curiously inert, fish. "Pretend blood," included in some of the packages, can be added for even greater verisimilitude. The consumer can choose among versions of Wonder World Aquarium that range from "My Pretty Mermaid" to "Piranha Attack" — the latter a scenario in which the pretend blood is doubtless a mandatory rather than optional ingredient.

Hasbro contracted out the manufacture of this remarkable product. Southern Clay Products Company was to sell and ship Laponite HB, a patented synthetic clay, to Cloud Corporation, which was to mix the Laponite with a preservative according to a formula supplied by Hasbro, pack the mixture in the packets that we mentioned, and ship them to affiliates of Hasbro in East Asia. The affiliates would prepare and package the final product — that is the aquarium, the packet of gel, and the plastic fish (and "pretend blood") — and ship it back to Hasbro in the United States for distribution to retailers.

The project was in operation by the middle of 1995. Hasbro would from time to time issue purchase orders for a specified number of large and small packets to Cloud, which would in turn order the quantity of Laponite from Southern Clay Products that it needed in order to manufacture the specified number of packets. The required quantity of Laponite depended not only on the number of large and small packets ordered by Hasbro but also on the formula that Hasbro supplied to Cloud specifying the proportion of Laponite in each packet. The formula was changed frequently. The less Laponite per packet specified in the formula, the more packets could be manufactured for a given quantity of the ingredient.

Early in 1997 Hasbro discovered that its East Asian affiliates, the assemblers of the final package, had more than enough powder on hand to supply Hasbro's needs, which were diminishing, no doubt because Wonder World Aquarium was losing market appeal. Mistakenly believing that Hasbro's market was expanding rather than contracting, Cloud had manufactured a great many packets of powder in advance of receiving formal purchase orders for them from Hasbro. Hasbro refused to accept delivery of these packets or to pay for them. Contending that this refusal was a breach of contract, Cloud sued Hasbro in federal district court in Chicago, basing jurisdiction on diversity of citizenship and seeking more than $600,000 in damages based mainly on the price of the packets that it had manufactured and not delivered to Hasbro and now was stuck with — for the packets, being usable only in Wonder World Aquaria, had no resale value. After a bench trial, the district judge ruled in favor of Hasbro.

Cloud does not quarrel with the district judge's findings of fact, but only with her legal conclusions. The governing law is the Uniform Commercial Code as interpreted in Illinois.

The original understanding between Hasbro and Cloud regarding Cloud's role in the Wonder World Aquarium project either was not a contract or was not broken — probably the former, as the parties had not agreed on the price, quantity, delivery dates, or composition of the packets. These essential terms were set forth in the purchase orders that Hasbro sent Cloud, confirming discussions between employees of Cloud and Kathy Esposito, Hasbro's employee in charge of purchasing inputs for the company's foreign affiliates. Upon receipt of a purchase order, Cloud would send Hasbro an order acknowledgment and would order from Southern Clay Products the quantity of Laponite required to fill the purchase order.

In October 1995, which is to say a few months after the launch of Wonder World Aquarium, Hasbro sent a letter to all its suppliers, including Cloud, that contained a "terms and conditions" form to govern future purchase orders. One of the terms was that a supplier could not deviate from a purchase order without Hasbro's written consent. As requested, Cloud signed the form and returned it to Hasbro. Nevertheless, to make assurance doubly sure, every time Hasbro sent a purchase order to Cloud it would include an acknowledgment form for Cloud to sign that contained the same terms and conditions that were in the October letter. Cloud did not sign any of these acknowledgment forms. The order acknowledgments that it sent Hasbro in response to Hasbro's purchase orders contained on the back of each acknowledgment Cloud's own set of terms and conditions — and the provision in Hasbro's letter and forms requiring Hasbro's written consent to any modification of the purchase order was not among them. There was a space for Hasbro to sign Cloud's acknowledgment form but it never did so. Neither party complained about the other's failure to sign the tendered forms.

Hasbro placed its last purchase orders with Cloud in February and April 1996. The orders for February specified 2.3 million small packets and 3.2 million large ones. For April the numbers were 1.5 and 1.4 million. Hasbro notified Cloud of the formula that it was to use in making the packets and Cloud ordered Laponite from Southern Clay Products accordingly.

Now as it happened Southern Clay Products was having trouble delivering the Laponite in time to enable Cloud to meet its own delivery schedule. In June 1996, amidst complaints from Hasbro's East Asian affiliates that they were running out of powder, and concerned about the lag in Laponite deliveries, Hasbro notified Cloud that it was to use a new formula in manufacturing the powder, a formula that required so much less Laponite that the same quantity would enable Cloud to produce a third again as many packets. Cloud determined that by using the new formula it could produce from the quantity of Laponite that it had on hand 4.5 million small and 5 million large packets, compared to the 3.8 and 3.9 million called for by the February and April orders but not yet delivered. Cloud had delivered 700,000 of the large packets ordered in February and April; that is why it had 7.7 million packets still to deliver under those orders rather than 8.4 million, the total number of packets ordered (2.3 + 3.2 + 1.5 + 1.4 = 8.4).

Although it had received no additional purchase orders, Cloud sent Hasbro an order acknowledgment for 4.5 million small and 5 million large packets with a delivery date similar to that for the April order, but at a lower price per packet, reflecting the smaller quantity of Laponite, the expensive ingredient in the powder, in each packet.

Cloud's acknowledgment was sent in June. Hasbro did not respond to it — at least not explicitly. It did receive it, however. And Kathy Esposito continued having e-mail exchanges and phone conversations with Cloud. These focused on delivery dates and, importantly, on the quantities to be delivered on those dates. Importantly because some very large numbers — much larger than the February and April numbers, numbers consistent however with Cloud's order acknowledgment sent to Hasbro in June — appear in these and other e-mails written by her. In two of the e-mails the quantity Cloud is to ship is described as "more or less depending on the formula," consistent with Cloud's understanding that if the formula reduced the amount of Laponite per packet Cloud should increase the number of packets it made rather than return unused Laponite to Southern Clay Products. A notation made in August by another member of Hasbro's purchasing department, Maryann Ricci — "Cloud O/S; 4,000,000 sm; 3.5 million lg." — indicates her belief that Cloud had outstanding ("O/S") purchase orders for 4 million small and 3.5 million large packets. These numbers were far in excess of the undelivered portions of the February and April orders; and since all the earlier orders had, so far as we can determine, already been filled and so were no longer outstanding, she must have been referring to the numbers in Cloud's June order acknowledgment.

The district judge, despite ruling for Hasbro, found that indeed "Hasbro intended to exceed the quantities of . . . packages it had ordered from Cloud in February and April of 1996," that "Hasbro was more concerned with prompt product than with the specific terms of its order[s]," and, most important, that "given Hasbro's repeated message that it could not get enough Laponite HB to fill its needs in a timely fashion, Cloud's decision to produce as many packets as possible appeared to be a safe course of action. Cloud was trying to keep pace with Hasbro's Laponite HB needs, a task made virtually impossible by the length of time it took Southern Clay to fill Cloud's Laponite HB orders." The judge even suggested that given Hasbro's desperation, Cloud could have persuaded Hasbro to execute additional purchase orders at prices equal to those in the February and April orders. Instead, rather than trying to take advantage of Hasbro's fix, Cloud reduced its price to reflect its lower cost. A curious consequence of the reduction, unremarked by the parties, is that even if Cloud has no contract remedy, it has (unless time barred) a remedy in quantum meruit for the benefit it conferred on Hasbro by voluntarily reducing the price specified in the February and April purchase orders.

When some months later Hasbro pulled the plug on Wonder World Aquarium, Cloud had not begun delivering any of the additional quantity that it had manufactured over and above the quantities called for in the February and April purchase orders.

Was Cloud commercially unreasonable in producing the additional quantity without a purchase order? If not, should the Uniform Commercial Code, which was intended to conform sales law to the customs and usages of business people, UCC §§ 1-102(2)(b), 1-105 comment 3; *In re Merritt Dredging Co.*, 839 F.2d 203, 206 (4th Cir. 1988); Kerry Lynn Macintosh, "Liberty, Trade, and the Uniform Commercial Code: When Should Default Rules Be Based on Business Practices?" 38 WM. & MARY L. REV. 1465, 1488–91 (1997), nevertheless condemn Cloud, as the district judge believed, for failing to request written purchase orders for the additional quantity that the change in formula enabled it to manufacture? Or was Hasbro contractually obligated to pay for that additional quantity?

The answers to these questions depend on whether there was a valid modification of the quantity specifications in the February and April purchase orders (obviously Hasbro cannot complain about the price modification!). The October letter provided that purchase orders could not be modified without Hasbro's written consent. Cloud signed the letter and so became bound by it, consideration being furnished by Hasbro's continuing to do business with Cloud. Hasbro's order acknowledgments accompanying its February and April purchase orders also provided that the orders could not be modified without Hasbro's written consent.

Cloud did not sign Hasbro's acknowledgments and its own acknowledgments omitted the provision requiring that any modification have Hasbro's written consent. But these facts have no significance. In the case of discrepant order and acceptance forms, if the acceptance merely adds a term, that term binds the offeror, UCC § 2-207(1); this modification of the common law's "mirror image" rule minimizes transaction costs by eliminating a negotiation over the additional term unless the offeror is unwilling to accede to the offeree's desire for it. But what if the term added by the acceptance contradicts a term in the offer? Then it doesn't become a part of the contract — that much is clear. § 2-207(2)(b). But is there a contract, and if so what are its terms? The UCC doesn't say, but the majority rule, and the rule in Illinois, is that the inconsistent terms cancel each other out and the court fills the resulting void with a term of its own devising. William B. Davenport, Daniel R. Murray & Donald R. Cassling, *Uniform Commercial Code with Illinois Code Comments* § 5/2-207, Illinois Code Comment 11, pp. 126–27 (Illinois Practice Series, vol. 2a, 1997).

In this case, however, there was neither a supplemental nor an inconsistent term in the acceptance; there was *no* term concerning modification, and in such a situation Hasbro's term is enforceable. *Earl M. Jorgensen Co. v. Mark Construction, Inc.*, 56 Haw. 466, 540 P.2d 978, 982–83 (1975); 1 JAMES J. WHITE & ROBERT S. SUMMERS, UNIFORM COMMERCIAL CODE 15–16 (4th ed. 1995). It is a case of different but not inconsistent terms, in which event the acceptance is effective to make a contract. UCC § 2-207(1). The offeree's silence is not interpreted as rejection in this situation because transaction costs would again be higher if the offeror had to quiz the offeree on whether every term in the offer not mentioned in the acceptance was acceptable to the offeree. Cloud, the offeree, knew that Hasbro wanted the modification provision and if this was unacceptable it should have said so.

For unexpressed reasons the district judge did not focus on the contractual provisions requiring that any modification of a purchase order be in writing. She considered only whether the UCC's statute of frauds required this, and ruled that it did. The quantity term in a contract for the sale of goods for more than $500 must be memorialized in a writing signed by the party sought to be held to that term, UCC § 2-201(1), and so, therefore, must a modification of that term. UCC § 2-209(3). However — and here we part company with the district judge — Kathy Esposito's e-mails, plus the notation that we quoted earlier signed by Maryann Ricci, another member of Hasbro's purchasing department, satisfy the statutory requirement. The UCC does not require that the contract itself be in writing, only that there be adequate documentary evidence of its existence and essential terms, which there was here. *Architectural Metal Systems, Inc. v. Consolidated Systems, Inc.*, 58 F.3d 1227, 1229–31 (7th Cir. 1995); *Monetti, S.P.A. v. Anchor Hocking Corp.*, 931 F.2d 1178, 1185 (7th Cir. 1991); *Axelson, Inc. v. McEvoy-Willis*, 7 F.3d 1230, 1233 n.6 (5th Cir. 1993).

But what shall we make of the fact that Kathy Esposito's e-mails contained no signature? The Electronic Signatures in Global and National Commerce Act, 15 U.S.C. § 7001, provides that in all transactions in or affecting interstate or foreign commerce (the transactions between Cloud and Hasbro were in interstate commerce and affected both interstate and foreign commerce), a contract or other record relating to the transaction shall not be denied legal effect merely because it is in electronic form. That would be conclusive in this case — had the e-mails been sent after the Act took effect in 2000. But they were sent in 1996. The Act does not purport to be applicable to transactions that occurred before its effective date, and, not being procedural, *compare Landgraf v. USI Film Products*, 511 U.S. 244, 275, 114 S. Ct. 1483, 128 L. Ed. 2d 229 (1994), it is presumed not to apply retroactively. *Johnson v. Ventra Group, Inc.*, 191 F.3d 732, 745 (6th Cir. 1999). But like the court in *Shattuck v. Klotzbach*, No. 011109A, 2001 WL 1839720, at *2–3 (Mass. Super. Dec. 11, 2001), we conclude without having to rely on the federal Act that the sender's name on an e-mail satisfies the signature requirement of the statute of frauds. *Toghiyany v. AmeriGas Propane, Inc.*, 309 F.3d 1088, 1091 (8th Cir. 2002), another e-mail case that does not cite the electronic signatures act (maybe because, as in this case, the contract predated the Act), tugs the other way. But it is unclear whether the court thought the absence of a signature fatal or thought that it was that absence combined with the absence of an essential term — the duration of the contract — that triggered the statute of frauds.

Neither the common law nor the UCC requires a *hand-written* signature, *Just Pants v. Wagner*, 247 Ill. App. 3d 166, 187 Ill. Dec. 38, 617 N.E.2d 246, 251 (1993); *Monetti, S.P.A. v. Anchor Hocking Corp., supra*, 931 F.2d at 1182; *Hillstrom v. Gosnay*, 188 Mont. 388, 614 P.2d 466, 469 (1980); Davenport, Murray & Cassling, *supra*, § 5/1-201, Illinois Code Comment 42, pp. 53–54; *cf. Restatement (Second) of Contracts* § 134, comment a (1981), even though such a signature is better evidence of identity than a typed one. It is not customary, though it is possible, to include an electronic copy of a handwritten signature in an e-mail, and therefore its absence does not create a suspicion of forgery or other fraud — and anyway an electronic copy of a signature could *be* a forgery.

The purpose of the statute of frauds is to prevent a contracting party from creating a triable issue concerning the terms of the contract — or for that matter concerning whether a contract even exists — on the basis of his say-so alone. That purpose does not require a handwritten signature, especially in a case such as this in which there is other evidence, and not merely say-so evidence, of the existence of the contract (more precisely, the contract modification) besides the writings. The fact that Cloud produced the additional quantity is pretty powerful evidence of a contract, *Consolidation*

Services, Inc. v. KeyBank National Ass'n, 185 F.3d 817, 821 (7th Cir. 1999); *Monetti, S.P.A. v. Anchor Hocking Corp.*, *supra*, 931 F.2d at 1183, as it would have been taking a terrible risk in doing so had it thought it would have no right to be paid if Hasbro refused to accept delivery but would instead be stuck with a huge quantity of a product that had no salvage value. Actually, in the case of a contract for goods specially manufactured by the buyer, partial performance by the seller takes the contract outside the statute of frauds, without more. UCC § 2-201(3)(a). This may well be such a case; but we need not decide.

The background to the modification — the fact that the parties had dealt informally with each other (as shown by their disregard of the form contracts), and above all that Hasbro plainly wanted more product and wanted it fast — is further evidence that had Cloud asked for a written purchase order in June 1996 for the additional quantity, Hasbro would have given it, especially since Cloud was offering a lower price.

There is more: "between merchants [a term that embraces 'any transaction with respect to which both parties are chargeable with the knowledge or skill of merchants,' UCC § 2-104(3)] if within a reasonable time a writing in confirmation of the contract and sufficient against the sender is received and the party receiving it has reason to know its contents, it satisfies the requirements of subsection 1 [the statute of frauds] . . . unless written notice of objection to its contents is given within 10 days after it is received." UCC § 2-201(2). Cloud sent an order acknowledgment, reciting the increased quantity, shortly after the oral modification, and Hasbro did not object within ten days. *Campbell v. Yokel*, 20 Ill. App. 3d 702, 313 N.E.2d 628, 628–31 (1974); *Klockner, Inc. v. Federal Wire Mill Corp.*, 663 F.2d 1370, 1374, 1376 (7th Cir. 1981); *Apex Oil Co. v. Vanguard Oil & Service Co.*, 760 F.2d 417, 423 (2d Cir. 1985).

So Hasbro's statute of frauds defense fails on a number of independent grounds. But what of the *contractual* requirement of the buyer's consent in writing to any modification? Could that stiffen the requirements of the UCC's statute of frauds? Parties are free to incorporate stronger conditions for contractual modification than the UCC provides: "A signed agreement which excludes modification or rescission except by a signed writing cannot be otherwise modified or rescinded, but except as between merchants such a requirement on a form supplied by the merchant must be separately signed by the other party." UCC § 2-209(2); *see Martinsville Nylon Employees Council Corp. v. NLRB*, 969 F.2d 1263, 1267 (D.C. Cir. 1992); *Wisconsin Knife Works v. National Metal Crafters*, 781 F.2d 1280, 1292 (7th Cir. 1986) (dissenting opinion); Frank A. Rothermel, Comment, "Role of Course of Performance and Confirmatory Memoranda in Determining the Scope, Operation, and Effect of 'No Oral Modification' Clauses," 48 U. Pitt. L. Rev. 1239, 1251–52 (1987). The UCC's statute of frauds requires only quantity terms to be in writing. The contractual requirement that the buyer's consent be in writing was not limited to quantity terms, but this makes no difference, since those are the terms in dispute.

Could the contractual statute of frauds (to speak oxymoronically) be broader in a different sense? Specifically, could "consent in writing" require an explicit written statement of consent, missing here, rather than merely an inference of consent from a writing or series of writings? Maybe, but Hasbro does not argue that the contractual statute of frauds in this case has any different scope from the statutory, though it seems highly unlikely that a no-oral-modification clause would be subject to the exception in section 2-201(2) (quoted earlier) to the statute of frauds. Such a clause is added to a contract when the parties want to draft their own statute of frauds, as they are permitted to do; and there is no reason to suppose that they would want to adopt wholesale the limitations that the UCC imposes on its own statute of frauds. If they wanted those limitations they wouldn't need their own, customized clause.

So we may set section 2-201(2) to one side. That leaves intact, however, Cloud's argument, which we have accepted, that there was adequate evidence of written consent to the modification. And it leaves intact still *another* alternative argument by

Cloud: "an attempt at modification" that does not satisfy the statute of frauds nevertheless "can operate as a waiver." § 2-209(4). The word "can" is key. To prevent the "attempt" provision from eviscerating the statute of frauds, the courts require that the attempting modifier, Cloud in this case, must show either that it reasonably relied on the other party's having waived the requirement of a writing, *Wisconsin Knife Works v. National Metal Crafters, supra*, 781 F.2d at 1286–87 (7th Cir. 1986); *American Suzuki Motor Corp. v. Bill Kummer, Inc.*, 65 F.3d 1381, 1386 (7th Cir. 1995); *contra, BMC Industries, Inc. v. Barth Industries, Inc.*, 160 F.3d 1322, 1333 (11th Cir. 1998), or that the waiver was clear and unequivocal. *In re Nitz*, 317 Ill. App. 3d 119, 250 Ill. Dec. 632, 739 N.E.2d 93, 103 (2000); *Lavelle v. Dominick's Finer Foods, Inc.*, 227 Ill. App. 3d 764, 169 Ill. Dec. 800, 592 N.E.2d 287, 291–92 (1992); *McElroy v. B.F. Goodrich Co.*, 73 F.3d 722, 724 (7th Cir. 1996); *Bank v. Truck Ins. Exchange*, 51 F.3d 736, 739 (7th Cir. 1995). This exception to the statute of frauds applies equally to the Abuyer's written consent provision of the parties' contracts, UCC § 2-209(4); *Wisconsin Knife Works v. National Metal Crafters, supra*, 781 F.2d at 1284–87, because waiver is a general doctrine of contract law rather than an appendage to the statute of frauds.

The district judge erred by requiring that Cloud show *both* reasonable reliance and that the waiver was clear and unequivocal. There was no clear and unequivocal waiver, but there was reliance. The judge *found* reliance. She found that Cloud had been acting in good faith in producing the additional quantity of packets because it reasonably believed that Hasbro wanted the additional quantity. But she concluded that Cloud had been unreasonable in relying on its reasonable belief because it could so easily have insisted on a written purchase order modifying the quantity terms in the February and April orders. Reasonableness, however, is relative to commercial practices and understandings rather than to the desire of judges and lawyers, reflecting their training and professional culture, to see a deal memorialized in a form that leaves no room for misunderstanding the legal consequences. The employees of Hasbro and Cloud who were responsible for the administration of the parties' contractual undertaking were not lawyers. Doubtless because of this, the parties had, as we have noted, been casual about documentation. Cloud had treated the purchase orders as sources of information on how much Hasbro wanted when and according to what formula, but had paid no attention to them as contracts containing terms and conditions that might bind it. Hasbro had treated Cloud's purchase-order acknowledgments with similar insouciance. The parties had a smooth working relationship the details of which were worked out in informal communications. With time of the essence and the parties on good terms and therefore careless or impatient with formalities, Cloud was reasonable in believing that *if* Hasbro didn't want to be committed to buying the additional quantity that it plainly wanted in the summer and autumn of 1996, it would so advise Cloud rather than leading Cloud down the primrose path. A practice, under the rubric of "course of dealing," can be evidence of what a contract requires, *see, e.g.*, UCC § 1-205; *Restatement (Second) of Contracts* § 223 (1981); *Frank Novak & Sons, Inc. v. Sommer & Maca Industries, Inc.*, 182 Ill. App. 3d 781, 131 Ill. Dec. 325, 538 N.E.2d 700, 703–05 (1989) — can even, under the rubric of "contract implied in fact," give rise to binding contractual obligations though no words are spoken. *Brines v. XTRA Corp.*, 304 F.3d 699, 703 (7th Cir. 2002).

Cloud could have been more careful. But a failure to insist that every i be dotted and t crossed is not the same thing as being unreasonable. In any event, to repeat an earlier point, Hasbro did give its written consent to the modification.

We conclude that the June modification was enforceable and we therefore reverse the judgment and remand the case for a determination of Cloud's damages.

REVERSED AND REMANDED.

NOTES AND QUESTIONS

1. Judge Posner introduces the next three topics that we will consider with respect to modifications: determining when the modification itself must satisfy the statute of frauds under § 2-209(3), determining the scope of the parties' ability to agree to a "no oral modification clause" pursuant to § 2-209(2), and the significance of the court's ability to find a "waiver" even in the absence of an enforceable modification under § 2-209(4) and (5).

2. The drafters of Article 2A used § 2-209 as a model, but they omitted (3). The Comment explains that this "provision was not incorporated as it is unfair to allow an oral modification to make the entire lease contract unenforceable." § 2A-208, Comment. Is this potentially harsh result another basis for reading § 2-209(3) differently?

PROBLEM 2-11

Synergy Manufacturing and Biotech Industries executed a written agreement which provided that Synergy would manufacture and deliver 10,000 custom embroidered cloth briefcases for Biotech's marketing department at a total cost of $50,000. Biotech subsequently discovered that Synergy's competitor would provide the same briefcases for $48,000, and so Biotech complains to Synergy about its pricing. Synergy orally agreed to charge only $48,000.

Is this oral modification enforceable? If opposing counsel argued that all modifications to contracts within the scope of § 2-201 must separately satisfy § 2-201, how would you argue against that position? Can you distinguish *Cloud* on the facts?

Would your answer change if Biotech and Synergy orally agreed that Biotech could pay the lower price if it agreed to purchase 20,000 briefcases?

3. "No Oral Modification" Clauses: The "Private" Statute of Frauds

Commercial parties wary of false allegations of modifications might want to limit their freedom of contract by requiring that all modifications be memorialized in a signed writing. Against a common law backdrop that was reluctant to enforce such limitations, § 2-209(2) ensures that such agreements are binding. Given the potential for abuse of less sophisticated parties, the rule offers the caveat that a non-merchant will not be held to this writing requirement if the clause is on a form supplied by the merchant, unless the non-merchant separately signs the requirement.

MORGAN LABORATORIES, INC. v. MICRO DATA BASE SYSTEMS, INC.
United States District Court, Northern District of California
39 U.C.C. Rep. Serv. 2d 319 (1997)

THELTON E. HENDERSON, Chief Judge, United States District Court.

The above captioned matter comes before the Court on defendant's motions to dismiss for improper venue and, in the alternative, for transfer pursuant to 28 U.S.C. § 1404(a).

FACTUAL BACKGROUND

Plaintiff Morgan Laboratories, Inc. ("Morgan") produces and sells software products aimed at the banking industry. Since August 1991, Morgan has incorporated into its software certain software modules produced by defendant Micro Data Base Systems, Inc. ("MDBS"). Morgan's right to copy and distribute the MDBS modules derives from a May 1991 licensing agreement between the parties.

Morgan and MDBS are now embroiled in a dispute arising out of their licensing relationship. Presently before the Court, however, is the preliminary question of where this dispute should be litigated. Morgan filed suit in San Francisco Superior Court on October 2, 1996. Eight days later, MDBS filed suit in the Northern District of Indiana. MDBS subsequently removed the California suit to federal court, and now brings the instant motions in an effort to transfer the litigation to Indiana.

LEGAL STANDARD

1. Motion to Dismiss for Improper Venue

It is well-established that parties may by contract designate the forum in which any litigation is to take place, and that litigation commenced elsewhere may be subject to dismissal for improper venue. . . . Forum selection clauses, moreover, are presumptively valid under federal law and parties seeking to avoid them bear a heavy burden when seeking an alternate venue. . . . In the Ninth Circuit, a district court must look to federal law for the governing standards with respect to the effect and validity of a forum selection clause. . . .

* * *

DISCUSSION

1. Motion to Dismiss for Improper Venue

Although forum selection clauses enjoy presumptive validity, MDBS has failed to demonstrate that its agreement with Morgan contains a forum selection clause. This failure is fatal to its motion to dismiss for improper venue.

It is undisputed that the explicit language of the May 1991 licensing agreement that governs the relationship between MDBS and Morgan does not include a forum selection clause. It does, however, include the following provision:

> This Agreement and the License Agreement for the System are the entire agreement between the MDBS and the Licensee regarding the subject matter; no verbal representations are binding; any amendment must be signed by MDBS and Licensee.

See MDBS IV Runtime License Agreement & 9. The parties do not dispute that Indiana has adopted the Uniform Commercial Code, including § 2-209(2):

> A signed agreement which excludes modification or rescision except by a signed writing cannot be otherwise modified or rescinded, but except as between merchants such a requirement on a form supplied by the merchant must be separately signed by the other party.

Indiana Code § 26-1-2-209(2). Accordingly, by the terms of the "no-modification-except-in-writing" clause included in paragraph 9 of the May 1991 agreement, the addition of a forum selection clause must appear in a signed writing in order to be part of the agreement between the parties.

Conceding that the May 1991 agreement contains no forum selection clause, MDBS argues that Morgan should be bound by the forum selection clause that appears in the "shrinkwrap license" that accompanies its software modules. This license is printed on the outside of the boxes in which MDBS ships its software modules. The first paragraph of the shrinkwrap license provides that the opening of the package indicates acceptance of the license terms, which include a forum selection clause designating Tippecanoe County, Indiana as the exclusive venue for disputes arising between the parties. It is undisputed that this shrinkwrap license has appeared on MDBS software modules shipped to Morgan since June 1992 and that Morgan employees have read the shrinkwrap licenses.

The enforceability of shrinkwrap licenses generally is a difficult question that the federal courts have only just begun to face squarely. . . . For purposes of the instant motions, however, the Court need not reach this thorny issue, because the parties in their May 1991 agreement explicitly precluded contract modifications that were not signed by both parties.

MDBS makes a number of ultimately unavailing arguments to overcome the "no-modification-except-in-writing" clause of the May 1991 agreement. First, it alleges that the terms of the shrinkwrap license do not "modify" the prior agreement, but rather constitute a "supplemental agreement" between the parties. To support this view, MDBS points out that paragraph 2.1 of the May 1991 agreement provides that Morgan "must be a licensed user of the System before entering into this Agreement." This language, according to MDBS, explicitly refers to and incorporates into the May 1991 agreement the terms of a prior "user license."

Assuming that paragraph 2.1 of the May 1991 agreement incorporated the terms of a prior user license, MDBS must show that the original user license included a forum selection clause or that the parties subsequently modified the original user license to include such a clause. At oral argument the Court inquired whether the user license in force prior to May 1991 contained such a clause. MDBS admitted that it had not submitted this original user license to the Court and that it did not know whether the license contained a forum selection clause. Because MDBS, as the moving party, bears the burden of demonstrating the existence of a forum selection clause, and because they have failed to produce the terms of the original user license, the Court must presume that the original user license did not include a forum selection clause.

With respect to subsequent modification of the original user license, MDBS offers the forum selection clauses that appeared in the shrinkwrap licenses that appeared on its software boxes *after* the May 1991 agreement went into effect. As noted earlier, however, these shrinkwrap licenses were not signed by Morgan, and thus cannot be read to modify the material terms of the May 1991 agreement or any "supplemental" terms that may have been incorporated into that agreement. The provisions of paragraph 9 of the May 1991 agreement, at the very least, evince an intention by the parties to bar unilaterally-presented, unsigned modifications of that agreement's material terms.

MDBS contends, notwithstanding the provisions of paragraph 9, that Morgan has modified the May 1991 agreement by its "course of conduct" in opening and using the software modules for nearly 4 years after the inclusion of the shrinkwrap license. As an initial matter, it is not at all clear that a "course of conduct" in this case should displace the "no-modification-unless-in-writing" provision of paragraph 9. *See Arizona Retail Sys. v. Software Link, Inc.*, 831 F. Supp. 759, 764 (D. Ariz. 1993) ("Section 2-209 requires assent to proposed modifications and . . . the assent must be express and cannot be inferred merely from a party's conduct in continuing with the agreement.").

Even assuming that a course of performance might modify the May 1991 agreement, however, MDBS states the issue too broadly. "Ordinarily, a 'course of dealing' or 'course of performance' analysis focuses on the actions of the parties *with respect to a particular issue*." Because this appears to be the first litigated dispute between these parties, there is simply no "course of performance" with respect to the forum selection clause. . . . ("Because this is the parties' first serious dispute, the parties have not previously taken any action with respect to the matters addressed by the warranty disclaimer and the limitation of liability terms of the box-top license.").

MDBS focuses next on Morgan's complaint, arguing that the complaint itself states that the May 1991 agreement has been modified by the course of performance between the parties. Morgan's complaint includes the following:

The [May 1991] agreement was also amended by further oral and written agreement of Morgan and MDBS, by their course of performance, and by amendments implied by contract. . . .

According to MDBS, this language estops Morgan from relying on the "no-modification-unless-in writing" clause to preclude a course of performance modification. This estoppel argument misses the point. As noted earlier, there has been absolutely no course of performance with respect to the forum selection clause. Although Morgan's pleadings may have opened the door for course of performance arguments, this opening provides no comfort to MDBS with respect to the forum selection provision in question.

In the final analysis, it is plain that the May 1991 agreement, even if it did incorporate the terms of a prior user license, did not include a forum selection clause. It is similarly plain that the May 1991 agreement provided that modifications to its terms must be in writing and signed by both parties. MDBS has failed to demonstrate that the parties modified their May 1991 agreement to include a forum selection clause, whether by signed writing or by course of performance. Although shrinkwrap licenses may, in some cases, be enforceable, . . . they do not trump explicit prior agreements where those agreements contain integration clauses and "no-modification-unless-in-writing" clauses. . . . As a result, this Court concludes that the agreement between the parties does not include a forum selection clause.

* * *

CONCLUSION

For the foregoing reasons, defendant MDBS' motions to dismiss for improper venue and to transfer pursuant to 28 U.S.C. § 1404(a) are HEREBY DENIED.

QUESTION

Return to the *Cloud* case, above. Judge Posner notes that the trial court decided the case based on § 2-209(3) and did not consider the independent significance, if any, of the no oral modification clause that is validated by § 2-209(2). Is there a difference between the provisions? How do these provisions relate to each other?

4. Distinguishing Waiver from Modification

The "private" statute of frauds poses the risk of harsh results and unfair dealing, no less than the statute of frauds. If parties orally agree to a modification in the course of performance, it would be potentially inequitable for one party to assert later that the original written agreement required that all modifications must be in writing to be enforceable. Just as § 2-201 generally provides various exceptions to the signed writing requirement of the statute of frauds, § 2-209(4) and (5) provide an important exception to the statute of frauds and private statute of frauds in the context of a purported modification. If an attempt at modification fails to satisfy the requirements of (2) or (3), and therefore is unenforceable as a modification, it may nevertheless operate as a waiver of rights, subject to retraction unless the other party has materially relied on the waiver so as to make a retraction unjust.

The statute does not resolve when an attempt at modification should operate as a waiver of rights, even though it fails to be effective as a modification. Article 29(2) of the CISG provides that a party may be "precluded by his conduct from asserting" that a no oral modification clause is enforceable, "to the extent that the other party has relied on that conduct." A number of courts have interpreted § 2-209 in this manner, concluding that an attempted modification should operate as a waiver only when there is reliance by the other party. A majority of courts, however, have determined that a party may waive its rights even if there is no enforceable modification and regardless of the other party's reliance on the waiver. It is important to keep in mind the difference between a waiver and a modification. A waiver is a relinquishment of a right, and may be retracted under § 2-209(5), whereas a modification is binding unless the parties again modify their agreement.

BMC INDUSTRIES, INC. v. BARTH INDUSTRIES, INC.
United States Court of Appeals, Eleventh Circuit
160 F.3d 1322 (1998)

TJOFLAT, Circuit Judge:

This appeal arises from a contract entered into between BMC Industries, Inc., and Barth Industries, Inc., for the design, manufacture, and installation of equipment to automate BMC's production line for unfinished eyeglass lenses. Eighteen months after the delivery date set out in the contract had passed, BMC filed suit against Barth for breach of contract. Barth, in turn, counterclaimed for breach of contract. BMC's suit also included a claim against Barth's parent company, Nesco, Inc. According to BMC, Nesco had orally promised to ensure Barth's completion of the contract, and therefore was liable under the theory of promissory estoppel for Barth's nonperformance.

A jury resolved the breach of contract and promissory estoppel issues in favor of BMC, and returned a verdict of $3 million against Barth and $2.1 million against Nesco. After denying Barth's and Nesco's alternative motions for judgment as a matter of law and for a new trial, the district court rendered judgment in accordance with the jury's verdicts, and Barth and Nesco appealed. We affirm the district court's decision denying Barth judgment as a matter of law. We conclude, however, that the court erroneously instructed the jury on the contract issues, and therefore vacate the judgment against Barth and remand the case for a new trial on these issues. As for Nesco, we conclude that the court should have granted Nesco judgment as a matter of law, and thus direct the district court to dismiss Nesco from this case.

I.

A.

BMC, through its Vision-Ease division, manufactures semi-finished polymer opthalmic lenses that are used in the production of eyeglasses. These lenses are created by an assembly-line process. First, an employee fills a mold assembly with a monomer fluid, and places the mold assembly on a conveyor. Next, the assembly is inspected and then heated and cured until the monomer solidifies into a plastic lens. Finally, the lens is removed from the mold assembly through a process called "de-clipping and de-gasketing"; an employee removes the spring clip holding the mold assembly together and slices open the rubber gasket that holds the lens. The lens is then packaged and sold to a finished eyeglass retailer.

In order to decrease labor costs, and thereby remain competitive with other lens manufacturers who were utilizing cheaper foreign labor, BMC decided to become the first company to automate portions of its lens manufacturing process. Consequently, in early 1986, BMC commissioned Barth to complete a preliminary design and feasibility study. Barth's subcontractor, Komech, finished the study in June 1986. Based on this study, Barth and BMC entered into a contract (the "Contract") which provided that Barth would "design, fabricate, debug/test, and supervise field installation and start up of equipment to automate the operations of mold assembly declipping, clip transport, mold assembly clipping, and mold filling." The Contract, which stated that it was governed by Florida law, listed a price of $515,200 and provided for delivery of four automated production lines by June 1987. The Contract also stated that time was of the essence.

On November 4, 1986, Barth and BMC executed a written amendment to the Contract, extending the delivery date by one month. In February 1987, Barth terminated Komech as design subcontractor, and hired another engineering company, Belcan, in its place. Belcan subsequently redesigned the automation equipment, which delayed Barth's progress and led the parties to execute the second (and last) written amendment, which extended the delivery date to "October 1987."

After this *second amendment*, Barth continued to experience technical problems and design difficulties that caused repeated delays. The parties did not extend the delivery date beyond October 1987 to accommodate these delays, however. Instead, Barth and BMC each demonstrated a willingness to continue performance under the Contract.

One such delay, for example, occurred in June 1987, when Belcan decided that the equipment design posed a risk of explosion because of the proximity of certain chemicals to electrical components. Although BMC perceived no such risk, it told Barth and Belcan to "go ahead" and redesign the equipment. Barth revised its estimated delivery schedule to account for the resulting delay, listing December 1987 as the new delivery deadline. It sent this schedule to BMC with a cover letter that stated: "Please look over the attached & let me know what you think." BMC's response, if any, is not contained in the record.

This design problem was only one of many technical difficulties that developed; other problems arose with the filling nozzles and mold assembly springs, among other components. Consequently, by October 1987, the amended Contract's delivery deadline, Barth estimated that it could not deliver the equipment until April 1988. BMC executives were still anxious, however, to continue the automation project. Thus, during the spring of 1988, although they protested Barth's failure to deliver the equipment on time, these executives encouraged Barth to continue working on the project.

In June 1988, Barth completed the four automated de-clip/de-gasket machines and delivered them to BMC. Without the entire automated system, however, BMC could not fully test these machines; the whole production line had to be in place.

By August 1988, BMC's mounting apprehension about Barth's ability to perform led it to seek assurance that Barth would be able to complete performance under the Contract. In an effort to obtain such assurance, BMC executives met with Robert Tomsich, a Barth officer (and director) who also served as Nesco's president. According to these executives, Tomsich ensured them that Barth would perform the Contract, that Nesco's resources were committed to the project, and that, in the future, BMC should deal directly with Nesco.

Although BMC had considered terminating the Contract and suing Barth for breach, BMC took neither step. Instead, it continued to lead Barth and Nesco to believe that it was determined to finish the project; BMC collaborated with Barth's engineers to overcome difficulties, suggested design changes, and asked Barth whether more money (presumably provided by BMC) would help it complete the equipment in less time.

By January 1989, Barth still had not produced a functioning automation system. Due to time and cost overruns, Barth had invested over $1 million of its own money in the project. BMC previously had agreed to compensate Barth for these additional expenses; consequently, during that month, Tomsich asked BMC for $250,000 to cover some of Barth's cost overruns. One month later, BMC responded with a $100,000 payment, along with a letter stating that BMC was "insisting on Barth's adherence to the projected schedule," and was "not waiving any rights or remedies" for any breach, including "Barth's failure to meet the delivery dates specified in the contract." Barth's latest schedule called for delivery in June 1989.

Barth's delays and setbacks continued throughout the spring of 1989; but while BMC encouraged Barth to carry on, and continued to cooperate with Barth's engineers to solve problems, BMC also became increasingly impatient. In March, and again in April 1989, BMC pointed out Barth's unacceptable failure to meet deadlines.

Near the end of May 1989, Barth notified BMC that it had finally completed the mold assembly filling machine and that it would deliver the equipment F.O.B. Barth's dock in accordance with the Contract. BMC refused delivery of the mold assembly filler, and instead filed this lawsuit on June 5, 1989.

B.

BMC's complaint contained fourteen counts. Seven of the counts were based on representations made by Barth and Nesco both prior to the formation of the Contract and during its performance, six of the counts sought to impose liability on Barth's and Nesco's successors in interest, and one count sought recovery against Barth's directors under the Delaware Corporate Code. By the time of the final pretrial conference, BMC's complaint had been reduced to three claims: breach of contract against Barth (count I), fraudulent misrepresentation against Barth (count II), and promissory estoppel against Nesco (count VIII).

BMC's breach of contract count alleged that the second written amendment to the Contract established October 1987 as the deadline for Barth's performance. Because Barth failed to deliver the automated equipment by that date, Barth was in default of its contractual obligations. BMC sought damages for Barth's breach in the sum of $6.4 million. Two separate injuries suffered by BMC comprised this measure of damages. First, BMC sought to recover the labor costs that it would have saved had it been able to use the automated equipment rather than pay employees to produce the lenses manually. Because BMC executives predicted that the automated equipment would have a useful life of ten years, BMC sought these lost labor savings for the ten year period from October 1987 until October 1997. Second, BMC sought compensation for what it termed the "working capital effect." This effect is an estimate of the money BMC lost because its capital was tied up paying higher labor costs rather than being used for investment or being used to pay off the company's debt (and thus reducing the interest BMC paid to its creditors).

As an affirmative defense to BMC's breach of contract claim, Barth asserted that BMC's conduct after the October 1987 delivery date had passed amounted to a waiver of the delivery date under Article 2 of the Uniform Commercial Code ("UCC"). Although Barth failed to deliver the machines by October 1987, Barth argued, BMC executives urged Barth to keep working, BMC engineers continued to assist Barth in overcoming technical problems, and BMC executives agreed to increase the purchase price. Therefore, Barth claimed, BMC waived its entitlement to delivery of the machines in October 1987.

Additionally, Barth counterclaimed against BMC for breach of contract. Barth repeated its argument that BMC's conduct amounted to a waiver of the October 1987 delivery date, and asserted that the delivery deadline therefore became indefinite. Because Barth tendered the machines within a reasonable amount of time, Barth substantially performed its contractual obligations. Consequently, Barth claimed, BMC's refusal to accept delivery of the machines in May 1989 constituted breach of the Contract. Barth sought damages totaling $1.13 million, which consisted of the original purchase price of $515,200 specified in the Contract, plus Barth's cost overruns that BMC had agreed to reimburse.

BMC's fraudulent misrepresentation count alleged that Barth induced BMC into signing the Contract by making several false representations. Among them were Barth's statements that it had experience in designing and manufacturing custom machinery similar to the automated equipment BMC sought to purchase, that it had the ability to design and manufacture the automated equipment, and that the equipment would function according to the specifications in the Contract. BMC sought judgment on this claim for compensatory damages in the sum of $6.4 million, as well as punitive damages.

As an affirmative defense, Barth responded that BMC fraudulently failed to inform Barth of problems BMC was unable to solve in its manual lens production process, and that BMC misrepresented that problems experienced by the automated equipment did not occur when BMC produced lenses manually. Barth claimed that it would not have entered into the Contract had BMC not made these misrepresentations; BMC's own fraud, therefore, barred BMC from recovery on its claims against Barth. Barth also counterclaimed against BMC for fraud, and sought both compensatory and punitive damages.

* * *

C.

On appeal, Barth contends that the district court erred when it concluded that the UCC did not apply to the Contract, and thus did not govern the waiver issue. Had the court applied the UCC, Barth argues, it would have concluded that BMC waived the October 1987 delivery date, and therefore breached the Contract by refusing to accept delivery in May 1989. Having reached that conclusion, the court would have granted Barth's motion for judgment as a matter of law on the breach of contract issues, and awarded Barth damages in the sum of $1.13 million. Assuming a dispute of material fact on the waiver issue, Barth contends alternatively that BMC's judgment on the breach of contract count should be vacated, and the case remanded for a new trial on that count and its breach of contract counterclaim.

Nesco contends that BMC's promissory estoppel claim is nothing more than a suit on an oral guarantee of a past-due obligation and, as such, is barred by the statute of frauds. Accordingly, the district court erred in denying its motion for judgment as a matter of law, and the case should be remanded with instruction that the court dismiss it from the case.

In part II.A [omitted] of this opinion, we consider whether the Contract was predominantly a transaction in goods (and thus governed by the UCC) or in services (and thus governed by the common law), and conclude that it was a transaction in goods. . . .

II.

* * *

B.

Having determined that the UCC governs this case, we must next apply Article 2's waiver provision to the Contract. . . .[42]

1.

Although the UCC does not specifically lay out the elements of waiver, we have stated that waiver requires "(1) the existence at the time of the waiver a right, privilege, advantage, or benefit which may be waived; (2) the actual or constructive knowledge thereof; and (3) an intention to relinquish such right, privilege, advantage, or benefit." . . . Conduct may constitute waiver of a contract term, but such an implied waiver must be demonstrated by clear evidence. . . . Waiver may be implied when a party's actions are inconsistent with continued retention of the right.

As an initial matter, we must determine whether, under the UCC, waiver must be accompanied by detrimental reliance. Although it is settled that waiver under Florida

---

[42] [17] The Contract included a provision requiring all modifications to be in writing. Although the parties therefore did not successfully modify the Contract, we apply Fla. Stat. ch. 672.209 to determine whether BMC's conduct constituted a waiver of the October 1987 delivery date.

common law must be supported by valid consideration or detrimental reliance, . . .
courts disagree on whether the UCC retains this requirement. We conclude, however,
that the UCC does not require consideration or detrimental reliance for waiver of a
contract term.

Our conclusion follows from the plain language of subsections 672.209(4) and (5).
While subsection (4) states that an attempted modification that fails may still constitute
a waiver, subsection (5) provides that the waiver may be retracted unless the
non-waiving party relies on the waiver. Consequently, the statute recognizes that
waivers may exist in the absence of detrimental reliance — these are the retractable
waivers referred to in subsection (5). Only this interpretation renders meaning to
subsection (5), because reading subsection (4) to require detrimental reliance for all
waivers means that waivers would *never* be retractable. *See Wisconsin Knife Works v.
National Metal Crafters*, 781 F.2d 1280, 1291 (7th Cir. 1986) (Easterbrook, J.,
dissenting) (noting that reading a detrimental reliance requirement into the UCC would
eliminate the distinction between subsections (4) and (5)). Subsection (5) would therefore
be meaningless.

At least one Florida court implicitly agrees with this conclusion; in *Linear Corp. v.
Standard Hardware Co.*, 423 So. 2d 966 (Fla. 1st DCA 1982), the court held that a
contract term had been waived despite the absence of any facts showing detrimental
reliance. The court in *Linear* addressed a contract between a manufacturer and a
retailer for the sale of electronic security devices. The contract included a provision
stating that the manufacturer would not repurchase any devices the retailer was unable
to sell, and another term providing that contract modifications must be in writing.
Despite this contractual language, the retailer filed suit claiming that the manufacturer
subsequently made an oral agreement to repurchase unsold devices, but failed to adhere
to this oral agreement.

Citing chapter 672.209(4), the court concluded that the parties' conduct demonstrated
that they had waived the requirement that modifications be in writing, and therefore
gave effect to the oral modification. . . . The court recognized this waiver despite the
apparent absence of any detrimental reliance by the retailer — in fact the court never
even mentioned any reliance requirement for waiver under the UCC. Consequently, the
court implicitly held that a contract term could be waived without the existence of
detrimental reliance by the non-waiving party.

Although other courts have held that waiver requires reliance under the UCC, those
courts have ignored the UCC's plain language. The leading case espousing this view of
waiver is *Wisconsin Knife Works v. National Metal Crafters*, 781 F.2d 1280 (7th Cir.
1986) (addressing section 2-209 of the model version of the UCC, from which Florida
adopted section 672.209 verbatim), in which a panel of the Seventh Circuit addressed a
contract that included a term prohibiting oral modifications, and considered whether an
attempted oral modification could instead constitute a waiver. Writing for the majority,
Judge Posner concluded that the UCC's subsection (2), which gives effect to "no oral
modification" provisions, would become superfluous if contract terms could be waived
without detrimental reliance. Judge Posner reasoned that if attempted oral modifications that were unenforceable because of subsection (2) were nevertheless enforced as
waivers under subsection (4), then subsection (2) is "very nearly a dead letter." *Id.* at
1286. According to Judge Posner, there must be some difference between modification
and waiver in order for both subsections (2) and (4) to have meaning. This difference is
waiver's detrimental reliance requirement.[43]

---

[43] [19] Contrary to our reasoning above, Judge Posner claims that reading a reliance requirement into
waiver under subsection (4) is not inconsistent with subsection (5). According to Judge Posner, subsection (5)
is broader than subsection (4), covering waivers other than mere attempts at oral modification. Judge Posner
argues as an example that subsection (5) covers express waivers that are written and signed. *See id.* at 1287.
In dissent, however, Judge Easterbrook convincingly dissects this argument. As Judge Easterbrook explains,

Judge Posner, however, ignores a fundamental difference between modifications and waivers: while a party that has agreed to a contract modification cannot cancel the modification without giving consideration for the cancellation, a party may unilaterally retract its waiver of a contract term provided it gives reasonable notice. The fact that waivers may unilaterally be retracted provides the difference between subsections (2) and (4) that allows both to have meaning. We therefore conclude that waiver under the UCC does not require detrimental reliance. Consequently, without reaching the issue of detrimental reliance, we consider whether BMC waived the Contract's October 1987 delivery date.

2.

Applying the elements of waiver to the facts before us, we hold as a matter of law that BMC waived the October 1987 delivery date. The October 1987 delivery date was a waivable contract right, of which BMC had actual knowledge. We also conclude that BMC's conduct impliedly demonstrated an intent to relinquish that right.

The most cogent evidence of this waiver is BMC's own representation of its relationship with Nesco. Throughout this litigation, BMC has maintained that Nesco, beginning in August 1988, "stepped in and promised to complete the project. In doing so, Nesco expressly represented that all of its resources were committed to the project, and instructed BMC to deal solely with Nesco." According to BMC, therefore, Nesco voluntarily became liable, in the fall of 1988, for Barth's completion of the project. By that time, however, the October 1987 delivery date had already passed. If, as BMC claims, the contract was already breached, then Nesco could never have performed its obligations; Nesco was in breach of its promise as soon as that promise was made, and could have been sued by BMC the next day. For Nesco's promise to have meaning, BMC must have given Barth and Nesco additional time to perform — in other words, BMC must have waived the October 1987 delivery date.

BMC argues, however, that while it agreed to delay enforcing its rights against Barth in return for Nesco's promise, it did not *waive* those rights. BMC's argument defies logic. According to this theory, BMC could sue Barth and Nesco at its whim. Consequently, Nesco miraculously could have completed the project the day after its promise, and still have been fully liable to BMC for Barth's breach of contract. Nesco had nothing to gain and everything to lose from such an agreement.

BMC's own complaint buttresses our conclusion that BMC waived the October 1987 delivery date. According to BMC's complaint, Nesco promised "that Barth would *meet dates*, performance and reliability criteria under the agreement, as amended," and that Nesco "ensured that the equipment was *timely* completed and delivered to BMC in Florida." (emphasis added). Because the October 1987 delivery date had already passed, however, Barth could not "meet dates" or "timely" complete the equipment unless the delivery date had been extended.

Furthermore, BMC's course of dealing with Barth evidenced BMC's waiver of the October 1987 delivery date, because BMC failed timely to demand compliance with that contract term or terminate the Contract and file suit. When a delivery date passes without the seller's delivery, the buyer must object within a reasonable time and warn the seller that it is in breach. . . .

Although BMC maintained at trial that Barth breached the contract as of October 1987, BMC did not tell Barth it intended to terminate the contract and hold Barth liable for the breach until May 1989. In fact, the earliest indication from BMC that it was

---

subsection (5) is narrower than subsection (4) — limiting the effect of waivers that are not detrimentally relied upon — not the reverse as Judge Posner claims. Furthermore, Judge Easterbrook demonstrates that subsection (5) cannot cover express written and signed waivers because such writings are not waivers, but rather effective written modifications under subsection (2). *See id.* at 1291 (Easterbrook, J., dissenting).

considering termination was August 1988, when BMC executives met with Tomsich to seek assurance that Barth would perform. As we have already stated, however, the result of that meeting was a waiver of the October 1987 delivery date, not a timely exercise of BMC's right to terminate the Contract. BMC did not warn Barth in earnest of its intent to terminate until February 1989, when BMC sent Barth a letter along with $100,000 of the $250,000 payment Tomsich had requested at the August 1988 meeting. This letter warned Barth that BMC was not waiving its rights and remedies for Barth's failure to meet contractual delivery dates. BMC warned Barth again in March when it sent a letter advising of its intent to "hold [Barth] responsible, both for the initial breach and for all failures to meet subsequently promised dates."

Until 1989, however, BMC continued to act as though both parties were bound by the Contract and that Barth was not in default of its obligations: the October 1987 delivery date passed without comment from BMC; engineers from BMC frequently provided advice or assistance to help Barth personnel overcome technical problems; BMC executives frequently visited Barth's production facilities and encouraged Barth to continue working to complete the equipment; BMC even continued to spend money on the project — in December 1987, over one month after the October 1987 delivery date had passed, BMC purchased an additional $71,075 worth of springs and tooling for the machines. In sum, rather than terminating the Contract, or at least warning Barth that it was in breach after the October 1987 delivery date had passed, BMC continued to act as though the Contract remained in effect.

This is not to say that BMC never complained that Barth had missed deadlines; BMC executives frequently expressed their concern and disappointment that the project was so far behind schedule. On April 5, 1988, for example, the Chairman, President, and CEO of BMC sent a letter to Barth in which he stated: "The project is well behind schedule, and each day of delay represents lost savings for Vision-Ease. I hope that Barth will exert every effort to ensure the speedy completion and installation of the equipment and avoid any further delay." But while BMC complained of delays, it never declared Barth in default or terminated the contract — instead, BMC told Barth to keep working. After Barth had spent an additional eighteen months of time and money and, according to Barth, was prepared to deliver the machines, however, BMC suddenly decided to terminate the Contract. This BMC could not do.

The UCC states that when a contractual delivery date is waived, delivery must be made within a reasonable time. *See* Fla. Stat. ch. 672.309(1) (1997); *KLT Indus., Inc. v. Eaton Corp.*, 505 F. Supp. 1072, 1079 (E.D. Mich. 1981). Consequently, because BMC waived the October 1987 delivery date, Barth was only obligated to deliver the machines within a reasonable time period. We remand this case to the district court for a new trial on the question of whether Barth tendered the machines within a reasonable time period.

*   *   *

NOTES AND QUESTIONS

1. The question of how best to interpret § 2-209 on waiver remains a source of controversy. The confusion is caused by competing arguments about whether a waiver under § 2-209(4) requires detrimental reliance, and also whether a waiver under § 2-209(4) is a waiver of the writing requirement, or a waiver of the right to enforce the particular term as originally agreed. As to the first problem, recall that Judge Posner more recently suggested in the *Cloud* case that the split of authority in effect creates an alternative test: to prove a waiver the party must show either "detrimental reliance" on the attempted modification, or a clear and unequivocal relinquishment of a right under the contract. Does this make sense, or must courts choose one way in which to interpret § 2-209(4)?

2. Is there a difference between an oral attempt to modify an agreement that is

unenforceable under § 2-209(2), and a course of performance that deviates from the original contract? The following problem explores this distinction.

PROBLEM 2-12

Bigelow Bikes and Sherman Manufacturing execute a written contract for sale that requires Sherman to ship 100 bicycle brake assemblies to Bigelow on the first day of each month for thirty-six (36) consecutive months. The written agreement also provided: "Any and all modifications of this agreement must be in writing and signed by both parties in order to be effective and binding on the parties."

First Scenario. Sherman called Bigelow one month before deliveries were scheduled to begin and requested a 15-day extension for the first delivery. Bigelow agreed during the phone call to receive the first shipment on the 15th of the month.

Has the contract been modified?

What is the effect of Bigelow immediately calling back and demanding that the first shipment arrive on the first day of the month?

What is the effect if Bigelow calls two weeks after the first phone call and demands the original shipment date (now just two weeks away), but by that time Sherman has reallocated its production schedule and incurred contractual liabilities to third parties?

Second Scenario. Sherman ships the first 12 installments an average of ten days late, but Bigelow does not protest. Can Bigelow sue Sherman for breach of contract? Must Bigelow accept all future deliveries 10 days late? Is this question governed by § 2-209 or by § 1-303?

Chapter 3
CONTRACT TERMS

If the parties have an enforceable agreement, the next task is to determine the terms of their agreement. This is not always an easy matter, given that Article 2 recognizes an enforceable agreement even if the parties have not agreed to all of the material terms. Article 2 provides a number of default rules, or "gap-fillers," that specify the term of the sales agreement if the parties have not agreed to that term. We begin by considering the important gap-filler provisions regarding price and payment. Next, we consider the Code's provisions regarding the quantity term. These latter rules are more like definitions of otherwise ambiguous terms, inasmuch as the parties must agree to a quantity for there to be a reasonable basis for affording a remedy, § 2-204(3), and must evidence their quantity term in a writing to satisfy the statute of frauds, § 2-201(1).

In the second section we cover warranties, which are particularly important terms in the agreement. Warranties are terms that pertain to the character of the goods, rather than non-goods related terms such as the delivery date. Article 2 recognizes express warranties, which are warranties created by the parties, but also implied warranties which are gap-filling provisions that must be overcome by disclaimers. Given the centrality of warranties to the agreement, it should come as no surprise that the rules surrounding warranties are quite complex.

A. GAP-FILLERS

Parties do not always expressly agree to all of the material terms governing their transaction. Failure to agree to a particular term may result from a variety of circumstances: the parties may have done a poor job of drafting a written memorial which serves as the complete and exclusive statement of the terms of the agreement for parol evidence rule purposes; they may not have understood the need for agreement on the term in question at the time of formation; a complex commercial agreement regarding long-term arrangements might not have been susceptible to detailed specification at the time of contracting; the parties may have been negligent or lazy in their negotiations; they may have determined that the transaction costs of reaching agreement on every detail exceeded the benefit of reaching such agreement; or they may simply have been unable to agree to a term that they decided might not be relevant to performance and decided to proceed without settling the matter.

The classical approach of the common law of contract was to conclude that there was no enforceable contract if any of the material terms were unclear, incomplete, or indefinite. In *Varney v. Ditmars*, 217 N.Y. 223, 228, 111 N.E. 822 (1916), the New York Court of Appeals observed that:

> It is elementary in the law that, for the validity of a contract, the promise, or the agreement of the parties to it must be certain and explicit, and that their full intentions may be ascertained to a reasonable degree of certainty. Their agreement must be neither vague nor indefinite, and, if thus defective, parol proof cannot be resorted to.

Article 2 departs substantially from this classical position. The drafters sought to accommodate the exigencies of modern commercial transactions and the proliferation of long-term agreements by requiring much less before recognizing a binding agreement. Section 2-204 states the Code's basic rule regarding contract formation: "A contract for sale of goods may be made in any manner sufficient to show agreement . . . ," and "[e]ven though one or more terms are left open, a contract for sale does not fail for indefiniteness if the parties have intended to make a contract and there is a reasonably certain basis for giving an appropriate remedy." Thus, the section establishes a two-part test that provides a relatively low threshold: the parties must have intended to contract, and they must have agreed to enough terms to permit the court to award an appropriate remedy.

The parties' intent to agree is a factual question that calls for an examination of the express agreement to terms, their conduct, and evidence of course of performance, course of dealing, and trade usage. If the trier concludes on the basis of this evidence that the parties have an agreement and they intended to be bound, the agreement will be enforced if it provides a reasonably certain basis for granting relief. At a minimum, it would appear that the parties must have agreed to a description of the goods that are the subject of the sale and a quantity, or it will be impossible to fashion a remedy. For example, no matter how persuasive the evidence that the parties intended to be bound to each other, there will be no enforceable agreement if they have agreed only to buy "some stuff." Of course, if many terms are undecided or unclear, the comment emphasizes that it is less likely that the parties have the requisite intent to be bound.

Because liability is assumed under § 2-204 with intent and a bare minimum of agreed terms, the drafters understood that it was necessary to provide guidance for courts adjudicating disputes in which one or more terms necessary to the dispute have not been agreed to by the parties. In many cases, Article 2 validates a delegation of power to one of the parties to specify the missing term. For example, it is permissible for the parties to agree that the buyer may select the color or size of the goods to be purchased, but the specification by the buyer "must be in good faith and within limits set by commercial reasonableness." § 2-311. In the case of a term that is left open by the parties, Article 2 provides the term through a series of "gap-filling" rules. These rules amount to default rules, in that they provide the terms of the contract only to the extent that the parties have not otherwise agreed. For example, if the parties have agreed to a contract for the sale of desks but have not yet agreed to the price to be charged, the price that will be enforced by the court is a "reasonable price at the time of delivery." § 2-305(1).

Article 2A deviates from the model of Article 2 by not providing gap-filling provisions, and the reason for this deviation is instructive. The drafters of Article 2A understood that lease transactions, unlike sales transactions, do not have set patterns that carry over from one lease to another. Without established business customs, the generic gap-filler provisions of "reasonable" do not work well. A reasonable sale price for goods may be reconstructed by reference to a market for the transfer of ownership of certain goods; however, a reasonable lease rental for the same goods would depend on other terms of the lease, such as length of rental and location of the goods. It would be reasonable to assume that the difficulty in specifying gap-filler rules might lead courts to be more wary of finding that the parties have agreed to a lease when there are material terms that have not been resolved by the parties.

Use the following problem to work through the basic rules of some of the gap-filler provisions of Article 2. We will then cover some of the gap-filling provisions in greater detail. As you will find, the gap-filler provisions do not supply the missing term as much as they instruct the court how to find the missing term embedded in the commercial circumstances surrounding the transaction.

PROBLEM 3-1

Byse Construction Company executed a written purchase order with Shelly Concrete, Inc., which provided in relevant part:

> Byse agrees to purchase 2,000 yards of concrete, per specifications 13.006–13.008, pertaining to Tower Project at Mill Street, and Shelly agrees to provide said concrete in timely fashion.

Assuming no other relevant facts or circumstances,

a. Do the parties have a contract for sale? *See* § 2-204.

b. Where will the goods be delivered? *See* § 2-308.

c. When must the goods be delivered? *See* § 2-309.

d. In what manner will the goods be delivered and tendered? *See* §§ 2-307, 2-311(1), 2-503.

e. What will Byse have to pay for the goods? *See* § 2-305.

f. What quality concrete must Shelly provide, if the specifications are silent as to quality? *See* § 2-314.

Now assume that Buyer and Seller have contracted in the past, and that their practice (and the practice in the industry generally) is that the concrete is "on call" for delivery to the particular project at the Seller's posted price at time of delivery; that is, Buyer will call each morning and request that a certain quantity of concrete be delivered for work on that day. Additionally, the specifications indicate that the concrete must pass certain performance tests in order to be acceptable. How would these facts alter your analysis?

1. Gap-Filling Rules for Price and Payment Terms

It may seem strange that parties would not agree to the price and payment terms. The following excerpt explains the practical considerations that may result in open price and payment terms, and provides an important conceptual explanation of the gap-filling approach of Article 2.

R. Duesenberg & L. King, Sales and Bulk Transfers Under the U.C.C.
§ 4.03[1] (1980)[1]

OPEN PRICE TERM

A significant term of any bargain for the sale of goods is the price. Goods cannot be sold without a price being set, although it is not necessary that the price be stated in terms of monetary value. A barter is as much controlled by Article 2 of the Code as is a sale for a dollar amount.

To say that price is a significant term of a contract is not the same as stating that it is an essential term, if by "essential" is meant that without it there is no enforceable agreement. True, many courts have said that a contract to be enforceable must contain all essential terms. But this is an abstraction which, when applied to concrete examples, fades in meaning. There are many situations where agreements for the sale and purchase of goods have been enforced, though no price was stated. Though there is considerable common-law background which has been hostile to open price agreements, the practical fact is that there are good commercial reasons for omitting a price term. If commercial justification for such omissions exists, it ought to follow that the expectations of parties to such agreements should not be frustrated by a principle of jurisprudence which condemns and makes unenforceable bargains which fail to set a price term.

Consistent with this position is the principle expressed in the general provision of the Code which recites that "even though one or more terms are left open, a contract for sale does not fail for indefiniteness if the parties have intended to make a contract and there is a reasonably certain basis for giving an appropriate remedy." [§ 2-204(3).]

Subsection (1) [of § 2-305] clearly announces that absence of a fixed price does not necessarily mean that an agreement is unenforceable. As such, it recognizes the commercial proposition that parties to a sales bargain may not wish, at the time of contracting, to shift the risks of market fluctuation by establishing at that time a price which is certain. The uncertainty created by this omission is not fatal under the Code. If the parties intend to enter a binding agreement, and an appropriate remedy can be given, then the basic test of the Code is satisfied. [§ 2-204(3).]

Many circumstances make it commercially desirable to leave the price term open, or

---

[1] Copyright 1980 by Matthew Bender & Co., Inc. Reprinted with permission.

to leave open certain components of the final price, such as a transportation allowance. Long-term agreements present the most dramatic example, since a fixed price over a number of years creates an enormous risk that as time passes either the seller or the buyer will be receiving too little or paying too much, as the case may be. Intelligent marketing negotiations make it imperative to provide for some method of adjustment in these contracts. And the more volatile a product is, the more important it becomes to provide for price alteration, upward or downward, even sometimes irrespective of the length of time over which the agreement is to be performed.

To accommodate these market conditions, the parties may simply leave the price term open, saying nothing about it. If this is the case, the Code provides that the price shall be a reasonable price at the time for delivery. This is not generally an advisable approach for buyer and seller to take, since it leaves open the question of what is the basis for determining reasonableness. The standard is subject to being determined by references not only to published prices, but by references to prices actually being paid on the open market. The two are not always the same. Also, questions of relevant market areas, contracts of like kind and quality, the relevance of custom and usage and course of performance, and other factors make it too easy for dispute to arise, thus potentially plunging the parties into the need for expensive litigation or arbitration to determine an applicable price.

More precise methods for determining price should be used. A frequent hedge against a rise or fall in value is to use an escalation clause based upon appropriate factors in reference to manufacturing. Raw materials cost, labor cost, and the cost of utilities and shipment are common factors in escalation clauses. Either the experience of the seller, or the fluctuations established nationally and published in government reports, may be used to determine the measure by which to make a price adjustment. Sellers are generally interested in hedging against the risk of increased production costs, and therefore are concerned more with price escalation upward. Buyers' interests are somewhat different; if consent to upward adjustment is insisted upon, a downward adjustment should be sought as a price for the concession. In negotiating escalation clauses, buyers especially should consider the effect of such clauses on the incentive of their sellers to keep costs down, and always consideration should be given to inserting a maximum adjustment percentage.

A well-drawn escalation clause should be based on obtainable standards. If the standards of the seller are used, the parties should establish a base from which to make the adjustment, and should also stipulate the elements to be considered in determining labor, shipment, raw materials, or other costs used in the escalation. While there is pre-Code litigation challenging — usually without success — the effectiveness of escalation clauses on the ground of uncertainty, there is no question but that under the Code such techniques for price establishment are valid. Such clauses fall within the scope of Subsection 2-305(1)(c), and its provision as to an outside "other standard."

As already observed, a variety of situations is possible in considering outside criteria for the determination of price. Both the criterion and the time for its application should be taken into account in the contract drafting. Should the time for establishing the price be the time of delivery, a certain fixed date for designated contract periods, or some other basis? In choosing a criterion, its possible disappearance before the time for using it arrives must also be assessed. Often, prices published in trade journals are used, in which case the basis for the journal publication becomes important, since it can always happen that these may change. Not only do they change, but sometimes their relevance or very existence may cease, in which case complex issues may arise, such as whether performance may be excused for impracticability. One such case has refused the defense, saying that when the external source fails, the Code requisite for applying a reasonable price governs.

Aside from external references, parties may agree that the price to be paid is that which is set by one of the parties to the contract, usually the seller. A provision of this character is often made to depend upon the seller's published or market price, in which event it is in fact an external standard to which reference is made, though the seller, a party to the contract, is able to alter that standard from time to time. Where the seller's list or market price is the basis for price determination, good faith is not likely to be a matter of great issue. A seller's market price is something which is relatively easy to determine. But where the seller simply has the right to establish the price, without reference to a published list or his "market," then good faith in setting it can be significant. Pre-Code cases sometimes took the position that if the price could be changed from time to time by either party — again, usually the seller — there was no mutuality in the bargain, and the agreement was unenforceable. But some cases imposed on this discretionary power a duty of good-faith performance. This is the test adopted by the Code, which imposes through § 2-305(2) the standard that the party fixing the price act in good faith.

Agreement to Agree on Price

Code rules regarding open price terms are subject to the provision that if "the parties intend not to be bound unless the price be fixed or agreed and it is not fixed or agreed there is no contract." [§ 2-305(4).] This is an important provision, designed to leave open the possibility that parties may agree to all the terms of a bargain but the price, and if they do not come to agreement concerning this, then they do not intend to be bound. On the surface, the provision conflicts with the language of § 2-305(1)(b), which states that a reasonable price is applicable if "the price is left to be agreed by the parties and they fail to agree." The key to understanding the distinction between these two provisions is intention, not in relation to price, but to the parties' mutual intention to be bound or not to be bound depending upon their agreeing to a price term. If the parties intend that a bargain has been entered, though the price is yet to be agreed, failure to agree on the price will not frustrate enforcement of the agreement. On the other hand, if they do not intend themselves bound to the terms of anything, unless they come to agreement on price, there is no contract until such an agreement is reached.

It is a question of fact whether the parties intend to be bound, leaving open only their subsequent agreement as to price, failing which a reasonable price would apply; or whether they intend no bargain until price agreement is reached. It is fair to say that the disposition of most pre-Code cases has been not to enforce bargains where the parties agreed that price or the method of payment was "to be agreed upon before delivery." The fact, however, that price or method of payment was "to be agreed upon" before delivery does not necessarily mean that the parties did not intend an otherwise binding agreement, the terms of which could be completed by a court's imposing a reasonable price. Through the years, there has been a common-law lack of sympathy for bargains leaving open important terms, and this judicial disposition carried over into cases where such terms were expressly left "to be agreed upon." There is no question, of course, that if the parties expressly provide that their failure to agree on price should have the consequence of no binding agreement, that such will be the result. In terms of contract drafting, it would be well for parties to state their intent, wherever it is provided that price is to be agreed upon. The impact of common-law history on decisions as they arise under the Code may be that courts will continue to construe most language of future mutual agreement as preventing the coming into being of an enforceable agreement. For this reason, to take advantage of the Code rule that an agreement to agree on prices does not necessarily render ineffective the bargain if subsequent agreement is not reached, but rather that a reasonable price is then applicable, parties should state their intentions clearly to be bound even if subsequent agreement between them as to the price of the goods is not forthcoming. Or, conversely, if their intention is not to be bound unless agreement is reached on price, then this should explicitly be stated. In view of the Code rules, however, to state baldly and without qualification that the price is to be agreed upon amounts to careless drafting, and inevitably creates a problem of construction which otherwise might easily be avoided.

PROBLEM 3-2

Betty and Sam agree that Betty will purchase Sam's used minivan for a price to be determined by Sam. The parties understand that Sam will ask around to determine a fair price. Soon thereafter, Sam decides not to sell his minivan. Sam tells Betty: "I won't set the price, and therefore we don't have a contract at all." What are Betty's rights under these circumstances?

What if Sam relents to Betty's assertion that they have a binding contract, but he sets the price for the minivan at 5 million dollars? What are Betty's rights under these circumstances?

SHELL OIL CO. v. HRN, INC.
Texas Supreme Court
144 S.W.3d 429 (2004)

CHIEF JUSTICE PHILLIPS delivered the opinion of the Court.

In this case, we must decide whether the price fixed by a refiner for the sale of its gasoline under an open-price-term contract with its dealers was in good faith as required by section 2.305(b) of the Texas Business and Commerce Code. The dealers claim that the refiner's pricing practices are forcing them out of business and therefore are not in good faith. The trial court concluded that the refiner had established its good faith as a matter of law, but the court of appeals reversed the summary judgment, concluding that circumstantial evidence raised a fact issue about the refiner's good faith. *HRN, Inc. v. Shell Oil Co.*, 102 S.W.3d 205 (Tex. App.—Houston [14th Dist.] 2003). Although the refiner's price was commercially reasonable when compared to the prices of other refiners in the relevant market, the court found some evidence in the record to suggest that the refiner's price might have been influenced by improper subjective motives such as the desire to force some of its dealers out of business. Because we conclude that the refiner established as a matter of law that its price was fixed in good faith as defined in the Code, we reverse the judgment of the court of appeals and render judgment that plaintiffs take nothing.

I.

Plaintiffs are several hundred lessee dealers in seventeen different states who lease service stations and buy gasoline from Shell, operating those stations as independent businesses.[2] Each dealer and Shell enter into two agreements: a Lease and a Dealer Agreement. Shell's relationship with its lessee dealers is also governed by the federal Petroleum Marketing Practices Act ("PMPA"), which regulates the grounds for termination and nonrenewal of petroleum franchise relationships. 15 U.S.C. §§ 2801–2806.

In the Dealer Agreement, each dealer agrees to buy Shell-branded gasoline from Shell at the "dealer prices . . . in effect" at the time of purchase. Shell's price to its dealers is referred to as the DTW ("dealer tank wagon") price because it includes delivery to the dealer's station by a Shell tanker truck. The DTW pricing provision is an "open price term" governed by section 2.305(b) of the Texas Business and Commerce Code (which corresponds to section 2-305(2) of the Uniform Commercial Code). Open-price-term contracts are commonly used in the gasoline refining and marketing industry due to price volatility.

---

[2] [1] For management and discovery purposes the trial court agreed to limit the initial trial to Houston Dealers only.

Shell markets gasoline to the public through a retail network that includes not only lessee dealers, but open dealers and company-operated stations as well. First, Shell acts as a franchisor, leasing service stations to franchisees such as the Dealers here that sell Shell-branded gasoline. Second, Shell sells Shell-branded gasoline directly to the public through company-operated stations. Finally, Shell sells branded and unbranded gasoline to jobbers. Some jobbers are wholesale distributors, selling Shell-branded and unbranded gasoline to stations operated by independent business owners. Other jobbers are also independent retail dealers, selling Shell-branded and unbranded gasoline directly to the public.

Jobbers operate fleets of trucks to pick up gasoline at refiners' terminals and distribute it to their own stations or to independent ones. Jobbers may have distribution agreements with several refiners simultaneously. Jobbers pay a "rack" price that is available for gasoline bought and picked up at Shell's terminals. The DTW price is typically higher than the rack price, although Shell does not set either price in relation to the other.

Shell's agreements with the Dealers prohibit them from selling any gasoline except Shell-branded gasoline. Although the contracts with the Dealers do not require them to buy Shell gasoline exclusively from Shell itself, agreements between Shell and its jobbers effectively eliminate the only major alternative source for Shell-branded gasoline. When a jobber sells gasoline to a Dealer, the jobber is retroactively charged the DTW price for that product, not the lower rack price it otherwise would pay.

The Dealers claim that Shell's pricing practices are forcing them out of business. Although Shell has the right under the Dealer Agreement to fix the DTW price at which the Dealers must buy its gasoline, all parties agree that it must exercise this right in good faith. *See* Tex. Bus. & Com. Code § 2.305(b). Dealers claim that Shell's DTW prices cannot be set in good faith because they are so high that they put Dealers at a competitive disadvantage. Dealers further assert that Shell's DTW pricing is part of a plan to replace them with company-operated outlets which are more profitable for Shell.

Shell moved for summary judgment on Dealers' good-faith pricing claims, contending that it was entitled to judgment as a matter of law because it charged a posted price applied uniformly to all Dealers and was a commercially reasonable price as well. Rather than contest the commercial reasonableness of Shell's DTW prices, Dealers argued that fact issues existed as to whether Shell had acted in bad faith by setting its DTW price with the subjectively improper motive of running Dealers out of business.

The trial court granted Shell's motion for summary judgment. The court of appeals reversed and remanded the case for trial, concluding that the Dealers had raised fact issues about Shell's subjective good faith when setting its DTW price. 102 S.W.3d 205.

II.

Most contracts for the sale of goods specify a price, but some do not because either the parties fail to consider the issue directly or purposefully leave it for later determination. When a contract for the sale of goods does not specify a price, section 2.305 of the Uniform Commercial Code supplies default rules for determining whether a contract exists and what the price should be. This section is one of a series of provisions in Article 2 of the Code that fill common "gaps" in commercial contracts.

In this instance, the Code imposes on Shell the obligation of good faith when fixing its DTW price under the Dealer Agreement, providing that "[a] price to be fixed by the seller or by the buyer means a price for him to fix in good faith." Tex. Bus. & Com. Code § 2.305(b). Good faith is defined elsewhere in the Code to mean "honesty in fact and the observance of reasonable commercial standards of fair dealing." *Id.*

§ 1.201(b)(20).[3] Official Comment 3 to section 2.305(b) further elaborates on the good faith requirement, creating a presumption in the normal case that a seller's posted price or price in effect is also a good faith price:

> 3. Subsection [b], dealing with the situation where the price is to be fixed by one party rejects the uncommercial idea that an agreement that the seller may fix the price means that he may fix any price he may wish by the express qualification that the price so fixed must be fixed in good faith. Good faith includes observance of reasonable commercial standards of fair dealing in the trade if the party is a merchant. (Section 2-103). *But in the normal case a "posted price" or a future seller's or buyer's "given price," "price in effect," "market price," or the like satisfies the good faith requirement.*

Tex. Bus. & Com. Code § 2.305 cmt. 3 (emphasis added). Despite this definition and comment, or perhaps because of them, Shell and the Dealers urge conflicting ideas about what good faith should mean in this case.

Shell argues that a good faith price, as section 2.305(b) requires, is one that is commercially reasonable and non-discriminatory. Because its DTW price fell within the range of DTW prices charged by other refiners in the relevant geographic markets (was commercially reasonable) and was applied uniformly among similarly-situated dealers (was non-discriminatory), Shell submits that summary judgment was appropriate. According to Shell, the chief concern of the drafters in adopting section 2.305(b) was to prevent suppliers from charging two buyers with identical pricing provisions different prices for arbitrary or discriminatory reasons. The drafters, however, also wished to minimize judicial intrusion into the setting of prices under open-price-term contracts. To balance these concerns, the drafters created a presumption under Official Comment 3 that a "posted price" or "price in effect" is a good faith price that may be rebutted only by evidence of discrimination. Shell asserts that because the Dealers brought forth no such evidence here, this is a normal case where the posted price or a price in effect is a good faith price under section 2.305.

The Dealers respond that Shell's concept of good faith and the "normal case" under section 2.305 is too narrow. They reject the notion that discriminatory pricing is the only way to rebut Comment 3's posted price presumption. Instead, the Dealers submit that the definition of good faith incorporates two elements: a subjective element, "honesty in fact," and an objective element, "the observance of reasonable commercial standards of fair dealing." *See* Tex. Bus. & Com. Code § 1.201(b)(20). They conclude that both elements must be satisfied before a case is considered normal and before the posted price presumption can apply.

III.

The Dealers rely extensively on the Fifth Circuit Court of Appeals' recent decision in *Mathis v. Exxon Corp.*, 302 F.3d 448 (5th Cir. 2002), which also involved open-price contracts between an oil refiner and its dealer/franchisees. Those dealers similarly complained that the refiner had breached its duty of good faith by purposefully setting its dealer price for gasoline at uncompetitively high levels to run them out of business. The *Mathis* court identified the central issue to be whether good faith required observance of both subjective and objective good faith in light of the apparent "safe harbor" described in Official Comment 3. *Id.* at 454–55. The refiner contended that a price fixed according to an established price schedule was within the safe harbor described in Comment 3. The court reasoned, however, that this safe harbor was not absolute because it applied only to "normal cases," or those cases in which an open price

---

[3] This definition was formerly limited to merchants, like Shell, but recent amendments to the Code have "brought the Article 2 merchant concept of good faith (subjective honesty and objective commercial reasonableness) into other Articles." *See* Tex. Bus. & Com. Code § 1.201(b)(20) cmt. 20.

term was set with subjective good faith. Thus, the court placed the following limitation on Comment 3's safe harbor:

> [Comment 3] avoids challenges to prices set according to an open price term, unless that challenge is outside the normal type of case. Although price discrimination was the type of aberrant case on the minds of the drafters, price discrimination is merely a subset of what constitutes such an aberrant case. Any lack of subjective, honesty-in-fact good faith is abnormal; price discrimination is only the most obvious way a price-setter acts in bad faith — by treating similarly-situated buyers differently.

Id. at 457. In support of its interpretation, the court cited *Nanakuli Paving & Rock Co. v. Shell Oil Co.*, 664 F.2d 772, 806 (9th Cir. 1981), and *Allapattah Serv., Inc. v. Exxon Corp.*, 61 F. Supp. 2d 1308, 1322 (S.D. Fla. 1999), *aff'd*, 333 F.3d 1248 (11th Cir. 2003).

The court of appeals in this case adopted the reasoning in *Mathis*, concluding that good faith under section 2.305 encompasses both subjective and objective elements. 102 S.W.3d at 214. Although a commercially reasonable price might establish the oil company's objective good faith, it would not alone be sufficient if there were also evidence that the company's price might have been influenced by its desire to replace franchisees with more profitable company-owned stores (a lack of subjective good faith). *Id.* at 214–15. Because the court concluded that the Dealers had presented sufficient circumstantial evidence on Shell's subjective intent to drive them out of business, it reversed the summary judgment. *Id.* at 215.

IV.

Most courts have rejected the approach of the Fifth Circuit and the court below in interpreting the good faith requirement of section 2.305. Instead, the majority of decisions suggest that a commercially reasonable DTW price, that is, one within the range of DTW prices charged by other refiners in the market, is a good faith price under section 2.305 absent some evidence that the refiner used pricing to discriminate among its purchasers. *See, e.g., Tom-Lin Enters., Inc. v. Sunoco, Inc.*, 349 F.3d 277, 281–83 (6th Cir. 2003); *Havird Oil Co. v. Marathon Oil Co.*, 149 F.3d 283, 290–91 (4th Cir. 1998); *Richard Short Oil Co. v. Texaco, Inc.*, 799 F.2d 415, 422 (8th Cir. 1986); *Wayman v. Amoco Oil Co.*, 923 F. Supp. 1322, 1332 (D. Kan. 1996), *aff'd mem.*, 145 F.3d 1347 (10th Cir. 1998); *T.A.M., Inc. v. Gulf Oil Corp.*, 553 F. Supp. 499, 509 (E.D. Pa. 1982); *Adams v. G.J. Creel & Sons, Inc.*, 320 S.C. 274, 465 S.E.2d 84, 86 (S.C. 1995). *But see Wilson v. Amerada Hess Corp.*, 168 N.J. 236, 773 A.2d 1121 (2001); *E.S. Bills, Inc. v. Tzucanow*, 38 Cal. 3d 824, 215 Cal. Rptr. 278, 700 P.2d 1280 (1985). As the court in *Wayman* observed, "[i]t is abundantly clear . . . that the chief concern of the UCC Drafting Committee in adopting § 2-305(2) was to prevent discriminatory pricing — i.e., to prevent suppliers from charging two buyers with identical pricing provisions in their respective contracts different prices for arbitrary or discriminatory reasons." *Wayman*, 923 F. Supp. at 1346–47.

The Dealers themselves concede that Shell is not obligated to price its gasoline with their interests in mind or to protect them from competition. They further explain that their theory in this case does not turn on the DTW price set by Shell but rather on the reason why Shell chose to charge that price. Likewise, the court of appeals concludes that this is not the normal case because the price, although commercially in line with that charged by other refiners to their lessee dealers, may have been motivated by an improper underlying purpose to eliminate some dealerships.

It is not apparent, however, why the intent behind a commercially reasonable, non-discriminatory price should matter for purposes of a breach of contract claim under section 2.305(b). Dealers do not contend that they are entitled to any particular price and do not disagree that Shell's DTW price is within the range charged by other refiners to their dealers. Thus, if these Dealers were charged the same DTW price by another refiner who did not have a similar plan to thin their ranks, presumably the price would pass muster under the Dealers' view of section 2.305. Premising a breach of contract claim solely on assumed subjective motives injects uncertainty into the law of contracts and undermines one of the UCC's primary goals — to "promot[e] certainty and predictability in commercial transactions." *Am. Airlines Employees Fed. Credit Union v. Martin*, 29 S.W.3d 86, 92 (Tex. 2000).

Beyond prohibiting discriminatory pricing, the drafters wished to minimize judicial intrusion into the setting of prices under open-price-term contracts. They understood that requiring sellers in open-price industries, such as the oil and gas industry, to justify the reasonableness their prices in order to satisfy section 2.305 would "mean[ ] that in every case the seller is going to be in a lawsuit" and that every sales contract would become "a public utility rate case." Walter D. Malcolm, *The Proposed Commercial Code: A Report on Developments from May 1950 Through February 1951*, 6 Bus. Law. 113, 186 (1951). The drafters reasonably foresaw that almost any price could be attacked, unless it benefitted from a strong presumption. Thus, they adopted a safe harbor, Comment 3's posted price presumption, to preserve the practice of using "sellers' standard prices" while seeking "to avoid discriminatory prices." *Id.; see also* Tex. Bus. & Com. Code § 2.305 cmt. 3.

The reasoning in *Mathis* and the court of appeals in this case negates the effect of Comment 3's "safe harbor" by concluding that circumstantial evidence of "[a]ny lack of subjective, honesty-in-fact good faith" is sufficient to create an "abnormal" case in which the posted-price presumption no longer applies. *See Mathis*, 302 F.3d at 457. The effect is to allow a jury to determine in every section 2.305(b) case whether there was any "improper motive animating the price-setter," even if the prices ultimately charged were undisputedly within the range of those charged throughout the industry. *Id.* at 454. This result appears to conflict with the drafters' desire to eliminate litigation over prices that are nondiscriminatory and set in accordance with industry standards. Although the subjective element of good faith may have a place elsewhere in the Code, *see, e.g., La Sara Grain Co. v. First Nat'l Bank*, 673 S.W.2d 558, 562–63 (Tex. 1984) (applying subjective good faith to a negotiable instrument), we do not believe this subjective element was intended to stand alone as a basis for a claim of bad faith under section 2.305. Rather, we conclude that allegations of dishonesty under this section must also have some basis in objective fact which at a minimum requires some connection to the commercial realities of the case. *See* 2 James J. White & Robert S. Summers, Uniform Commercial Code § 17.6 at 167 (4th ed. 1995) (noting that "the subjective rule never prevailed in Article 2 with respect to merchants" and that in "various other articles of the Code there has been a movement from subjective to objective definitions of good faith").

* * *

V.

The Dealers maintain, however, that even though Shell used a posted price it nevertheless violated its duty of good faith by setting its DTW price too high with the conscious intention of driving some of its franchisees out of business. And the court of appeals agreed that there was enough circumstantial evidence to raise a fact issue about Shell's subjective motives and therefore its good faith. According to the court, this evidence generally included: (1) the DTW price itself, which was on the high end of the wholesale pricing spectrum; (2) the "captive" nature of relationship between Shell and its franchisees; and (3) the general decline in the business fortunes of Shell franchisees. 102 S.W.3d at 214–15.

Shell argues that these circumstantial factors are either irrelevant, unrelated to Shell's pricing, or unsupported by the record. Shell submits that there is no evidence that its DTW price caused any particular Dealer to fail or be uncompetitive in the market. And even if there were evidence of this, Shell submits it would not raise a fact issue about its good faith because section 2.305 does not require a competitive price or the lowest price available. Moreover, Shell argues that the fact that some franchisees have experienced declining sales, lost money, or gone out of business does not raise a fact issue about whether Shell had a bad-faith plan to price them out of business. Instead, Shell suggests that market forces beyond its control are at the root of these problems. Shell points out that the Dealers' own expert agreed that the lessee dealer is "a class of trade whose economic viability is dying" due to broader market forces, including the entry of mass merchandisers into gasoline retailing.

We agree with Shell that the court of appeals' list of circumstantial factors are not evidence that Shell lacked good faith when fixing its DTW price. The DTW price, the captive nature of the franchisee relationship, and the business losses suffered by the Dealers are variations of the same theme: Shell's DTW price is too high for the Dealers to compete with other gasoline retailers. But good faith under section 2.305(b) does not mandate a competitive price for each individual Dealer, nor could it. The competitive circumstances of each Dealer in the same pricing zone may vary from station to station, and yet Shell must treat them all the same.

The court of appeals, however, suggests that because the Dealers paid more than most of the other gasoline retailers in Houston, the DTW price itself is some evidence of Shell's subjective bad faith. 102 S.W.3d at 214 ("73–80% of [the Dealers'] Houston competition paid rack price — or lower — for gas. . . ."). We cannot agree that a relatively high, yet commercially reasonable, price is evidence of bad faith. A good-faith price under section 2.305 is not synonymous with a fair market price or the lowest price available. *TCP Indus., Inc. v. Uniroyal, Inc.*, 661 F.2d 542, 548 (6th Cir. 1981); *Harvey v. Fearless Farris Wholesale, Inc.*, 589 F.2d 451, 461 (9th Cir. 1979); *see also* 1 JAMES J. WHITE & ROBERT S. SUMMERS, UNIFORM COMMERCIAL CODE § 3–8, at 150 (4th ed. 1995) ("Note that the section says 'a reasonable price' and not 'fair market value of the goods.' These two would not be identical.").

Each Dealer contractually agreed to buy gasoline at the DTW price applicable only to Shell-branded lessee-dealers. The court of appeals' wholesale cost analysis indiscriminately compares Shell's DTW price to prices available to other classes of trade, with different contractual buying arrangements. Included in the comparison are branded and unbranded jobbers who pick up their gasoline at terminals, open dealers who own their own premises, and company-owned stores operated by other refiners. Evidence that different prices are available to different classes of trade is not evidence of bad faith under section 2.305. *See Ajir v. Exxon Corp.*, No. C 93-20830, 1995 WL 261412, at *4 (N.D. Cal. May 2, 1995) ("The existence of different prices for different classes of trade is not sufficient to demonstrate that [a refiner] is overcharging plaintiffs for gasoline."), *aff'd*, 185 F.3d 865 (table), 1999 WL 393666 (9th Cir. 1999); *Exxon Corp. v. Superior Court of Santa Clara County*, 51 Cal. App. 4th 1672, 60 Cal. Rptr. 2d 195, 205 (1997) (same).

Moreover, the court's description of the Dealers as " 'captive buyers' required to purchase Shell-branded gas at Shell's price" is not evidence of bad faith or an abnormal case within the meaning of Comment 3. 102 S.W.3d at 214. Dealers are only "captive" as a result of their own choice to become Shell-branded lessee dealers, which involved their agreement to buy gasoline from Shell at the DTW price, rather than at rack or some other price. That is the nature of a long-term franchise. Such "captivity" is therefore the "normal" case.

Because the summary judgment evidence establishes that Shell's posted price was both commercially reasonable and fairly applied to the Dealers, we reverse the judgment of the court of appeals and render judgment that the plaintiffs take nothing.

QUESTIONS

1. Is the court on solid ground to conclude that the language of an Official Comment provides a "safe harbor" that effectively amends the statutory definition of good faith?

2. Can you make the case for HRN stronger by assuming additional facts regarding subjective bad faith, or has the court shut the door to any such arguments? Can you re-formulate HRN's claims in terms of objective bad faith?

2.   Quantity Terms

Although Article 2 provides rules to fill the gaps in otherwise enforceable agreements, you will recall that the quantity term is the only term that must appear in the writing that satisfies the statute of frauds rule of § 2-201(1), and that an agreed quantity term is certainly necessary to provide a basis upon which a remedy could be fashioned. A "reasonable" price can be used if the parties fail to agree to a price term, but there are no similar objective standards for establishing a missing quantity term. Although technically not a gap-filling provision because the parties must agree to the quantity, § 2-306 performs an important function by validating output and requirement contracts by providing a definition of these terms that ensures that they operate as definite quantity terms for the purpose of finding an enforceable agreement. Section 2-306(1) provides that "output" and "requirements" are quantity terms that render an agreement enforceable; § 2-306(2) delineates the rights and duties of the parties in an exclusive dealing arrangement.

a.   Output and requirements contracts

At common law, the agreement to sell one's "output" of a good, or to purchase one's "requirement" for a good, was highly suspect. A traditional argument was that such an agreement lacked mutuality, because the seller unilaterally could determine its "output," and the buyer could unilaterally determine its "requirements." Section 2-306(1) eliminates the potential that this argument might carry the day. Note how § 2-306(1) defines the obligations of the parties to such contracts, so as to establish mutuality of obligation.

CANUSA CORP. v. A & R LOBOSCO, INC.
United States District Court, Eastern District of New York
986 F. Supp. 723 (1997)

MEMORANDUM AND ORDER

TRAGER, District Judge.

This diversity action for breach of contract raises a surprisingly novel question: what is the effect of an estimate in an output contract when the supplier produces less than the stated estimate? I conclude that New York law would hold that good faith, rather than the stated estimate, would control whether a breach has occurred.

Background

Plaintiff Canusa seeks damages for lost sales as a result of an alleged breach of contract by defendants Lobosco as well as attorneys' fees in connection with an equipment lease to Lobosco. The case was tried without a jury, where the following facts are found.

Plaintiff Canusa is a Maryland corporation that recycles and brokers waste paper. A&R Lobosco ("Lobosco") is a New York corporation that receives, collects, cleans, and resells this recyclable paper to paper mills or brokers like Canusa. Michael Lobosco is A&R Lobosco's president.

In late 1992, Lobosco entered into an agreement with the City of New York to accept 850 tons per week (3,400–3,500 tons per month) of material to be recycled. *See* Trial Tr. (Tr.) at 233; Def.'s Ex. A, "Agreement and Bid Specifications" at B-7. To handle this paper, Lobosco needed a bailer, a piece of equipment to process and bale the recyclable paper. At about the same time, Canusa heard from a third party also in the paper recycling business that Lobosco had obtained a City contract and might be looking for a baler. *See* Tr. at 337–39. Lobosco had put down a deposit on a baler with another firm, but ultimately decided to enter into an arrangement with Canusa because Canusa would finance the baler, while the other arrangement obligated Lobosco to obtain separate financing. *See id.* at 237. Canusa's president, Bruce Fleming, testified that Canusa only enters into baler financing agreements to obtain a steady supply of paper. Fleming testified that Canusa obtains 30% of its paper from contract sources like Lobosco and obtains the balance in the spot market. Of that 30%, approximately half, or 15% of Canusa's total supply of waste paper comes from agreements similar to the one Canusa had with Lobosco.

Lobosco began receiving recyclables from the City in January of 1993; later that month, Michael Lobosco entered into negotiations with David Knight, a Canusa vice president, for a baler. *See id.* at 236. On March 15, 1993, the parties entered into an Equipment Lease secured by a personal guarantee signed by Michael Lobosco. *See* Pl.'s Ex. 1 ("Equipment Lease"); Pl.'s Ex. 2 ("Personal Guarantee"). Among other things, the Equipment Lease provided that the lessee (Lobosco) would be liable for costs, fees and reasonable attorneys' fees for any action taken to preserve Canusa's rights. *See* Pl.'s Ex. 1, & 14.

The lease also provided that Lobosco was to pay rent, but did not specify an amount. The lease did, however, refer to an "Output Agreement" ("Agreement") that the parties had entered into on March 1, 1993. *See* Tr. at 56. Thus, Lobosco would finance the baler by supplying Canusa with paper, which would then be credited to its account. Michael Lobosco testified that under these agreements Lobosco was to pay $1,551.00/week toward the baler; any amounts of paper sent in excess of that would be credited to Lobosco's account. *See id.* at 240. Michael Lobosco also testified that he was aware that Canusa would resell his paper to third parties. *See id.* at 238.

The Agreement (captioned an "Output Agreement") recited that the parties were entering into an output contract with a five-year term, but it also contained language stating that Lobosco would initially ship 1100 tons per month of number 8 quality old news print (ONP 8) per month to Canusa in 1993, and 1500 tons per month thereafter (1994–97). Both parties presented evidence that they understood this number to mean the minimum number of tons Lobosco was obligated to provide to Canusa. *See* Tr. at 123, 241. The Agreement also provided that the price per ton of ONP would be set each month between the parties and defined acceptable ONP. Fleming described ONP 8 as "anything that normally comes in a household newspaper." Tr. at 36. Materials that have no relationship to paper, such as garbage, masonry, metal, etc., are called prohibitives. Materials that are acceptable in small amounts are called outthrows. Examples of outthrows include Sunday newspaper magazines and coupon circulars. *See id.* Some paper products, most notably telephone books, are also considered prohibitives. The Agreement specified that no prohibited materials would be accepted, and that total outthrows could not exceed one quarter of one percent (.25%) by weight. *See* Pl.'s Ex. 3 & 8. The Equipment Lease and Guarantee provided for the application of Maryland law, while the Agreement provided for the application of New York law.

From the beginning, the relationship was a rocky one. Canusa provided documentation demonstrating the actual tons of material shipped to it from 1993 to May 1994, Lobosco's last shipment date. Only in the very first month of the contract, April 1993, did Lobosco come close to the estimate in the Agreement, shipping 942 tons.

Michael Lobosco gave several reasons for his firm's inability to meet the schedule set in the Agreement. First, he stated that the materials from the City had a much higher proportion of garbage than what he had previously obtained from similar programs in the suburbs. *See* Tr. at 245. Second, he noted that he did not always get the amount promised under the City contract. *See id.* He also testified, without contradiction, that of the material he received from the City, ultimately 28% was convertible into ONP 8. Michael Lobosco derived this figure as follows: he testified that 30% of each load from the City consisted of prohibitives such as garbage, thus leaving 70% of the initial amount. Of this remainder, Lobosco estimated that 40% of it was ONP 8. *See id.* at 266. During this time, Lobosco also received about 150 tons per month of newspaper from other sources. *See id.* at 292.

At the same time Lobosco was not meeting the specification of the Agreement, it was shipping another paper product to Mandala Recycling. *See* Tr. at 265; Pl.'s Exs. 15, 29–32. Lobosco testified that this product contained "50–60%" newspaper. *See* Tr. at 265. There was no direct testimony by the buyer or the seller as to the outthrow content of this proprietary package, which was to be sent overseas, but the principal of Mandala, Stephen Batty, testified that he was allowed "a little more latitude" in the material that he shipped to Indonesia. *See id.* at 223.[4]

Beginning in September 1993, after a series of attempts to have Lobosco's output conform to ONP 8, Canusa offered to modify the Agreement. Specifically, Canusa offered to accept 500 tons per month of ONP 7/8 (also known as "export news") instead of the higher quality ONP 8. *See* Ex. 49-A, (Ltr. from David Knight to Mike Lobosco dated December 13, 1993); Ex. 49-B (Ltr. from David Knight to Ken Knigan of Lobosco dated September 13, 1993). Michael Lobosco never signed this agreement; however, he testified that he acted pursuant to his understanding of it. *See* Tr. at 261. Lobosco also testified that he told Knight not to ship this product to a newsprint mill because it would be rejected, but that Knight went ahead and did so. *See id.* Knight's testimony was similar, except that Knight stated that the material was rejected because it had rotted due to moisture. *See id.* at 146, 157–58. In the month following this amendment (October, 1993), the amount of paper Lobosco shipped to Canusa almost doubled.

Although Lobosco had shipped 440 tons in January of 1994, that number decreased to 270 in February and zero in March. In January 1994, Canusa offered to accept a "baler fee" payment of $3.00 per ton, relieving Lobosco of any obligation under the Agreement. *See* Pl.'s Ex. 50 (Ltr. from Canusa to Lobosco dated January 25, 1994). In March 1994, Canusa again offered to modify the Agreement. Lobosco would pay, in addition to the regular baler payment, $3,000.00 per month. This amount was computed on the basis of a $2 per ton profit on the 1500 tons that Lobosco was to have shipped to Canusa. In return, Canusa would release Lobosco from its obligation under the Output Agreement. *See* Pl.'s Ex. 52 (Ltr. from Canusa to Lobosco dated March 30, 1994). Lobosco never accepted this proposal. *See* Tr. at 51–52. Canusa filed its complaint on June 27, 1994.

Canusa sought damages for breach of contract, fraudulent inducement, and replevin of the baler. The parties entered into a stipulation of partial settlement on June 30, 1994, which provided that Lobosco would purchase the baler from Canusa, settling the replevin and rent claims, but that Canusa reserved all of its other rights under the Equipment Lease, guarantee, and Agreement. *See* Pl.'s Ex. 4 (Stipulation of Partial

---

[4] [3] Canusa argues that the material sold to Mandala should be considered as the equivalent of ONP 8 even though Canusa admits that its outthrow content may have exceeded the requirements for ONP 8 by a considerable margin (10% versus .25%). In support of this argument, Canusa produced evidence from an inspection firm (SGS) which certified to the destination country (Indonesia) that the bales sold to Mandala and shipped from Lobosco's premises were exportable recycled paper. *See* Tr. at 310–33. For reasons explained in the "Damages" section of this opinion, *infra* at 733, Canusa is not entitled to damages based upon Lobosco's sales to Mandala.

Settlement). At trial, Canusa's fraudulent inducement claim was dismissed; thus, only the action for breach of contract under the Agreement and fees and costs associated with the replevin action remain to be decided.

Discussion

A. Breach

In this diversity action, the parties do not dispute that New York law governs the question of breach of the Agreement, while Maryland law governs the Equipment Lease and Guarantee. Under New York law, because the Agreement is a contract for the sale of goods, it is governed by New York's version of the Uniform Commercial Code ("UCC").

Canusa contends that Lobosco breached its contract by failing to meet the minimum set forth in the Agreement. Lobosco contends that there was no breach because it supplied Canusa with all the ONP 8 that it produced. The initial dispute, then, is over the meaning of an estimate in an output contract. Canusa argues that under the Agreement it is entitled to the minimum tonnage specified, while Lobosco argues that output agreements like this one are subject only to the requirement of good faith. Significantly, Canusa did not offer any evidence to prove, nor advance the theory at trial, that this contract was a fixed quantity contract; indeed, it would be difficult to do so given the document itself. In fact, Knight testified at trial that Canusa subsequently changed its contracts to supply contracts to ensure that it would receive a specified amount. *See* Tr. at 167–69; Def.'s Ex. F. Thus, there is no dispute that the Agreement is an output contract; the issue is what weight should be given to the Agreement's estimate.

Output contracts are governed by § 2-306, which provides in part:

> A term which measures the quantity by the output of the seller or the requirements of the buyer means such actual output or requirements as may occur in good faith, except that no quantity unreasonably disproportionate to any stated estimate or in the absence of a stated estimate to any normal or otherwise comparable prior output or requirements may be tendered or demanded.

N.Y. UCC § 2-306(1) (McKinney 1993). Prior to the introduction of the UCC, estimates in output contracts were just that: estimates. *See Orange and Rockland Utils., Inc. v. Amerada Hess Corp.*, 59 A.D.2d 110, 115, 397 N.Y.S.2d 814 (2d Dep't 1977). Comment 3 to § 2-306 provides: "Any minimum or maximum set by the agreement shows a clear limit on the intended elasticity. In similar fashion, the agreed estimate is to be regarded as a center around which the parties intend the variation to occur." N.Y. UCC § 2-306, cmt. 3 (McKinney 1993). In contrast, comment 2 states: "The essential test is whether the party is acting in good faith." *Id.*, cmt. 2. Taken together, these comments do not provide much guidance as to the importance of the estimate in a reduced output context, because the weight given an estimate in an output or requirement contract usually only becomes an issue in the context of an increase, either in the seller's output or in the buyer's demand. The former case is illustrated by *Philadelphia Corp. v. Niagara Mohawk Power Corp.*, 207 A.D.2d 176, 621 N.Y.S.2d 237 (3d Dep't 1995). There, the court held that the plaintiffs, who sought to increase their electrical output, could not "increase their electrical output beyond the reasonable expectations of the parties as quantified by the stated estimates." *Id.* at 179, 621 N.Y.S.2d 237 (citation and footnote omitted). In *Orange and Rockland Utilities*, the court held that in a rising market the doubling of an estimated demand for fuel oil under a fixed price contract was unreasonably dispropor- tionate. *See* 59 A.D.2d at 115, 397 N.Y.S.2d 814.

Because these decisions do not address the concerns that arise in the specific factual context of this case they are inapposite. Three cases do, however, shed light on this issue.

* * *

The second relevant case is *Empire Gas Corp. v. American Bakeries Co.*, 840 F.2d 1333 (7th Cir. 1988). In *Empire Gas*, the parties entered into a requirements contract to convert several thousand of defendant's vehicles to gas; the defendant never converted a single vehicle under the contract. On appeal, the defendant contended it was error for the trial judge to read § 2-306 verbatim to the jury, because the "unreasonably disproportionate" language, without explanation, might effectively have produced a directed verdict for plaintiff, since taking nothing under the contract could easily be "unreasonably disproportionate." Writing for the court, Judge Posner held that when a buyer takes less, rather than more than the stated estimate in a requirements contract, the unreasonably disproportionate provision of § 2-306 does not apply, and the sole test is good faith. *See id.* at 1339. Thus, a buyer could reduce his or her requirements to zero under a requirements contract, provided that he or she did so in good faith. *See id.* at 1338.

The court began its analysis of the disproportionate proviso by noting that case law distinguishes between overdemanding and underdemanding cases, and that at common law the sole test of underdemanding was good faith. *See id.* at 1337 (citing cases). The court then read the statute to mean that the "unreasonably disproportionate" language as providing a specific articulation of good faith, the general standard, in the context of an overdemanding case. *See id.* at 1338. Thus, the "unreasonably disproportionate" language of § 2-306(1) has no application in the context of an underdemanding case.

At least one circuit court has adopted the reasoning of *Empire Gas* in a factual setting similar to this case. In *Atlantic Track & Turnout Co. v. Perini Corp.*, 989 F.2d 541 (1st Cir. 1993), Perini had contracted to remove material as part of a railroad track rehabilitation project, and then sought to sell this material to Atlantic Track. Perini supplied on 15% of the material estimated in Atlantic Track's purchase orders because the rehabilitation contract was modified and then terminated, and because some of the material from the project was contaminated and apparently unusable. Atlantic Track argued that under § 2-306, Perini was obligated to provide material in conformity with the estimates in plaintiff's purchase orders, which also stated that Perini was to furnish "all available material." *Id.* at 542–43. Rejecting this argument, the First Circuit held that the unreasonably disproportionate language of § 2-306 does not apply to an output contract where the seller tenders less than the estimate, and that the sole test in this context is good faith. *See id.* at 544–45. In reaching its conclusion, the court first adopted the reasoning in *Empire Gas* that the "unreasonably disproportionate" language represented a specified articulation of good faith, and that a requirements contract "represents a risk allocation." *Id.* at 544 (citing *Empire Gas*, 840 F.2d at 1340). Interpreting Massachusetts law, the court went on to hold that the risk allocation rationale articulated in *Empire Gas* "supports different treatment of cases such as the present one, in which the seller in an output contract tenders less than the stated estimate, from cases in which the seller tenders more." *Atlantic Track*, 989 F.2d at 545 (citation omitted). Here, "the output contract allocates to the buyer the risk of a change in the seller's business that makes continuation costly, while the seller assumes the risk of a less urgent change in circumstances." *Id.*

Although *Atlantic Track* is not controlling . . . the reasoning . . . is compelling here. . . . In a requirements contract, the seller takes the risk that the buyer may in good faith reduce its requirements to zero. Given the premise that a seller will want to maximize its output, the good faith standard provides a sufficient test to measure a reducing seller's performance against. *See HML Corp. v. General Foods Corp.*, 365 F.2d 77, 81 (3d Cir. 1966) (applying New York law). So too, in an output contract, the buyer takes the risk that the seller may reduce its production to zero. . . . Applying good faith rather than an estimate does not give the seller an unbargained for advantage; rather, it merely preserves the essential character of contracts that lack a fixed term, albeit through the somewhat elusive concept of good faith. . . .

Moreover, a mechanical adherence to the estimate in the contract would essentially convert all output contracts with an estimate into fixed contracts. The fallacy of this proposition is illustrated by this case: having bargained for the flexibility of an output contract, Canusa now seeks to treat it as a fixed goods contract. An output agreement is not transformed into a fixed quantity contract by the insertion of an estimate. Thus, where an output contract provides for a certain amount of goods to be produced, the appropriate test for a seller's reduction in output is good faith rather than the estimate in the contract.[5]

After discounting the estimate in the Agreement as the appropriate yardstick, the baseline for the defendant's good faith must be set at Michael Lobosco's own estimate of the ONP 8 he could produce from the City's material, because Canusa failed to establish any other basis. Despite being given the opportunity, Canusa did not offer *any* evidence of other percentages of ONP production from *any* city's recycling program. Measured by its own standard, however, Lobosco's performance does not comport with good faith. When asked why he failed to produce ONP 8 in quantities consistent with his own production estimate, Michael Lobosco's only explanation was that it would have taken more time to sort the material. *See* Tr. at 298. The fact that it would cost more to clean the material to reach the ONP 8 standard does not demonstrate good faith; nor does it provide an excuse . . . especially where there is no showing that the additional costs would not have made the contract unprofitable. Thus, because Lobosco failed to supply the ONP 8 that its president testified it could produce, it breached the Output Agreement.

Lobosco did not raise the defense of waiver at trial. Even if it had, Canusa's efforts to work with Lobosco is not a waiver of the good faith requirement, because a party need not terminate the contract, but may instead seek to resolve the problem.

The only issue remaining is at what point can it be said that Lobosco breached the contract. Although an earlier date can be supported by the record, it would appear that as late as October 1993, Lobosco was seeking to resolve his differences with Canusa. In that month, he sent substantially more than the minimum requirement and double the previous month. In November, shipment began to deteriorate again, never to recover. Therefore, the breach can fairly be ascribed as occurring in November 1993, and damages will be calculated from that date.

---

[5] [5] An alternative analysis under common law principles of contract law would reach the same result. As a matter of law, the contract is ambiguous because there is more than one reasonable reading of it. *See Breed v. Insurance Co. of N. Am.*, 46 N.Y.2d 351, 355, 413 N.Y.S.2d 352, 385 N.E.2d 1280 (N.Y. 1978). Although the parties to a contract "may not create an ambiguity merely by urging conflicting interpretations of their agreement . . . if ambiguity exists, then extrinsic evidence of the parties' intent may be looked to as an aid to construing the contractual language." *Sayers v. Rochester Tel. Corp. Supplemental Management Pension Plan*, 7 F.3d 1091, 1095 (2d Cir. 1993) (citations omitted) (construing New York law); *see also John Hancock Mut. Life Ins. Co. v. Amerford Int'l Corp.*, 22 F.3d 458, 461 (2d Cir. 1994). Moreover, this Agreement does not contain a merger clause. Therefore, extrinsic evidence is admissible as an aid to interpretation.

Testimony taken at the trial clearly demonstrated that the figure placed in the Agreement was based solely on the figure from the City contract. *See* Tr. at 240–41. Furthermore, Michael Lobosco testified that although he gave Knight the tonnage figure from Lobosco's contract with the City, it was Canusa that specified the tonnage figures in the Agreement. In this context, the pertinent interpretive principle is the rule that "[i]n cases of doubt or ambiguity, a contract must be construed most strongly against the party who prepared it, and favorably to a party who had no voice in the selection of its language." *Jacobson v. Sassower*, 66 N.Y.2d 991, 993, 499 N.Y.S.2d 381, 489 N.E.2d 1283 (N.Y. 1985) (citation omitted). As a result, the estimate in the Agreement cannot be seen as controlling.

* * *

PROBLEM 3-3

Bob's Bakery, Inc. has a fleet of 3,000 trucks that distribute its bakery products throughout the United States. Bob's entered into a contract with Shelly's Gas Conversion, Inc. to purchase conversion kits enabling the trucks to run on propane fuel instead of gasoline. Bob's explained that it was attempting to cut operating expenses, and Shelly's provided information regarding projected cost savings (assuming the current costs of propane gas and gasoline). The written agreement between the parties included the following clause:

> Quantity. Bob's will purchase approximately 3,000 conversion units, more or less, depending on its requirements at the time.

The parties agree that the contract is a requirements contract governed by § 2-306.

First Scenario: A sudden interruption of the mideast oil supply drives crude oil prices significantly higher in the succeeding two months. Consequently, a shortage of the propane conversion units develops, driving their prices much higher. Bob's places an order for 5,000 units. Subsequent discovery reveals that Bob's is planning to sell approximately 2,000 units to members of its trade organization at a modest markup. Is Shelly's breaching the contract if it refuses to deliver more than 3,000 units at the contract price?

Second Scenario: Discovery during litigation revealed that Bob's order was increased because it intended to stockpile 2,000 units for future use as the fleet was expanded.

Third Scenario: Within three weeks of signing the agreement, Bob's decides that conversion savings were not sufficient to counter the costs of conversion and maintenance, and the inconvenience of using an alternative fuel. Bob's decides not to convert any of its trucks to propane fuel. Bob's advises Shelly's that it requires no units under their contract. Has Bob's breached its contract?

b. Duties under exclusive dealing agreements

When one party has agreed to deal exclusively with another party, that party is at increased risk. In the famous case of *Wood v. Lucy, Lady Duff-Gordon*, 222 N.Y. 88, 118 N.E. 214 (1917), Judge Cardozo found that by securing Lady Duff-Gordon's promise to permit Wood the exclusive right to market her name to promote the sale of various goods, Wood impliedly promised to use reasonable efforts to market products with her endorsement. Section 2-306(2) codifies this ruling by providing that in an exclusive dealing arrangement, the party who is exclusively bound is owed a duty of "best efforts" by the other party. It will come as no surprise that the scope of "best efforts" has been litigated in a number of cases.

BLOOR v. FALSTAFF BREWING CORP.
United States Court of Appeals, Second Circuit
601 F.2d 609 (1979)

FRIENDLY, Circuit Judge:

This action, wherein federal jurisdiction is predicated on diversity of citizenship, 28 U.S.C. § 1332, was brought in the District Court for the Southern District of New York, by James Bloor, Reorganization Trustee of Balco Properties Corporation, formerly named P. Ballantine & Sons (Ballantine), a venerable and once successful brewery based in Newark, N.J. He sought to recover from Falstaff Brewing corporation (Falstaff) for breach of a contract dated March 31, 1972, wherein Falstaff bought the Ballantine brewing labels, trademarks, accounts receivable, distribution systems and other property except the brewery. The price was $4,000,000 plus a royalty of fifty cents on each barrel of the Ballantine brands sold between April 1, 1972, and March 31, 1978.

Although other issues were tried, the appeals concern only two provisions of the contract. These are:

8. *Certain Other Covenants of Buyer.*

 (a) After the Closing Date the [Buyer] will use its best efforts to promote and maintain a high volume of sales under the Proprietary Rights.

* * *

 2(a)(v) [The Buyer will pay a royalty of $.50 per barrel for a period of 6 years], provided, however, that if during the Royalty Period the Buyer substantially discontinues the distribution of beer under the brand name "Ballantine" (except as the result of a restraining order in effect for 30 days issued by a court of competent jurisdiction at the request of a governmental authority), it will pay to the Seller a cash sum equal to the years and fraction thereof remaining in the Royalty Period times $1,100,000, payable in equal monthly installments on the first day of each month commencing with the first month following the month in which such discontinuation occurs. . . .

Bloor claimed that Falstaff had breached the best efforts clause, 8(a), and indeed that its default amounted to the substantial discontinuance that would trigger the liquidated damage clause, 2(a)(v). In an opinion that interestingly traces the history of beer back to Domesday Book and beyond, Judge Brieant upheld the first claim and awarded damages but dismissed the second. Falstaff appeals from the former ruling, Bloor from the latter. Both sides also dispute the court's measurement of damages for breach of the best efforts clause.

 We shall assume familiarity with Judge Brieant's excellent opinion, 454 F. Supp. 258 (S.D.N.Y. 1978), from which we have drawn heavily, and will state only the essentials. Ballantine had been a family owned business, producing low-priced beers primarily for the northeast market, particularly New York, New Jersey, Connecticut and Pennsylvania. Its sales began to decline in 1961, and it lost money from 1965 onwards. On June 1, 1969, Investors Funding Corporation (IFC), a real estate conglomerate with no experience in brewing, acquired substantially all the stock of Ballantine for $16,290,000. IFC increased advertising expenditures, levelling off in 1971 at $1 million a year. This and other promotional practices, some of dubious legality, led to steady growth in Ballantine's sales despite the increased activities in the northeast of the "nationals" which have greatly augmented their market shares at the expense of smaller brewers. However, this was a profitless prosperity; there was no month in which Ballantine had earnings and the total loss was $15,500,000 for the 33 months of IFC ownership.

 After its acquisition of Ballantine, Falstaff continued the $1 million a year advertising program, IFC's pricing policies, and also its policy of serving smaller accounts not solely through sales to independent distributors, the usual practice in the industry, but by use of its own warehouses and trucks — the only change being a shift of the retail distribution system from Newark to North Bergen, N.J., when brewing was concentrated at Falstaff's Rhode Island brewery. However, sales declined and Falstaff claims to have lost $22 million in its Ballantine brand operations from March 31, 1972, to June 1975. Its other activities were also performing indifferently, although with no such losses as were being incurred in the sale of Ballantine products, and it was facing inability to meet payrolls and other debts. In March and April 1975, control of Falstaff passed to Paul Kalmanovitz, a businessman with 40 years experience in the brewing industry. After having first advanced $3 million to enable Falstaff to meet its payrolls and other pressing debts, he later supplied an additional $10 million and made loan guarantees, in return for which he received convertible preferred shares in an amount that endowed him with 35% of the voting power and became the beneficiary of a voting trust that gave him control of the board of directors.

Mr. Kalmanovitz determined to concentrate on making beer and cutting sales costs. He decreased advertising, with the result that the Ballantine advertising budget shrank from $1 million to $115,000 a year. In late 1975, he closed four of Falstaff's six retail distribution centers, including the North Bergen, N.J. depot, which was ultimately replaced by two distributors servicing substantially fewer accounts. He also discontinued various illegal practices that had been used in selling Ballantine products. What happened in terms of sales volume is shown in plaintiff's exhibit 114 JY. With 1974 as a base, Ballantine declined 29.72% in 1975 and 45.81% in 1976 as compared with a 1975 gain of 2.24% and a 1976 loss of 13.08% for all brewers excluding the top 15. Other comparisons are similarly devastating, at least for 1976.[6] Despite the decline in the sale of its own labels as well as Ballantine's, Falstaff, however, made a substantial financial recovery. In 1976, it had net income of $8.7 million and its year-end working capital had increased from $8.6 million to $20.2 million and its cash and certificates of deposit from $2.2 million to $12.1 million.

Seizing upon remarks made by the judge during the trial that Falstaff's financial standing in 1975 and thereafter "is probably not relevant" and a footnote in the opinion, 454 F. Supp. at 267 n.7,[7] appellate counsel for Falstaff contend that the judge read the best efforts clause as requiring Falstaff to maintain Ballantine's volume by any sales methods having a good prospect of increasing or maintaining sales or, at least, to continue lawful methods in use at the time of purchase, no matter what losses they would cause. Starting from this premise, counsel reason that the judge's conclusion was at odds with New York law, stipulated by the contract to be controlling. . . .

We do not think the judge imposed on Falstaff a standard as demanding as its appellate counsel argues that he did. Despite his footnote 7, he did not in fact proceed on the basis that the best efforts clause required Falstaff to bankrupt itself in promoting Ballantine products or even to sell those products at a substantial loss. He relied rather on the fact that Falstaff's obligation to "use its best efforts to promote and maintain a high volume of sales" of Ballantine products was not fulfilled by a policy summarized by Mr. Kalmanovitz as being:

We sell beer and you pay for it. . . .

We sell beer, F.O.B. the brewery. You come and get it.

— however sensible such a policy may have been with respect to Falstaff's other products. Once the peril of insolvency had been averted, the drastic percentage reductions in Ballantine sales as related to any possible basis of comparison required Falstaff at least to explore whether steps not involving substantial losses could have been taken to stop or at least lessen the rate of decline. The judge found that, instead of doing this, Falstaff had engaged in a number of misfeasances and nonfeasances which could have accounted in substantial measure for the catastrophic drop in Ballantine sales . . . , see 454 F. Supp. at 267–72. These included the closing of the North Bergen depot which had serviced "Mom and Pop" stores and bars in the New York metropolitan area; Falstaff's choices of distributors for Ballantine products in the New Jersey and

---

[6] [5] Falstaff argues that a trend line projecting the declining volume of Ballantine's sales since 1966, before IFC's purchase, would show an even worse picture. We agree with plaintiff that the percentage figures since 1974 are more significant; at least the judge was entitled to think so.

[7] [6] "Even if Falstaff's financial position had been worse in mid-1975 than it actually was, and even if Falstaff had continued in that state of impecuniosity during the term of the contract, performance of the contract is not excused where the difficulty of performance arises from financial difficulty or economic hardship. As the New York Court of Appeals stated in *407 E. 61st St. Garage, Inc. v. Savoy Corp.*, 23 N.Y.2d 275, 281, 296 N.Y.S.2d 338, 344, 244 N.E.2d 37, 41 (1968):

'(W)here impossibility or difficulty of performance is occasioned only by financial difficulty or economic hardship, even to the extent of insolvency or bankruptcy, performance of a contract is not excused.' (Citations omitted.)"

particularly the New York areas, where the chosen distributor was the owner of a competing brand; its failure to take advantage of a proffer from Guinness-Harp Corporation to distribute Ballantine products in New York City through its Metrobeer Division; Falstaff's incentive to put more effort into sales of its own brands which sold at higher prices despite identity of the ingredients and were free from the $.50 a barrel royalty burden; its failure to treat Ballantine products evenhandedly with Falstaff's; its discontinuing the practice of setting goals for salesmen; and the general Kalmanovitz policy of stressing profit at the expense of volume. In the court's judgment, these misfeasances and nonfeasances warranted a conclusion that, even taking account of Falstaff's right to give reasonable consideration to its own interests, Falstaff had breached its duty to use best efforts. . . .

Falstaff levels a barrage on these findings. The only attack which merits discussion is its criticism of the judge's conclusion that Falstaff did not treat its Ballantine brands evenhandedly with those under the Falstaff name. We agree that the subsidiary findings "that Falstaff but not Ballantine had been advertised extensively in Texas and Missouri" and that "[i]n these same areas Falstaff, although a 'premium' beer, was sold for extended periods below the price of Ballantine," while literally true, did not warrant the inference drawn from them. Texas was Falstaff territory and, with advertising on a cooperative basis, it was natural that advertising expenditures on Falstaff would exceed those on Ballantine. The lower price for Falstaff was a particular promotion of a bicentennial can in Texas, intended to meet a particular competitor.

However, we do not regard this error as undermining the judge's ultimate conclusion of breach of the best efforts clause. While that clause clearly required Falstaff to treat the Ballantine brands as well as its own, it does not follow that it required no more. With respect to its own brands, management was entirely free to exercise its business judgment as to how to maximize profit even if this meant serious loss in volume. Because of the obligation it had assumed under the sales contract, its situation with respect to the Ballantine brands was quite different. The royalty of $.50 a barrel on sales was an essential part of the purchase price. Even without the best efforts clause Falstaff would have been bound to make a good faith effort to see that substantial sales of Ballantine products were made, unless it discontinued under clause 2(a)(v) with consequent liability for liquidated damages. *Cf. Wood v. Duff-Gordon*, 222 N.Y. 88, 118 N.E. 214 (1917) (Cardozo, J.). Clause 8 imposed an added obligation to use "best efforts to promote and maintain a *high* volume of sales. . . ." (Emphasis supplied.) Although we agree that even this did not require Falstaff to spend itself into bankruptcy to promote the sales of Ballantine products, it did prevent the application to them of Kalmanovitz' philosophy of emphasizing profit *uber alles* without fair consideration of the effect on Ballantine volume. Plaintiff was not obliged to show just what steps Falstaff could reasonably have taken to maintain a high volume for Ballantine products. It was sufficient to show that Falstaff simply didn't care about Ballantine's volume and was content to allow this to plummet so long as that course was best for Falstaff's overall profit picture, an inference which the judge permissibly drew. The burden then shifted to Falstaff to prove there was nothing significant it could have done to promote Ballantine sales that would not have been financially disastrous.

[Ed. Note: The court then approved the trial judge's method for computing royalties on the lost sales.]

Affirmed.

NOTES AND QUESTIONS

1. Note that in *Bloor* the "best efforts" obligation was imposed by a clause in the agreement between the parties. Section 2-306(2) requires that the parties use their best efforts in an exclusive dealing contract, "unless otherwise agreed." In *HML Corp. v. General Foods Corp.*, 365 F.2d 77 (3d Cir. 1966), the court found that there was no

obligation to use "best efforts." In that case, the contract contained an integration clause. The agreement's failure to provide that the defendant would use his best efforts and energy to promote the product indicated to the court that no such obligation existed. Because the evidence showed that the defendant was greatly concerned about the plaintiff's obligation to market the product, the court decided that the omission of a best efforts clause was an indication that the parties had "otherwise agreed." Moreover, knowledgeable commercial attorneys representing both parties had drafted the agreement. Does this case make sense in light of the role of gap-filling provisions?

2. Is *Bloor* a § 2-306(1) or § 2-306(2) case? What was the source of the "best efforts" obligation: the contract, § 2-306(2), or both? Would the same analysis pertain regardless of the source of the best efforts obligation?

MDC CORP. v. JOHN H. HARLAND CO.

United States District Court, Southern District of New York

228 F. Supp. 2d 387 (2002)

OPINION AND ORDER

MUKASEY, Chief Judge.

In this diversity action, plaintiffs Artistic Greetings, Inc. ("Artistic") and MDC Corporation, Inc. ("MDC") sue John H. Harland Company ("Harland"), seeking a judgment declaring that a covenant not to compete in an agreement between Harland and Artistic is enforceable against Artistic only and unenforceable against MDC or any other party. Harland counterclaims, alleging breach of contract against Artistic and tortious interference with a contract against MDC. Artistic and MDC move to dismiss the counterclaims pursuant to Fed. R. Civ. P. 12(b)(6). For the reasons stated below, the motion is denied.

I.

The following facts are alleged in the complaint and the amended answer and counterclaims ("Counterclaims"); the facts taken from the counterclaims are accepted as true for the purposes of this motion. Harland sells checks and other financial forms to financial institutions. Harland is a Georgia corporation and maintains its principal place of business in Decatur, Georgia. Artistic sells checks directly to consumers. Artistic is a Delaware corporation and maintains its principal place of business in Joppa, Maryland. MDC, through its divisions and subsidiaries, prints and sells checks, postage stamps, credit cards, and transaction services. MDC is organized under the laws of Ontario, Canada and maintains its principal place of business in Toronto, Canada.

Harland and Artistic entered into three written agreements on or about August 29, 1996 ("the Agreements") — a Master Agreement, a Fulfillment Agreement, and an Agreement to Purchase Equipment ("Equipment Agreement"). Under the Fulfillment Agreement, Artistic agreed to purchase its requirements of checks from Harland during the term of the Agreements and Harland agreed to supply Artistic's check requirements for direct sale to consumers.

Section 8.2 of the Master Agreement bars Harland from competing with Artistic in the direct mail market. Section 8.2(a) provides that:

neither [Harland] nor any of its Affiliates shall engage, directly or indirectly, on its own account, or as a shareholder, agent, officer, director, partner or joint venturer in any corporation or business entity, in any business engaged in the direct mail marketing of checks and/or direct mail sale of checks from, at or into the United States (a "Competing Business"), nor within the same area to lend money or otherwise furnish services to any Competing Business.

* * *

Section 8.2(b) restricts Harland from entering the consumer check business by giving Artistic the right to buy any competing business acquired by Harland within 15 days of the acquisition. (Master Agreement § 8.2(b).) Section 8.2(c), in addition to granting Artistic an option to buy Harland's interest in The Check Store, Inc. ("CSI") for any price that a third party might offer Harland, also permits Harland to maintain its ownership interest in CSI provided that CSI:

> place only such advertising as shall have been committed prior to the date of this Agreement, which in any event shall not exceed $500,000, any other advertising of any kind by CSI shall be prohibited and [Harland] will use its reasonable best efforts to cause CSI to cancel and/or terminate any committed advertising which can be terminated without penalty; and to not expand its business in any way beyond the servicing of initial orders and reorders. . . .

In addition to placing restrictions on Harland, Section 8.2(a) also identifies certain Harland businesses that the Master Agreement does not cover:

> Notwithstanding the foregoing, nothing in this Agreement shall restrict the right of [Harland] to continue to conduct its business as presently conducted which involves relationships with: (a) catalog companies which place, and/or distribute catalogs containing; ads for distinctive, premium priced checks which are produced and designed by [Harland]; (b) large affinity groups which sell ad space in their publications in which [Harland] advertises such affinity group's specialty checks; (c) third party marketing groups which promote distinctive, premium priced checks and whereby [Harland] provides entry, printing and customer service for such groups; (d) financial software companies where [Harland] provides private label order fulfillment and direct mail campaigns to those companies' customers; and (e) direct mail companies where [Harland] provides order fulfillment and/or provides supplies.

Artistic and Harland also included the following "Covenant not to Compete" in Section 8.2 of the Master Agreement, which restricts Artistic's ability to enter supply relationships with banks:

> For the period from the Closing Date to eighteen (18) months following the termination of the Fulfillment Agreement, [Artistic] agrees that, without the consent of [Harland], neither [Artistic] not any of its affiliates shall engage, directly or indirectly, on its own account, or as a shareholder, agent, officer, director, partner or joint venturer in any corporation or business entity, in any business engaged in the entering into of direct contractual relationships with banking institutions . . . to supply check products to customers of such banking institutions in the United States.

Pursuant to agreements dated December 21, 1997, MDC, through its subsidiaries, acquired Artistic. At the time of the acquisition, MDC knew of Artistic's obligations under the three agreements, and it accepted and adopted the Agreements when and after it acquired Artistic. Although Harland and Artistic initially expected Artistic's check requirements to increase substantially during the term of the agreements, Artistic did not increase its purchases from Harland. Instead, at the behest of MDC, Artistic diverted its check sales to other affiliates of MDC and dramatically reduced its check product purchases from Harland. Additionally, at the behest of MDC, Artistic decreased the frequency of advertising for its check products in favor of increased advertising for the check products of affiliates. As a result, Harland has not recouped the cost of equipment purchased from Artistic.

Upon learning of MDC's planned acquisition of Artistic in 1997, Harland gave notice to MDC of an alleged anticipatory breach of the Agreements. Harland informed MDC that Harland would consider any agreement by MDC or any of its subsidiaries or divisions to supply checks to U.S. banking institutions to be a "clear violation" of the covenant not to compete and that Harland would seek to enjoin performance under any such agreement.

Artistic and MDC filed the initial complaint in this action on June 28, 2001. The complaint seeks a declaration that the covenant not to compete in § 8.2(d) of the Master Agreement is enforceable only against Artistic, an injunction barring any attempt by Harland to enforce § 8.2(d) of the Master Agreement against any person other than Artistic, and MDC's and Artistic's costs and reasonable attorney's fees. Harland counterclaims, alleging breach of contract against Artistic on two grounds: breach of the implied obligation to use best efforts in an exclusive dealing contract and breach of the implied covenant of good faith in a requirements contract. Harland also alleges that MDC tortiously interfered with its contract with Artistic. Artistic and MDC now move, pursuant to Fed. R. Civ. P. 12(b)(6), to dismiss Harland's counterclaims on the ground that they fail to state a claim upon which relief can be granted. The parties agree that New York law controls and that this court has personal jurisdiction over the parties.

* * *

III.

Harland first alleges that Artistic breached the Agreements by violating the covenant of best efforts that is implied at law in an exclusive dealing contract. New York's version of the Uniform Commercial Code ("UCC") governs contracts for the sale of goods. *Canusa Corp. v. A & R Lobosco, Inc.*, 986 F. Supp. 723, 727 (E.D.N.Y. 1997). Under the UCC, "[a] lawful agreement by either the seller or the buyer for exclusive dealing in the kind of goods concerned imposes unless otherwise agreed an obligation by the seller to use best efforts to supply the goods and by the buyer to use best efforts to promote their sale." N.Y. UCC § 2-306(2) (McKinney 2001). On its face, this provision could be interpreted to mean that any party to a requirements contract has an implied obligation to use best efforts, because a requirements contract obligates the buyer to buy exclusively from a particular supplier. *See* 1 W. HAWKLAND, UCC SERIES § 2-306:3 (2001) ("By their very nature, output and requirements contracts involve exclusive dealing."). However, an Official Comment to section 2-306 indicates that the duty to use best efforts applies only to buyers who receive the benefit of an exclusive commitment from a supplier, and not to buyers that merely commit to purchase from a single seller. *See* N.Y. UCC § 2-306, cmt. 5 ("Under such contracts the *exclusive agent* is required, although no express commitment has been made, to use reasonable effort and due diligence in the expansion of the market or the promotion of the product, as the case may be.") (emphasis added).

The relatively sparse case law interpreting section 2-306(2) of the UCC supports the conclusion that the duty to use best efforts applies to exclusive agents only, and not to all requirements buyers. *See Tigg Corp. v. Dow Corning Corp.*, 962 F.2d 1119, 1125 (3d Cir. 1992); *Gestetner Corp. v. Case Equip. Co.*, 815 F.2d 806, 811 (1st Cir. 1987); *Kubik v. J. & R. Foods of Or., Inc.*, 282 Or. 179, 183, 577 P.2d 518, 520 (1978). In distinguishing between pure requirements contracts and exclusive agency agreements under section 2-306(2), courts have reasoned that when a requirements contract does not obligate the supplier to sell particular goods to one customer alone, the buyer's efforts (or lack thereof) do not necessarily affect the supplier. If the buyer reduces its requirements, the supplier can solicit orders from other buyers. *See Tigg*, 962 F.2d at 1125. On the other hand, in an exclusive dealing arrangement, when the supplier has only one customer in a designated market, that customer's requirements represent all of the supplier's sales in that market. *See id.*

Artistic contends that Harland's best efforts claim should be dismissed based on Section 8.2 of the Master Agreement. Section 8.2(a) prevents Harland from engaging in the direct mail marketing or sale of checks in the United States. Section 8.2(b) restricts Harland from entering the consumer check business by acquisition, and Section 8.2(c) imposes strict limits on Harland's subsidiary CSI's advertising and marketing to consumers. At the same time, as Section 8.2(a) makes explicit, Harland may maintain supply relationships with catalog companies that market premium checks, "large affinity groups" to which Harland sells specialty checks, "third party marketing groups" to which Harland provides entry, printing, and customer service, "financial software companies where [Harland] provides private label order fulfillment and direct mail campaigns to those companies' customers" and "direct mail companies where [Harland] provides order fulfillment and/or provides supplies."

According to Artistic, because Section 8.2(a) permits Harland to maintain these discrete supply relationships, Artistic is not Harland's exclusive agent and therefore has no implied obligation to use best efforts in promoting Harland's products. Harland, however, contends that Section 8.2, with its severe restrictions on Harland's direct marketing and sales of checks, has made Artistic Harland's exclusive sales outlet to check customers in the direct channel of distribution.

To grant Artistic's motion to dismiss, this court would have to conclude that, as a matter of law, a requirements contract that allows a supplier to sell goods to any party other than the designated buyer is not an exclusive dealing contract for the purposes of N.Y. UCC § 2-306(2). That is different from holding that an exclusive dealing contract does not exist where a manufacturer maintains the right to sell products generally to other customers after meeting a particular customer's requirements. *See Logan Co. v. BRT Corp.*, No. 91-851, 1992 U.S. Dist. LEXIS 15255 (E.D. Pa. Oct. 7, 1992) (refusing to infer a "best efforts" obligation where a manufacturer could sell scanners to other customers after selling 50 scanners to a single buyer). Here, pursuant to Section 8.2 of the Master Agreement, Harland has agreed to forego competition in a specified market. Without any additional evidence as to the commercial impact of this provision, to grant Artistic's motion to dismiss would be to conclude that the contract creates no "exclusive dealing" arrangement between Harland and Artistic no matter how much the restrictions on Harland's direct sales affect its business, and despite the preclusion of Harland from competing in the direct mail market.

New York pre-Code law, as well as cases from other jurisdictions interpreting section 2-306(2), counsel against such a brittle interpretation of "exclusive dealing." In *Wood v. Lucy, Lady Duff-Gordon*, 222 N.Y. 88, 118 N.E. 214 (1917) (Cardozo, J.),[8] a sales agent sued his principal for breach of contract, claiming that the principal violated his exclusive right to place the principal's endorsements on the designs of others. The principal defended on the ground that there was no consideration for her promise of exclusivity because the agent had made no express commitment to market the designs. Rejecting the principal's argument, the Court found that the principal's promise was supported by consideration, because the agent had promised implicitly to use reasonable efforts to market the principal's endorsements. To reach this conclusion, the Court did not simply focus on the exclusive privilege granted to the agent to promote the

---

[8] [3] It is widely recognized that section 2-306(2) of the UCC codified the New York Court of Appeals's holding in *Wood. See* N.Y. UCC § 2-306 annots. (McKinney 2002) ("Subsection (2) is apparently based on *Wood v. Lucy, Lady Duff-Gordon.*"); *Tigg*, 962 F.2d at 1125 (treating the statutory provision and the holding in *Wood* as equivalent); *Fusion, Inc. v. Neb. Aluminum Castings*, No. 95-2366, 1997 U.S. Dist. LEXIS 1163, 1997 WL 51227, at *19 (D. Kan. Jan. 23, 1997) (describing section 2-306(2) as a codification of *Wood*'s implied covenant to use best efforts); *Flight Concepts Ltd. v. Boeing Co.*, 819 F. Supp. 1535, 1552 (D. Kan. 1993) (treating the statutory provision and the holding in *Wood* as equivalent); *Feld v. Henry S. Levy & Sons, Inc.*, 37 N.Y.2d 466, 470, 335 N.E.2d 320, 322, 373 N.Y.S.2d 102, 105 (1975) ("Section 2-306 is consistent with prior New York case law."); *Beautis Prods. Co. v. Chromatic Corp.*, 1978 WL 23479 (N.Y. Sup. Ct. July 6, 1978) (treating the statutory provision and the holding in *Wood* as equivalent). The Court's suggestion in *Fakhoury Enterprises v. J.T. Distributors*, No. 94 Civ. 2729, 1997 U.S. Dist. LEXIS 7667, 1997 WL 291961, at *3 (S.D.N.Y. June 2, 1997), that "unlike the *Wood* case itself, which relied on a number of circumstances to support an inference of an implied promise, under the UCC, an obligation is implied by the existence of an exclusivity term alone," is inconsistent with this substantial authority.

principal's endorsements of clothing designs. Rather, the Court also emphasized that the agent formed a business for the sole purpose of promoting Lady Duff-Gordon and that Lady Duff-Gordon's compensation for her endorsements was based solely on the profits resulting from the agent's efforts. After declaring that, "[w]e are not to suppose that one party was to be placed at the mercy of the other," the Court found that "without an implied promise, the transaction cannot have such business efficacy as both parties must have intended that at all events it should have," *Wood*, 222 N.Y. at 91, 118 N.E. at 214 (citations omitted).

Cases interpreting section 2-306(2) also suggest that, for the purpose of deciding whether to impose an implied best efforts obligation on a buyer of goods, an exclusive dealing relationship should not be mechanically defined as a relationship in which a supplier has only one outlet for every good that it produces. Courts have supplied a term calling for best efforts where buyers were given an exclusive right to sell a supplier's product in a prescribed territory. *See Fusion, Inc. v. Neb. Aluminum Castings*, No. 95-2366, 1997 U.S. Dist. LEXIS 1163, 1997 WL 51227, at *20 (D. Kan. Jan. 23, 1997); *Jo-Ann, Inc. v. Alfin Fragrances, Inc.*, 731 F. Supp. 149, 158 (D.N.J. 1989); *Thermal Systems of Ala., Inc. v. Sigafoose*, 533 So. 2d 567, 571 (Ala. 1988); *Rocka v. Gipson*, 3 Ark. App. 293, 625 S.W.2d 558 (Ark. Ct. App. 1981). In each of these cases, the supplier relied on a distributor in a specified territory only; if the distributor did not perform, the supplier could sell goods to any outlet outside the territory. In *Fusion*, moreover, the supplier was allowed to bypass its exclusive agent to deal directly with individual "house accounts," and yet the Court imposed a best efforts obligation on the agent. *Fusion*, 1997 U.S. Dist. LEXIS 1163, 1997 WL 51227, at *20.

Finally, in *Tigg*, the requirements contract (that the Court interpreted to include an implied obligation to use best efforts) allowed the supplier Tigg to sell to other buyers if Dow Corning failed to buy a specified minimum number of units. *See Tigg*, 962 F.2d at 1125. Nevertheless, the Court, reasoning that the provision allowing Tigg to sell products to other buyers became effective only if Dow Corning failed to buy the mandatory minimum number of units, concluded that the contract was an exclusive dealing arrangement and that Dow Corning had an implied obligation to use best efforts in promoting Tigg's goods. *Id.* at 1125–26. The *Tigg* Court thus supplied a best efforts term in favor of a manufacturer whose exclusive dealing obligation arose only after the buyer purchased a specified number of units. Here, by contrast, the exclusive dealing obligation in the direct mail market is binding without regard to any minimum purchase by Artistic.

The common thread linking *Wood*, the territorial exclusivity cases, and *Tigg* is that these courts have not framed the inquiry, as Artistic would have this court do, as whether a supplier has no potential outlets other than a single designated buyer. Rather, in determining whether an exclusive dealing arrangement exists, these courts have focused on the hold that one commercial party has over another in a particular market.

Artistic's proposed interpretation of the exclusive dealing requirement of section 2-306(2) as a requirement that the contract preclude any supply relationship with other parties is too rigid. To impose a best efforts obligation on Artistic, Harland must demonstrate that Section 8.2 of the Master Agreement puts Harland "at the mercy of" Artistic in a particular market. Although Harland may not be able to make this showing, this court cannot decide, based on the pleadings and the text of the Agreements alone, that the Agreements do not constitute an exclusive dealing arrangement.

IV.

Harland alleges also that Artistic breached the Agreements by violating the covenant of good faith that is implied at law in a requirements contract for the sale of goods. Under New York law, every contract includes an implied covenant of good faith. *See, e.g., Apfel v. Prudential-Bache Sec., Inc.*, 183 A.D.2d 439, 439, 583 N.Y.S.2d 386, 387 (1st Dep't 1992), *modified on other grounds and aff'd*, 81 N.Y.2d 470, 600 N.Y.S.2d 433, 616

N.E.2d 1095 (1993). This implied covenant is not distinct from the underlying contract, *see Geler v. Nat'l Westminster Bank USA*, 770 F. Supp. 210, 215 (S.D.N.Y. 1991), nor can it imply new or inconsistent terms into the contract, *see Bibeault v. Advanced Health Corp.*, No. 97 Civ. 6026, 1999 U.S. Dist. LEXIS 7173, 1999 WL 301691, at *8 (S.D.N.Y. May 12, 1999). Thus, "[a]s a general rule, '[t]he cause of action alleging breach of [the implied covenant] is duplicative of a cause of action alleging breach of contract.' " *OHM Remediation Servs. Corp. v. Hughes Envtl. Sys., Inc.*, 952 F. Supp. 120, 124 (S.D.N.Y. 1997) (quoting *Apfel*, 183 A.D.2d at 439, 583 N.Y.S.2d at 387). To the extent that Harland's good faith claim rests on Artistic's alleged breach of its implied best efforts obligation (*see* Counterclaims ¶41 ("Artistic has breached its . . . good faith and cooperation obligations to Harland . . . by failing to use its best efforts.")), the claim is duplicative.

If Harland claimed only that Artistic breached its implied covenant of good faith by failing to use best efforts, Harland's good faith claim would be facially insufficient. However, Harland alleges also that, by reducing its orders and diverting business to affiliates of MDC, Artistic breached the implied covenant of good faith that section 2-306(1) imposes on requirements buyers. . . .

Applying the plain language of the provision, courts have held uniformly that a buyer may not in good faith demand disproportionately *more* than the buyer's anticipated requirements, as measured by a stated estimate or normal or otherwise comparable prior requirements. *See Empire Gas Corp. v. Am. Bakeries Co.*, 840 F.2d 1333, 1337 (7th Cir. 1988) ("This limitation is fairly easy to understand when the disproportion takes the form of the buyer's demanding more than the amount estimated. If there were no ceiling, and if the price happened to be advantageous to the buyer, he might increase his 'requirements' so that he could resell the good at a profit."); *Orange and Rockland Utils., Inc. v. Amerada Hess Corp.*, 59 A.D.2d 110, 114, 397 N.Y.S.2d 814, 818 (2d Dep't 1977) (applying New Jersey law) ("There is . . . a good deal of pre-Code case law on the requirement of 'good faith'. It is well settled that a buyer in a rising market cannot use a fixed price in a requirements contract for speculation.").

However, courts have had difficulty applying section 2-306(2) to cases in which a buyer seeks to obtain *less* than an anticipated or normal quantity of goods. On its face, the "unreasonably disproportionate" provision appears to apply to increases and decreases alike, as it does not distinguish between the buyer who raises his require-ments and the buyer who lowers them. Further, there is language in the Official Comments pointing to symmetrical treatment of overdemanding and underdemanding cases: "the agreed estimate is to be regarded as a center around which the parties intend the variations to occur." N.Y. UCC § 2-306, cmt. 3.

On the other hand, another Official Comment states that "good faith variations from prior requirements are permitted even when the variation may be such as to result in discontinuance." N.Y. UCC § 2-306, cmt. 2. Because a reduction of orders to zero would be, under many circumstances, unreasonably disproportionate to prior output or requirements, this comment suggests that the proviso does not apply when a require-ments buyer decreases its orders. Comment 2 is also consistent with the common law approach, *see HML Corp. v. Gen. Foods*, 365 F.2d 77, 81 (3d Cir. 1966) (applying New York pre-Code law) ("[T]he seller assumes the risk of all good faith variations in the buyer's requirements even to the extent of a determination to liquidate or discontinue the business."), from which section 2-306(1) was not intended to depart, *see id.*, n.5; Note, *Requirements Contracts: Problems of Drafting and Construction*, 78 HARV. L. REV. 1213, 1220 (1965).

Two state appellate courts have applied this part of section 2-306(1) to deviations both above and below stated estimates. *See Simcala, Inc. v. Am. Coal Trade, Inc.*, 821 So.2d 197 (Ala. 2001); *Romine v. Savannah Steel Co.*, 117 Ga. App. 353, 354, 160 S.E.2d 659, 660–61 (1968). However, most authorities, including several circuit courts, have declined to apply it to decreases in orders and held instead that a requirements buyer may decrease its orders, as long as it does so in good faith. *See Brewster of Lynchburg, Inc. v. Dial Corp.*, 33 F.3d 355, 365 (4th Cir. 1994); *Empire Gas*, 840 F.2d at 1337–38; *R.A. Weaver and Assocs., Inc. v. Asphalt Constr., Inc.*, 587 F.2d 1315, 1322 (D.C. Cir. 1978).

The one court that has directly applied New York's version of section 2-306(1) to requirements contracts has also exempted decreases in orders from the "unreasonably disproportionate" proviso and concluded that "when a buyer takes less than the stated estimate in a requirements contract, the sole test is good faith." *Dienes Corp. v. Long Island R.R.*, No. 01 Civ. 4272, 2002 U.S. Dist. LEXIS 6824, 2002 WL 603043, at *5 (E.D.N.Y. Mar. 19, 2002). Moreover, another federal court, applying New York law to output contracts, borrowed directly from *Empire Gas*'s analysis of requirements contracts to conclude that, "in an output contract, the buyer takes the risk that the seller may reduce its production to zero." *Canusa Corp. v. A & R Lobosco, Inc.*, 986 F. Supp. 723, 729–30 (E.D.N.Y. 1997).

Finally, without specifically addressing the asymmetry between the treatment of increases and decreases in orders, several courts applying New York law have found that a requirements buyer need only act in good faith when reducing its purchases under a requirements contract. *E.g., Laing Logging, Inc. v. Int'l Paper Co.*, 228 A.D.2d 843, 846, 644 N.Y.S.2d 91, 94 (3d Dep't 1996); *Abrasive-Tool Corp. v. Cystic Fibrosis Found.*, No. 88 Civ. 1314S, 1991 U.S. Dist. LEXIS 7198, 1991 WL 97445, at *4 (W.D.N.Y. May 6, 1991).

For a breach of contract claim based on section 2-306(1) of the UCC to succeed, therefore, the plaintiff must demonstrate more than that the defendant reduced its buying under a requirements contract. Ultimately, Harland must demonstrate that Artistic had no legitimate business reason for reducing its orders. *See NCC Sunday Inserts, Inc. v. World Color Press, Inc.*, 759 F. Supp. 1004, 1009 (S.D.N.Y. 1991) (applying Illinois' version of the UCC) ("In resolving the question of good faith, there is no established standard. . . . The proper inquiry requires an analysis of the buyer's subjective motives to determine if it had a legitimate business reason for eliminating its requirements, as opposed to a desire to avoid its contract."); *see also Brewster*, 33 F.3d at 365–66 (finding that a party to a requirements contract is not acting in bad faith if it has a business reason for scaling back its requirements); *Empire Gas*, 840 F.2d at 1339 (same).

Artistic contends that Harland's good faith claim should be dismissed because Harland and Artistic could have put a minimum requirements term in the contract, but chose not to do so. However, this argument ignores the relevant authority discussed above, under which a good faith term is implied in requirements contracts, notwithstanding the absence of a mandatory minimum. By alleging that Artistic has drastically reduced its check requirements as part of a concerted plan to divert purchases from Harland, Harland has adequately pleaded bad faith, and is entitled to prove that Artistic had no legitimate business reason for reducing its purchases.

* * *

For the reasons stated above, plaintiffs' motion to dismiss defendant's counterclaims for failure to state a claim is denied.

QUESTIONS

1. What is the difference between a requirements contract and an exclusive dealing contract? Can an output contract be an exclusive dealing contract? What is the seller's interest in an exclusive dealing contract?

2. Note the first three words of subsection 2-306(2). The enforcement of output, requirements, or other exclusive dealing contracts is also affected by federal and state antitrust laws. Such arrangements may violate § 3 of the Clayton Act, 15 U.S.C. § 14;

the Sherman Act, 15 U.S.C. §§ 1, 2; or the Federal Trade Commission Act, 15 U.S.C. § 45.

PROBLEM 3-4

Briganti, Inc. operates a business known as the Crushed Toast Company. Semolina Products, Inc. is engaged in the wholesale bread baking business. The parties entered into a written contract under which the defendant agreed to sell, and the plaintiff to purchase, "all bread crumbs produced by Semolina in its factory at 115 Thames Street, Brooklyn, New York." The parties further agreed that the contract was to "be deemed automatically renewed thereafter for successive renewal periods of one year" with each party reserving the right to cancel by giving not less than six months' notice to the other by certified mail.

The term "bread crumbs" is a term of art that refers to a product manufactured from stale or imperfect loaves of bread by removing the labels, processing the bread through two grinders, inserting the bread into a drum in an oven for toasting, and, finally, bagging the finished product. Unused bread that has not been cut and toasted in this manner would not be considered "bread crumbs."

Semolina sold to Briganti over 250 tons of bread crumbs, but Semolina ceased bread crumb production on May 15, 2008 without any notice to Briganti. Semolina's comptroller testified that the oven was too large for the toasting drum, and therefore, that the operation was "very uneconomical." However, he also admitted that Semolina took no steps to obtain equipment that could operate economically. Semolina completely dismantled the oven in the summer of 2008, and used the space previously occupied by the oven as a computer room. It appears, without dispute, that Semolina indicated to Briganti at different times that Semolina would resume bread crumb production if Briganti agreed to modify the contract price from 6 cents per pound to 7 cents per pound. After the crumb making machinery was dismantled, Semolina sold its stale and imperfect loaves of bread to animal food manufacturers.

Semolina contends that the contract did not require it to manufacture bread crumbs, but merely required that it sell any manufactured bread crumbs to Briganti. Briganti argues that Semolina breached its agreement by ceasing production of the bread crumbs.

Does this problem raise issues under § 2-306(1), § 2-306(2), or both? How would you analyze the problem?

B. WARRANTIES

Warranty terms relate to the character or quality of the goods being sold. An agreement that seller's light bulbs will burn for at least 10,000 hours is a warranty; an agreement that the light bulbs will be delivered on June 1 is not a warranty, although it is a term of the agreement. Article 2 provides that the parties may agree to warranty terms, called express warranties, but it also provides certain warranties as "gap-fillers" that are implied, but may be disclaimed by agreement. We consider each warranty in turn.

1. Express Warranties

Section 2-313(1) provides that express warranties may be created by an affirmation of fact, promise, description, sample, or model. It might be more accurate to term these "agreed" warranties, as they do not require formal words, nor even an express agreement that a warranty is created. Section 2-313(2) distinguishes express warranties from "an affirmation merely of the value of the goods," or "merely the seller's opinion or commendation of the goods." In the first section, we consider whether an express warranty has been created, or whether the claimed warranty is nothing more than salesmanship by the seller. In the second section, we consider the import of the elusive requirement that the express warranty "becomes part of the basis of the bargain," as specified in § 2-313.

a. Creation of an express warranty

Section 2-313 clearly signals an intention to break away from formal requirements for the creation of a warranty. As a result, like most issues under Article 2, the analysis largely is factual in nature. Determine whether the following cases provide sufficient guidance for investigating the facts to determine, if a warranty has been created by the seller.

EWERS v. EISENZOPF

Wisconsin Supreme Court

276 N.W.2d 802 (1979)

COFFEY, Justice.

The plaintiff-appellant appeals from a judgment dismissing his action against the owner of the Verona Rock Shop. The plaintiff brought the action seeking to recover damages for the death of 17 tropical fish in his salt water aquarium. The action was commenced in the small claims court of Dane county, County Judge Harry E. Larsen, presiding. The county court dismissed the case and made a finding that neither an express nor an implied warranty was created in the purchase of certain sea shells, coral and a driftwood branch from the rock shop. The judgment appealed to the circuit court for Dane county was affirmed by Circuit Judge Michael B. Torphy, presiding.

The plaintiff-appellant, an aquarium hobbiest, purchased a salt water aquarium and fish in June 1975. The defendant-respondent, the proprietor of the Verona Rock Shop, sold an assortment of rocks, jewelry, lapidary supplies, novelties, and sea shells. On August 10th of 1975, the plaintiff selected several sea shells, a piece of coral and a driftwood branch at the defendant's shop for use in his aquarium. Before paying for the merchandise, Ewers' friend asked the sales clerk if the items selected were "suitable for placement in a salt water aquarium." The part-time sales clerk with 3 years' experience at the rock shop replied "They had come from salt water and that they were suitable for salt water aquariums, if they were rinsed." The plaintiff purchased the items and returned to his home where he rinsed the shells, coral, and branch for twenty minutes in a salt and tap water solution. Within one week after placing the shells, coral, and branch in the tank, the plaintiff's 17 fish died.

The plaintiff discussed this problem with Ed Duren who owns the hobby shop where the plaintiff had purchased the aquarium and fish. Duren, after inspecting the tank, found the water polluted. He testified that he removed several sea shells from the tank and upon examination found they emitted a toxic odor. Duren stated at trial it was his opinion that the fish died as a result of this toxic matter released into the water by the decay of the creatures inhabiting the shells and coral. Duren explained that the decaying matter can be removed from the shells and coral by a week-long cleansing process which consists of soaking the items in boiling water.

The trial court dismissed the small claims action on each ground of express and implied warranty. . . . Dealing with the express warranty claim, the trial court said:

> . . . I cannot find that there was an express warranty in this case upon a fish hobbiest . . . asking a young clerk whether . . . shells . . . were suitable for use in a salt water aquarium and gave the reply that they were suitable, if properly rinsed. I cannot find that that constitutes an express warranty that these . . . shells . . . were expressly warranted to be suitable for the type of fish and the type of aquarium this plaintiff had.

The decision of the circuit court in affirming the trial court, notes the testimony of Mr. Duren stating that the shells should have been voided of decaying organic matter before being placed in the aquarium. The circuit court summarily affirmed the lower court's opinion on the implied warranty issue and stated, in reference to an express warranty:

" . . . Neither the questions nor the answers to them are so clear and definite so as to constitute such a warranty."

"Suitability for usage in a salt water tank is not so concise as to promise suitability with any or all such fish and plants as might be placed in such a tank. (It might even be argued, however, that the answer to the question put was not in error for the method described by Duren for curing shells is little more than an extended rinsing or soaking.)"

Issues:

1. Whether the seller's statement that certain goods were "suitable for salt water aquariums, if they were rinsed" constitutes an express warranty under sec. 402.313, Stats.?

2. Whether there is an implied warranty: fitness for a particular purpose pursuant to sec. 402.315, Stats., when a seller is asked whether the items the buyer selected are "suitable for placement in a salt water aquarium?"

The Uniform Commercial Code's provision relating to the creation of an express warranty in a sales transaction has been codified in sec. 402.313, Wis. Stats. . . .

It should be pointed out that although sec. 402.313(2) does not require the magic words of "warrant" or "guarantee" to establish an express warranty, a buyer has the burden of proving the purchase was consummated on the basis of factual representations regarding the "title, character, quantity, quality, identity, or condition of goods." *A.A. Baxter Corp. v. Colt Industries, Inc.*, 10 Cal. App. 3d 144, 88 Cal. Rptr. 842, 847 (1970); *see Hagenbuch v. Snap-On-Tools Corp.*, 339 F. Supp. 676, 680 (D.C.N.H. 1972).

In the present case, the circuit court found that an express warranty was not made as the plaintiff's question and the sales clerk's answer were not "so clear and definite so as to constitute a warranty." However, sec. 402.313(1), Stats., does not require a warranty to be stated with any degree of preciseness, only that the seller's statements are an affirmation of fact "that the goods shall conform to the affirmation or promise." Sec. 402.313(1), Stats. Further, it has already been noted that "No technical or particular words need be used to constitute an express warranty, yet whatever words are used must substantially mean the seller promises or undertakes to insure that certain facts are, or shall be, as he represents them." *Naaf v. Griffitts*, 201 Kan. 64, 439 P.2d 83, 85 (1968). In the case before us, the statement by the sales clerk that the shells, coral and branch were "suitable for salt water aquariums, if they were rinsed" is an affirmation of fact regarding the quality and condition of the goods sold.

The second element required to establish an express warranty is that the affirmation of fact pertaining to the goods being purchased must become "a basis of the bargain." Sec. 402.313(1), Stats. The statutory language "a *basis* of the bargain" does not require the affirmation to be the sole basis for the sale, only that it is *a* factor in the purchase. The official Uniform Commercial Code Comments to § 2-313 explains that the seller's intent to establish a warranty and the buyer's reliance on the affirmation are not determinative as to whether the representation is a basis of the bargain:

"No specific intention to make a warranty is necessary, if any of these factors is made part of the basis of the bargain. In actual practice affirmations of fact made by the seller about the goods during a bargain are regarded as part of the description of those goods; hence no particular reliance on such statements need be shown in order to weave them into the fabric of the agreement. Rather, any fact which is to take such affirmations, once made, out of the agreement requires clear affirmative proof. The issue normally is one of fact." *See Sessa v. Riegle*, 427 F. Supp. 760 (E.D. Pa. 1977) and "Express Warranties and Greater

Consumer Protection from Sales Talk" 50 Marq. L. Rev. 88 (1966).

In *Pritchard v. Liggett & Myers Tobacco Co.*, C.A. 1965, 350 F.2d 479, *cert. den.*, 382 U.S. 987, *opinion amended*, 370 F.2d 95, *cert. den.*, 386 U.S. 1009, it was recognized that the seller's intent and the buyer's reliance were irrelevant to a determination of whether an express warranty had been made. The Court set forth a workable test for finding whether an express warranty has been created:

> "The true test is not whether the seller actually intended to be bound by his statement but rather whether he made an affirmation of fact *the natural tendency of which was to induce the sale and which did in fact induce it.*" *Id.* at 487. (emphasis supplied.)

In this appeal the plaintiff purchased the shells, coral, and branch for use in his aquarium. Certainly, the sales clerk's representations regarding the suitability of the goods induced Ewers to purchase the shells, coral, and branch, for if these items were not suitale for the fish tank the plaintiff would not have consummated the transaction.

Additionally, we cannot agree with the circuit court that the curing or cleansing process detailed by Edward Duren to make the shells satisfactory for use is the same as the colloquial meaning of the word "rinsed." Had the seller more thoroughly described the required cleansing process of submerging the items in boiling water for a period of a week, we would be reaching a different result and affirming the judgments of the lower courts. But in the instant case, the goods did not and could not conform to the seller's affirmation of suitability for their intended use, even though the plaintiff followed the seller's vague directions regarding the cleansing process.

We hold the seller's statements constituted an express warranty when the seller specifically stated the merchandise would be suitable for use in the aquarium after rinsing. Therefore, the buyer in this particular fact situation is entitled to recover as the terms of the warranty were not fulfilled. The fact that the defendant's shop does not primarily cater to buyers of aquarium equipment and that the shop owner is relatively inexperienced in the field, does not relieve him of liability. In *Cagney v. Cohn*, 13 U.C.C. Rep. 998 (D.C.S. Ct. 1973), the seller's lack of experience in the field was held inconsequential to the determination of whether a warranty was made during the sale of a defective motorcycle, the court stating:

> "The particular statements made during the sales negotiations and the surrounding circumstances of this sale have been carefully considered by the Court, since the defendant seller is neither a motorcycle expert nor a dealer. Nevertheless, such a lay status does not exempt the defendant from § 2-313 of the Uniform Commercial Code."

> "Section 2-313 addresses itself to assertions made by the seller which become part of the basis of the bargain. Paragraph 8 of the official comments to § 2-313 states that it must be determined '[w]hat statements of the seller have in the circumstances and objective judgment become part of the basis of the bargain?' And in answer thereto, the commentators declare that 'all of the statements of the seller do so, unless good reason is shown to the contrary.'"

Id. at 1003. The record in this case is void of any indication that the purchaser did not exercise good judgment in purchasing the merchandise based upon the seller's representations.

* * *

Courts of this state should carefully consider and evaluate the circumstances surrounding transactions where there is a claim made of an express warranty in a sale. Judicial decisions must not inhibit the free flow of relevant information between the buyer and the seller. Nevertheless, a merchant must be cautious in going beyond "puffing" in making claims and representations about their product. Further, the seller must give specific directions when he claims the goods are suitable for an intended and limited use. A merchant's vague or incomplete directions will induce the purchase of merchandise and often these directions are as misleading as when erroneous affirmations of fact are given. A merchant who knows the limitations of his product will bear no liability, as long as he is truthful and accurate in his representations to the consumer.

. . . Judgment reversed and cause remanded for proceedings consistent with this opinion.

CALLOW, Justice (Dissenting).

In reversing the trial court, the majority finds the seller's statement that the rocks would be suitable for use in the plaintiff's salt water aquarium if rinsed to be an affirmation of fact which became the basis of the bargain, creating an express warranty under sec. 402.313, Stats. The majority holds: (1) there was an express warranty; and (2) the seller breached the warranty. In my opinion, the record supports neither conclusion.

The trial court and the circuit court on appeal found that the seller's statement did not constitute an express warranty. The trial court did not set forth its reasoning in detail, but one may infer that it believed the statement to be too vague to constitute an affirmation of fact forming the basis of the bargain within the meaning of sec. 402.313, Stats. The circuit court explicitly determined that "[n]either the questions nor the answers to them are so clear or definite so as to constitute such a warranty."

Ordinarily, the question whether a statement constitutes an express warranty is a question of fact. . . . Thus, trial court's finding should not be upset, unless against the great weight and clear preponderance of the evidence. . . . Where the evidence admits of more than a single inference, we must accept the inferences drawn by the trial court. . . . I believe the majority ignores these principles in reaching its decision. Here, the buyer asked the sales clerk in a rock shop if the items he selected were suitable for a salt water aquarium, without mentioning fish. Her answer, "yes, if they were rinsed," was a qualified and conditional response. Therefore, the buyer was put on notice that the items purchased were not suitable for that purpose in their existing state. The buyer elected not to pursue further inquiry to determine why the items were not suitable for use in a salt water tank in their present condition, did not ask the seller to what extent rinsing was necessary nor what rinsing accomplished to make them suitable for his intended use, did not ask about their effect on fish, and did not specify that his was a closed system aquarium.

This case concerns a merchant dealing in rocks not aquarium accessories. There is no holding out of special expertise on the subject of aquarium supplies by the seller. Between buyer and seller, the only one having any apparent experience with an aquarium is the buyer. The record conclusively shows the seller stated the items were not usable in a salt water aquarium, unless they were rinsed. The sale occurred notwithstanding this admonition. We do not have an affirmation of fact, but instead a cautionary instruction. The buyer bought the items accepting the obligation to do that which would be necessary to make them usable. Since the items were acknowledged by both parties to be unusable for the buyer's purpose in the form in which they were offered for sale, it was the buyer's duty to pursue an inquiry as to the reasons they were unsuitable for his purpose and to seek reasonably specific instructions concerning the treatment necessary to make them usable. Such information was reasonably available. After the fish died, upon inquiry plaintiff was told by Edward Duren, the proprietor of the store where he bought his fish and fish tank, that these items are made usable by extended rinsing and soaking.

Thus, the evidence amply supports a finding that there was no affirmation of fact by the seller becoming part of the bargain. I believe the majority recognizes as much in the last paragraph of the opinion: "A merchant's vague or incomplete directions will induce the purchase of merchandise and often these directions are as misleading *as when erroneous affirmations of fact are given*." (Emphasis added.) I believe sec. 402.313, Stats., requires "erroneous affirmations of fact," and nothing less, as a condition precedent to recovery. If ever a seller was caught between a rock and a hard place, this is the classic case. Here, there was a vague exchange which should have put the buyer on notice that the goods were unsuited in their present state for the intended use. The trial court's finding is supported by the record.

The majority's second holding — that the warranty was breached — is equally unsound. Because the trial court and circuit court on appeal found that there was no warranty, there was no need for these courts to reach the question of breach. The circuit court did state, however:

> Suitability for usage in a salt water tank is not so concise as to promise suitability with any or all such fish and plants as might be placed in such a tank. *(It might even be argued, however, that the answer to the question put was not in error for the method described by Duren for curing shells is little more than an extended rinsing or soaking.)*

(Emphasis added.) In making what amounts to a finding of fact that the warranty was breached, the majority compounds the error of determining that there was an express warranty in the inconclusive exchange between the plaintiff and the defendant's sales clerk: Where there is no definite affirmation of fact, how is one to determine that there has been a breach of the supposed warranty? I agree with the trial court's suggestion that a reasonable person might conclude that the seller's general admonition was correct. If anything, the buyer failed to comply with the condition of any "affirmation."

Assuming there was an express warranty, as the majority holds, the evidence does not show that the defendant breached it. The rocks and shells would have been suitable for the plaintiff's use had the plaintiff rinsed them in the manner he later ascertained to be appropriate. My view of the record would be different had there been an express trial court finding that plaintiff fully complied with the condition.

A "yes but" or a "no unless" representation by a seller should shift the burden to the buyer to get the specifics of the treatment necessary to make the item usable for the buyer's purposes. Unless he does, he buys at his peril. If instructions to make the item adaptable are given by the seller to the buyer, the buyer must show reasonable conformance with the instructions before he makes out a prima facie case of breach. Such a requirement will cause consideration by both parties of the potential problems involved in the qualified usability. Since the buyer is in the best position to know the specific use contemplated, it should be his duty to seek specific instructions on making the item adaptable.

The trial court and the circuit court on appeal found that no promise or affirmation of fact was made by the seller to the buyer which formed the basis for the bargain under sec. 402.313, Stats. That finding is not against the great weight and clear preponderance of the evidence. The buyer, having specific notice of unsuitability, bought at his peril and should suffer the consequential loss. Moreover, the evidence shows no breach of any representation. The trial court properly dismissed the action.

I am hereby authorized to state that DAY, J., joins in this dissenting opinion.

QUESTIONS

1. In *Sessa v. Riegle*, 427 F. Supp. 760 (E.D. Pa. 1977), *aff'd*, 568 F.2d 770 (3d Cir. 1978), the seller of a horse represented that the animal was a "good one" and "sound." The court concluded that the seller's words constituted an opinion or commendation rather than an express warranty. Whether the language constitutes a warranty or mere opinion or commendation depends on the circumstances of the sale and the type of goods sold. Because horses are fragile creatures, susceptible to myriad maladies, detectable and undetectable, the court found that it was customary in the horse trade for sellers not to give a warranty, except in special circumstances, and that the buyer protected itself by examining the horse at the point of sale. Does this case provide any

additional guidance in how courts distinguish between express warranties and mere "puffing" or "sales talk"?

2. In *Ewers*, what effect did the clerk's caution that the rocks should be rinsed have on the creation of the warranty? Does such a cautionary statement place the buyer on notice that further investigation is required?

ENGLAND v. LEITHOFF
Nebraska Supreme Court
323 N.W.2d 98 (1982)

WHITE, Justice.

This is an appeal in a law action from the judgment of the District Court for Buffalo County, Nebraska, in favor of the plaintiff-appellee for $1,789.03 and costs of $427.06. The District Court affirmed the judgment of the Buffalo County Court. The errors assigned are essentially that the decision is contrary to the law and is not supported by the evidence.

*   *   *

The suit arose out of the purchase by the plaintiff, James England, of eight bred gilts (female pigs). The sale took place on April 21, 1979. The seller of the gilts was the defendant, Robert A. Leithoff. England purchased the gilts in response to an advertisement Leithoff ran in the Grand Island Independent newspaper. England contacted Leithoff and the price was fixed at $1,760 for all eight, or $220 each. England testified that Leithoff informed him "that he had got them from a friend auctioneer of his and I said if these come off of the salebarn or out of the salebarn, I don't want them and upon his answer, they had not come from a salebarn." England testified that if he had known the gilts had been sold at a sale barn, he would not have purchased them. The gilts had, in fact, been purchased by Leithoff at a sale barn in Sargent, Nebraska, on April 13, 1979. The gilts appeared to be healthy on delivery on April 21, 1979, and were placed on clean ground at England's farm. The first gilt delivered on April 24, 1979, within 3 days of the purchase, and all 9 pigs were dead at birth. Four more gilts delivered within 24 hours and all pigs were born dead. Eleven pigs were ultimately delivered alive from the eight gilts.

Shortly after the delivery of the first gilt, England contacted Robert Hinke, a livestock equipment dealer from Axtell, Nebraska. Hinke testified that he was born and raised on a farm and had raised hogs practically all his life. Further, he had been a partner with a veterinarian and had worked as a veterinarian's assistant, assisting in diagnosis and treatment of diseases of hogs. Hinke testified that he had attended seminars run by veterinarians from Iowa State University and Purdue University relating to animal care, and has read extensively on the subject. Hinke drove to the England farm and observed the gilts that had just given birth to the dead pigs. He observed excessive saliva at the mouth and heavy mucous drainage of the vagina, and the piglets were premature, gaunt, and their hair was shorter than normal. Over objection, he was allowed to testify that the gilts were suffering from a swine disease called leptospirosis. Hinke took two of the dead piglets to Dr. Glen Nickelson of the Holdrege Veterinary Clinic. Dr. Nickelson examined the pigs internally and externally, and observed that the lungs were flat, indicating that the pigs were born dead. Hinke related his observations of the gilts. Dr. Nickelson testified that in his opinion the gilts suffered from leptospirosis, a disease that destroys the value of gilts as breeding stock and results in either aborted dead pigs or stunted pigs that fail to gain weight or reach market weight as do pigs born of healthy gilts. He further testified that leptospirosis has an incubation period of from 5 to 21 days, and that the gilts suffered from the disease at the time they were delivered to the England farm.

Hinke further testified that hog producers would not purchase gilts from a sale barn because "Where they run so many hogs through salebarns, it is inevitable that you can

. . . that you can take hogs that are well and run them through a salebarn and they will pick up a disease from the manure if nothing else in the pens and the alleys and therefore farmers who buy breeding stock . . . there are very few that I know of that would even take the risk of buying from a salebarn for brood stock in hogs." Hinke further testified that he would never recommend to a customer to buy gilts from a sale barn, and that, in view of the risk, his opinion of the value of a bred sow from a sale barn was that "they would have to pay me to take a bred sow out of a salebarn."

England introduced a regulation of the state Department of Agriculture adopted April 14, 1975, pursuant to Neb. Rev. Stat. §§ 54-1157 to 54-1186, 54-1701 to 54-1711, and 54-2001 to 54-2019 (Reissue 1978), which provides at (3)(c)(i)(E):

> Swine released from a market or concentration point shall be confined on the premises of the purchaser for thirty (30) days separate from all other swine. . . .

Although plaintiff urges that a private cause of action is created by the regulation in favor of purchasers from buyers who violate this regulation, in view of our decision here we need not pass on the point, and do not do so. Neb. UCC § 2-313 (Reissue 1980) provides:

> (1) Express warranties by the seller are created as follows: (a) Any affirmation of fact or promise made by the seller to the buyer which relates to the goods and becomes part of the basis of the bargain creates an express warranty that the goods shall conform to the affirmation or promise.

In discussing actions on warranties arising under Neb. UCC §§ 2-313, 2-314, and 2-315 (Reissue 1980), WHITE & SUMMERS, UNIFORM COMMERCIAL CODE § 9-1 at 326 (2d ed. 1980), observes that a lawyer with a warranty case:

> First . . . must prove that the defendant made a warranty, express or implied, under 2-313, 2-314, or 2-315. Second, he must prove that the goods did not comply with the warranty, that is, that they were defective at the time of the sale. Third, he must prove that his injury was caused, "proximately" and in fact, by the defective nature of the goods. . . . Fourth, he must prove his damages.

England brought suit on the theory of breach of an express warranty, and not fraud. The trial court found and the evidence supports the finding that Leithoff warranted that the gilts did not come from a sale barn. However, it is not sufficient that a statement is made in connection with a contract for the sale of goods; the statement, in order to constitute an express warranty, must be "related to the goods." Subsection (1)(b) of § 2-313 provides:

> Any description of the goods which is made part of the basis of the bargain creates an express warranty that the goods shall conform to the description.

Larutan Corp. v. Magnolia Homes Manuf. Co., 190 Neb. 425, 209 N.W.2d 177 (1973).

Is a representation that farm animals came from a private source and not from a public market related to the goods? We are persuaded by the reasoning of the Kansas Supreme Court in *Young & Cooper, Inc. v. Vestring*, 214 Kan. 311, 521 P.2d 281 (1974). In that case, the seller brought suit to recover the purchase price of cattle. The jury returned a verdict for the seller and the buyers appealed, urging that the trial court erred in refusing to instruct the jury on its claim that the seller made express warranties concerning the cattle, which were not true. Among the representations made at trial, according to the testimony of the buyers, were "That the cows were a choice quality Angus breeding herd; it was their second calf crop; they were *all one brand of cattle* . . . they originated from San Angelo, Texas, (which according to the [buyers] indicated good quality cattle). . . ." *Id.* at 315, 521 P.2d at 285. The cattle had a disappointing calving season, and after testing a number of them were discovered to have brucellosis. While testing the cows, the veterinarian discovered that 43 of the 450 cows bore Louisiana ear tags. The area in San Angelo, Texas, was shown to be a modified brucellosis-free zone.

In reversing the trial court and remanding for a new trial, the Kansas Supreme Court observed:

> There was evidence from which the jury could find that this herd of cows was not as expressly warranted. There was abundant evidence that the herd in question was not a stable, or one brand herd. Forty-three head of animals in this herd tested by the veterinarians were found to have originated in Louisiana, and they were traced to be transient heifers in Louisiana. There was also evidence of fresh brands on these cows in the pasture at the time they were tested, indicating that cows had been recently added to the herd prior to purchase by the Vestrings.

*   *   *

> Oral representations that a herd of cows possesses these qualities are representations of fact which constitute express warranties.

Id. at 326–27, 521 P.2d at 292–93.

Although the facts indicate other and more sweeping representations than present in this case, nevertheless, the clear holding of the Kansas Supreme Court is that representations of origin of livestock made in the course of the sale of livestock are express warranties relating to the livestock. "One of the primary tests of whether a given representation is a warranty or a mere expression of opinion is whether the seller assumed to assert a fact of which the buyer was ignorant or whether the seller merely expressed a judgment about a matter as to which each party could be expected to have an opinion." Annot., 94 A.L.R.3d 729, 730 (1979).

"It is the general rule of law that a warranty is express when the seller makes an affirmation with respect to the article to be sold, pending the agreement of sale, upon which it is intended that the buyer shall rely in making the purchase." *Naaf v. Griffitts*, 201 Kan. 64, 66, 439 P.2d 83, 85 (1968).

Here, both parties testified that Leithoff led England to believe that the gilts were not from a sale barn. England also testified that he would not have purchased the gilts if he knew they came from a sale barn because "I didn't want anything that was brought through a salebarn."

We believe, as did the trial court, that Leithoff led England to believe that he was buying gilts that had not come from a sale barn and that this constitutes an affirmation of fact with respect to the gilts which was part of the basis of the bargain. England relied on Leithoff's representations when he purchased the gilts.

The evidence supports the decision of the trial court. The proximate cause of the damages was adequately shown. Relying on Leithoff's representations, England purchased bred gilts that were suffering from leptospirosis. The incubation period coincides with the time Leithoff purchased the gilts from the sale barn. There was also testimony that the risk of contracting the disease is increased by exposure to a public market.

The defendant does not assign the amount of damages as error. We can find no error in the trial court's decision; therefore we affirm.

AFFIRMED.

QUESTIONS

1. Did Leithoff make a promise to England about the gilts? Is a promise necessary to create an express warranty? How does the court distinguish between a warranty and a "mere expression of opinion"? Would an express warranty arise if a buyer stated, "this truck will certainly be able to pull my trailer," and the seller responded, "I agree, that truck will pull that trailer"?

2. Assume that England had proved that the gilts, in fact, were purchased at a sale barn, but that the incubation period for the infection as measured from the date of

delivery to the sale barn had not passed. Alternatively, assume that England had kept the pigs at a stockyard for a week after the purchase. What effect would these new facts, if any, have on a breach of warranty claim? Which of the four elements of a warranty claim cited by the court would be affected by these new facts?

b. Part of the basis of the bargain

It is not enough that the seller create an express warranty through its language or conduct; § 2-313 provides that a warranty is not enforceable as such unless it "becomes part of the basis of the bargain." Some early courts assumed that some measure of reliance by the buyer was necessary to make the warranty effective as part of the basis of the bargain, but modern courts have rejected this reading as being inconsistent with the purposes of § 2-313. Read the following case and determine what, if anything, replaces reliance as the guiding determinant of what has become part of the basis of the bargain.

RITE AID CORP. v. LEVY-GRAY
Maryland Court of Appeals
894 A.2d 563 (2006)

Battaglia, J.

In the case *sub judice*, a jury returned a verdict against Rite Aid Corporation, the petitioner, for breach of express warranty based on a package insert that it generated and provided with a prescription pharmaceutical, doxycycline, directing the respondent, Ellen Levy-Gray, to "take with food or milk if upset stomach occurs." Because, based on the facts of the instant case, we determine that the jury reasonably could infer that the language "take with food or milk if upset stomach occurs" constitutes an express warranty under Maryland Code (1975, 2002 Repl. Vol.), Section 2-313 of the Commercial Law Article, we affirm the judgment of the Court of Special Appeals.

Background

On October 25, 2000, Dr. Ronald Geckler, the head of Infectious Diseases at Mercy Medical Center, diagnosed Ms. Levy-Gray with Lyme disease and gave her a prescription for doxycycline, a drug that is part of the group of Tetracycline-based drugs. Dr. Geckler informed Ms. Levy-Gray that while taking doxycycline she could not continue nursing her son, but provided no other instructions as to how she should take the doxycycline. Ms. Levy-Gray filled her prescription at the Rite Aid Pharmacy # 4465, located at 12224 Tullamore Road, in Timonium, Maryland, which she stated she chose because of prior dealings with that store, as well as the fact that Rite Aid was a national chain of pharmacies. Rite Aid obtained the doxycycline at issue from Watson Laboratories, Inc. of Corona, California (Watson), which is not a party to this action. Watson shipped the doxycycline in bottles containing 500 capsules and included an eight-page pamphlet which the manufacturer had submitted to the United States Food and Drug Administration (FDA) and which had been approved by that agency as "labeling" for that prescription drug. The pamphlet from Watson provided in pertinent part:

> If gastric irritation occurs, it is recommended that doxycycline be given with food or milk.

The doxycycline received by Ms. Levy-Gray was accompanied by an instruction and information pamphlet, known as a "patient package insert" (PPI), entitled "Rite Advice." The "Rite Advice" pamphlet was drafted for Rite Aid by First Data Bank Corporation, which is not a party to the case *sub judice*. The cover page of the pamphlet informed readers: "Inside is everything you need to know about your prescription. It covers everything in writing from dosage to side effects. If you have any questions, just ask your pharmacist." The inside of the pamphlet stated, in part:

IMPORTANT NOTE: THE FOLLOWING INFORMATION IS IN-
TENDED TO SUPPLEMENT, NOT SUBSTITUTE FOR, THE EXPER-
TISE AND JUDGMENT OF YOUR PHYSICIAN, PHARMACIST OR
OTHER HEALTHCARE PROFESSIONAL.

IT SHOULD NOT BE CONSTRUED TO INDICATE THAT USE OF
THE DRUG IS SAFE, APPROPRIATE, OR EFFECTIVE FOR YOU.

CONSULT YOUR HEALTHCARE PROFESSIONAL BEFORE USING
THIS DRUG.

*   *   *

HOW TO TAKE THIS MEDICATION: Take each dose with a full glass of
water (4 oz. or 120 ml) or more. Do not lie down for at least 1 hour after taking
this drug. Take with food or milk if stomach upset occurs unless your doctor
directs you otherwise. Avoid taking antacids, containing magnesium, aluminum
or calcium, sucralfate, iron preparations, or vitamin (zinc) products within 2–3
hours of taking this medication. These products bind with the medication
preventing its absorption. . . .

*   *   *

The information in this leaflet may be used as an educational aid. This
information does not cover all possible uses, actions, precautions, side effects, or
interactions of this medicine. This information is not intended as medical advice
for individual problems[.]

Ms. Levy-Gray took the first dose of doxycycline on October 26 with water. According
to Ms. Levy-Gray's testimony, the following day she started taking the medication with
milk because she had experienced an upset stomach. While continuing to take the drug,
Ms. Levy-Gray also consumed a large quantity of dairy products including eight to ten
glasses of milk per day, macaroni and cheese, grilled cheese sandwiches, yogurt, ice
cream, and cottage cheese, as she testified, in an effort to maintain her breast milk to
resume nursing her son after her treatment ended. During this time, according to Ms.
Levy-Gray's testimony, she experienced no alleviation of her symptoms from Lyme
disease.

Upon advice from her brother, a urological oncologist, Ms. Levy-Gray stopped taking
the doxycyline with dairy products. Although Ms. Levy-Gray's symptoms improved
within two or three days of discontinuing consumption of dairy products in conjunction
with the doxycycline, she did not fully recover and was referred by Dr. Christine
Lafferman, her internist, to Dr. Charles A. Haile, the Chief of Medical Staff and Chief
of the Division of Infectious Diseases at Greater Baltimore Medical Center, who is board
certified in internal medicine and infectious diseases. Ms. Levy-Gray met with Dr. Haile
on December 28, 2000. When a second six-week course of doxycycline failed to
ameliorate Ms. Levy-Gray's symptoms, Dr. Haile diagnosed her with post-Lyme
syndrome, which is a chronic autoimmune response in which patients experience
symptoms that mimic Lyme disease without an active bacterial infection.

On November 2, 2001, Ms. Levy-Gray filed a complaint in the Circuit Court for
Baltimore County against Rite Aid seeking relief based on the theories of negligence,
product liability, failure to warn, negligent misrepresentation, and breach of express
warranty. Her husband asserted a claim for loss of consortium. Ms. Levy-Gray alleged
that her consumption of milk and other various dairy products while taking the
doxycycline, consistent with the information provided by Rite Aid, reduced the
absorption of the drug and prevented it from operating as effectively as possible,
thereby proximately causing her post-Lyme syndrome.

On December 10, 2001, Rite Aid filed a motion to dismiss the complaint for failure to state a claim upon which relief could be granted because the statements contained in the "Rite Advice" pamphlet did not constitute an express warranty and the fact that the particular Rite Aid store involved in the case was not a proper party to the suit. The court granted the motion with respect to the Rite Aid store and denied the motion regarding the express warranty issue on February 25, 2002. Rite Aid thereafter filed a motion for summary judgment arguing that it could not be held liable under negligence, strict liability, or breach of express warranty under the facts of the case *sub judice*. On January 10, 2003, the trial judge denied the motion. Ms. Levy-Gray subsequently filed an amended complaint, which increased the *ad damnum* clause for compensatory damages to $2,500,000 and added a claim for $8,000,000 in punitive damages.

On May 20, 2003, the trial in the Circuit Court of Baltimore County before Judge John F. Fader II commenced and lasted seven days, wherein the jury heard copious testimony from expert witnesses called by both parties. Rite Aid's experts testified that the absorption of doxycycline might have been reduced by up to twenty percent when taken with milk or other dairy products, but that the reduction was clinically insignificant because the recommended dosage provided more of the drug than was necessary to treat the infection. Conversely, Ms. Levy-Gray's experts testified that doxycycline should not have been taken with dairy products and that Ms. Levy-Gray's consumption of milk with her medication caused her continued Lyme disease symptoms.

At the close of evidence, Judge Fader permitted the case to go to the jury on the theories of negligence and breach of express warranty and dismissed the remainder of the claims. The court presented the jury with the following instructions:

* * *

There is also a cause of action for express warranty, again, focusing on the Rite Aid advice. That is the contract type of action. An express warranty is a representation about a product by the seller to a buyer when the buyer relies upon the representation in purchasing the product. Any statement of fact made by the seller to the buyer about the product is an express warranty that the product conforms to the statement or promise made. The promise or statement may be oral or in writing. No particular words are necessary to create an express warranty, nor is it necessary that the seller use formal words such as warranty or guarantee or that the seller have a specific intention to make a warranty.

The attorneys are going to talk to you about that Rite Aid Rite Advice pamphlet. The Plaintiffs are going to say and argue to you that this constituted an express warranty. The Defendants are going to refer to the same paper and argue to you that it did not.

You will see the pamphlet, the warranty, and listen to the differences of opinion, factual and expert witnesses and then we ask you to answer this second question alleging breach of warranty: Do you find in favor of Rite Aid Corporation or in favor of Ellen R. Levy-Gray.

The jury found in favor of Rite Aid on the negligence claim and found in favor of Ms. Levy-Gray with respect to the breach of express warranty claim in the amount of $250,000. After the Circuit Court denied Rite Aid's post-judgment motions including a motion for judgment n.o.v., Rite Aid filed a notice of appeal with the Court of Special Appeals seeking review of the jury's determination that it was liable for breach of express warranty, and Ms. Levy-Gray filed a cross-appeal premised upon her assertion that the trial court erred in failing to give the jury an instruction on Rite Aid's failure to warn her about the contraindication of doxycycline and calcium containing products.

In a published opinion, the Court of Special Appeals determined that Ms. Levy-Gray established reliance on the information contained in the "Rite Advice" pamphlet due to her course of dealing with the pharmacy and her continued confidence in Rite Aid to provide facts concerning her prescription that were not furnished by her physician. *Rite*

Aid Corporation v. Levy-Gray, 162 Md. App. 673, 691–92, 876 A.2d 115, 126 (2005). Moreover, the Court of Special Appeals held that the statement in the "Rite Advice" pamphlet stating that doxycycline should be taken with food or milk in the event of upset stomach is a representation that a characteristic of doxycycline is that it is compatible with food or milk. The intermediate appellate court concluded that the issue of whether the general disclaimer accompanying the information in the "Rite Advice" pamphlet took doxycycline's compatibility with dairy out of the bargain was a question of fact for the jury to decide. The Court of Special Appeals also held that Ms. Levy-Gray did not have to be aware of the express warranty at the time of her purchase from Rite Aid for the warranty to be effective. Thus, the court determined that Rite Aid expressly warranted that doxycycline could be taken with milk without altering the drug's efficacy. Based on its analysis of the issues presented by Rite Aid, the Court of Special Appeals concluded that it did not have to address the question raised by Ms. Levy-Gray in her cross-appeal.

On July 18, 2005, Rite Aid filed a petition for writ of certiorari with this Court and presented the following questions for our review:

1. Whether a pharmacy can be held liable on a theory of express warranty for information and advice furnished with a prescription drug;

2. Whether instructions on how to use a product, delivered to the customer after the product is paid for, which the customer is unaware of prior to the sale and which makes no promise of the product's performance, fulfills the requirements for an express warranty under Section 2-313 of Maryland's Commercial Law Article that the statement be "an affirmation of fact or promise made by the seller that relates to the goods" and that the affirmation be "part of the basis of the bargain."

On September 8, 2005, we granted the petition and issued the writ. *Rite Aid v. Levy-Gray*, 388 Md. 673, 882 A.2d 286 (2005). We conclude that under the facts present in the case at bar, Rite Aid may be held liable for breach of express warranty. Moreover, we determine that, under the circumstances of the case *sub judice*, the jury reasonably could infer that the instruction "take with food or milk if upset stomach occurs" in the "Rite Advice" pamphlet constitutes an express warranty under Maryland Code (1975, 2002 Repl. Vol.), Section 2-313 of the Commercial Law Article. Therefore, we affirm the judgment of the Court of Special Appeals.

Discussion

Rite Aid argues that the statements contained in the "Rite Advice" pamphlet cannot be part of the basis of the bargain because the decision to purchase the doxycycline was based solely on the advice of Ms. Levy-Gray's prescribing physician and that it is protected from liability due to the "learned intermediary" doctrine, which governs the relationship between physicians, patients, and pharmacists. Rite Aid also contends that the statements about doxycycline contained in the "Rite Advice" pamphlet were not part of the basis of the bargain because Ms. Levy-Gray did not receive them and was not aware of their existence until after the sale was completed. Rite Aid asserts that the advice to take doxycycline with milk if the stomach is upset unless otherwise directed by a physician is not an affirmation about the drug that can give rise to an express warranty because it was not a statement that use with milk was invariably appropriate for all consumers.

Conversely, Ms. Levy-Gray contends that the statements contained in the "Rite Advice" pamphlet were part of the basis of the bargain because of her previous course of dealing with Rite Aid and her reliance on the information that she received from Rite Aid. Ms. Levy-Gray also argues that the advice to "[t]ake with food or milk if stomach upset occurs, unless your doctor directs you otherwise" is an affirmation that doxycycline is compatible with milk and can give rise to an express warranty. She asserts that Rite Aid not only warranted that doxycycline was compatible with milk, but also expressly warranted the completeness and correctness of its information and advice contained in the "Rite Advice" pamphlet.

Can Rite Aid Be Held Liable for Breach of Express Warranty

The threshold issue that we must address is Rite Aid's argument that the sale of pharmaceuticals is qualitatively different from the sale of other goods, such that pharmacies cannot be held liable for breach of express warranties under the Uniform Commercial Code. Although courts in our sister jurisdictions consistently have declined to impose the Uniform Commercial Code implied warranties of fitness and merchantability because they have determined that the prescribing of medication is an aspect of the delivery of medical services, *see Elsroth v. Johnson & Johnson*, 700 F. Supp. 151 (S.D.N.Y. 1988); *Coyle v. Richardson-Merrell, Inc.*, 526 Pa. 208, 584 A.2d 1383 (1991); *Murphy v. E.R. Squibb & Sons, Inc.*, 40 Cal. 3d 672, 221 Cal. Rptr. 447, 710 P.2d 247 (1985), Rite Aid has failed to produce a single case that stands for the proposition that pharmaceuticals may not be the subject of an express warranty.

* * *

A prescription drug satisfies the definition of "goods" as explicated in Maryland Code . . . Prescription drugs are "movable at the time of identification to the contract for sale." Moreover, there is no reasonable basis upon which to distinguish between prescription drugs and other goods under the Uniform Commercial Code with respect to express warranties. Thus, because drugs are goods subject to sale, they may potentially be the subject of an express warranty. *See, e.g., Batiste v. American Home Prods. Corp.*, 32 N.C. App. 1, 231 S.E.2d 269 (1977) (holding that a drug manufacturer's sale of drugs to a plaintiff would fall within the purview of the UCC). Therefore, in light of the absolute lack of authority for distinguishing between prescription drugs and other goods for express warranty purposes, we conclude that we are not precluded as a matter of law from affirming the jury's verdict against Rite Aid on the basis of breach of express warranty.

* * *

The Statement at Issue Constituted An Express Warranty

[Ed. Note: The court then quotes § 2-313 and Comments 3 and 7.]

In the case *sub judice*, Ms. Levy-Gray alleges that the language "take [doxycycline] with food or milk if stomach upset occurs, unless your doctor directs you otherwise" constitutes an affirmative statement by Rite Aid that the doxycycline is compatible with the simultaneous consumption of milk or other dairy products, which constitutes an express warranty. Conversely, Rite Aid asserts that the information at issue cannot be considered an express warranty because it is derived from the FDA-approved language developed by the manufacturer of the doxycycline and was presented with the statement that "it should not be construed to indicate that use of the drug is safe, appropriate, or effective for you."

The similarity between Rite Aid's advice and that of Watson does not preclude Rite Aid's statement from constituting a warranty on its part. The language was Rite Aid's, and it was in no way attributed to Watson. Ms. Levy-Gray would necessarily assume that the advice was entirely that of Rite Aid. The jury reasonably could infer that Rite Aid represented to Ms. Levy-Gray that the doxycycline was compatible with milk consumption.

Moreover, we decline to hold that a general disclaimer would preclude any express warranty in this case as a matter of law, because a reasonable consumer could conclude that the general statement did not negate the effect of the more specific assertion as to the administration of the doxycycline when the entire document is read as a whole. From the language of the "Rite Advice" pamphlet, the jury could reasonably infer from the evidence introduced that the phrase "take with food or milk if upset stomach occurs," although not guaranteeing effectiveness, affirmed that milk would not adversely impact the efficacy of the drug. The issue of fact concerning the interplay between the general disclaimer and the administration instruction was properly before the jury and we must give deference "to the inferences a fact-finder may draw." *State v. Smith*, 374 Md. 527, 534, 823 A.2d 664, 668 (2003).

An affirmation of fact must become "part of the basis of the bargain" for the statement to be considered an express warranty. The term "bargain" is not defined in the Uniform Commercial Code, but is itself used in the definition of "agreement" in Maryland Code (1975, 2002 Repl. Vol.), Section 1-201(3) of the Commercial Law Article, which provides in pertinent part:

> "Agreement" means the bargain of the parties in fact as found in their language or by implication from other circumstances including course of dealing or usage of trade or course of performance as provided in Titles 1 through 10 of this article.

Rite Aid argues that for an affirmation to become "part of the basis of the bargain," the affirmation must be a negotiated term of the agreement, or the consumer must at least have been aware of its existence prior to the consummation of the deal. Based on the circumstances surrounding most purchases in modern commercial dealing, we disagree.

Official Comment 7 to Section 2-313 provides, "[t]he precise time when words of description or affirmation are made or samples are shown is not material. The sole question is whether the language . . . [is] fairly to be regarded as part of the contract." Md. Code (1975, 2002 Repl. Vol.), § 2-313 official cmt. 7 of the Commercial Law Article. The clear implication of Official Comment 7 is that express warranties may be formed prior to the completion of the sale or even after the sale has been consummated. What is paramount is the relationship between the sale of the goods and the affirmations made by the seller. Various commentaries on the Uniform Commercial Code have similarly recognized the reality that warranties are often given at the time of the sale such that the buyer does not become aware of their terms until after the sale is finished:

> As it is common knowledge that sellers will deliver written warranties after the contract has been made, some courts are recognizing that later statements found in these writings are part of the basis of the bargain.

3 Lary Lawrence, *Anderson on the Uniform Commercial Code*, § 2-313:66 at 60 (3d ed. 2002); *see also* James J. White & Robert S. Summers, *Uniform Commercial Code*, § 9-5 at 354–55 (5th ed. 2000).

We agree with the analysis explicated in *Murphy v. Mallard Coach Co.*, 179 A.D.2d 187, 582 N.Y.S.2d 528 (N.Y. App. Div. 3d Dep't 1992), in which the court rejected an argument identical to that presented by Rite Aid:

> [W]e believe that while the warranty was technically handed over *after* plaintiffs paid the purchase price, the fact that it was given to plaintiffs at the time they took delivery of the motor home renders it sufficiently proximate in time so as to fairly be said to be part of the basis of the bargain (*compare*, UCC 2-313, comment 7; 1 White and Summers, Uniform Commercial Code, § 9-5 at 448–455 [3d ed.]; *cf.*, *Marine Midland Bank v. Carroll*, 98 A.D.2d 516, 471 N.Y.S.2d 409). To accept the manufacturer's argument that in order to be part of the basis of the bargain the warranty must actually be handed over during the negotiation process so as to be said to be an actual procuring cause of the contract, is to ignore the practical realities of consumer transactions wherein the warranty card generally comes with the goods, packed in the box of boxed

items or handed over after purchase of larger, non-boxed goods and, accordingly, is not available to be read by the consumer until after the item is actually purchased and brought home. Indeed, such interpretation would, in effect, render almost all consumer warranties an absolute nullity.

Id. at 531.

This position also was adopted by the United States District Court for the Southern District of Indiana in *In re Bridgestone/Firestone, Inc. Tires Prods. Liability Litigation*, 205 F.R.D. 503 (S.D. Ind. 2001), *rev. on other grounds*, 288 F.3d 1012 (7th Cir. 2002). . . . [T]he court determined that the interpretation urged by the defendants in *In re Bridgestone/Firestone*, and by Rite Aid before this Court, " 'would, in effect, render almost all consumer warranties an absolute nullity,' inasmuch as it is common practice for warranty booklets to be provided to consumers inside the sealed box in which a product is packaged, or, in the case of vehicles, in the glove box of a new car upon delivery." *Id.* at 527 n. 31 (citation omitted).

* * *

Rite Aid attempts to distinguish these cases by arguing that the warranties were expressly labeled as such and that the warranties were actually remedial promises under Official Comment 11 to Section 2-313, which provides in pertinent part:

A promise about the quality or performance characteristics of the goods creates an express warranty if the other elements of a warranty are present, whereas a promise by which the seller commits itself to take remedial action upon the happening of a specified event is a remedial promise. The distinction has meaning in the context of the statute of limitations.

* * *

The concept of remedial promise is dealt with in a separate subsection to make clear that it is a concept separate and apart from express warranty and that the elements of an express warranty, such as basis of the bargain, are not applicable.

3 Lary Lawrence, *Anderson on the Uniform Commercial Code*, § 2-313:339 (3d ed. Supp. 2005).

We are not persuaded by Rite Aid's argument. Under the plain language of Maryland Code (1975, 2002 Repl. Vol.), Section 2-313(2) of the Commercial Law Article, "[i]t is not necessary to the creation of an express warranty that the seller use formal language such as 'warrant' or 'guarantee' or that he have a specific intention to make a warranty." Thus, the fact that the assertions contained in the "Rite Advice" pamphlet did not include language expressly indicating that the information listed therein was a warranty does not preclude a finding that it gave rise to an express warranty.

Furthermore, Rite Aid's reliance on Official Comment 11 to Section 2-313 of the Uniform Commercial Code, as enunciated in Anderson on the Uniform Commercial Code, is misplaced. The Maryland General Assembly has not adopted Official Comment 11 as part of the Official Comment that accompanies the Uniform Commercial Code in the Commercial Law Article, nor has the Legislature enacted any statute that recognizes "remedial promises" as distinct from express warranties. Moreover, the cases at issue analyze the terms of the written warranties in terms of express warranties, not "remedial promises." Thus, the reasoning remains persuasive.

Rite Aid also relies on the "learned intermediary" doctrine, which applies to the tripartite relationship between the drug manufacturer, the prescribing physician, and the patient, as supporting the proposition that pharmacists cannot be held liable for the breach of express warranty because the patient is presumed to have relied upon the advice rendered by her physician.

* * *

Although we adopted the "learned intermediary" doctrine in *People's Serv. Drug Stores* with respect to the ordinary pharmacist-patient relationship wherein the pharmacist merely fills the prescription as ordered by the physician, we decline to extend the doctrine to those cases in which the pharmacy is disseminating information concerning the properties and efficacy of a prescription drug. To extend the defense to the facts of the instant case to insulate the pharmacy from the consequences of its affirmative decision to distribute information and instructions contained that provide direction to the patients in a patient package insert is without legal justification. Therefore, we decline to hold as a matter of law that the "learned intermediary" doctrine precludes a pharmacy from being held liable for breach of express warranty when it provides a package insert that could provide the basis for such a warranty.

We cannot agree with Rite Aid's proposition that Ms. Levy-Gray relied solely on the expertise of Dr. Geckler, her prescribing physician, to describe the appropriate manner in which to take doxycycline as a matter of law. Dr. Geckler testified that he relied on Rite Aid to provide the necessary information to Ms. Levy-Gray. Based on Dr. Geckler's testimony that he did not provide Ms. Levy-Gray with guidance as to the administration of the doxycycline, the jury reasonably could have inferred that Ms. Levy-Gray similarly relied on the information furnished by Rite Aid with respect to doxycycline's characteristics and how it should be taken. Moreover, the jury further could have inferred from the evidence presented at trial that the language contained in the "Rite Advice" pamphlet encouraged Ms. Levy-Gray to rely on the information contained therein based upon its assertion on the cover that "[i]nside is everything that you need to know about your prescription;" thus, the statement "take with food or milk if upset stomach occurs" had the effect of warranting that for the duration of Ms. Levy-Gray's doxycycline treatment the doxycycline will not be adversely affected by her consumption of milk. Based on the facts of the case *sub judice*, the jury reasonably could have inferred that Ms. Levy-Gray relied on the veracity of Rite Aid's affirmation each time she took the dose of doxycycline with milk.

Conclusion

We determine that under the facts of the case at bar, pharmacies may be held liable for breach of express warranty under the Uniform Commercial Code. Furthermore, because we conclude that a jury reasonably could infer that Ms. Levy-Gray relied on the instruction "take with food or milk if upset stomach occurs" as an affirmation that doxycycline is compatible with dairy such that it became part of the basis of the bargain, and that therefore, the statement constituted an express warranty under Maryland Code (1975, 2002 Repl. Vol.), Section 2-313 of the Commercial Law Article, we affirm the judgment of the Court of Special Appeals.

JUDGMENT OF THE COURT OF SPECIAL APPEALS AFFIRMED. COSTS IN THIS COURT AND IN THE COURT OF SPECIAL APPEALS TO BE PAID BY THE PETITIONER.

Dissenting Opinion by HARRELL, J. which RAKER, J., Joins.

After searching this record in vain to locate a legally cognizable express warranty in Rite Aid's instructions to Ms. Levy-Gray for taking doxycycline, "[t]ake each dose with a full glass of water . . . [or] [t]ake with food or milk if stomach upset occurs unless your doctor directs you otherwise," I respectfully dissent.

A.

The pharmaceutical instruction for the modality of ingesting doxycycline if upset stomach occurred did not constitute an express warranty because the instructions were not part of the basis of the bargain and may not be said fairly to be part of the contract of sale. This Court has not analyzed before the "basis of the bargain" requirement of

§ 2-313(1)(a) and (b). The Majority's interpretation of § 2-313(1) disposes of this statutory requirement all together by its effective holding that an express warranty existed in the instructions contained in an enclosed pamphlet of drug information read by the purchaser after the purchase of the drug, but which would not have been a factor in the decision to buy even had she read it before the sale. The medication instruction, regardless of whether Ms. Levy-Gray knew of it before the purchase, could not have been part of the basis of the bargain between Rite Aid and her because it was neither a dickered term nor part of the contract. Ms. Levy-Gray purchased doxycycline because her doctor advised her to purchase it.[9] Thus, even assuming the instruction was a representation to Ms. Levy-Gray that the intended operative medicinal effectiveness of taking doxycycline was compatible with concurrent milk consumption at some level at the time of ingestion of the pill, as the Majority opinion characterizes it, the statement was not a representation that became part of the basis of the bargain as required by § 2-313(1).

A pharmacy should not be subject to liability, at least under a breach of express warranty theory, regarding statements about prescription drugs it dispenses on a doctor's order. As the United States District Court for the Southern District of New York aptly noted in its well-reasoned decision, *In Re Rezulin*, pharmacies do not play the role of retail merchant when selling prescription drugs to patients. *In Re Rezulin*, 133 F. Supp. 2d at 291–92 ("Patients who purchase prescription drugs from pharmacists do not negotiate or bargain with the pharmacist about the suitability of the product."). Every state appellate court that has considered whether to hold pharmacies liable under a breach of warranty theory with respect to the operative properties of prescription drugs also has declined to do so. . . . Instead, prescription drug sales are attributable to the advice of the patient's physician. Hence, the purchase of prescription drugs is fundamentally different from the purchase of other consumer goods. Because patients generally do not base their decision to purchase a prescription medication on the instructions for its consumption or use or any information contained in the informational pamphlet accompanying the prescription drug, such information is not part of the basis of the bargain, and, therefore, no express warranty is created thereby.

The more appropriate theory of liability under which pharmacies may be held accountable for the instructions for use of a prescription medication is negligence. *See* Restatement (Third) of Torts: Products Liability § 6(e)(2) (1998) (providing that a retail seller of a prescription drug is subject to liability for harm caused by the drug if "at or before the time of sale or other distribution of the drug [] the retail seller or other distributor fails to exercise reasonable care and such failure causes harm to persons").[10] The purpose of the theory of liability for breach of an express warranty is not served by applying it to a pharmacy because a pharmacy does not make representations that induce patients to purchase a particular prescription drug. If a pharmacy breaches a duty to the buyer to provide the drug indicated on the prescription or supplies inaccurate instructions, then it may be held liable in negligence. In Ms. Levy-Gray's case, she failed to convince the jury that Rite Aid was negligent, an issue not preserved for appeal (although she effectively may have convinced the Majority that Rite Aid was negligent).

---

[9] [3] Ms. Levy-Gray's prescribing physician testified that had Ms. Levy-Gray asked him, he would have given the same advice to take the doxycycline with food or milk if upset stomach occurred when taking it with water only. Of even greater factual significance is the absence of any discussion between Ms. Levy-Gray and the Rite Aid pharmacist regarding her intended additional consumption of atypical amounts of dairy products during the on-going period of time she was taking the medication, over and above a mere glass of milk with each pill.

[10] [5] Even under a negligence theory of recovery, Comment h and Illustration 4 to Restatement (Third) of Torts: Prod. Liab. § 6 notes that courts have limited the tort liability of intermediary parties, including pharmacies, by holding "that they should be permitted to rely on the special expertise of manufacturers, prescribing and treating health-care providers, and governmental regulatory agencies."

The Majority opinion cites, as authorities found persuasive by it for its interpretation of § 2-313(1) that "basis of the bargain" does not require the buyer to be aware of the alleged warranty representation during the negotiation of the bargain, a multitude of cases regarding consumer goods like motor homes (e.g. *Murphy v. Mallard Coach Co.*, 179 A.D.2d 187, 582 N.Y.S.2d 528 (N.Y. App. Div. 1992)) and hay-baling chemicals (e.g. *Bigelow v. Agway*, 506 F.2d 551 (2d Cir. 1974)), none of which require a prescription by a physician (or anything remotely analogous) in order to purchase. Majority slip op. at 18–22. These cases are not persuasive authority here because we are dealing with the purchase of a prescription medication from a pharmacy, which is a fundamentally different sale of goods. Unlike the buyer of a motor home, for example, who relies upon the affirmations of fact and descriptions by the motor home retailer when making the purchase, a buyer of prescription drugs does not rely upon representations of the pharmacy when deciding to purchase the drug prescribed by a physician. In addition, the instructions for taking the medication (which, even when followed, may not work as intended for each patient's particular condition and diet) indicating to take it with food or milk if upset stomach occurs is quite different from a warranty policy or card that a mobile home is free of defects and which promises to repair or replace the goods.

The Majority opinion also relies on Official Comment 7 to § 2-313, which states:

> The precise time when words of description or affirmation are made or samples are show is not material. The sole question is whether the language or samples or models are *fairly to be regarded as part of the contract.* If language is used after the closing of the deal (as when the buyer when taking delivery asks and receives an additional assurance), the warranty becomes a modification, and need not be supported by consideration if it is otherwise reasonable and in order (Section 2-209). (Emphasis added).

Majority slip op. at 17–18. Applying this reasoning, I conclude that it would not be fair to regard the instructions for use of a prescription medication as "part of the contract" because it is not the kind of affirmation of fact or description as to the prescription medication that would be a factor in a patient's decision to purchase the medication from the pharmacy. If the patient reads the instructions for use provided by the pharmacy, while standing at the pharmacy counter, and decides that he or she is in doubt and may no longer wish to purchase the medication, the patient more properly would need to return to the prescribing physician to discuss any concerns and possibly obtain a new prescription more suited to his or her particular circumstances.

*   *   *

NOTES AND QUESTIONS

1. Do the majority and dissent reach different results after applying the same test, or do they apply different tests?

2. Should a pharmacy that sells a prescription drug that fails to conform to warranties be treated differently from a pharmacy that sells shampoo that fails to conform to warranties? How would you respond to Rite Aid's claim that its documentation in no way led to the sale of the drug, which can be authorized only by a physician? How would you respond to Rite Aid's claim that it is the physician who should be held liable for the injury in this case?

3. Professor John Murray has argued that the "part of the basis of the bargain" test makes sense only if courts recognize that Article 2 has expanded the concept of "bargain." He urges courts to apply this test by keeping the following in mind:

> It has long been unclear whether "basis of the bargain" in Uniform Commercial Code (U.C.C.) Section 2-313(1) incorporates a reliance test. . . .

*   *   *

. . . The test which courts must use is a familiar test: What are the reasonable expectations of the buyer? The reasonable expectations of the buyer are not relegated to those induced by the seller's promise. Nor are they relegated to those expectations which the buyer also relied upon in making the purchase. Rather they are those expectations created by all of the "affirmation of fact made by the seller about the goods during a bargain." Since the duration of the bargain in Article 2 transcends the classical concept of bargain, this test will protect those reasonable expectations that a seller's statements create, regardless of when those statements were made or when the buyer learned of them.

* * *

Consider a situation where the seller makes a statement, for the first time, after a sale is concluded. This is the typical postformation statement outlined in Comment 7 to section 2-313. These postformation statements clearly fall within the suggested test. For example, suppose a seller makes a statement relating to the performance capability of a computer after it is purchased and delivered to a buyer. The buyer has a reasonable expectation that the statement is true. Moreover, all the reasons for protecting this reasonable expectation are clearly present. The buyer may forgo other opportunities which he does not even consciously consider as a result of the seller's statement. He may attempt to operate the computer according to the seller's representation and suffer some measurable loss. If the seller's statement is not enforceable, the inevitable result will be an impairment of facilitation of business arrangements. Finally, the seller's defense, in which he asserts an excuse based on the timing of his statement, would manifest obvious bad faith.

Next, consider the situation in which the seller makes a preformation statement that the buyer does not learn of until after the goods are purchased and delivered. One should initially note that this situation is virtually indistinguishable from a postformation warranty. To make it a warranty under Comment 7, the buyer would only have to ask the seller about the matter contained in the pre-existing statement and have the seller restate it. Distinguishing between a statement that the seller merely restates and a statement that the seller does not restate is antagonistic to the express antitechnical nature of Article 2.

* * *

These preformation statements, later heard by the buyer, are also subject to the same dangers as postformation statements. Suppose the seller has made written statements about the goods contained in a publication — for example, an owner's manual — that the buyer reads only after the goods are purchased and delivered. The manual contains a statement of various features of the goods that the buyer was not aware of prior to the purchase. Although the buyer was not specifically aware of these features prior to the sale, even before purchasing the buyer reasonably expected any statements by the seller in such a publication to be true. The buyer will not expect the product to have only those features that he or she remembers it has from reading the owner's manual. The buyer will feel oppressed and unfairly surprised if the goods do not contain the features represented in the sales literature. If the product does not meet the standards set forth in the owner's manual, the buyer will not only be disappointed, but may also forbear other opportunities that are immeasurable. Moreover, the buyer may rely upon the seller's statement in attempting to use the goods pursuant to the statement, resulting in personal injury or economic loss. If courts recognized the seller's defense that the statement cannot be a warranty because the buyer read the statement only after purchase, business arrangements would be seriously impaired. If every preformation statement had to be read or heard, if every examination of a sample or model had to be meticulously complete, and if no postformation statement in any form could be trusted, buyers would be forced to incredible cautionary efforts before concluding the technical contract of sale. Finally, a seller's defense based on the buyer's lack of awareness violates the UCC's requirement of good faith. Does this analysis reduce "part of the basis of the bargain" to a nullity? Clearly not. One should not read Section 2-313 under this analysis as making any statement relating to the goods an express warranty, regardless of when it is made. The comments to section 2-313 indicate that the seller may show that the statements were not express warranties by "clear affirmative proof" or "good reason" is evidence of the withdrawal of the statement prior to the closing of the deal. For example, if the seller has made a statement relating to one model of goods, and the buyer indicates an interest in another model, the seller's statement that the second model does not have the feature attributed to the first is an obvious withdrawal of the express warranty.

Other illustrations of statements which do not meet the "basis of the bargain" test include a seller's statement that the buyer knows is untrue. If an expert buyer examines the goods and discovers that the seller's statements are untrue, such a buyer cannot reasonably expect the goods to conform to the statements. A description of the goods or performance specification appears, on its face, to be an obvious statement of fact relating to the goods. Yet, if there is clear, affirmative proof that the parties did not regard that statement as anything more than an aspiration — a hope, target, or goal — the buyer should have no reasonable expectation with respect to that stated specification.

While these illustrations do not exhaust the possible variations of a seller's statements that do not become part of the basis of the bargain, they do emphasize the narrow scope of escape from the broad, reasonable expectations of the buyer. Yet, even under a "rebuttable presumption" test, such as White and Summers suggest, it will be difficult for a seller to prove that his or her statements are not express warranties. Certainly, the comments to section 2-313 strongly suggest that escape from the basis of the bargain will be unusual. Most important, these illustrations of statements that are not within the basis of the bargain, together with the numerous illustrations of statements that are part of the basis of the bargain, indicate that the suggested test is workable.

To determine what is or what is not part of the basis of the bargain by determining the reasonable expectations of the buyer is not a mechanical test. Yet, no test can be mechanical if the essential question is the determination of the bargain-in-fact of the parties. It is a question of fact. But it is not a more difficult question than innumerable other questions of fact which courts decide comfortably and with familiarity. Like all such questions, there will be difficult cases and there will be dissenting views. A reasonable expectation test, however, is no more difficult than either a reliance or inducement test. In making this determination of fact, a court must consider all of the circumstances surrounding the transaction, not restricting itself to classical concepts of contract or bargain.

John E. Murray, Jr., *"Basis of the Bargain": Transcending Classical Concepts*, 66 Minn. L. Rev. 283 (1982).[11]

4. Recall the "terms later" contracts in the previous chapter. Sellers argued, often successfully, that buyers should be bound to "shrinkwrap terms" that they received after agreeing to purchase the product regardless of whether the buyer actually read the term. Should warranty terms be treated any differently? If a purchaser of a

---

[11] Copyright 1982. All rights reserved. Reprinted with permission of the author and the Minnesota Law Review.

computer will be bound to an arbitration clause that arrives with the goods and is never read by the buyer, why shouldn't Ms. Levy-Gray be able to sue for breach of warranty even if she never read the pamphlet that was included in the bag with her prescription?

PROBLEM 3-5

Betty owns a store in a dangerous part of town. Betty has been robbed several times, but she refuses to purchase a firearm, and she cannot afford to hire a private security service. Betty received a brochure in the mail from Safety First, the manufacturer of "Stop-M-Dead," a hand-held mace weapon. Betty contacted Safety, who sent a representative to the store and sold 2 units to Betty. Two weeks after the purchase Betty was robbed by 2 armed gunmen. Betty fired her Stop-M-Dead at the robber in front of her (4 feet away) hitting him in the face, and then fired at the robber standing by the doorway (20 feet away), but the spray did not reach the second robber. Neither robber was incapacitated and Betty was shot by both before they escaped. Betty sued on account of her personal injuries, alleging that they were consequential damages of Safety's breach of warranty (*see* § 2-715(2)(b)).

What are Betty's arguments that express warranties made by the Safety were breached, assuming the following additional facts:

1. The brochure reads in part as follows:

> Stop-M-Dead: stops them in their tracks! The spray rapidly vaporizes on the assailant's face, effecting instantaneous incapacitation. . . . The effectiveness is the result of a unique incapacitating formula projected in a shotgun-like pattern that instantly causes extreme tearing, and a stunned, winded condition. . . . Fires accurately up to 10 feet.

2. Safety's representative told Betty: "This stuff is great. It's better than having a gun because this really zaps 'em."

3. Safety's representative told Betty: "Stop-M-Dead will do just that: you won't have to worry about the assailant while the police are on their way. Of course, Stop-M-Dead is no guarantee, because anything can happen in a panic-filled moment. But, it is the best chance that you will have."

4. Safety's representative produced a bottle and asked Betty to shoot at a Bulls' Eye that was placed about 25 feet away. Betty found the product easy to aim, and quickly hit the mark.

5. When the two cans were delivered, Betty used one of them to repeat the Bulls' Eye test before paying Safety's representative.

6. Just after Betty paid the money and received the units, she asked Safety's representative how many times the unit can be fired. "Don't worry," the representative responded, "there are at least 10 full-strength shots in there."

2. Implied Warranty of Merchantibility

In addition to the express warranties that govern the specific agreement of the parties, Article 2 recognizes several "gap-filling" warranties that are part of the agreement of the parties unless they are excluded or modified by agreement. Section 2-314 provides that if the seller is "a merchant with respect to goods of that kind," then "a warranty that the goods shall be merchantable is implied in a contract for their sale." This tautology, that a merchant will be expected to sell goods of the quality sold by merchants, obviously calls for a fact-intensive inquiry, guided by the criteria of § 2-314(2)(a)–(f).

The first problem posed by § 2-314 is determining the level of quality that is required by the term "merchantable." Does the statute, or the cases interpreting it, provide any real guidance beyond the general requirement that the goods "at least" must "pass without objection in the trade"?

DEMPSEY v. ROSENTHAL
New York City Civil Court
468 N.Y.S.2d 441 (1983)

DAVID B. SAXE, Judge.

The novel issue that I am asked to resolve in the context of this Small Claims proceeding is as follows: Is a consumer who purchases a dog with one undescended testicle entitled to damages amounting to a refund of the amount paid on the ground that the dog is defective and therefore non-merchantable?

The essential facts are these: While passing by the American Kennels pet stores on May 20, 1983, at 786 Lexington Avenue in Manhattan, Ms. Ruby Dempsey, a Huntington, Long Island school teacher, decided to investigate the purchase of a poodle.

Apparently overcome by the beauty of a four-and-one-half pound, nine-week-old puppy, a pedigreed white poodle, Ms. Dempsey paid over $541.25 to the store and became the proud owner of a new pet whom she named Mr. Dunphy.

Five days after purchase, Mr. Dunphy was examined at the Animal Clinic of New York by veterinarian, Dr. Malcolm A. Kram. Dr. Kram's findings were succinct: " . . . While the dog appears in good physical health I have found him to be a unilateral cryptorchid. This is considered to be a congenital defect . . . ."

A unilateral cryptorchid is a dog with one undescended testicle. Ms. Dempsey was outraged and demanded a full refund from American Kennels. "It's defective," she exclaimed in court, referring to the hapless Mr. Dunphy. "I assumed it would be suitable for breeding but it's defective — it can't breed," she continued.

On July 5, 1983, Mr. Dunphy was again examined at the Animal Clinic — this time by veterinarian Dr. Marco Zancope. Dr. Zancope confirmed the diagnosis of his colleague, viz., that Mr. Dunphy had only one normally descended testicle. Over the defendant's objection, Ms. Dempsey returned Mr. Dunphy to the store and again demanded a refund. The store refused. A suit was begun.

At trial, Ms. Dempsey relied on the testimony of her two expert witnesses, Drs. Kram and Zancope who reiterated the contents of their reports — that Mr. Dunphy had only one descended testicle, and also upon her belief, that due to this condition, the dog could not be properly bred.

When called as a witness, Dr. Kram acknowledged that the dog was in good health. Additionally, he stated that the level of fertility was about the same for a dog with Mr. Dunphy's condition as compared with one with two normally descended testicles. Indeed, he stated that the condition might be later reversible with the "dropping" of the other testicle. The condition was, he continued, a genetic defect and a future litter would likely carry this trait. Finally, he stated, a dog with this condition could not be a show dog. Mr. Dunphy was not offered in evidence.

American Kennels, in defense, relies on the wording of its contract of sale and upon the expert testimony of its veterinarian, Dr. Richard Holmes, who examined the dog (it was returned to the store by Ms. Dempsey and never picked up by her) on July 15, 1983. At the time of the examination, Dr. Holmes found both testicles in the scrotum. "The right testicle is higher than the left but is scrotal. Both normal size and shape," he wrote.

Ms. Dempsey, however, still concerned presumably about this condition arising in future litters, insisted that the dog was still objectionable and pressed for a refund.

The contract of sale provides the consumer with rights to a full refund upon return of the pet "if your veterinarian finds within two weeks of sale that your pet is sick as to be unfit for purchase." But, that was not the case here. Neither of the veterinarians who appeared for Ms. Dempsey found Mr. Dunphy to be "sick as to be unfit for purchase."

The contract of sale also provides a 60-day health guarantee to the buyer with a right to exchange the pet within 60 days of purchase if the veterinarian finds anything wrong with the pet.

The clause continues:

> . . . in such case it will be exchanged for another pet of equal value of the customer's choice at once or when available provided a letter from the examining veterinarian is presented as evidence of the pet's illness and the pet is returned within the guarantee period.

This provision does not aid the claimant here because it provides for an exchange of pets (not a refund) and more importantly, it appears to be triggered only upon the discovery of some illness by the veterinarian. The heading of the clause is "60 day Health Guarantee" and thus bears out this conclusion.

Thus, whatever rights may expressly exist under the contract of sale, they are not of a nature to mandate the return of her purchase price.

The inquiry turns next to the applicability of one or more of the implied warranties which arise in connection with modern sales transactions under Article 2 of the Uniform Commercial Code. Mr. Dunphy, a pet dog, is considered a "good" as defined by UCC Sec. 2-105. *See Key v. Bagen*, 136 Ga. App. 373, 221 S.E.2d 234 (1975).

*   *   *

Here, it cannot be disputed that the vendor, American Kennels, is a merchant in the business of regularly selling dogs and other pets.

UCC § 2-314(2) sets forth a complex definition of merchantability with six standards. These standards are designed to be minimal requirements since goods are required to "at least" conform with all of the tests to be "merchantable" (*see* Comment 6 to UCC Sec. 2-314).

The first test of merchantable quality is whether the goods "pass without objection in the trade under the contract description" (UCC Sec. 2-314(2)(a)). This standard effectively sums up all of the various "definitions" of merchantable quality since the principal function of the warranty of merchantability has been to give legal effect to a buyer's reasonable expectations based on trade understanding of the quality of goods normally supplied under such a contract. (51 N.Y. Jur., *Sales* Sec. 176).

*   *   *

Would a dog with one undescended testicle pass without objection in the trade? A review of some of the authoritative case law may be instructive. In *Sessa v. Riegle*, 427 F. Supp. 760 (E.D. Pa. 1977), *aff'd*, 568 F.2d 770 (3rd Cir. 1978), a buyer of a race horse (Tarport Conaway) brought an action against the seller to recover for breach of an express warranty and implied warranties after the horse was found to suffer from tendinitis and thrombosis of the iliac arteries causing intermittent claudication. The court found for the seller. With respect to the contention that the implied warranty of merchantability was breached, the Court said [at 770]:

> Even with tendinitis and intermittent claudication Tarport Conaway met this standard. The tendinitis was merely temporary and of no long term effect. The intermittent claudication did not prevent him from becoming a creditable if unspectacular race horse. After rest and recuperation, he won three races in thirteen starts in 1975. Certainly he did not live up to Sessa's hopes for a preferred pacer, but such disappointments are an age old story in the horse racing business. Anyone who dares to deal in standard breeds know that whether you pay $2500.00 or $250,000.00, a given horse may prove to be a second Hambletonian or a humble hay burner. Consequently, since Tarport Conaway was able to hold his own with other standard breds, he was reasonably fit for the ordinary purposes for which race horses are used, and was merchantable.

See also Agoos Kid Co. v. Blumenthal Import Corp., 282 Mass. 1, 6, 184 N.E. 279, 281 (1933).

Unlike the condition in *Sessa v. Riegle, supra*, the condition here is apparently permanent and would be passed on to future generations of Mr. Dunphy's offspring. Under the circumstances, I believe it to be a reasonable conclusion that a unilateral cryptorchid would not pass without objection in the trade. I conclude that Mr. Dunphy was not a merchantable dog.

*   *   *

FORD v. MILLER MEAT CO.
California Court of Appeal
33 Cal. Rptr. 2d 899 (1994)

Sonenshine, Associate Justice.

Grace Joyce Ford appeals judgments in favor of Miller Meat Company (Miller) and Alpha Beta Company (Alpha Beta) in a nonjury trial. Ford sought to recover damages for injuries sustained when she bit into a fragment of bone contained in ground beef purchased at an Alpha Beta supermarket.

We affirm. Our Supreme Court in *Mexicali Rose v. Superior Court* (1992) 1 Cal. 4th 617, 4 Cal. Rptr. 2d 145, 822 P.2d 1292, articulated principles of liability in the context of a diner's injuries caused by food served in a restaurant. *Mexicali Rose* expressly limited its holding "to commercial restaurant establishments" (*id.* at p. 619, fn. 1, 4 Cal. Rptr. 2d 145, 822 P.2d 1292), where the patron plays no part in preparation of the food and thus has little, if any, opportunity to examine the ingredients for the presence of potentially harmful substances. We find *Mexicali Rose*'s reasoning of even greater force where there has been a retail sale of meat to a consumer who herself has prepared the injurious food.

Factual and Procedural Background

On January 30, 1989, Ford bought packaged ground beef from Alpha Beta, took it home and, while she was browning it for tacos, removed a small portion to taste. She bit down on something hard and damaged a tooth. When she spit out the meat, she observed a "tiny" bone fragment which she estimated could have been up to a quarter of an inch at its largest diameter. She sued Alpha Beta and Miller, the meat supplier, alleging causes of action for strict product liability, breach of warranty and negligence. The parties waived a jury and proceeded to trial in November 1992.

The issues of liability and damages were bifurcated. Ford's entire liability case consisted of her own testimony. She presented no evidence against Miller, and its motion for nonsuit was granted. Alpha Beta's meat manager, Jeff Bear, testified Miller supplies prepackaged ground beef in four-pound rolls. Alpha Beta removes the meat from the packages, regrinds it and repackages it for sale. In the typical regrinding process, the meat handler breaks the ground beef into handful-size pieces, visually inspects them and places them in a grinder. The meat is reground into a "mush," and then machine-compacted through a steel plate perforated by holes three to four millimeters in diameter. The ground beef emerges in the tubular, spaghetti-like strands familiar to consumers. Although it is not absolutely impossible that anything larger than three or four millimeters will pass through the steel plate, it is "very unlikely." The meat handler observes the entire operation, from start to finish. The grinder is not left unattended. The reground meat is packaged in styrofoam and sealed in plastic wrap for sale in the Alpha Beta market.

At the conclusion of the above testimony, the court gave judgment in favor of Alpha Beta. It found the theories of strict liability and breach of implied warranty did not apply. As for negligence, it stated, "It seems . . . if we look at the totality of the situation here, that the plaintiff has not met its [sic] burden. . . . The description of [the bone fragment] by the plaintiff indicates that she probably was in error in describing the size of it. From what appears to be the only source of processing ground meat, it would have had to have been smaller than [one-quarter of an inch]. [¶] According to my quick calculations, a three to four millimeter aperture would mean that the bone fragment would have to be within one-eighth of an inch or smaller. That is, the court [will] not find under those circumstances that anyone would have a reasonable expectation of having such small particles of bone removed from hamburger."

Discussion

*   *   *

The court found Ford must have overestimated the size of the bone fragment which could not have been larger than one-eighth of an inch. We are bound by that factual determination and do not reweigh the evidence or reassess issues of credibility. (*Orange County Employees Assn. v. County of Orange* (1988) 205 Cal. App. 3d 1289, 1293–1294, 253 Cal. Rptr. 584.)

I.

Plaintiff's first argument is: (1) Under *Mexicali Rose v. Superior Court, supra*, 1 Cal. 4th 617, 4 Cal. Rptr. 2d 145, 822 P.2d 1292, injury-producing foreign substances in food give rise to claims for strict liability and breach of warranty, but natural substances do not. (2) The bone fragment Ford bit into cannot be deemed a natural substance because ground beef is pulverized and there is nothing natural about its containing pieces of bone large enough to produce an injury. (3) Since the bone fragment is not natural, it is foreign; therefore (a) it renders the ground beef defective, subjecting Alpha Beta to strict liability, and (b) it renders the ground beef unfit for consumption, subjecting Alpha Beta to liability for breach of the warranty of fitness. (4) The court erred in eliminating Ford's theories of strict liability and breach of the implied warranty.

Ford misconstrues *Mexicali Rose*, in which the plaintiff sued a restaurant for negligence, strict liability and breach of the implied warranty, alleging he suffered throat injuries from a one-inch chicken bone contained in a chicken enchilada. The trial court overruled the restaurant's demurrer to the complaint; the Court of Appeal issued a writ of mandate directing the lower court to sustain the demurrer. The Supreme Court affirmed the judgment of the Court of Appeal insofar as its order eliminated the causes of action for strict liability and breach of the implied warranty. (It reversed with regard to the negligence theory of liability, a point which will be discussed more fully below.)

At the outset, the *Mexicali Rose* court noted it had granted review for the purpose of reexamining the foreign-natural test of *Mix v. Ingersoll Candy Co.* (1936) 6 Cal. 2d 674, 59 P.2d 144, which held there could be no tort or implied warranty liability for injuries caused by substances natural to the food served. (*Mexicali Rose v. Superior Court, supra*, 1 Cal. 4th 617, 619, 4 Cal. Rptr. 2d 145, 822 P.2d 1292.) In a discussion tracing the nearly 60-year history of food product suits, the court observed the more recent cases tended to reject the rigid foreign-natural test in favor of a reasonable expectations test, under which the substances "natural to the preparation of the food served" are to be anticipated and thus do not render the food unfit or defective. (*Id.* at p. 630, 4 Cal. Rptr. 2d 145, 822 P.2d 1292.)

Discarding the foreign-natural rule of *Mix* in favor of the reasonable expectation test, the *Mexicali Rose* court stated, "First, whether bones or other injurious substances ought to be anticipated in a particular dish becomes a question for the trier of fact, unless as a matter of law the food was fit for consumption because the substance was natural to the food served. [Citation.] Second, and more important, this reasonable expectation test focuses not on the components of the dish, but on the final item sold to the consumer and the expectations that are engendered by the type of dish and the type of preparation used in making the dish." (*Ibid.*)

Most significantly to Ford's claim, *Mexicali Rose* departs from the foreign-natural rule *only* to the extent it bars a negligence claim, *not* to the extent it precludes actions for strict liability and breach of warranty. (*Mexicali Rose v. Superior Court, supra*, 1 Cal. 4th 617, 632, 4 Cal. Rptr. 2d 145, 822 P.2d 1292.) With regard to the latter two theories of recovery, *Mexicali Rose* holds: "If the injury-producing substance is natural to the preparation of the food served, it can be said that it was reasonably expected by its very nature and the food cannot be determined unfit or defective. A plaintiff in such a case has no cause of action in strict liability or implied warranty." (*Id.* at p. 633, 4 Cal. Rptr. 2d 145, 822 P.2d 1292.)

Confronted with this unequivocal holding, Ford protests the bone fragment was not *natural* to the "pulverized" ground beef, but *Mexicali Rose* answers this claim as well. It expressly adopts the reasoning of an out-of-state case, *Loyacano v. Continental Insurance Company* (La. Ct. App. 1973) 283 So.2d 302, which is indistinguishable from Ford's case. In *Loyacano*, the plaintiff purchased ground beef wrapped in a plastic-bottom container wrapped with clear cellophane. She took it home, refrigerated it for a couple of days, and then used it to make hamburger patties. After browning the patties, she broke off a small piece, bit into a bone fragment and broke her tooth. The *Loyacano* court noted it cannot be said, as a matter of general knowledge, that ground beef should not contain any pieces of bone (*Loyacano v. Continental Insurance Company, supra*, 283 So.2d 302, 305), thus strict liability or breach of warranty may not be imposed "except insofar as a foreign object would be concerned." (*Ibid.*)

Clearly, under *Mexicali Rose*, a bone fragment remains a natural substance under the foreign-natural distinction. Therefore, the trial court correctly determined Ford could not recover on theories of strict liability or breach of implied warranty.

QUESTIONS

1. What is the "trade" in which the dog in *Dempsey* would not "pass without objection"? What is the "ordinary purpose" for an animal purchased at the pet store? If virtually all of the customers purchasing animals from American Kennels purchase them for household pets, and if Mr. Dunphy would pass without objection as an animal suitable for a household pet, would this eliminate Ms. Dempsey's claim for breach of implied warranty?

2. The *Ford* court does not analyze the case in light of the language of § 2-314. Use the statutory language and comments to justify the result in the case.

3. As a general rule, plaintiffs will use tort theories such as strict liability for defective products that cause bodily injury. The *Ford* case provides a good example of a plaintiff seeking relief in both tort and under the contract principles of Article 2. In some cases, this is simply careful, all-inclusive pleading, but in other cases there may be a problem with the tort theories that require the plaintiff to seek damages under Article 2. Should Article 2 abandon this field to tort law, or is there a continuing role for the law of warranties?

PROBLEM 3-6

Bjorn purchased a new car from Smiley's Auto, Inc. Three years later, Bjorn brings suit alleging that rust spots are developing around the tail light modules and over the rear wheel wells. At the time of suit, the vehicle has been driven 86,000 miles without any major mechanical problems. Bjorn alleges that the premature rusting constitutes a violation of the implied warranty of merchantability. Will Bjorn prevail?

PROBLEM 3-7

Brenda purchased a four-year-old pick-up truck for use in her commercial landscaping business. She purchased the truck from Spanky's Used Cars, a dealer that purports to have the county's largest selection of used vehicles. Brenda finds soon after the purchase that the truck frame is bent, causing difficulty in steering when she is carrying a heavy load, as well as uneven wear on the tires. Brenda sues Spanky's for breach of the implied warranty of merchantability. Should Brenda prevail?

PROBLEM 3-8

Sure Cast is a manufacturer engaged in the production of cast iron products. Burke's Supplies owns a store that sells equipment and supplies to contractors who plant trees. Burke's brought a hoedad collar (used to secure the metal blade of a forestry planting tool to a wooden handle) to Sure Cast and asked if Sure Cast could duplicate the casting for an impact forestry tool that occasionally strikes rocks or roots. Sure Cast stated that, although it had never manufactured hoedad collars, it could make the casting for Burke's. Sure Cast suggested that a durable iron be used. Burke's purchased 1,000 specially manufactured hoedad collars from Sure Cast.

Problems arise when Burke's customers return many of the tools after the hoedad collars break. Burke's sues Sure Cast for breach of the implied warranty of merchantability. Analyze whether Sure Cast is a merchant, and determine whether the specially manufactured hoedad collars are unfit for their ordinary purpose.

Does Burke's have other theories of recovery if it is unable to prevail on a breach of the warranty of merchantability?

PROBLEM 3-9

Bonita was a life-long smoker of cigarettes manufactured by the Smithfield Tobacco Company. Bonita developed lung cancer and died as a result of her disease. Her husband and son sued Smithfield for breach of implied warranty, arguing that Smithfield sold an unmerchantable product to Bonita. Specifically, they argue that the cigarettes sold by Smithfield were inherently unhealthy and unsafe. Additionally, they argue that Smithfield manipulated the nicotine content of its cigarettes through chemical processes, to ensure that smokers became addicted to their product. They claim that the nicotine-enhanced cigarettes were unmerchantable. Will these claims prevail?

3.   Implied Warranty of Fitness for Particular Purpose

Section 2-315 implies another warranty in the absence of contrary agreement, namely a warranty that goods will be fit for the particular purpose for which they are purchased, if the seller has reason to know that the buyer is relying on the seller's skill or judgment to furnish goods suitable for this purpose. The implied warranty of fitness for particular purpose is different in several important respects from the implied warranty of merchantability. First, under § 2-315, there is no requirement that the seller be a merchant. Also, under § 2-315, the focus shifts from supplying goods fit for the ordinary purpose of such goods to supplying goods fit for the particular buyer's purpose.

LEWIS v. MOBIL OIL CORP.
United States Court of Appeals, Eight Circuit
438 F.2d 500 (1971)

GIBSON, Circuit Judge.

In this diversity case the defendant appeals from a judgment entered on a jury verdict in favor of the plaintiff in the amount of $89,250 for damages alleged to be caused by use of defendant's oil.

Plaintiff Lewis has been doing business as a sawmill operator in Cove, Arkansas, since 1956. In 1963, in order to meet competition, Lewis decided to convert his power equipment to hydraulic equipment. He purchased a hydraulic system in May 1963, from a competitor who was installing a new system. The used system was in good operating condition at the time Lewis purchased it. It was stored at his plant until November 1964, while a new mill building was being built, at which time it was installed. Following the installation, Lewis requested from Frank Rowe, a local Mobil Oil dealer, the proper hydraulic fluid to operate his machinery. The prior owner of the hydraulic system had used Pacemaker oil supplied by Cities Service, but plaintiff had been a customer of Mobil's for many years and desired to continue with Mobil. Rowe said he didn't know what the proper lubricant for Lewis' machinery was, but would find out. The only information given to Rowe by Lewis was that the machinery was operated by a gear-type pump; Rowe did not request any further information. He apparently contacted a Mobil representative for a recommendation, though this is not entirely clear, and sold plaintiff a product known as Ambrex 810. This is a straight mineral oil with no chemical additives.

Within a few days after operation of the new equipment commenced, plaintiff began experiencing difficulty with its operation. The oil changed color, foamed over, and got hot. The oil was changed a number of times, with no improvement. By late April 1965, approximately six months after operations with the equipment had begun, the system broke down, and a complete new system was installed. The cause of the breakdown was undetermined, but apparently by this time there was some suspicion of the oil being used. Plaintiff Lewis requested Rowe to be sure he was supplying the right kind of oil. Ambrex 810 continued to be supplied.

From April 1965 until April 1967, plaintiff continued to have trouble with the system, principally with the pumps which supplied the pressure. Six new pumps were required during this period, as they continually broke down. During this period, the kind of pump used was a Commercial pump which was specified by the designer of the hydraulic system. The filtration of oil for this pump was by means of a metal strainer, which was cleaned daily by the plaintiff in accordance with the instruction given with the equipment.

In April 1967, the plaintiff changed the brand of pump from a Commercial to a Tyrone pump. The Tyrone pump, instead of using the metal strainer filtration alone, used a disposable filter element in addition. Ambrex 810 oil was also recommended by Mobil and used with this pump, which completely broke down three weeks later. At this point, plaintiff was visited for the first time by a representative of Mobil Oil Corporation, as well as a representative of the Tyrone pump manufacturer.

On the occasion of this visit, May 9, 1967, plaintiff's system was completely flushed and cleaned, a new Tyrone pump installed, and on the pump manufacturer's and Mobil's representative's recommendation, a new oil was used[12] which contained certain chemical additives, principally a "defoamant." Following these changes, plaintiff's

---

[12] [1] Upon recommendation of Mobil, Plaintiff used Mobil's DTE 23 and Del Vac Special after the second Tyrone was installed in May 9, 1967, until July 25, 1967, when plaintiff changed to Pacemaker XD-15. All of the above oils contained certain chemical additives for anti-wear, anti-oxidation and anti-foaming.

system worked satisfactorily up until the time of trial, some two and one-half years later.

Briefly stated, plaintiff's theory of his case is that Mobil supplied him with an oil which was warranted fit for use in his hydraulic system, that the oil was not suitable for such use because it did not contain certain additives, and that it was the improper oil which caused the mechanical breakdowns, with consequent loss to his business. The defendant contends that there was no warranty of fitness, that the breakdowns were caused not by the oil but by improper filtration, and that in any event there can be no recovery of loss of profits in this case.

I. THE EXISTENCE OF WARRANTIES

Defendant maintains that there was no warranty of fitness in this case, that at most there was only a warranty of merchantability and that there was no proof of breach of this warranty, since there was no proof that Ambrex 810 is unfit for use in hydraulic systems generally. We find it unnecessary to consider whether the warranty of merchantability was breached, although there is some proof in the record to that effect, since we conclude that there was a warranty of fitness.

Plaintiff Lewis testified that he had been a longtime customer of Mobil Oil, and that his only source of contact with the company was through Frank Rowe, Mobil's local dealer, with whom he did almost all his business. It was common knowledge in the community that Lewis was converting his sawmill operation into a hydraulic system, Rowe knew this, and in fact had visited his mill on business matters several times during the course of the changeover. When operations with the new machinery were about to commence, Lewis asked Rowe to get him the proper hydraulic fluid. Rowe asked him what kind of a system he had, and Lewis replied it was a Commercial pump type. This was all the information asked or given. Neither Lewis nor Rowe knew what the oil requirements for the system were, and Rowe knew that Lewis knew nothing more specific about his requirements. Lewis also testified that after he began having trouble with his operations, while there were several possible sources of the difficulty, the oil was one suspected source, and he several times asked Rowe to be sure he was furnishing him with the right kind.

Rowe's testimony for the most part confirmed Lewis'. It may be noted here that Mobil does not contest Rowe's authority to represent it in this transaction, and therefore whatever warranties may be implied because of the dealings between Rowe and Lewis are attributable to Mobil. Rowe admitted knowing Lewis was converting to a hydraulic system and that Lewis asked him to supply the fluid. He testified that he did not know what should be used and relayed the request to a superior in the Mobil organization, who recommended Ambrex 810. This is what was supplied.

When the first Tyrone pump was installed in April 1967, Rowe referred the request for a proper oil recommendation to Ted Klock, a Mobil engineer. Klock recommended Ambrex 810. When this pump failed a few weeks later, Klock visited the Lewis plant to inspect the equipment. The system was flushed out completely and the oil was changed to DTE-23 and Del Vac Special containing several additives. After this, no further trouble was experienced.

This evidence adequately establishes an implied warranty of fitness. Arkansas has adopted the Uniform Commercial Code's provision for an implied warranty of fitness. . . . Under [§ 2-315], there are two requirements for an implied warranty of fitness: (1) that the seller have "reason to know" of the use for which the goods are purchased, and (2) that the buyer relies on the seller's expertise in supplying the proper product. Both of these requirements are amply met by the proof in this case. Lewis' testimony, as confirmed by that of Rowe and Klock, shows that the oil was purchased specifically for his hydraulic system, not for just a hydraulic system in general, and that Mobil certainly knew of this specific purpose. It is also clear that Lewis was relying on

Mobil to supply him with the proper oil for the system, since at the time of his purchases, he made clear that he didn't know what kind was necessary.

Mobil contends that there was no warranty of fitness for use in his particular system because he didn't specify that he needed an oil with additives, and alternatively that he didn't give them enough information for them to determine that an additive oil was required. However, it seems that the circumstances of this case come directly within that situation described in the first comment to this provision of the Uniform Commercial Code:

> 1. Whether or not this warranty arises in any individual case is basically a question of fact to be determined by the circumstances of the contracting. Under this section the buyer need not bring home to the seller *actual knowledge of the particular purpose* for which the goods are intended or of his reliance on the seller's skill and judgment, if the circumstances are such that the seller has reason to realize the purpose intended or that the reliance exists.

7C Ark. Stat. Ann. § 85-2-315, Comment 1 (1961) (emphasis added). Here Lewis made it clear that the oil was purchased for his system, that he didn't know what oil should be used, and that he was relying on Mobil to supply the proper product. If any further information was needed, it was incumbent upon Mobil to get it before making its recommendation. That it could have easily gotten the necessary information is evidenced by the fact that after plaintiff's continuing complaints, Mobil's engineer visited the plant, and, upon inspection, changed the recommendation that had previously been made.

Additionally, Mobil contends that even if there were an implied warranty of fitness, it does not cover the circumstances of this case because of the abnormal features which the plaintiff's system contained, namely an inadequate filtration system and a capacity to entrain excessive air. There are several answers to this contention. First of all, the contention goes essentially to the question of causation — i.e., whether the damage was caused by a breach of warranty or by some other cause — and not to the existence of a warranty of fitness in the first place. Secondly, assuming that certain peculiarities in the plaintiff's system did exist, the whole point of an implied warranty of fitness is that a product be suitable for a specific purpose, and that a seller should not supply a product which is not so suited. Thirdly, there is no evidence in the record that the plaintiff's system was unique or abnormal in these respects. It operated satisfactorily under the prior owner, and the new system has operated satisfactorily after it was adequately cleaned and an additive type oil used.

While we will discuss these problems more completely in the question of causation, it may be briefly noted here that the proof shows that plaintiff's filtration system was installed and maintained in strict accordance with the manufacturer's recommendations, that this was a standard system, and that any hydraulic system has a certain unavoidable capacity to entrain air. While a "perfect" system which is run 24 hours a day might not have any air in it, in actual practice there are at least two sources of air. One is from minute leaks in "packing glands." The other source arises from the fact that when the system is shut down, as at night and over the lunch hour, as well as for repairs, the oil drains out of the system and into the reservoir. When the system is started up again, air which has entered the system to replace the drained oil must be dissipated. This dissipation occurs by running the system for a few minutes and is affected by the capacity of the oil to rid itself of air bubbles. It is sufficient to note here that there was no evidence that the plaintiff's system was in any way unique in this respect. Thus, Mobil's defense that there was no warranty of fitness because of an "abnormal use" of the oil is not appropriate here.

II. BREACH OF WARRANTY AS THE CAUSE OF PLAINTIFF'S DAMAGE

The primary controversy in this case is whether the damage done to the plaintiff's hydraulic system was caused by the defendant's breach of warranty in failing to provide a proper oil. This issue primarily presents a question of the sufficiency of the evidence to support the jury's verdict that the cause of the plaintiff's damage was the use of Ambrex 810 and that Ambrex 810 was an improper oil for his system. Of course, on appeal the evidence must be viewed in the light most favorable to the jury verdict, and we think there was sufficient evidence to support the verdict on the breach of warranty issue. An understanding of the evidence in this case will be facilitated by a brief explanation of each party's theory of the cause of damage.

Plaintiff's theory was that the damage was caused by pump cavitations induced by the failure of the oil to expurgate air bubbles quickly enough from its body, and that this characteristic of the oil could have been prevented by the addition of proper additives, principally a defoamant additive, but also anti-wear, anti-oxidation, and anti-rust additives.

Pump cavitation occurs when air bubbles in the body of the oil are sucked into the pump along with the hydraulic fluid. The moving parts within the pump have very small tolerances and must be kept lubricated at all times by the hydraulic fluid. Due to the exceedingly high pressures within the pump, when there are air bubbles in the fluid, they become compressed into larger bubbles and at some point interfere with the lubricating qualities of the oil, permitting the metal parts of the pump to come in contact. When this contact occurs, small metal pieces flake off and get into the fluid, which then disperses these metal contaminants throughout the system. These metal particles can in turn be responsible for causing other problems in the system which would result in the introduction of atmospheric contamination — i.e., dirt — into the system. As the metal particles, plus the other contamination, are circulated throughout the system by means of the hydraulic fluid and returned to the pump intake, serious damage is caused to the pump which cannot tolerate these contaminants.

According to the plaintiff's theory, this process can be prevented by the addition of an anti-foamant additive in the oil which aids it in expurgating air quickly so that air bubbles are not sucked into the pump in the first place.

Defendant's theory of the cause of damage was that plaintiff failed to maintain his equipment properly, failed to have a proper filtration system, and failed to flush the system after pump failures. Defendant also contested plaintiff's allegations that a defoamant additive in the oil would prevent damage from pump cavitation.

[Ed. Note: The court determined that there was adequate proof in the record to sustain the jury's verdict on the breach of warranty issue.]

* * *

PROBLEM 3-10

Burnes, Inc. manufactures electrical heating elements that are embedded in a rubber-like material that is flexible and can be adapted to numerous shapes. Burnes requires an adhesive to affix this material to aluminum frames that will be specially manufactured to meet its customers' requirements. Burnes contacts Stickum, a commercial adhesives dealer, and requests an adhesive that would affix pliable material to aluminum and can withstand temperatures up to 300 degrees Fahrenheit. Stickum advises Burnes to purchase XR-23, and Burnes does so.

First Scenario. Soon, Burnes discovers that its customers are returning its products regularly, complaining that the adhesive was not holding sufficiently. Does Burnes have a viable claim against Stickum under § 2-315?

Second Scenario. When Burnes' customers complain, Burnes complains to Stickum and then learns that the adhesive breaks down in the presence of strong electrical currents. The parties then discover that the electrical charge required to heat the pads was sufficient to break down the adhesive. Had Stickum been advised of the specific conditions under which the adhesive would be used, it would have known that XR-23 would not be suitable. Does Burnes have a viable claim against Stickum under § 2-315?

Third Scenario. Assume that when Burnes contacted Stickum it requested XR-23, based on promotional materials that it had received in the mail. After Stickum asked about the application, Burnes said that it needed the adhesive to affix pliable pads to aluminum frames that might reach 300 degrees generated by an electrical current running through the pad. Stickum's sales representative then said, "You've asked for the right product." Does Burnes have a viable claim against Stickum under § 2-315?

4. Extended Warranties

DRAVO EQUIPMENT CO. v. GERMAN
Oregon Court of Appeals
698 P.2d 63 (1985)

ROSSMAN, JUDGE.

Plaintiff appeals from an adverse judgment in this action to foreclose a nonpossessory lien. The sole issue is whether defendants German and Hunter were entitled to raise an express warranty as a defense when they were not parties to it. We hold that privity is not required to recover economic loss on an express warranty. Accordingly, we affirm.

Plaintiff is an equipment company which operates out of Medford. It sold a used tractor with a rebuilt engine to defendants Brooks, Boyer and Bismark (BB & B) in April 1979. BB & B obtained an express warranty on the tractor's engine, which provided: "This price includes new, rebuilt engine and to carry 1500 hours of 100 percent engine warranty." The trial court found that the warranty, which was written in longhand on a standard sales agreement, was a separately bargained for contractual right and was not just incidental to the purchase of the tractor. The agreement was silent as to the transferability of the warranty.

In January 1980, BB & B sold their rock crushing business, including the tractor, to defendants German and Hunter (defendants), who thereafter operated the business as Modoc Rock. During the course of negotiating the sale, defendants were shown a copy of the engine warranty by BB & B. Defendant German testified that, after the negotiations, it was his understanding that the warranty was valid for 1500 hours and that he and Hunter checked the hour meter to make sure that the engine was still within the warranty period.

Ultimately, the tractor engine seized up and was taken by defendants to plaintiff for repairs. From the beginning, defendants were adamant that any repairs were covered by the warranty. Plaintiff's employees deny ever having conceded that point to defendants. In any event, the nature of the engine malfunction was quite serious. Owing to the importance of repairing the tractor as quickly as possible, it was decided to replace the engine with a rebuilt one. After that was completed, defendants refused to pay. Plaintiff offered to accept 50 percent as payment, but that offer was refused also. Defendants regained possession of the tractor and, sometime later, plaintiff filed a nonpossessory lien and initiated this suit against BB & B and defendants. Defendants raised the warranty as a defense and counter-claimed for damage to their credit reputation. The trial judge found that defendants were entitled to enforce the warranty and, accordingly, ruled that plaintiff was not entitled to recover anything against defendants or BB & B. The judge also ruled against defendants on their counterclaim.

On appeal, plaintiff urges that defendants were not entitled to enforce the warranty, because they were not privy to the transaction in which the warranty was given. Thus, the single issue we need to address is whether privity of contract is required to enforce an express warranty in order to recover for purely economic loss. The issue is new to the Oregon courts. The Oregon Uniform Commercial Code contains certain provisions relating to warranties. ORS 72.3180 provides:

A seller's warranty whether express or implied extends to any natural person who is in the family or household of his buyer or who is a guest in his home if it is reasonable to expect that such person may use, consume or be affected by the goods and who is injured in person by breach of the warranty. A seller may not exclude or limit the operation of this section.

Under this section, a seller's warranty extends beyond the buyer only in cases involving personal injuries and then only to a limited number of people. However, that limitation is not dispositive. It is important to note that the official commentary to the UCC provides at subparagraph (3):

ORS 72.3180 expressly includes as beneficiaries within its provisions the family, household, and guests of the purchaser. Beyond this, the section is neutral and is not intended to enlarge or restrict the developing case law on whether the seller's warranties, given to his buyer who resells, extend to other persons in the distributive chain.

Accordingly, we need to look at the case law to ascertain whether the warranty in this case can extend to remote purchasers like defendants. In *Hupp Corp. v. Metered Washer Service*, 256 Or. 245, 472 P.2d 816 (1970), the court addressed whether

. . . an ultimate purchaser can recover economic loss upon the theory of implied warranty against a manufacturer although the property was not purchased directly from the manufacturer but through an intermediate seller.

256 Or. at 247. The court concluded that he could not. The same issue arose in *Davis v. Homasote Company*, 281 Or. 383, 574 P.2d 1116 (1978). In that case, an owner of an apartment complex installed a sub-floor building material manufactured by the defendant, which was supposed to be weather proof and act as a sound buffer. The material, which was purchased through a distributor and not directly from the defendant, allegedly did not perform as promised. The plaintiff brought an action against the manufacturer for breach of implied warranties of fitness and merchantability. The claims were dismissed by the trial court. The Supreme Court adhered to its rule that privity of contract is essential before a purchaser can recover economic loss from a manufacturer for breach of an implied warranty. 281 Or. at 386.

These two cases represent the current status of the law in Oregon. No appellate case has overruled the requirement for privity in a breach of implied warranty case where damages for economic loss were sought. Although defendant's loss was economic, we do not believe that the rule developed for implied warranties is necessarily applicable to the express warranty in the case.

Implied warranties are imposed on the seller. They arise from the circumstances of a transaction as a matter of law. *See* ORS 72.3140 and 72.3150. Accordingly, it makes sense, when not dealing with personal injuries that implied warranties should not extend beyond the transaction in which the law imposes them. By contrast, express warranties are created by the express representations of the seller. *See* ORS 72.3130. A seller, as the master of a warranty's destiny, is free to make it as broad or as narrow as it chooses. Express warranties can be limited in effect, duration and transferability. Because the seller is free to create an express warranty in any fashion it chooses, there is no reason why the warranty should not extend to remote purchasers when it is not so limited.

The express warranty in this case provided that the tractor engine was guaranteed for 1500 hours. Its enforceability was not expressly limited to BB & B, nor did plaintiff restrict its transferability. The only limiting factor was its duration. Defendants' purchase of the tractor and the engine breakdown clearly occurred within that time limit. Given the unrestricted terms of the warranty, there appears to be no reason why it cannot be enforced by defendants.[13]

WHITE & SUMMERS, UNIFORM COMMERCIAL CODE § 11-5 (1980), says that, unless a buyer can show actual reliance on express representations by the remote seller, the buyer cannot maintain an action for breach of an express warranty to recover direct economic loss (*i.e.*, loss of the bargain) in the absence of privity. *See also Randy Knitwear, Inc. v. American Cyanamid Com.*, 11 N.Y.2d 5, 226 N.Y.S.2d 363, 181 N.E.2d 399 (1962). Even if that were the rule, which we need not decide, defendants did rely on plaintiff's express representations. They were shown a copy of the warranty that expressly warranted the tractor engine for 1500 hours and they checked to make sure that the engine was still within that period. Plaintiff's warranty was relayed to defendants by BB & B, but plaintiff created the warranty and was free to limit it in any way it chose. The warranty was not limited, and defendants' reliance on it was reasonable.

We hold that defendants were entitled to enforce the express engine warranty, even though they were not in privity and their loss was only economic.

Affirmed.

NOTES AND QUESTIONS

1. What basis of distinction does the court formulate between express and implied warranties? Is the distinction convincing? For what purpose did the court draw the distinction? Should it matter that §§ 2-318 and 2A-216 do not so distinguish between express and implied warranties?

2. The court noted that "[E]xpress warranties can be limited in effect, duration and transferability." Is that true of implied warranties as well?

3. The drafters of § 2A-216 explain that their adjustment of the language in § 2-318 was intended to give effect to the comments to § 2-318. Were the drafters successful? Was this a clarification of the law, or a change in the law?

PROBLEM 3-11

In 1968, Bluto Construction Company entered into a contract with Swift to build a ham canning facility. A substantial amount of scaffolding equipment was needed for the job, and Bluto decided to lease the scaffolding rather than buy it. Bluto investigated the availability of the equipment and read a brochure that was printed by Morris Mfg. and had the name of Lysander Scaffolding stamped on it. The brochure described the scaffolding that Morris Mfg. manufactured as being sufficient to meet the requirements of the job and indicated that Lysander Scaffolding offered it for lease. Lysander had purchased the scaffolding and used Morris' brochure for promotional purposes. Bluto decided to lease the scaffolding from Lysander.

The scaffold equipment was used to support the roof deck cement pour. While the cement was being poured, the scaffolding collapsed. Although no employees were injured, the roof and a substantial part of the building were destroyed.

Answer the following questions:

1. Can Bluto recover from Morris Mfg. for a breach of warranty? Consider each alternative of § 2-318.

---

[13] [4] Of course, we can envision a situation when extending the warranty to a remote purchaser would so change the character and nature of the seller's performance that it would be beyond the seller's contemplation when it made the warranty. For example, had BB & B been a non-industrial consumer, its subsequent sale of the tractor to defendants for use in a rock crushing business might have dictated a different result. Under those circumstances, the more intensive use to which the tractor would have been put by defendants would have been far different than what plaintiff and BB & B originally bargained for. However, that is not the case here, where defendants' use of the tractor was identical to BB & B's.

2. What effect, if any, would the alternatives listed in § 2A-216 have on this problem? Assume one of Bluto's employees was injured. Would Article 2A help this employee recover from Morris?

3. Compare the alternatives of § 2-318 with the corresponding alternatives of § 2A-216. What are the differences? Will courts find it easier to expand coverage under § 2A-216 than they have under § 2-318? Can a lessor provide a warranty to the lessee but disclaim or limit it as to the classes of individuals described § 2A-216? Is the treatment of this issue the same under § 2-318?

The following case is indicative of a trend to extend warranty rights to consumers against remote manufacturers, even when the consumer does not suffer a personal injury. Is the court's analysis of § 2-318 persuasive in light of the historical context described by the court?

HYUNDAI MOTOR AMERICA, INC. v. GOODIN
Indiana Supreme Court
822 N.E.2d 947 (2005)

BOEHM, Justice.

We hold that a consumer may sue a manufacturer for economic loss based on breach of the implied warranty of merchantability even if the consumer purchased the product from an intermediary in the distribution chain. There is no requirement of "vertical" privity for such a claim.

Facts and Procedural Background

On November 18, 2000, Sandra Goodin test drove a Hyundai Sonata at AutoChoice Hyundai in Evansville, Indiana. The car was represented as new and showed nineteen miles on the odometer. Goodin testified that when she applied the brakes in the course of the test drive she experienced a "shimmy, shake, pulsating type feel." The AutoChoice salesperson told her that this was caused by flat spots on the tires from extended inactivity and offered to have the tires rotated and inspected. After this explanation, Goodin purchased the Sonata for $22,710.00.

The manufacturer, Hyundai, provided three limited warranties: 1 year/12,000 miles on "wear items;" 5 years/60,000 miles "bumper to bumper;" and 10 years/100,000 miles on the powertrain.[14] Hyundai concedes that brake rotors, brake calipers, and brake caliper slides were subject to the 5 year/60,000 mile warranty covering "[r]epair or replacement of any component originally manufactured or installed by [Hyundai] that is found to be defective in material or workmanship under normal use and maintenance." To claim under this warranty, a vehicle must be serviced by an authorized Hyundai dealer who is then reimbursed by Hyundai for any necessary parts or labor.

Three days after the car was purchased, Goodin's husband, Steven Hicks, took it back to AutoChoice for the promised tire work. Goodin testified that she continued to feel the shimmy but did nothing further for a month. On December 22, she took the car to a different Hyundai dealer, Bales Auto Mall, in Jeffersonville, Indiana, for an

---

[14] [1] On the "Buyers Order," AutoChoice Hyundai included the following pre-printed language in capital letters:

ALL WARRANTIES, IF ANY, BY A MANUFACTURER OR SUPPLIER OTHER THAN DEALER ARE THEIRS, NOT DEALER'S, AND ONLY SUCH MANUFACTURER OR OTHER SUPPLIER SHALL BE LIABLE FOR PERFORMANCE UNDER SUCH WARRANTIES, UNLESS DEALER FURNISHES BUYER WITH A SEPARATE WRITTEN WARRANTY MADE BY DEALER ON ITS OWN BEHALF. DEALER HEREBY DISCLAIMS ALL WARRANTIES, EXPRESS OR IMPLIED, INCLUDING ANY IMPLIED WARRANTIES OF MERCHANTABILITY OR FITNESS FOR A PARTICULAR PURPOSE, ON ALL GOODS AND SERVICES SOLD BY DEALER. . . .

unrelated problem and also made an appointment six days later for Bales to inspect the brakes. Bales serviced the brake rotors for warping, but on May 1, 2001, Goodin returned to Bales complaining that the vehicle continued to vibrate when the brakes were applied. Bales found the rotors to be out of tolerance and machined them. Eighteen days later Goodin again returned to Bales, reporting that she still felt vibrations and for the first time also heard a "popping" noise. Goodin told the service advisor at Bales that she thought there may be a problem with the suspension, and Bales changed and lubed the strut assembly. Eleven days later Goodin once more brought the car to Bales reporting continued shimmy and also a "bed spring type" noise originating from the brakes. The Bales mechanic was unable to duplicate the brake problem, but balanced and rotated the tires as Goodin had requested. One week later Goodin returned to Bales where she and Jerry Hawes, Bales's Service Manager, test drove the Sonata. The brake problem did not occur during the test drive, but Hawes identified a noise from the direction of the left front tire and repaired the rubber mounting bracket.

Goodin told Hawes that the brake problem had occurred about seventy percent of the time. The problem was worse when it was wet or cool, was consistently occurring when she drove down a steep hill near her home, and was less frequent when a passenger's weight was added. Goodin made arrangements to leave the car with Hawes at Bales, but, according to Hawes, over a several day period he could not duplicate the symptoms Goodin reported.

On August 24, 2001, Goodin took her car back to her original dealer, AutoChoice, reporting that the brakes "squeak and grind when applied." Goodin left the car with AutoChoice where the left front rotor was machined and loose bolts on the front upper control arm were tightened. Goodin testified that after this five-day procedure the brakes began to make the same noises and vibrations even before she arrived home.

In October 2001 Goodin hired an attorney who faxed a letter to Hyundai Motor America giving notice of her complaint and requesting a refund of the purchase price. On November 13, 2001, Goodin filed a complaint against Hyundai Motor America, Inc. alleging claims under the Magnuson-Moss Warranty Act, 15 U.S.C. §§ 2301–2312, for breach of express warranty, breach of implied warranty, and revocation of acceptance. On April 23, 2002, in anticipation of litigation, Goodin hired William Jones to inspect her car. Jones noted that the odometer read 57,918 miles and the car was still under warranty. Jones drove the car approximately five miles and found "severe brake pulsation on normal stops" which "was worse on high speed stops." Although he did not remove the tires to inspect the brake rotors, Jones opined that the rotors were warped and defective or there was "a root cause that has not been discovered and corrected by the repair facilities." His ultimate conclusion was that the "vehicle was defective and unmerchantable at the time of manufacture and unfit for operation on public roadways." Three weeks later, after the 5 year/60,000 mile warranty had expired, Goodin's husband, Hicks, replaced the rotors with new rotors from a NAPA distributor.[15] After this repair, according to Hicks, the pulsation went from "very bad" to "mild" and "less frequent."

Steven Heiss, District Parts and Service Manager for Hyundai Motor America served as the liaison between Hyundai and the dealers and provided warranty training. If a dealer is not performing repairs correctly, Hyundai, through its liaisons, addresses the problem. Heiss inspected Goodin's Sonata on October 21, 2002. At that point the Sonata had been driven 77,600 miles. He testified that during his twenty-three mile test drive he neither heard the noise described by Goodin nor felt any vibration from the brakes. However, Heiss did hear a "droning noise" which he later concluded was due to a failed left rear wheel bearing. He regarded this as a serious problem and not one

---

[15] [2] Hicks is an A.C. Certified Master Engine Machinist and Diesel Fuel Technician who had been trained in brakes during his certification process.

caused by abuse or misuse of the vehicle. The wheel bearing would have been covered by the 5 year/60,000 mile warranty. Before his inspection, Heiss had been told that the rotors had been changed by Hicks five months earlier, and when Heiss measured the rotors he found that they were out of standard. Heiss testified a miscast from the factory was one of a number of possible reasons for damaged rotors.

At the conclusion of a two day trial, the jury was instructed on all claims. Over defendants' objection, the instructions on implied warranties made no reference to a privity requirement. The jury returned a verdict for Hyundai on Goodin's breach of express warranty claim, but found in favor of Goodin on her claim for breach of implied warranty of merchantability. Damages of $3,000.00 were assessed and Goodin's counsel was later awarded attorneys' fees of $19,237.50 pursuant to the fee shifting provisions of the Magnuson-Moss Warranty Act.

Hyundai orally moved to set aside the verdict as contrary to law on the ground that Goodin purchased the car from AutoChoice and therefore did not enjoy vertical privity with Hyundai. The court initially denied that motion, but the following day set aside the verdict, holding lack of privity between Goodin and Hyundai precluded a cause of action for breach of implied warranty. Goodin then moved to reinstate the verdict, and, after briefing and oral argument, the trial court granted that motion on the ground that Hyundai was estopped from asserting lack of privity.

Hyundai appealed, asserting: (1) it was not estopped from asserting a defense of lack of privity; and (2) lack of vertical privity barred Goodin's recovery for breach of implied warranty of merchantability. The Court of Appeals agreed on both points, holding that Hyundai was not estopped from asserting that privity was an element of Goodin's prima facia case, and, because privity was lacking, Goodin did not prove her case. *Hyundai Motor Am., Inc. v. Goodin*, 804 N.E.2d 775, 781 (Ind. Ct. App. 2004). The Magnuson-Moss Warranty Act looks to state law for the contours of implied warranties. The Court of Appeals was "not unsympathetic" to Goodin's claims but regarded itself as bound by a footnote in *Martin Rispens & Son v. Hall Farms, Inc.*, 621 N.E.2d 1078, 1084 n. 2 (Ind. 1993), where this Court stated: "In Indiana, privity between the seller and the buyer is required to maintain a cause of action on the implied warranties of merchantability." *Id.* at 784. We granted transfer. *Hyundai Motor Am., Inc. v. Goodin*, 812 N.E.2d 808 (Ind. 2004).

Vertical Privity

A. The Relationship Between Federal and State Law in Claims

Based on Implied Warranty of Merchantability

This case is brought under a federal statute. The Magnuson-Moss Warranty Act, 15 U.S.C. §§ 2301–2312 (2000), provides a federal right of action for consumers to enforce written or implied warranties where they claim to be damaged by the failure of a supplier, warrantor, or service contractor to comply with any obligation under that statute or under a written warranty, implied warranty, or service contract. The Act also limits the extent to which manufacturers who give express warranties may disclaim or modify implied warranties, but looks to state law as the source of any express or implied warranty. *Schimmer v. Jaguar Cars, Inc.*, 384 F.3d 402, 405 (7th Cir. 2004). As the Seventh Circuit recently put it: "because §§ 2308 and 2304(a) do not modify, or discuss in any way, a state's ability to establish a privity requirement, whether privity is a prerequisite to a claim for breach of implied warranty under the Magnuson-Moss Act therefore hinges entirely on the applicable state law." *Voelker v. Porsche Cars N. Am., Inc.*, 353 F.3d 516, 525 (7th Cir. 2003).

Goodin's claim is for breach of the implied warranty of merchantability, not for violation of any substantive provision of the federal statute. Accordingly, her claim lives or dies on the resolution of an issue of state law, specifically whether Indiana requires privity between buyer and manufacturer for a claim of breach of implied warranty.

B. Standard of Review

Hyundai does not dispute that under circumstances applicable here Indiana recognizes implied warranties of fitness for a particular purpose and implied warranties of merchantability. Ind. Code §§ 26-1-2-314, 315 (2003). Rather, Hyundai contends that under Indiana law, a buyer must be in vertical privity with a seller to impose liability on the seller for breach of an implied warranty. Whether Indiana law requires privity to sustain an action for breach of an implied warranty is purely a question of law and therefore is reviewed under a de novo standard. *See Griffith v. State*, 788 N.E.2d 835, 839 (Ind. 2003). An implied warranty of merchantability imposed by operation of law is to be liberally construed in favor of the buyer. *Frantz v. Cantrell*, 711 N.E.2d 856, 859 (Ind. Ct. App. 1999).

C. Origins of Privity

Indiana has adopted the Uniform Commercial Code, notably its provision that: "A warranty that the goods shall be merchantable is implied in a contract for their sale if the seller is a merchant with respect to goods of that kind. . . ." Ind. Code § 26-1-2-314(1) (2004). Hyundai asserts, and the Court of Appeals found, Indiana law requires vertical privity between manufacturer and consumer when economic damages[16] are sought. *Hyundai*, 804 N.E.2d at 783. Goodin argues that traditional privity of contract between the consumer and manufacturer is not required for a claim against a manufacturer for breach of the implied warranty of merchantability, especially if the manufacturer provides a Magnuson-Moss express warranty with the product.

Privity originated as a doctrine limiting tort relief for breach of warranties. The lack of privity defense was first recognized in *Winterbottom v. Wright*, 10 M. & W. 109, 152 Eng. Rep. 402 (Ex. 1842). 2 HAWKLAND, U.C.C. SERIES, § 2-318:1 at 771 (2001). In that case, the court sustained a demurrer to a suit by an injured coachman for breach of warranty by a third party who contracted with the owner to maintain the coach. In this century, however, *MacPherson v. Buick Motor Co.*, 217 N.Y. 382, 111 N.E. 1050 (1916), and *Henningsen v. Bloomfield Motors, Inc.*, 32 N.J. 358, 161 A.2d 69 (1960), established that lack of privity between an automobile manufacturer and a consumer would not preclude the consumer's action for personal injuries and property damage caused by the negligent manufacture of an automobile. "Vertical" privity typically becomes an issue when a purchaser files a breach of warranty action against a vendor in the purchaser's distribution chain who is not the purchaser's immediate seller. HAWKLAND, *supra*, at 771. Simply put, vertical privity exists only between immediate links in a distribution chain. *Rheem Mfg. Co. v. Phelps Heating & Air Conditioning, Inc.*, 714 N.E.2d 1218, 1228 n. 8 (Ind. Ct. App. 1999). A buyer in the same chain who did not purchase directly from a seller is "remote" as to that seller. *Id.* "Horizontal" privity, in contrast, refers to claims by non-purchasers, typically someone who did not purchase the product but who was injured while using it. 1 JAMES J. WHITE & ROBERT S. SUMMERS, UNIFORM COMMERCIAL CODE 585 (4th ed.1995). Goodin purchased her car from a dealership and is thus remote from the manufacturer and lacks "vertical" privity with Hyundai.

---

[16] [4] In *Reed v. Central Soya Co., Inc.*, 621 N.E.2d 1069, 1074 (Ind. 1993), this Court defined economic damages under Indiana law as "the diminution in the value of a product and consequent loss of profits because the product is inferior in quality and does not work for the general purposes for which it was manufactured and sold." In this case, Goodin seeks only direct economic damages the decreased value of the Sonata by reason of the allegedly defective brakes. Goodin seeks the difference between the actual value of the goods accepted and the value they would have had if they had been as warranted. *See* I.C. § 26-1-2-714(2). Damages can also be measured by the cost of replacement or the cost of repair. *Rheem Mfg. Co. v. Phelps Heating & Air Conditioning, Inc.*, 746 N.E.2d 941, 955–56 (Ind. 2001).

"Although warranty liability originated as a tort doctrine, it was assimilated by the law of contracts and ultimately became part of the law of sales." HAWKLAND, *supra*, at 771. But "privity is more than an accident of history. It permitted manufacturers and distributors to control in some measure their risks of doing business." Richard W. Duesenberg, *The Manufacturer's Last Stand: The Disclaimer*, 20 BUS. LAW 159, 161 (1964). Because vertical privity involves a claim by a purchaser who voluntarily acquired the goods, it enjoys a stronger claim to justification on the basis of freedom of contract or consensual relationship. It nevertheless has come under criticism in recent years, and this is the first opportunity for this Court to give full consideration to this issue.

D. Indiana Case Law

Although this Court did not address the issue, even before the Products Liability Act, both the Court of Appeals and federal courts applying Indiana law held that a claimant was not required to prove privity to succeed in a personal injury action in tort based on breach of implied warranties. *Lane v. Barringer*, 407 N.E.2d 1173, 1175 (Ind. Ct. App. 1980); *Dagley v. Armstrong Rubber Co.*, 344 F.2d 245, 252 (7th Cir. 1965) (drawing support from *J.I. Case Co. v. Sandefur*, 245 Ind. 213, 221–22, 197 N.E.2d 519, 523 (1964)); *Neofes v. Robertshaw Controls Co.*, 409 F. Supp. 1376, 1379 (S.D. Ind. 1976). Three federal court decisions drew on these decisions to conclude that privity of contract is not required in Indiana to maintain a cause of action for personal injury based on breach of an implied warranty. *See Filler v. Rayex Corp.*, 435 F.2d 336, 337–38 (7th Cir. 1970) (Indiana law does not require privity between manufacturer and plaintiff under theories of implied warranty, strict liability or negligence); *Dagley*, 344 F.2d at 254; *Karczewski v. Ford Motor Co.*, 382 F. Supp. 1346, 1352 (N.D. Ind. 1974).

However, several Court of Appeals decisions subsequently held that recovery of economic loss for alleged failure of the expected benefit of the bargain based on breach of implied warranty under the UCC required a buyer to be in privity of contract with the seller. *See Candlelight Homes, Inc. v. Zornes*, 414 N.E.2d 980, 982 (Ind. Ct. App. 1981); *Lane*, 407 N.E.2d at 1173; *Richards v. Goerg Boat & Motors, Inc.*, 179 Ind. App. 102, 384 N.E.2d 1084 (1979). *Corbin v. Calico Industries*, 748 F.2d 411, 415 (7th Cir. 1984), took the view that "[s]ubsequent Indiana cases have shed new light on Indiana's interpretation of implied warranty under the UCC, thus making it clear that privity is indeed required."

* * *

Indiana law, as developed in the Court of Appeals, has already eroded the privity requirement to some degree. In *Thompson Farms, Inc. v. Corno Feed Products, Inc.*, 173 Ind. App. 682, 366 N.E.2d 3 (1977), the Court of Appeals permitted the plaintiff to recover on an implied warranty where it was shown that the contractual arrangements between the manufacturer and the dealer who sold to the plaintiff created an agency relationship; and the manufacturer's agents participated significantly in the sale both through advertising and personal contact with the buyer. Under those circumstances the Court of Appeals held that the manufacturer was a "seller" within the meaning of Indiana Code section 26-1-2-314. *Richards*, 179 Ind. App. at 112, 384 N.E.2d at 1092, involved a defective boat sold by a dealer where the manufacturer's agents also engaged in personal contact with the buyer by giving demonstrations and attempting to adjust the loss after the sale. The Court of Appeals then, following *Thompson Farms, Inc.*, held that the participation in the sale by the manufacturer was sufficient to bring it into the transaction as a seller within the requirements of Indiana Code section 26-1-2-314. However, if the plaintiff could not show perfect vertical privity or an exception to the rule, then the plaintiff could not prove the claim. *Candlelight Homes*, 414 N.E.2d at 982.

E. Statutory Developments in Indiana

The Product Liability Act, Indiana Code § 34-20-2-1 *et seq.* (1999), does not require a personal injury plaintiff to prove vertical privity in order to assert a products liability claim against the manufacturer. *See Lane*, 407 N.E.2d at 1175. Even before the Product Liability Act in 1978, the requirement of privity of contract in warranty actions in Indiana began to erode in 1963 with the passage of the Uniform Commercial Code under section 2-318:

> A seller's warranty whether express or implied extends to any natural person who is in the family or household of his buyer or who is a guest in his home if it is reasonable to expect that such person may use, consume or be affected by the goods and who is injured in person by breach of the warranty. A seller may not exclude or limit the operation of this section.

I.C. § 26-1-2-318. Section 2-318 was taken verbatim from the UCC as originally prepared by the Uniform Code Committee Draftsmen in 1952. It eliminated "horizontal" privity as a requirement for warranty actions. However, that version of 2-318 took no position on the requirement of vertical privity. WHITE & SUMMERS, *supra*, at 586.

The purpose of the original version of section 2-318, which remains unchanged in Indiana today, was to give standing to certain non-privity plaintiffs to sue as third-party beneficiaries of the warranties that a buyer received under a sales contract. HAWKLAND, *supra*, at 769. That version of section 2-318 provided only that the benefit of a warranty automatically extended to the buyer's family, household, and houseguests. *Id., supra*, at 775. It was intended to, and did, accomplish its goal of "freeing any such beneficiaries from any technical rules as to [horizontal] privity." UCC § 2-318 cmt. 2. Some states refused to enact this version of section 2-318, and others adopted non-uniform versions of the statute. HAWKLAND, *supra*, at 777. In 1966, in response to this proliferation of deviant versions of a purportedly uniform code, the drafters proposed three alternative versions of section 2-318. Only California, Louisiana, and Texas have failed to adopt one of these three versions of section 2-318.

The majority of states, including Indiana, retained or adopted the 1952 version of section 2-318, which now appears in the Uniform Commercial Code as "Alternative A." Alternative B provides that "any natural person who may reasonably be expected to use, consume or be affected by the goods and who is injured in person by breach of warranty" may institute a breach of warranty action against the seller. UCC § 2-318 cmt. 3. Alternative B expands the class of potential plaintiffs beyond family, household, and guests, and also implicitly abolishes the requirement of vertical privity because the seller's warranty is not limited to "his buyer" and persons closely associated with that buyer. *See* HAWKLAND, *supra*, at 789. Alternative B is applicable only to claims for personal injury.

> Because Alternatives A and B of 2-318 are limited to cases where the plaintiff is "injured in person," they do not *authorize* recovery for such loss. But neither do they *bar* a non-privity plaintiff from recovery against such a remote manufacturer for direct economic loss. . . . Thus, Alternatives A and B of 2-318 do not prevent a court from abolishing the *vertical* privity requirement even when a non-privity buyer seeks recovery for direct economic loss.

WHITE & SUMMERS, *supra*, at 593 (emphasis in original).

Alternative C is the most expansive in eliminating the lack-of-privity defense. WHITE & SUMMERS, *supra*, at 593; HAWKLAND, *supra*, at 792. It provides that: "A seller's warranty whether express or implied extends to any person who may reasonably be expected to use, consume or be affected by the goods and who is injured by breach of the warranty." HAWKLAND, *supra*, at 769. Alternative C expands the class of plaintiffs to include other non-purchasers such as the buyer's employees and invitees, and bystanders. Jane M. Draper, Annotation, *Third-Party Beneficiaries of Warranties Under UCC*

§ 2-318, 100 A.L.R.3d 743 at §§ 5–6 (1980). Alternative C also eliminates the vertical privity requirement, but is not restricted to "personal" injury. Because Alternative C refers simply to "injury," plaintiffs sustaining only property damage or economic loss in some states have been held to have standing to sue under this language. *See, e.g., Milbank Mut. Ins. Co. v. Proksch,* 309 Minn. 106, 244 N.W.2d 105 (1976) (allowing purchaser's father to recover for residential property damage caused when their Christmas tree caught fire). This is consistent with the stated objective of the drafters that the third alternative follow "the trend of modern decisions as indicated by RESTATEMENT OF TORTS 2D § 402A (Tentative Draft No. 10, 1965) in extending the rule beyond injuries to the person." HAWKLAND, *supra,* at 770; *But see Nebraska Innkeepers, Inc. v. Pittsburgh-Des Moines Corp.,* 345 N.W.2d 124, 129 (Iowa 1984) (holding Alternative C did not permit non-privity plaintiffs to seek recovery solely for economic loss).

The commentaries to the UCC were careful to explain that these alternatives were not to be taken as excluding the development of the common law on the issue of vertical privity:

> [Alternative A] expressly includes as beneficiaries within its provisions the family, household and guests of the purchaser. Beyond this, the section in this form is neutral and is not intended to enlarge or restrict the developing case law on whether the seller's warranties, given to his buyer who resells, extend to other persons in the distributive chain.

U.C.C. § 2-318, cmt. n. 3.

F. Privity as an Obsolete Requirement as Applied to Consumer Goods

There is a split of authority in other jurisdictions with similar or identical versions of section 2-318 on the availability of implied warranty claims by remote purchasers, particularly if only economic loss is claimed, as in the present case. Courts of other jurisdictions that have retained or adopted Alternative A note that the statute speaks only to horizontal privity, and is silent as to vertical privity. . . . As the Pennsylvania Supreme Court put it: "Merely to *read* the language [of § 2-318] is to demonstrate that the code simply fails to treat this problem. . . . There thus is nothing to prevent this court from joining in the growing number of jurisdictions which, although bound by the code, have nevertheless abolished vertical privity in breach of warranty cases." . . . Indiana has not legislated on this issue since 1966 when the UCC adopted these three alternatives. More recently, the "Buyback Vehicle Disclosure" statute eliminated the lack-of-privity defense for actions under that section. *See* I.C. § 24-5-13.5-13(c) (1995). In short, the General Assembly in keeping Alternative A left to this Court the issue of to what extent vertical privity of contract will be required.

Courts that have abolished vertical privity have cited a variety of reasons. Principal among these is the view that, in today's economy, manufactured products typically reach the consuming public through one or more intermediaries. As a result, any loss from an unmerchantable product is likely to be identified only after the product is attempted to be used or consumed. . . . Others have cited the concern that privity encourages thinly capitalized manufacturers by insulating them from responsibility for inferior products. . . . Yet others have focused on the point that if implied warranties are effective against remote sellers it produces a chain of lawsuits or cross-claims against those up the distribution chain. . . .

Finally, some jurisdictions have abolished privity in warranty actions where only economic losses were sought based on the notion that there is "no reason to distinguish between recovery for personal and property injury, on the one hand, and economic loss on the other." . . . A variance on this theme is the view that abolishing privity "simply recognizes that economic loss is potentially devastating to the buyer of an unmerchantable product and that it is unjust to preclude any recovery from the manufacturer for such loss because of a lack of privity, when the slightest physical injury can give rise to strict liability under the same circumstances." . . . One court preserving the privity requirement expressed the view that "there may be cases where the plaintiff may be unfairly prejudiced by the operation of the economic loss rule in combination with the privity requirement." . . .

In Indiana, the economic loss rule applies to bar recovery in tort "where a negligence claim is based upon the failure of a product to perform as expected and the plaintiff suffers only economic damages." . . . Possibly because of the economic loss rule, Goodin did not raise a negligence claim here. Furthermore, at oral argument Goodin's attorney pointed to the warranty disclaimer in the Buyer's Order as a bar to Goodin's ability to sue her direct seller, AutoChoice, which could then have sued Hyundai for reimbursement. This disclaimer, Goodin contends, precluded a chain of claims ultimately reaching the manufacturer. Therefore, Goodin claims that if this Court does not abolish the vertical privity requirement she will be left without a remedy for Hyundai's breach of its implied warranty of merchantability, and Hyundai's implied warranty becomes nonexistent in practical terms.

The basis for the privity requirement in a contract claim is essentially the idea that the parties to a sale of goods are free to bargain for themselves and thus allocation of risk of failure of a product is best left to the private sector. Otherwise stated, the law should not impose a contract the parties do not wish to make. The Court of Appeals summarized this view well:

> Generally privity extends to the parties to the contract of sale. It relates to the bargained for expectations of the buyer and seller. Accordingly, when the cause of action arises out of economic loss related to the loss of the bargain or profits and consequential damages related thereto, the bargained for expectations of buyer and seller are relevant and privity between them is still required.

> Implied warranties of merchantability and fitness for a particular use, as they relate to economic loss from the bargain, cannot then ordinarily be sustained between the buyer and a remote manufacturer.

Richards, 179 Ind. App. at 112, 384 N.E.2d at 1092 (citations omitted). We think that this rationale has eroded to the point of invisibility as applied to many types of consumer goods in today's economy. The UCC recognizes an implied warranty of merchantability if "goods" are sold to "consumers" by one who ordinarily deals in this product. Warranties are often explicitly promoted as marketing tools, as was true in this case of the Hyundai warranties. Consumer expectations are framed by these legal developments to the point where technically advanced consumer goods are virtually always sold under express warranties, which, as a matter of federal law run to the consumer without regard to privity. 15 U.S.C. § 2310. Magnuson-Moss precludes a disclaimer of the implied warranty of merhantability as to consumer goods where an express warranty is given. 15 U.S.C. § 2308. Given this framework, we think ordinary consumers are entitled to, and do, expect that a consumer product sold under a warranty is merchantable, at least at the modest level of merchantability set by UCC section 2-314, where hazards common to the type of product do not render the product unfit for normal use. *Cf. Allgood v. R.J. Reynolds Tobacco Co.*, 80 F.3d 168, 171 (5th Cir. 1996) (under Texas law, only actual sellers are liable, not trade associations nor public relations agents who play a role in distribution. "Even where a party has promoted a product, and made promises regarding that product, if the party is not the actual seller a claim for breach of warranty will not lie.").

Even if one party to the contract—the manufacturer—intends to extend an implied warranty only to the immediate purchaser, in a consumer setting, doing away with the **privity requirement** for a product subject to the Magnuson-Moss Warranty Act, rather **than rewriting** the deal, simply gives the consumer the contract the consumer expected.

The manufacturer, on the other hand is encouraged to build quality into its products. To the extent there is a cost of adding uniform or standard quality in all products, the risk of a lemon is passed to all buyers in the form of pricing and not randomly distributed among those unfortunate enough to have acquired one of the lemons. Moreover, elimination of privity requirement gives consumers such as Goodin the value of their expected bargain, but will rarely do more than duplicate the Products Liability Act as to other consequential damages. The remedy for breach of implied warranty of merchantability is in most cases, including this one, the difference between "the value of the goods accepted and the value they would have had if they had been as warranted." 714 I.C. § 26-1-2-714(2). This gives the buyer the benefit of the bargain. In most cases, however, if any additional damages are available under the UCC as the result of abolishing privity, Indiana law would award the same damages under the Products Liability Act as personal injury or damage to "other property" from a "defective" product. *Gunkel v. Renovations, Inc.*, 822 N.E.2d 150, 2005 WL 236630 (Feb. 01, 2005).

For the reasons given above we conclude that Indiana law does not require vertical privity between a consumer and a manufacturer as a condition to a claim by the consumer against the manufacturer for breach of the manufacturer's implied warranty of merchantability.

Conclusion

The judgment of the trial court is affirmed.

5. Seller's Exclusion or Modification of Warranties

One of the primary functions of contracting is to carefully limit the scope of one's obligations, exercising what is sometimes termed the "freedom from contract." Sellers are particularly concerned about their warranty obligations, which go to the heart of their commitment to the buyer, and so they seek to ensure that they are not warranting more than they wish to be held accountable for providing. First, a seller might be concerned about the implied warranties in certain cases. For example, a seller that is reselling used goods may not be willing to warrant that the goods are merchantable, at least not without increasing the price to reflect increased expenditures to assess the goods and to provide self-insurance for the goods that will be returned as defective. Because the implied warranties of merchantability and fitness for particular purpose are default provisions rather than mandatory provisions, they may be disclaimed entirely or modified in scope by agreement. Section 2-316 provides detailed rules for sellers seeking to exclude implied warranties.

In a related vein, sellers may be worried that their sales department will promise the moon to a buyer in order to make the sale, resulting in an express warranty that the goods cannot meet. Consider the problems facing a car dealership if its salesperson eagerly describes a vehicle to prospective buyers as being the "safest car on the road according to government crash statistics." If this statement of fact is untrue (and is regarded as an affirmation of fact rather than mere commendation), the dealership may be bound to an express warranty by its sales agent. However, § 2-316(1) clearly provides that a seller may not negate or limit an express warranty in the same manner that it may exclude or modify an implied warranty. Once a seller creates an express warranty, it cannot be taken out of the deal by a disclaimer. However, the statute cross-references the parol evidence rule, and Comment 2 explains that a seller concerned about unauthorized express warranties is protected by the parol evidence rule.

The first case provides an overview of these two strategies for limiting the seller's warranty obligations, and the succeeding cases provide more details about the requirements of § 2-316. After reading these cases and reading the Code language carefully, you should be prepared to work through the problems.

L.S. HEATH & SON v. AT & T INFORMATION SYSTEMS
United States Court of Appeals, Seventh Circuit
9 F.3d 561 (1993)

CUDAHY, Circuit Judge.

L.S. Heath & Sons (Heath) brought this action against AT & T Information Systems (AT & T) alleging, *inter alia*, that AT & T breached implied and express warranties and committed common-law and statutory fraud in the sale of a computer network. The suit was removed to federal court and AT & T counterclaimed on the contract. The district court granted summary judgment in favor of AT & T on its counterclaims and subsequently granted summary judgment against Heath on each of its claims. We have jurisdiction pursuant to 28 U.S.C. §§ 1332 & 1291. We affirm in part, reverse in part and remand.

I.

Heath is a manufacturer of chocolate products, incorporated and with its principal place of business in Illinois. In 1984, Heath decided that its current computer system was becoming outmoded and resolved to upgrade and enhance its computer and telecommunications capabilities. It therefore established an executive committee to research the needs of the company and to solicit sales proposals from interested vendors. Honeywell, IBM and AT & T were among the vendors submitting bids.

AT & T is a Delaware corporation with its principal place of business in New Jersey. In 1984, AT & T was just entering the computer market and, in preparing its bid, spent a great deal of time gathering information about Heath and Heath's computer and telecommunication needs. Two representatives of AT & T were instrumental in working with Heath and in preparing AT & T's proposal — Account Executive Tim Keith and Technical Consultant Ed Hein. On August 3, 1984, AT & T presented its final Recommendation and Proposal (Recommendation) to the executive committee. The Recommendation restated Heath's eight main objectives[17] and provided that "[s]tarting with a System 75 as the backbone we will progressively build to a complete intregated [*sic*] data processing and voice/data communications network that satisfies all of your aforementioned objectives. AT & T can make this statement — AT & T-IS can provide from *one* source all of your voice and data needs."

The Recommendation then went on to propose a phased implementation schedule

---

[17] [1] Heath's main objectives, as restated in AT & T's Recommendation, were as follows:

INTERACTIVE SYSTEM — To convert from a primarily batch mode system to an interactive system providing on-line real time information input, processing and output.

DISTRIBUTED PROCESSING — To provide for processing, storage and access at the West Plant and other designated locations to allow for main CPU shut down while maintaining processing capability. Through the System 75, each of the distributed processors will still be able to access and update the main CPU during normal office hours.

REAL TIME INFORMATION AVAILABILITY — To provide on-line access to actual current information for designated personnel.

OPEN ARCHITECTURE — To initially install a system that will facilitate future growth, enhancements and additions without a major equipment or software change.

GROWTH — To implement a system capable of expansion to support your increasing voice and data requirements.

PORTABILITY — To build the new system around hardware and software that can be interchanged and, if necessary, can be economically physically moved.

PHASED TRANSITION — A must. Any provided system will be implemented in logical phases that will allow budgeting, program assurance, new user training and be responsive to your developing needs.

PARTNERSHIP/ONE VENDOR — To form an ongoing partnership with *one vendor* to plan and implement an integrated information system.

whereby the network would be assembled and programmed in six phases. By the sixth phase of implementation, to be completed by February 1, 1986, the network would consist of a 3–2 computer processor at Heath's plant, with the larger 3–5 processor to be located at the office facility; a System 75 to link the computers to the users; a protocol converter to enable the AT & T network to communicate with Heath's existing IBM System 3 computer; 3 printers and 17 terminals; and numerous software applications.

Heath agreed to the design, and a two-page Master Agreement was signed by the parties in September and October of 1984. The Master Agreement did not identify any prices, products, services, software, applications or systems, but simply stated that the agreement would cover all future purchases.

AT & T began to install the system and Heath ordered supplemental equipment as recommended by AT & T. For each piece of equipment purchased, Heath would sign a Computer Systems Amendment for the specific products purchased. In all, there were six such amendments, involving at least 35 additional products.

In 1985, the project was progressing relatively smoothly, and AT & T approached Heath about using Heath and its computer system in a national advertising campaign consisting of print and video advertisements. The advertisements and brochures emphasized the benefits and flexibility of the integrated voice/data system AT & T was providing Heath. For instance, the magazine ad run by AT & T featured Heath executives explaining why Heath selected AT & T's System 75, stating that "the system [AT & T] proposed could easily accommodate internal growth and technological change . . . [and] [w]e can expand our system, add new products, and incorporate new technology as it becomes available. . . ." The AT & T brochures also stated that "AT & T is designing and installing a fully integrated communications and information system custom-tailored to Heath's long-term needs."[18]

In 1986, however, the project apparently began experiencing difficulties. It was determined that the 3–5 processor did not have sufficient memory to perform the tasks desired by Heath and the processor was upgraded to a larger 3–15. Even with this upgrade, however, Heath's review of the system suggested that the processor was undersized to perform all of the desired applications and that the strain on the processor's capacity caused the system to slow down when in use. There were also problems with the protocol converter used to communicate between the new system and Heath's old IBM System 3.

By the end of 1987, the system was still not working as Heath had anticipated. Therefore, on December 23, 1987, Heath served notice on AT & T and formally demanded a cure within seven days or it would revoke its acceptance of the computer and sue for incidental and consequential damages. When AT & T did not respond to the demand for a cure, Heath informed AT & T on January 4, 1988, that it was formally revoking its acceptance.

Heath then filed this suit in Illinois state court on January 20, 1988, and AT & T removed the action to federal court on diversity grounds. Heath's First Amended Complaint raised eight causes of action against AT & T: (1) breach of implied warranty of fitness for a particular purpose; (2) breach of implied warranty of merchantability; (3) breach of express warranties as to the ability of AT & T's equipment and software to meet Heath's objectives. . . .

* * *

---

[18] [2] The record also contains an article published in late 1984 or early 1985 in *Focus*, an internal AT & T publication, entitled *A Sweet Mixture: An Integrated Voice and Data System*, detailing the selling of the System 75 to Heath by AT & T.

B. *Breach of Warranty Claims*

The district court granted summary judgment against Heath's breach of warranty claims on the ground that all warranties except those expressly contained in the agreement had been disclaimed by the provision to that effect in the Master Agreement. The court concluded that the Master Agreement was an integrated document because it contained a merger clause. The only express warranty found in that document, according to the court, was AT & T's representation that the equipment would be in good working order in accordance with AT & T specifications. The court then held that, because there was no evidence that the equipment was not in good working order — only evidence that it could not perform as promised — summary judgment was appropriate.

Heath contends that summary judgment was not warranted because the agreement between the parties extended beyond the provisions of the Master Agreement and included AT & T's promises before and after the Master Agreement was signed. Heath maintains that there is a genuine factual dispute whether the parties intended the Master Agreement to be the complete and exclusive statement of their agreement. Heath insists that the Master Agreement cannot be a complete statement of the agreement because that document omits basic and essential items of information. According to Heath, the Recommendation indicates that the parties intended that AT & T provide a fully integrated, custom-tailored information system meeting all of Heath's stated objectives. Because the Recommendation is part of the agreement between the parties, Heath argues, the district court was remiss in not considering the express warranties found in that document.

Heath relies principally on *Sierra Diesel Injection Service, Inc. v. Burroughs Corp.*, 890 F.2d 108 (9th Cir. 1989). In that case, a buyer of computer hardware and software received a letter from the seller stating that its computer could "put your inventory, receivables, and invoicing under complete control." *Id.* at 110. The buyer purchased the computer and signed various form contracts for the hardware, software and maintenance service. When the computer did not perform the invoicing and accounting functions for which it was purchased, the buyer brought suit alleging that the computer company breached the express warranties found in the initial letter as well as the implied warranty of merchantability. The court held that the form contracts did not represent the entire agreement between the parties, despite the existence of a merger clause, but that representations made in the letter were part of the agreement. The court concluded that the disclaimer of warranty in the printed form contracts was ineffective to void the express warranties in the letter. Further, because the disclaimer was not conspicuous, it was also ineffective to void the implied warranty of merchantability.

Consistent with *Sierra Diesel*, we believe that in the present case genuine issues of fact exist to preclude summary judgment on the breach of express warranty claim. On the other hand, summary judgment was proper on the implied warranty claims. Under the UCC parol evidence rule,

> a writing intended by the parties as a final expression of their agreement . . . may not be contradicted by evidence of any prior agreement or of a contemporaneous oral agreement but may be explained or supplemented . . . by evidence of consistent additional terms unless the court finds the writing to have been intended also as a complete and exclusive statement of the terms of the agreement.

N.J. Rev. Stat. § 12A:2-202. We find initially that the parties did not necessarily intend the Master Agreement to reflect the complete agreement between the parties simply because they included the merger clause. To be sure, the presence of a merger clause is strong evidence that the parties intended the writing to be the complete and exclusive agreement between them, but such a clause is not dispositive. *Sierra Diesel*, 890 F.2d at 112; R. ANDERSON, UNIFORM COMMERCIAL CODE, § 2-202:25 (1983). In order to determine whether the parties intended a writing to be the complete and exclusive agreement between them, a court must compare the writing with the prior negotiations. *Atlantic Northern Airlines, Inc. v. Schwimmer*, 96 A.2d 652, 656, 12 N.J. 293 (1953). If the allegedly integrated writing does not, without reference to another document or other coordinating information, reveal what the basic transaction entailed, then the writing is not integrated. *Sierra Diesel*, 890 F.2d at 113.

Based on this reasoning, the Master Agreement clearly fails to reflect the complete agreement between the parties. The Master Agreement omits subject matter; it does not identify any prices, products, services, software applications or configurations. Further, contrary to AT & T's contentions, the Master Agreement does not reflect the complete agreement even when considered together with the System Amendments.[19] Neither the Master Agreement nor its Amendments reflect the fact that the parties intended for AT & T to custom-tailor and install for Heath a fully integrated information system which would solve specific problems and perform specific applications. Indeed, under AT & T's theory, it could have ended its relationship with Heath without breaching the contract after performing on the *first Amendment*, since the Master Agreement does not articulate what products and services must ultimately be included in the Amendments. If nothing else, it would seem that the parties would have opted for a contractual arrangement less open-ended than that contemplated by the Master Agreement and Amendments if they merely wished to ensure the delivery of discrete products and services unrelated to some larger goal.

The Recommendation, with its detailed discussion of this information and with a specific time frame for implementing and completing the proposed transaction, provides the terms the Master Agreement and Amendments lack. For purposes of summary judgment, however, we do not have to conclude definitively that the Recommendation is part of the agreement, but simply must find, as we do, that the Master Agreement and System Amendments do not reflect the complete and exclusive agreement between the parties.

Although we do not conclude that the Recommendation is part of the agreement — a question we leave for the trier of fact — we shall assume, *arguendo*, that key terms contained in the Recommendation do constitute part of the agreement between Heath and AT & T. We then find that AT & T's statement that its "complete integrated [sic] data processing and voice/data communications network [will] satisf[y] all of your [Heath's] aforementioned objectives," may amount to an express warranty. For § 12A:2-313 provides that express warranties are created when:

---

[19] [5] AT & T argues that the Master Agreement and System Amendments together constitute the final agreement between the parties based on case law stating that documents that refer to or incorporate each other must be analyzed together. Appellee Pet. at 5–6. Such reference or incorporation is not clearly evidenced by the Master Agreement's integration clause. The integration clause contained in the Master Agreement is as follows:

> THIS IS THE ENTIRE AGREEMENT BETWEEN THE PARTIES WITH RESPECT TO THE PRODUCTS AND SERVICES HEREUNDER AND SUPERSEDES ALL PRIOR AGREEMENTS, PROPOSALS OR UNDERSTANDINGS WHETHER WRITTEN OR ORAL.

It is not entirely clear exactly what the subject of the sentence, "THIS," refers to. "THIS" may refer to the Master Agreement alone or to the Agreement together with the Amendments or "THIS" may include other documents. The Master Agreement, if it refers to or incorporates the System Amendments at all, does so by declaring its application "to any order for the provision or sale of products and services to Customer [Heath] by AT & T-IS which is placed by Customer on or after the date Customer signs this Agreement." Appellee B.R. at 25 (quoting from Master Agreement). That is, even though the Master Agreement does not appear to use the word "amendments," the Master Agreement arguably governs the sale of specific products and services contemplated in each of the Amendments because Heath placed these sales "on or after" the date it signed the Agreement. The Amendments reference the Master Agreement more explicitly, each stating that "Customer Requests the Provision of the Following Products Subject to the Terms and Conditions of the Above-Referenced Contract. . . ." *Id.* at 26 (quoting from Systems Amendments).

Any affirmation of fact or promise made by the seller to the buyer which relates to the goods and becomes part of the basis of the bargain creates an express warranty that the goods shall conform to the affirmation or promise.

A statement can amount to a warranty, even if unintended to be such by the seller, "if it could fairly be understood . . . to constitute an affirmation or representation that the [product] possesse[s] a certain quality or capacity relating to future performance." *Gladden v. Cadillac Motor Car Div., General Motors Corp.*, 416 A.2d 394, 396, 83 N.J. 320 (1980). The statement made in the Recommendation clearly could be understood as an assurance that the computer network sold to Heath would perform up to certain standards — in particular, that it would satisfy all of Heath's objectives in purchasing the network. And there is no question that such assurances had a "natural tendency" to induce Heath to select AT & T for its computer and telecommunications needs and, thus, were a significant part of the basis of the bargain. *Id.*

AT & T, however, relies upon the disclaimer provision in the Master Agreement and contends that, even if those assurances in the Recommendation could be considered express warranties, they were effectively disclaimed. But under UCC § 2-316, a warranty disclaimer inconsistent with an express warranty is inoperative. N.J. Rev. Stat. 12A:2-316; *Gladden*, 416 A.2d at 398; *accord Sierra Diesel*, 890 F.2d at 113.

*   *   *

With respect to the breach of implied warranty claims, however, we agree with the district court that the disclaimer was effective. The implied warranty of merchantability may be disclaimed if the word "merchantability" is used in the written document and is "conspicuous." This means "that a reasonable person against whom it is to operate ought to have noticed it." *Gindy Mfg. Corp. v. Cardinale Trucking Corp.*, 268 A.2d 345, 349, 111 N.J. Super. 383 (1970). In general, a disclaimer is conspicuous if it is in larger print or otherwise appears in contrasting type or color. *Id.* To disclaim the implied warranty of fitness for a particular purpose, on the other hand, the writing need not specifically mention "fitness for a particular purpose" but the disclaimer must be conspicuous.

The disclaimer in the Master Agreement provides in capital letters under the heading

"WARRANTY EXCLUSIONS FOR TERM PLANS OR PURCHASE":

EXCEPT AS SPECIFICALLY MADE HEREIN, AT & T-IS AND ITS AFFILIATED SUBCONTRACTOR AND SUPPLIERS MAKE NO WAR-RANTIES, EXPRESS OR IMPLIED, AND SPECIFICALLY DISCLAIM ANY WARRANTY OF MERCHANTABILITY OR FITNESS FOR A PAR-TICULAR PURPOSE.

This writing specifically mentions "merchantability" and, although not required, also mentions "fitness for a particular purpose." In addition, the use of capital letters under the black-letter heading **"WARRANTY EXCLUSIONS"** makes the writing conspicuous. This seems especially true given Heath's sophistication in commercial dealings. *See H.B. Fuller Co. v. Kinetic Sys., Inc.*, 932 F.2d 681, 689 (7th Cir. 1991) (applying Wisconsin law). Therefore, we conclude that the provision of the Master Agreement amounted to a valid disclaimer of the implied warranties of merchantability and fitness for a particular purpose and that summary judgment as to these counts was appropriate.

*   *   *

CATE v. DOVER CORP.
Texas Supreme Court
790 S.W.2d 559 (1990)

DOGGETT, Justice.

We consider the enforceability of a disclaimer of implied warranties. The trial court upheld the disclaimer and granted summary judgment in favor of Dover Corporation. The court of appeals affirmed. 776 S.W.2d 680. We reverse the judgment of the court of appeals and remand this cause to the trial court for further proceedings consistent with this opinion.

In September 1984, Edward Cate, doing business as Cate's Transmission Service, purchased from Beech Tire Mart three lifts manufactured and designed by Dover Corporation to elevate vehicles for maintenance. Despite repairs made by Beech and Dover, the lifts never functioned properly. Dover contends that Cate's subsequent claim against it for breach of the implied warranty of merchantability is barred by a disclaimer contained within a written, express warranty.

This warranty is set forth on a separate page headed in blue half inch block print, with the heading: "YOU CAN TAKE ROTARY'S NEW 5-YEAR WARRANTY AND TEAR IT APART." The statement is followed by bold black type stating, "And, when you are through, it'll be just as solid as the No. 1 lift company in America. Rotary." The text of the warranty itself is in black type, contained within double blue lines, and appears under the blue three-eighths inch block print heading "WARRANTY." The disclaimer of implied warranties, although contained in a separate paragraph within the warranty text, is in the same typeface, size, and color as the remainder of the text. [Ed. Note: The Appendix to the case is a reproduction of the warranty and disclaimer described in the opinion]

An implied warranty of merchantability arises in a contract for the sale of goods unless expressly excluded or modified by conspicuous language. Tex. Bus. & Com. Code Ann. §§ 2.314(a), 2.316(b) (Vernon 1968). Whether a particular disclaimer is conspicuous is a question of law to be determined by the following definition:

> A term or clause is conspicuous when it is so written that a reasonable person against whom it is to operate ought to have noticed it. A printed heading in capitals (as: NON-NEGOTIABLE BILL OF LADING) is conspicuous. Language in a body of a form is conspicuous if it is larger or of other contrasting type or color. But in a telegram, any stated term is conspicuous.

Id. § 1.201(10). Further explanation is provided by comment 10 thereto:

> This [section] is intended to indicate some of the methods of making a term attention-calling. But the test is whether attention can reasonably be expected to be called to it.

In interpreting this language, Dover argues that a lesser standard of conspicuousness should apply to a disclaimer made to a merchant, such as Cate. Admittedly, an ambiguity is created by the requirement that disclaimer language be conspicuous to "a reasonable person *against whom it is to operate.*" Comment 10, however, clearly contemplated an objective standard, stating the test as "whether attention can reasonably be expected to be called to it."

We then turn to an application of an objective standard of conspicuousness to Dover's warranty. The top forty percent of the written warranty is devoted to extolling its virtues. The warranty itself, contained within double blue lines, is then set out in five paragraphs in normal black type under the heading "WARRANTY." Nothing distinguishes the third paragraph, which contains the exclusionary language. It is printed in the same typeface, size and color as the rest of the warranty text. Although the warranty in its entirety may be considered conspicuous, the disclaimer is hidden among attention-getting language purporting to grant the best warranty available.[20]

Dover cites *Ellmer v. Delaware Mini-Computer Systems, Inc.*, 665 S.W.2d 158 (Tex. App.—Dallas 1983, no writ), as authority for imposing a subjective standard of conspicuousness. In finding a disclaimer conspicuous, that court did look to the circumstances surrounding the transaction. That particular language, however, was in bold print, unlike the language under review here. Nor did that court give consideration to the effect of comment 10. Nevertheless, to the extent that *Ellmer* may be read as imposing a subjective standard, we disapprove it.

Although this is a case of first impression in Texas, the facts here parallel those reviewed in other states. In *Massey-Ferguson, Inc. v. Utley*, 439 S.W.2d 57, 59 (Ky. Ct. App. 1969), a disclaimer hidden under the heading "WARRANTY and AGREEMENT" was found not to be conspicuous:

> It is true that the *heading* was in large, bold-face type, but there was nothing to suggest that an exclusion was being made; on the contrary, the words of the headings indicated a *making* of warranties rather than a *disclaimer*.

(Emphasis in original.) Similarly, in *Hartman v. Jensen's, Inc.*, 277 S.C. 501, 289 S.E.2d 648 (1982), the court found that placing a disclaimer under the bold heading "Terms of Warranty" failed to alert the consumer to the fact that an exclusion was intended. Dover's disclaimer similarly fails to attract the attention of a reasonable person and is not conspicuous.

*   *   *

Dover argues that even an inconspicuous disclaimer should be given effect because Cate had actual knowledge of it at the time of the purchase. Because the object of the conspicuousness requirement is to protect the buyer from surprise and an unknowing waiver of his or her rights, inconspicuous language is immaterial when the buyer has actual knowledge of the disclaimer. This knowledge can result from the buyer's prior dealings with the seller, or by the seller specifically bringing the inconspicuous waiver to the buyer's attention. The Code appears to recognize that actual knowledge of the disclaimer overrides the question of conspicuousness. For example, Section 2.316(b) does not mandate a written disclaimer of the implied warranty of merchantability but clearly provides that an oral disclaimer may be effective. Similarly, Section 2.316(c)(3) allows an implied warranty to be excluded or modified by methods other than a conspicuous writing: course of dealing, course of performance, or usage of trade. When the buyer is not surprised by the disclaimer, insisting on compliance with the conspicuousness requirement serves no purpose. *See* R. ANDERSON, UNIFORM COMMERCIAL CODE § 2-316:49–50 (1983). The extent of a buyer's knowledge of a disclaimer of the implied warranty of merchantability is thus clearly relevant to a determination of its enforceability. *See Singleton v. LaCoure*, 712 S.W.2d 757, 759 (Tex. App.—Houston [14th Dist.] 1986, writ ref'd n.r.e.) (relying in part on buyer's acknowledgment to enforce disclaimer). The seller has the burden of proving the buyer's actual knowledge of the disclaimer.

As this is a summary judgment case, the issue on appeal is whether Dover met its burden by establishing that there exists no genuine issue of material fact thereby entitling it to judgment as a matter of law. *City of Houston v. Clear Creek Basin Authority*, 589 S.W.2d 671, 678 (Tex. 1979). All doubts as to the existence of a genuine

---

[20] [1] Justice Grant's dissent in the court of appeals correctly characterizes the warranty as follows:

> Dover has cleverly buried the disclaimer provision within language that strongly suggests a warranty that greatly benefits the consumer. The bold print language suggests that warranties were included rather than excluded. *See Mallory v. Conida Warehouses, Inc.*, 134 Mich. App. 28, 350 N.W.2d 825 (1984).

776 S.W.2d at 685.

issue of material fact are resolved against the movant, and we must view the evidence in the light most favorable to the Petitioner. *Great American Reserve Ins. Co. v. San Antonio Plumbing Supply Co.*, 391 S.W.2d 41, 47 (Tex. 1965). In support of its claim that Cate had actual knowledge of the disclaimer, Dover relies on Cate's deposition testimony, as follows:

Q: Do you know, or do you remember what kinds of warranties you received when you bought the lifts?

A: I may be wrong, but I think it was a five year warranty.

Q: What was your understanding of that warranty?

A: Any problems would be taken care of within the five year period.

Q: Do you know if that warranty was from Beech Equipment, or from Dover?

A: I believe it was from Dover.

Q: Did you receive any written documentation in regard to that warranty?

A: Yes, ma'am.

Although it is clear that Cate understood the warranty to extend for only five years, it is not clear that he understood any other limitations or exclusions. Merely providing a buyer a copy of documents containing an inconspicuous disclaimer does not establish actual knowledge. Dover has failed to establish that as a matter of law Cate had actual knowledge of the disclaimer.

We hold that, to be enforceable, a written disclaimer of the implied warranty of merchantability made in connection with a sale of goods must be conspicuous to a reasonable person. We further hold that such a disclaimer contained in text undistinguished in typeface, size or color within a form purporting to grant a warranty is not conspicuous, and is unenforceable unless the buyer has actual knowledge of the disclaimer. For the reasons stated herein, we reverse the judgment of the court of appeals and remand to the trial court for further proceedings consistent with this opinion.

APPENDIX

YOU CAN TAKE ROTARY'S NEW 5-YEAR WARRANTY AND TEAR IT APART.

And, when you're through, it'll be just as solid as the No. 1 lift company in America. Rotary. Not so with some of the other companies. They may offer you a multi-year warranty, too. But you're likely to discover it's limited to parts only.

And, hidden in all the mumbo-jumbo, you may find out—too late—that their beautifully worded "warranty" doesn't even cover major components... like power units. So what you really have is a great warranty that covers almost nothing.

We at Rotary are proud of the surface lift products we manufacture. And we don't have to "play it safe" when it comes to guaranteeing them. Here's what our new 5-year warranty says:

WARRANTY

All Rotary Surface Mounted Lifts are guaranteed to the original owner for five years from invoice date. Rotary Lift Division here after is known as "The Company". The Company shall replace for the full five years those parts returned to the factory which prove upon inspection by the Company to be defective. The Company shall pay for reasonable costs of transportation and labor for replacement of said parts for the first 12 months only. Purchaser will bear costs of transportation and labor for parts returned after the first year and the remainder of this warranty. This warranty shall not apply unless the product is installed, used and maintained in accordance with the Company's specifications as set forth in the Company's installation, operation and maintenance instructions.

This warranty does not cover normal maintenance or adjustments, damage or malfunction caused by improper handling, installation, abuse, misuse, negligence or carelessness of operation.

This warranty is exclusive and is in lieu of all other warranties expressed or implied including any implied warranty of merchantability or any implied warranty of fitness for a particular purpose, which implied warranties are hereby expressly excluded.

The remedies described are exclusive and in no event shall the Company be liable for special, consequential or incidental damages for the breach of or delay in performance of the warranty.

This warranty shall be governed by the State of Indiana, and shall be subject to the exclusive jurisdiction of the Court of the State of Indiana in the County of Jefferson.

American made

Rotary®

Exhibit A

Spears, Justice, concurring.

Although I concur in the court's opinion, I write separately to declare that the time has come for the legislature to consider the realities of the marketplace and prohibit all disclaimers of the implied warranties of merchantability and fitness.

These implied warranties, created by common-law courts long before the adoption of the UCC, developed to protect purchasers from losses suffered because of "the frustration of their expectations about the worth, efficacy, or desirability" of a product. W. Keeton, Prosser and Keeton on the Law of Torts § 95A (5th ed. 1984). Implication of these warranties into every goods contract, without regard to the parties' actual assent to their terms, served "to police, to prevent, and to remedy" unfair consumer transactions. Llewellyn, *On Warranty of Quality, and Society*, 39 Colum. L. Rev. 699, 699 (1936); *Humber v. Morton*, 426 S.W.2d 554, 557–58 (Tex. 1968). These implied warranties also serve other important purposes: they create incentives to produce and market higher quality products; they discourage shoddy workmanship and unethical trade practices; and they place responsibility on those who profit from the sale of goods, have the greatest control over the products, and are better able to bear the risk of loss. *See Humber*, 426 S.W.2d at 562; *Decker & Sons v. Capps*, 139 Tex. 609, 610, 164 S.W.2d 828, 829 (1942). Section 2-316 of the UCC, however, subverts all of these purposes by giving sellers almost unlimited license to disclaim implied warranties.

We live in an age when sellers of goods "saturate the marketplace and all of our senses" with the most extraordinary claims about the worth of their products. Anderson, *The Supreme Court of Texas and the Duty to Read the Contracts You Sign*, 15 Tex. Tech. L. Rev. 517, 544 (1984); *Henningsen v. Bloomfield Motors, Inc.*, 32 N.J. 358, 161 A.2d 69, 84 (1960). Yet, the same sellers under the *carte blanche* granted them by section 2-316 of the UCC refuse to guarantee and indeed expressly disclaim that their products are merchantable or even fit for their intended purposes. Under section 2-316, not much is actually required for an effective disclaimer. To disclaim the implied warranty of merchantability the seller need only include the word "merchantability" in a conspicuous fashion. Tex. Bus. & Com. Code Ann. § 2.316(b) (Vernon 1968). To disclaim the implied warranty of fitness the seller must use a writing and must make the disclaimer conspicuous. *Id.* at § 2.316(b). No particular form of words is needed to disclaim an implied warranty of fitness, nor does section 2.316 require the buyer to be actually aware of the disclaimer before it will be enforced. All implied warranties can be disclaimed by the mere inclusion of expressions like "as is" or "with all faults." *Id.* at § 2.316, comment 1. Finally, as today's majority makes clear, section 2.316 does not even require the disclaimer to be conspicuous if the buyer's actual knowledge of the disclaimer can be shown.

By establishing specific "requirements" for disclaimers, section 2.316 ostensibly "seeks to protect a buyer from unexpected and unbargained language of disclaimer." Tex. Bus. & Com. Code § 2.316, comment 1 (Vernon 1968). In reality, however, section 2.316 completely undermines implied warranties. Implicitly, section 2.316 adopts the position that disclaimers should be enforced because society benefits when parties to a contract are allowed to set *all* the terms of their agreement. The problem with this position, and with section 2.316 generally, is twofold: it ignores the fact that governmental implication of protective terms into private contracts is commonplace (e.g. the implied warranties of merchantability and fitness); and, more importantly, it rests on the faulty premise that contractual disclaimers are generally freely bargained for elements of a contract.

Freedom of contract arguments generally, and section 2.316 specifically, presuppose and are based on "the image of individuals meeting in the marketplace" on equal ground to negotiate the terms of a contract. Rakoff, *Contracts of Adhesion: An Essay in Reconstruction*, 96 Harv. L. Rev. 1174, 1216 (1983). At one time, this image may have accurately reflected marketplace realities. However, the last half of the twentieth century has witnessed "the rise of the corporation" and, increasingly, the displacement of physical persons as sellers in consumer and commercial contracts. Phillips, *Unconscionability and Article 2 Implied Warranty Disclaimers*, 62 CHI.-KENT L. REV. 199, 239 (1985). This development has led to innumerable situations in which consumers deal from an unequal bargaining position, the most prominent example being the ubiquitous standard form contract which is now used by most sellers of goods and which invariably contains an implied warranty disclaimer. *See Melody Home Mfg. Co. v. Barnes*, 741 S.W.2d 349, 355 (Tex. 1987); *Henningsen*, 161 A.2d at 86–89; Slawson, *Standard Form Contracts and Democratic Control of Lawmaking Power*, 84 HARV. L. REV. 529, 529 (1971) ("standard form contracts probably account for more than ninety-nine percent of all the contracts now made"); L. VOLD, HANDBOOK OF THE LAW OF SALES 447 (2d ed. 1959) (dramatic rise in corporate power has yielded the standard form contract whose terms are drafted by the seller and usually contain implied warranty disclaimers).

The great majority of buyers never read an implied warranty disclaimer found in a standard form contract. Even when implied warranty disclaimers are read, their legal significance is not generally understood. Such disclaimers include unfamiliar terminology (e.g. "implied warranty of merchantability"), and comprehending their legal effect requires one not only to understand what substantive rights are involved, but also to grasp that these rights have been lost via the disclaimer. Phillips, *Unconscionability and Article 2 Implied Warranty Disclaimers*, 62 CHI.-KENT L. REV. 199, 243 (1985); *see also* Federal Trade Commission, Facts for Consumers (Mar. 23, 1979) (more than 35% of those surveyed mistakenly believed that an "as is" disclaimer meant the dealer would have to pay some, if not all, costs if a car broke down within 25 days of a sale). Finally, even if a buyer reads and understands an implied warranty disclaimer, chances are he will be without power to either strike these terms or "shop around" for better ones. If the buyer attempts the former, he will likely run into an employee who is unauthorized to alter the form contract; if he attempts the latter, he will likely confront a competitor who offers substantially the same form terms. *Henningsen*, 161 A.2d at 87. In short, the "marketplace reality" suggests that freedom of contract in the sale of goods is actually nonexistent; a buyer today can either take the contract with the disclaimer attached or leave it and go without the good.

Increasingly, the courts and legislatures of other states have acted to ameliorate or to avoid entirely the harsh consequences wrought by section 2.316. Several courts have refused to enforce disclaimers, on public policy grounds, unless the disclaimer sets forth the particular qualities and characteristics of fitness being waived, is clearly brought to the buyer's attention and is expressly agreed to by the buyer. . . .

A number of other courts have found even conspicuous disclaimers to be unconscionable under section 2-302 of the UCC, despite the disclaimer's compliance with § 2-316. . . .

Several states have gone even further by enacting protective legislation which forbids implied warranty disclaimers or by repealing section 2-316 of the Code. . . .

Finally, the federal Magnuson-Moss Warranty Act places severe limits on the seller's ability to disclaim implied warranties in the sale of consumer goods. 15 U.S.C. § 2301-12 (1982). The Act's most important clause essentially provides that *if* a seller gives a written express warranty, he cannot disclaim the implied warranties. *Id.* § 2308(a). The Act effectively prohibits the common practice of a seller boldly announcing an express warranty of limited value and then disclaiming the more valuable implied warranties, leaving the consumer with a delusive remedy at best.

*   *   *

The realities of the modern marketplace demand that the legislature prohibit implied warranty disclaimers by repealing section 2-316 of the UCC. Without such action, Texas courts will be forced to rely on "covert tools," such as the unconscionability provision in section 2-302 or the "conspicuous" requirement in section 2-316, to reach a just and fair result in disclaimer suits. When these tools are used, guidance, predictability and consistency in the law is sacrificed, while limited judicial resources are spent policing unjust bargains that could have been avoided. Were it up to the judicial branch, the courts could declare such disclaimers void as against public policy. If the legislature has the interests of Texas citizens at heart, it will repeal section 2-316 because, no matter how conspicuous, such disclaimers are abusive of consumers.

MAUZY, J., joins in this concurring opinion.

RAY, Justice, concurring and dissenting.

I concur in that portion of the court's opinion requiring that a written disclaimer of the implied warranty of merchantability must be conspicuous to a reasonable person. I write separately, however, to take issue with the court's immediate erosion of that standard by permitting a showing of actual knowledge of the disclaimer to override a lack of conspicuousness.

The statute, on its face, provides for no actual knowledge exception. There is no room for judicial crafting of those omitted by the legislature. I would hold that the extent of a buyer's knowledge of a disclaimer is irrelevant to a determination of its enforceability under Section 2.316(b) of the UCC.

The effect of actual knowledge is subject to debate among leading commentators on commercial law. The purpose of the objective standard of conspicuousness adopted by the court today reflects the view that "the drafters intended a rigid adherence to the conspicuousness requirement in order to avoid arguments concerning what the parties said about the warranties at the time of the sale." J. WHITE AND R. SUMMERS, UNIFORM COMMERCIAL CODE § 12-5 (2d ed. 1980). An absolute rule that an inconspicuous disclaimer is invalid, despite the buyer's actual knowledge, encourages sellers to make their disclaimers conspicuous, thereby reducing the need for courts to evaluate swearing matches as to actual awareness in particular cases. *See* W. POWERS, TEXAS PRODUCTS LIABILITY LAW § 2.0723 (1989). Today's decision condemns our courts to a parade of such cases.

DEMPSEY v. ROSENTHAL
New York City Civil Court
468 N.Y.S.2d 441 (1983)

DAVID B. SAXE, Judge

[Ed. Note: The facts of this case involving "Mr. Dunphy," the "unmerchantable" dog, are set out in Section III.B.2, above.]

Finally, an examination or an opportunity to examine the disputed goods may result in a denial of the warranty claim.

* * *

The comment to [§ 2-316(3)(b)] emphasizes the importance of "[t]he particular buyer's skill and the normal method of examining goods in the circumstances. . . ." As a recognized authority states:

> The comment then suggests a distinction between professional and nonprofessional buyers. For example, a governmental agency buying magnetic tape "as a farmer purchasing feeder pigs" will be held to have assumed the risk for any defects that professionals in their respective fields should have discovered upon examination. On the other hand, a layman purchasing an automobile cannot be expected to be able to discover subtle mechanical and design defects. Absent unusual circumstances, we expect that most courts would be reluctant to find that an examination by a consumer has excluded all implied warranties.

WHITE AND SUMMERS, UNIFORM COMMERCIAL CODE, *supra*, p. 452.

The question posed then was Mr. Dunphy's condition a defect capable of being discovered by a consumer. Ms. Dempsey testified that she had previously owned two poodles. Their gender is not known. Nor is it known how thorough an examination she gave Mr. Dunphy prior to purchase. Although five days after sale her veterinarian determined the condition, it is unclear if she ought to have discovered the condition herself. There were no evident warnings that Mr. Dunphy had one undescended testicle. This condition appears not to have been readily observable to Ms. Dempsey. A manual manipulation of the scrotal area would appear to be the only means of properly verifying this condition. I find that Ms. Dempsey did not know this, nor should she be chargeable with knowledge of this fact.

In short, I hold that the type of examination that would be undertaken by a casual buyer (such as Ms. Dempsey) of a male puppy during the period leading up to sale is not of a nature which would under normal and reasonable circumstances, lead a consumer to manually manipulate the scrotal area, thereby possibly determining that one testicle was undescended. That being said, my holding that the implied warranty of merchantability has been breached remains intact.

* * *

A judgment for the claimant in the amount of $541.25 shall be entered by the clerk.

PROBLEM 3-12

First Scenario. Broadleaf Contracting is a landscape contractor. Stable Fork Trucks, Inc. sells new and factory-reconditioned fork trucks. Broadleaf purchased a fork truck from Stable to move supplies in its yard and to load its delivery trucks. However, the fork truck proved to be an endless source of problems, and after three weeks Broadleaf quit using the machine and demanded compensation from Stable. There is no dispute that Stable is a merchant for purposes of this transaction, and that the fork truck is unmerchantable. However, Stable denies liability under § 2-314 on the basis that it properly excluded the implied warranty of merchantability. Stable's sales representative will testify that Broadleaf's purchasing agent was informed the forklift was factory-reconditioned and could not be guaranteed, and that the purchasing agent understood that the bargain price was conditioned on the lack of any guarantee as to quality of the fork truck.

The Purchase Order provided by Stable is a single sheet of paper with terms printed on both sides of the page. The preprinted form on the front includes spaces into which the parties inserted the model number of the fork truck, the price, the delivery date, the buyer's name, and other negotiated terms. At the bottom of the page, the following statement appears: "THIS PURCHASE IS SUBJECT TO THE STANDARD TERMS AND CONDITIONS ON THE REVERSE SIDE." The reverse side of the page is titled, "STANDARD TERMS AND CONDITIONS," and contains 14 numbered paragraphs. Paragraph 8 on the reverse side is entitled, "Warranties," and it includes the sentence: "EXCEPT AS SPECIFICALLY PROVIDED IN THIS ORDER, THERE ARE NO WARRANTIES, EXPRESS OR IMPLIED. THE WARRANTY OF MERCHANTABILITY IS EXPRESSLY DISCLAIMED."

The Purchase Order was signed at the bottom of the front side of the document by Broadleaf's purchasing agent, who admits receiving the document but does not remember looking at the back of the document. The purchasing agent denies that Stable's sales representative disclaimed all warranties, and alleges that he only understood that the typical express warranties relating to new equipment would not be available with the factory-reconditioned product.

A. Is Stable subject to the implied warranty of merchantability, or does the Purchase Order protect Stable from liability?

B. If the Purchase Order doesn't satisfy the requirements of § 2-316, does Stable have any other arguments to avoid liability?

C. Even if the Purchase Order satisfies the requirements of § 2-316, can Broadleaf argue successfully that the disclaimer is unenforceable?

Second Scenario. Broadleaf also purchased a reconditioned fork truck to move pallets of sod in connection with its lawn service business. Broadleaf decided to purchase Model 86 only after Stable's sales representative assured Broadleaf that the equipment was capable of lifting and moving 1,500 pounds of unevenly stacked sod on a wooden pallet. Broadleaf's purchasing agent signed a Purchase Order that then was counter-signed by Stable's sales representative. This Purchase Order provided as follows (with the underlined portions typed onto the form):

> WARRANTIES. Buyer hereby agrees and understands that it is purchasing Model 86 — fork truck AS IS, WHERE IS. Buyer also agrees and acknowledges that neither Stable Fork Trucks, Inc., nor its employees, agents and representatives, have made any representations or statements about the equipment except as is specifically provided in this purchase order. Buyer also agrees and understands that there are no warranties beyond those appearing in this purchase order, and that all implied warranties are disclaimed.

The Purchase Order makes no reference to the lifting capacity, nor to the ability of the equipment to lift an unevenly stacked, dense load such as a pallet of sod.

Two weeks later, Broadleaf's driver is injured when the fork truck topples over while moving a 1,400 pound pallet of sod. Broadleaf seeks recovery on two grounds: first, that there was a breach of the express warranty regarding the capabilities of the forklift; second, that there was a breach of the implied warranty of merchantability.

Argue on behalf of Stable that it has successfully disclaimed liability for these warranties.

Chapter 4
TITLE

Sales law is closely related to property law. A sales agreement is a contract to transfer ownership in tangible property. Consequently, identifying the owner of title to property has substantial significance in a sales course. In this chapter, we consider several important issues relating to title. First, we discuss timing issues related to determining when title passes from the seller to the buyer. Next, we will consider the seller's power to transfer good title if the seller has void or voidable title. In the final section, we consider the interplay between the title provisions of Article 2 and more specific Certificate of Title statutes relating to items such as automobiles.

A. LOCATION OF TITLE

In pre-Code days, the concept of title served as a "jack-of-all-trades" in sales law. One had only to decide who had title, and then the answers would neatly follow to such diverse questions as where the risk of loss lay, whether the seller could maintain an action for the price, whether the buyer could replevy the goods, or whether the seller's or buyer's creditors could levy on the goods. For Karl Llewellyn, however, the neatness of such a singularity of issue was not worth its price:

> The quarrel thus is, first, with the use of Title for purposes of decision as if the *location* of Title *were* determinable with certainty; and second, with the insistence on reaching for a single lump to solve all or most of the problems between seller and buyer — and even in regard to third parties.[1]

Thus, when the drafting of the Code began, Llewellyn was convinced that the time had come to scrap title as a means to resolve sales controversies. The unpredictability of application and emptiness of rational content of the concept of title led Llewellyn to conclude that title should not play a role in substantive sales law.

Making the most of their opportunity, Llewellyn and his crew of drafters made the bold move of replacing the role of title with specific rules premised on considerations peculiar to the problem at hand. For example, the Code prescribes a separate set of rules on risk of loss (*see* UCC §§ 2-509 & 2-510), a buyer's right to replevin (*see* UCC § 2-716), or a seller's right to recover the full price (*see* UCC § 2-709). The one-test-fits-all approach of pre-Code law has been discarded, but the drafters did not completely ignore the concept of title: Section 2-401 provides rules for determining who has title, if that issue is relevant. The rules should be consulted only if a Code "provision refers to such title" (UCC § 2-401) or when "situations are not covered by the other provisions of this Article and matters concerning title become material" (UCC § 2-401). The reference in the official comment to the class of relevant title situations serves only to remind one that title will no longer be used to solve *sales* problems. Of course, it is still important in its own right to determine who owns the goods. Section 2-401 comment 1 provides:

> This section, however, in no way intends to indicate which line of interpretation should be followed in cases where the applicability of "public" regulation depends upon a "sale" or upon location of "title" without further definition. . . .
> It is, therefore, necessary to state what a "sale" is and when title passes under this Article in case courts deem any public regulation to incorporate the defined term of the "private" law.

Article 4(b) of the CISG makes it clear that the Convention is not concerned with "the effect which the contract may have on the property in the goods sold." Thus, the Convention, like the UCC, rejects the arbitrary nature of the property or title-analysis approach to sales problems. Rather, the specific provisions that govern the rights and

---

[1] Karl N. Llewellyn, *Through Title to Contract and a Bit Beyond*, 15 N.Y.U. L.Q. Rev. 159, 216 (1938).

obligations of the parties were formulated based on policy considerations that take into account the commercial setting of international sales transactions.

MEINHARD-COMMERCIAL CORP. v. HARGO WOOLEN MILLS
New Hampshire Supreme Court
300 A.2d 321 (1972)

GRIMES, J.

The issue presented by this case is the correctness of the master's rulings as to who has ownership or title in the disputed goods. Hargo Woolen Mills, Inc., and its wholly-owned subsidiary, Wallisford Mills, Inc., were respectively the seller and the manufacturer of woolen cloth. Meinhard-Commercial Corporation, the factor for and principal secured creditor of Hargo, instituted equity receivership proceedings against Hargo and Wallisford. On December 15, 1967, the Superior Court, Cheshire County, appointed a receiver who took possession of Hargo's and Wallisford's assets.

Shabry Trading Co. was in the business of trading waste material, and for over ten years prior to the receivership had sold card waste, used in the production of cloth, to Hargo.

On or about May 17, 1966, Shabry shipped and invoiced to Hargo twenty-four bales of card waste. Hargo did not wish to purchase the material at that time and so on May 24, 1966, Shabry and Hargo made an oral agreement whereby Hargo was to store the goods on its premises but was not to pay for or be charged for the goods until Hargo returned the invoice for the goods to Shabry. Shabry marked the invoice "Pro-forma" and returned it to Hargo. This invoice fixed the price at which these bales could be purchased by Hargo. In September of 1966, Hargo notified Shabry that it could use eight bales. Shabry invoiced them as of the original invoice date of May 17, 1966. Hargo had this revised to September since the parties had agreed Hargo was to be billed only at the time it used the goods. Hargo then used the goods and Shabry received part payment for the eight bales (the balance being lost to Shabry as a general creditor in the receivership).

The remaining sixteen bales were never used by or billed to Hargo except upon the "pro-forma" invoice of May 17. The receiver took possession of the bales on or about December 15, 1967. Shabry on February 21, 1968, demanded possession of the sixteen bales from the receiver, claiming that Hargo never owned the bales since title was retained by Shabry until use of the bales by Hargo. The receiver sold the sixteen bales, and pursuant to the final decree by the Superior Court in the receivership proceedings on March 27, 1969, a sum of $7,500 covering the value of the bales was delivered by the receiver to a joint account of Shabry's and Meinhard's counsel, subject to further proceedings of the Superior Court to determine Shabry's claim. This final decree also found Meinhard the holder of a first lien against all of Hargo's inventory and proceeds thereof and as such the residuary beneficiary of all of Hargo's funds, credits and deposits after payment of certain specific items, none of which are in issue here except for the purported claim of Shabry. The court obliged Meinhard to defend the claim of Shabry on behalf of Hargo's receiver. There was no evidence that Meinhard relied on the card waste as belonging to Hargo in extending its credit.

Meinhard and Shabry subsequently appeared before a master to settle the issue of whether Shabry had retained title to the sixteen bales of card waste prior to Hargo's receivership or whether title had passed to Hargo prior to receivership. The master found as a matter of law under RSA 382-A:1-201(37) and 2-401(1) that when Shabry delivered the bales to Hargo, title passed to Hargo and a security interest was concurrently created for Shabry. Shabry, never having perfected his security interest in the goods prior to appointment of the receiver, was left in the status of an unsecured creditor of Hargo.

The master found as a matter of fact that Hargo and Shabry believed and intended that title to the sixteen bales would not pass until Hargo notified Shabry of their use. Hargo was under no obligation to buy and Shabry was free to sell the goods to other buyers. Hargo never took the sixteen bales into its inventory and the bales were separately stored and distinctly marked as not being included in Hargo's general raw materials inventory.

The master's report was approved by the Superior Court. . . .

The utilization of the concept of title in sales transactions is not novel, nor is the misconception and the misuse of it. Learned Hand has said: " '[T]itle' is a formal word for a purely conceptual notion; I do not know what it means and I question whether anybody does, except perhaps legal historians." *In re Lake's Launft Inc.*, 79 F.2d 326, 328–29 (2d Cir. 1935) (dissenting opinion). Prior to the Uniform Commercial Code, the Uniform Sales Act accepted the common-law notion that title determination was the main solvent of sales problems. The UCC deliberately de-emphasizes this view. RSA 382-A:2-101. The Code supplants many title-determined issues with specific Code provisions to determine the rights and duties of the buyer and seller, such as risk of loss (RSA 382-A:2-509 and 2-510), insurable interest (RSA 382-A:2-501), suit of third parties (RSA 382-A:2-722), buyer's rights on seller's insolvency (RSA 382-A.2-709), and buyer's right to replevy identified goods (RSA 382-A:2-716). Despite its minimization of the title concept, the Code does recognize situations where the lack of any other legal tool requires the courts to fall back on the eternal title question of mine or thine. The Code, therefore, provides a catch-basin rule (RSA 382-A.2401) that applies only when the more specific Code provisions fail to deal with the issue. The case before us was decided below with resort to this catch-basin rule, the pertinent portion of which reads as follows: "Any retention or reservation by the seller of the title (property) in goods shipped or delivered to the buyer is limited in effect to a reservation of a security interest. *Subject to these provisions* . . . , title to goods passes from the seller to the buyer in any manner and on any conditions explicitly agreed on by the parties." RSA 382-A:2-401(1) (emphasis added).

The master correctly interpreted this provision to disallow in a sales situation the parties' intent to govern where title lay in a sale situation. Although the parties agree to reserve title in the seller after delivery of the goods to the buyer, the statutory language of "Subject to" clearly subjects the parties' title agreement to the previous sentence's mandate that a seller may only retain a security interest after delivery to the buyer. *Providence Electric Co., Inc. v. Sutton Place, Inc.*, 161 Conn. 242, 287 A.2d 379 (1971); *see Annot.*, 17 A.L.R.3d 1010, 1081 (1968).

However, since RSA 382-A:2-401 speaks only in terms of buyers and sellers, we believe it does not apply to the transaction between these parties. RSA 382-A:2-103(1)(d) defines seller as "unless the context otherwise requires . . . (1)(d) 'Seller' means a person who sells or contracts to sell goods." A buyer is defined in RSA 382-A:2-103(1)(a) as "unless the context otherwise requires . . . (1)(a) 'Buyer' means a person who buys or contracts to buy goods." To determine the meaning of these sections, we refer to the definition of sale and contract for sale in RSA 382-A:2-106(1). " 'Contract for sale' includes both a present sale of goods and a contract to sell goods at a future time. A 'sale' consists in the passing of title from the seller to the buyer for a price. (*See* RSA 382-A:2-401)." For RSA 382-A:2-401(1) to apply, we must, therefore, first find that the transaction between the supplier, Shabry, and the manufacturer, Hargo, was a sale. *Columbia International Corp. v. Kempler*, 46 Wis. 2d 550, 175 N.W.2d 465 (1970).

Whether this transaction was a sale or some other type of transaction is a question of the intent of the parties, which is a question for the trier of fact to determine. . . . Under the Code, there must still be a meeting of minds between the parties before there is a contract. . . . The master found in the parties' requests for findings and rulings that the factual understanding between Hargo and Shabry contemplated no passage of title until Shabry was notified of Hargo's intention to use the goods and Shabry thereafter invoiced the goods to Hargo. The master also found that Hargo was never obligated to purchase and Shabry could have sold the goods to other buyers. Furthermore, the master specifically rejected the request for a finding of fact that Hargo's and Shabry's transaction constituted a sale of inventory to Hargo, and he also specifically found that the explicit agreement made between Shabry and Hargo contemplated no sale of goods until Hargo's election to buy and Shabry's invoicing of the goods.

Given these findings, it is clear that the parties' agreement concerning the delivered card waste created no contract for sale by the passage of title for a price. The parties showed no intent to pass title. No title may pass for a price without commitment of the buyer to pay the price. *See* Duesenberg & King, *Bender's U.C.C. Service: Sales & Bulk Transfers*, § 13.03[4](d)(i) at 13–26 (1972). The mere fact that goods are delivered to the premises of a prospective buyer does not in and of itself create a sale, where neither party considered it a sale. . . .

The parties did agree as to the placement of the goods on Hargo's premises and Shabry did make an offer on the pro-forma invoice of a price if Hargo wished to buy. The parties' course of dealings in card waste helps us interpret the meaning of this agreement. RSA 382-A:1-205(1) and 1-201(3). The record shows that Shabry's previous dealings with Hargo involved completed sales when the goods were delivered. When Shabry sent Hargo the contested card waste, Hargo, already possessing a card waste surplus, did not want to buy. Hargo, in accord with their prior course of dealing, intended to return the card waste; but Shabry, wishing to avoid the high cost of warehouse storage of card waste, offered to let Hargo retain possession of the goods and buy them only as Hargo had use for them at the price of the pro-forma invoice. Hargo accepted this storage offer and marked and stored Shabry's card waste independent of its other goods. This agreement contravened the old sale-on-delivery course of dealing between the parties and indicated this was a special new deal that did not purport to be a sale until further action by Hargo on Shabry's offer. Hargo was nothing more than a bailee with an option to buy if the goods were not sold to others. . . .

The performance of the parties also sheds light on their agreement. *Cf.* RSA 382A:2-208(1). When Hargo needed eight bales of the card waste, he notified Shabry, who separately invoiced the eight bales to Hargo at the pro-forma invoice price, and Hargo thereafter paid for the goods. The clear notification and separate invoicing show that Shabry had not previously relinquished ownership of the bales to Hargo. All that Shabry had relinquished was possession of goods for his own benefit to save storage costs and for the benefit of Hargo if it should need the goods. This course of performance also shows Shabry had made Hargo an offer at the pro-forma invoice price with specific instructions as to how Hargo could accept this offer. When Hargo decided to buy the eight bales, they were invoiced as of that time instead of as of the date the twenty-four bales were stored with Hargo.

We find from the master's finding of the express terms of the parties' agreement, from the parties' course of dealing, and from the parties' course of performance, that the parties agreed only as to storage of the goods with Hargo for their mutual benefit. No sale was made until Shabry's offer was accepted by Hargo through notification of intent to use. No such acceptance occurred with respect to the sixteen bales at issue here.

The master assumed the parties transacted a sale when he held the issue of title to the sixteen bales of card waste rests on RSA 382-A:2-401. The master's findings of fact buttressed by the evidence in the record are inconsistent with his application of the law. Since the master's findings of fact are supported in the record, they are binding on appeal.

We, therefore, hold that, since there was no sale, title to these goods cannot be determined by RSA 382-A.2-401 and, since no other provisions of the Code apply, the rights of the parties are determined by the law of contracts. *See* RSA 382-A:2-102; RSA

382-A:1-103. The master found the parties' stated intentions to be that title to these sixteen bales never passed to Hargo. We, therefore, hold that title remained in Shabry and that the receiver wrongfully withheld return of the sixteen bales to Shabry.

Exceptions of Shabry Trading Co. sustained; remanded.

QUESTIONS

1. The special master found that UCC § 2-401(1) governed the transaction. Does that provision state that a seller cannot sell goods to a buyer and retain the title to the goods until he is paid? If this is a correct reading of § 2-401(1), what assurance does the seller have that he will be paid? The special master ruled that Shabry had a security interest in the goods, yet Shabry still lost its right to the card waste. Why?

2. According to the court's opinion, what type of arrangement existed between Shabry and Hargo: A sales contract? A security agreement? A bailment? Consider the factors that the court considered in determining that Shabry had title to the card waste. Would the court's conclusion have been different if Shabry had agreed that Hargo had a first option to purchase the bales?

A NOTE ON SECURITY INTERESTS

The security interest discussed in § 2-401(1) is subject to Article 9, even though it arises under Article 2. There are several other security interests arising under Article 2 or 2A, and UCC § 9-110 provides for the mesh of these interests with the rules contained in Article 9. Although these Article 2 and 2A security interests appear similar to their Article 9 counterparts, to a large degree, they are non-consensual and based on the notion of possession. Thus, if the seller, buyer, or lessee who claims a security interest gives up possession of the goods, he loses his security interest unless he obtains a security agreement from the other party. The best example of a security interest that arises solely through the rules of Article 2 is contained in § 2-505. When a seller ships goods under reservation of title pursuant to § 2-505, he reserves a security interest. Section 2-711(3) provides that on rightful rejection or justifiable revocation of acceptance, a buyer has a security interest in goods in his possession for the payment of their price and any reasonable expenses. Section 2A-508 gives a lessee a security interest when the lessee rightfully rejects or revokes acceptance of the goods.

The counseling point of § 9-110 is that although Article 9 governs these transactions, these security interests are exempt from certain provisions of the secured transactions article provided that the debtor obtains possession of the goods. Once that occurs, the attachment, perfection, and enforcement rules of Article 9 apply *in toto*.

PROBLEM 4-1

Biederman Printing agreed to purchase 1,000 tons of printing paper each month from Saffron Pulp Products, for the price of $400 per ton. Biederman ordered 38 pound paper with clay in the top sheet to produce an extra smooth finish; this product is known as "liner board." Saffron, generally, produced only 44 pound paper, but it agreed to adjust its production machinery once each month in order to produce the liner board for Biederman in a single run.

Biederman was a newly-formed business. Consequently, it did not have the operating capital to pay for the monthly shipment upon delivery, nor was Saffron interested in permitting Biederman to take the paper and process it without paying for the paper. Moreover, Saffron did not want to allocate space in its production facility to store the monthly run of liner board for Biederman's use during the month. To resolve this problem, the parties agreed that Saffron would produce a month's supply of liner board and immediately transfer it to a warehouse owned by Biederman. They also agreed that Biederman would process the paper for end users and deliver it as it was ordered by its customers, and that Biederman then would notify Saffron by fax that it had used part of the shipment. Saffron then would issue an original bill of lading and invoice recognizing the sale of the paper that had been used by Biederman and providing for full payment within 10 days.

Biederman's business went from bad to worse. Its customers were slow to make payment from the outset, and ultimately they stopped ordering sufficient quantities of paper. Eventually, Biederman was forced to file for bankruptcy. At the time of the filing, Biederman had 4,000 tons of liner board that had accumulated in its warehouse. Saffron demanded that the bankruptcy trustee return this paper to Saffron, alleging that Saffron still owned the paper because title did not pass to Biederman until it used the paper and was invoiced by Saffron. If a court finds that Biederman has title to the paper, it will be sold and the proceeds used to pay Biederman's creditors in accordance with the Bankruptcy Code rules regarding priorities. Saffron is not a secured creditor, and so it will receive very little, if anything, from the bankruptcy estate.

Does Saffron have title to the 4,000 tons of paper, entitling it to obtain the paper from the possession of the bankruptcy estate?

B. POWER TO TRANSFER TITLE

Section 2-403 of the Code governs the extent to which a seller of goods can transfer title to the goods. This section of the Code establishes the general principles concerning power to transfer and delineates the protections afforded good faith purchasers for value in several areas that caused problems under prior law. Additionally, § 2-403 protects purchasers who buy out of inventory and in the ordinary course of business. UCC § 2-403, comment 2. We consider these two primary features of the provision in turn.

If a purchaser does not fall within the protection of § 2-403, he may maintain a claim for breach of warranty of good title under UCC § 2-312. Although § 2-403 served as the model for § 2A-304, the provisions of the Article 2 analogue were significantly revised in Article 2A to reflect leasing practices and to take into account certificate of title statutes. The comments to § 2A-304 outline the differences between sales and lease transactions and describe the section's operation when there is a subsequent lease by a lessor. Section 2A-305 is a companion to § 2A-304 and states the rule with respect to the leasehold interest obtained by a buyer or sublessee from a lessee of goods under an existing lease. Generally, under both §§ 2A-304 and 2A-305, the subsequent lessee, or the buyer or sublessee obtains the interest in the goods that the lessor or lessee had power to transfer. For a discussion of the problems those two Article 2A provisions may cause secured creditors of the lessor or lessee, see Harris, *The Rights of Creditors Under Article 2A*, 39 ALA. L. REV. 803 (1988).

1. Transferring Voidable Title

Generally, one who purchases goods obtains all the title which the transferor has or has the power to transfer. This rule has two aspects. One is the "derivation" principle of *nemo dat quod non habet* (one cannot give what one does not have). *Nemo dat* dictates that the transferee takes its interest subject to all third-party claims and interests that were enforceable against the transferor. The second aspect of the rule is commonly referred to as the "shelter" principle. When the transferor has priority over third-party claims, the transferee will enjoy that same priority. The contract of sale, however, may state that the purchaser is buying only a limited or fractional interest in the goods; under such a contract, the purchaser obtains "less title" than the transferor had the power to transfer.

Although the foregoing rules governing the transfer of title provide common sense protections to the purchaser, the remaining provisions of subsection (1) of § 2-403 afford protections to the purchaser that might appear unusual. Even if the transferor's title is voidable (e.g., if the transferor acquired title from a minor), the transferor has the power to transfer good title to a good faith purchaser for value. To claim this protection successfully, the purchaser must be able to demonstrate both that he purchased in good faith and that he purchased for value. Next, subsection (1) resolves four specific transfer of title issues which were problematic under prior law. UCC § 2-403, comment 1. Each of these issues involves the power of a purchaser to transfer good title to the purchased goods subsequent to the delivery of those goods to him. The purchaser acquires the power to transfer good title to a good faith purchaser for value even though: (1) the transferor from whom the purchaser obtained the goods was deceived as to the identity of the purchaser; (2) the purchaser obtained delivery of the goods in exchange for a check that was subsequently dishonored; (3) the purchaser acquired the goods in a transaction that was supposed to be a "cash sale," but the price was not actually paid; and (4) the purchaser obtained delivery of the goods by fraud that is punishable as larcenous under the criminal law. Though § 2-403 is concerned with protecting the good faith purchaser for value in each of these situations, it is important to recognize that the original transferor in each of these transactions is not left without a remedy; rather, the original transferor usually has recourse against the party who obtained title by any of these dubious means before conveying the goods. Of course, whether such recourse is likely to be of any real value is another matter entirely.

KOTIS v. NOWLIN JEWELRY, INC.
Texas Court of Appeals
844 S.W.2d 920 (1992)

DRAUGHN, J.

Eddie Kotis appeals from a judgment declaring appellee, Nowlin Jewelry, Inc., the sole owner of a Rolex watch, and awarding appellee attorney's fees. . . . We affirm.

On June 11, 1990, Steve Sitton acquired a gold ladies Rolex watch, President model, with a diamond bezel from Nowlin Jewelry by forging a check belonging to his brother and misrepresenting to Nowlin that he had his brother's authorization for the purchase. The purchase price of the watch, and the amount of the forged check, was $9,438.50. The next day, Sitton telephoned Eddie Kotis, the owner of a used car dealership, and asked Kotis if he was interested in buying a Rolex watch. Kotis indicated interest and Sitton came to the car lot. Kotis purchased the watch for $3,550.00. Kotis also called Nowlin's Jewelry that same day and spoke with Cherie Nowlin.

Ms. Nowlin told Kotis that Sitton had purchased the watch the day before. Ms. Nowlin testified that Kotis would not immediately identify himself. Because she did not have the payment information available, Ms. Nowlin asked if she could call him back. Kotis then gave his name and number. Ms. Nowlin testified that she called Kotis and told him the amount of the check and that it had not yet cleared. Kotis told Ms. Nowlin that he did not have the watch and that he did not want the watch. Ms. Nowlin also testified that Kotis would not tell her how much Sitton was asking for the watch.

John Nowlin, the president of Nowlin's Jewelry, testified that, after this call from Kotis, Nowlin's bookkeeper began attempting to confirm whether the check had cleared. When they learned the check would not be honored by the bank, Nowlin called Kotis, but Kotis refused to talk to Nowlin. Kotis referred Nowlin to his attorney. On June 25, 1990, Kotis' attorney called Nowlin and suggested that Nowlin hire an attorney and allegedly indicated that Nowlin could buy the watch back from Kotis. Nowlin refused to repurchase the watch.

After Sitton was indicted for forgery and theft, the district court ordered Nowlin's Jewelry to hold the watch until there was an adjudication of the ownership of the watch. Nowlin then filed suit seeking a declaratory judgment that Nowlin was the sole owner of the watch. Kotis filed a counterclaim for a declaration that Kotis was a good faith purchaser of the watch and was entitled to possession and title of the watch. After a bench trial, the trial court rendered judgment declaring Nowlin the sole owner of the watch. The trial court also filed Findings of Fact and Conclusions of Law.

In point of error one, Kotis claims the trial court erred in concluding that Sitton did not receive the watch through a transaction of purchase with Nowlin, within the meaning of Tex. Bus. & Com. Code Ann. § 2.403(a). . . .

Kotis contends there is evidence that the watch is a "good" under the UCC, there was a voluntary transfer of the watch, and there was physical delivery of the watch. Thus, Kotis maintains that the transaction between Sitton and Nowlin was a transaction of purchase such that Sitton acquired the ability to transfer good title to a good faith purchaser under § 2.403. . . .

Neither the code nor case law defines the phrase "transaction of purchase." "Purchase" is defined by the code as a "taking by sale, discount, negotiation, mortgage, pledge, lien, issue or reissue, gift, or any other voluntary transaction creating an interest in property." Tex. Bus. & Com. Code Ann. § 1.201(32) (Vernon 1968). Thus, only voluntary transactions can constitute transactions of purchase.

Having found no Texas case law concerning what constitutes a transaction of purchase under § 2.403(a), we have looked to case law from other states. Based on the code definition of a purchase as a voluntary transaction, these cases reason that a thief who wrongfully takes the goods against the will of the owner is not a purchaser. *See Suburban Motors, Inc. v. State Farm Mut. Automobile Ins. Co.*, 218 Cal. App. 3d 1354, 268 Cal. Rptr. 16, 18 (Cal. Ct. App. 1990); *Charles Evans BMW, Inc. v. Williams*, 196 Ga. App. 230, 395 S.E.2d 650, 651–52 (Ga. Ct. App. 1990); *Inmi-Etti v. Aluisi*, 63 Md. App. 293, 492 A.2d 917, 922 (Md. App. 1985). On the other hand, a swindler who fraudulently induces the victim to deliver the goods voluntarily is a purchaser under the code. *Inmi-Etti*, 492 A.2d at 922; *Williams*, 395 S.E.2d at 652.

In this case, Nowlin's Jewelry voluntarily delivered the watch to Sitton in return for payment by check that was later discovered to be forged. Sitton did not obtain the watch against the will of the owner. Rather, Sitton fraudulently induced Nowlin's Jewelry to deliver the watch voluntarily. Thus, we agree with appellant that the trial court erred in concluding that Sitton did not receive the watch through a transaction of purchase under § 2.403(a). We sustain point of error one.

In point of error two, Kotis contends the trial court erred in concluding that, at the time Sitton sold the watch to Kotis, Sitton did not have at least voidable title to the watch. In point of error nine, Kotis challenges the trial court's conclusion that Nowlin's Jewelry had legal and equitable title at all times relevant to the lawsuit. The lack of Texas case law addressing such issues under the code again requires us to look to case law from other states to assist in our analysis.

In *Suburban Motors, Inc. v. State Farm Mut. Automobile Ins. Co.*, the California court noted that § 2.403 provides for the creation of voidable title where there is a voluntary transfer of goods. 268 Cal. Rptr. at 18. Section 2.403(a)(1)–(4) set forth the types of voluntary transactions that can give the purchaser voidable title. Where goods are stolen such that there is no voluntary transfer, only void title results. *Id.* at 19; *Inmi-Etti*, 492 A.2d at 921. Subsection (4) provides that a purchaser can obtain voidable title to the goods even if "delivery was procured through fraud punishable as larcenous under the criminal law." Tex. Bus. & Com. Code Ann. § 2.403(a)(4) (Vernon 1968). This subsection applies to cases involving acts fraudulent to the seller such as where the seller delivers the goods in return for a forged check. *See Inmi-Etti*, 492 A.2d at 921. Although Sitton paid Nowlin's Jewelry with a forged check, he obtained possession of the watch through a voluntary transaction of purchase and received voidable, rather than void, title to the watch. Thus, the trial court erred in concluding that Sitton received no title to the watch and in concluding that Nowlin's retained title at all relevant times. We sustain points of error two and nine.

In point of error three, Kotis claims the trial court erred in concluding that Kotis did not give sufficient value for the watch to receive protection under § 2.403, that Kotis did not take good title to the watch as a good faith purchaser, that Kotis did not receive good title to the watch, and that Kotis is not entitled to the watch under § 2.403. In points of error four through eight, Kotis challenges the trial court's findings regarding his good faith, his honesty in fact, and his actual belief, and the reasonableness of the belief, that the watch had been received unlawfully.

Under § 2.403(a), a transferor with voidable title can transfer good title to a good faith purchaser. Tex. Bus. & Com. Code Ann. § 2.403(a) (Vernon 1968). Good faith means "honesty in fact in the conduct or transaction concerned." Tex. Bus. & Com. Code Ann. § 1.201(19) (Vernon 1968). The test for good faith is the actual belief of the party and not the reasonableness of that belief. *La Sara Grain v. First Nat'l Bank*, 673 S.W.2d 558, 563 (Tex. 1984).

Kotis was a dealer in used cars and testified that he had bought several cars from Sitton in the past and had no reason not to trust Sitton. He also testified that on June 12, 1990, Sitton called and asked Kotis if he was interested in buying a Ladies Rolex. Once Kotis indicated his interest in the watch, Sitton came to Kotis's place of business. According to Kotis, Sitton said that he had received $18,000.00 upon the sale of his house and that he had used this to purchase the watch for his girlfriend several months before. Kotis paid $3,550.00 for the watch. Kotis further testified that he then spoke to a friend, Gary Neal Martin, who also knew Sitton. Martin sagely advised Kotis to contact Nowlin's to check whether Sitton had financed the watch. Kotis testified that he called Nowlin's after buying the watch.

Cherie Nowlin testified that she received a phone call from Kotis on June 12, 1990, although Kotis did not immediately identify himself. Kotis asked if Nowlin's had sold a gold President model Rolex watch with a diamond bezel about a month before. When asked, Kotis told Ms. Nowlin that Sitton had come to Kotis' car lot and was trying to sell the watch. Ms. Nowlin testified that Kotis told her he did not want the watch because he already owned a Rolex. Ms. Nowlin told Kotis that Sitton had purchased the watch the day before. Kotis asked about the method of payment. Because Ms. Nowlin did not know, she agreed to check and call Kotis back. She called Kotis back and advised him that Sitton had paid for the watch with a check that had not yet cleared. When Ms. Nowlin asked if Kotis had the watch, Kotis said no and would not tell her how much Sitton was asking for the watch. Ms. Nowlin did advise Kotis of the amount of the check.

After these calls, the owner of Nowlin's asked his bookkeeper to call the bank regarding Sitton's check. They learned on June 15, 1990 that the check would be dishonored. John Nowlin called Kotis the next day and advised him about the dishonored check. Kotis refused to talk to Nowlin and told Nowlin to contact his attorney. Nowlin also testified that a reasonable amount to pay for a Ladies President Rolex watch with a diamond bezel in mint condition was $7,000.00–$8,000.00. Nowlin maintained that $3,500.00 was an exorbitantly low price for a watch like this.

The trier of fact is the sole judge of the credibility of the witnesses and the weight to be given their testimony. . . . Kotis testified that he lied when he spoke with Cherie Nowlin and that he had already purchased the watch before he learned that Sitton's story was false. The judge, as the trier of fact, may not have believed Kotis when he said that he had already purchased the watch. If the judge disbelieved this part of Kotis' testimony, other facts tend to show that Kotis did not believe the transaction was lawful. For example, when Kotis spoke with Nowlin's, he initially refused to identify himself, he said that he did not have the watch and that he did not want the watch, he refused to divulge Sitton's asking price, and he later refused to talk with Nowlin and advised Nowlin to contact Kotis' attorney. Thus, there is evidence supporting the trial court's finding that Kotis did not act in good faith.

There are sufficient facts to uphold the trial court's findings even if the judge had accepted as true Kotis' testimony that, despite his statements to Nowlin's, he had already purchased the watch when he called Nowlin's. The testimony indicated that

Kotis was familiar with the price of Rolex watches and that $3,550.00 was an extremely low price for a mint condition watch of this type. An unreasonably low price is evidence the buyer knows the goods are stolen. . . . Although the test is what Kotis actually believed, we agree with appellee that we need not let this standard sanction willful disregard of suspicious facts that would lead a reasonable person to believe the transaction was unlawful. . . . Thus, we find sufficient evidence to uphold the trial court's findings regarding Kotis' lack of status as a good faith purchaser. We overrule points of error three through eight. . . .

We affirm the trial court's judgment.

PROBLEM 4-2

Ted Thomas went to Sherman's Farm Supply and selected a John Deere combine. Thomas told Sherman's that he was representing Victoria Vict, who would be purchasing the combine. Sherman's created a customer purchase order and a variable loan contract and security agreement that listed Victoria Vict as the purchaser. Thomas said that he would bring the paperwork to Vict for her signature. Instead, Thomas forged Vict's signature on all the paperwork and returned it to the dealer. Sherman's then delivered the combine to Vict's property, not knowing that Vict was out of town for the week. Thomas removed the combine from Vict's property without the knowledge of Sherman's or Vict.

Thomas took the combine to Bob's Tractor Sales, where he sought to borrow money against the value of the combine. Instead, Bob's suggested that he enter into a retail installment sales contract that purported to represent the sale of the combine from Bob's to Thomas. Thomas was paid a lump sum by Bob's, but then was obligated under the sales contract to make monthly payments to Bob's. Bob's immediately assigned the loan agreement to Quick Credit Company. Thomas took the lump sum payment and left town immediately. When Thomas failed to make his first payment, Quick Credit repossessed the combine.

Meanwhile, Vict had been receiving notices of late payment from Sherman's, which she attributed to shoddy bookkeeping. When Sherman's attempted to repossess the combine, it learned that Vict had never authorized the paperwork relating to the sale, had never received possession of the combine, and did not know the location of the combine.

Sherman's seeks to recover the value of the combine from Quick Credit. Quick Credit claims that Bob's was a good faith purchaser for value that acquired title to the combine because Thomas had voidable title. Quick Credit claims that it has full rights in the combine as a result.

Should Sherman's prevail in its claim that Quick Credit has no rights in the combine?

2. Transferring Title of Entrusted Goods

The purpose of subsections (2) and (3) of § 2-403 is to protect purchasers who buy out of inventory and in the ordinary course of business. UCC § 2-403, comment 2. Although the type of purchase protected by these subsections is similar to the protection of a good faith purchaser for value under subsection (1), the requirements of "buyer in the ordinary course of business" are more specific. See UCC § 1-201(9). Thus, under these subsections, the Code attempts to eliminate the protection of those purchasers who managed to "fit into" the loose interpretations of good faith purchaser for value under prior law. UCC § 2-403, comment 3. Subsections (2) and (3) provide that when one who has title to goods entrusts the goods to a merchant who deals in goods of that kind, the merchant has the power to transfer all the rights of the entruster to a buyer in the ordinary course of business. The merchant has that power to transfer such title once the goods have been delivered to him and the owner has acquiesced in the merchant's retention of possession of the goods. To be considered a "merchant who deals in goods of that kind," one regularly must engage in selling goods of that kind. *See Toyomenka, Inc. v. Mount Hope Finishing Co.*, 432 F.2d 722, 727 (4th Cir. 1970). As with subsection (1), the purpose is to protect the purchaser in the ordinary course of business, and the owner's remedy, if he has been wronged, is against the merchant to whom he entrusted the goods. The hypothetical case is the jeweler who sells a watch that has been left with him for repair. The purchaser of the entrusted watch is protected by subsections (2) and (3).

PEREZ-MEDINA v. FIRST TEAM AUCTION, INC.
Georgia Court of Appeals
426 S.E.2d 397 (1992)

Andrews, J.

Perez-Medina brought this trover action against First Team Auction alleging that First Team Auction refused to relinquish possession of a tractor owned by him. Perez-Medina appeals from the trial court's order granting summary judgment in favor of First Team Auction, and denying his motion for summary judgment.

Construed in favor of appellant as the party opposing summary judgment, the evidence reflects that Perez-Medina bought the tractor at an auction for $66,500. At the auction, appellant met Julio Lara, who was bidding on the same tractor. At a second auction the same day, appellant purchased certain equipment for the tractor. He met Lara again at the second auction, and the two agreed that Lara would install the equipment on the tractor. With Perez-Medina's knowledge and consent, Lara took possession of the tractor, and moved it to his place of business for this purpose. About four months later, Perez-Medina went to Lara's place of business, and paid him $10,000 to install the equipment. Appellant testified that the business where the tractor was located appeared to him to be a repair shop rather than a business dealing in heavy equipment. Other undisputed evidence showed that Lara operated a business in which he regularly bought and sold heavy equipment like the tractor at issue at auctions conducted by First Team Auction and others, and in other business transactions. Subsequently, without appellant's knowledge or consent, Lara represented to First Team Auction that he was the owner of the tractor free and clear of any liens, and put the tractor up for sale at an auction conducted by First Team Auction. After the auction failed to produce an adequate bid for the tractor, Lara negotiated a sale of the tractor to First Team Auction for about $54,000. The tractor was sold without appellant's knowledge or consent, and appellant received no part of the sales proceeds. The tractor was thereafter sold by First Team Auction to a tractor dealer, who sold it to a consumer. When the sales were made, neither First Team Auction, nor the subsequent purchasers had any knowledge of appellant's interest in the tractor. After Lara's conversion of the tractor was discovered, the subsequent purchasers after First Team Auction returned the purchase price and tractor, culminating in First Team Auction's return of the purchase price, and acceptance of the tractor back from its purchaser.

O.C.G.A. § 11-2-403 provides that: "(2) Any entrusting of possession of goods to a merchant who deals in goods of that kind gives him power to transfer all rights of the entruster to a buyer in ordinary course of business. (3) 'Entrusting' includes any delivery and any acquiescence in retention of possession regardless of any condition expressed between the parties to the delivery or acquiescence and regardless of whether the procurement of the entrusting or the possessor's disposition of the goods have been such as to be larcenous under the criminal law." Thus, the issue becomes whether Lara was a "merchant" under O.C.G.A. § 11-2-104(1) to whom appellant "entrusted" the tractor within the meaning of O.C.G.A. § 11-2-403(2), (3). If so, then Lara was empowered to transfer appellant's ownership interest in the tractor to a "buyer in ordinary course of business" as defined in O.C.G.A. § 11-1-201(9). Accordingly, if First Team Auction retained the status of a buyer in ordinary course of business, appellant cannot prevail in the present trover action because he would lack title or right of possession to the tractor as against First Team Auction. *Perimeter Ford v. Edwards*, 197 Ga. App. 747, 748, 399 S.E.2d 520 (1990).

1. In his first enumeration of error, appellant contends the trial court erred by determining that Lara was a "merchant." A " '[m]erchant' means a person who deals in goods of the kind or otherwise by his occupation holds himself out as having knowledge or skill peculiar to the practices or goods involved in the transaction. . . ." O.C.G.A. § 11-2-104. The evidence is undisputed that Lara was known by First Team Auction and others as a regular dealer buying and selling heavy equipment. Moreover, appellant met Lara at an auction, where Lara was bidding on the tractor at issue. After meeting Lara again at another such auction the same day, appellant hired him to install equipment on the tractor, and authorized him to take immediate possession of the tractor for this purpose. Appellant contends that Lara is not a "merchant" because he did not know he was a dealer in heavy equipment. This contention is based on his observation of Lara's place of business, which he visited about four months after placing the tractor in Lara's possession. Appellant concluded that the business appeared to him to be a place to make repairs, rather than a business dealing in heavy equipment.

The primary rationale behind the entrusting provisions of O.C.G.A. § 11-2-403 is aimed at protecting the buyer who purchases the entrusted goods in the ordinary course of business. *Simson v. Moon*, 137 Ga. App. 82, 85, 222 S.E.2d 873 (1975). Thus, "the owner takes the risk by placing or leaving his chattel with a merchant of his own choosing who could convert or otherwise misdeal it. . . . The protection afforded the purchaser is merely a special application of the broad equitable principle that where one of two innocent persons must suffer loss by reasons of the fraud or deceit of another, the loss should rightly fall upon him by whose act or omission the wrongdoer has been enabled to commit the fraud." (citations omitted). *Id.* at 85–86. Nevertheless, given that the entrusting provisions of the statute operate only where the goods have been placed with a "merchant," it is reasonable to conclude that the statute requires, from an objective viewpoint, that the entruster know, or in the exercise of reasonable diligence should know, that he placed the goods with one who might reasonably appear to third persons to be a dealer in the type of goods in question. *See* ANDERSON, UNIFORM COMMERCIAL CODE, 3d ed., *Sales*, § 2-403:34. It follows that the entrustment provisions of O.C.G.A. § 11-2-403 do not operate in the context of a casual sale, where the entruster places the goods in the possession of one who exhibits no objective indicia of being a dealer in the kind of goods in question.

Here, the record supports the trial court's conclusion, as a matter of law, that Lara was a merchant dealing in the kind of goods at issue. Appellant met Lara at an auction at which Lara was bidding on the tractor at issue. Appellant later met Lara at a similar auction, agreed for Lara to install equipment on the tractor, and placed the tractor in Lara's possession. When appellant visited Lara four months later, he contends the place where Lara kept the tractor impressed him as a repair shop. Other undisputed testimony from First Team Auction and others engaged in the buying and selling of heavy equipment, shows that Lara held himself out as a merchant in the business of buying and selling the kind of goods at issue, and regularly bought and sold such goods at auctions and in other business transactions. The evidence established, as a matter of law, that First Team Auction and other third parties knew Lara was a dealer in the type of goods in question, and that appellant knew, or should have known, that Lara might reasonably appear to third parties to be such a dealer.

2. Secondly, appellant argues that he did not "entrust" the tractor to Lara. The trial court also properly concluded that appellant "entrusted" the tractor to Lara as defined by O.C.G.A. § 11-2-403 (2), (3). "[S]ubsection (3) [of the statute] specially includes *any* delivery and acquiescence in possession, and encompasses possession regardless of any condition or limitation expressed between the parties." (citations omitted). *Perimeter Ford, supra* at 749. Under the statute, the tractor was "entrusted" despite the fact that

it was placed in Lara's possession only for the purpose of installing equipment for appellant rather than for sale. *See Simson, supra* (after entruster placed truck in possession of dealer for purpose of repairs, dealer's unauthorized sale of truck to a buyer in the ordinary course of business was effective to convey the entruster's ownership interest); *Christopher v. McGehee*, 124 Ga. App. 310, 311, 183 S.E.2d 624 (1971). Under the statute, "[appellant's] acquiescence in leaving the [tractor] with [Lara] amounts to an estoppel, which is the underlying principle of [O.C.G.A. § 11-2-403(2) and (3)]." *Simson, supra* at 85; *see* ANDERSON, UNIFORM COMMERCIAL CODE, 3d ed., *Sales*, §§ 2-403:42, 2-403:43 (under the entrustment provisions of O.C.G.A. § 11-2-403, it is immaterial why possession of the goods was left with the merchant-seller, or that sale of the goods was not authorized by the entruster); *compare Sylvester Motor & Tractor Co. v. Farmer's Bank of Pelham*, 153 Ga. App. 614, 615, 266 S.E.2d 293 (1980) (although noting the goods were not "entrusted" to the dealer for sale, the holding appears to ultimately rest on the conclusion that the purchaser from the dealer was not a buyer in the ordinary course of business). Accordingly, Lara was empowered to transfer appellant's ownership interest to a buyer in the ordinary course of business. *Classic Cadillac v. World Omni Leasing*, 199 Ga. App. 115, 117, 404 S.E.2d 452 (1991); *Perimeter Ford, supra* at 750.

3. In his third enumeration, appellant contends the trial court erred in ruling that First Team Auction was a buyer in the ordinary course of business. A "buyer in ordinary course of business" is defined by O.C.G.A. § 11-1-201(9) as "a person who in good faith and without knowledge that the sale to him is in violation of the ownership rights or security interest of a third party in the goods buys in ordinary course from a person in the business of selling goods of that kind. . . ." The record shows that First Team Auction, which bought, sold, and conducted an auction business in goods of this kind, knew Lara was in the business of buying and selling heavy equipment, and had dealt with Lara on a regular basis. There is no evidence that First Team Auction, as a dealer itself, failed to reasonably inquire into Lara's interest in the tractor, nor do we find any peculiar circumstances about the sale sufficient to raise a question of fact as to whether there was a good faith purchase. *See Perimeter Ford, supra* at 750. Prior to First Team Auction's purchase of the tractor, Lara executed a standard pre-auction document declaring that he had ownership interest in the tractor and could sell it free of all liens. There is no requirement that the sale of the tractor be evidenced by a bill of sale or other proof of ownership. *See Brown v. Allen*, 203 Ga. App. 894, 895, 418 S.E.2d 153 (1992). As a buyer in the ordinary course of business, First Team Auction received from Lara all of appellant's ownership interest in the tractor under O.C.G.A. § 11-2-403. *Perimeter Ford, supra*. On the present facts, the risk of the loss caused by Lara's conversion, as between appellant and First Team Auction, is borne by appellant. *See Benton v. Duvall Livestock Marketing*, 201 Ga. App. 430, 411 S.E.2d 307 (1991). Consequently, there was no error in the trial court's grant of summary judgment in favor of First Team Auction.

4. Finally, appellant contends the trial court erred in denying his motion for summary judgment because, even if First Team Auction was a buyer in the ordinary course of business when it originally purchased from Lara, it could not occupy that status when, after learning of Lara's conversion, it repurchased the tractor from its subsequent good faith purchaser with knowledge of appellant's interests. By returning the purchase price and reobtaining the tractor, First Team Auction accomplished a rescission of the sale rather than a repurchase, and thus continued to occupy the status of a good faith buyer in the ordinary course of business. *See Charles Evans BMW v. Williams*, 196 Ga. App. 230, 233, 395 S.E.2d 650 (1990). The trial court properly denied appellant's motion for summary judgment.

Judgment affirmed.

PROBLEM 4-3

Shady Yacht Sales and Marina operates a business on the Gulf Coast of Florida. Shady sells new and used luxury yachts, services and repairs yachts, and also leases stalls for owners who wish to dock their yachts at the Marina. Ben Hadd decided to purchase a yacht, and so he visited the Marina. Ben wasn't impressed with the used yachts in Shady's inventory, and he mentioned that a yacht docked at the Marina would be "perfect" for him. Shady immediately said that the owner had consigned the yacht for sale, and concluded a deal with Ben. Ben paid cash and took delivery of the yacht one week later.

Ben later discovered that the yacht that he obtained from Shady was owned by Charisse Elgin. Shady knew that Charisse was in Europe for two months and had sold her yacht with the intention of filing a false theft report to generate an insurance recovery. This scheme, as you might expect, quickly unraveled. Charisse demanded that Ben return her yacht. Ben responded that he had purchased the yacht in good faith, and that it was now his property.

Who holds title to the yacht? Would your answer change if Charisse had delivered her yacht to Shady for servicing and repairs, and it was sold from Shady's dry dock facility where it stored used yachts in its sales inventory?

C. THE INTERPLAY BETWEEN ARTICLE 2 AND CERTIFICATE-OF-TITLE STATUTES

Title disputes that would otherwise be decided solely under Article 2 will sometimes involve automobiles or other goods covered by a certificate-of-title statute. Questions are bound to arise if the party who claims to have received good title by virtue of being a good faith purchaser under § 2-403(1), or a buyer in ordinary course of business under § 2-403(2), fails to comply with all of the transfer requirements of the certificate-of-title law. When the application of Article 2 and the title statute produce different results, the proper resolution will depend on the wording of the certificate-of-title statute. Generalizing in this area has been complicated by the fact that there were two uniform certificate-of-title acts (*see* Uniform Motor Vehicle Certificate of Title and Anti-Theft Act, 11A U.L.A. 175 (1995 & Supp. 2001); Uniform Vehicle Code (1968)). There is now a third uniform act known as the Uniform Certificate of Title Act ("UCOTA"), *available at* http://www.law.upenn.edu/bll/archives/ulc/ucota/2005final.htm. Moreover, there are a variety of non-uniform acts. Professor Christina L. Kunz has suggested that notwithstanding their differences, the statutes fall into three groups: excepting, invalidating, and nondirective.

(1) The excepting CTA provisions include, with or without minor language changes, subsection (e) of [the Uniform Motor Vehicle Certificate of Title and Anti-Theft Act (UMVCTA)] section 14 or [the Uniform Vehicle Code (UVC)] section 3-112. The excepting CTAs state that if certain procedures are not followed in the transfer of a motor vehicle, then, except as between the parties, the transfer is ineffective.

(2) The invalidating CTA provisions, while not modeled after either of the two uniform acts, also contain language that would seem to require judicial invalidation of any motor vehicle transfer when the parties fail to comply with statutory procedures. The major difference between excepting CTAs and invalidating CTAs is the scope of the invalidating effect.

(3) The nondirective CTA provisions require compliance by the parties, but do not explicitly spell out the effect on title if the parties fail to comply.

Christina L. Kunz, *Motor Vehicle Ownership Disputes Involving Certificate-of-Title Acts and Article Two of the U.C.C.*, 39 Bus. Law. 1599, 1606 (1984). Professor Alvin C.

Harrell, who was the Reporter for the committee responsible for drafting UCOTA, describes the treatment of good faith purchasers and buyers in ordinary course of business:

The UCC recognizes that buyers purchasing goods in the ordinary course of business from merchants who deal in goods of that kind customarily expect to acquire the goods free from claims of the seller's creditors (*see* UCC section 9-320). The UCC also recognizes that an owner of goods who delivers those goods to a merchant who deals in goods of that kind (e.g., in a consignment or other bailment) has reason to expect that the goods may be sold in the ordinary course of the merchant's business (*see* UCC section 2-403(2)). This "entrusting" rule subordinates the bailor's rights to those of a buyer in ordinary course of business (BIOCOB). There are similar rules for lessees in the ordinary course under UCC Article 2A.

These UCC rules recognizing the primacy of a BIOCOB in merchant sales transactions are fundamental and essential to the smooth functioning of retail markets. Any other rule would require retail buyers of goods to conduct a title and lien search before making routine transactions, effectively converting common sales of goods transactions into the equivalent of a real estate sales transaction (with title and lien searches, title insurance, a closing agent, escrow period, closing costs, etc.). This is simply not practical for sales of goods.

Moreover, in most sales of goods transactions, the BIOCOB has no practical means to protect against the risk of a bailment since bailments are not subject to any system of public recordation. Thus, unlike real estate transactions, the most elaborate closing process would not protect a BIOCOB against the claims of a bailor. In contrast, the bailor can easily protect himself or herself against the risk of a bailee selling to a BIOCOB by exercising caution about delivering goods to a bailee who is a merchant selling goods of that kind. The difficulty of protecting a BIOCOB from claims of a bailor, the relative ease with which a bailor can protect himself or herself from the obvious risk of sale by a merchant bailee, and the need to maintain a smooth-functioning and efficient retail system for sales of goods constitute strong public policy reasons in support of the UCC rules, which are basic law in all the states. UCOTA conforms to those rules at sections 18 and 19.

UCC section 1-201(9) defines BIOCOB and makes clear that this status requires a sale that "comports with the usual or customary practices in the kind of business in which the seller is engaged or with the seller's own usual or customary practices." There can be no doubt that, in retail sales of vehicles by dealers, it is customary for the buyer to drive away from the sale in the vehicle being purchased without receiving the CT. UCOTA recognizes this, consistent with the UCC definition at section 1-201(9), by specifying at section 19(c) that execution of the CT is not a requirement for BIOCOB status. This again is the rule in a majority of jurisdictions and is essential for consistency with the UCC.

As noted, a few jurisdictions have authority to the contrary, apparently based on isolated cases or transactions involving cars that were sold without authorization after being entrusted to a dealer. For the most part, this authority is aberrational and does not reflect a sound analysis of the UCC. These cases are not a basis for either contradicting clear and long-established UCC principles, changing the law in the majority of the states, or imposing significant new costs and burdens on common retail sales transactions. Nor is it apparent why these issues should be of any interest to unaffected parties such as title offices. Of course, if a state (and its title office) considers the issue carefully and decides that retail buyers purchasing vehicles from dealers in that state should not be accorded the protections of a BIOCOB, it is a simple matter to modify UCOTA accordingly in that state. However, in most states, that would significantly reduce consumer protections, contradict the UCC, create both external and internal conflicts in state law, and increase the cost, uncertainty, and complexity of vehicle sales transactions, all at no apparent benefit to the office, dealers, most consumers, or secured parties.

Your author is aware of arguments that buyers who purchase vehicles without a CT should be given BIOCOB status only if, for example, it is a new vehicle without a CT; the dealer is properly licensed; or (as in California) the vehicle was entrusted to the dealer for the purpose of sale. Two final, basic points need to be emphasized with regard to these arguments: (1) Any of these rules would place on the buyer an untenable burden to make legal judgments as to technical issues that cannot be firmly resolved without a law suit; and (2) by depriving buyers in customary transactions of BIOCOB status, these rules would not only subordinate these buyers to the dealer's entrustor but would also subordinate the buyer to the dealer's inventory loan. This would essentially wipe out the ability of ordinary buyers to obtain clear title in the purchase of vehicles from dealers, regardless of whether there was an entrustment. Obviously, this solution would require a fundamental and far-reaching reconsideration of basic issues in sales and secured transactions law.

Alvin C. Harrell, *The Uniform Certificate of Title Act: Myths and Realities*, U.C.C. L.J., Summer 2006, at 1.

If the title dispute involves aircraft, the Federal Aviation Act requires that transfers be recorded in compliance with its provisions. *See* 49 U.S.C. § 44108 (1994). In *Philko Aviation, Inc. v. Shacket*, 462 U.S. 406, 76 L. Ed. 2d 678, 103 S. Ct. 2476 (1983), the Supreme Court adopted what might be described as a two-step approach to title transfers similar to that advocated by Professor Kunz. Before the purchaser is entitled to claim the protection of the good faith purchase provisions of the UCC, she must first satisfy the transfer requirements of the federal statute.

GODFREY v. GILSDORF
Nevada Supreme Court
476 P.2d 3 (1970)

Thompson, J.

This case involves the interplay between our motor vehicle licensing and registration law and the entrustment provisions of the Uniform Commercial Code. As will be seen, each party, seller and buyer, acted in good faith. Each is innocent of any wrongdoing. Unfortunately, one of them must sustain a loss due to an unprincipled used car dealer. The thrust of the ruling below placed that loss upon the seller, a determination with which we agree. However, other aspects of the judgment are incorrect and must be adjusted to conform with established law.

This is a replevin action to recover possession of a used automobile. It was commenced by the seller, Godfrey, against the buyer, Gilsdorf, who had purchased the vehicle from a used car dealer to whom the seller had entrusted it for sale. The facts are stipulated. Godfrey was the registered owner of a 1967 Toyota. The legal owner was Commercial Credit Corporation who held title as security for the balance ($1,187.03) of a debt owing it by Godfrey. Godfrey removed the license plates and certificate of registration from the car and delivered the vehicle for sale to a used car dealer, Auto Center. Gilsdorf saw the car at Auto Center and arranged to buy it. He made a downpayment of $300, signed a car purchase order, and received possession of the Toyota to which was affixed the pink copy of the statutory Dealer's Report of Sale. He then borrowed $1,600 from Allstate Credit Corporation, gave a chattel mortgage as security, and inquired of Allstate whether he should get the title certificate. Allstate advised him not to worry about it since Auto Center would mail the certificate to Allstate directly. Gilsdorf then delivered Allstate's draft for $1,600 to Auto Center together with his personal check for $726.50 and received in return the green copy of Dealer's Report of Sale. He submitted the latter document to the Motor Vehicle Department and was issued license plates and a registration certificate as allowed by NRS 482.400(2) and 482.215.

Meanwhile, Godfrey noticed that his car was not on the Auto Center lot and made inquiry. He was told that the car was sold and payment would be forthcoming when the check cleared the bank. The money was never paid him. Auto Center ceased doing business. Several weeks later Godfrey paid his debt to Commercial Credit ($1,187.03) and received the title certificate to the Toyota. The value of the car when delivered to Auto Center was $2,550 and its reasonable rental value was $150 per month.

When this replevin action was commenced, Godfrey obtained possession of the car by resort to the provisional remedy of claim and delivery. . . . Gilsdorf, the defendant, had used the car for eight months. The complaint requested alternative relief, delivery of the car or its value in case delivery could not be had, and damages for its unlawful detention. . . . Gilsdorf, by counterclaim, sought to compel Godfrey to transfer the title certificate to him.

The seller, Godfrey, plaintiff below and appellant here, insists that title to a motor vehicle can only be transferred in accordance with the motor vehicle licensing and registration law, and not otherwise. That law requires the legal owner (in this instance, Commercial Credit Corporation) and the transferee (Allstate Credit Corporation who financed a major portion of the purchase for Gilsdorf) "to write their signatures with pen and ink upon the certificate of ownership issued for such vehicle, together with the residence address of the transferee in the appropriate places provided upon the reverse side of the certificate." NRS 482.400. Thereafter, one of them must deliver the certificate of title to the Department of Motor Vehicles. NRS 482.426. Since the purpose of the statute is to provide a fast and simple way to determine ownership and to prevent fraud and theft, strict compliance is essential. Exceptions should not be allowed, for to do so would frustrate the realization of an important legislative purpose and policy. This contention carries considerable force and may not lightly be cast aside.

On the other hand, the buyer Gilsdorf, defendant below and respondent here, urges that the entrustment provisions of the Uniform Commercial Code, NRS 104.2403(2), (3) create an estoppel against the seller to assert title to the car. Moreover, he argues that the buyer, in these circumstances, acquired the automobile free of the security interest of Commercial Credit Corporation. NRS 104.9307. In persuasive fashion, he presses the following. The seller entrusted his car to a merchant who deals in cars and, in the words of the UCC "gave him the power to transfer all rights of the entrustor to a buyer in the ordinary course of business." NRS 104.2403(2). Gilsdorf was a "buyer in the ordinary course of business." NRS 104.1201(9). He bought a used car from a person in the business of selling used cars, and bought it in good faith without knowledge of the ownership rights of a third party, Commercial Credit Corporation. He arranged immediate financing for the car and paid cash to the dealer. He inquired as to title and was assured by the dealer and by Allstate who financed the purchase for him, that title would be taken care of by having the dealer send it to Allstate. He had the car registered in his name and paid for the license plates. Finally, the buyer stresses the fact that the seller set in motion the chain of events which led to the sale of the car and should bear the loss incurred from the misconduct of the dealer whom he selected. We turn to resolve these opposing views.

1. The licensing and registration provisions of the vehicle code are essentially police regulations and strict compliance with them appears to be the prevailing view. *State v. Glenn*, 423 S.W.2d 770 (Mo. 1968). The underlying policy and purpose of that regulatory scheme are best promoted by such a view. It does not follow, however, that those purposes are subverted by the application of an estoppel theory to a business transaction falling within the entrustment provisions of the UCC. As we see it, the relevant provisions of the two codes can exist side by side with meaning given to each

and without doing violence to either, and we should so construe them. *Bodine v. Stinson*, 85 Nev. 657, 461 P.2d 868 (1969).

When the used car dealer sold the Toyota to Gilsdorf, the Commercial Credit Corporation enjoyed a perfected security interest in that vehicle, to wit, legal title. At that point, the purchaser, under the entrustment provisions of NRS 104.2403(2), acquired only the rights of the entruster-seller subject to the security interest of Commercial Credit. At least, such appears to be the case if we look only to 104.2403(2). However, sections of the UCC found elsewhere, particularly 104.2103(d) defining "seller," and 104.9307 of Article 9, may be construed to mean that the buyer took the car free of the perfected security interest of Commercial Credit. We need not resolve this problem in the case at hand since the seller, Godfrey, paid off his debt to Commercial Credit, and acquired the ownership certificate before filing suit. Thus, we are concerned only with the propriety of applying an estoppel against the seller to achieve the purposes of 104.2403(2), (3).

Illinois estopped the seller and protected the buyer in similar circumstances, and placed its decision mainly upon the entrustment provisions of the UCC. *Humphrey Cadillac & Oldsmobile Co. v. Sinard*, 229 N.E.2d 365 (Ill. App. 1967). Oklahoma agrees. *Medico Leasing Co. v. Smith*, 457 P.2d 548 (1969).

In summary, we find, as did the court below, that Godfrey entrusted his car to a merchant who deals in cars. The merchant was empowered to transfer Godfrey's rights to a buyer in the ordinary course of business and did so. We conclude that the principle of estoppel precludes Godfrey from asserting his later-acquired title against Gilsdorf who purchased in good faith, for value and without notice of the then existing security interest of Commercial Credit Corporation.

2. In a replevin action, the judgment must be in the alternative, that is, for the return of the property or its value in case a return cannot be had. NRS 17.120; *Ex parte Havas*, 78 Nev. 237, 371 P.2d 30 (1962). The prevailing party does not have the option to take judgment for the value of the property absolutely. *Lambert v. McFarland*, 2 Nev. 58 (1866).

The judgment entered below for the defendant-buyer upon his counterclaim was not an alternative judgment, but merely sought to give him the value of the car. This was error. However, this error was not assigned on the buyer's cross-appeal from the judgment, nor by the seller in his appeal therefrom. Apparently, the seller wishes to retain the car which he secured by the provisional remedy of claim and delivery, and the buyer is content to recover the value instead of the car itself. Since error as to the form of the judgment was not asserted, we shall not disturb the matter.

The stipulated value of the car was $2,550, and judgment should have been entered for the defendant in that amount. However, the court erroneously reduced that sum by the rental value of the car during the eight months when the defendant used it. Since the court found that the defendant owned the car, there was no basis for charging him with the rental value thereof. In this regard, the judgment is modified with direction to enter an amended judgment in accordance herewith.

Affirmed as modified.

PROBLEM 4-4

Mary Theroux rented a Lexus automobile from Orbit Car Rentals under an assumed name and then failed to return the car. Theroux traveled to a neighboring state and obtained a title for the Lexus by using forged signatures of fictitious parties to make it appear that Orbit had sold the car to her at an auction. Theroux listed the car for sale in a local newspaper, and signed the title over to Dermot Vessey in exchange for a cashier's check in the amount of $43,000. Before completing the purchase, Vessey took the certificate of title to a friend who was a car salesman and confirmed that the title was legitimate and had been issued by the state. Theroux then vanished.

Orbit located the car and repossessed it, asserting its rights as owner of the vehicle. Vessey brought suit to replevy the car from Orbit. He argued that he had valid title to the Lexus, and he also argued that he was a bona fide purchaser for value who acted in good faith.

Should Vessey prevail?

Chapter 5

DELIVERY OBLIGATIONS AND RISK OF LOSS

After the parties have concluded an enforceable agreement the seller is obligated to perform by tendering the goods to the buyer. In this chapter, we consider the risk that the goods will be damaged or destroyed prior to their tender to the buyer, and the allocation of the resulting loss. The risk of loss rules are keyed to the seller's tender obligation under the contract. A series of rules in § 2-509 generally provides that the risk of loss shifts from the seller to the buyer when the seller has successfully tendered the goods to the buyer. In the first section, we review Article 2's gap-filling provisions regarding the seller's tender obligations, namely, the terms regarding the time, place, and manner of delivery. Next, we work through the risk of loss rules in § 2-509 in the order that they appear in that section. Finally, we consider the effect of a party's breach on the risk of loss rules, as articulated in § 2-510.

A. TIME AND PLACE OF DELIVERY

The delivery term is a key provision of any sales or lease contract. Questions arise in every transaction as to where, when, and how the goods are to be delivered. Most contracts will contain a clear, concise delivery term that answers these questions, solving the delivery problem. In some instances, however, the parties either will fail to provide the delivery term or will state one that is ambiguous or meaningless. In the event that the parties have not agreed to delivery terms, Article 2 provides gap-filling rules against which the seller's performance will be judged.

Read UCC §§ 2-301, 2-308(1), 2-309(1), and 2-503. These sections set out the delivery obligations of the seller. "Delivery" contemplates the seller's physical transfer of the goods to the buyer. Subsection (1) of § 2-308 provides that, absent contrary agreement, the seller has no obligation to transport the goods to the buyer; the buyer must pick up the goods at the seller's place of business. The following cases review Article 2's gap-filling provisions regarding time and place of delivery.

BEIRIGER & SONS IRRIGATION, INC. v. SOUTHWEST LAND CO.
Colorado Court of Appeals
705 P.2d 532 (1985)

STERNBERG, JUDGE.

By contract entered into in mid-March 1982, Beiriger and Sons Irrigation, Inc. (seller), sold, and Southwest Land Company (purchaser), purchased, a sprinkler system to be used in irrigation Southwest's land. The contract price was $103,209, of which the purchaser paid $32,000 down, with the balance payable upon delivery. Because of design problems, the system did not become operational until July 4, 1982. The purchaser, therefore, refused to pay the balance due. Thereafter, the seller sued for the remainder of the contract price, and the purchaser counter-claimed seeking damages for expenses incurred in modifying the water delivery system, in moving obstacles from the path of the sprinkler, and for crop and fertilizer losses.

The trial court awarded the seller the balance due on the contract price, but gave the purchaser a set-off in the amount of $17,349.80, for the expenses incurred in correction of the inoperable design. The court dismissed the other counterclaims, finding that under the circumstances, the delivery date was not untimely, and there was insufficient evidence to establish that the purchaser's moving expenses were properly attributable to the seller. We affirm.

The parties agree that no specific date was set for delivery, but they anticipated that the system would be used in conjunction with the 1982 crop. After encountering many difficulties in installation, the sprinklers finally became fully operational on July 4, 1982.

At trial, the evidence established that in order to mature, oats must be sown by June 1. However, as a result of the delay in getting the sprinkler operational, the purchaser did not sow a crop of oats until the end of June. The crop was harvested in October, but because it had not matured, the harvest was used as hay. The purchaser claimed the difference in the value of the mature oats and oats as hay, as well as losses for topsoil erosion and fertilizer as consequential damages caused by the seller's failure to have the sprinkler system operative before July 4.

We agree with the trial court's conclusion that, inasmuch as there was no agreement between the parties for a specific delivery date, the purchaser is not entitled to damages for crop loss, fertilizer loss, and loss of topsoil.

There was no evidence presented that the seller knew that oats was the 1982 crop on which the sprinkler was to be used or that such crop had to be planted by June 1. Although there was evidence that sometime during May, the seller became aware that the purchaser was concerned about when the system would be completed, no agreement as to a delivery date was shown.

The purchaser is correct that, under either the Uniform Commercial Code or common law, where no delivery date is specified, a reasonable date will be furnished by the court. . . . However, there is no evidence that the date of delivery was unreasonable under the circumstances. That the date of delivery did not meet expectations of the purchaser does not necessarily make it either unreasonable or untimely.

The court did not award damages because it did not find the delivery untimely, noting that it would have found otherwise had the parties contracted for a specific date of delivery, or had they made an understanding of the purchaser's needs apparent. Under these circumstances, we perceive no error in this ruling. The other contentions of error are without merit.

The judgment is affirmed.

SUPERIOR BOILER WORKS, INC. v. R.J. SANDERS, INC.
Rhode Island Supreme Court
711 A.2d 628 (1998)

FLANDERS, Justice.

In this case, we consider the enforceability of a seller's original estimated time for it to ship its manufactured product to a commercial buyer. More specifically, the dispositive issue is whether the seller's original estimate of a four-week shipping period should be deemed binding upon the seller (1) when the buyer's ultimate order for the goods was not released until later in the seller's season, (2) when the seller's shipment conditions materially changed in the interim, (3) when the seller's final acceptance of the buyer's order specified a longer shipping date, and (4) when the buyer failed to come forward with evidence indicating that this longer shipping date was commercially unreasonable. For the reasons discussed below, we hold that the earlier estimate did not become a part of the ultimate sales contract in this case and, therefore, it was unenforceable against the seller.

The buyer, defendant R.J. Sanders, Inc. (Sanders), appeals from a Superior Court motion justice's entry of summary judgment in favor of the seller, plaintiff Superior Boiler Works, Inc. (Superior). Superior sued Sanders for breach of contract and, alternatively, for quantum meruit in connection with Superior's delivery of three boiler units to Sanders for a purchase price of $145,827. Sanders contends that it was error to grant summary judgment to Superior. However, in opposing Superior's summary-judgment motion, Sanders failed to adduce competent evidence showing that the longer shipping date was commercially unreasonable. As a result, we affirm the Superior Court's judgment and deny this appeal.

Facts and Travel

The following facts appear from the materials submitted in support of and in opposition to Superior's motion for summary judgment. Sanders was a Rhode Island corporation engaged in the installation of large heating systems. Superior was a Kansas corporation in the business of manufacturing and selling commercial boilers. In 1990, Sanders was working on the construction of a federal prison camp in West Virginia. On March 27, 1990, in response to specifications provided by Sanders, Superior issued a proposal setting out specifications for a so-called Seminole boiler and indicating an estimated delivery time of four weeks. Language printed on the proposal stated that "[t]he specified time of delivery is approximate * * *. The indicated date of shipment is our present best estimate of the approximate date when the material should be ready for shipment, and necessarily, is subject to cause or delay outside of our own management or control." The proposal also stated that any resulting contract would be governed by Kansas law. On June 5, 1990, the seller's agent, Atkinson & Lawrence, Inc. (Atkinson), wrote to Sanders, stating, "In discussing the importance of quick delivery with Superior, they indicate that they will be able to ship in four weeks and possibly three. We will review our pricing and give you our best numbers within the next couple days."

Two days later, Superior issued another proposal (second proposal) for the sale of its Seminole boilers, setting a price of approximately $156,000 for three units. This second proposal again indicated a four-week estimated shipping timeframe but retained the earlier caveat that "[t]he specified time of delivery is approximate." In addition, the second proposal stated, "This proposal must be *accepted* within thirty (30) days from the date hereof, otherwise this proposal is withdrawn." (Emphasis added.) Kansas law was again to govern any ensuing agreement.

Eleven days after the second proposal, Sanders issued a purchase order (purchase order) for three Seminole boilers signed by one John Burde and dated June 18, 1990. The purchase order was date-stamped June 20, 1990, contains the price $145,000 (some $11,000 less than the second proposal), and adds the condition "All as per plans and specifications (section 15557), pending government approval." This purchase order, however, said nothing about what jurisdiction's law should govern any later dispute arising between the parties.

On June 25, 1990, Atkinson wrote to Superior, conveying that Sanders had contacted him and now wanted to substitute Industrial Combustion (IC) burners for use in the boilers instead of the Gordan-Piatt burners originally specified. Two days later Atkinson again communicated with Superior, stating that Superior should "quote a price for the boilers less burners." On June 29, Sanders issued a second purchase order (amended purchase order) requesting that Superior amend Sanders' previous purchase order by adding $867 to the purchase price to reflect the change of burner units from Gordan-Piatt to IC. This purchase-order amendment carried the notation "Date Required: 4 Weeks" but was unsigned. On July 19, over three weeks after the amended purchase order was initially issued, Atkinson returned this document for Sanders' signature. On that very same day and while acting as an agent for Superior, Atkinson submitted specifications for the boilers to the prison project's government engineers for their approval. Atkinson's communication to the government engineers contained the notation "We have received your comments on the boiler submittal. These will be acted upon."

The next day Atkinson wrote to Sanders, stating that the specifications had been submitted to the government engineers and added, "We have received your fax forwarding preliminary approval on the boilers. We will ask the factory to respond to the relocation of the control panel * * *. The system should have modulating feedwater controls and motorized valves. This change is easily made now." On July 20, the following day, the government engineers gave their final oral approval of the specifications, and Sanders released the purchase order.

Finally, on August 6, 1990, Superior issued a sales order for the three Seminole boilers (now with IC burners) for a price matching the amended purchase-order price of $145,827. However, instead of a four-week delivery schedule, Superior's August sales order indicated a shipping date of October 1, 1990. In support of its summary-judgment motion, Superior submitted an affidavit of its national sales manager, Gregory Call (Call). His affidavit alleged that the longer delivery timeframe was necessary and reasonable because Superior had received a seasonal influx of other boiler orders while Sanders was changing various specifications and other details of its order during June and July. As a result, he claimed, Superior's previous estimate of a four-week delivery window was no longer feasible after Sanders released its ultimate purchase order following the government's July 20 approval of the specifications. Call also insinuated that Superior had been unable to begin manufacturing the boilers until it had received final approval from the government engineers for the various specification changes requested by Sanders. According to Call, Superior did not receive that approval until July 20, 1990.

At some point following the issuance of Superior's August 6 sales order, Sanders apparently telephoned Superior with regard to the October 1 shipping date. However, because Sanders submitted no documents, affidavits, or other competent evidence memorializing that communication, the record does not reflect when or how this communication occurred or what was said by the participants. The record does suggest, however, that some sort of communication occurred because on September 6, 1990, Atkinson forwarded the following response to Sanders:

> "John, I'm sorry to say that we cannot improve shipment on any of the boilers for the above job. Scheduled shipment remains week of 9/24. During the time that there was indecision about burner selection and other details, Superior received a large influx of orders and therefore could not meet original commitment. Delays in releasing orders this time of year carry that risk."

At this point, Sanders apparently contacted the Federal Bureau of Prisons to inform it of a potential delay in the installation of the boilers. But a government-contract specialist responded to Sanders on August 28, 1990, and indicated that the Bureau of Prisons was unmoved by Sanders' problem in obtaining an earlier delivery of the boilers: "The Government's original position remains unchanged regarding the significance of a completion date. This contract was awarded to R.J. Sanders in good faith and your compliance with its terms is imperative. Corrective action on your behalf is required to comply with the projects [sic] final completion date of October 5, 1990."

Superior ultimately shipped the boilers on or about October 1 and they arrived at the West Virginia site on October 5. However, having anticipated that the boilers would not be completely installed by the government's mandated completion date of October 5, Sanders had already arranged for temporary rental boilers to be trucked to the site and hooked up to supply heat in the interim. After the arrival and installation of Superior's boilers, Sanders tendered the contract price of $145,827 in substantial part, less $45,315.85 in "backcharges." Sanders claims these charges were the reasonable costs it incurred as a result of Superior's failure to meet its original contractual commitment to a four-week shipment period.[1]

Superior thereafter filed this lawsuit, seeking the unpaid balance of the contract price and relying upon breach of contract and quantum meruit theories. In due course, Superior filed a motion for summary judgment, and both sides submitted memoranda attaching the various documents to which we have previously made reference. After a hearing, a Superior Court motion justice granted the motion, and judgment entered for Superior in the principal amount of $45,867 plus interest for a total judgment of $94,253.50. Sanders appealed the grant of summary judgment to this court. Following a

---

[1] A $500 discrepancy remains unexplained by the parties.

prebriefing conference, we ordered the parties to show cause why the appeal should not be summarily decided. After hearing oral argument and reviewing the parties' memoranda, we conclude that no cause has been shown and proceed to resolve the appeal without further briefing and argument.

*   *   *

The Parties' Summary-Judgment Submissions

In its memorandum in support of summary judgment, Superior advanced two alternate arguments. First, Superior contended that it delivered the boilers on time because its October 1 delivery date was reasonable in light of industry standards and therefore, satisfied the delivery terms of the agreement. However, Superior failed to articulate its position with regard to exactly when the parties entered into an enforceable contract relating to the boilers or why no precise delivery date had been agreed upon. Alternatively, Superior contended that even if the four-week delivery period that it had originally proposed somehow became a term of the contract, Sanders' acquiescence to the delay in shipment operated to waive its objection to any breach by Superior.

In support of its motion, Superior submitted the Call affidavit and attached thereto numerous documents relating to the purchase and sale of the boilers. Sanders filed a memorandum opposing the summary-judgment motion that was unaccompanied by any affidavit. However, Sanders did attach several documents relating to the boilers and to the prison-construction project. Because these particular documents are important to the parties' negotiation of the boiler-purchase agreement and to the underlying federal-prison project, and because neither party objected to the Superior Court's consideration of these documents, we are satisfied they would have been competent and admissible as evidence at trial. *See* R.I. R. Evid. 901(b)(4).[2]

Sanders also backed its opposition to the motion by referring to the various documents discussed in the Call affidavit that were attached to Superior's summary-judgment memorandum. As stated above, a party opposing summary judgment need not come forward with any evidence of its own (whether in the form of discovery materials, affidavits, or other forms of evidence) if the materials submitted by the movant reveal a factual dispute or indicate that the movant is not entitled to judgment as a matter of law. However, because we conclude that Sanders failed to adduce any evidence at all with respect to a critical issue in this case, we conclude that the summary judgment was properly granted.

Analysis

. . . .

In the usual case, the question of what constitutes a reasonable time under the UCC is one for the finder of fact to determine from the nature, the purpose, and the

---

[2] [3] We note that unauthenticated documents merely attached to a legal memorandum are not usually "competent evidence" worthy of consideration by the court in ruling on a motion for summary judgment. Documents typically must be properly authenticated in order to qualify as admissible evidence. *See* R.I. R. Evid. 901. In connection with a summary-judgment motion, this task can be accomplished in the usual course by submitting an affidavit of a person with personal knowledge of the documents who can attest to their authenticity and qualify them as admissible evidence. Although this particular procedure was not followed by either party in this case, neither side objected to the court's consideration of the proffered documents. A party's failure to move to strike or to make some other objection to an opponent's summary-judgment submission waives that issue for purposes of any later appeal. *See* 11 Moore's Federal Practice § 56.14[2][c], at 56–184 (1997). Moreover, document authenticity need not be established by any particular means, *see* R.I. R. Evid. 901 advisory comm. note (a), and may be accomplished by any of the methods enumerated in Rule 901 or 902.

circumstances surrounding the transaction, including the parties' course of dealing, usages of trade in the pertinent industry, or the parties' course of performance. *See* § 6A-1-204(2); 1 ANDERSON § 1-204:8 (generally improper to enter summary judgment on such questions). Here, Superior, as the movant for summary judgment, submitted the Call affidavit. Call averred that "[b]ased upon my experience [as national sales manager for a boiler manufacturer], one of the most common causes for delayed delivery of boilers is the purchaser's failure to approve final orders early in the year since approvals received later in the year are subject to a longer shipping date." Call further alleged that a seasonal flood of orders did indeed deluge Superior in July and August such that by early August, "the estimated ship date was October 1." Although Call does not specifically contend that the October 1 ship date was reasonable in light of these circumstances, that is a fair inference to be drawn from his affidavit.

In response, Sanders offered absolutely no affidavit or other competent evidence concerning the reasonableness of the October 1 delivery date. Although Sanders did produce a copy of the apparent rebuff it received from the government contract officer concerning the October 5 final completion date for the prison project, it provided no competent evidence tending to show that Superior was aware of this deadline or that it knew that the Bureau of Prisons had refused to extend the project's completion date. And although another document originating from Atkinson shows that Superior was aware in early June of "the importance of quick delivery," here too, there is no indication that Superior knew that "quick delivery" meant no longer than four weeks or that the boilers had to be delivered and installed before Sanders' undisclosed October 5 deadline with the Bureau of Prisons.

Thus, because Superior met its initial burden to show that it was entitled to judgment as a matter of law on undisputed facts, the burden lay on Sanders to counter this showing with contrary evidence indicating that a genuine issue of material fact existed concerning the reasonableness of the longer shipping period specified in the August 6 sales order. Because Sanders did not meet this challenge and failed to satisfy its burden as the nonmoving party, the hearing justice properly granted summary judgment in favor of Superior. *See Bourg v. Bristol Boat Co.*, 705 A.2d 969 (R.I. 1998) (defendant boatbuilder's failure to adduce any competent evidence that a promissory-note obligation had been modified warranted summary judgment).

Conclusion

For the foregoing reasons, the appeal is denied, and the Superior Court's judgment is affirmed.

NOTES AND QUESTIONS

1. What does the word *tender* mean? How does a seller tender delivery of the goods if the contract has no delivery terms?

2. The parties in the *Beiriger* case failed to state a specific delivery date in their contract. How did the court determine the delivery provision?

3. Effective delivery requires such notification to the buyer as to enable it to take delivery. An improper notification causes a defective tender of delivery and may be a breach of contract by the seller. Comment 5 to § 2-309 explains that "[t]he obligation of good faith under this Act requires reasonable notification before a contract may be treated as breached because a reasonable time for delivery or demand has expired." Therefore, "[w]hen both parties let an originally reasonable time go by in silence, the course of conduct under the contract may be viewed as enlarging the reasonable time for tender or demand of performance." Comment 6 adds that "[e]ffective communication of a proposed time limit calls for a response, so that failure to reply will make out acquiescence." A buyer may request more information or object to the delivery notice; however, "[o]nly when a party insists on undue delay or on rejection of

the other party's reasonable proposal is there a question of flat breach." UCC § 2-309, comment 6.

B. CONTRACTS INVOLVING CARRIAGE OF THE GOODS

Where the seller is required or authorized to send the goods to the buyer (i.e., the contract involves carriage of the goods), the basic default rule is that delivery occurs when and where the seller hands the goods over to the carrier for transmission to the buyer. These contracts are typically referred to as "shipment" contracts. *See* UCC § 2-503 and Comment 5. However, some contracts require the seller to deliver the goods at a particular destination, and are appropriately called "destination" contracts.

Section 2-504 specifies that a seller has three obligations under a shipment contract. It must: (1) put the goods in the possession of a carrier and make a reasonable contract for their transportation; (2) obtain and promptly tender documents necessary for the buyer to obtain possession of the goods or that are otherwise required by the sales agreement or usage of trade; and (3) promptly notify the buyer of the shipment.

In the absence of an agreement, the seller may choose any reasonable carrier, routing, and other arrangements. Section 2-504(a) is intended to make it clear that whether the shipment is at the seller's or the buyer's expense, and unless otherwise agreed, the seller must make all reasonable arrangements for the safe transportation of the goods so that they will arrive at the destination in substantially the same condition in which they were shipped. The seller is relieved of this obligation only when the buyer is in a position to make these arrangements, and the seller gives him reasonable notice that he should do so. *See* § 2-504, comment 3.

Unless otherwise agreed, acceptable means of notification of shipment under § 2-504(c) are the sending of an invoice under open credit shipments and prompt forwarding of documents under documentary contracts. The sending of a straight bill of lading is not required unless the buyer has a claim against the carrier for loss or damage. Notification by wire or cable is only required if a term requiring such notification is included in the agreement. *See* § 2-504, comment 5.

Section 2-504 also provides that the seller's failure to fulfill his obligations to put the goods in the possession of a carrier, to make a contract for their transportation, and to notify the buyer of their shipment constitute grounds for rejection of the goods only if material delay or loss results from the failure. The burden, however, is on the seller to show that events justifying rejection did not occur subsequent to his error. *See* § 2-504, comment 6.

In many cases, the parties will specify the place of delivery and the seller's related duties by using a mercantile trade term. The original drafters of the Code realized that many of the terms had recognized meaning in the business community. Accordingly, §§ 2-319 through 2-324 were drafted to define the terms according to their accepted meaning. However, these sections are no longer an accurate reflection of the current commercial understanding of these terms. This means that these terms must be interpreted in light of any applicable trade usage, course of dealing, or course of performance.

In particular, it is anticipated that courts will rely heavily on the *Incoterms* as a source of meaning, and it is likely that many parties will choose to incorporate these definitions in their agreements. The *Incoterms* are produced by the International Chamber of Commerce (ICC) and were first published in 1936. The most recent version is *Incoterms* 2000. Although there are 13 different *Incoterms*, they can be divided into four principal categories, one for each of different first letters of the constituent terms E, F, C, and D. Each category of terms, ranging from E through D, represent a gradual increase in the responsibility of the seller. The distinctions within each category often distinguish between traditional waterway transport (by ship) and other means of transportation, including multi-modal transportation (e.g., by truck, then train, then ship).

The "*Ex Works*" terms require the seller to tender the goods by placing them at the buyer's disposal, without any obligation on the seller's part to transfer possession of the goods to a carrier. For example, the term *Ex Factory* requires the seller to tender the goods at its factory. The "*Free*" terms require the seller to commence the process of getting the goods in transit. For example, the term *Free Alongside Ship* requires the seller to deliver the goods alongside a named ship in a certain port, as arranged by the buyer. The "*Cost*" terms require the seller to arrange for certain transportation details and to pay costs related to the transportation. For example, the term *Carriage and Insurance Paid To* term requires the seller to arrange for the transportation of the goods, and to pay transportation and insurance costs to deliver the goods, although the seller is not responsible for the arrival of the goods. The "*Destination*" terms require the seller to arrange details for transportation to the destination and to pay related costs. For example, the term *Delivered Ex Ship* requires the seller to arrange and pay for the transportation to a named port, and to make the goods available to the buyer on board ship at the destination port.

The following *Incoterm* introduces you to the manner in which these important commercial terms are defined. The "Free on Board" term is a classic example of a "shipment" term, in that the seller is not obligated to tender the goods at a specified destination.

International Chamber of Commerce, *Incoterms*
(2000 ed.) (Publication No. 560)[3]

FREE ON BOARD (named port of shipment)

"Free on Board" means that the seller delivers when the goods pass the ship's rail at the named port of shipment. This means that the buyer has to bear all costs and risks of loss of or damage to the goods from that point. The FOB term requires the seller to clear the goods for export. This term can be used only for sea or inland waterway transport. If the parties do not intend to deliver the goods across the ship's rail, the FCA [Ed. note: "Free Carrier"] term should be used.

A. The Seller's Obligations

A1 Provision of goods in conformity with the contract

The seller must provide the goods and the commercial invoice, or its equivalent electronic message, in conformity with the contract of sale and any other evidence of conformity which may be required by the contract.

A2 Licences, authorizations, and formalities

The seller must obtain at his own risk and expense any export licence or other official authorization and carry out, where applicable, all customs formalities necessary for the export of the goods.

A3 Contracts of carriage and insurance

[No obligation.]

---

[3] Incoterms 2000 TM, R. ICC Publication No. 560(E) — ISBN 92.842.1199.9. Published in its official English version by the International Chamber of Commerce, Paris. Copyright 1999 — International Chamber of Commerce (ICC). Available from ICC Publishing SA, 38 Cours Albert 1er, 75008, Paris, France and www.iccbooks.com.

A4 Delivery

The seller must deliver the goods on the date or within the agreed period at the named port of shipment and in the manner customary at the port on board the vessel nominated by the buyer.

A5 Transfer of risks

The seller must, subject to the provisions of B5, bear all risks of loss of or damage to the goods until such time as they have passed the ship's rail at the named port of shipment.

A6 Division of costs

The seller must, subject to the provisions of B6, pay

— all costs relating to the goods until such time as they have passed the ship's rail at the named port of shipment; and

— where applicable, the costs of customs formalities necessary for export as well as all duties, taxes, and other charges payable upon export.

A7 Notice to buyer

The seller must give the buyer sufficient notice that the goods have been delivered in accordance with A4.

B. The Buyer's Obligations

B1 Payment of the price

The buyer must pay the price as provided in the contract for sale.

B2 Licences, authorizations, and formalities

The buyer must obtain at his own risk and expense any import licence or other official authorization and carry out, where applicable, all customs formalities for the import of the goods and, where necessary, for their transit through any country.

B3 Contracts of carriage and insurance

a) Contract of carriage: The buyer must contract at his own expense for the carriage of the goods from the named port of shipment.

b) Contract of insurance: No obligation.

B4 Taking delivery

The buyer must take delivery of the goods when they have been delivered in accordance with A4.

B5 Transfer of risks

The buyer must bear all risks of loss or damage to the goods

— from the time they have passed the ship's rail at the named port of shipment; and

— from the agreed date or the expiry date of the agreed period for delivery which arise because he fails to give notice in accordance with B7, or because the vessel nominated by him fails to arrive on time, or is unable to take the goods, or closes for cargo earlier than the time notified in accordance with B7, provided, however, that the goods have been duly appropriated to the contract, that is to say, clearly set aside or otherwise identified as the contract goods.

B7 Notice to seller

The buyer must give the seller sufficient notice of the vessel name, loading point, and required delivery time.

We will return to the FOB *Incoterm* in the context of determining which party bears the risk of loss.

C. RISK OF LOSS

1. Risk of Loss in the Absence of Breach

The two principal questions that we address in this section are: (1) what is risk of loss, and (2) what are the Code rules affecting risk of loss? The first question has a relatively straightforward answer. Risk of loss determines who (the seller or buyer) bears the loss if the goods are damaged or destroyed through no fault of either the seller or the buyer. Fire, theft, and flooding are dangers that can damage or destroy the goods specified in the agreement. For example, goods in the seller's warehouse may be damaged by a flood, or goods in transit may be destroyed by fire. If the seller bears the risk of loss, it must deliver a new shipment of conforming goods. If the buyer bears the risk of loss, it must pay for the goods despite their destruction. Thus, the party that bears the risk of loss should maintain insurance on the goods.

Recall from Chapter 4 that the concept of title to the goods is de-emphasized by Article 2. The comment to § 2-101 notes that the "legal consequences are stated as following directly from the contract and action taken under it without resorting to the idea of when property or title passed or was to pass as being the determining factor." Risk of loss is one of the important legal issues that formerly was closely connected to the location of title in the goods, but now is divorced from title. Under pre-Code law, risk of loss usually shifted from seller to buyer at the same time that the title or "property" in the goods passed. The defect with this approach was that the point in time at which title passed often was vague and difficult to identify. Moreover, the passage of title often was unrelated to the commercial realities of the transaction; thus, risk of loss could be placed on a seller or buyer without any particular justification. Rather than "title," the Code assigns risk of loss to a seller or buyer based on readily ascertainable facts that relate to the policy decision to link risk of loss to factors such as which party controls the goods and is better able to avoid a loss, which party is best able to insure against loss, and the normal expectations of a businessperson in the circumstances. The comments to § 2-509 make it clear that the Code's rules, rather than the title concept, control the risk of loss issue. The underlying theory of § 2-509 concerning risk of loss is the adoption of the contractual approach rather than an arbitrary shifting of the risk with the "property of goods."

The following summary explains the principles involved in the risk of loss question and examines the Code's approach to the issue in some detail. Use this discussion to help you work through the statutory provisions.

Underlying Principles of Risk of Loss Rules

The goals of the risk of loss rules in the Uniform Commercial Code are: (1) clarity; (2) conformity to common assumptions; (3) reduction of avoidable losses; and (4) encouragement of efficient breaching behavior. Clarity is necessary because it allows the merchant to purchase insurance and factor that risk into the price. Sellers include the risk of loss in the price they ultimately charge to consumers. Insurance spreads the risk among many parties which allows the seller to charge less to the consumer. Vague liability rules prevent insurers from accurately assessing risk, leading to a less accurate assessment of premiums. Risk averse sellers will overestimate their liability and pay the excessive premium, passing the cost on to the consumer.

In addition to increasing a seller's insurance premium, vague rules increase bargaining cost to the extent that the risk of loss term must be negotiated in the contract to offset the default rule's lack of clarity. Bargaining cost decreases when default rules conform to common assumptions, which make them acceptable to the parties. Finally, parties in control of goods are best able to avoid losses. They also are in a better position to calculate risk and obtain insurance on the goods. It is efficient, therefore, to place liability on the party who has control of the goods and is best able to avoid loss or bear its cost.

Overview of UCC Risk of Loss Provisions

The UCC provisions that deal with risk of loss are §§ 2-509 and 2-510. Section 2-509, which has four subsections, applies when there has been no breach of contract. The first subsection of § 2-509 covers the risk of loss when the seller is authorized to use a carrier to deliver the goods. If the parties have not agreed otherwise, or the agreement is ambiguous, risk of loss is presumed to pass from buyer to seller when the seller delivers the goods to the carrier. This is known as a shipment contract. In the alternative contract, known as a destination contract, the seller bears the risk of loss until the seller tenders delivery at the destination.

The second subsection contemplates transactions in which a bailee has possession of the goods, with ownership passing from buyer to seller without the goods being moved. The buyer will not bear the risk of loss until it receives a negotiable document of title. If the transaction does not involve any documents, the buyer bears the risk of loss when the bailee acknowledges the buyer's ownership and right of possession in the goods.

The third subsection of § 2-509 covers all other transactions. This subsection differentiates between merchants and non-merchants. A merchant seller bears the risk of loss until the buyer receives the goods; it is sufficient for a non-merchant seller to tender delivery to the buyer, which means that the non-merchant has only to notify the buyer that conforming goods are available.

In addition to the first three subsections, § 2-509(4) allows parties to negotiate around the default risk of loss provisions. Parties do not use this provision often, so courts require the parties to state specifically that they are making an alternative agreement. Alternative agreements may be made through course of performance, course of dealing, and usage of trade.

Applying § 2-509 to Consumer Transactions

Consumer transactions pose particular challenges to the risk of loss provisions in the Uniform Commercial Code now that electronic contracting has made it easy for consumers to purchase goods from remote sellers who must ship the goods to the consumer. Because § 2-509(1) presumes that a contract is a shipment contract unless explicitly stated otherwise, a consumer buying goods electronically often will bear the risk of loss as soon as the Internet retailer delivers the goods to a carrier. Consumers, however, do not expect to bear the risk of loss for goods they have neither seen nor received, and are unlikely to insure the goods. The risk of loss rule, therefore, does not conform to common assumptions or encourage efficient breaching behavior in consumer contracting. The Code drafters could not contemplate the rise of the Internet and the effect it would have on consumer purchasers.

Courts still may be able to place the risk of loss on e-sellers because § 2-509(1) requires that the goods be "duly delivered" to the carrier, and under § 2-504, sellers do not duly deliver goods until the seller gives the buyer all the documents the buyer needs to take possession of the goods and notifies the buyer promptly that the goods have shipped. With the speed of electronic transactions, sellers may ship the goods on the same day that the buyer purchases them. However, sellers now often send e-mail confirmations that the goods have been delivered to the carrier and provide information to the buyer about how to track the progress of the shipment. In these cases, it would appear that the seller effectively transfers the risk upon release of the goods to the carrier and sending e-mail notice to the buyer.

Courts may attempt to use the risk of loss provisions to protect consumers who purchase goods electronically. It would effectuate the purposes of the UCC if courts presumed a destination contract when a merchant sells goods to a consumer. The merchant is more likely and better able to insure the goods and to avoid loss. Such a rule would conform more closely to common assumptions, prevent avoidable losses, and encourage efficient breaching behavior. It is also important to remember that virtually, no major Internet seller would attempt to enforce the risk of loss rules if goods were damaged during shipment to a consumer, and so, customer relations objectives often will prevent unfair surprise.

a.   Risk of loss under "shipment" contracts

We begin with the rules of § 2-509(1)(a) regarding contracts which require the seller only to ship the goods, rather than to deliver them at a particular destination. The next case applies the UCC risk of loss provision in the absence of applicable mercantile terms.

WILSON v. BRAWN OF CALIFORNIA, INC.
California Court of Appeal, First Appellate District
33 Cal. Rptr. 3d 769 (2005)

The San Francisco Superior Court entered judgment against Brawn of California (Brawn), a mail order company, ruling that Brawn had engaged in a deceptive business practice by charging its customers an "insurance fee" of $1.48 with every order placed. The ruling presumed that Brawn, rather than its customers, bears the loss of risk in transit, so that its customers received nothing of value in return for paying the fee. The court also awarded plaintiff litigation expenses in the amount of $24,699.21 and attorney fees in the amount of $422,982.50.

We reverse, concluding that Brawn did not bear the risk of loss of goods in transit under the applicable Commercial Code sections discussed below.

Background

Brawn markets clothing through its catalogs and over the Internet. When a customer places an order, Brawn packages it, and holds it at its warehouse, where it is picked up by a common carrier and delivered to the customer, using an address provided by the customer. At all times relevant, the terms of Brawn's mail order form required the customer to pay the listed price for the goods purchased, plus a delivery fee and a $1.48 "insurance fee." As to the last, the form recited: "INSURANCE: Items Lost or Damaged in Transit Replaced Free." Brawn based the insurance fee on the costs to it of replacing any goods lost in transit, and Brawn did indeed replace, without further cost to the customer, any goods that had been lost in transit. Brawn rarely, if ever, sold its goods to a customer unwilling to pay the insurance fee.

On February 5, 2002, and again on February 7, 2002, plaintiff Jacq Wilson (plaintiff) purchased items from Brawn's catalogue, each time paying the insurance fee. On February 13, 2002, Wilson, acting on behalf of himself and all other similarly situated persons, brought suit against Brawn, contending that in charging the fee, Brawn violated the Unfair Competition Law, Business and Professions Code section 17200 et. seq., prohibiting unfair competition, and Business and Professions Code section 17500 et seq., prohibiting false advertising.

Plaintiff's suit was premised on the theory that by charging customers an insurance fee, Brawn suggested to them that they were paying for and receiving a special benefit-insurance against loss in transit-when in fact, customers did not need insurance against loss in transit because Brawn already was required to pay for that loss as a matter of law. The trial court agreed, finding that irrespective of the insurance fee, Brawn bore the risk of loss of goods in transit, reasoning that the fee was an "illusory" benefit. The court found that Brawn's customers were likely to be deceived by the insurance fee, and that Brawn therefore had engaged in a deceptive business practice, entitling its customers to restitution.

Standard of Review

Our decision is based on our construction and application of statutory law, and not on any disputed issue of fact. Questions of law, such as statutory interpretation or the application of a statutory standard to undisputed facts, are reviewed de novo. (*Harustak v. Wilkins* (2000) 84 Cal. App. 4th 208, 212, 100 Cal. Rptr. 2d 718.)

Discussion

Neither party has cited any significant source of law concerning mail order sales or the risk of loss in mail order consumer sales, resting their contentions on provisions of the Commercial Code. As the Commercial Code, and the cases cited there, typically involve arm's-length sales between fairly sophisticated parties, the fit is not perfect. Nonetheless, there appears to be little legislation or case law specifically concerned with mail order sales or risk of loss in consumer sales contracts, and we, too, turn to the Commercial Code's provisions.

Commercial Code section 2509 sets forth the general rules for determining which party bears the risk of loss of goods in transit when there has been no breach of contract. Subdivision (1) of section 2509 provides, as relevant: "(1) Where the contract requires or authorizes the seller to ship the goods by carrier [¶] (a) If it does not require him to deliver them at a particular destination, the risk of loss passes to the buyer when the goods are duly delivered to the carrier . . . ; but [¶] (b) If it does require him to deliver them at a particular destination and the goods are there duly tendered while in the possession of the carrier, the risk of loss passes to the buyer when the goods are there duly so tendered as to enable the buyer to take delivery."

Shipment Contract or Destination Contract

Official Code comment 5 to Uniform Commercial Code § 2-503, concerning the seller's manner of tendering delivery, explains: "[U]nder this Article the 'shipment' contract is regarded as the normal one and the 'destination' contract as the variant type. The seller is not obligated to deliver at a named destination and bear the concurrent risk of loss until arrival, unless he has specifically agreed so to deliver or the commercial understanding of the terms used by the parties contemplates such a delivery." (Official Comments on U. Com. Code, Deering's Ann. Cal. U. Com. Code (1999 ed.) foll. § 2503, p. 198.) Of course, a seller will have to provide the carrier with shipping instructions. It follows that a contract is not a destination contract simply because the seller places an address label on the package, or directs the carrier to "ship to" a particular destination. "Thus a 'ship to' term has no significance in determining whether a contract is a shipment or destination contract for risk of loss purposes." (*Eberhard Manufacturing Company v. Brown* (1975) 61 Mich. App. 268, 232 N.W.2d 378, 380.) The point is illustrated in *La Casse v. Blaustein* (1978) 93 Misc. 2d 572, 403 N.Y.S.2d 440, where the plaintiff, a student in Massachusetts, purchased 23 pocket calculators by telephone from a New York manufacturer. The method of shipment was left to the seller, but the plaintiff wrote a check to cover postage, and directed the seller to ship the goods to the plaintiff's residence. The court held: "Under the Uniform

Commercial Code, the sales contract which provides for delivery to a carrier is considered the usual one and delivery to a particular destination to a buyer the variant or unusual one. [Citations.] In view of the foregoing, the request of the plaintiff's letter to ship to his residence is insufficient to convert the contract into one requiring delivery to a destination rather than one to a carrier. The request was nothing more than a shipping instruction and not of sufficient weight and solemnity as to convert the agreement into a destination contract." (*Id.* at p. 442.) Similarly, in *California State Electronics Assn. v. Zeos Internat. Ltd.* (1996) 41 Cal. App. 4th 1270, 49 Cal. Rptr. 2d 127, one of the few California cases discussing the issue, the court held: "The evidence showed that Zeos's sales operation consists of telephone orders which are shipped at the buyer's expense via an overnight express service. The paperwork Zeos prepares and sends to the buyer, with the goods or shortly after their shipment, contains no provision requiring Zeos to deliver the goods to the buyer. These facts plainly mark Zeos's terms as 'shipment' contracts, which is the presumptive form." (*Id.* at p. 1277, 49 Cal. Rptr. 2d 127.)[4]

In addition, although the risk of loss does not necessarily pass at the same time title to the goods passes, Commercial Code section 2401, subdivision (2)(a), provides that "[i]f the contract requires or authorizes the seller to send the goods to the buyer but does not require him to deliver them at [a] destination, title passes to the buyer at the time and place of shipment." This section, therefore, also distinguishes between the seller's obligation to deliver goods to a carrier, and the seller's obligation to deliver goods to the buyer.

It is not at all uncommon for a contract to shift the risk of loss to the buyer at the point at which the seller delivers the goods to a common carrier, while calling for the seller to pay for delivery and insurance. . . .

Other evidence, while not determinative, is consistent with the conclusion that Brawn, at least, intended the contracts to be shipment contracts. Brawn's own insurance covers goods lost while in Brawn's possession, but does not cover goods destroyed or lost after the goods left Brawn's physical possession. Brawn pays California use tax, rather than sales tax, on the theory that the goods were "sold" when they left Brawn's place of business, located outside of California. Brawn records the revenue for the goods sold at the point of shipment, and removes the goods from its inventory at the time of shipment.

In sum, nothing in Brawn's conduct, and nothing in the delivery or insurance terms of Brawn's mail order forms, suggests that it was offering anything other than a standard, C.I.F.-type shipment contract, which the customers agreed to when they used Brawn's mail order form to purchase goods.

. . . .

Conclusion

The judgment is reversed. The order awarding litigation expenses and attorney fees is reversed. Brawn is awarded its costs on appeal.

---

[4] [1] While *Merchants Acceptance, Inc. v. Jamison* (1999) 752 So. 2d 422 reasoned that a contract was a destination contract because it contained a term specifying the buyer's street address as the place of delivery, the author of 3a-8 Sales and Bulk Transfers Under the UCC cites *Jamison* as an illustration of a simple mistake courts occasionally make. (Bender's UCC Service, Duesenberg et al., 3a-8 Sales & Bulk Transfers, § 8.02, fn. 9.)

We concur: Marchiano, P.J., and Swager, J.

PROBLEM 5-1

Schön Wines, a German wine producer and exporter, agreed to sell 1,000 cases of wine to Barry's Wholesale Wines, a wholesaler of wines located in Miami, Florida, under the following term: "price $90,000 FOB Rotterdam; payment to be made against Negotiable Bill of Lading and related documents specified in Attachment C." On November 29, Schön consolidated the order in a container with other wine for shipment from Rotterdam to Miami on board the MS München. The ship left port on December 2, and was lost at sea with all cargo on December 8.

On December 10, Barry's designated bank received the documents specified in the contract, including the Negotiable Bill of Lading that entitled Barry to possession of the goods. Barry immediately arranged for insurance on the goods. On December 14, Schön informed Barry that the goods were lost at sea, stated that it had performed all its obligations under the contract, and demanded payment. Barry refused to pay for the wine that it did not receive. Who should prevail? Can Barry claim that it had a right under § 2-513 to inspect the wine before paying the contract price?

b. Risk of loss under "destination" contracts

If the seller has agreed to deliver the goods to a particular destination and to tender them to the buyer at that place, the risk of loss does not shift to the buyer until the point in time when the goods are "there duly so tendered." § 2-509(1)(b). Consider whether this test applies in the following problem, and if so, how the test would be applied.

PROBLEM 5-2

Singleton's Encyclopedia solicited Brian Wilson by mail to purchase its complete 48 volume encyclopedia for $2,500. Brian returned the enclosed "agreement," with a $100 check as a deposit. The form provided that Singleton would deliver the encyclopedias to the address listed on the form as "delivery address," at which time, monthly payments of $100 would become due. Brian listed his home address information in the area designated "delivery address." In a separate part of the form, Brian listed his P.O. Box as his "mailing address."

On May 1, Singleton shipped the goods by US Mail, but due to an error by Singleton, they were delivered to his P.O. Box. Brian received a notice in his P.O. Box on May 9 that he had several parcels from Singleton waiting for him, but he ignored the notice because he was beginning to reconsider the wisdom of purchasing the encyclopedias. On May 14, a partial roof collapse led to the destruction of the encyclopedias in the post office.

Singleton sued for the balance of the purchase price, but Brian argued that the encyclopedias were not tendered at his home address, and therefore, that the risk of loss remained with Singleton at the time of the casualty. Which party should prevail?

c. Risk of loss when goods are in the possession of a bailee

The issue of risk of loss when the goods are in the hands of a bailee and are to be delivered without being moved is governed by § 2-509(2). A good illustration is the case where a party sells one hundred television sets which are in storage in Ace Warehouse. The sale occurs on May 1, and both parties understand that the televisions will remain in Ace Warehouse for six months, until buyer needs them for the Christmas season. The issue crystallizes when, on May 20, the warehouse and the televisions are destroyed by fire. Which party bears the risk of loss? The Code instructs the parties to look to the bailee and his response to the sale. If the bailee has given the seller a negotiable warehouse receipt (a negotiable document of title is defined in § 7-104), then the risk of loss passes when the document is transferred. If no negotiable document of title was issued by the bailee, then risk passes either: (1) after the bailee has acknowledged the buyer's rights to the goods, or (2) after the seller has given the buyer a non-negotiable document or a written direction to the bailee to deliver to the buyer. Note, however, that § 2-503(4)(b) requires that in the case of the non-negotiable document or direction to the bailee, the risk of loss does not pass until the buyer has had a reasonable time to present the document or written directions to the bailee. Read § 2-503(4).

d.   Risk of loss in the absence of agreement: the default rule

Section 2-509(4) provides a strong reiteration of a basic theme in Article 2: the parties' freedom of contract is broad and courts will enforce their agreements. In the absence of a specific agreement as to risk of loss, we have seen that when parties agree to certain delivery terms, they in effect are agreeing to the applicable risk of loss rule set forth in § 2-509. If the parties enter into a shipment contract, for example, the risk of loss passes under the rule set forth in § 2-509(1)(a). But if the parties have not specifically agreed to a risk of loss provision, and their agreement as to tender and delivery does not trigger the rules under § 2-509(1) or (2), the code provides a default rule in § 2-509(3). Consider how this rule is applied in the next two cases.

HAWKINS v. FEDERATED MUTUAL INSURANCE COMPANY
United States District Court, Northern District of Mississippi
1996 U.S. Dist. LEXIS 21436 (1996)

MEMORANDUM OPINION

ALEXANDER, Magistrate Judge.

. . . .

FACTUAL SUMMARY

West is a merchant dealing in the sale of farm equipment. On November 8, 1993, Hawkins contracted ("the sales contract") to purchase a rice combine and rigid platform implement ("the equipment") from West for $61,500.00. Hawkins paid part of the purchase price as a down payment, and both parties to the transaction agreed that West would arrange actual delivery of the equipment to Hawkins. It is undisputed that neither party breached the sales contract.

On November 8, 1993, Hawkins secured financing for the balance of the purchase price of the equipment through a credit agreement ("the credit agreement") with Deere Credit Services, Inc. ("DCS"). As a condition for the financing, Hawkins purchased a physical damage insurance policy covering the equipment from John Deere Insurance Company ("JDIC"). At the time of the transaction, Federated insured West under a commercial package policy, which included an equipment dealer's stock floater form providing coverage for loss of West's stock merchandise under certain conditions.

On or about November 16, 1993, prior to physical delivery of the equipment to Hawkins but while the insurance policies of both Hawkins and West were in effect, a fire destroyed the equipment while it was stored in the possession of G & S Flying Service in Louisiana. Hawkins and West seek the court's interpretation of the risk of loss provision in the credit agreement and a judgment declaring whether Federated or JDIC is liable for the loss.

. . . .

DISCUSSION

For the most part, the defendants do not disagree about what law controls, thus, this opinion focuses only on the points of contention. Ultimately, this case turns on whether the risk of loss of the equipment had passed to Hawkins from West at the time of the fire. The parties agree that the court must resolve this controversy by looking to the law of Mississippi. The section of Mississippi's version of the Uniform Commercial Code which governs allocation of the risk of loss in the absence of breach of contract provides that in a situation such as the one before the court, "the risk of loss passes to the buyer on his receipt of the goods if the seller is a merchant. . . ." Miss. Code Ann. § 75-2-509(3) (1981). However, the statute further provides that this general rule is "subject to contrary agreement of the parties. . . ." Miss. Code Ann. § 75-2-509(4) (1981). Both parties cite *Everhard Manufacturing Company v. Brown*, 232 N.W.2d 378, 380 (Mich. App. 1975), in support of the position that the parties to a sales transaction may mutually agree to shift risk of loss. Because West is a merchant and physical delivery had not occurred as of the date of the fire, Federated acknowledges that "[a]t first glance, it would appear that West bore the risk of loss. . . ." Federated asserts that there was indeed a contrary agreement, however, which shifted the risk of loss to Hawkins.

Clearly, the "parties" to whom the statute refers are the buyer and seller-in this case, Hawkins and Federated because they were the only parties to the sales contract regarding the purchase of the equipment at issue. The sales contract itself does not contain a risk of loss provision, but the November 8, 1993 credit agreement expressly provides as follows:

> RISK OF LOSS AND OTHER AGREEMENTS: I will bear the risk of loss or damage to the Goods and my debt to you will not be reduced if the goods are lost or damaged.

Federated contends that this provision in the credit agreement constitutes a "contrary agreement" for purposes of § 75-2-509(4), and it asserts Hawkin's subsequent purchase of the physical damage insurance policy from JDIC is further evidence that the parties mutually agreed to shift the risk of loss. Therefore, Federated contends, JDIC should be liable for the loss as Hawkins' insurer. JDIC disagrees that Hawkins and West reached a "contrary agreement" which would shift the risk of loss, thus, JDIC contends the risk remained with West, and Federated should be liable for the loss.

Defendants both address two particular cases in stating their respective positions. In *Hayward v. Postma*, 188 N.W.2d 31, 720–21 (Mich. App. 1971), fire destroyed a boat prior to delivery to the buyer, and the court found it necessary to construe a Michigan statute identical to the one at issue in the case *sub judice*. The court held that the risk of loss had not passed to the buyer simply because boilerplate language in a security agreement provided that the buyer was to "at all times, keep the Goods in first class order and repair [and] fully insured against loss, damage, theft, and other risks. . . ." *Id.* at 722. Federated attempts to distinguish *Hayward* because the buyer in that case was an "average consumer," while Hawkins is "a large-scale, agricultural businessman and he purchased the JDIC policy to insure against the risk assumed." JDIC counters that the *Hayward* court based its decision not on the buyer's inexperience, but primarily on the fact that the language in the security agreement was too vague to constitute a "contrary agreement" within the meaning of the statute sufficient to shift the risk of loss prior to delivery of the boat.

JDIC cites *Caudle v. Sherrard Motor Company*, 525 S.W.2d 238 (Tex. App. 1975), in support of its position that risk of loss had not effectively passed to Hawkins at the time of the fire. In *Caudle*, the buyer contracted to buy a house trailer that was subsequently stolen from the seller's premises prior to delivery. *Id.* at 239. Again, addressing a statute identical to Mississippi's § 75-2-509, the Texas court held that a clause in the sales contract providing that "no loss, damage, or destruction of [the trailer] shall release buyer from his obligation" under the contract was insufficient to rise to the level of a "contrary agreement" which would override the general rule that risk of loss passes to the buyer only upon his receipt of the goods. *Id.* at 240. JDIC emphasizes that the *Caudle* court read the specific contractual provision and the sales contract as a whole "intend[ing] to fix responsibility for loss after the [buyer] had taken possession of the trailer." *Id.* Federated attempts to distinguish *Caudle* because the provision in that case was somewhat vague, while the provision in the instant credit agreement is clearly denoted as a "RISK OF LOSS" provision, contending that it thus clearly and unequivocally represents an agreement to shift the risk prior to delivery of the equipment.

The court is convinced, having read the parties' briefs and the applicable law, that JDIC's position is the better one in the situation before the court, and it is dispositive of this controversy. The *Caudle* court wisely held that "[a] contract which shifts the risk of loss to the buyer before he receives the merchandise is so unusual that a seller who desires to achieve this result must clearly communicate his intent to the buyer." *Id.*, citing *Hayward*, 188 N.W.2d at 33. While Federated places considerable emphasis on the fact that no explicit term in the risk of loss provision before the court made shifting of the risk effective only upon delivery, it is more telling that the provision makes no reference to delivery *at all*. This is simply not the sort of "clear and unequivocal language" which the *Caudle* court reasoned necessary to shift the risk of loss to an unsuspecting buyer. "To hold otherwise would be to set a trap for the unwary." *Hayward*, 188 N.W.2d at 725. This court must use restraint in inferring that an arguably ambiguous contractual provision shifted the risk of loss to a buyer such as Hawkins. *See Galbraith v. American Motorhome Corp.*, 545 P.2d 561, 563 (Wash. App. 1976). In Federated's brief in support of its response to JDIC's cross-motion for summary judgment, Federated states that "[i]f the risk of loss is to shift to the buyer only upon receipt of the goods, then the contract should say so." While technically accurate, Federated's statement fails to fully articulate the applicable law: Because "a contract which shifts the risk of loss to the buyer before he receives the goods is so unusual that a seller who wants to achieve this result must make his intent very clear to the buyer," *Hayward*, 188 N.W.2d at 33, if a credit agreement, such as the one in this case, which the seller executes as agent of the lender, is to shift the loss *from the seller* to the buyer, instead of *from the intended lender* to the buyer, the contract must be clear and unequivocal. The result which Federated seeks here cannot be reached by means of inferential language in an instrument which is clearly intended to govern the relationship between lender and borrower, not the relationship between buyer and seller. There simply was no clear risk-shifting agreement between Hawkins and West, thus, the risk of loss prior to delivery remained upon West in accordance with § 75-2-509(3). JDIC is entitled to summary judgment in its behalf.

. . . .

O.C.T. EQUIPMENT, INC. v. SHEPHERD MACHINERY CO.
Oklahoma Court of Civil Appeals
95 P.3d 197 (2004)

Defendant/Appellant Shepherd Machinery Co. (Shepherd) appeals from summary judgment granted in favor of Plaintiff/Appellee O.C.T. Equipment, Inc. (O.C.T.). A tractor which O.C.T. agreed to buy from Shepherd was damaged while in the possession of a bailee. The damage occurred before the bailee had acknowledged O.C.T.'s right to possession and before the tractor was made ready for delivery. We find the undisputed facts show that the risk of loss remained on Shepherd at the time the tractor was damaged. We therefore affirm summary judgment directing Shepherd to refund the purchase price to O.C.T.

After the tractor was damaged, O.C.T. refused delivery and sought reimbursement of the $42,000 it had paid for the tractor. Shepherd refused to refund the purchase price. O.C.T. then filed its Petition alleging that Shepherd breached the contract. O.C.T. sought recision of the contract as well as damages and attorney fees. In its Answer, Shepherd asserted that it was not liable because at the time the tractor was damaged, the risk of loss had passed to O.C.T.

The parties' primary dispute was who bore the risk of loss at the time the tractor was damaged. O.C.T. also argued that it had a right to reject nonconforming goods regardless of the risk of loss, but as will be explained, ultimately the issue is resolved under the risk of loss provisions of the Uniform Commercial Code. The trial court found in favor of O.C.T. and awarded $42,500, the price O.C.T. had paid Shepherd for the tractor.

The parties' competing motions for summary judgment, along with responses and replies, show no dispute of material fact. The parties do not dispute that O.C.T. sought to purchase tractors from Caterpillar, which directed O.C.T. to Shepherd. Mike Clark of O.C.T. called Shepherd December 14, 1998 to inquire about tractors then owned by Caterpillar.[5] Shepherd's employee David Solem met Clark at the Keen Transport yard in Santa Paula, California on December 16, 1998. A Keen employee showed the tractors to Clark. Clark agreed at that time to purchase four tractors, including the tractor which is the subject of this suit, serial number JAK0012531. The invoice for the tractors indicated that each would be equipped with EROPS, pat blade, and winch.[6] A fifth tractor was later added to the order and its serial number was hand-written on the invoice. The parties do not dispute that at the time Clark agreed to buy the tractors, tractor JAK0012531 did not have a winch installed and that it was agreed the winch would be installed before delivery. Although it is not included in the written invoice, the parties do not dispute that they also agreed that the tractors would be painted yellow before delivery.

Shepherd faxed the invoice to O.C.T. and O.C.T. wired payment for the tractors to Shepherd December 22, 1998. The tractors remained at Keen from the time Clark viewed them and agreed to purchase them. Shepherd sent instructions to Keen not to release any of the tractors to O.C.T.'s carrier until Keen had received a bill of lading for each tractor and a verbal release from one of two Shepherd employees. Shepherd sent O.C.T. a fax dated December 23, 1998 which stated that four of the tractors, including tractor JAK0012531, would be ready for pickup December 28, 1998. Shepherd does not dispute that on December 21, 1998, O.C.T. contacted Shepherd to ask that each of the tractors be checked for antifreeze levels, because of O.C.T.'s concern about the tractors going through high elevations en route to Oklahoma. Shepherd employee Solem contacted Keen and asked for the antifreeze readings. Keen sent Shepherd a listing of the tractor serial numbers showing the antifreeze readings for all the tractors O.C.T. had agreed to buy, but the list showed that tractor JAK0012531 had no antifreeze reading. Solem called Keen December 28, 1998 and asked Keen to recheck tractor JAK0012531 for antifreeze.

A bill of lading in the record shows that tractor JAKOO12598 was picked up by O.C.T.'s carrier at Keen December 30, 1998. Keen contacted Shepherd December 31, 1998 to inform Shepherd that during the night between December 30 and December 31, 1998, a security guard at Keen had driven tractor JAK0012531. At the time the security guard drove tractor JAK0012531, it had no antifreeze/coolant in it and the engine was burned up and ruined. Shepherd then called O.C.T. December 31, 1998 to inform O.C.T. of the damage to tractor JAK0012531. Solem indicated that at that time he also informed O.C.T. that O.C.T. owned tractor JAK0012531 and would have to work with

---

[5] [2] Caterpillar sold the tractors to Shepherd for resale to O.C.T.

[6] [3] The invoice is stamped with the words "as is where is" and Shepherd also argued that such language absolved it of responsibility. Those words apply to any warranty on the goods; they do not alter the risk of loss provisions of the UCC.

Keen to resolve the damage. O.C.T. refused to take delivery of the damaged tractor.[7] After Shepherd and O.C.T. could not agree on who bore the risk of loss to the tractor, and Shepherd refused to refund O.C.T.'s payment for the tractor, O.C.T. filed its Petition.

The UCC provision pertinent to this case is 12A O.S.2001 § 2-509(2). That subsection provides:

> § 2-509 Risk of Loss in the Absence of Breach
>
> *   *   *
>
> (2) Where the goods are held by a bailee to be delivered without being moved, the risk of loss passes to the buyer
>
> > (a) on his receipt of a negotiable document of title covering the goods; or
> >
> > (b) on acknowledgment *by the bailee* of the buyer's right to possession of the goods; or
> >
> > (c) after his receipt of a nonnegotiable document of title or other written direction to deliver, as provided in subsection 4(b) of Section 2-503.[8]

Shepherd asserts that § 2-509(2)(b) is applicable to this case and that its application requires a finding that O.C.T. bore the risk of loss at the time of the damage. Shepherd's primary contention is that Shepherd, the seller, acknowledged to Keen, the bailee, that O.C.T., the buyer, had the right to possession of the tractors and that § 2-509(2)(b) was therefore met in this case and the risk of loss had transferred to O.C.T. at the time tractor JAK0012531 was damaged. We note the evidence shows only that Shepherd informed Keen in writing that a bill of lading and verbal release (from Shepherd) were required before delivery of each tractor to O.C.T.'s carrier. More importantly, however, it is immaterial what Shepherd communicated to Keen. The plain language of § 2-509(2)(b) requires acknowledgment *by the bailee* of the buyer's right to possession.

Judge Posner, writing for the Seventh Circuit Court of Appeals, has explained that under § 2-509(2)(b), even acknowledgment by the bailee, but only to the seller, is insufficient to transfer the risk of loss. *See Jason's Foods, Inc. v. Peter Eckrich & Sons, Inc.*, 774 F.2d 214 (7th Cir. 1985). In *Jason's Foods*, Jason's Foods agreed to sell to Eckrich 38,000 pounds of ribs. The ribs were stored by a bailee — an independent meat storage facility. Under the sales agreement, delivery would be made by transferring the ribs from Jason's account ledger at the storage facility to Eckrich's account at the facility, without moving the ribs. Jason's asked the storage facility to move the ribs from Jason's account to Eckrich's. The facility clerk noted the transfer on the books immediately. Eckrich did not receive a receipt, and did not know the transfer had been made until 11 days later. In the meantime, the ribs were destroyed by a fire at the storage facility. The parties disputed when the risk of loss transferred. Jason's contended the risk transferred to Eckrich on the date the clerk transferred the ribs to Eckrich's account, because on that date, Jason's lost ownership and control over the ribs.

---

[7] [5] Bills of lading in the record show that O.C.T. took possession of the other tractors in the agreement.

[8] [6] Section 2-503(4)(b) provides for the manner of tender of delivery and provides:

> (4) Where goods are in the possession of a bailee and are to be delivered without being moved
>
> *   *   *
>
> (b) tender to the buyer of a nonnegotiable document of title or of a written direction to the bailee to deliver is sufficient tender unless the buyer seasonably objects, and receipt by the bailee of notification of the buyer's rights fixes those rights as against the bailee and all third persons; but risk of loss of the goods and of any failure by the bailee to honor the nonnegotiable document of title or to obey the direction remains on the seller until the buyer has had a reasonable time to present the document or direction, and a refusal by the bailee to honor the document or to obey the direction defeats the tender.

Eckrich argued that it should not bear the risk of loss of ribs it did not know it owned or controlled.

The court explained that under § 2-509(2), risk of loss is not related to title, but rather shifts when the transfer is acknowledged. *Id.* at 217. The court then considered to whom the statute required acknowledgment be made. Judge Posner opined that there would be little purpose in acknowledging to the seller the buyer's right to possession, particularly because the seller has informed the bailee of the buyer's right to possession and necessarily already has such knowledge. *Id.* The court noted that § 2-503(4)(a) also indicates that acknowledgment by the bailee of the buyer's right to possession is a method of tendering goods sold without being moved. But, that section likewise fails to indicate to whom the bailee must make the acknowledgment. *Id.* The court noted, however, that the corresponding provision of the Uniform Sales Act, which preceded the UCC, provided that acknowledgment must be made to the buyer, and the UCC comments following § 2-503 state that the section was not intended to change the Uniform Sales Act provision. *Id.* Additionally, the court noted that the comments to § 2-509 indicate that in the circumstance of delivery without moving goods in the possession of a bailee, the rules on manner of tender apply on the issue of risk of loss. *Id.* The court deduced that acknowledgment by the bailee to the buyer is required for tender, and likewise for transfer of the risk of loss. *Id.* The court noted that the acknowledgment need not be in writing, and the court declined to answer whether the pertinent date is when a written acknowledgment is mailed or when it is received, because it found that issue had not been raised by the parties. *Id.* at 218.

We find the reasoning in *Jason's Foods* persuasive. And, the case on which Shepherd relies does not suggest another holding. In *Whately v. Tetrault*, 29 Mass. App. Dec. 112, 5 U.C.C. Rep. Serv. 838 (1964), the plaintiff owned a boat and trailer which were kept in a storage facility. The defendant's agent met with the plaintiff and agreed to purchase the boat and trailer on behalf of the defendant. The agent and the plaintiff then went together to the storage facility where the plaintiff explained to the clerk that the boat and trailer had been sold and told him the agent could arrange to pick up the boat and trailer. The agent and clerk at that time agreed to have the boat and trailer picked up the following day. When the defendant went to the bailee's facility the next day as agreed, the trailer was missing.

The dispute in *Whately* was over who bore the risk of the loss of the trailer. The court found that the bailee had acknowledged the defendant's right to possession of the trailer to the defendant's agent when the two arranged for the time to pick up the boat and trailer. *Id.* at 840. The court also held that because of the acknowledgment by the bailee, there had been a tender of delivery under § 2-503(4)(a). *Id.* The court found that nothing remained for the plaintiff seller to do under the agreement because he had been paid, he had informed the bailee of the sale, and the bailee had acknowledged to the defendant buyer his right to possession of the trailer. The court concluded that the risk of loss therefore had transferred to the buyer at the time of the loss. *Id.* We agree that acknowledgment from the bailee to the buyer is required by § 2-509(2)(b) to transfer the risk of loss to the buyer in the case of goods in the possession of the bailee held to be delivered without being moved.

In anticipation of this interpretation of the statute, Shepherd argued in its Reply to O.C.T.'s Response to Shepherd's Motion for Summary Judgment that Keen had communicated to O.C.T. about O.C.T.'s carrier picking up the tractors. The record contains no evidence to support this assertion. The record contains no bill of lading for tractor JAK0012531. We recognize the Seventh Circuit's holding that an acknowledgment is not required to be in writing, but the record contains no evidence that Keen ever gave O.C.T. verbal or written acknowledgment that O.C.T. had the right to possession of tractor JAK0012531. Indeed, Solem's affidavit makes clear that all communications from Keen were made to Solem at Shepherd, who then passed the information on to O.C.T. Solem's affidavit indicates these communications regarded the coolant readings and then the damage to the tractor; nothing in Solem's affidavit purports to show that Keen acknowledged O.C.T.'s right to possession by communication passed via Shepherd, even if such indirect acknowledgment could operate to transfer the risk of loss.

Shepherd's argument, that its release of a different tractor, which O.C.T. picked up December 30, 1998, somehow operated as an acknowledgment by Keen to O.C.T. of O.C.T.'s right to possession of *all* of the tractors at that time, is unsupported. Particularly where the undisputed evidence shows that tractor JAK0012531 was not in fact ready for pick up according to the parties' agreement because coolant had not been added to it. O.C.T. employee Clark's affidavit states that *Shepherd informed O.C.T.* on December 23, 1998 that tractor JAK0012531 would be ready for transport December 28, 1998 and that O.C.T. arranged for transport of the equipment for December 30, 1998. However, tractor JAK0012531 was in fact not ready for transport on December 28 or December 30, 1998, because it did not have coolant in it. Solem's affidavit shows that Shepherd continued to direct Keen's actions toward tractor JAK0012531, particularly directing Keen to check the coolant level in the tractor, at the time it was damaged. This fact is important because of the written evidence that Shepherd directed Keen not to release the tractors without a bill of lading and verbal release. It is unreasonable to assume that Shepherd would have given the verbal release of tractor JAK0012531 when Shepherd was still directing Keen to make checks and repairs to that tractor, and which clearly were not completed at the time of the damage. Additionally, it would be unreasonable to say that a bailee could make an acknowledgment and effectively pass the risk of loss before the object of the agreement is conforming. The record contains no legitimate evidence that Keen gave O.C.T. acknowledgment of its right to possession of the tractors as required by § 2-509(2)(b).

Similarly, we dispense with Shepherd's contention that O.C.T. owned the tractor at the time of the damage because O.C.T. inspected the tractors December 16 and mailed payment before the damage occurred. O.C.T. asserts that § 2-513 provides that a buyer has a right before payment or acceptance to inspect the goods. Shepherd contends that this allows but one inspection *either* before payment or before acceptance, and that O.C.T. inspected the goods when it agreed to purchase them. Shepherd's contention ignores the language of § 2-512(2) that payment does not constitute an acceptance of goods or impair the buyer's right to inspect or any other buyer's remedy. It is undisputed that when O.C.T.'s representative looked at the tractors December 16 (which Shepherd refers to as an inspection), the parties then agreed that Shepherd would make several changes to the tractors before delivery. It is unreasonable to assert that if Shepherd had failed to install the winch or had failed to paint the tractors, O.C.T. would still have been forced to accept delivery of the non-conforming tractors. More importantly, we rely, as the courts in *Jason's Foods* and *Whately* did, on § 2-503 regarding time of tender of delivery in the case of goods held by a bailee for delivery without being moved. That section requires acknowledgment from the bailee to the buyer of the buyer's right to possession before tender of delivery can be found.

. . . .

PROBLEM 5-3

Borghese Construction company reached an oral agreement with Sanchez Concrete Distributors to purchase one of its mixing trucks. Borghese's President, Brenda Borghese, drove to Sanchez's place of business and paid the full purchase price. Sanchez's President handed her the keys and said, "It's yours." However, Brenda does not have the necessary driver's license to operate the vehicle on the street, and so she states that she will have one of her drivers return on the following morning to pick up the truck. That night, the truck is stolen by some rowdy teens and is totaled when they drive it into the side of the local high school building.

Who bears the risk of loss at the time of the theft?

2. Effect of Breach on Risk of Loss

When one party to a contract breaches that contract, § 2-510 attempts to place the cost of the breach on the breaching party. Section 2-510(1) keeps the risk of loss on the seller when it delivers nonconforming goods. The risk of loss does not pass to the buyer until the seller cures the defect or delivers conforming goods. If the buyer already has accepted the goods, but then rightfully revokes acceptance, the buyer "may to the extent of any deficiency in his effective insurance coverage treat the risk of loss as having rested on the seller from the beginning." § 2-510(2). When the buyer repudiates or breaches the contract in any way after conforming goods have been identified to the contract and before the risk of loss has passed to the buyer, § 2-510(3) stipulates that the buyer must bear any losses that occur within a commercially reasonable time that the seller's insurance will not cover.

The results under § 2-510(1) are efficient. By placing the risk of loss on the seller for shipping nonconforming goods, it creates an incentive for sellers to make sure the goods are conforming before they ship them. Buyers do not have to bear the risk of loss of goods for which they did not contract.

Once the buyer has accepted the goods, allocating the risk of loss becomes more complicated. The buyer has control and possession of the goods, which makes the buyer better able to protect them and more likely to insure them. The Code drafters, however, did not want to make the buyer responsible for the seller's breach. In order to balance these two competing principles, § 2-510(2) leaves the seller responsible for any losses that are not covered by the buyer's insurance. This rule still creates an incentive for sellers to ship conforming goods.

However, some might argue that § 2-510(3) allocates risk improperly because it discourages efficient breaches. The breaching buyer is responsible for any deficiency in the seller's insurance. In addition to calculating the risk of the breach, then, the buyer must also determine the risk of loss unconnected to the breach. This forces the buyer to inflate the cost of breaching, which may cause an inefficient allocation of resources. Section 2-510(3) would allocate the risk of loss more efficiently if it held buyers responsible only for losses that occurred after the risk of loss would have passed had the buyer not breached. Buyers would be able to benefit from the seller's insurance coverage. This would place information costs on the buyer to discover what, if any, insurance the seller possess, but it would allow the buyer to assess the cost of breach more accurately.

BERRY v. LUCAS
Oregon Court of Appeals
150 P.3d 424 (2006)

This appeal arises from a contract dispute regarding a manufactured home placed on a lot in Bandon, Oregon. Following a bench trial, the trial court entered a judgment in favor of plaintiffs and awarded damages of $6,535. Defendant appeals and, for the reasons discussed below, we affirm.

. . . .

The contract consisted of a printed form (front and back) and three exhibits. Defendant agreed as part of the contract to deliver and set up the manufactured home on a lot owned by plaintiffs in Bandon, Oregon. The parties contemplated that plaintiffs would be receiving a home suitable for occupancy. The contract provided that plaintiffs would pay 50% down and the balance on delivery. * * *

As part of the contract, the parties certified that the terms printed on the back side of the contract were part of the contract, and furthermore, plaintiffs acknowledged by signing the contract that they had read and understood the contract and received a copy of the contract.

Plaintiffs mailed a check for one-half of the purchase price to defendant in September 2002 and mailed a check for the remaining balance in early November.

The manufactured home was delivered in two sections to plaintiffs' lot on November 15, 2002, and placed on a concrete slab that had been constructed by plaintiffs' contractor. About a month later — before the home had been completed and prepared for occupancy — it suffered severe storm damage. The trial court found:

> "As of that date, the carpet inside the home had not been laid, railings remained to be installed, sheet rock still needed to be installed, and exterior siding on the west end had not yet been installed. * * * [T]he home was not ready to be moved into because set up work remained to be done by the defendant, and its agent, both inside and outside the home. The carpet work, the railings, the sheet rock, and the exterior siding were the responsibility of defendant. Neither party had insurance on the manufactured home as of the date of the storm damage. Plaintiffs paid a contractor $6535 to repair the damage."

Plaintiffs filed this action to recover the repair bill plus lost wages of $350. They first alleged that defendants violated the Unlawful Trade Practices Act (UTPA). In a second count, plaintiffs alleged that the damage to the manufactured home "was sustained after the manufactured home was shipped to the specified destination but before Defendants could tender delivery or Plaintiffs could inspect and potentially accept the goods." Plaintiffs alleged that defendant refused to repair the wind and rainwater damage and that plaintiffs therefore had to incur the expense of having the repair performed.

. . . .

As a general matter, Oregon's codification of the Uniform Commercial Code (UCC) governs sales contracts of the type involved here. But, "[t]he effect of provisions of the Uniform Commercial Code may be varied by agreement, except as otherwise provided in the Uniform Commercial Code." ORS 71.1020(3); *see also* ORS 72.5090(4) (regarding the provision addressing risk of loss in the absence of breach, "[t]he provisions of this section are subject to contrary agreement of the parties"). Defendant acknowledges the general applicability of the UCC, but argues that a provision of the contract governs the risk of loss in this case and is dispositive. We begin with that argument.

Paragraph 12 of the sales contract states:

> "**INSURANCE**. Buyer understands that Buyer is <u>not</u> covered by insurance on the unit purchased until accepted by an insurance company, and Buyer agrees to hold Dealer harmless from any and all claims due to loss or damage prior to acceptance of insurance coverage by an insurance company."

(Underscoring and boldface in original.) Defendant argues that paragraph 12 addresses risk of loss and that resort to the UCC provisions regarding risk of loss therefore is unnecessary. It argues that paragraph 12 "effectively allocates the risk of loss to the buyer before complete performance of the contract." According to defendant, the risk of loss under paragraph 12 had passed to plaintiffs at the time of the storm damage.

In interpreting a contract, we first examine the text and context to determine if the contract is ambiguous. *Batzer Construction, Inc. v. Boyer*, 204 Ore. App. 309, 317–18, 129 P.3d 773, *rev den*, 341 Ore. 366 (2006). Whether a contract is ambiguous presents a question of law. *Id.* at 317. In addition to examining the text and context of the provision, the court, in determining whether the contract is ambiguous, is also to consider extrinsic evidence of "the circumstances underlying the formation of the contract." *Id.* at 317. Finally, if the "provision remains ambiguous after the first two steps have been followed, the court relies on appropriate maxims of construction" to determine the provision's meaning. *Yogman v. Parrott*, 325 Ore. 358, 364, 937 P.2d 1019 (1997).

Paragraph 12 does not, on its face, address risk of loss. It follows a heading that reads, "Insurance." Its text focuses on the effect of insurance coverage, not a time in the transaction that will shift the risk of loss from seller to buyer. Moreover, as plaintiff points out, at the time the parties entered into the contract, the manufactured home had not yet been constructed by the manufacturer. According to plaintiff,

> "it seems nonsensical and illogical to force the Plaintiff to bear the risk of loss for a manufactured home that had yet to be manufactured and yet to be placed in the control of the Defendant. * * * It also seems untenable to force the Plaintiff to bear the risk of loss when the Defendant and Defendant's agents are still working on setting up the manufactured home, in accordance with their contractual duties."

Although we are not convinced that paragraph 12 addresses risk of loss, the provision arguably is ambiguous in that regard. That is, it could be read to place the risk of loss on the buyer from the time the contract is signed. Or, as plaintiff argues, it could be read to simply not address risk of loss at all. The parties point to no extrinsic evidence that resolves the ambiguity or that sheds light on the parties' intention. In light of the provision's ambiguity, we proceed, then, to ascertain the provision's meaning by applying maxims of construction.

Two maxims apply to the provision at issue here. First, it is a basic tenet of contract law that ambiguous language in a contract is construed against the drafter of the contract. *Hill v. Qwest*, 178 Ore. App. 137, 143, 35 P.3d 1051 (2001). Here, the form contract was provided by defendant, and applying that maxim leads to the conclusion that the parties did not intend to reallocate the risk of loss by the paragraph relating to insurance.

The second relevant maxim is one that is more specific to the situation involved here. That maxim is that, to allocate risk of loss in a manner different from that contemplated by the UCC, "the parties must expressly shift the risk of loss and such a shift will not readily be inferred." *Galbraith v. American Motorhome Corporation*, 14 Wn App 754, 757–58, 545 P.2d 561, 563 (1976); *see also McKenzie v. Olmstead*, 587 N.W.2d 863, 865 (Minn Ct App 1999) ("The implications of any contrary agreement regarding allocation of the risk of loss * * * should be explicit and understood by both parties."). Moreover, insurance provisions in a contract — such as a provision that the buyer must insure a yacht while the seller was installing options after receiving the boat from the manufacturer — have been held not to allocate the risk of loss contrary to the relevant UCC provision. *Hayward v. Postma*, 31 Mich. App. 720, 724, 188 N.W.2d 31, 33 (1971). Rather, as the *Hayward* court held, "we feel that a contract which shifts the risk of loss to the buyer before he receives the goods is so unusual that a seller who wants to achieve this result must make his intent very clear to the buyer." *Id.*

Applying those two maxims, and considering the text in context, we conclude that the parties did not intend to vary the risk of loss from that provided in the UCC. We turn, accordingly, to the UCC provision governing risk of loss.

Risk of loss in this case is governed by ORS 72.5090, which provides, in part:

> (1) Where the contract requires or authorizes the seller to ship the goods by carrier:
>
> . . . .
>
> (b) *If it does require the seller to deliver them at a particular destination and the goods are there duly tendered while in the possession of the carrier, the risk of loss passes to the buyer when the goods are there duly so tendered as to enable the buyer to take delivery.*
>
> . . . .
>
> (3) In any case not within subsection (1) or (2) of this section, the risk of loss passes to the buyer on receipt by the buyer of the goods if the seller is a merchant; otherwise, the risk passes to the buyer on tender of delivery.

(4) The provisions of this section are subject to contrary agreement of the parties and to the provisions of ORS 72.3270 on sale on approval and ORS 72.5100 on effect of breach on risk of loss.

(Emphasis added.) The contract between plaintiffs and defendant required defendant to deliver the manufactured home to plaintiffs' lot and to set it up. The transaction thus is governed by ORS 72.5090(1)(b). In short, the "goods" that plaintiffs purchased consisted of a complete manufactured home, placed on their lot, and ready for occupancy.

At the time of the storm damage, defendant had not supplied the goods that it had agreed to tender. Rather, it had provided an as — yet incomplete manufactured home. Under ORS 72.5090(1)(b), risk of loss passes to the buyer only after the goods are "duly so tendered as to enable the buyer to take delivery." ORS 72.5030(1) provides, in part, that "[t]ender of delivery requires that the seller put and hold *conforming goods* at the buyer's disposition and give the buyer any notification reasonably necessary to enable the buyer to take delivery." (Emphasis added.) And under ORS 72.1060(2), "Goods or conduct including any part of a performance are 'conforming' or conform to the contract when they are in accordance with the obligations under the contract."

Here, although defendant had partially performed under the contract, it had not tendered delivery of a completed manufactured home by putting conforming goods at plaintiffs' disposition. Simply put, defendant had not — at the time that the damage occurred — tendered delivery of the goods for which plaintiffs had contracted. And because, under ORS 72.5090(1)(b), the risk of loss is on the seller until such tender has occurred, the risk remained on defendant at the time the storm damaged the manufactured home. It follows that the trial court correctly entered judgment in favor of plaintiffs.

Courts applying other states' versions of the UCC have reached the same conclusion — although not necessarily following the exact route we have. *Moses v. Newman*, 658 S.W.2d 119 (Tenn Ct App 1983), is the case most factually similar to this one. As in this case, the seller had agreed to provide a mobile home and to set it up on the buyer's lot. As in this case, the home was delivered to the lot but, before the seller could complete the set-up, a windstorm destroyed the home. Although the court analyzed the liability issue under UCC § 2-510 (codified in Oregon as ORS 72.5100), its analysis was analogous to ours. It concluded that, although the buyer had placed certain items of personal property in the home before it was destroyed, the buyer had not accepted delivery of the home at that time. *Id.* at 122. Moreover, the court explained that the risk of loss had not passed from the seller to the buyer at the time the goods were destroyed:

> "In this case, plaintiff contracted for a habitable mobile home plus the installation. Accordingly, since the loss occurred before the installation was complete, the defendant had not delivered conforming goods which would shift the risk of loss to plaintiff."

Id.

Similarly, in *Southland Mobile Home Corporation v. Chyrchel*, 255 Ark 366, 500 S.W.2d 778 (1973), the plaintiff purchased a mobile home from the defendant. After delivering the mobile home and placing it in position, the defendant hooked up the sewer and gas connections, but did not complete other connections. *Id.* at 367, 500 S.W.2d at 779. Before the connections were completed, an explosion occurred and extensively damaged the mobile home. *Id.* at 368, 500 S.W.2d at 779. In addressing the risk of loss issue, the Arkansas Supreme Court rejected the argument "that the sale was complete before the fire and the risk of loss had passed to the buyer." *Id.* at 371, 500 S.W.2d at 781. The court concluded that the risk of loss never passed to the buyer because the seller had not delivered conforming goods. *Id. at 372, 500 S.W.2d at 782.*

Other courts, albeit in somewhat different factual contexts, have reached the same result. *See, e.g., In re Thomas*, 182 BR 347, 349 (SD Fla 1995) (buyer purchased pool heater under contract that included installation; seller dropped heater off on buyer's driveway, from where it was stolen; United States Bankruptcy court concluded that unit never was "delivered," so that risk of loss remained on seller); *William F. Wilke, Inc. v. Cummins Diesel Engines, Inc.*, 252 Md 611, 618, 250 A.2d 886, 890 (1969) (contract called for purchase, installation, and field testing of diesel generator; damage occurred after generator was installed, but before other obligations were performed; the court held, "[W]e have no difficulty in holding that the delivery of the generator to the job site, while identifying the goods to the contract, did not amount to a delivery of goods or the performance of obligations conforming to the contract. It could not constitute such a delivery and performance until the generator had been installed, started up, and field tests completed.").

In sum, because plaintiffs contracted for a completed manufactured home and no such home had been delivered at the time the windstorm damage occurred, the risk of loss was still on defendant at that time. Accordingly, the trial court correctly found in favor of plaintiffs and awarded damages.

Affirmed.

NOTE

The most difficult issues raised by § 2-510 are whether: (1) the goods are "conforming" (subsection (1)), (2) the buyer has rightfully revoked acceptance (subsection (2)), or (3) the buyer has repudiated or is otherwise in breach. These issues are discussed in the next chapter.

PROBLEM 5-4

Shiraz Novelties agrees to sell 10,000 paper hats to Blow Out Parties, Inc. for $1 each. The agreement stipulates that the hats will be made available at Shiraz's warehouse on or before August 5, 1992, for Blow Out to pick up. The parties further agree that Blow Out is to pick up the goods within five (5) days after Shiraz makes them available.

On August 5, 1992, Shiraz notified Blow Out that conforming hats had been identified to the contract and were available for pickup during normal business hours. On August 10, 1992, Shiraz notified Blow Out that it still was holding the goods but demanded that Blow Out immediately pick them up and pay for them. On August 15, 1992, Shiraz notified Blow Out that it considered Blow Out to be in breach of their agreement.

On September 15, 1992, a fire at Shiraz's warehouse completely destroyed the hats identified to the contract. Shiraz recovered $5,000 from its insurer on account of the loss of the hats.

At the time of the fire, who bore the risk of loss under § 2-509?

Does § 2-510 alter the result of § 2-509? What factors would you need to consider in applying the rule of § 2-510?

Chapter 6
REPUDIATION, EXCUSE, AND BREACH

Unfortunately, not all sales transactions conclude without dispute. In this chapter we cover issues relating to a party's anticipatory repudiation of its obligations under the agreement, the ability of a party to claim an excuse for nonperformance due to impracticability, and the general breach provisions as expressed in the concepts of rejection, acceptance, and revocation of acceptance. In the next chapter, we survey the remedies available to an aggrieved party.

A. REPUDIATION AND EXCUSE

Before the seller tenders the goods, circumstances may change so as to make it unprofitable, difficult, or even impossible for one party to perform. This may lead the party to disclaim its obligations, or to advise the other party that it will be unable to perform. The party facing the changed circumstances might also claim that its failure to perform is excused. In this section, we consider how Article 2 defines a party's anticipatory repudiation of its obligations under the agreement, and the available excuses for non-performance.

1. Anticipatory Repudiation and Adequate Assurance of Due Performance

In the course of commercial transactions, it may come to the attention of one of the parties that the other party either cannot or will not perform as provided in the contract. If, for example, the seller is not scheduled to make the agreed-upon delivery until June 30, but on April 10 the seller clearly repudiates its obligations, commercial efficiency is undermined by requiring the buyer to wait until June 30 to protect itself. This is particularly true in volatile markets because quick action by the buyer can mitigate losses. Without the doctrine of anticipatory repudiation, however, the buyer would have to wait until June 30 to know for sure that the seller breached the agreement.

Article 2 addresses repudiation in §§ 2-609, 2-610, and 2-611. You will see that §§ 2-610 and 2-611 state the general rule regarding repudiation and the ability to retract a repudiation. Section 2-609 represents an innovation in Article 2 by permitting a party having "reasonable grounds for insecurity" about the other's performance to demand in writing "adequate assurance of due performance." The other party's failure to provide such assurances is deemed a repudiation. In effect, then, § 2-609 permits a party to "smoke out" an impending breach in circumstances where the other party has not yet clearly and unequivocally repudiated.

IN RE CHATEAUGAY CORP.
United States District Court, Southern District of New York
11 UCC Rep. Serv. 2d 506 (1989)

. . . .

OPINION

ROBERT J. WARD, District Judge.

Diamond Gateway Coal Company ("Diamond Gateway") appeals from an order of the bankruptcy court expunging and disallowing its claim against The LTV Corporation ("LTV") and LTV Steel Company Inc. ("LTV Steel") (collectively, "Debtors"). After a hearing on Debtors' Objection to Claims of Diamond Gateway, the bankruptcy court ruled that Diamond Gateway, prior to the institution of the bankruptcy proceeding, had repudiated the contract upon which it based its claims against Debtors. The court therefore entered an order expunging and disallowing Diamond Gateway's claim, and this appeal followed. For the reasons set forth below, the order of the bankruptcy court is reversed and the case is remanded for further proceedings consistent with this opinion.

BACKGROUND

1. *The Agreement*

The facts underlying this appeal are not in dispute. On October 31, 1980, Diamond Gateway and the predecessor of LTV Steel entered into a fifteen-year coal supply agreement (the "Agreement") pursuant to which Diamond Gateway was to sell coal to LTV Steel from a large underground mine located in Greene County, Pennsylvania (the "Gateway Mine"). Record on Appeal at 280 ("Record"). Under the Agreement, LTV is guarantor of LTV Steel's performance. *Id.* at 124. Clause 2 of the contract provides that LTV Steel purchase from Diamond Gateway, each year, an amount of clean coal "equivalent to the quantity produced by processing 450,000 tons of Raw Coal" from the Gateway Mine through a designated coal cleaning plant. *Id.* at 74.

. . . .

Under the Agreement, in the event that LTV Steel in any Coal Year takes less than 75% of the quantity of coal specified in Clause 2 (minus allowances for failure to take coal for reasons of force majeure), Diamond Gateway has the right, pursuant to Clause 17, to terminate the Agreement. The Agreement provides that, should Diamond Gateway choose to exercise this termination option, the liability of both parties extends only up until the point of termination of the Agreement. *Id.* at 119.

2. *The Dispute*

By letter dated May 24, 1985, LTV Steel notified Diamond Gateway that, beginning June 1, 1985, LTV Steel would "not accept shipments of Gateway coal until further notice." *Id.* at 198. The letter further stated that "Clause 15 of the [Agreement] covers *Liquidated Damages for Failure to Take Specified Quantities.* Liquidated damages are handled at the end of each coal year." *Id.* (emphasis in original).

In response to this communication, Diamond Gateway took the position, in a letter dated August 12, 1985 (the "August 12 Letter"), that it did "not agree that Section 15 may be unilaterally invoked by LTV to avoid its obligation to take delivery of Clean Coal. . . ." *Id.* at 159. The letter informed LTV Steel that Diamond Gateway "must consider LTV's stated intent not to take delivery of Clean Coal on and after October 1, 1985 as a breach and repudiation of its obligations under the Coal Supply Agreement." *Id.* Based upon this interpretation of the Agreement, Diamond Gateway requested adequate assurance of performance by LTV Steel. Nonetheless, Diamond Gateway made it clear that it "was, and is, prepared to supply LTV on and after October 1, 1985 with Clean Coal as required under Section 2 of the Coal Supply Agreement." *Id.*

LTV Steel responded in a letter dated September 11, 1985 clarifying its position with regard to future coal deliveries. LTV Steel informed Diamond Gateway that it had "not determined never to take Clean Coal under the Coal Supply Agreement," but only that it would not take any coal during October 1985, and that Diamond Gateway would be kept advised of its plans for subsequent months. LTV Steel disputed Diamond Gateway's right to request assurance that LTV Steel would always take delivery of coal rather than electing to pay liquidated damages under Clause 15 of the Agreement, but assured Diamond Gateway that it would continue to perform under the Agreement. *Id.* at 161.

Subsequently, LTV Steel informed Diamond Gateway that it wished to take delivery of Clean Coal under the Agreement for the month of November 1985. *Id.* at 304. By letter dated October 15, 1985, LTV Steel stated that it would "look upon any failure of delivery as a significant and substantial breach by Diamond Gateway of its obligations under the Coal Supply Agreement." *Id.*

In response to this demand for Clean Coal, Diamond Gateway, in a letter dated October 25, 1985 (the "October 25 Letter"), reiterated its belief that it had the right to request adequate assurance of performance under Section 2-609 of the Uniform Commercial Code. Despite this position, Diamond Gateway attempted to accommodate LTV Steel by reaffirming its intention to perform under the Agreement pending a resolution of the parties' dispute. The letter stated, in part:

> First, Diamond Gateway will deliver to LTV Steel Clean Coal as requested in your letter of October 15, 1985, under, and in accordance with, the price, quantity, and other terms of the Coal Supply Agreement. Second, Diamond Gateway is willing to deliver Clean Coal under the Coal Supply Agreement with our commitment that any Clean Coal taken and paid for by LTV Steel would not be the subject of any lawsuit or other action by Diamond Gateway. *Third, Diamond Gateway will continue to make deliveries of Clean Coal under the Coal Supply Agreement, as LTV Steel interprets the Agreement;* provided, however, that Diamond Gateway will not forfeit either its right to obtain a determination of the issues [in dispute] or any rights that may flow therefrom.

Record at 163 (emphasis added). In a subsequent letter dated October 29, 1985 (the "October 29 Letter"), Diamond Gateway reaffirmed its opinion that the failure of LTV Steel to provide adequate assurance of performance would constitute a repudiation by LTV Steel of the Agreement, but stated that Diamond Gateway remained "ready, willing and able to deliver Clean Coal for November and thereafter under and pursuant to the Coal Supply Agreement pending a determination of the issues" in dispute between the parties. *Id.* at 164.

LTV Steel responded to this communication, in a letter dated October 30, 1985, by asserting that "Diamond Gateway is in breach of its obligations under the Coal Supply Agreement," and that LTV Steel saw "no need for further communications on this subject at this time." *Id.* at 166.

In November 1985, Diamond Gateway filed "two lawsuits seeking a declaration of the parties' respective rights under the Coal Supply Agreement." Record at 3 (Joint Stipulation of the Parties, filed April 1, 1987). In each suit, Diamond Gateway sought a declaration of the parties' rights and obligations under the Agreement and, in the event Diamond Gateway's interpretation of the Agreement prevailed, damages for breach of the Agreement by Debtors.

Also in November, Diamond Gateway sent to LTV Steel an invoice, pursuant to Clause 15 of the Agreement, for liquidated damages for Coal Year 1985. LTV Steel responded to this invoice, in part, with the proviso: "We consider your invoice to be an acknowledgment that the Gateway Coal Supply Agreement is in effect." Record at 18.

On December 13, 1985, LTV Steel stated by letter to Diamond Gateway that it would "resume taking delivery of Clean Coal under the Coal Supply Agreement (Gateway) in January, 1986." *Id.* at 202. In reply, Diamond Gateway stated in a letter dated December 17, 1985 ("the December 17 Letter"):

> Pursuant to your request of December 13, 1985, Diamond Gateway Coal Company will, for the month of January, 1986, deliver Clean Coal to LTV Steel Company, Inc., pursuant to the Coal Supply Agreement.

Id. at 203. Because LTV Steel had informed Diamond Gateway that this request for Clean Coal did not imply any commitment on the part of LTV Steel to take delivery, rather than pay damages under Clause 15 of the Agreement, for any subsequent month, the December 17 Letter made clear that the January deliveries would "be made without prejudice to, and under a reservation of, Diamond Gateway's rights as more particularly set forth in [the federal and state lawsuits]." *Id.*

In order to comply with LTV Steel's request for Clean Coal under the Agreement for the month of January 1986, Diamond Gateway was obligated to reopen the Gateway Mine, which had been closed since July 1985. *Id.* at 284. During January 1986, Diamond Gateway delivered to LTV Steel 29,980 tons of Clean Coal in thirty separate barge lot installments. This was the total amount requested by LTV Steel. *Id.* at 202. LTV Steel accepted delivery of all thirty installments of Clean Coal, *Id.* at 285, stating in a letter to Diamond Gateway dated January 13, 1986 that "LTV Steel's position is that we have ordered coal for January under and in accordance with the Coal Supply Agreement, and we are pleased that you are responding to our request." *Id.* at 204. The amount paid by LTV Steel for the coal, pursuant to the pricing and premium provisions of the Agreement, was approximately three times the market price for January 1986 coal. *Id.* at 357.

No further Clean Coal was requested by LTV Steel from Diamond Gateway, and on July 17, 1986, Debtors filed a petition for reorganization under chapter 11 of the Bankruptcy Code. Subsequently, the parties entered into a Joint Application and Stipulation (the "Joint Stipulation") for an order authorizing Debtors to reject the contract pursuant to 11 U.S.C. § 365(a).[1] The Joint Stipulation was adopted and approved by the bankruptcy court in an order dated April 27, 1987. It expressly provided that it was "without prejudice to any claim or defense which has been or may be asserted" in the state and federal lawsuits concerning the continued validity of the Agreement.

Diamond Gateway thereafter filed a timely notice of claim against Debtors based upon Debtors' rejection of the Agreement, and Debtors filed an objection to Claims of Diamond Gateway. A hearing was held in the bankruptcy court, after which the Debtors' Objection to Claims was sustained and the claim ordered expunged.

3. *The Bankruptcy Court Decision*

The bankruptcy court correctly determined that three issues necessitated resolution in order for the court to rule on Debtors' Objection to Claims of Diamond Gateway: (1) whether LTV Steel breached the Agreement by failing to take delivery of coal rather than pay liquidated damages under Clause 15; (2) if LTV Steel did not breach the Agreement by the foregoing actions, whether Diamond Gateway through its several letters and by institution of two lawsuits repudiated the Agreement; and (3) whether in either case the Agreement was reinstated by LTV Steel's subsequent acceptance of and payment for Clean Coal in January 1986.

After an oral argument during which no factual dispute was presented, the bankruptcy court decided the issues "as if [they] were presented on a motion for summary judgment." *Id.* at 233. The bankruptcy court held that, under the Agreement, LTV Steel was entitled to elect to pay liquidated damages rather than take delivery of Clean Coal, and thus, had not breached the Agreement either by failing to take delivery of coal, or by refusing to provide assurances of future performance under UCC 2-609. The bankruptcy court construed Clause 15 of the Agreement, in the context of the document as a whole, as constituting a "take-or-pay" option for LTV Steel, under which LTV Steel could discharge its performance obligation either by taking delivery of Clean Coal, or by paying the liquidated damages specified in that clause. *See* Record at 466

---

[1] [4] Section 365(a) provides, in pertinent part: . . . the trustee, subject to the court's approval, may assume or reject any executory contract or unexpired lease of the debtor. 11 U.S.C. § 365(a). Under section 365(g), the rejection of an executory contract constitutes a breach except in certain enumerated circumstances not present in this case.

(Conclusion of Law no. 4, January 5, 1989 order).

Turning to the issue of repudiation, the bankruptcy court found that Diamond Gateway's letters to LTV Steel of August 12, October 25, October 29, and December 17 of 1985, combined with the commencement of two lawsuits against Debtors, constituted a repudiation of the Agreement by Diamond Gateway prior to the filing of the Chapter 11 petition by Debtors. *See* Record at 467 (Conclusion of Law no. 8, January 5, 1989 order). The bankruptcy court further found that the subsequent actions of the parties did not serve to reinstate the Agreement. *See* Record at 525 (Conclusion of Law no. 2, April 18, 1989 order).

DISCUSSION

. . . .

2. *The Merits*

The bankruptcy court correctly determined that, under the terms of the Agreement, LTV Steel was entitled to elect to pay the amount specified in Clause 15 without thereby breaching the Agreement. Record at 530 (Conclusions of Law nos. 3 & 4, January 5, 1989 order).

. . . .

The bankruptcy court erred, however, in its determination that Diamond Gateway, by advancing an erroneous interpretation of the Agreement while still promising full performance, anticipatorily repudiated the Agreement. Under the law of Pennsylvania, the test for determining whether an anticipatory repudiation has occurred is strict. According to the Pennsylvania Supreme Court, "to constitute anticipatory breach under Pennsylvania law, there must be 'an absolute and unequivocal refusal to perform or a distinct and positive statement of an inability to do so.'" *2401 Pennsylvania Ave. v. Federation of Jewish Agencies*, 507 Pa. 166, 489 A.2d 733, 736 (1985) (quoting *McClelland v. New Amsterdam Casualty Co.*, 322 Pa. 429, 185 A. 198 (1936)). The Uniform Commercial Code, in comment 1 to section 2-610,[2] "appears to retain the common law requirement that a statement of intention not to perform must be positive and unequivocal." J. WHITE & R. SUMMERS, UNIFORM COMMERCIAL CODE 239 (3d ed. 1988).

Similarly, "a demand for greater performance than agreed upon constitutes a repudiation 'when under a fair reading it amounts to a statement of intention not to perform except on conditions which go beyond the contract.'" *Id.* at 238–39 (quoting UCC § 2-610 comment 2). In either situation — whether a simple statement of intent not to perform, or a statement of intent not to perform except upon a condition which goes beyond the contract — the pivotal inquiry must be whether there was manifested the requisite intention not to perform under the contract. It is this necessary element which is lacking under the facts of the present case.

In each of the four letters cited by the bankruptcy court as evidencing Diamond Gateway's purported repudiation of the Agreement, Diamond Gateway made clear its continued willingness to perform under the Agreement as interpreted by LTV Steel pending resolution of the parties' dispute. At no time did Diamond Gateway state an intention not to perform, and it certainly did not do so with the clarity and unequivocalness required under Pennsylvania law.

In the August 12 Letter, Diamond Gateway requested adequate assurance of future performance from LTV Steel, and stated its belief that LTV Steel's interpretation of the Agreement was erroneous and would constitute a breach of the Agreement if LTV steel

---

[2] [7] Comment 1 to section 2-610 states that "anticipatory repudiation centers upon an overt communication of intention or an action which renders performance impossible or demonstrates a clear determination not to continue with performance."

continued to act upon it. The letter ended: "I trust that we will continue to work together in a spirit of mutual cooperation, but LTV's refusal to take Clean Coal causes us grave concern." Although Diamond Gateway was mistaken in its belief that it was entitled, under the UCC, to request assurance of performance from LTV Steel, nowhere did the August 12 Letter state that Diamond Gateway intended not to perform under the contract. On the contrary, the August 12 Letter made clear that Diamond Gateway "was, and is, prepared to supply LTV on and after October 1, 1985 with Clean Coal as required under Section 2 of the Coal Supply Agreement."

Similarly, the October 25 Letter did not contain any clear statement of an intention not to perform under the Agreement. It contained, in fact, a clear statement of a continued willingness to perform despite any disagreement between the parties as to the proper interpretation of Clause 15. The letter stated: " . . . Diamond Gateway will continue to make deliveries of Clean Coal under the Coal Supply Agreement, as LTV Steel interprets the Agreement. . . ." Diamond Gateway's reservation of the right to obtain a determination of the disputed issue in no way negates this clear statement that it would perform. *See, e.g., Bill's Coal Company v. Board of Public Utilities*, 682 F.2d 883 (10th Cir. 1982), *cert. denied*, 459 U.S. 1171, 74 L. Ed. 2d 1014, 103 S. Ct. 816 (1983) (urging of erroneous interpretation of contractual clause, even if done in bad faith, did not amount to anticipatory repudiation where neither party's performance under the contract was thereby affected).

The October 29 Letter again made clear that Diamond Gateway remained "ready, willing and able" to perform under the Agreement pending a resolution of the disputed issues. Finally, the last of the four letters found by the bankruptcy court to constitute "elements" of Diamond Gateway's repudiation — the December 17 Letter — nowhere stated an intention on the part of Diamond Gateway not to perform, but instead, informed LTV Steel that it would deliver the coal ordered by LTV Steel for the month of January 1986 "pursuant to the Coal Supply Agreement." Further evidencing its intent to continue to supply Clean Coal under the Agreement, Diamond Gateway, at great expense, reopened the Gateway Mine, which had been closed prior to the request for January coal.

Appellees argue that, by interpreting Clause 15 in the way that it did, Appellant stated an intent not to perform except on a condition which went beyond the contract. According to this argument, by requiring LTV Steel to give up its "pay" option to which it was entitled under the Agreement, Diamond Gateway conditioned its performance and thereby committed an anticipatory breach. This argument is misdirected. Although Diamond Gateway did press an erroneous interpretation of the Agreement, it never stated that it would not fully perform under the Agreement *as interpreted by LTV Steel*, pending a resolution of the dispute. Diamond Gateway did not, as required for a repudiation to have occurred, state an "intention not to perform except on conditions which go beyond the contract." UCC § 2-610, comment 2. As the official comment to § 2-610 makes clear:

> Under the language of this section, a demand by one or both parties for more than the contract calls for in the way of counter-performance is not in itself a repudiation nor does it invalidate a plain expression of desire for future performance.

Id. Thus, the mere demand that LTV Steel renounce its "pay" option, not coupled with a statement of intention not to perform unless LTV Steel acceded to this demand, did not amount to a repudiation of the Agreement by Diamond Gateway. *Cf. e.g., 2401 Pennsylvania Avenue Corp. v. Federation of Jewish Agencies*, 507 Pa. 166, 489 A.2d 733 (1985) (statements refusing to acknowledge validity of lease insufficient to meet requirement for anticipatory repudiation of absolute and unequivocal refusal to perform); *Oak Ridge Construction Co. v. Tolley*, 351 Pa. Super. 32, 504 A.2d 1343 (1985) (letter stating that charges for work performed were "in dispute or disagreement" and requesting resolution under arbitration clause was not a repudiation, where letter did not contain an unequivocal refusal to pay the charges); *Copylease Corp. of America v. Memorex Corporation*, 403 F. Supp. 625 (S.D.N.Y. 1975) (statements that contract not binding, not coupled with statement of intent not to perform, did not amount to anticipatory repudiation).

Finally, Appellees argue that Diamond Gateway repudiated the Agreement by filing the state and federal lawsuits seeking damages for the alleged breach of the Agreement by LTV Steel. The Court rejects this argument. As noted above, unless the actions of Diamond Gateway implied a clear and unequivocal intention not to perform its obligations under the contract, no repudiation can have occurred. As the Court of Appeals for the Tenth Circuit has stated in a similar context:

> If a seller's interpretation of a termination clause is ludicrous, the buyer should ignore it; if the interpretation might prevail in a court of law, the seller has a right to urge it.

Bill's Coal Company v. Board of Public Utilities, 682 F.2d 883, 886 (10th Cir. 1982).

That Diamond Gateway's interpretation of the Agreement would not have prevailed does not transform a clear statement of willingness to perform pending determination of the issues into an anticipatory repudiation of the Agreement. If such were the case, a party believing the other party to a contract to be in breach would have no recourse other than risking breach itself in the event it mistakenly pressed any claim. Appellees have not cited any case to this Court in which the filing of a lawsuit alone was held to constitute a repudiation, and this Court declines to so hold.

The Court need not address the issue of reinstatement of the Agreement, since it finds that the Agreement was not repudiated in the first instance by Diamond Gateway.

CONCLUSION

. . . .

It is so ordered.

QUESTION

Are §§ 2-610 and 2A-402 drafted so loosely that a party may be able to find evidence of the other party's repudiation too easily? Would the provisions work better if they incorporated a requirement that the party in receipt of a communication it deems to represent an anticipatory repudiation notify the sender that it considers the communication to be a repudiation? How would you draft a new subsection of §§ 2-610 and 2A-402 to effect that result?

HORNELL BREWING CO. v. SPRY
New York Supreme Court
664 N.Y.S.2d 698 (1997)

. . . .

LOUISE GRUNER GANS, Justice.

Plaintiff Hornell Brewing Co., Inc. ("Hornell"), a supplier and marketer of alcoholic and non-alcoholic beverages, including the popular iced tea drink "Arizona," commenced this action for a declaratory judgment that any rights of defendants Stephen A. Spry and Arizona Tea Products Ltd. to distribute Hornell's beverages in Canada have been duly terminated, that defendants have no further rights with respect to these products, including no right to market and distribute them, and that any such rights previously transferred to defendants have reverted to Hornell.

In late 1992, Spry approached Don Vultaggio, Hornell's Chairman of the Board, about becoming a distributor of Hornell's Arizona beverages. Vultaggio had heard about Spry as an extremely wealthy and successful beer distributor who had recently sold his business. In January 1993, Spry presented Vultaggio with an ambitious plan for distributing Arizona beverages in Canada. Based on the plan and on Spry's reputation, but without further investigation, Hornell in early 1993 granted Spry the exclusive right to purchase Arizona products for distribution in Canada, and Spry formed a Canadian corporation, Arizona Iced Tea Ltd., for that express purpose.

Initially, the arrangement was purely oral. In response to Spry's request for a letter he needed to secure financing, Hornell provided a letter in July 1993 confirming their exclusive distributorship arrangement, but without spelling out the details of the arrangement. Although Hornell usually had detailed written distributorship agreements and the parties discussed and exchanged drafts of such an agreement, none was ever executed. In the meantime, Spry, with Hornell's approval, proceeded to set himself up as Hornell's distributor in Canada. During 1993 and until May 1994, the Hornell line of beverages, including the Arizona beverages, was sold to defendants on 10-day credit terms.

In May 1994, after an increasingly problematic course of business dealings, Hornell *de facto* terminated its relationship with defendants and permanently ceased selling its products to them.

The problem dominating the parties' relationship between July 1993 and early May 1994 was defendants' failure to remit timely payment for shipments of beverages received from plaintiff. Between November and December 1993, and February 1994, defendants' unpaid invoices grew from $20,000 to over $100,000, and their $31,000 check to Hornell was returned for insufficient funds. Moreover, defendants' 1993 sales in Canada were far below Spry's initial projections.

In March and April 1994, a series of meetings, telephone calls, and letter communications took place between plaintiff and defendants regarding Spry's constant arrearages and the need for him to obtain a line and/or letter of credit that would place their business relationship on a more secure footing. These contacts included a March 27, 1994 letter to Spry from Vanguard Financial Group, Inc. confirming "the approval of a $1,500,000 revolving credit facility" to Arizona Tea Products Ltd., which never materialized into an actual line of credit; Spry sent Hornell a copy of this letter in late March or early April 1994.

All theses exchanges demonstrate that during this period plaintiff had two distinct goals: to collect the monies owed by Spry, and to stabilize their future business relationship based on proven, reliable credit assurances. These exchanges also establish that during March and April, 1994, Spry repeatedly broke his promises to pay by a specified deadline, causing Hornell to question whether Vanguard's $1.5 million revolving line of credit was genuine.

On April 15, 1994, during a meeting with Vultaggio, Spry arranged for Vultaggio to speak on the telephone with Richard Worthy of Metro Factors, Inc. The testimony as to the content of that brief telephone conversation is conflicting. Although Worthy testified that he identified himself and the name of his company, Metro Factors, Inc., Vultaggio testified that he believed Worthy was from an "unusual lending institution" or bank which was going to provide Spry with a line of credit, and that nothing was expressly said to make him aware that Worthy represented a factoring company. Worthy also testified that Vultaggio told him that once Spry cleared up the arrears, Hornell would provide Spry with a "$300,000 line of credit, so long as payments were made on a net 14 day basis." According to Vultaggio, he told Worthy that once he was paid in full, he was willing to resume shipments to Spry "so long as Steve fulfills his requirements with us."

Hornell's April 18, 1994 letter to Spry confirmed certain details of the April 15 conversations, including that payment of the arrears would be made by April 19, 1994. However, Hornell received no payment on that date. Instead, on April 25, Hornell received from Spry a proposed letter for Hornell to address to a company named "Metro" at a post office box in Dallas, Texas. Worthy originally sent Spry a draft of this letter with "Metro Factors, Inc." named as the addressee, but in the copy Vultaggio received the words "Factors, Inc." were apparently obliterated. Hornell copied the draft letter on its own letterhead and sent it to Metro over Vultaggio's signature. In relevant part, the letter stated as follows:

Gentlemen:

Please be advised that Arizona Tea Products, Ltd. (ATP), of which Steve Spry is president, is presently indebted to us in the total amount of $79,316.24 as of the beginning of business Monday, April 25, 1994. We sell to them on "Net 14 days" terms. Such total amount is due according to the following schedule:

*   *   *

Upon receipt of $79,316.24. (which shall be applied to the oldest balances first) by 5:00 P.M. (EST) Tuesday, May 2, 1994 by wire transfer(s) to the account described below, we shall recommence selling product to ATP on the following terms:

1) All invoices from us are due and payable by the 14th day following the release of the related product.

2) We shall allow the outstanding balance owed to us by ATP to go up to $300,000 so long as ATP remains "current" in its payment obligations to us. Wiring instructions are as follows:

*   *   *

Hornell received no payment on May 2, 1994. It did receive a wire transfer from Metro of the full amount on May 9, 1994. Upon immediate confirmation of that payment, Spry ordered 30 trailer loads of "product" from Hornell, at a total purchase price of $390,000 to $450,000. In the interim between April 25, 1994 and May 9, 1994, Hornell learned from several sources, including its regional sales manager Baumkel, that Spry's warehouse was empty, that he had no managerial, sales, or office staff, that he had no trucks, and that in effect, his operation was a sham.

On May 10, 1994, Hornell wrote to Spry, acknowledging receipt of payment and confirming that they would extend up to $300,000 of credit to him, net 14 days cash "based on your prior representation that you have secured a $1,500,000. US line of credit." The letter also stated,

Your current balance with us reflects a 0 balance due. As you know, however, we experienced considerable difficulty and time wasted over a five-week time period as we tried to collect some $130,000 which was 90–120 days past due.

Accordingly, before we release any more product, we are asking you to provide us with a letter confirming the existence of your line of credit as well as a personal guarantee that is backed up with a personal financial statement that can be verified. Another option would be for you to provide us with an irrevocable letter of credit in the amount of $300,000.

Spry did not respond to this letter. Spry never even sent Hornell a copy of his agreement with Metro Factors, Inc., which Spry had signed on March 24, 1994 and which was fully executed on March 30, 1994. On May 26, 1994, Vultaggio met with Spry to discuss termination of their business relationship. Vultaggio presented Spry with a letter of agreement as to the termination, which Spry took with him but did not sign. After some months of futile negotiations by counsel this action by Hornell ensued.

. . . .

Notwithstanding the parties' conflicting contentions concerning the duration and termination of defendants' distributorship, plaintiff has demonstrated a basis for lawfully terminating its contract with defendants in accordance with section 2-609 of the

Uniform Commercial Code. Section 2-609(1) authorizes one party upon "reasonable grounds for insecurity" to "demand adequate assurance of due performance and until he receives such assurance . . . if commercially reasonable suspend any performance for which he has not already received the agreed return." The Official Comment to section 2-609 explains that this

> section rests on the recognition of the fact that the essential purpose of a contract between commercial men is actual performance and they do not bargain merely for a promise, or for a promise plus the right to win a lawsuit and that a continuing sense of reliance and security that the promised performance will be forthcoming when due, is an important feature of the bargain. If either the willingness or the ability of a party to perform declines materially between the time of contracting and the time for performance, the other party is threatened with the loss of a substantial part of what he has bargained for. A seller needs protection not merely against having to deliver on credit to a shaky buyer, but also against having to procure and manufacture the goods, perhaps turning down other customers. Once he has been given reason to believe that the buyer's performance has become uncertain, it is an undue hardship to force him to continue his own performance.

McKinney's Consolidated Laws of NY, Book 62 1/2, UCC § 2-609 Official Comment 1, at 488.

Whether a seller, as the plaintiff in this case, has reasonable grounds for insecurity, is an issue of fact that depends upon various factors, including the buyer's exact words or actions, the course of dealing or performance between the parties, and the nature of the sales contract and the industry. WHITE & SUMMERS, UNIFORM COMMERCIAL CODE, *supra* § 6-2 at 286; *see also, Phibro Energy, Inc. v. Empresa De Polimeros De Sines Sarl*, 720 F. Supp. 312, 322 (S.D.N.Y. 1989); *S & S Inc. v. Meyer*, 478 N.W.2d 857, 863 (Iowa App. 1991); *AMF, Inc. v. McDonald's Corp.*, 536 F.2d 1167, 1170 (7th Cir. 1976). Subdivision (2) defines both "reasonableness" and "adequacy" by commercial rather than legal standards, and the Official Comment notes the application of the good faith standard. WHITE & SUMMERS, *id.*, at 287; McKinney's Consolidated Laws of NY, Book 62 1/2, UCC § 2-609 Official Comment at 488, 489; *Turntables, Inc. v. Gestetner*, 52 A.D.2d 776, 382 N.Y.S.2d 798 (1st Dep't 1976).

Once the seller correctly determines that it has reasonable grounds for insecurity, it must properly request assurances from the buyer. Although the Code requires that the request be made in writing, UCC § 2-609(1), courts have not strictly adhered to this formality as long as an unequivocal demand is made. WHITE & SUMMERS, UNIFORM COMMERCIAL CODE, *supra* § 6-2 at 288; *see, e.g., ARB, Inc. v. E-Systems, Inc.*, 663 F.2d 189 (D.C. Cir. 1980); *Toppert v. Bunge Corp.*, 60 Ill. App. 3d 607, 18 Ill. Dec. 171, 377 N.E.2d 324 (1978); *AMF, Inc. v. McDonald's Corp., supra.* After demanding assurance, the seller must determine the proper "adequate assurance." What constitutes "adequate" assurance of due performance is subject to the same test of commercial reasonableness and factual conditions. MCKINNEY'S CONSOLIDATED LAWS OF NY, Book 62 1/2, UCC § 2-609 Official Comment at 489.

Applying these principles to the case at bar, the overwhelming weight of the evidence establishes that at the latest, by the beginning of 1994, plaintiff had reasonable grounds to be insecure about defendants' ability to perform in the future. Defendants were substantially in arrears almost from the outset of their relationship with plaintiff, had no financing in place, bounced checks, and had failed to sell even a small fraction of the product defendant Spry originally projected.

Reasonable grounds for insecurity can arise from the sole fact that a buyer has fallen behind in his account with the seller, even where the items involved have to do with separate and legally distinct contracts, because this "impairs the seller's expectation of due performance." MCKINNEY'S CONSOLIDATED LAWS OF NY, Book 62 1/2, UCC § 2-609

Official Comment 2, at 488; *see also Waldorf Steel Fabricators, Inc. v. Consolidated Systems, Inc.*, 1996 WL 480902 (S.D.N.Y.) (n.o.r.); *Turntables, Inc. v. Gestetner, supra; American Bronze Corp. v. Streamway Products*, 8 Ohio App. 3d 223, 456 N.E.2d 1295 (1982).

Here, defendants do not dispute their poor payment history, plaintiff's right to demand adequate assurances from them, and that plaintiff made such demands. Rather, defendants claim that they satisfied those demands by the April 15, 1994 telephone conversation between Vultaggio and Richard Worthy of Metro Factors, Inc., followed by Vultaggio's April 18, 1994 letter to Metro, and Metro's payment of $79,316.24 to Hornell, and that thereafter, plaintiff had no right to demand further assurance.

The court disagrees with both plaintiff and defendants in their insistence that only one demand for adequate assurance was made in this case to which there was and could be only a single response. Even accepting defendants' argument that payment by Metro was the sole condition Vultaggio required when he spoke and wrote to Metro, and that such condition was met by Metro's actual payment, the court is persuaded that on May 9, 1994, Hornell had further reasonable grounds for insecurity and a new basis for seeking further adequate assurances.

Defendants cite WHITE & SUMMERS, UNIFORM COMMERCIAL CODE, § 6-2 at 289, for the proposition that "[i]f a party demands and receives specific assurances, then absent a further change of circumstances, the assurances demanded and received are adequate, and the party who has demanded the assurances is bound to proceed." Repeated demands for adequate assurances are within the contemplation of section 2-609. *See* MCKINNEY'S CONSOLIDATED LAWS OF NY, Book 62 1/2, UCC § 2-609 Official Comment at 490.

Here, there was a further change of circumstances. Vultaggio's reported conversation with Worthy on April 15 and his April 25 letter to Metro both anticipate that once payment of defendants' arrears was made, Hornell would release *up to* $300,000 worth of product on the further condition that defendants met the 14 day payment terms. The arrangement, by its terms, clearly contemplated an opportunity for Hornell to test out defendants' ability to make payment within 14-day periods.

By placing a single order worth $390,000 to $450,000 immediately after receipt of Metro's payment, Spry not only demanded a shipment of product which exceeded the proposed limit, but placed Hornell in a position where it would have *no* opportunity learn whether Spry would meet the 14-day payment terms, before Spry again became indebted to Hornell for a very large sum of money.

At this point, neither Spry nor Worthy had fully informed Hornell what assurance of payment Metro would be able to provide. Leaving aside the question whether the factoring arrangement with Metro constituted adequate assurance, Hornell never received any documentation to substantiate Spry's purported agreement with Metro. Although Spry's agreement with Metro was fully executed by the end of March, Spry never gave Hornell a copy of it, not even in response to Hornell's May 10, 1994 demand. The March 27, 1994 letter from Vanguard coincided with the date Spry signed the Metro agreement, but contained only a vague reference to a $1.5 million "revolving credit facility," without mentioning Metro Factors, Inc. Moreover, based on the Vanguard letter, Hornell had expected that payment would be forthcoming, but Spry once again offered only excuses and empty promises.

These circumstances, coupled with information received in early May (on which it reasonably relied) that Spry had misled Hornell about the scope of his operation, created new and more acute grounds for Hornell's insecurity and entitled Hornell to seek further adequate assurance from defendants in the form of a documented line of credit or other guarantee. *Cf. Creusot-Loire Int'l Inc. v. Coppus Engineering Corp.*, 585 F. Supp. 45, 50 (S.D.N.Y. 1983). Defendants' failure to respond constituted a repudiation of the distributorship agreement, which entitled plaintiff to suspend performance and terminate the agreement. UCC § 2-609(4); *Turntables, Inc. v. Gestetner, supra;*

Creusot-Loire Int'l v. Coppus Engineering Corp., supra; AMF, Inc. v. McDonald's Corp., supra; ARB, Inc. v. E Systems, Inc., supra; Toppert v. Bunge Corp., supra; Waldorf Steel Fabricators, Inc. v. Consolidated Systems, Inc., supra.

Even if Hornell had seen Spry's agreement with Metro, in the circumstances of this case, the agreement did not provide the adequate assurance to which plaintiff was entitled in relation to defendants' $390,000 to $450,000 order. Spry admitted that much of the order was to be retained as inventory for the summer, for which there would be no receivables to factor within 14 days. Although the question of whether every aspect of Hornell's May 10 demand for credit documentation was reasonable is a close one, given the entire history of the relationship between the parties, the court determines that the demand was commercially reasonable. This case is unlike *Pittsburgh-Des Moines Steel Co. v. Brookhaven Manor Water Co.*, 532 F.2d 572 (7th Cir. 1976), cited by defendants, in that plaintiff's demand for credit assurances does not modify or contradict the terms of an elaborated written contract.

The court notes in conclusion that its evaluation of the evidence in this case was significantly influenced by Mr. Spry's regrettable lack of credibility. *See Spanier v. New York City Transit Authority*, 222 A.D.2d 219, 634 N.Y.S.2d 122 (1st Dept 1995). The court agrees with plaintiff, that to an extent far greater than was known to Hornell in May 1994, Mr. Spry was not truthful, failed to pay countless other creditors almost as a matter of course, and otherwise engaged in improper and deceptive business practices.

For the foregoing reasons, it is hereby

ORDERED and ADJUDGED that plaintiff Hornell Brewing Co., Inc. have a declaratory judgment that defendants Stephen A. Spry and Arizona Tea Products, Ltd. were duly terminated and have no continuing rights with respect to plaintiff Hornell Brewing Co.'s beverage products in Canada or elsewhere.

PROBLEM 6-1

Sure Cast agrees to manufacture 1,000 cast iron forestry tools known as hoedad collars for Burke's Supply. Payment in full is due from Burke's thirty days after delivery and acceptance of the goods. After Sure Cast commences performance, it learns from other merchants in the trade that Burke's is experiencing substantial financial difficulties that threaten Burke's business. Upon further inquiry, Sure Cast learns that some of Burke's suppliers are receiving payments late, that Burke's has recently changed banks and is rumored to be "overextended" as a result of substantial loans used to fund its business expansion, and Burke's market for selling its products has worsened since the time that Burke's entered into the contract. The word on the street is that Burke's will be lucky to survive this financial distress. Sure Cast is concerned by all of these developments and calls Burke's. Burke's tells Sure Cast that it has not yet defaulted on any of its obligations, although it admits that some "temporary business disturbances" have caused some late payments to its suppliers. Burke's emphasizes that it will be harmed if Sure Cast delays performance or defaults. Burke's admits that it does not have substantial cash on hand at the moment, but states that it has a number of ready cash buyers for the hoedad collars manufactured by Sure Cast, and that it fully expects that immediate sales will more than cover the cost of the Sure Cast contract.

Sure Cast is considering refusing to ship the goods to Burke's, on the theory that Burke's has made clear that Sure Cast is running a substantial risk of not being paid. How do you advise Sure Cast?

2. Excuse for Nonperformance

Just as § 2-302 provides a type of safety valve that empowers judges to refuse to enforce agreed terms that are "unconscionable" at the time the contract is made, the Code provisions concerning excuse and commercial impracticability provide the courts a means to adjust or abrogate altogether the bargain of the parties in light of changes in circumstances after contracting. The crucial inquiry turns on the statutory reference to "impracticability" and the public policies that should attend construction of that term, for in every impracticability case there is one litigant that wants the court to enforce the bargain of the parties and an opposing litigant trying to invoke the deal-avoidance techniques provided in the Code. Consider Professor Gillette's remarks and determine how his perspective might illuminate the cases and problems that follow.

Gillette, *Commercial Rationality and the Duty To Adjust Long-Term Contracts*
69 MINN. L. REV. 521 (1985)[3]

Negotiating Uncertainty in Long-Term Contracts

Whenever two parties enter into a long-term sales agreement, there is a possibility that a subsequent event will occur that is not in the agreement. That event may make the contract much more profitable for one party and much less profitable for the other party. The party for whom the agreement is no longer beneficial may seek to revoke the contract by using the doctrines of frustration, mistake, or impracticability. Courts traditionally have construed these doctrines narrowly and have been reluctant to release parties from their contractual duties. Section 2-615 was drafted to provide courts with a greater degree of flexibility in allowing parties to revoke their agreements. Section 2-615 is based upon the supposition that the parties did not allocate the risk that this particular event would occur, assumed that the event would not occur, and the event has made performance impracticable for one of the parties.

Some commentators have used the flexibility in § 2-615 to argue that courts should require the party who profited from the event to adjust the agreement for the benefit of the other party. These commentators contend that neither party agreed to bear the risk of the unforeseen event, so it would be unfair to make one party bear all of the costs. Modification of the contract would spread the risk fairly between both parties.

Even if a contingency is not addressed explicitly in the contract, it is not necessarily unforeseen. The parties may have recognized the risk, but they may have decided that it was too remote to justify the time and cost of allocating the risk. They may have decided to forego bargaining and, if the remote event occurs, let the loss fall where it may. When the parties rationally have agreed (albeit implicitly) in this manner, the party who profits from the changed circumstances will have a strong argument that it should be allowed the benefit of its bargain without being forced to adjust the agreement for the benefit of the losing party.

PROBLEM 6-2

Showy Cars is a dealer in antique Rolls Royce automobiles. Brendan recently came into a sizable inheritance and decided to indulge himself by purchasing his "dream car." Brendan and Showy quickly reach an agreement for a specified car on Showy's lot, and they then reduce the agreement to a signed writing. Brendan agrees to return on the following day to pay the $285,000 purchase price and to accept delivery of the car. On the following day, Brendan arrived with the required check in hand only to find that vandals had scaled the six-foot fence surrounding Showy's lot and totaled several cars on the lot, including the car that Brendan had agreed to purchase.

Can Brendan sue Showy for breach of contract?

CHAINWORKS, INC. v. WEBCO INDUSTRIES, INC.
United States District Court, Western District of Michigan
2006 U.S. Dist. LEXIS 9194 (2006)

Bell, Chief J.

This dispute arises out of a requirements contract for steel tubing between Plaintiff Chainworks, Inc., and Defendant Webco Industries, Inc., governed by the Uniform Commercial Code. Chainworks seeks a declaration that it has not breached the contract and does not owe approximately $300,000 billed by Webco. The central issue in this case concerns Webco's ability to pass on certain additional costs incurred during the course of the contract. Although Webco offers a variety of creative arguments in support of its position, the Court is not persuaded from the view that this is a simple breach of contract case in which the parties agreed to a fixed and certain price for Chainworks' product requirements for an entire calendar year. As such, Webco could not unilaterally impose a new contract price. Accordingly, for the reasons stated below, Chainworks' motion for summary judgment is granted.

I.

Webco is a steel tubing manufacturer and supplier. Chainworks is a commercial broker of steel tubing which acts as an intermediary between Webco and third-party purchasers. The parties have had a commercial relationship since 1999. This case arises out of the parties' contract for 2004. In November 2004, Webco sent a memorandum regarding pricing for the 2004 calendar year. The memorandum provided price quotations for two types of steel tubing and specified that the prices were "[f]irm for the period 1/1/04 through 12/31/04." Thereafter, following the federal government's removal of steel tariffs on foreign-made steel, Chainworks president, Andy Hinkley, inquired as to whether Webco's 2004 pricing would be affected. Jeff Williams, Webco's vice president of OEM sales, replied,

> The lifting of tariffs is seen as having no effect for the next 12-months. The worldwide market has shifted into a higher gear. Supplies are tightening and pricing is rising — mills now have all customers on allocation. We believe the economy, domestically and internationally, will continue to strengthen and demand, domestically and internationally, will continue to rise.

> The result is that this will have no effect on our thinking for SSID tubing in 2004.

Exhibit I, Pl.'s Br. Summ. J. (Docket # 46). Following this exchange, on December 8, 2003, Chainworks issued a blanket purchase order incorporating the fixed prices provided by Webco. The blanket purchase order specified that it was a "requirements based blanket order." Under this arrangement, Chainworks would make purchases as its needs dictated throughout the year pursuant to the blanket purchase order and Webco would ship manufactured steel tubing to Chainworks' third-party purchaser (Tenneco Canada, Inc.). The blanket purchase order also incorporated Chainworks' published terms and conditions.

During the first week of January, 2004, Webco shipped the first series of steel products to Tenneco. Following the shipment, Webco mailed an invoice to Chainworks seeking payment at the price quoted in both Webco's initial price quotation and Chainworks' blanket purchase order. Webco's invoice also included its own conditions of sale. The conditions of sale included a paragraph stating: "All base prices, together with related extras and deductions, are subject to change without notice, and all orders are accepted subject to prices in effect at the time of shipment." Exhibit Q (the "price adjustment clause"), Def.'s Res. Br. (Docket # 57). Shortly after sending the invoice, Webco notified Chainworks that it was monitoring "dramatic developments in the steel industry" that were creating a "tight steel availability situation as well as dramatically higher prices." Exhibit D, Def.'s Answer (Docket # 6). These "dramatic developments" eventually manifested themselves through a market shift that caused prices to soar. As a result, Wheeling Pittsburgh, Webco's supplier, imposed a raw material surcharge on all steel products and demanded payment by Webco in order to continue the production and shipment of steel. Exhibit B, Def.'s Res. Br. In response, Webco attempted to pass on the surcharge to Chainworks. On January 27, 2004, Jeff Williams notified Andy Hinkley that Webco would be assessing a surcharge on steel products shipped to Chainworks effective February 1, 2004. Webco advised that "[i]n order . . . to maintain an uninterrupted supply of material to Chainworks; I must have, in writing, your acceptance of these charges." Exhibit G, Def.'s Res. Br.

Throughout February, Webco sought Chainworks' acceptance of the surcharge, warning "[i]f Chainworks does not wish to pay the surcharge, we will advise our material supplier that Webco cannot pay the surcharge for Chainworks raw material and we anticipate they will refuse to ship." Exhibit B, Def.'s Res. Br. On March 1, 2004, Hinkley sent the following memorandum to Williams:

> In the interest of maintaining an uninterrupted supply of your products for our customers, we feel that we have no other option but to accept the steel surcharge that you intend to impose on us, as described in your letter dated January 27, 2004. We sincerely hope that you will reconsider straddling us with these additional financial burdens, as we are not likely to obtain similar accommodation from our customers.
>
> Given the current lack of alternatives and in the interest of mitigating our losses, we are making this concession under duress and reserve all rights and remedies that we may otherwise have under our original agreement.

Exhibit S, Pl.'s Br. Summ. J. Thereafter, Webco sent monthly notices of the surcharge amount to be applied to future shipments. Exhibits K — R, Pl.'s Br. Summ. J. Between March and August, Chainworks continued to authorize the manufacture and shipment of products to Tenneco as needed.

On August 23, 2004, Williams notified Hinkley that, in addition to the raw material surcharge, Webco was raising the price of its steel tubing products. Exhibit O, Pl.'s Br. Summ. J. Again, Williams cautioned that "Webco must have your agreement to accept this price revision or we will not be able to continue to order raw material or accept future releases for shipment." *Id.* In a nearly identically worded memorandum to the March 1, 2004 letter, Hinkley agreed to the price increases, explaining that Chainworks believed it was conceding under duress and in order to mitigate its losses. Exhibit T, Pl.'s Br. Summ. J. Once again, Hinkley advised that Chainworks "reserve[d] all rights and remedies that we may otherwise have under our original agreement." *Id.* Thereafter, Chainworks again authorized Webco to manufacture and ship products to Tenneco through December.

Beginning in September and continuing through December, the parties attempted to negotiate a contract for the following year. Although the parties' discussed pricing arrangements for 2005, both parties agree that a contract was never entered into. In addition to the contract negotiations, in December 2004, Chainworks requested that three steel product shipments be sent to Chainworks' warehouse, rather than directly to Tenneco's facility.

On January 7, 2005, Chainworks notified Webco that it had entered into a requirements contract for 2005 with a Korean supplier and would not continue its relationship with Webco. Upon receipt of the final invoice for 2004, Chainworks discounted all surcharges and price increases assessed during the year from its final payment. This amounted to $301,949.78. The parties do not dispute that the amount allegedly owed only encompasses surcharges and price increases assessed during 2004. Chainworks contends that it is not required to pay this amount under the 2004 contract and seeks a declaratory judgment on this issue. Conversely, the failure to pay this amount provides the basis for Webco's counterclaim for breach of contract against Chainworks. Webco also alleges counterclaims for account stated, unjust enrichment, promissory estoppel, and fraudulent and/or negligent misrepresentation. The counterclaims stem from Chainworks' failure to inform Webco that it did not intend to enter into a contract for 2005 as well as Chainworks' alleged stock-piling of products at the end of 2004. Before the Court is Chainworks' motion for summary judgment on its declaratory judgment claim and on Webco's counterclaims.

. . . .

III. Statute of Frauds.

A. Chainworks' Breach of Contract Claim

In its breach of contract claim, Chainworks alleges that Webco breached the 2004 contract by unilaterally imposing the surcharges and price increase. Chainworks' position can be summed up in a relatively simple fashion: a deal is a deal. That is, the parties agreed to a contract that would provide Chainworks with all the steel tubing it required during 2004 at a fixed price. When Webco sought to increase that price, it breached the contract. Accordingly, Chainworks seeks a declaration that it has fulfilled the terms of the original contract and, thus, does not owe the remaining balance.

Against this simple, straightforward analysis, Webco has offered numerous creative arguments, based on various provisions of the UCC and common law, in an attempt to justify its actions and avoid summary judgment. Webco's arguments include the following: 1) that under UCC § 2-207, the parties' contract included a term permitting Webco to alter the contract price, 2) that Chainworks' agreed to the surcharges and price increases, and 3) that the impracticability defense under UCC § 2-615 applies and permits Webco's failure to abide by the original, fixed contract price. Finally, Webco also alleges that Chainworks is barred from any recovery because it did not properly provide notice that it considered the price increase a breach of contract.

After reviewing the record in this case, the parties' briefs, and hearing oral argument, the Court is led to the conclusion that Chainworks' view is correct, as a matter of law, and summary judgment should be entered in its favor on the breach of contract claim. Webco's arguments to the contrary are unavailing. At its essence, this is a simple breach of contract case. The parties entered into a contract under which Webco agreed to provide all of Chainworks' steel tubing needs for 2004 in exchange for a fixed price. After this contract was entered into, Webco attempted to unilaterally alter the price. This was a clear breach of contract and Chainworks is not required to pay the additional cost unilaterally imposed by Webco. A review of Webco's arguments to the contrary reveals that each lacks merit.

. . . .

3. Impracticability

Webco next argues that the surcharge and price increase were permissible because unforeseen market conditions rendered its performance impracticable under the original contract. Section 2-615 of the UCC allows a seller to raise impracticability as a defense in a sales contract. Mich. Comp. Laws § 440.2615; *Cleveland-Cliffs Iron Co. v. Chicago & North Western Transp. Co.*, 581 F. Supp. 1144, 1151 (W.D. Mich. 1984) (Hillman, J.). Section 2-615 provides in pertinent part:

> Delay in delivery or non-delivery in whole or in part by a seller who complies with paragraphs (b) and (c) is not a breach of his duty under a contract for sale if performance as agreed has been made impracticable by the occurrence of a contingency the nonoccurrence of which was a basic assumption on which the contract was made or by compliance in good faith with any applicable foreign or

domestic governmental regulation or order whether or not it later proves to be invalid.

Mich. Comp. Laws § 440.2615. A party asserting the impracticability defense must prove the following: 1) that an unforeseeable event occurred; 2) the nonoccurrence of the event was a basic assumption underlying the agreement; and 3) the event rendered performance impracticable. *Roth Steel Prods. v. Sharon Steel Corp.*, 705 F.2d 134, 149 (6th Cir. 1983) (interpreting Ohio's version of the UCC).

Webco argues that the dramatic rise in the market price for steel in early 2004 was not foreseeable and rendered its performance under its contract with Chainworks impracticable. Webco does not argue that it was unable to deliver product, that it was unable to obtain quality materials, or that there was a severe shortage of available material. Rather, it argues only that, due to the industry-wide surcharge, the cost to procure raw materials rose dramatically. It is abundantly clear to the Court, however, that increased cost, without more, does not support a claim of impracticability. *See Roth Steel Prods.*, 705 F.2d at 149 n.34 ("Increases in the cost of production, however, do not, absent more, support a claim of commercial impracticability."); *Bernia Dist., Inc. v. Bernia Sewing Mach. Co.*, 646 F.2d 434, 439–40 (10th Cir. 1981) ("[C]ost increases alone, though great in extent, do not render a contract impracticable."); *Transatlantic Financing Corp. v. United States*, 363 F.2d 312, 319 (D.C. Cir. 1966); *Eastern Airlines, Inc. v. Gulf Oil Corp.*, 415 F. Supp. 429, 439–40 (S.D. Fla. 1975); Official Comment 4, Mich. Comp. Laws § 440.2615. Moreover, Webco has failed to demonstrate that the shift in the market price was the result of an unforeseen contingency.

The undisputed evidence before the Court shows that the parties knew that the steel market was volatile and that an increase in raw material costs was foreseeable. First, Chainworks has provided a series of press releases from various steel companies announcing the imposition of surcharges due to the increase in raw material costs. *See* Exhibit F, Pl.'s Reply Br. The press releases were issued during December 2003, prior to Webco's acceptance, and explain that the surcharges are being assessed due to rapid increases in raw material prices. Further, the releases describe "recent volatility" in the steel market, a "perfect storm in the market," "enormous cost pressures" on all steel producers, and that "the major topic of conversation in and around the U.S. steel industry" is the rapid increase in raw material costs. The sheer number of press releases filed in this case illustrates that the upward volatility of the market was clearly apparent prior to Webco's acceptance of Chainworks' offer. Further, as a sophisticated business entity and member of the steel industry, Webco was certainly aware of these volatile market conditions and the steps that steel companies were taking in response.

In fact, there is undisputed evidence in the record that Webco was aware of the volatility in the marketplace prior to entering into the contract with Chainworks. In an email dated December 4, 2003, Jeff Williams stated "[t]he worldwide market has shifted into a higher gear. *Supplies are tightening and pricing is rising* — mills now have all customers on allocation." Exhibit I, Pl.'s Br. Summ. J. (emphasis added). Nevertheless, Williams concluded that Webco's fixed pricing for 2004 would remain unchanged. *Id.*

Second, the parties' previous dealings also indicate that they understood that raw material pricing could fluctuate. In mid-2002, the parties attempted to negotiate a long-term agreement that included a pricing adjustment clause that would allow the contract price to rise or fall if the raw material price rose above or fell below a certain percentage of the original contract price. Exhibit E, F, Pl.'s Br. Summ. J. While the parties' negotiations did not result in a long term contract, the discussion of a pricing adjustment clause indicates that the parties were well aware that raw material pricing could fluctuate during the course of their dealings with each other. This is further evidence that the increase in raw material costs was foreseeable prior to the parties' contract.[4]

In response to this evidence, Webco has offered a selection of news articles that it contends shows that the price increase did not occur until January 2004, after the parties entered into their contract. *See* Exhibit T, Pl.'s Res. Br. Rather than creating a genuine issue of fact for trial, the articles simply reinforce the conclusion that the raw material cost increase was foreseeable before the parties' contract. While the articles do indicate that steel pricing increased during January and February 2004, they also describe the historical volatility of the steel market as far back as 1995. According to the articles, steel pricing has fluctuated throughout the late 1990's and into 2003. This is simply further evidence that a market shift was foreseeable prior to the parties' agreement.

Webco has failed to allege a triable issue with respect to the foreseeability of the increased costs. The evidence demonstrates that, prior to the parties' contract, both Webco and Chainworks understood that the steel market was volatile and that steel manufacturers were imposing surcharges due to raw material price increases. Based on this evidence, it is clear that the increased costs incurred by Webco were not unforeseeable and do not support the assertion of the impracticability defense. At best, the evidence shows that while increased costs were foreseeable, Webco either misjudged or did not anticipate the *degree* of the increase. In the midst of this volatile market climate, the parties agreed to a contract that provided for the payment of a fixed, certain price. Webco cannot, after the fact, alter the contract based on impracticability simply because it may have misread the market and entered into a contract which became a greater financial burden than originally expected. *Neal-Cooper Grain Co. v. Texas Gulf Sulfur Co.*, 508 F.2d 283, 294 (7th Cir. 1974) ("The buyer has a right to rely on the party to the contract to supply him with goods regardless of what happens to the market price. That is the purpose for which such contracts are made."); Mich. Comp. Laws § 440.2615 Official Comment 4 ("Neither is a rise or a collapse in the market in itself a justification, for that is exactly the type of business risk which business contracts made at fixed prices are intended to cover."); 1 J. WHITE & R. SUMMERS, UNIFORM COMMERCIAL CODE § 3–10 (4th ed. 1995) (discussing increased costs as a basis for impracticability under § 2-615 and concluding "[i]n our judgment an increase in price, even a radical increase in price, is the thing that contracts are designed to protect against.").

. . . .

5. Conclusion

. . . .

. . . Accordingly, Chainworks' motion for summary judgment on its breach of contract claim is granted and the Court will enter an order declaring that Chainworks does not owe the total amount of the surcharges and price increase.

. . . .

NORTHERN INDIANA PUBLIC SERVICE CO. v. CARBON COUNTY COAL CO.
United States Court of Appeals, Seventh Circuit
799 F.2d 265 (1986)

POSNER, Circuit Judge.

These appeals bring before us various facets of a dispute between Northern Indiana Public Service Company (NIPSCO), an electric utility in Indiana, and Carbon County

---

[4] [9] Moreover, as Chainworks' points out, the negotiation and rejection of the pricing adjustment clause also indicates that the non-occurrence of a market shift was not a "basic assumption on which the contract was made." Mich. Comp. Laws § 440.2615(a). To the contrary, by rejecting the adjustment clause in favor of fixed pricing, the parties assumed the risk that the price could rise or fall during the contract's duration.

Coal Company, a partnership that until recently, owned and operated a coal mine in Wyoming. In 1978, NIPSCO and Carbon County signed a contract whereby Carbon County agreed to sell and NIPSCO to buy, approximately 1.5 million tons of coal every year for 20 years, at a price of $24 a ton, subject to various provisions for escalation which by 1985, had driven the price up to $44 a ton.

NIPSCO's rates are regulated by the Indiana Public Service Commission. In 1983, NIPSCO requested permission to raise its rates to reflect increased fuel charges. Some customers of NIPSCO opposed the increase on the ground that NIPSCO could reduce its overall costs by buying more electrical power from neighboring utilities for resale to its customers and producing less of its own power. Although the Commission granted the requested increase, it directed NIPSCO, in orders issued in December 1983 and February 1984 (the "economy purchase orders"), to make a good faith effort to find, and wherever possible buy from, utilities that would sell electricity to it at prices lower than its costs of internal generation. The Commission added ominously that "the adverse effects of entering into long-term coal supply contracts which do not allow for renegotiation and are not requirement contracts, is a burden which must rest squarely on the shoulders of NIPSCO management." Actually, the contract with Carbon County did provide for renegotiation of the contract price — but one-way renegotiation in favor of Carbon County; the price fixed in the contract (as adjusted from time to time in accordance with the escalator provisions) was a floor. And the contract was indeed not a requirements contract: it specified the exact amount of coal that NIPSCO must take over the 20 years during which the contract was to remain in effect. NIPSCO was eager to have an assured supply of low-sulphur coal and was therefore willing to guarantee both price and quantity.

Unfortunately for NIPSCO, however, as things turned out, it was indeed able to buy electricity at prices below the costs of generating electricity from coal bought under the contract with Carbon County; and because of the "economy purchase orders," of which it had not sought judicial review, NIPSCO could not expect to be allowed by the Public Service Commission to recover in its electrical rates the costs of buying coal from Carbon County. NIPSCO therefore decided to stop accepting coal deliveries from Carbon County, at least for the time being; and on April 24, 1985, it brought this diversity suit against Carbon County in a federal district court in Indiana, seeking a declaration that it was excused from its obligations under the contract either permanently or at least until the economy purchase orders ceased preventing it from passing on the costs of the contract to its ratepayers. In support of this position, it argued that the contract violated section 2(c) of the Mineral Lands Leasing Act of 1920, 30 U.S.C. § 202, because of Carbon County's affiliation with a railroad (Union Pacific), and that in any event, NIPSCO's performance was excused or suspended — either under the contract's *force majeure* clause or under the doctrines of frustration or impossibility — by reason of the economy purchase orders. On May 17, 1985, Carbon County counterclaimed for breach of contract and moved for a preliminary injunction requiring NIPSCO to continue taking delivery under the contract. On June 19, 1985, the district judge granted the preliminary injunction, from which NIPSCO has appealed. Also on June 19, rejecting NIPSCO's argument that it needed more time for pretrial discovery and other trial preparations, the judge scheduled the trial to begin on August 26, 1985. Trial did begin then, lasted for six weeks, and resulted in a jury verdict for Carbon County of $181 million. The judge entered judgment in accordance with the verdict, rejecting Carbon County's argument that in lieu of damages, it should get an order of specific performance requiring NIPSCO to comply with the contract. Upon entering the final judgment, the district judge dissolved the preliminary injunction, and shortly afterward, the mine — whose only customer was NIPSCO — shut down. NIPSCO has appealed from the damage judgment, and Carbon County from the denial of specific performance and from the district judge's order staying execution of the damage judgment without requiring NIPSCO to post a bond guaranteeing payment of the judgment should NIPSCO lose on appeal.

We are left with the following issues to decide: (1) whether the district judge abused his discretion in refusing to give NIPSCO more time to prepare for trial, (2) whether the contract was unenforceable as a violation of the Mineral Lands Leasing Act, (3) whether NIPSCO's obligations under the contract were excused or suspended by virtue of either the *force majeure* clause or (4) the doctrines of frustration or impracticability, (5) whether Carbon County was entitled to specific performance of the contract, and (6) whether NIPSCO should be required to post a bond in order to be allowed to stave off the execution of the damage judgment until the appellate process is over.

. . . .

4. The district judge refused to submit NIPSCO's defenses of impracticability and frustration to the jury, ruling that Indiana law does not allow a buyer to claim impracticability and does not recognize the defense of frustration. Some background (on which see FARNSWORTH, CONTRACTS §§ 9.5–9.7 (1982)) may help make these rulings intelligible. In the early common law, a contractual undertaking unconditional in terms was not excused merely because something had happened (such as an invasion, the passage of a law, or a natural disaster) that prevented the undertaking. *See Paradine v. Jane*, Aleyn 26, 82 Eng. Rep. 897 (K.B. 1647). Excuses had to be written into the contract; this is the origin of *force majeure* clauses. Later, it came to be recognized that negotiating parties cannot anticipate all the contingencies that may arise in the performance of the contract; a legitimate judicial function in contract cases is to interpolate terms to govern remote contingencies — terms the parties would have agreed on explicitly if they had had the time and foresight to make advance provision for every possible contingency in performance. Later still, it was recognized that physical impossibility was irrelevant, or at least inconclusive; a promisor might want his promise to be unconditional, not because he thought he had superhuman powers but because he could insure against the risk of nonperformance better than the promisee, or obtain a substitute performance more easily than the promisee. *See Field Container Corp. v. ICC*, 712 F.2d 250, 257 (7th Cir. 1983); HOLMES, THE COMMON LAW 300 (1881). Thus, the proper question in an "impossibility" case is not whether the promisor could not have performed his undertaking but whether his nonperformance should be excused because the parties, if they had thought about the matter, would have wanted to assign the risk of the contingency that made performance impossible or uneconomical to the promisor or to the promisee; if to the latter, the promisor is excused. Section 2-615 of the Uniform Commercial Code takes this approach. It provides that:

> delay in delivery . . . by a seller . . . is not a breach of his duty under a contract for sale if performance as agreed has been made impracticable by the occurrence of a contingency the non-occurrence of which was a basic assumption on which the contract was made. . . .

Performance on schedule need not be impossible, only infeasible — provided that the event which made it infeasible was not a risk that the promisor had assumed. Notice, however, that the only type of promisor referred to is a seller; there is no suggestion that a buyer's performance might be excused by reason of impracticability. The reason is largely semantic. Ordinarily, all the buyer has to do in order to perform his side of the bargain is pay, and while one can think of all sorts of reasons why, when the time came to pay, the buyer might not have the money, rarely would the seller have intended to assume the risk that the buyer might, whether through improvidence or bad luck, be unable to pay for the seller's goods or services. To deal with the rare case where the buyer or (more broadly) the paying party, might have a good excuse based on some unforeseen change in circumstances, a new rubric was thought necessary, different from "impossibility" (the common law term) or "impracticability" (the Code term, picked up in RESTATEMENT (SECOND) OF CONTRACTS § 261 (1979)), and it received the name "frustration." Rarely is it impracticable or impossible for the payor to pay; but if something has happened to make the performance for which he would be paying worthless to him, an excuse for not paying, analogous to impracticability or impossibility, may be proper. *See* RESTATEMENT, *supra*, § 265, comment a.

The leading case on frustration remains *Krell v. Henry*, 2 K.B. 740 (C.A.). Krell rented Henry a suite of rooms for watching the coronation of Edward VII, but Edward came down with appendicitis and the coronation had to be postponed. Henry refused to pay the balance of the rent and the court held that he was excused from doing so because his purpose in renting had been frustrated by the postponement, a contingency outside the knowledge, or power to influence, of either party. The question was, to which party did the contract (implicitly) allocate the risk? Surely Henry had not intended to insure Krell against the possibility of the coronation's being postponed, since Krell could always relet the room, at the premium rental, for the coronation's new date. So Henry was excused.

NIPSCO is the buyer in the present case, and its defense is more properly frustration than impracticability; but the judge held that frustration is not a contract defense under the law of Indiana. He relied on an Indiana Appellate Court decision which indeed so states, *Ross Clinic, Inc. v. Tabion*, 419 N.E.2d 219, 223 (Ind. App. 1981), but solely on the basis of an old decision of the Indiana Supreme Court, *Krause v. Board of Trustees*, 162 Ind. 278, 283–84, 70 N.E. 264, 265 (1904), that doesn't even discuss the defense of frustration and anyway precedes by years the recognition of the defense by American courts. At all events, the facts of the present case do not bring it within the scope of the frustration doctrine, so we need not decide whether the Indiana Supreme Court would embrace the doctrine in a suitable case.

For the same reason, we need not decide whether a *force majeure* clause should be deemed a relinquishment of a party's right to argue impracticability or frustration, on the theory that such a clause represents the integrated expression of the parties' desires with respect to excuses based on supervening events; or whether such a clause either in general or as specifically worded in this case covers any different ground from these defenses; or whether a buyer can urge impracticability under section 2-615 of the Uniform Commercial Code, which applies to this suit. Regarding the last of these questions, although the text says "seller," Official Comment 9 to the section says that in some circumstances "the reason of the present section may well apply and entitle the buyer to the exemption," and many courts have done just that. *See, e.g.*, *Nora Springs Coop. Co. v. Brandau*, 247 N.W.2d 744 (Iowa 1976); *Lawrance v. Elmore Bean Warehouse, Inc.*, 108 Idaho 892, 894, 702 P.2d 930, 932 (Idaho Ct. App. 1985); *Northern Illinois Gas Co. v. Energy Coop., Inc.*, *supra*, 122 Ill. App. 3d at 954, 461 N.E.2d at 1060 (1984). The rub is that Indiana has not adopted the "Official Comments" to the UCC. It has its own official comments, and they seem critical of Official Comment 9: "Comment 9 discusses 'exemption' for the buyer, but the text of the section is applicable only to sellers." Burns Ind. Stat. Ann. § 26-1-2-615, Ind. Comment. It may be, therefore, that buyers cannot use section 2-615 in Indiana. But it is not clear that this has substantive significance. Section 1-103 of the Uniform Commercial Code authorizes the courts to apply common law doctrines to the extent consistent with the Code — this is the basis on which NIPSCO is able to plead frustration as an alternative defense to section 2-615; and the essential elements of frustration and of impracticability are the same. With section, 2-615 compare RESTATEMENT, *supra*, §§ 261 (impossibility/impracticability) and 265 (frustration); and see *id.*, § 265, comment a. NIPSCO gains nothing by pleading section 2-615 of the Uniform Commercial Code as well as common law frustration, and thus, loses nothing by a ruling that buyers in Indiana cannot use section 2-615.

Whether or not Indiana recognizes the doctrine of frustration, and whether or not a buyer can ever assert the defense of impracticability under section 2-615 of the Uniform Commercial Code, these doctrines, so closely related to each other and to *force majeure* as well, see *International Minerals & Chemical Corp. v. Llano, Inc.*, 770 F.2d 879, 885–87 (10th Cir. 1985), cannot help NIPSCO. All are doctrines for shifting risk to the party better able to bear it, either because he is in a better position to prevent the risk from materializing or because he can better reduce the disutility of the risk (as by insuring) if the risk does occur. Suppose a grower agrees before the growing season to sell his crop to a grain elevator, and the crop is destroyed by blight and the grain elevator sues. Discharge is ordinarily allowed in such cases. *See, e.g., Matousek v. Galligan*, 104 Neb. 731, 178 N.W. 510 (1920); *Pearce-Young-Angel Co. v. Charles R. Allen, Inc.*, 213 S.C. 578, 50 S.E.2d 698 (1948); *cf. Olbum v. Old Home Manor, Inc.*, 313 Pa. Super. 99, 459 A.2d 757 (1983). The grower has every incentive to avoid the blight; so if it occurs, it probably could not have been prevented; and the grain elevator, which buys from a variety of growers not all of whom will be hit by blight in the same growing season, is in a better position to buffer the risk of blight than the grower is.

Since impossibility and related doctrines are devices for shifting risk in accordance with the parties' presumed intentions, which are to minimize the costs of contract performance, one of which is the disutility created by risk, they have no place when the contract explicitly assigns a particular risk to one party or the other. As we have already noted, a fixed-price contract is an explicit assignment of the risk of market price increases to the seller and the risk of market price decreases to the buyer, and the assignment of the latter risk to the buyer is even clearer where, as in this case, the contract places a floor under price but allows for escalation. If, as is also the case here, the buyer forecasts the market incorrectly and therefore, finds himself locked into a disadvantageous contract, he has only himself to blame and so cannot shift the risk back to the seller by invoking impossibility or related doctrines. *See* FARNSWORTH, *supra*, at 680 and n.18; WHITE & SUMMERS, HANDBOOK OF THE LAW UNDER THE UNIFORM COMMERCIAL CODE 133 (2d ed. 1980). It does not matter that it is an act of government that may have made the contract less advantageous to one party. *See, e.g., Connick v. Teachers Ins. & Annuity Ass'n*, 784 F.2d 1018, 1022 (9th Cir. 1986); *Waegemann v. Montgomery Ward & Co.*, 713 F.2d 452, 454 (9th Cir. 1983). Government these days is a pervasive factor in the economy and among the risks that a fixed-price contract allocates between the parties is that of a price change induced by one of government's manifold interventions in the economy. Since "the very purpose of a fixed price agreement is to place the risk of increased costs on the promisor (and the risk of decreased costs on the promisee)," the fact that costs decrease steeply (which is in effect what happened here — the cost of generating electricity turned out to be lower than NIPSCO thought when it signed the fixed-price contract with Carbon County) cannot allow the buyer to walk away from the contract. *In re Westinghouse Electric Corp. Uranium Contracts Litigation*, 517 F. Supp. 440, 453 (E.D. Va. 1981); *cf. Neal-Cooper Grain Co. v. Texas Gulf Sulphur Co.*, 508 F.2d 283, 293 (7th Cir. 1974). To summarize, the appeal from the grant of the preliminary injunction is dismissed as moot; the other orders appealed from are affirmed. No costs will be awarded in this court, since we have turned down Carbon County's appeals as well as NIPSCO's.

SO ORDERED.

QUESTIONS

1. Why couldn't NIPSCO prevail by arguing that its performance was rendered impracticable "by compliance in good faith with any applicable . . . governmental regulation," as provided in § 2-615(a)?

2. As the preceding cases demonstrate, impracticability (by express provision of Articles 2 and 2A), frustration (per § 1-103, by operation of supplementary principles), and force majeure (by contract provision) all address, depending on the court's view, at least similar and perhaps identical concerns. How are the three interrelated? That is, do

they overlap to such an extent that something is "crowded-out," or could they be viewed as concerning related, but distinct, issues?

PROBLEM 6-3

Stargaze Farms cultivates roses in Southern California that are renowned and highly sought after. Boron Group is a large insurance company interested in entering a float in the annual New Year's Day Rose Bowl Parade. Boron reaches an agreement with Stargaze to purchase 10,000 carnation roses to be grown on Stargaze's property for use in constructing its parade float.

First Scenario: Assume that half of Stargaze's growing field is rendered unusable for that year when a small asteroid slams into the earth. Stargaze plans to cultivate the roses on the remaining half of its field. Stargaze informs you that it has four corporate customers, each of whom have contracted to purchase 10,000 carnation roses. However, due to the meteor strike, Stargaze's output this year will only be 20,000 roses rather than 40,000 roses.

What do you advise Stargaze to do? What are Boron's rights in this situation?

Second Scenario: Now assume that after the parties entered into their contract, the parade is cancelled by local government ordinance due to a severe oil shortage caused by tensions in the Middle East; television coverage will be limited to the football game.

Boron calls you and asks if it still must purchase the 10,000 carnation roses. Stargaze has already informed Boron that the price of roses has plummeted, and that there is no possibility of reselling the flowers to another purchaser for a reasonable price. The roses are ready for delivery.

What do you tell Boron?

B.   TENDER AND BREACH

If there has been no repudiation or justified refusal to perform, the seller will tender goods. In the event that the seller's tender is nonconforming (for example, if the delivery is late, the goods are not as specified in the agreement, etc.), the seller would be breaching its obligations. However, the Code provides a somewhat complicated vocabulary to deal with the respective rights and obligations of the parties upon tender.

The correlative rights and duties regarding tender can be summarized briefly, and are set out in greater detail below. The seller has the obligation to make a "perfect tender," which means that substantially complying with the contract requirements is not sufficient. If a seller fails to make a perfect tender, the buyer has the right to "reject" the goods, which effectively pushes them back to the seller and relieves the buyer of any further obligation for the moment. However, the seller then has a right to "cure" the rejected shipment under certain circumstances, which is accomplished by tendering conforming goods to the buyer.

Despite a non-conforming tender, the buyer might "accept" the goods (either purposefully or inadvertently). If it accepts, under certain circumstances the buyer may "revoke" the acceptance and have the same rights as if it had rejected the goods. If the buyer has finally accepted nonconforming goods, it loses the right to force the goods back to the seller, but it does have the right to sue for damages. After Professor Whaley's introduction to these issues, the following subsections walk through this chronological sequence of tender, rejection, cure, acceptance, and revocation.

1.   Proper Tender

Whaley, *Tender, Acceptance, Rejection, And Revocation — The U.C.C.'s "TARR"-Baby*
24 DRAKE L. REV. 52, 52, 78 (1974)[5]

If a lawyer's practice occasionally leads him into the Uniform Commercial Code (UCC), he may find himself facing the Code's rules concerning tender, acceptance, rejection, and revocation. These rules, found in Article 2, Part 6 of the UCC, will hereafter be referred to acronymously as the "TARR" sections. As the lawyer looks at the TARR sections, he may conclude that they state absolutes he may rely on to solve his dilemma. Under section 2-601, the seller must make a "perfect" *tender*. If he does not, buyer may *reject* for any reason, or buyer may *accept* the defective tender and sue for breach of warranty. If buyer accepts and *then* discovers a substantial non-conformity, buyer may *revoke* his acceptance *vis-a-vis* section 2-608. But, like Chandler's tar-baby, the TARR sections do not quite deliver the clean result they promise on first examination. As a result of court construction and supplementary Code provisions, seller's tender can be quite imperfect and still not give buyer a right of rejection. And buyer's post-tender remedies (rejection, acceptance plus warranty breach damages, and revocation of acceptance) depend upon his careful compliance with statutory duties or they are lost.

The Code's TARR rules are complicated and frequently ambiguous, but they have not proved insurmountable to courts bent on doing justice to the parties before them. It is a rare TARR decision that offends the reader's sensibilities. The attorney faced with a TARR problem should stop and ask himself questions that have to do with the basic equities of the situation. Has the client behaved in a commercially-reasonable fashion? Both the attorney for the seller and the buyer should begin their analysis of TARR cases by asking why the buyer *really* rejected/revoked? If it was because he was truly unhappy with the goods, he will probably win the lawsuit unless his standards are unreasonably high. But if it was because the market was dropping and he wanted out of what had become a financially-unprofitable deal, the buyer stands little chance of finding legal solace in the UCC In the *Zoss* case, the seller's attorney at one point, wrote the Zosses and suggested that the reason they wanted out of the contract was that they had found they could not afford a sports car (they were outraged at the suggestion). Had this been true they would have been ill-advised to sue. The reader who reviews this article will note how often I refer to "common sense" as the quasi-legal test for the courts' resolution of these issues. Only after an attorney has gotten the answers to the basic "common sense" questions can he or she look to the TARR sections of the Uniform Commercial Code and find something other than a tar-baby.

That predisposition, focus on the underlying equities, goes a long way toward making the tender, acceptance, rejection, and revocation provisions of Articles 2 and 2A accessible. So long as you may refer to your sense of equity in order to see whether a statutory analysis reaches the proper result, you can develop some degree of confidence through the apposite provisions.

a.   The "perfect tender" rule

You might recall from contracts that a party is not relieved of its obligation to perform under a contract if the other party has tendered substantial performance. Article 2 rejects the notion of substantial performance as a general rule, and adopts what is known as the "perfect tender" rule. As you might expect, there are statutory-based exceptions and judicial exceptions to this rule.

ALASKA PACIFIC TRADING CO. v. EAGON FOREST PRODUCTS, INC.
Washington Court of Appeals
933 P.2d 417 (1997)

. . . .

FACTS

ALPAC and Eagon are both corporations engaged in importing and exporting raw logs. In April 1993, Setsuo Kimura, ALPAC's president, and C.K. Ahn, Eagon's vice president, entered into a contract under which ALPAC would ship about 15,000 cubic meters of logs from Argentina to Korea between the end of July and the end of August 1993. Eagon agreed to purchase the logs. In the next few months, the market for logs began to soften, making the contract less attractive to Eagon. ALPAC became concerned that Eagon would try to cancel the contract. Kimura and Ahn began a series of meetings and letters, apparently in an effort to assure ALPAC that Eagon would purchase the logs.

At Eagon, the home office was troubled by the drop in timber prices and initially withheld approval of the shipment. Ahn sent numerous internal memoranda to the home office to the effect that the corporation may not wish to go through with the deal, given the drop in timber prices, but that accepting the logs was "inevitable" under the contract. On August 30, Ahn sent a letter to the home office stating that he would attempt to avoid acceptance of the logs, but that it would be difficult and suggesting that they hold ALPAC responsible for shipment delay.

On August 23, Eagon received a faxed latter from ALPAC suggesting that the price and volume of the contract be reduced. Eagon did not respond to the fax. During a business meeting soon after, Kimura asked Ahn whether he intended to accept the logs. Ahn admitted that he was having trouble getting approval. Kimura thereafter believed that Eagon would not accept the shipment.

ALPAC eventually canceled the vessel that it had reserved for the logs because it believed that Eagon was canceling the contract. The logs were not loaded or shipped by August 31, 1993, but Ahn and Kimura continued to discuss the contract into September. On September 7, Ahn told Kimura that he would continue to try to convince headquarters to accept the delivery. Ahn also indicated that he did not want Kimura to sell the logs to another buyer. The same day, Ahn sent a letter to Eagon's head office indicating that "the situation of our supplier is extremely grave" and that Eagon should consider accepting the shipment in September or October.

By September 27, ALPAC had not shipped the logs. It sent a final letter to Eagon stating that Eagon had breached the contract because it failed to take delivery of the logs. Eagon's president, L.R. Haan, responded to the letter, stating that there was "no contract" because ALPAC's breach excused Eagon's performance. ALPAC filed a complaint for breach of contract in King County Superior Court. Eagon brought a motion for summary judgment, arguing that it did not breach but that ALPAC breached by failing to deliver the logs. The trial court granted the motion and dismissed ALPAC's claims. ALPAC's motion for reconsideration was denied.

DISCUSSION

. . . .

ALPAC Breached by Failing to Timely Deliver Logs

ALPAC's first contention is that it did not breach the contract by failing to timely deliver the logs because time of delivery was not a material term of the contract. ALPAC relies on common law contract cases to support its position that, when the parties have not indicated that time is of the essence, late delivery is not a material breach which excuses the buyer's duty to accept the goods. *See Cartozian & Sons, Inc. v. Ostruske-Murphy, Inc.*, 64 Wn.2d 1, 390 P.2d 548 (1964); *Scott Paper Co. v. City of Anacortes*, 90 Wn.2d 19, 578 P.2d 1292 (1978).[6] However, as a contract for the sale of goods, this contract is governed by the Uniform Commercial Code, Article II (UCC II) which replaced the common law doctrine of material breach, on which ALPAC relies, with the "perfect tender" rule. Under this rule, "if the goods or the tender of delivery fail in any respect to conform to the contract, the buyer may . . . reject the whole." RCW 62A.2-601(a). Both the plain language of the rule and the official comments clearly state that, if the tender of the goods differs from the terms of the contract in any way, the seller breaches the contract and the buyer is released from its duty to accept the goods. *Moulton Cavity & Mold, Inc. v. Lyn-Flex Indus., Inc.*, 396 A.2d 1024 (Me. 1979) (holding that the "perfect tender" rule applies to time of tender). ALPAC does not dispute that the contract specified a date for shipment or that the logs were not shipped by that date. Thus, under the applicable "perfect tender" rule, ALPAC breached its duty under the contract and released Eagon from its duty to accept the logs.

NOTES AND QUESTIONS

1. Is the perfect tender rule of § 2-601 efficient? When might it yield wasteful results?

2. What good policy reasons militate in favor of a perfect tender rule with regard to the sale of goods? Are those same policies served, and to the same extent, in a lease contract? *See* UCC § 2A-509(1). Would it matter whether the lessor generally rented used goods rather than new goods?

3. Under the CISG, once the seller has delivered the goods, the buyer has an immediate right to declare the contract avoided only if there has been a fundamental breach. Thus, the buyer's right to undo the transaction and throw the goods back on the seller will turn on the degree of injury caused by the non-conformity. *See* CISG Article 49(1). Obviously, this approach is less protective of the buyer's interests than is UCC § 2-601, which permits a buyer to reject and cancel the contract if the goods deviate from the contract "in any respect."

The Article 25 definition of "fundamental breach" is applicable to both sellers and buyers and is one of the key concepts on which the remedial structure of the CISG is built. Although Article 25 is merely a definition article, it is central to the application of other articles of the CISG. Thus, "fundamental breach" triggers the aggrieved party's right to terminate the contract under Article 49 (avoidance by the buyer), Article 64 (avoidance by the seller), Article 51(2) (avoidance by the buyer when the seller has delivered only a part of the goods or only a part of the goods is non-conforming), Article 72 (avoidance for anticipatory breach), and Article 73 (avoidance in the case of an installment contract). The concept is also significant in determining whether a buyer is entitled to the remedy of specific performance under Article 46 and in allocating the risk of loss following casualty to the goods. *See* Article 70.

---

[6] [2] ALPAC also cites to RCW 62A.2-504, and several cases applying that section, for the proposition that the seller's breach must cause material delay or loss before the buyer's performance is excused. But that provision refers only to forming a proper shipment contract or notifying the buyer that the goods have been shipped. It does not negate the perfect tender rule. ALPAC also cites to several cases which purport to excuse the seller from complying with the perfect tender rule. For example, it cites *D.P. Technology Corp. v. Sherwood Tool, Inc.*, 751 F. Supp. 1038 (D. Conn. 1990), for the proposition that the perfect tender rule does not apply to the time of delivery. Because Connecticut follows the minority rule which requires a showing of prejudice, *D.P. Tech.* does not apply here. ALPAC also cites *Ramirez v. Autosport*, 88 N.J. 277, 440 A.2d 1345 (1982), which holds that, while the perfect tender rule applies, the seller has the right to cure within a reasonable time before the contract is terminated. However, ALPAC does not argue that it attempted to cure; thus, *Ramirez* is inapplicable.

b.   Qualifying the perfect tender rule

Most courts find that the perfect tender rule of Article 2 is not subject to exception, except as expressly provided in Article 2. However, some courts have responded to harsh results by fashioning exceptions. Is the following case persuasive? Is there a better argument to support the court's holding?

DP TECHNOLOGY v. SHERWOOD TOOL, INC.
United States District Court, District of Connecticut
751 F. Supp. 1038 (1990)

NEVAS, District Judge.

In this action based on diversity jurisdiction, the plaintiff seller, D.P. Technology ("DPT"), a California corporation, sues the defendant buyer, Sherwood Tool, Inc. ("Sherwood"), a Connecticut corporation, alleging a breach of contract for the purchase and sale of a computer system. Now pending is the defendant's motion to dismiss, pursuant to Rule 12(b)(6), Fed. R. Civ. P., for failure to state a claim upon which relief can be granted. For the reasons that follow, the defendant's motion to dismiss is denied.

I.

A.

The facts of this case can be easily summarized. On January 24, 1989, the defendant entered into a written contract to purchase a computer system, including hardware, software, installation, and training, from the plaintiff. The complaint alleges that the computer system was "specifically" designed for the defendant and is not readily marketable. The contract, executed on January 24, 1989, incorporates the delivery term set forth in the seller's Amended Letter of January 17, 1989 stating that the computer system would be delivered within ten to twelve weeks. The delivery period specified in the contract ended on April 18, 1989. The software was delivered on April 12, 1989 and the hardware was delivered on May 4, 1989. On May 9, 1989, the defendant returned the merchandise to the plaintiff, and has since refused payment for both the software and the hardware. Thus, the plaintiff alleges that the defendant breached the contract by refusing to accept delivery of the goods covered by the contract while the defendant argues that it was rather the plaintiff who breached the contract by failing to make a timely delivery.

*   *   *

II.

Because the contract between the parties was a contract for the sale of goods,[7] the law governing this transaction is to be found in Article 2 of the Uniform Commercial Code ("UCC"); Conn. Gen. Stat. §§ 42a-2-101 *et seq.* In its motion to dismiss, the defendant argues that the plaintiff fails to state a claim upon which relief can be granted because the plaintiff breached the contract which provided for a delivery period of ten to twelve weeks from the date of the order, January 24, 1989. Since the delivery period ended on April 18, 1989, the May 4 hardware delivery was 16 days late. The defendant contends that because the plaintiff delivered the hardware after the contractual deadline, the late delivery entitled the defendant to reject delivery, since a seller is required to tender goods in conformance with the terms set forth in a contract. UCC § 2-301; Conn. Gen. Stat. § 42a-2-301.

---

[7] [4] Computer systems, including software, have been interpreted to be goods rather than services and thus subject to the Uniform Commercial Code. [Citations omitted.]

In its memorandum in opposition, the plaintiff contends that the defendant waived the original delivery schedule. The plaintiff points to its allegation in the complaint that it designed and developed the computer system pursuant to the contract, Complaint ¶ 3-6. and argues that, in designing and developing a "specifically designed" computer system, consultations with the defendant took place which resulted in adjustment of the delivery schedule, and that the defendant waived the 10–12 week delivery requirement. In *Bradford Novelty Co. v. Technomatic*, 142 Conn. 166, 170, 112 A.2d 214, 216 (1955) (pre-Code), where the buyer acquiesced to a delay in delivery, the court found that the buyer "by its conduct, waived its right to strict compliance with the provisions of the contract as to time of performance." In the instant case, however, the plaintiff failed to allege its waiver claim in the complaint. Consequently, the defendant's motion to dismiss cannot be denied on a claim of waiver.

The plaintiff also states that even if the computers were delivered late, the buyer could not reject the goods pursuant to Conn. Gen. Stat. § 42a-2-602 because the parties had an installment contract. The plaintiff contends that the contract was an installment one, which authorizes the delivery of goods in separate lots to be separately accepted, as illustrated by the separate deliveries of software and hardware. A buyer may reject an installment only if the non-conformity substantially impairs the value of the goods. Conn. Gen. Stat. § 42a-2-612(2)–(3). The defendant has not asserted that the late delivery substantially reduced the computer system's value. Since the allegations in the complaint must be construed in favor of the nonmoving party in a motion to dismiss, if an installment contract was alleged, then UCC Section 2-601 would be superseded by UCC Section 2-612. However, the complaint lacks any reference to an installment contract. Therefore, the defendant's motion to dismiss cannot be denied on the grounds that there was an installment contract.

In addition, the plaintiff argues that the defendant relies on the perfect tender rule, allowing buyers to reject for any nonconformity with the contract. Plaintiff points out that the defendant has not cited one case in which a buyer rejected goods solely because of a late delivery, and that the doctrine of "perfect tender" has been roundly criticized. While it is true that the perfect tender rule has been criticized by scholars principally because it allowed a dishonest buyer to avoid an unfavorable contract on the basis of an insubstantial defect in the seller's tender, *Ramirez v. Autosport*, 88 N.J. 277, 283–85, 440 A.2d 1345, 1348–49 (1982); *Moulton Cavity & Mold, Inc. v. Lyn-Flex Indus., Inc.*, 396 A.2d 1024, 1027 (Me. 1979); E. PETERS, COMMERCIAL TRANSACTIONS 33–37 (1971) (even before enactment of the UCC, the perfect tender rule was in decline), the basic tender provision of the Uniform Commercial Code continued the perfect tender policy developed by the common law and embodied in the Uniform Sales Act. Section 2-601 states that with certain exceptions, the buyer has the right to reject "if the goods or the tender of delivery fail *in any respect* to conform to the contract." (emphasis supplied). Conn. Gen. Stat. § 42a-2-601. The courts that have considered the issue have agreed that the perfect tender rule has survived the enactment of the Code. *See, e.g.*, . . . *Moulton Cavity & Mold, Inc. v. Lyn-Flex Indus., Inc.*, 396 A.2d 1024, 1027–28 (1979) (holding that the doctrine of substantial performance "has no application to a contract for the sale of goods"). . . .

These courts have thus found that the tender must be perfect in the context of the perfect tender rule in the sense that the proffered goods must conform to the contract in every respect. Connecticut, however, appears in this regard to be the exception. Indeed, in the one Connecticut case interpreting 2-601, *Franklin Quilting Co., Inc. v. Orfaly*, 1 Conn. App. 249, 251, 470 A.2d 1228, 1229 (1984), in a footnote, the Appellate Court stated that "the 'perfect tender rule' requires a *substantial nonconformity* to the contract before a buyer may rightfully reject the goods." *Id.* at 1229 n.3, citing WHITE & SUMMERS, UNIFORM COMMERCIAL CODE (2d Ed.), section 8-3 (emphasis supplied). Thus, the Connecticut Appellate Court has adopted "the White and Summers construction of 2-601 as in substance a rule that does not allow rejection for insubstantial breach such as a short delay causing no damage." *Id.* (3d Ed.) section 8-3. *See also National Fleet Supply,*

Inc. v. Fairchild, 450 N.E.2d 1015, 1019 n.4 (Ind. App. 1983) (despite UCC's apparent insistence on perfect tender, it is generally understood that rejection is not available in circumstances where the goods or delivery fail in some small respect to conform to the terms of the sales contract (citing WHITE & SUMMERS)); *McKenzie v. Alla-Ohio Coals, Inc.*, 29 U.C.C. Rep. Serv. 852, 856–57 (D.D.C. 1979) (there is substantial authority that where a buyer has suffered no damage, he should not be allowed to reject goods because of an insubstantial nonconformity).

As noted above, a federal court sitting in diversity must apply the law of the highest court of the state whose law applies. Since this court has determined that Connecticut law governs, the next task is to estimate whether the Connecticut Supreme Court would affirm the doctrine of substantial nonconformity. . . . As noted, the weight of authority is that the doctrine of substantial performance does not apply to the sale of goods. However, as noted by White and Summers, in none of the cases approving of perfect rather than substantial tender was the nonconformity insubstantial, such as a short delay of time where no damage is caused to the buyer. WHITE & SUMMERS, UNIFORM COMMERCIAL CODE (3d Ed.), section 8-3 n.8. In the instant case, there is no claim that the goods failed to conform to the contract. Nor is there a claim that the buyer was injured by the 16-day delay. There is, however, a claim that the goods were specially made, which might affect the buyer's ability to resell. Thus, Connecticut's interpretation of 2-601 so as to mitigate the harshness of the perfect tender rule reflects the consensus of scholars that the rule is harsh and needs to be mitigated. Indeed, Summers and White state that the rule has been so "eroded" by the exceptions in the Code that "relatively little is left of it; the law would be little changed if 2-601 gave the right to reject only upon 'substantial' non-conformity," especially since the Code requires a buyer or seller to act in good faith. R. SUMMERS & J. WHITE, UNIFORM COMMERCIAL CODE (3d Ed. 1988), 8–3, at 357. *See also Alden Press Inc. v. Block & Co., Inc.*, 123 Ill. Dec. 26, 30, 173 Ill. App. 3d 251, 527 N.E.2d 489, 493 (1988) (notwithstanding the perfect tender rule, the reasonableness of buyer's rejection of goods and whether such rejection of goods is in good faith are ultimately matters for the trier of fact); *Printing Center of Texas v. Supermind Pub. Co.*, 669 S.W.2d 779, 784 (Tex. App. 1984) (if the evidence establishes any nonconformity, the buyer is entitled to reject the goods as long as it is in good faith); *Neumiller Farms, Inc. v. Cornett*, 368 So. 2d 272, 275 (Ala. 1979) (claim of dissatisfaction with delivery of goods so as to warrant their rejection must be made in good faith, rather than in an effort to escape a bad bargain). A rejection of goods that have been specially manufactured for an insubstantial delay where no damage is caused is arguably not in good faith.

Although the Connecticut Supreme Court has not yet addressed the issue of substantial nonconformity, it has stated, in a precode case, *Bradford Novelty Co. v. Technomatic*, 142 Conn. 166, 170, 112 A.2d 214, 216 (1955), that although "[t]he time fixed by the parties for performance is, at law, deemed of the essence of the contract," where, as here, goods have been specially manufactured, "the time specified for delivery is less likely to be considered of the essence . . . [since] in such a situation there is a probability of delay, and the loss to the manufacturer is likely to be great if the buyer refuses to accept and pay because of noncompliance with strict performance." *Id. But see Marlowe v. Argentine Naval Comm'n*, 808 F.2d 120, 124 (D.C. Cir. 1986) (buyer within its rights to cancel a contract for 6-day delay in delivery since "time is of the essence in contracts for the sale of goods") (citing *Norrington v. Wright*, 115 U.S. 188, 203, 29 L. Ed. 366, 6 S. Ct. 12, 14 (1885) ("In the contracts of merchants, time is of the essence.")

After reviewing the case law in Connecticut, this court finds that in cases where the nonconformity involves a delay in the delivery of specially manufactured goods, the law in Connecticut requires substantial nonconformity for a buyer's rejection under 2-601, and precludes a dismissal for failure to state a claim on the grounds that the perfect tender rule, codified at 2-601, demands complete performance. Rather, Connecticut law requires a determination at trial as to whether a 16-day delay under these facts constituted a substantial nonconformity.

Conclusion

For the foregoing reasons, the defendant's rule 12(b)(6) motion to dismiss this one count complaint is denied.

SO ORDERED

c. The "substantial performance" standard in installment contracts

Article 2 provides an exception to the perfect tender rule in the case of installment contracts. As you read the next case, consider the characteristics of installment sales that provide the basis for refusing to permit the seller to impose nonconforming goods on a buyer in a single delivery contract, but permitting that right to the seller under certain circumstances in installment contracts. Keep in mind that the measure of the seller's right to compel the buyer's acceptance of the goods is a correlative to the buyer's duty to accept.

PHOENIX COLOR CORP. v. KRAUSE AMERICA, INC.
United States Court of Appeals, Fourth Circuit
25 F. Appx. 133 (2001)

. . . .

Before WILKINSON, CHIEF JUDGE, and WILLIAMS and MOTZ, CIRCUIT JUDGES.

OPINION

PER CURIAM.

Phoenix Color Corporation filed suit against Krause America, Inc., from which it purchased eight technologically advanced printing plate-making machines. Phoenix Color asserted claims for breach of warranty and breach of contract based on alleged defects in the first three machines. The district court awarded Phoenix Color $1,899,257.00 in damages as a result of pre-trial orders and the jury's findings, but refused to grant prejudgment interest. Krause America appeals and Phoenix Color cross-appeals. For the reasons that follow, we affirm the judgment of the district court.

I.

Phoenix Color Corporation is a manufacturer in the high resolution printing industry. It produces books and book components, including book jackets, paperback covers, and pre-printed case covers. The production process begins in the pre-press department with the creation of images on printing plates. The plates are then mounted onto a printing press to generate repeat impressions of the plated image. Until recently, such plates were prepared through the use of film. The advent of computer-to-plate ("CTP") technology, however, has rendered film unnecessary in the production of printing plates. The technology uses computer-guided lasers, allowing printers to burn images directly from computer files onto the plates. This reduces press down time and improves image quality over that produced with film.

This diversity action arises out of Phoenix Color's purchase of eight CTP plate-making machines from Krause America, Inc. in October 1997, for a price of approximately $3.5 million. As a result of alleged chronic failures and defects in the first three such machines Krause America installed at Phoenix Color's facilities ("CTP 1, 2, and 3"), as well as Krause America's refusal to take back the machines, Phoenix Color filed suit in the Circuit Court of Maryland for Washington County. It asserted claims for breach of warranty and breach of contract. Krause America removed the case to the United States District Court for the District of Maryland. It also filed counterclaims for breach of contract and anticipatory breach of contract based on Phoenix Color's failure to pay the full price for previously installed CTP machines and its refusal to accept future deliveries on order. After extensive discovery, the parties filed cross-motions for summary judgment.

On January 3, 2000, the district court granted Phoenix Color partial summary judgment. In relevant part, the court first held that Phoenix Color did not make an effective rejection of CTP 1, 2, or 3 under § 2-602 of the Connecticut version of the Uniform Commercial Code ("UCC"). Second, the court determined that Phoenix Color failed to provide timely notice necessary to revoke its acceptance of CTP 1, 2, and 3 under § 2-608. Third, the court concluded that defects in CTP 1, 2, and 3 resulted in breach of the implied warranty of merchantability under § 2-314. Fourth, the court held that the parties had entered into an installment contract under § 2-612 for the sale of eight CTP machines. Fifth, the court concluded that the jury would have to decide whether the problems with CTP 1, 2, and 3 so substantially impaired the value of the entire contract as to constitute breach of the whole contract, justifying Phoenix Color's cancellation of the remaining orders for five machines. Finally, the court held that Phoenix Color did not violate the UCC's obligation of good faith and was not conspiring with the substitute supplier it eventually engaged.

In response to Phoenix Color's motion for reconsideration, the district court held that Phoenix Color had properly revoked acceptance of CTP 1, 2, and 3. The court further amended its ruling in response to Krause America's request for further reconsideration, holding that CTP 1 was not part of the installment contract and that the jury would have to decide whether the final two machines ordered by Phoenix Color ("CTP 7 and 8") were part of the installment contract. The court also granted Phoenix Color's motion *in limine* to preclude the introduction of evidence of its contracts with a substitute supplier of CTP equipment.

After a seven-day trial, the jury determined that CTP 7 was part of the installment contract, but that CTP 8 was not. The jury also found that the defective performance of CTP 2 and 3 substantially impaired the value of the entire contract. As a result of its pre-trial orders and the jury's findings, the district court awarded Phoenix Color damages in the amount of $1,899,257.00, but refused to grant Phoenix Color prejudgment interest. The court also denied Phoenix Color's post-trial motion for judgment as a matter of law on the jury's exclusion of CTP 8 from the installment contract.

Krause America appeals various pre-trial orders and the final judgment. Phoenix Color cross-appeals the exclusion of CTP 8 from the installment contract and the denial of prejudgment interest.

II.

A.

Krause America first appeals the district court's determination as a matter of law that the CTP contracts signed by Phoenix Color and Krause America in October 1997 constituted an installment contract under § 2-612. Krause America observes that the parties executed a total of ten separate contracts for three different models of the Krause America CTP machine to be delivered to plants in six different states, and only five of these contracts were executed in October 1997. Krause America further submits that each contract consisted of an independent set of documents and was separately negotiated by the parties, and that the district court ignored the "singleness of the document and the negotiation" requirement of Comment 3 to § 2-612. Finally, Krause

America asserts that the court incorrectly resorted to modification of contract principles in holding both that CTP 1 was not part of the installment contract, and that the jury would have to determine whether CTP 7 and 8 were part of the installment contract.

We disagree. An installment contract "is one which requires or authorizes the delivery of goods in separate lots to be separately accepted." § 2-612(1). The court below reasoned that

> although there were eight separate specification sheets and quote forms, all of them grew out of a common set of negotiations, and all were executed in October, 1997, as a package deal. Under these circumstances, it is clear to the Court that common and commercial sense require this contract to be considered as an installment contract under Section 2-612. This is, in fact, precisely the sort of situation to which Section 2-612 was intended to apply, *viz.*, where a seller makes a series of deliveries over a period of time and the cumulation of nonconformities so impairs the value of the continuing relationship as to justify the buyer's excuse from continuing to be required to buy under the contract.

The district court was correct in so holding. Comment 1 to § 2-612 states that "[t]he definition of an installment contract" includes "installment deliveries tacitly authorized by the circumstances or by the option of either party." After reviewing the record, we agree that an installment contract existed under the "circumstances" of this case. The first purchase order signed by the parties expressly stated that Phoenix Color was agreeing "to allow KRAUSE AMERICA to supply all CTP systems to all [of its] facilities predicated upon [the] success of [the] 1st installation." The record further reveals that: (1) the parties negotiated with the common understanding that Krause America would be Phoenix Color's sole supplier; (2) Krause America extended price discounts because Phoenix Color was purchasing all of its CTP machines from Krause America; (3) the delivery schedule was set out in advance; (4) the model and design specifications of the machines were similar; (5) those specifications arose from the parties' recognition of Phoenix Color's particular needs; and (6) when Phoenix Color's needs changed, the parties responded by modifying their agreement. When something looks like an installment contract and walks like an installment contract, we find ourselves unable to conclude that it is not.

Krause America's arguments to the contrary are unpersuasive. We do not read Comment 3 to § 2-612 as imposing a strict "singleness of the document and the negotiation" requirement as a necessary condition for the existence of an installment contract. This is because Comment 3 explicitly addresses itself to the question of whether clauses in contracts such as " 'each delivery is a separate contract' " should be given "their legalistically literal effect," and concludes that they should not. But because such a clause is not at issue here, nothing in Comment 3 is dispositive of the relevant inquiry in this case.

As the district court correctly observed, the separate paperwork and purchase documents completed by the parties for the various machines did not preclude the formation of an installment contract because § 2-612's definition of "contract" is quite expansive. It is defined to mean "the total legal obligation which results from the parties' agreement as affected by this title and any other applicable rules of law." § 1-201(11). The parties' "agreement" is in turn defined to mean "the bargain of the parties in fact as found in their language or by implication from other circumstances including course of dealing or usage of trade or course of performance." § 1-201(3). Nowhere in these definitions is there a requirement of a single document or negotiation. And other courts agree that § 2-612 does not impose such a severe restriction. *See, e.g., Cassidy Podell Lynch, Inc. v. Snydergeneral Corp.*, 944 F.2d 1131, 1146–47 (3d Cir. 1991) (holding that twenty-three purchase orders "made up a single installment contract").

In addition, even limiting our focus to Comment 3, it states that not only the "singleness of the document and the negotiation," but also the "sense of the situation" should "prevail over any uncommercial and legalistic interpretation." The "sense of the situation" in this case causes us to conclude that the parties created and later modified an installment contract.

. . . .

C.

Krause America also claims that the court erred in holding as a matter of law that Phoenix Color made a justifiable revocation of acceptance of CTP 1, 2, and 3 under § 2-608, entitling it to a return of the purchase price paid for those machines under § 2-711. Krause America argues that the extensive productivity of CTP 1, 2, and 3 contradicts the court's ruling that nonconformities substantially impaired their value to Phoenix Color.

Based on the record before us, we disagree. In relevant part, § 2-608(1) provides that "[t]he buyer may revoke his acceptance of a lot or commercial unit whose nonconformity substantially impairs its value to him." Applying this section, the district court did not mince words in announcing its factual findings:

> The record is replete with overwhelming evidence that the delivered presses suffered from design defects that caused extraordinary amounts of down time, that required almost constant attention from both plaintiff's and defendants' personnel, and that rendered them unmerchantable. Indeed, the record contains numerous statements from defendants' personnel as to design and/or manufacturing defects in the presses. Defendants' evidence adduced in opposition is entirely too weak for any reasonable fact-finder to find in its favor.

The court reiterated that "[t]here is no question, in light of Krause documents admitting that the machines experienced continuing difficulties due at least in part to design and manufacturing defects, as amply chronicled in the record, that the machines did not conform to the contract."

We have reviewed the same record, and we conclude that the evidence of substantial impairment found by the district court is in fact there. As one example among many, Krause America's own head service technician confirmed the existence of "a combination of both design, and manufacturing faults, which while not major, routinely require the attention of a technician." Numerous service reports, telephone calls, and on-site repair efforts document the multitude of mechanical problems with the machines. The down time that resulted ultimately required rerouting of Phoenix Color's pre-press work from CTP to traditional film-based plate-making. We therefore have no doubt that the district court was correct in holding as a matter of law that nonconformities substantially impaired the value of CTP 1, 2, and 3 to Phoenix Color.

D.

. . . .

III.

For the foregoing reasons, the judgment of the district court is *AFFIRMED*.

NOTE AND QUESTION

Professor Benfield and Chancellor Hawkland suggest that the distinction between the perfect tender rule of § 2-601 and the substantial performance rule of § 2-612 may be understood as, in a rough way, maintaining a distinction Llewellyn considered to have commercial significance: the difference between the buyer's needs and expectations when the buyer is purchasing for resale (akin to § 2-612) and when the buyer is purchasing as the ultimate consumer of the goods (§ 2-601). *See* M. BENFIELD & W. HAWKLAND, SALES: CASES AND MATERIALS 344 (2d ed. 1986), *citing* Llewellyn, *On*

Warranty of Quality and Society II, 37 COLUM. L. REV. 341, 388–89 (1937). To what extent do §§ 2-601 and 2-612 give effect to the middleman-ultimate consumer dichotomy posited by Llewellyn? The issue of conforming tender is brought into sharper focus in the next section.

2. Rejection

GARFINKEL v. LEHMAN FLOOR COVERING CO.
New York District Court, Second District
302 N.Y.S.2d 167 (1969)

FRANCIS J. DONOVAN, J.

Plaintiff seeks to recover the sum of $1,363.63 which was paid to the defendant for floor covering. The covering was installed on the floors March 8, 1967. Immediately the plaintiff noticed an unsightly condition and called it to the attention of the defendant.

On two occasions, representatives of the defendant called at the plaintiff's home and worked on the carpet in an attempt to correct the condition.

The expert who testified on behalf of the defendant, described the condition as pressure bands caused by pressure when the carpeting was on the roller.

The expert said that the condition was corrected but that, on a later inspection, he found a condition which he attributed to wear or traffic causing differences in color or shading and perhaps a flattening out or crushed appearance. It was his opinion that the latter condition was normal with velvet carpet of the kind in suit.

The plaintiff testified that the condition which had been originally reported, examined, and worked on by the defendant, continued throughout.

On this issue, the court accepts the testimony of the plaintiff. Therefore, it follows that the pressure band condition was never corrected and the merchandise was defective. There were continual complaints to the defendant. On April 12, 1967, plaintiff's attorney wrote to the defendant rejecting the merchandise and demanding its removal.

The defendant failed to remove it. On August 15, 1967, a formal letter was sent by certified mail to the defendant, again demanding that it be removed and the purchase price refunded. Nevertheless, the defendant has failed to take any action. The merchandise is substantially defective and the plaintiff is entitled to have the purchase price refunded unless he has in some way prejudiced that right by retaining the carpet which is still on his floor and in use.

The defendant contends that such use bars a rescission, citing *Chalfin v. Fried & Sons* (97 N.Y.S.2d 643 [Appellate Term, 2d Dept.]) and *Alexander Carpet Co. v. Worms* (53 N.Y.S.2d 4 [Appellate Term, 1st Dept.]). Plaintiff relies on the Uniform Commercial Code.

The cited cases antedate the enactment of the Uniform Commercial Code. Section 2-602 of the Uniform Commercial Code provides that the buyer, if he has possession of the goods, is under a duty after rejection to "hold them with reasonable care for seller's disposition for a time sufficient to permit the seller to remove them; but the buyer has no further obligations with regard to goods rightfully rejected." It follows that the plaintiff was then permitted to retain the goods at his home awaiting removal by the seller and had no further obligation if the rejection was within a reasonable time and he had notified the seller.

The court finds as a fact that the rejection was justified; that it was made within a reasonable time and that proper notification was given to the seller.

The need for this provision of the Uniform Commercial Code has been apparent in this court for some time. Many cases were brought where a merchant delivered defective merchandise, bulky in character, expensive to transport and store. He then left the defective merchandise and refused to remove it. This placed the consumer in a dilemma. If the consumer removes and returns the goods, it is an expensive proposition. He is out of pocket money, in addition to the loss of his purchase price, in exchange for the gamble of recovering some of it by court action. On the other hand, if he retains the merchandise in his home, he loses the right to rescind the contract and his purchase money is gone. In return, he has to seek the right to damage for which he will need expensive expert testimony.

It is the opinion of the court that one of the beneficial purposes intended by the new commercial code was to put the burden on the merchant where the goods are defective and he is given proper notice of the defect. He delivered the goods and it is fair that he should remove them or let them remain at his peril.

Judgment for plaintiff for the sum of $1,363.63, with interest from March 8, 1967.

NOTES AND QUESTIONS

1. The court explains the reason for the rule of § 2-602 in terms of potential prejudice to consumers. Is the section a consumer protection provision? In the principal case, after what period of time would you be comfortable advising your client to rip out the floor-covering and throw it in the dumpster? Ever? Would the financial means of your client be a pertinent consideration?

2. As noted in the preceding section of this chapter, "[t]he burden is on the buyer to establish any breach with respect to the goods accepted." The same rule applies in lease transactions. *See* UCC § 2A-516(3)(c). By negative interference, we may safely assume that once the buyer rightfully rejects, the burden is on the seller to prove that the tender was conforming. Is that distinction concerning imposition of the burden of proof of damages appropriate? Consider the remarks of Circuit Judge J. Joseph Smith, of the United States Court of Appeals for the Second Circuit in *Miron v. Yonkers Raceway, Inc.*, 400 F.2d 112, 120 (2d Cir. 1968):

> Thus, if [the buyer] had carried out the customary inspection and accepted the horse, and the defect allegedly rendering [the horse] unsound at the time of sale were a defect not discoverable by inspection on the day of the sale, we may presume the District Court would not have placed the burden of proof on [the buyer], and would have said that he had "revoked his acceptance."

Consider whether that observation is consistent with the best commercial principles. What does it suggest about the relationship among acceptance, rejection, and revocation of acceptance? Your understanding of these issues will be enhanced after you cover the revocation of acceptance materials in this chapter. It is worthwhile, however, at this juncture, to develop a critical sense of the legal incidents attending the three alternatives.

PROBLEM 6-4

Bonanza Electronics has 500 retail stores across the country. It reaches an agreement with Shell Electronics to purchase 10,000 units of the latest generation DVD player manufactured by Shell. Consider whether Bonanza may reject the tender in the following scenarios:

1. On May 1, the 10,000 units arrive at Bonanza's central warehouse facility. Bonanza receives the goods and inspects them. The units are individually-boxed for retail sale, ten units are placed in a single crate for shipment purposes, and ten crates are strapped to a wooden pallet for loading and unloading. Bonanza discovers that one of the pallets was mishandled during shipping, and there are gouges in the crates on one side. Bonanza rejects the entire pallet that has damage (100 units), and accepts the rest of the shipment. Shell argues that the rejection is wrongful because only one unit on the pallet sustained any damage,

although several of the crates were damaged.

2. Assume that since the time of contracting, an entirely new technology is announced that vastly improves the quality of DVD players, while also lowering their price. Bonanza understands that it will suffer substantial losses if it purchases and resells the Shell DVD players. When the complete shipment arrives on May 1, Bonanza carefully inspects each individual unit. Bonanza discovers that one unit has a large visible scratch on the plastic casing, and that another unit does not work properly. Bonanza promptly notifies Shell that it is rejecting the entire shipment.

3. The parties have agreed that Bonanza will receive ten monthly shipments of 1,000 units each. On May 1, the first shipment of 1,000 units (10 pallets) arrives by truck. Bonanza inspects the goods and discovers that one crate was damaged by water, and the 10 units packed in this crate are not in salable condition. Bonanza suspects that Shell is not a reliable supplier and wants to minimize its dealings with Shell. Can Bonanza reject the May 1 shipment in its entirety? Can Bonanza reject Shell's performance of the entire contract?

3. Seller's Right to Cure a Rejected Tender

The perfect tender rule has the potential to be harsh: even a minor nonconformity gives the buyer the opportunity to walk away from the deal. To balance this duty, Article 2 confers a right on sellers to cure non-conforming tenders and a duty on buyers to accept the "cure," thereby keeping the agreement alive. Section 2-508(1) is relatively easy to understand: if the buyer rejects a non-conforming tender before the time for performance has expired, the seller may make a conforming tender within the contract time upon seasonable notification to the buyer of its intention to do so. Under this rule, the buyer obtains a conforming tender within the contract time, and therefore, should not be permitted to cancel the contract.

However, § 2-508(2) is more difficult to apply. If the time for performance has expired, the seller nevertheless is afforded a "further reasonable time to substitute a conforming tender," if the seller "had reasonable grounds to believe" that the tender would be acceptable, "with or without money allowance," so long as the seller gives seasonable notice to the buyer.

T & S BRASS & BRONZE WORKS, INC. v. PIC-AIR, INC.
United States Court of Appeals, Fourth Circuit
790 F.2d 1098 (1986)

BUTZNER, Senior Circuit Judge.

In this diversity action for conversion and counterclaim for breach of contract, Pic-Air, Inc., appeals a judgment holding it liable to T & S Brass and Bronze Works, Inc., for $22,000, and holding T & S liable to Pic-Air for $14,931. We affirm the magistrate's judgment with but slight modification.

I.

In February 1981, T & S Brass, a supplier of plumbing fixtures, paid Pic-Air $22,000 for the design and manufacture of tooling to be used to cast zinc faucet handles for T & S. The tooling, which T & S owned, remained in the possession of Pic-Air, enabling it to produce handles for T & S under subsequent purchase orders.

In February 1983, T & S and Pic-Air contracted for the purchase of 52,500 faucet handles to be cast from the tooling. The handles were to be delivered by Pic-Air in four installments, beginning May 6, 1983. The contract specified that time was of the essence and that Pic-Air could not subcontract without first notifying T & S. The contract also provided that Pic-Air would deliver the tooling to T & S on demand.

On March 28, Pic-Air informed T & S by telephone that until T & S paid an outstanding invoice and agreed to pay an increased price for the handles, Pic-Air would not begin production. T & S agreed orally to both requests, and on March 30, Pic-Air ordered production to begin. T & S paid the invoice the following day.

On April 7, Pic-Air assured T & S that the May 6 installment would be delivered on time. Soon thereafter T & S learned that Pic-Air had subcontracted to a manufacturer in Taiwan, and in a letter dated April 14, T & S informed Pic-Air that the subcontracting violated the contract. Four days later, T & S confirmed its oral agreement to pay the increased purchase price.

On April 21, Pic-Air notified T & S that the May 6 installment would not be delivered on time unless T & S agreed to pay the cost of air freight. Because delay would substantially disrupt its business, T & S agreed to pay for air freight and demanded assurance that subsequent installments would be on time. On April 26, Pic-Air gave the requested assurance, but on May 5 it notified T & S that the second installment of handles would not arrive on time unless T & S again agreed to pay for air freight. T & S agreed. Both the first and second installments arrived on time and were accepted.

On June 22, T & S received a third installment of more than 20,000 handles. The following day T & S phoned Pic-Air, informing it that at least 40 percent of the handles were unacceptably scratched and requesting return of the tooling. On June 27, representatives from Pic-Air came to T & S to examine the handles and discuss the problem. At this meeting T & S offered to sort the handles and return those that it could not use, charging Pic-Air for the costs of sorting. Alternatively, T & S offered to allow Pic-Air employees to sort the handles at the T & S facility. T & S told Pic-Air that it intended to change vendors, and it again demanded return of the tooling.

On June 29, Pic-Air notified T & S that the "slight imperfections" in the handles did not justify rejection and that Pic-Air did not authorize T & S to sort the handles. Pic-Air reiterated this position in a telex of July 5. Pic-Air did not respond to the demand for the tooling's return. T & S sorted the handles and used about half of them. In the later part of July, Pic-Air, without acknowledging that any of the parts were defective and without offering to pay sorting costs, asked T & S to return those handles that T & S claimed were defective. Pic-Air told T & S that its Taiwan subcontractor would replace the handles if in fact they were defective. T & S declined to return the handles on these terms.

On August 4, Pic-Air advised T & S that, because T & S had not paid for the prior three installments or for the air freight, Pic-Air would ship the outstanding fourth installment C.O.D., upon T & S's authorization.

By letter of August 8, Pic-Air for the first time acknowledged that improper packaging had caused scratches on some of the handles and again asked T & S to return the handles that it deemed defective. Pic-Air proposed that it would then determine whether or not these handles were defective and would replace the defective ones. Pic-Air expressly refused to pay the costs of sorting the handles. T & S did not return the defective handles.

On September 15, T & S filed this action against Pic-Air for conversion of the tooling. T & S sought damages of $22,000, the quoted purchase price for the tooling. Pic-Air counterclaimed for the air freight charges, the contract price of the three delivered installments, and the contract price on the fourth installment, which was never shipped.

The magistrate found that Pic-Air had converted the tooling as of April 14, 1983, the date of T & S's letter informing Pic-Air that it had breached the clause prohibiting subcontracting without prior notice. The magistrate entered judgment against Pic-Air for $22,000, plus prejudgment interest dating from April 14. The magistrate ruled that T & S was not liable for the air freight charges or for the price of the installment not shipped. The magistrate ruled that T & S's liability of $21,998 for the three delivered installments should be reduced by $6,792 for the defective handles and by $275 for the cost of sorting, resulting in a judgment against T & S of $14,931. The magistrate authorized T & S to sell the defective handles for scrap and apply the proceeds to Pic-Air's account if Pic-Air elected not to take possession of the handles in 60 days. Pic-Air appeals.

* * *

III.

Pic-Air asserts that the magistrate erred in ruling that T & S was entitled to a setoff for the price of the defective handles and for the cost of sorting these handles from acceptable ones.

The magistrate found that 10,955 handles were defective. This finding, supported by testimony from the supervisor of quality control at T & S, is not clearly erroneous. The court properly concluded that T & S had rightfully rejected the defective handles. *See* UCC 2-601(c) (1978) (buyer's right on receiving nonconforming tender to accept some of the goods and reject the rest).

Pic-Air contends, however, that even if the handles were defective, T & S's failure to return them deprives it of a setoff. Pic-Air relies on two related theories to reach this conclusion. First, it argues that T & S's failure to return the handles constituted acceptance or waiver, making T & S liable for the contract price of the entire installment. Secondly, Pic-Air contends that the failure to return the defective handles prevented cure, estopping T & S from objecting to the defects.

Pic-Air relies mistakenly on *C.W. Anderson Hosiery Co. v. Dixie Knitting Mills, Inc.*, 204 F.2d 503 (4th Cir. 1953), for the proposition that T & S accepted the handles and waived their defects by failing to return them. *Anderson Hosiery* explains that a buyer waives objections to defective goods by failing to "offer to rescind by returning the goods or placing them at the seller's disposal." 204 F.2d at 505, *quoting Reliance Varnish Co. v. Mullins Lumber Co.*, 213 S.C. 84, 95, 48 S.E.2d 653, 658 (1948). Similarly, the Uniform Commercial Code provides that upon rejecting goods a buyer must "hold them with reasonable care at the seller's disposition for a time sufficient to permit the seller to remove them." UCC § 2-602(2)(b) (1978). The buyer has no further obligations with respect to rightfully rejected goods. UCC § 2-602(2)(c) (1978).

The magistrate found that T & S had placed the goods at Pic-Air's disposal by inviting Pic-Air to inspect and sort the goods at T & S's facility. We agree that this invitation fulfilled T & S's immediate obligation to the seller. Consequently, T & S's failure to return the goods upon rejecting them was not acceptance or waiver.

Moreover, the magistrate correctly ruled that T & S was entitled to retain the defective handles after sorting them from the acceptable handles, because T & S held a security interest in the handles for the cost of inspecting and sorting them. The Code provides that a buyer has a security interest in rightfully rejected goods, to the extent of any expenses of inspection. Exercising this right, the buyer "may hold such goods" or may sell them. UCC § 2-711(3) (1978); *Baeza v. Robert E. Lee Chrysler, Plymouth, Dodge, Inc.*, 279 S.C. 468, 472 n.1, 309 S.E.2d 763, 766 n.1 (App. 1983) (dictum); *see also* UCC § 2-715(1) (1978) (buyer's incidental damages for nonconforming goods include expenses of inspection).

Pic-Air contends that T & S's right to hold the rejected goods was subject to Pic-Air's right to cure. Pic-Air argues that, by failing to return the defective handles, T & S prevented Pic-Air from cure and therefore waived the right to object to defects.

As we pointed out, the magistrate properly found that T & S had rightfully rejected the defective handles. Pic-Air's tender of the third installment was nonconforming. A seller's right to cure a nonconforming tender is defined in two subsections of the Code. If the time for the seller's performance has not yet expired, the seller may notify the buyer of intent to cure and may then cure within the time of performance specified in the contract. UCC § 2-508(1) (1978). In this case, the third installment was due on July 6. Because Pic-Air did not cure by this date, this provision of the Code does not apply.

If the time for performance has passed, the seller's right to cure is limited. The seller must reasonably believe at the time of tender that the goods will be acceptable. After learning of the nonconformity, the seller must seasonably notify the buyer of intent to substitute a conforming tender. Upon satisfying these two requirements, the seller may then have a reasonable further time to substitute a conforming tender. UCC § 2-508(2) (1978).

We assume that Pic-Air reasonably believed at the time of tender that the handles would be acceptable, because T & S had accepted prior installments. Pic-Air received notice of rejection on June 23 and inspected the shipment a few days later. Nevertheless, Pic-Air never unequivocally told T & S that it intended to cure. On June 29 and again on July 5, Pic-Air informed T & S that the handles were not defective. In late July and again in early August, Pic-Air conceded that some handles were scratched. But it neither acknowledged nonconformity nor undertook responsibility to cure, suggesting instead that its subcontractor would replace any handles that were in fact defective. Pic-Air cannot now insist on its right to cure, having never acknowledged the defects nor promised to cure them. *See Stephenson v. Frazier*, 399 N.E.2d 794, 797–98 (Ind. App. 1980) (seller's right to cure depends on seller's notifying buyer of intent to cure).

Pic-Air contends, however, that T & S could no longer rightfully retain the handles deemed defective after Pic-Air instructed T & S to return them.

We believe that T & S's refusal to follow these instructions did not constitute acceptance or waiver. The Code provides that a buyer's duty with respect to rightfully rejected goods in the buyer's possession is "to follow any reasonable instructions received from the seller with respect to the goods." This duty is subject to the buyer's security interest for inspection costs. Moreover, the seller's "instructions are not reasonable if on demand indemnity for expenses is not forthcoming." UCC § 2-603(1) (1978). Beginning on June 29, Pic-Air consistently refused to pay the expenses of sorting. Pic-Air reiterated this refusal in the August 8 letter of instructions. Because Pic-Air's instructions were unreasonable as a matter of law, T & S was not required to follow them. We conclude that T & S did not waive its right to object to the defects by continuing to hold the rejected handles rather than incur the additional expense of returning them, with no assurance of reimbursement. *See Deaton, Inc. v. Aeroglide Corp.*, 99 N.M. 253, 657 P.2d 109, 113–14 [35 U.C.C. Rep. Serv. 130] (1982) (buyer was not required to return defective goods on which it held a security interest, because seller did not tender the entire amount secured).

In sum, we hold that T & S rightfully rejected the defective handles, and it did not waive the right to object to their defects by refusing to return the handles. Consequently, the magistrate properly allowed a setoff for the defective handles and the cost of sorting them.

* * *

IV.

Pic-Air contends that its possession of the tooling after June 23 was not conversion. Pic-Air argues that it could properly retain the tooling until it had fulfilled the purpose of the bailment. Consequently, Pic-Air argues, it rightfully retained the tooling for the purpose of curing the defective installment.

Pic-Air's argument fails, both under the common law of bailments and under the Uniform Commercial Code. At common law, a bailee may make a qualified refusal to return the bailed item if the purpose of the bailment has not yet been fulfilled. But a bailee seeking to rely on a qualified refusal cannot thereby avoid liability for conversion unless he immediately communicates to the bailor the reason for the refusal to return the bailed item. *See, e.g., Stein v. Mauricio*, 580 S.W.2d 82, 83 (Tex. Civ. App. 1979); *White v. Goldberg*, 12 N.J. Super. 122, 79 A.2d 95 (1951); RESTATEMENT (SECOND) OF TORTS § 241(b) (1965). Pic-Air did not notify T & S that it was retaining the tooling for the purpose of curing the June 22 shipment. Consequently, Pic-Air cannot avoid liability for conversion on this ground.

The same analysis applies to Pic-Air's right to cure under the Code. A seller's right to cure after the time for performance has passed depends on the seller's both notifying the buyer of intent to cure and curing within a reasonable time. UCC § 2-508(2) (1978). Because Pic-Air did not preserve its right to cure by timely notice and cure, Pic-Air's continued possession of the tooling constitutes conversion.

The party suing for conversion has the right to elect return of the chattel or damages. *Reynolds v. Philips*, 72 S.C. 32, 34, 51 S.E. 523, 524 (1905); *see also Alderman v. Cooper*, 257 S.C. 304, 310, 185 S.E.2d 809, 811 (1971). T & S elected damages.

In South Carolina, the trier of fact has discretion to assess as damages for conversion the highest value of the property up to the time of trial. *Causey v. Blanton*, 281 S.C. 163, 166, 314 S.E.2d 346, 348 (App. 1984). The magistrate's award of $22,000, the purchase price of the tooling as originally quoted to T & S, did not abuse his discretion.

The judgment is affirmed, save that interest on Pic-Air's liability of $22,000 for conversion will run from June 23, 1983, the date of demand.

NOTES AND QUESTIONS

1. Pic-Air argued that the buyer's failure to return the goods constituted acceptance, and that T & S's failure to return the handles deprived Pic-Air of its right to cure. In response, T & S argued that it properly retained possession of the handles by virtue of its security interest in the goods. How is a court to distinguish between acceptance and rejection followed by the buyer's continued possession of the goods in order to protect its security interest in them? *Compare Bowen v. Young*, 507 S.W.2d 600 (Tex. Civ. App. 1974) (buyer's continued possession of nonconforming mobile home constituted acceptance), *with Jorgensen v. Pressnall*, 274 Or. 285, 545 P.2d 1382 (1976) (buyer's continued possession of mobile home constituted preservation of the collateral securing buyer's § 2-711(3) security interest in goods with regard to which acceptance had been rightfully revoked).

Section 2A-508(5) provides a lessee who has rejected or justifiably revoked acceptance of leased goods a security interest in those goods. How would the lessee foreclose that security interest? Could the lessee effectively sell goods that belong to the lessor? Would that be consistent with the division of property rights represented by a lease contract?

2. The *Pic-Air* court notes that the seller's right to cure would be dependent upon the seller having afforded the buyer a notice of an intent to cure. What were the consequences of the seller's failure to provide that notice in the principal case? What does this suggest would be a prudent practice when counsel is consulted in such circumstances? What problem might there be with recklessly notifying the buyer that your client, the seller, is retrieving goods in order to effect cure?

3. What is the duration of the right to cure? *See Peter Pan Seafoods, Inc. v. Olympic Foundry Co.*, 17 Wash. App. 761, 565 P.2d 819 (1977) (a six-month warranty period provided the duration period during which the seller would have a § 2-508(1) right to cure). Consider also, the remarks of Professor Jacqueline Kanovitz in *The Seller Fiddles and the Clock Ticks: Seller's Cure and the U.C.C. Statute of Limitations*, 60 NOTRE DAME L. REV. 318 (1985). She suggests four theories that buyers may use to avoid the § 2-725 statute of limitations bar to actions against a seller of nonconforming goods who has attempted but failed to cure the nonconformity: (1) the "future performance" exception within § 2-725; (2) postponement of accrual of cause of action until an exclusive repair remedy has failed of its essential purpose; (3) application of

estoppel principles pursuant to § 1-103 when the seller has induced the buyer to delay legal action while the seller attempts to effect cure; and (4) buyer's avoidance of the § 2-725 limitations period by operation of the exception provided in subsection 2-725(4), under which the statute might be tolled while efforts at cure are ongoing.

4. The CISG provisions on "cure" by the seller are designed to respond to problems which arise when the seller tenders non-conforming goods or documents. Essentially, cure is one of the several devices which the CISG offers to keep the contract intact, thus avoiding the economic waste that inevitably results from the needless destruction of a contractual relationship. Cure does this by giving the seller a second chance to comply with the contract. In so doing, the CISG resembles both the UNIDROIT Principles (*see* Article 7.1.4) and the UCC (*see* § 2-508). The articles on cure may be considered separately from the viewpoint of (1) cure within the time specified for performance and (2) cure thereafter.

Article 34 (documents) and Article 37 (goods) provide that the seller may cure any non-conformity in the tender up to the delivery date in the contract. These articles aid the seller only if the exercise of this right does not cause the buyer "unreasonable inconvenience or unreasonable expense." If the non-conformity is in the goods, the seller may cure by either repair or replacement. It should be noted that there is no express requirement that the seller notify the buyer of his intention to cure. Failure to do so, however, may preclude cure if it causes the buyer "unreasonable inconvenience or unreasonable expense." Of course, even an effective cure will not deprive the buyer of its right to recover for any losses caused by the original non-conformity.

Article 48(1) allows the seller to remedy any defect in the goods or documents after the date for delivery. This opportunity for a second tender is sharply limited; the seller must cure without unreasonable delay and without causing the buyer unreasonable inconvenience or "uncertainty of reimbursement by the seller of expenses advanced by the buyer." If the seller notifies the buyer of his intention to cure and requests that the buyer inform him if the time period within which the proposed cure will be effected is acceptable, the buyer's failure to respond will preclude a later claim that cure within this period of time amounted to an "unreasonable delay" under paragraph (1). *See* Article 48(2). Moreover, even if the seller's notice says nothing about a response, it is assumed to include such a request if a time for performance is indicated. *See* Article 48(3).

MERCURY MARINE v. CLEAR RIVER CONSTRUCTION CO.

Mississippi Supreme Court
839 So. 2d 508 (2003)

En Banc.

Waller, Justice, for the court:

. . . .

FACTS AND PROCEDURAL HISTORY

Nicholas Travis, president of Clear River Construction Company, is involved in the competitive saltwater fishing of king mackerel. Realizing competitive saltwater fishing was expensive, Travis contacted Charles Henderson of Atlantic Marine Brokers in Waveland, Mississippi, in September of 1997 and proposed that Mercury Marine, a division of Brunswick Corporation, and World Cat Boats sponsor Travis in Division 7 of the Southern Kingfish Association. Mercury Marine accepted and made Travis a member of its Saltwater Pro Team. As one of approximately 1100 members in Mercury Marine's promotional programs, Travis would receive a substantial discount on Mercury Marine motors in exchange for Travis's promoting of its products by, for example, wearing Mercury Marine logo shirts and including the motors in promotional photographs.

Travis purchased a new World Cat catamaran boat for $ 52,359.50 and two new 1998 200-horsepower Mercury Mariner Offshore motors for $ 13,862.00 (slightly above dealer cost) and a $ 300 freight charge to transport the motors to World Cat's facilities in Greenville, North Carolina, for installation. Travis wanted to purchase Mercury Marine's new Optimax motors but was informed that Mercury Marine was having problems with the development of the Optimax motors at the time. The Mariner motors carried a typical repair or replace express warranty stating:

> Claim shall be made under this warranty by delivering the Product for inspection to a Mercury Marine dealer authorized to service the Purchaser's Product. If Purchaser cannot deliver the Product to such authorized dealer, he may give notice in writing to the company. We shall then arrange for the inspection and repair, provided such service is covered under this warranty. Purchaser shall pay for all related transportation charges and/or travel time.

Travis took delivery of the boat and motors on November 18, 1997, and planned to travel to Wilmington, North Carolina, for the Southern Kingfish Association National Championship. A mechanic for Atlantic Marine Brokers traveled from Waveland to Greenville to assist in the installation and informed Travis when he took delivery that the motors had not been pre-run. Travis and the mechanic launched the boat in a nearby lake and realized that one of the motors would not run. Since the mechanic did not have the proper equipment to diagnose or repair the problem, Travis traveled to Crocker Marine, Mercury Marine's dealer in Wilmington. When Crocker Marine was unable to repair the motor, Travis traveled to another Mercury Marine dealer in Sneads Ferry, North Carolina, which was able to repair the problem, a defective throttle position indicator, as per the warranty. As a result, Travis was unable to "pre-fish," meaning scout for prime fishing areas prior to the tournament, and did not place.

The next problem with the motors occurred on August 7, 1998, during the GMC Gulf Coast Tournament at Dauphin Island, Alabama. In the meantime, nearly ten months had elapsed, and Travis had competed in four tournaments without any motor trouble. Specifically, the lower unit, or gear case, on the same motor which had malfunctioned earlier failed while Travis was fishing 83 miles offshore. After motoring back to shore on one motor, Travis had the lower unit replaced at Ed's Marine in Jackson at Mercury Marine's expense per the warranty. An inspection noted abnormal wear on the lower unit of the other motor which had yet to fail but was likewise replaced under the warranty. Travis had the two defective lower units rebuilt at his expense so that he could have them as spares. Mercury Marine usually kept the parts replaced under its warranties but allowed Travis to keep the old lower units and have them rebuilt.

Finally, on Friday, August 28, 1998, while pre-fishing in the Gulf of Mexico in preparation for the Cypress Cove Tournament, a rod bearing in the other motor failed thereby totally disabling it. Travis spoke with Joe Berkley, an employee of Dan Shad, head of Mercury Marine's promotional engine program, via cell phone from the Gulf requesting that they find a nearby mechanic or a spare motor. Travis likewise demanded that Mercury Marine air-freight a motor from its headquarters in Fond du Lac, Wisconsin, to Venice, Louisiana, for installation so that he could compete in the tournament. Berkley informed Travis that Mercury Marine would be unable to assist him as such and that he would have to take the motor to a Mercury Marine dealer for repair as required by the warranty.

Not being able to find a Mercury Marine dealer which would repair the motor that Friday night or the next morning, Travis traveled to a Yamaha dealership in New Orleans, Louisiana, which worked throughout the night installing a pair of new Yamaha outboard motors on Travis's World Cat boat. Travis spent over $ 21,000 on the Yamahas and returned to Venice to compete. The Mercury Marine motors had been operated approximately 132 hours and were subsequently repaired.

. . . .

DISCUSSION

I. WHETHER MERCURY MARINE WAS GIVEN A REASONABLE OPPORTUNITY TO CURE.

Mercury Marine first argues that Travis failed to afford it a reasonable opportunity to cure the motors' defects. By purchasing the Yamaha motors on the same day as the malfunction of the Mercury Marine motor and filing suit to recover the cost of the Yamaha motors, Mercury Marine contends that Travis failed to satisfy a legal prerequisite to recovery, namely, cure. Travis responds that the Mercury Marine motors failed on three different occasions and that Mercury Marine was given a reasonable opportunity to cure the defect each time, even the final time.

In *Fitzner Pontiac-Buick-Cadillac v. Smith*, 523 So. 2d 324 (Miss. 1988), Smith purchased a used car and sued the dealer alleging breach of express and implied warranties when the car experienced problems with, among other things, an intake gasket, transmission, and radiator. Rather than bringing the car to Fitzner for repair, Smith unconditionally insisted that the contract for the car be deemed rejected and that he be given his money back. 523 So. 2d at 328. In reversing and rendering a jury verdict in favor of Smith for the purchase price of the car, we noted the following regarding a seller's right to cure:

> We recognize that a strict reading of the cure provisions of *Miss. Code Ann.* § 75-2-508 (1972) reveals no explicit application to the revocation situation with which we are here concerned. *The law's policy of minimization of economic waste strongly supports recognition of a reasonable opportunity to cure.* Though the express language of Section 75-2-508 does not apply here, cure is not excluded by Section 75-2-608. By analogy to Section 75-2-508 and in furtherance of the policy justification undergirding that statute and our common law doctrine of cure in contracts generally, we recognize that, before Smith was entitled to get his money back, Fitzner had a right to a reasonable opportunity to cure the vehicle's deficiencies.

523 So. 2d at 328 n.1 (citations omitted & emphasis added).

We agree with Mercury Marine that Travis should have brought the malfunctioning motor to a Mercury Marine dealer for repair according to the warranty. The two prior defects had been repaired under the warranty without question. Also, the third and final malfunction occurred on a motor that had yet to experience problems. The fact is that the same thing never broke twice over the ten months Travis used the motors, and there was never any indication that Mercury Marine would not repair the broken rod bearing. Mercury Marine should have been allowed to cure the defective motor. *See Tucker v. Aqua Yacht Harbor Corp.*, 749 F. Supp. 142 (N.D. Miss. 1990) (applying Mississippi law) (finding that in a case which was instituted while repairs were being made to piston defect on boat motor, manufacturer should have been allowed to cure and thus, could not be held liable for breaches of express and implied warranties).

Also, this case is readily distinguishable from our prior opinions in which we found that the right to cure was not unlimited in the wake of repeated deficiencies and repeated attempts at repair. *Guerdon Indus., Inc. v. Gentry*, 531 So. 2d 1202 (Miss. 1988) (finding right to cure not unlimited in case where seller made ten attempts to repair a mobile home's defects in a five-month period); *Rester v. Morrow*, 491 So. 2d 204 (Miss. 1988) (holding likewise in a case where plaintiff's Renault automobile experienced problems with its electrical system, air conditioner, and oil indicator gauge justified buyer's revocation of acceptance).

. . . .

CONCLUSION

We find that Travis did not provide Mercury Marine a reasonable opportunity to cure the broken rod bearing. There was also no failure of the repair or replace warranty's essential purpose or breaches of the implied warranties of merchantability or fitness for a particular purpose. The evidence is insufficient to sustain the jury's verdict. Therefore, the Rankin County Court judgment entered in accordance with a $ 30,000 jury verdict and the judgment of the Rankin County Circuit Court are reversed, and judgment is hereby rendered in favor of Mercury Marine, finally dismissing the complaint and this action with prejudice.

PROBLEM 6-5

Slipright is a retailer of various lubrication products and Burgess is a manufacturing company. Slipright agrees to sell a lubricating oil with a rating of 6 ("R-6" oil) to Burgess.

First Scenario: At the time for performance, Slipright's shipping department sends R-7 oil to Burgess due to a temporary shortage of R-6 oil in its inventory. R-7 oil is slightly more expensive than R-6 oil. R-7 has the same general manufacturing applications as R-6 oil, but is regarded as a superior product overall. With the shipment, Slipright notifies Burgess of the substitution and indicates that no extra charge will be levied. Slipright is willing to ship the more expensive product because prices in the industry have generally declined by 10 percent since the date of the parties' agreement.

Slipright is unaware that Burgess recently purchased machines from a new manufacturer, and that these new model machines absolutely require the use of R-6 oil. Burgess rejects the R-7 oil when it arrives. The time for Slipright's performance has passed, but Slipright offers to purchase R-6 oil on the spot market and ship it to Burgess immediately. Burgess refuses Slipright's offer and purchases its R-6 oil at a lower price from another supplier.

Slipright sues Burgess for breach, arguing that Burgess refused to allow Slipright to effect a cure of its admittedly nonconforming tender. What should you argue on behalf of Slipright?

Second Scenario: Now assume that Slipright knows that Burgess can only use R-6 oil in its machines. On the date for delivery under the contract, Slipright's shipping department pulls the contract quantity out of inventory and delivers it to Burgess in late afternoon. Upon arrival, Burgess discovers that the sealed cartons marked "R-6" in fact contain bottles of "R-7" oil. Slipright discovers that the machine that marks the packing cartons was improperly coded one evening, resulting in the mis-labeled packaging and the shipment of the wrong oil. Slipright immediately apologizes to Burgess, agrees to deliver R-6 oil the following morning, and also agrees to pick up the R-7 oil at its own expense. However, Burgess tells Slipright, "you've blown it. We're not waiting around for you to get this order right." Burgess refuses the substitute shipment and purchases R-6 oil from another retailer at a 10% savings due to price decreases since the date of contracting with Slipright.

Slipright sues Burgess for breach, arguing that Burgess refused to allow Slipright to effect a cure of its admittedly nonconforming tender. How should you argue on behalf of Slipright?

4. Acceptance

Section 2-606 makes clear that a buyer can accept goods by inadvertence. Commercial efficiency demands that the buyer act promptly and prior to altering the condition of the goods if it wishes to force the seller to take back the goods. Once the buyer has accepted the goods its rights and duties change dramatically. First, the buyer is obligated to pay the purchase price. Second, the burden of proving nonconformity in the tender for purposes of recovering damages shifts to the buyer. In the words of Ellen Peters, a former Yale Law School Professor and later Chief Justice of the Connecticut Supreme Court, "The buyer's acceptance of goods, despite their alleged nonconformity, is a watershed." *Stelco Indus., Inc. v. Cohen*, 182 Conn. 561, 563, 438 A.2d 759 (1980).

PROBLEM 6-6

Sanchez Fabrications agreed to specially manufacture lead covered tanks to exacting standards supplied by the buyer, Buto Chemicals. Sanchez encountered various problems in manufacturing the tanks, but all delays were waived by Buto in recognition of the difficulty in achieving the desired results. On May 1, Buto's agent visited Sanchez's facility and inspected the tanks. The agent noted a number of small deficiencies remaining to be corrected, but stated that Buto would bring a truck on May 4 to pick up the goods. On May 2, Buto cancelled the contract without providing any reason. Sanchez argues that the tanks had been accepted by Buto despite the few remaining deficiencies that were to be corrected, and despite the fact that the final fine-tuning of the units would take place after installation.

If Buto has accepted the tanks, it is obligated to pay the contract price and must bear the burden of proving that the goods were non-conforming. § 2-607(1), (4). Argue on behalf of Sanchez that Buto has accepted the tanks.

5.   Revocation of Acceptance

The buyer's right to revoke acceptance may go a long way toward tipping the balance of rights and duties in sales and lease transactions in favor of buyers. The buyer's right to revoke acceptance is a statutory expansion of the common law (and statutory) right to rescind. It effectively continues the right to rescind beyond acceptance. But more profoundly, unlike the common law right to rescind, the buyer does not forfeit its claim to damages. A buyer could revoke acceptance and also recover damages (e.g., for breach of warranty) rather than settle for a rescission of the sales or lease contract. This difference is analogous to the difference between tort recovery (out of pocket, to return the parties to the position they were in before the transaction) and contract recovery (expectation damages, the benefit of the bargain).

NATIONAL EASTERN CORP. v. VEGAS FASTENER MFG
United States District Court, District of Connecticut
59 UCC Rep. Serv. 2d 330 (2006)

RULING ON PLAINTIFF'S MOTION FOR SUMMARY JUDGMENT

ARTERTON, J.

. . . .

I. FACTUAL BACKGROUND

The undisputed facts show that plaintiff National Eastern was a subcontractor to Cianbro Corporation ("Cianbro") providing stainless steel products for Cianbro's construction of the Tomlinson Bridge, located in New Haven, Connecticut, for the Connecticut Department of Transportation. In September 2001, National Eastern entered into a contract with Vegas Fastener for the purchase of various materials (including nuts and bolts) of Type 316 steel. Vegas Fastener thereafter provided materials to National Eastern with two Certificates of Compliance stating that the materials met the specification for Type 316 steel, along with test results.

In actuality, and unbeknownst to National Eastern when it accepted the materials, most of the materials supplied by Vegas Fastener were not of Type 316 steel, but of

Type 304. After Cianbro used the materials in the bridge project, it was discovered that the materials had corroded, and as a result, it was also discovered that they were non-conforming to state specifications. The Connecticut Department of Transportation, as owner of the bridge project, demanded that the nonconforming materials be removed and replaced with the specified Type 316 steel products. Cianbro, as the general contractor on the project, bore the costs of removal and replacement and passed on the costs to plaintiff in the form of back charges. Plaintiff challenged the amount of these back charges in an arbitration, which determined that Cianbro was entitled to $98,146.00 in back charges. Defendant does not dispute, or offer any evidence to contest, that it received notice of nonconformity within a reasonable time after plaintiff's discovery, but only asserts that plaintiff's statement that National Eastern and Cianbro contacted the defendant "almost immediately" upon discovery of the nonconformity is an opinion, not a statement of fact.

. . . .

III. DISCUSSION

A. Breach of Contract Claim (Count I)

Because the parties' contract was one for the sale of goods, Article 2 of the Uniform Commercial Code ("UCC"), Conn. Gen. Stat. § 42a-2-101 *et seq.*, applies. Plaintiff argues that defendant is liable for plaintiff's damages caused by the nonconformity of the materials tendered pursuant to UCC § 2-601, which provides that if goods tendered "fail in any respect to conform to the contract, the buyer may (a) reject the whole; or (b) accept the whole; or (c) accept any commercial unit or units and reject the rest," *see* Conn. Gen. Stat. § 42a-2-601, and UCC §§ 2-607(3), 2-714, which provide that where a tender has been accepted and the buyer has notified the seller within a reasonable time after it discovered or should have discovered any breach, the buyer "may recover as damages for any nonconformity of tender the loss resulting in the ordinary course of events from the seller's breach." *See* Conn. Gen. Stat. §§ 42a-2-607(3), 42a-2-714(1).

Defendant believes that UCC § 2-608 applies, and argues that plaintiff may only recover damages for a nonconformity that substantially impaired the value of the goods to plaintiff. Because defendant proffers an expert opinion regarding the similarity of Types 304 and 316 steel, it contends that a genuine issue of material fact exists as to whether the value of the goods to plaintiff was substantially impaired because it can prove that the Type 304 goods and Type 316 goods were substantially similar for the purposes used.

The UCC provides multiple remedies for buyers of nonconforming goods. First, a buyer may reject a tender of goods at the outset if those goods "fail in any respect to conform to the contract." *See* Conn. Gen. Stat. § 42a-2-601. If the buyer has already accepted the goods, as here, the buyer may revoke his acceptance pursuant to UCC § 2-608 and recover the contract purchase price, or the buyer may elect to sue for damages resulting from the non-conformity pursuant to UCC § 2-607(3). *See* Conn. Gen. Stat. §§ 42a-2-607(3), 608; *Comind, Companhia de Sequros v. Sikorsky Aircraft*, 116 F.R.D. 397, 410–11 (D. Conn. 1987) (describing the various recovery options available to a buyer of nonconforming goods); *Superior Wire & Paper Prods., Ltd. v. Talcott Tool & Machine, Inc.*, 184 Conn. 10, 13–14, 441 A.2d 43, 45 (Conn. 1981) ("If the buyer can demonstrate that he has been damaged by the nonconformity of the goods that he has accepted, he is entitled to recover such damages as he can prove. . . . Alternatively, if the buyer can demonstrate that the goods are substantially nonconforming, he is entitled, with some qualifications, to revoke his acceptance and recover the purchase price."). Whether a buyer who has accepted nonconforming goods chooses to revoke his acceptance or to sue for damages, that buyer is required to give notice to the seller "within a reasonable time after he discovers or should have discovered" the nonconformity. *See* Conn. Gen. Stat. §§ 42a-2-607(3), 608; *Superior Wire*, 184 Conn. at 12–16, 441 A.2d at 45–47.

If the buyer attempts to revoke its acceptance of the goods pursuant to UCC § 2-608, it must "show that their 'nonconformity substantially impairs [their] value to [it]' and that they were initially accepted because the buyer reasonably expected the seller to cure any defects or because the buyer could not immediately discover such defects." *Superior Wire*, 184 Conn. at 16, 441 A.2d at 46 (citing Conn. Gen. Stat. § 2-608). Alternatively, a buyer who has accepted the goods may sue for damages under UCC §§ 2-607(3) and 2-714(1) for losses shown to result from "*any* nonconformity of tender." Conn. Gen. Stat. § 2-714(1) (emphasis added).

In this case, National Eastern could not return the goods upon discovery of nonconformity because they were already used in the bridge project, and does not seek to revoke its acceptance of the goods and recover the purchase price, effectively rescinding the contract, but rather seeks to recover consequential damages for the losses it incurred as a result of the nonconformity. Thus, this claim for damages for breach of contract is one pursuant to UCC §§ 2-607(3) and 2-714, and not UCC § 2-608. *See Superior Wire* and *Comind, supra.* Accordingly, the substantial impairment requirement of UCC § 2-608 is not applicable to plaintiff's claim. Because plaintiff's claim is one for damages, plaintiff may recover losses resulting from "any nonconformity," *see* Conn. Gen. Stat. § 42a-2-714(1), and is not required to meet "the higher standard of showing that the nonconformity of the goods 'substantially impairs their value to [it],'" which is the statutory standard governing revocation of acceptance."[8] *See Stelco Indus., Inc. v. Cohen*, 182 Conn. 561, 564, 438 A.2d 759, 761 (Conn. 1980) (citing Conn. Gen. Stat. § 42a-2-608).

UCC § 2-714, Conn. Gen. Stat. § 42a-2-714, provides:

> Where the buyer has accepted goods and given notification as provided in subsection (3) of section 42a-2-607 he may recover as damages for any nonconformity of tender the loss resulting in the ordinary course of events from the seller's breach as determined in any manner which is reasonable.

Conn. Gen. Stat. § 42a-2-714(1). The section further provides that "[i]n a proper case any incidental and consequential damages under [Section 2-715] may also be recovered." *See* Conn. Gen. Stat. § 42a-2-714(3). Thus, pursuant to UCC §§ 2-607 and 2-714, in order to recover damages for the nonconformity of the goods supplied to plaintiff, plaintiff must prove: (1) that within a reasonable time after it discovered or should have discovered any breach it notified defendant of the breach, *see* Conn. Gen. Stat. § 42a-2- 607(3); and (2) that plaintiff suffered losses in the ordinary course of events resulting from defendant's breach. *See* Conn. Gen. Stat. § 42a-2-714(1).

In this case, defendant has admitted that it provided non-conforming goods to the plaintiff under to their contract, in that it provided materials made of Type 304 steel, and not of Type 316 steel as specified. Moreover, as discussed above, while defendant denies that plaintiff notified it "almost immediately," defendant does not rebut plaintiff's evidence of notification within a "reasonable time" after discovery by offering any evidence to contradict Mr. Muckenhirn's statement that defendant was notified of the

---

8 [6] Even if plaintiff were required to show that the nonconformity resulted in a substantial impairment of the value of the goods to plaintiff, plaintiff meets this higher standard. Defendant's arguments that the Type 304 and Type 316 steel are substantially similar for the purposes supplied, and that there is a genuine issue of material fact as to whether materials of Type 316 steel would also have corroded as did the Type 304 materials, are inapposite. The value of the goods to plaintiff was substantially impaired not because the Type 304 materials corroded, but because the Type 304 materials were not the Type 316 materials specified by plaintiff in its contract with defendant and required by Cianbro and the Connecticut Department of Transportation for the bridge project, and thus the Connecticut Department of Transportation and Cianbro were entitled to charge plaintiff for the removal and replacement of the nonconforming materials.

nonconformity "immediately upon its discovery." Thus, there is no disputed issue of material fact from which a jury could conclude that plaintiff is not entitled to damages flowing from defendant's tender of nonconforming goods.

As noted above, while the parties' briefing disputed the actual amount of damages, the arbitration commenced by National Eastern against Cianbro challenging the back charges amount has now concluded, entitling Cianbro to back charge plaintiff $98,146.00 for the nut and bolt removal and replacement. Defendant is thus liable to plaintiff for consequential damages incurred by plaintiff as a result of the nonconformity in the amount of $98,146.00. Plaintiff is also awarded prejudgment interest at a rate of 10 percent, from the time Cianbro deducted costs for removal/replacement from amounts otherwise due to plaintiff.

* * *

WILK PAVING, INC. v. SOUTHWORTH-MILTON, INC.
Vermont Supreme Court
649 A.2d 778 (1994)

* * *

Before ALLEN, C.J., and GIBSON, DOOLEY, MORSE and JOHNSON, JJ.

ALLEN, Chief Justice.

Defendant Southworth-Milton, Inc., appeals from a judgment in favor of plaintiff, Wilk Paving, Inc., in the amount of the purchase price of an asphalt roller that plaintiff had purchased from defendant. After a bench trial, the court ruled that plaintiff was entitled to revoke acceptance and effectively had revoked acceptance under the Uniform Commercial Code (UCC), see 9A V.S.A. §§ 2-101 to 2-725 (Article 2, Sales). We affirm.

On October 10, 1989, plaintiff purchased the roller, relying in part on representations in a brochure provided by defendant that the machine was versatile, well-suited for plaintiff's typical paving jobs, reliable, and easy to maintain. As part of the purchase contract, defendant warranted repair and replacement of defective parts for one year and disclaimed all other warranties. On December 8, 1989, plaintiff discovered that the right rear vibratory motor was leaking oil and that the electrical system required repair. Plaintiff was advised to deliver the roller to defendant's place of business, and on December 18, 1989, the repair work was done to correct the foregoing problems. In addition, defendant replaced a blown fuse, tightened loose hydraulic lines that were leaking oil, resealed a hydraulic feedline to the vibratory motor, and gave the roller a general tune-up. Thereafter, plaintiff did not use the roller until the spring, when weather permitted resumption of paving projects.

On June 7, 1990, oil was observed to be leaking from the brake housing, requiring replacement of the housing and seals. On June 21, 1990, defendant found that the front drive motor was leaking oil from the parking brake piston. On June 29, 1990 the water pump seal was leaking and required disassembly, cleaning, and resealing. On August 16, 1990, the starter failed because of loose wiring in the principal wiring harness and starter. On August 28, 1990, the oil plug broke off, causing oil to leak over the surface of the pavement being applied. As a result, plaintiff had to replace the affected surface. All but the last of these problems were reported to defendant. Plaintiff also complained that the problems with the internal hydraulics made it difficult to drive the roller onto a trailer for transporting.

In September 1990, plaintiff's president informed defendant that he no longer wanted the machine and requested a return of the purchase price, less a reasonable rental fee for the time plaintiff used the roller during the summer. In November 1990, the roller was parked in plaintiff's lot and covered with a tarp. Examinations of the roller by experts in 1992 in preparation for trial disclosed that it was still leaking oil.

After trial, plaintiff was awarded the purchase price of the roller, but was denied recovery for consequential damages. . . .

On appeal, defendant contends that it was not afforded an opportunity to cure the roller's defects, that plaintiff failed to prove a nonconformity sufficient to create a right of revocation of acceptance, and that any such right to revoke was waived when plaintiff continued to use the roller. . . .

On review, this Court will not disturb the trial court's findings of fact or conclusions of law unless the party challenging them demonstrates they are clearly erroneous. V.R.C.P. 52(a); *Estate of Sawyer v. Crowell*, 151 Vt. 287, 291, 559 A.2d 687, 690 (1989). Findings of fact will stand if supported by any reasonable and credible evidence, even if contrary evidence exists. *Community Feed Store v. Northeastern Culvert Corp.*, 151 Vt. 152, 155, 559 A.2d 1068, 1069 (1989).

I.

A.

Defendant first argues that plaintiff should be barred from any recovery for revoking acceptance without first giving defendant an opportunity to cure defects in the roller. As a general rule, once a buyer accepts tender the buyer must, within a reasonable time after discovery of a breach, notify the seller of the breach or be barred from any remedy. 9A V.S.A. § 2-607(3)(a). This notice requirement affords a seller the opportunity to cure the claimed defects or minimize the buyer's losses. *Desilets Granite Co. v. Stone Equalizer Corp.*, 133 Vt. 372, 375, 340 A.2d 65, 67 (1975). The right to cure has limits, however: "[t]he buyer . . . is not bound to permit the seller to tinker with the article indefinitely in the hope that it may ultimately be made to comply with the warranty." *Orange Motors of Coral Gables, Inc. v. Dade County Dairies, Inc.*, 258 So. 2d 319, 321 (Fla. Dist. Ct. App. 1972).

The record amply supports the trial court's conclusion that defendant had a reasonable opportunity to cure but failed to do so. The court's findings are based on evidence that a series of mechanical problems plagued the roller from the start of plaintiff's ownership. Almost without exception, plaintiff reported the problems to defendant, who, at various times over nine months, attempted repairs sufficient to keep the roller working as promised. Under the circumstances of this case, plaintiff afforded defendant adequate opportunity to make good on its representations before revoking acceptance.

B.

Defendant next asserts that plaintiff failed to prove a nonconformity sufficient to create a right of revocation. Revocation of acceptance is governed by UCC § 2-608(1), which provides:

> The buyer may revoke his acceptance of a . . . commercial unit whose non-conformity substantially impairs its value to him if he has accepted it
>
> . . . .
>
> (b) without discovery of such non-conformity if his acceptance was reasonably induced either by the difficulty of discovery before acceptance or by the seller's assurances.

9A V.S.A. § 2-608(1).

Defendant argues that the warranty was not breached because each oil leak was from a different seal, and defendant repaired or was prepared to repair all such leaks within the warranty period. The trial court took a broader view of the evidence, and concluded that defendant breached the express warranty that the roller required only simple and light maintenance, was ideal for base surface application, and would perform exceptionally well on plaintiff's usual jobs. This conclusion is amply supported by the findings with respect to the deficiencies. A seller cannot bar revocation by repairing or agreeing to repair numerous defects; at some point a buyer may say "enough is enough" and revoke acceptance. *Rester v. Morrow*, 491 So. 2d 204, 210 (Miss. 1986). Defendant's argument that it never repaired or replaced the same part twice is not persuasive because the string of malfunctions substantially impaired the value of the roller. Moreover, the breakdowns undermined plaintiff's confidence in the ability of the machine to do the job. In light of these findings, the court reasonably concluded that the roller did not conform to defendant's warranties, notwithstanding defendant's repair efforts.

C.

Defendant also contends that plaintiff waived any right to revoke acceptance by continuing to use the roller after giving notice of revocation. Defendant asserts that the trial court erred in finding that revocation occurred in November 1990, when the machine was parked, and in finding that the roller was used only once thereafter, inadvertently, by one of plaintiff's employees. According to defendant, plaintiff revoked acceptance in June 1990, when plaintiff's president telephoned the manufacturer and offered to pay a reasonable rental fee in exchange for a return of the roller. The record shows, however, that after additional repairs during the summer of 1990, this offer was communicated to the defendant on August 27, 1990. Plaintiff's president testified that he made the call "to see what they wanted to do for me." In late September, plaintiff's president just demanded the return of his money. The court found that defendant made repairs to the roller during the summer of 1990 and continued to assure plaintiff that the problems would be corrected up to and after revocation. In August 1990, plaintiff's mechanic replaced a broken oil plug, a burnt-out starter and wiring. Plaintiff's president testified that the roller was used on two subsequent jobs in October of that year.

A buyer who revokes acceptance has the same rights and duties with regard to the goods involved as if they had been rejected. 9A V.S.A. § 2-608(3). With limited exceptions, a buyer's exercise of ownership after rejection is wrongful as against the seller. *Id.* § 2-602(2)(a); see *id.* § 2-603(1) (buyer under duty to attempt to sell rejected perishable goods on seller's account if seller has no agent or place of business at market of rejection), *id.* § 2-604 (if seller gives no instructions within reasonable time after buyer's rejection, buyer may store, reship, or sell on seller's account). Nevertheless, continued use of goods whose acceptance has been revoked does not vitiate the revocation if the use was reasonable. *McCullough v. Bill Swad Chrysler-Plymouth, Inc.*, 5 Ohio St. 3d 181, 449 N.E.2d 1289, 1292 (1983). Reasonable use is a question of fact that depends on whether: (1) the seller tendered instructions concerning return of the rejected goods upon notice of the revocation; (2) business needs or personal circumstances compelled the buyer's continued use; (3) the seller continued to offer assurances that the nonconformities would be cured or that the buyer would be recompensed for dissatisfaction and inconvenience during the period of continued use; (4) the seller acted in good faith; and (5) the seller suffered undue prejudice as a result of the continued use. *Id.* 449 N.E.2d at 1293.

The court found that the continued use after revocation was a good faith attempt to mitigate damages, that defendant continued to assure plaintiff that repairs would be successful and that the use was reasonable under the circumstances. The record does not disclose any instructions by the defendant to plaintiff regarding permanent return of the roller, or evidence of prejudice from continued use. We agree with the trial court that the use of the roller during the month of October, after buyer had given notice, was not unreasonable. Therefore, plaintiff's post-revocation use did not waive the revocation of acceptance.

. . . .

Affirmed.

NOTE AND QUESTIONS

Sections 2-608 and 2A-517 both provide that a buyer or lessee may revoke acceptance if the goods tendered are non-conforming to the degree that the non-conformity substantially impairs the value of the goods to the buyer/lessee. Does the court describe that as an objective or subjective standard? Can the two standards be interrelated? Could they possibly not be, as a practical matter?

PROBLEM 6-7

Selig Carpet Warehouse, Inc. entered into a contract to "lease" floor covering to BEF Realty Co. for use in a new apartment complex built by BEF. The contract provided that Selig would deliver and install vinyl tile and carpeting within ten days of BEF notifying Selig that a particular phase of the complex had been completed. Five days after BEF notified Selig that phase one was complete, Selig installed the floor covering. Ten days thereafter, employees at BEF inspected the goods and the work, and, quite by accident, discovered that the carpeting was not in fact stain resistant, as Selig had assured BEF it would be. BEF then demanded that Selig remove all of the carpeting and replace it with a more stain-resistant product. Selig, though disposed to refuse BEF's request, has called you to get a sense of the law governing the controversy. After reading § 2A-513(2), outline the discussion that you would have with the officers of Selig when they come to meet with you.

PROBLEM 6-8

Return to the facts of Problem 6-6. If Buto is determined to have "accepted" the lead-covered tanks, can it argue that it revoked its acceptance on the following day?

PROBLEM 6-9

Byte Computer, Inc. purchased regrind plastic pellets from Sally's Plastic Supply, Inc. for use in molding computer cabinets for its customers. "Regrind" is plastic that has been molded at least one time before and then has been scrapped and ground for use again. Sally's warranted that products molded from the pellets would withstand temperatures of at least 205 degrees. Sally's had no knowledge of Byte's intended customers or final use for the product.

As was common in the industry, Sally's forwarded a sample to Byte to test whether the pellets were relatively free of contamination and would mold properly. No manufacturer in Byte's industry has the facilities to perform any other tests on the sample submitted. Byte approved the sample and received the full shipment from Sally's.

Byte molded all of the pellets into computer cabinets and then shipped them to its customer for painting. When exposed to 150 degree temperatures during the painting process, the computer cabinets warped. Byte immediately informed Sally's of the problem and demanded that new pellets be sent immediately. Sally's instructed Byte to return the material. With Sally's permission, Byte reground the cabinets at a cost of $1,000 because it made shipping much less expensive and resale by Sally's much easier.

Analyze whether Byte can properly reject the pellets; if not, can Byte revoke acceptance of the pellets?

6.   Right of Inspection; Timing of Rejection or Revocation

As you have seen, the timing of the buyer's actions is crucial for determining whether the buyer has effectively rejected or revoked acceptance. In this final section, we focus on the timing questions as a way to summarize the preceding material.

GNP COMMODITIES, INC. v. WALSH HEFFERNAN CO.
Illinois Appellate Court
420 N.E.2d 659 (1981)

SULLIVAN, Presiding Justice:

Defendants appeal from a judgment for plaintiffs, after a jury trial, in an action to recover damages in the sale of nonconforming frozen pork bellies. They contend that (1) the trial court should not have permitted plaintiff to file a jury demand after defendants withdrew their jury demand prior to the retrial of the case; (2) plaintiff's rejection or revocation of acceptance of the goods did not occur within a reasonable time; (3) plaintiff had no right to revoke acceptance since the value of the goods to plaintiff was not substantially impaired; and (4) the trial court improperly instructed the jury that the sole measure of damages was the return of the purchase price. The record discloses that the plaintiff is a commodity trader, a member of the Chicago Mercantile Exchange (Exchange) and, at the time of the transaction with defendants, a hedger and speculator in frozen pork bellies. Its activities included the purchase and sale of pork bellies (referred to as "actual" or "cash" product) and the Exchange traded futures contracts for the purpose of speculating on the difference between the actual product and the futures market. It accomplished this by a technique called "hedging," which involved the purchase of the actual product and the sale of futures against it.

Myron Rosenthal, president of plaintiff, was responsible for buying the actual product through a public meat broker and selling the corresponding futures contract on the Exchange. He testified that he never bought nondeliverable frozen bellies during the hedging season, which was from November through August, and that bellies frozen after November 1 were important to a hedger such as plaintiff because they afforded the option of delivering the actual product against the futures position.

On March 27, 1974, Rosenthal received a telephone call from Eugene Figurelli, the agent for defendant Walsh Heffernan Company (Walsh), a public meat broker, which in turn was the agent that conducted the transaction for the seller of the bellies, defendant Florence Beef Company (Florence). The meat broker assists potential customers by obtaining offerings of fresh or frozen products from sellers who pay for the broker's services, and he is responsible for obtaining necessary information (including freeze dates) from the seller for the buyer.

In the March 27 telephone call, Figurelli asked Rosenthal if he was interested in purchasing five loads of frozen pork bellies, and Rosenthal replied that he was, depending on the freeze date, price, manufacture and location. Figurelli called back within 20 minutes and reported that the bellies were frozen on February 1, 1974, or later, were priced at 43 1/2 cents per pound, and that the weight met Exchange specifications for delivery. Rosenthal told Figurelli that he would purchase those five loads and asked if Figurelli could obtain five more loads which were more "desirable"; that is, either fresh or frozen within the last 15 days. Figurelli later called Rosenthal and told him that he had five more loads priced at 44 cents per pound which would meet Rosenthal's specifications, and he assured Rosenthal that all 10 loads complied with Exchange requirements for delivery.

It appears from the testimony that a party planning to deliver the actual product as protection against a futures contract deliverable between February and August of a given year must comply with Exchange regulations, the most important of which concerns the freeze date and requires that bellies must have been frozen no earlier than the preceding November 1, or must have been accumulating in the freezer not earlier than October 16 with other product and frozen not earlier than November 1. Freeze dates are significant because after bellies have been in the freezer for several months, there is a progressively greater chance of deterioration. Bellies frozen before November 1 are not deliverable against futures short sales starting the following February. To a hedger, therefore, bellies frozen before November 1 have no value, especially between February and August, and thus there is always a price differential between old and new bellies.

Three or four days after the transaction between Rosenthal and Figurelli, Walsh sent plaintiff written confirmations for each of the 10 loads. These revealed that the seller was defendant Florence and included the weight of each load, the storage locations, and the storage companies' lot numbers, but they did not disclose the dates that the product first went into the freezers. Plaintiff paid a total of $164,368.39 for the 10 loads.

Rosenthal and Figurelli communicated every 5 to 10 days for about six weeks in April and May. When freeze dates were mentioned, Figurelli continually assured Rosenthal, "It's okay, it's just a matter of confirming which dates got on which loads." He did not, however, give Rosenthal the exact freeze dates but said they were February 1, 1974, or later. Rosenthal testified that he had no reason to doubt Figurelli's word since there had been no problems dealing with him in the past.

In late May, Rosenthal requested an inspection by the Exchange so that the bellies could be delivered against a futures contract, if necessary. About June 8 or 9, Rosenthal received the first inspection report from the Exchange for loads one and two. They did not pass inspection, since the bellies had been frozen prior to November 1, 1973, and thus were not deliverable. Plaintiff then tried to return the bellies to defendants, but they refused to cancel the transaction. Eventually it was determined that nine of the 10 loads were frozen before November 1973, and were not deliverable. Plaintiff then sold those nine loads on the open market for 21 cents per pound. The tenth load, which was frozen prior to March 1, 1974, was deliverable and was sold for 45 1/2 cents per pound. Plaintiff's proceeds for the 10 loads came to $87,984.16; storage costs were $5,000.

The record further discloses that loads one and two, which defendants sold to plaintiff, were originally owned by Pacific Trading Company (Pacific), which had inadvertently failed to sell them in 1973 and then sold them on January 4, 1974, through Figurelli to Florence. Two months later, on March 19, defendants sold the first five loads (including the Pacific loads) to Murlas Brothers Commodities (Murlas), also through Figurelli. The confirmations on that sale recited that the bellies were frozen in November 1973 or later, but did not provide all the usual information which Figurelli promised to supply later. Murlas had purchased the five loads for November 1 and later freeze so that the bellies could be deliverable on the Exchange and, when the information was not provided, Murlas returned the five loads to Florence on March 26. They were then sold to plaintiff on March 27 through Figurelli.

Plaintiff sued both defendants, alleging breach of contract, fraud and misrepresentation, wilful and wanton fraud and misrepresentation against each, and also breach of fiduciary duty against Walsh. A count alleging breach of warranty was dismissed. The jury found both defendants liable and assessed plaintiff's damages in the full amount claimed of $81,384.15. The jury also answered two special interrogatories in the affirmative, finding that defendants either singly or together knowingly misrepresented the age of the meat to plaintiff at the time of the sale and that the agreement between the parties specified that the 10 loads were to have been February 1, 1974, freeze or later.

Opinion

Defendants next contend that plaintiff did not reject the pork bellies or revoke acceptance of them within a reasonable time. They argue that plaintiff's conduct was unreasonable because plaintiff indicated no intention to inspect the goods and because information about their condition was readily available.

The record discloses that plaintiff purchased the bellies at the end of March 1974, but did not inspect them until May of that year. Thereafter, plaintiff notified defendants that the goods were nonconforming and unsuccessfully sought to return them. The jury was instructed as to plaintiff's theories that the goods were rejected within a reasonable time and that acceptance was revoked within a reasonable time after discovery of the nonconformity. The issue that is raised, therefore, is whether plaintiff's conduct was reasonable within the framework of those theories.

The Uniform Commercial Code (the Code) provides generally that an action is to be judged as reasonable depending on the nature, purpose and circumstances of such action (Ill. Rev. Stat. 1979, ch. 26, par. 1-204(2)), and in each case that determination rests with the trier of fact (*see Heller v. Sullivan* (1978), 57 Ill. App. 3d 190, 372 N.E.2d 1036; *Sauers v. Tibbs* (1977), 48 Ill. App. 3d 805, 363 N.E.2d 444; *Boysen v. Antioch Sheet Metal, Inc.* (1974), 16 Ill. App. 3d 331, 306 N.E.2d 69). Consistent with that standard, section 2-602(1) provides in relevant part that "[r]ejection of goods must be within a reasonable time after their delivery or tender." (Ill. Rev. Stat. 1979, ch. 26, par. 2-602(1).) Similarly, section 2-608(2) provides in relevant part:

"Revocation of acceptance must occur within a reasonable time after the buyer discovers or should have discovered the ground for it and before any substantial change in condition of the goods which is not caused by their own defects. It is not effective until the buyer notifies the seller of it." (Ill. Rev. Stat. 1979, ch. 26, par. 2-608(2).)

It is also well established that a jury's finding will not be disturbed on review unless so unreasonable as to be against the manifest weight of the evidence. (*Russo v. Checker Taxi Co.* (1978), 67 Ill. App. 3d 379, 385 N.E.2d 33; *Papageorgiou v. F.W. Woolworth Co.* (1978), 66 Ill. App. 3d 873, 383 N.E.2d 1346.) In the case before us, we believe that the finding of liability under either theory is not against the manifest weight of the evidence.

We note that the courts may permit buyers to delay inspection until they are ready to resell or use the goods if there is proof of custom or trade usage. In this regard, section 1-205(2) of the Code provides in relevant part:

"A usage of trade is any practice or method of dealing having such regularity of observance in a place, vocation or trade as to justify an expectation that it will be observed with respect to the transaction in question." (Ill. Rev. Stat. 1979, ch. 26, par. 1-205(2).)

An example in this regard is *La Villa Fair v. Lewis Carpet Mills, Inc.* (1976), 219 Kan. 395, 548 P.2d 825, where the buyer arranged with the seller to have 21 rolls of carpeting delivered to a warehouse to be stored pending the outcome of a strike affecting the buyer's customer. Evidence was presented of an industrial practice for a wholesaler-retailer not to inspect large orders of carpeting upon delivery and that the carpeting would normally be stored until ready for use rather than to unroll it immediately for inspection of concealed defects. Based upon this practice, the court held that a 9-month delay by plaintiff in bringing defects to the seller's attention was not unreasonable. Similarly, in *La Nasa v. Russell Packing Co.*, (7th Cir. 1952), 198 F.2d 992, the buyer purchased lard for its baking business. Although 27 of 80 drums had been used before it was determined that the lard had spoiled, the court permitted the buyer to rescind the contract, holding that the buyer was entitled to rely upon the custom of the baking industry not to test standard baking ingredients before using them and to make refunds for any ingredients which proved defective when used. The common factor in the above cases is that the courts permitted delay in inspection when a course of dealing or usage of trade was established.

From the testimony in the instant case, it appears that no physical transfer of meat occurred, as the delivery was accomplished by documents in the form of written confirmations; that in the meat industry inspection is not made until the buyer is ready to deliver the pork bellies from the warehouse against a short sale futures contract on the Exchange; and that the broker is relied upon for information as to freeze dates. We think this testimony established a trade usage permitting delay of inspection until the buyer is prepared to resell the product, and that this usage was a relevant consideration in the jury's decision that rejection or revocation of acceptance occurred within a reasonable time.

Concerning the rejection theory, it appears that some two months after the date of purchase, upon learning that loads one and two did not meet Exchange specifications, plaintiff promptly telephoned Walsh and sought to return the bellies. The record discloses no denial by defendants that those goods were nonconforming, that they did not receive prompt notification thereof, or that they refused to give plaintiff satisfaction. In the light thereof and considering the trade usage as set forth above, we believe that the combination of plaintiff's refusal to keep the delivered goods and its notice to defendants that plaintiff would not keep them are ample support for the finding that rejection came within a reasonable time.

The cases cited by defendants do not support their position that rejection was not timely. In *Miron v. Yonkers Raceway, Inc.* (2d Cir. 1968), 400 F.2d 112, the seller sued the buyer of a horse and the raceway which acted as the seller's agent in the auction sale of the horse. It was customary in purchasing a racehorse for the buyer's veterinarian or trainer to examine the horse's legs for fractures, but the buyer did not have the horse examined on the date of sale and testified only that the horse was unsound on the day after. The seller testified that the horse was sound at the time of sale, and it was held that where an injury to a horse's leg could have been discovered by the inspection customarily made at the time of sale, the buyer's attempted rejection 24 hours later was unreasonable. In the instant case, however, there was a usage of the futures trade permitting plaintiff to delay inspection of pork bellies until the date of delivery against a futures contract. *Goodlatte v. Acme Sales Corp.* (1923), 229 Ill. App. 610, cited by defendants, is also distinguishable. There, the goods were delivered at the end of April and defendant did not make payment on the due date of June 1 because it was having " 'a good deal of trouble' " with the goods. (229 Ill. App. 610, 612.) The first notice of nonconformity, however, was not given until June 29 and rejection took place on September 12. The court stated that "[t]here is no reason why the goods could not have been examined shortly after they were received by the defendant. This not having been done, it was in no position to reject them on September 12." (229 Ill. App. 610, 615.) In the present case, by contrast, plaintiff notified Walsh immediately upon learning that the goods were nonconforming rather than waiting 2 1/2 months, as the buyer did in *Goodlatte.*

Contrary to defendants' position, we think that the cases upon which they rely actually stand for the principle that all the circumstances, including the conduct of the parties and what was said, are to be considered in determining whether the buyer waited an unreasonably long time to reject the goods.

With respect to revocation of acceptance, we initially note that the jury could reasonably have inferred from the facts that the transaction had reached a stage beyond the time for rejection and thus that the goods had been accepted. (See Ill. Rev. Stat. 1979, ch. 26, par. 2-606.) In this regard, the focus of our inquiry is, like that of rejection, whether or not the record supports the finding that revocation occurred in a timely manner. Section 2-608(1)(b) of the Code provides:

> "(1) The buyer may revoke his acceptance of a lot or commercial unit whose non-conformity substantially impairs its value to him if he has accepted it
>
> . . . .
>
> (b) without discovery of such non-conformity if his acceptance was reasonably induced either by the difficulty of discovery before acceptance or by the seller's assurances." (Ill. Rev. Stat. 1979, ch. 26, par. 2-608(1)(b).)

Section 2-608(2) provides in relevant part that "[r]evocation of acceptance must occur within a reasonable time after the buyer discovers or should have discovered the ground for it. . . ." (Ill. Rev. Stat. 1979, ch. 26, par. 2-608(2).) Thus, the reasonable time for revocation of acceptance may be extended if the defect is difficult to discover or if the seller gives continuous assurances.

The record here indicates that the nonconformity was difficult to discover because the pork bellies were warehoused and because the transaction was completed through written confirmations. Testimony was also introduced that it was not customary for hedgers on the Exchange to inspect an actual product since the broker is responsible for ascertaining freeze dates and, in addition, there was ample evidence that defendants knew plaintiff was a hedger and speculator in frozen pork bellies and purchased actual product as protection against futures positions. Moreover, it appears clear that plaintiff was induced to accept the goods by Figurelli's continuous assurances that the goods met the freeze date specified in the contract. It is also significant that the jury especially found that defendants knowingly misrepresented the age of the bellies, and this is evident from defendants' transaction with Murlas involving five of the 10 loads one week earlier, in which defendant told Murlas that the pre-November 1 freeze date was post-November 1 freeze. Those misrepresentations supported the finding that defendants had engaged in the active concealment from plaintiff of the true freeze dates. We believe also that plaintiff's refusal to keep the goods and his prompt notification to Walsh are equally as important in determining timely revocation of acceptance, as in the case of timely rejection. Taking all of these factors into consideration, it seems clear that the jury was justified in concluding that the 2-month hiatus between the purchase and revocation of acceptance was reasonable.

Contrary to defendants' position that revocation must take place immediately upon purchase, the case law supports the view that depending on the circumstances, several weeks or months may elapse before revocation of acceptance. In *Ed Fine Oldsmobile, Inc. v. Knisley* (Del. Super. 1974), 319 A.2d 33, a buyer purchased an automobile which did not meet his expectations or the dealer's representations. Instead of rejecting the car, the buyer continued to bring it to the dealer who promised to make necessary repairs. The court found that the buyer was persuaded by the seller's assurances to withhold revocation for several months and that, even though the vehicle had been driven over 1500 miles, the buyer had had little opportunity for inspection since the car was frequently being repaired. In that situation, revocation of acceptance was held to be timely.

Similarly, in *Birkner v. Purdon* (1970), 27 Mich. App. 476, 183 N.W.2d 598, the buyer revoked acceptance of Christmas trees within one month. Testimony showed that immediate discovery of defect was difficult because of the time required for the trees to open up after being flattened in transit, and that on several occasions the seller had assured the buyer of the good quality of the trees. The court held that revocation was within a reasonable time. In *Parker v. Johnston* (1968), 244 Ark. 355, 426 S.W.2d 155, the seller fraudulently misrepresented the past profits of a vending machine business and the value of juke boxes, cigarette and pinball machines, which comprised the main assets of the business. The court held that the buyer's right to rescission was not waived by his having made 2 of 36 payments on the principal under the contract before becoming convinced of the misrepresentation. The court stated that inducement to retain the goods because of the seller's assurances may permit revocation of acceptance a substantial time after receipt of the goods.

Having found above that inspection could be delayed by virtue of the trade usage, we see no merit in defendants' contention that changes in the buyer's circumstances relative to market factors is an unfair criterion to determine reasonable time for revocation of acceptance. The record indicates that the futures season terminated with the August delivery month, so that the longest period for buyers to hold goods before having to inspect them would be from November 1, the earliest freeze date, through August. Plaintiff's ordering the inspection in May suggests that it acted consistently with the trade usage and that it recognized the possibility of delivering bellies against a futures contract. As the record also makes clear, defendants were familiar with the practices of the Exchange and with plaintiff's activities thereon. Therefore, since defendants were aware of these uncertainties occurring in the regular course of business, they cannot assert unfairness.

Defendants further suggest that since plaintiff purchased the goods pursuant to documents of title, it had no right of inspection and thus no right to reject or revoke acceptance. Defendants failed, however, to raise this point either at trial or in their post-trial motion and have thereby waived it on appeal. An issue not raised by appellant at trial cannot be considered for the first time on appeal (*Kravis v. Smith Marine, Inc.* (1975), 60 Ill. 2d 141, 324 N.E.2d 417; *Woman's Athletic Club v. Hulman* (1964), 31 Ill. 2d 449, 202 N.E.2d 528), and an argument not raised by post-trial motion also will not be considered on appeal (*Burgdorff v. International Business Machines Corp.* (1979), 74 Ill. App. 3d 158, 392 N.E.2d 183; *Domena v. Prince* (1977), 52 Ill. App. 3d 462, 367 N.E.2d 717; Ill. Rev. Stat. 1979, ch. 110A, par. 366(b)(2)(iii)).

In any event, although section 2-513(3)(b) of the Code precludes the buyer's inspection of goods before payment therefor (Ill. Rev. Stat. 1979, ch. 26, par. 2-513(3)(b)), it does not foreclose inspection after payment. It has been held that in a sale through documents of title, if goods for which the buyer must pay the purchase price before inspection are nonconforming, the buyer may recover the price he has paid. (*Price v. Neiman Brothers Co.* (1926), 240 Ill. App. 157; *also see* Ill. Ann. Stat., ch. 26, par. 2-513, Illinois Code Comment, at 409 (Smith-Hurd 1963).) Here, plaintiff made no attempt to inspect the goods prior to payment. The written confirmations were sent three days after the oral agreement was reached, and at that time title to the pork bellies was transferred and payment of the purchase price was made by sight drafts and warehouse receipts. Plaintiff ordered the inspection almost two months later. Therefore, section 2-513(3)(b) is inapplicable.

Finally, in support of their contention that rejection or revocation of acceptance was not timely, defendants make several factual assertions which are unsupported in the record. First, they assert that plaintiff had no desire to inspect the goods because it had entered into a so-called "bastard hedge," whereby nondeliverable pork bellies were purchased to offset a futures trade on the purchaser's books with no intention that the actual product be delivered against a futures trade. However, the jury found that the contract was for deliverable bellies, and defendants do not contest that finding. In addition, there was uncontradicted testimony by Rosenthal that he never bought actual product for a bastard hedge during the hedging season from November through August. Second, defendants assert that plaintiff could have ascertained the freeze dates from the broker, the seller, or the warehouse. The testimony consistently showed, however, that the buyer depends upon the broker to provide such information, and the jury apparently was so persuaded in finding that defendants had knowingly misrepresented the age of the bellies as post-November 1 freeze or later. Third, defendants assert that a warehouse receipt for one of the loads contained the pre-November 1 freeze date and thereby put plaintiff on notice of the nonconformity. However, there is no indication of such receipt in the record. Fourth, defendants assert that because the written confirmations did not specify a freeze date, they were ambiguous and should have put plaintiff on notice. The record clearly indicates, however, that Figurelli continually assured plaintiff that the freeze dates were in compliance with the contract and, because it was the broker's responsibility to provide that information, the time for putting plaintiff on notice was extended.

Concerning defendants' assertion that plaintiff made a substantial profit on the futures market and thereby failed to act in good faith (*see* Ill. Rev. Stat. 1979, ch. 26, par. 1-203), we note that defendants did not raise that issue at trial or by post-trial motion and thus have waived it on appeal. Nevertheless, there is no indication in the record that plaintiff knew or suspected that any of the freeze dates were pre-November 1 and merely waited for inspection until the market had dropped. Rather, it appears that plaintiff ordered the inspection in due course in anticipation of possible delivery. Even if plaintiff made a profit on futures contracts for pork bellies, we see no reason why the collateral source rule should not apply to bar defendants from reducing damages by proof that plaintiff has been compensated from a source to which they have not contributed. *See Cereal Byproducts Co. v. Hall* (1958), 16 Ill. App. 2d 79, 147 N.E.2d 383, *aff'd* (1958), 15 Ill. 2d 313, 155 N.E.2d 14; *also see Hanover Shoe, Inc. v. United Shoe Machinery Corp.* (M.D. Pa. 1965), 245 F. Supp. 258, *aff'd* (1968), 392 U.S. 481.

We recognize that rejection and revocation of acceptance were intended by the drafters of the Code to be theoretically distinct concepts. (*See* Ill. Ann. Stat., ch. 26, par. 2-602, Illinois Code Comment, at 428 (Smith-Hurd 1963).) Our reading of the case law suggests, however, that the courts have not always taken to this dichotomy (*see, e.g., Don's Marine, Inc. v. Haldeman* (Tex. Civ. App. 1977), 557 S.W.2d 826), nor does the instant case present an array of facts which fits neatly within one theory or the other. We think those facts are such that, viewed from one perspective, the jury could reasonably conclude that rejection would be the proper label for plaintiff's actions but, when viewed from another, it would constitute revocation of acceptance. A finding under either of the alternatives would not be contrary to the manifest weight of the evidence.

Defendants next contend that plaintiff was not entitled to revoke acceptance since the pork bellies sold to plaintiff were of sufficiently high quality so as not to be substantially impaired in value. They maintain that there is no significant difference between a pork belly frozen February 1, 1974 — which was what plaintiff ordered — and one frozen before November 1 of the preceding year, and thus they argue that they substantially complied with plaintiff's needs. Plaintiff argues, on the other hand, that it was entitled to revoke acceptance since the bellies were not deliverable against a futures contract — the type most often used in plaintiff's business — and therefore, the value of the goods to plaintiff was substantially impaired.

Revocation of acceptance due to substantial impairment is governed by section 2-608(1) of the Code, which provides in relevant part:

> "The buyer may revoke his acceptance of a lot or commercial unit whose non-conformity substantially impairs its value to him. . . ." (Ill. Rev. Stat. 1979, ch. 26, par. 2-608(1).)

The import of this section depends on the reference "to him," which suggests that impairment is to be measured in terms of the particular needs of the buyer. (*See* Ill. Ann Stat., ch. 26, par. 2-608, Illinois Commercial Code Comment, at 464 (Smith-Hurd 1963).) Thus, one buyer may find goods to be satisfactory despite minor defects, whereas another buyer because of his particular circumstances would find them unacceptable. In order to revoke acceptance, therefore, the buyer must present objective evidence showing that with respect to his own needs, the value of the goods was substantially impaired (*Sauers v. Tibbs* (1977), 48 Ill. App. 3d 805, 363 N.E.2d 444; *Overland Bond & Investment Corp. v. Howard* (1972), 9 Ill. App. 3d 348, 292 N.E.2d 168; *also see Barrington Homes of Florida, Inc. v. Kelley* (Fla. App. 1975), 320 So. 2d 841) and not merely that he thought or believed the value was impaired (*Hays Merchandise, Inc. v. Dewey* (1970), 78 Wash. 2d 343, 474 P.2d 270). What constitutes substantial impairment is determined by the trier of fact. *Boysen v. Antioch Sheet Metal, Inc.; Hays Merchandise, Inc. v. Dewey; see Campbell v. Pollack* (1966), 101 R.I. 223, 221 A.2d 615; *Rozmus v. Thompson's Lincoln-Mercury Co.* (1966), 209 Pa. Super. 120, 224 A.2d 782.

We think it clear from the record here that plaintiff wanted bellies deliverable against a futures contract and planned to resell them on the market; that there was a price differential between deliverable and nondeliverable product caused by the decline in value in direct proportion to age; and that nine of the loads were so old as to be nondeliverable. Additionally, it is implicit in its verdict that the jury found the price differential between deliverable and nondeliverable bellies to have substantially impaired the value of the merchandise to plaintiff, and we do not believe this finding was against the manifest weight of the evidence.

The question of substantial impairment has been considered by several courts. In *Sauers v. Tibbs*, plaintiff revoked acceptance of a mobile home which was infested with beetles. The court stated that with respect to revocation, the effect of impairment on the user and not the dollar value of repairs is crucial in establishing substantial impairment. In *Stamm v. Wilder Travel Trailers* (1976), 44 Ill. App. 3d 530, 358 N.E.2d 382, plaintiff complained of a number of minor defects in the new trailer he purchased, but presented no evidence as to costs of repairs. There was defense testimony that the defects could be repaired in one hour at a cost of $10, and that plaintiff brought the trailer in for repairs but when he was told that a couple of days would be needed to do the work, he left and did not return. It appears that plaintiff took a trip with the trailer despite the defects. Finding the defects to have minimal impact on plaintiff, the court held that substantial impairment had not been proved. In *Overland Bond & Investment Co. v. Howard*, the buyer told the seller he was a salesman and needed his car daily. On the first day the buyer used the car, the transmission fell out and it took nine days to repair. Then the gas line clogged and the brakes failed, requiring more repairs, but the seller did nothing for three weeks despite telling the buyer the repairs would be made. Finding that the car was so hazardous to drive that its value to the buyer was substantially impaired, the court held that revocation of acceptance was justified. In the light of the foregoing, we believe that plaintiff here has presented sufficient objective facts showing substantial impairment in the value of the goods to him.

Defendants' final contention is that as several theories of liability were advanced, the trial court erred by instructing the jury that the proper measure of damages was the difference between the purchase price and the amount paid to plaintiff for resale of the goods plus storage costs. Plaintiff maintains that each theory upon which liability is predicated permits recovery of the purchase price. Count I alleged that the goods were nonconforming and that plaintiff was entitled to reject them. Counts II and VI alleged that defendants were guilty of fraudulent misrepresentation. Count III alleged breach of contract. Count IV charged defendant Walsh with breach of fiduciary duty. Count VII, in repeating Count VI, also alleged wilful and wanton conduct by defendants.

The trial court instructed the jury as follows:

"If you decide for the plaintiff on the question of liability, you must then fix the amount of damages to which the plaintiff is entitled, which you are hereby directed to fix as the difference between the purchase price and the amount for which the plaintiff sold the goods plus storage charges you find the plaintiff incurred."

Defendants urge, however, that the trial court should have instructed the jury on the measure of damages in accordance with section 2-714(1) of the Code, which provides:

"Where the buyer has accepted goods and given notification (subsection (3) of Section 2-607) he may recover as damages for any non-conformity of tender the loss resulting in the ordinary course of events from the seller's breach as determined in any manner which is reasonable." Ill. Rev. Stat. 1979, ch. 26, par. 2-714(1).

Defendants' position lacks merit for several reasons. First of all, the record does not indicate that an instruction as to section 2-714(1) was tendered. If a party does not tender an instruction, the trial court's failure to give it cannot be claimed as error on appeal. (Ill. Rev. Stat. 1979, ch. 110A, par. 366(b)(2)(i).) Second, defendants have referred us to nothing in the record which would support giving an instruction under section 2-714(1). Unless the record includes some evidence to support the theory set out in a tendered instruction, the trial court is not required to give it. (*Figarelli v. Ihde* (1976), 39 Ill. App. 3d 1023, 351 N.E.2d 624; *Biggerstaff v. New York, Chicago & St. Louis R. Co.* (1957), 13 Ill. App. 2d 85, 141 N.E.2d 72.) Third, it is apparent that section 2-714(1) applies after the time for rejection and revocation of acceptance has passed (Ill. Ann. Stat., ch. 26, par. 2-714, Illinois Commercial Code Comment, at 574 (Smith-Hurd

1963)), and defendants have failed to show that such was the fact here. We find, therefore, that section 2-714(1) is inapplicable, and the trial court was not required to give such instruction.

Moreover, by their failure to object to the damages instruction at the instructions conference, defendants have waived any right to raise that issue on appeal. *Saunders v. Schultz* (1960), 20 Ill. 2d 301, 170 N.E.2d 163; *Onderisin v. Elgin, Joliet & Eastern Ry. Co.* (1959), 20 Ill. App. 2d 73, 155 N.E.2d 338. In any event, the instruction that the trial court gave was not inconsistent with section 2-714(1). Section 1-106(1) of the Code provides that remedies are to be liberally administered to the end that the aggrieved party may be placed in as good a position as if the other party had fully performed (Ill. Rev. Stat. 1979, ch. 26, par. 1-106(1); *see McGrady v. Chrysler Motors Corp.* (1977), 46 Ill. App. 3d 136, 360 N.E.2d 818) and, in view of this Code policy, we believe the manner in which damages were assessed in the instant case was reasonable. We note in addition that, contrary to defendants' assertion, the damage instruction did not assume as true any version of disputed facts which the jury should be expected to resolve. Rather, the instruction stated that the fixing of damages was conditioned by the finding of liability. *Cf. Pioneer Hi-Bred Corn Co. v. Northern Illinois Gas Co.* (1975), 61 Ill. 2d 6, 329 N.E.2d 228.

With respect to rightful rejection (Ill. Rev. Stat. 1979, ch. 26, par. 2-602) and justifiable revocation of acceptance (Ill. Rev. Stat. 1979, ch. 26, par. 2-608), the buyer's remedies are governed by section 2-711 of the Code, which provides in relevant part:

> "(1) Where . . . the buyer rightfully rejects or justifiably revokes acceptance then with respect to any goods involved, . . . the buyer may cancel. . . .

> (3) On rightful rejection or justifiable revocation of acceptance a buyer has a security interest in goods in his possession or control for any payments made on their price and any expenses reasonably incurred in their inspection, receipt, transportation, care and custody and may hold such goods and resell them in like manner as an aggrieved seller (Section 2-706)." (Ill. Rev. Stat. 1979, ch. 26, par. 2-711(1), (3).)

The aggrieved seller's right to resell is governed by section 2-706(1), which provides in relevant part:

> "Where the resale is made in good faith and in a commercially reasonable manner the seller may recover the difference between the resale price and the contract price together with any incidental damages allowed under the provisions of this Article (Section 2-710), but less expenses saved in consequence of the buyer's breach." Ill. Rev. Stat. 1979, ch. 26, par. 2-706(1).

Consistent with these Code provisions, it is our view here that plaintiff rightfully rejected or justifiably revoked acceptance and notified defendants in a timely manner that it was cancelling the contract. Also, since possession or control passed to plaintiff through the documentary sale, plaintiff had a security interest in the goods for payments made on the purchase price and any reasonably incurred expenses including care and custody of the goods. The record does not reveal and defendants give no indication that plaintiff did not sell the goods in a commercially reasonable manner. To the contrary, there was testimony that the price received for the nine nondeliverable loads was the best plaintiff could get, and it sought to recover the difference between the contract price and the resale price, together with incidental damages in the form of storage costs. (*Cf. American Paper & Pulp Co. v. Denenberg* (3d Cir. 1956), 233 F.2d 610.) Under section 2-710 of the Code, incidental damages includes expenses for care and custody of the goods. (*Also see Durfee v. Rod Baxter Imports, Inc.* (Minn. 1978), 262 N.W.2d 349; *Welken v. Conley* (N.D. 1977), 252 N.W.2d 311; *Mobile Home Sales Management, Inc. v. Brown* (1977), 115 Ariz. 11, 562 P.2d 1378.) We believe, therefore, that the measure of damages instruction comports with the Code requirements. Also, inasmuch as the contract in question involved the sale of goods, damages for the breach thereof are governed by the Code, so that we need not consider the question of damages for breach of contract under the common law.

Concerning damages where fraud is involved, the Code permits an aggrieved buyer to cancel the contract and recover the purchase price. Section 2-721 provides:

> "Remedies for material misrepresentation or fraud include all remedies available under this Article for non-fraudulent breach." (Ill. Rev. Stat. 1979, ch. 26, par. 2-721.)

Under sections 2-711(1), (3), 2-706(1), and 2-710, cancellation of the contract and recovery of the purchase price less proceeds from the resale plus storage costs are available as the measure of damages for fraud. (*See Calloway v. Manion* (5th Cir. 1978), 572 F.2d 1033; *Lanners v. Whitney* (1967), 247 Ore. 223, 428 P.2d 398; Ill. Ann. Stat., ch. 26, par. 2-721, Illinois Code Comment, at 605–06 (Smith-Hurd 1963).) The damages instruction is therefore consistent.

Additionally, the Code does not supersede the common law right of an aggrieved buyer in an action for fraud to rescind the contract and recover the purchase price. Although the Code abandons the concept of rescission for those of rejection and revocation (*Calloway v. Manion*; *Lawner v. Engelbach* (1969), 433 Pa. 311, 249 A.2d 295), it has been held that an action for fraud is still available outside the Code (*Calloway v. Manion*; *City Dodge, Inc. v. Gardner* (1974), 232 Ga. 766, 208 S.E.2d 794; *see* Ill. Rev. Stat. 1979, ch. 26, par. 1-103). One remedy generally available to the defrauded party is to elect to repudiate the transaction and be placed in status quo. (*Walsh v. Oberlin* (1971), 2 Ill. App. 3d 987, 276 N.E.2d 728; *Meneghin v. Thunander* (1962), 36 Ill. App. 2d 452, 184 N.E.2d 753.) Hence, in the present case, plaintiff would be properly compensated through the damages formula ordered by the trial court, that is, by repudiating the contract and recovering the consideration given less proceeds from the resale plus storage costs. *See Hey v. Duncan* (7th Cir. 1926), 13 F.2d 794; *Johnston v. Shockey* (1929), 335 Ill. 363, 167 N.E. 54.

Finally, the measure of damages for breach of fiduciary duty, like that in an action for fraud, entitles the purchaser to recover the purchase price. It is well settled that transactions of parties standing in a fiduciary relationship will be set aside where reasonable suspicion exists that the confidence had been abused. (*Moehling v. W.E. O'Neil Construction Co.* (1960), 20 Ill. 2d 255, 170 N.E.2d 100; *Lerk v. McCabe* (1932), 349 Ill. 348, 182 N.E. 388; *Spindler v. Krieger* (1958), 16 Ill. App. 2d 131, 147 N.E.2d 457.) Thus, it would appear that the contract between plaintiff and defendants was voidable and plaintiff was entitled to be placed in the position it occupied prior to the transaction. We hold, therefore, that the trial court's instruction on damages was not in error.

For the reasons stated, the judgment and the award of damages are *affirmed*.

NOTES AND QUESTIONS

1. Usually the inspection issue in a case concerns whether the inspection occurred within a "reasonable time." Because the right to reject turns on timely action, if the buyer is slow to inspect, it will be deemed to have accepted the goods. As we have seen, this precludes the buyer from forcing the goods back on the seller, and leaves the buyer with recourse only to revoking acceptance or suing for damages.

2. In *GNP Commodities*, how did the court determine whether a reasonable time had passed before the inspection of the pork bellies occurred? Note the court's discussion of the plaintiff's right to reject and recognize how the court must analyze the inspection issue in deciding whether the plaintiff has properly rejected. Why is the inspection of the goods so closely tied to rejection?

3. The defendant contended that since the plaintiff purchased the goods pursuant to documents of title, it had no right to inspect. What was the defendant's basis for this

contention? What was the court's response to the argument?

PROBLEM 6-10

Shirley's Wholesale in Atlanta contracts to sell one hundred televisions to Boyle's Department Store in Nashville, Tennessee. The televisions are to be shipped F.O.B. Atlanta for arrival date of June 1. The televisions arrive in a carton on Friday, June 1. Boyle's receiving supervisor does not look at the televisions until Wednesday, June 6, when he uncrates five sets for display in the store. At this time he discovers that the televisions have problems with the vertical-hold adjustment. Can Boyle's return the televisions?

Chapter 7
REMEDIES

This chapter begins by reviewing general remedies provisions, and then covers the remedies provisions of Article 2 in the basic order they are presented in the Code: first, the remedies available to aggrieved sellers, followed by the remedies available to aggrieved buyers. This approach has the advantage of focusing on the relationship between the remedial options available to a particular party, and raising the issue of when the party is free to choose between different remedies. However, this approach has the unfortunate effect of de-emphasizing the parallel structure of buyer's and seller's remedies. For example, the buyer is afforded the right in certain circumstances to compel the seller to deliver the goods, § 2-716, and the seller is afforded the right in certain circumstances to compel the buyer to pay the price of the goods, § 2-709. It is instructive to consider how these two "specific performance" remedial provisions are similar, and to note the basis for any differences. As you analyze the remedy provisions of Article 2 you should pay particular attention to the underlying guiding principles of Part 7 that manifest themselves in the parallel structure of buyers' and sellers' remedies. It is also important to keep in mind the Code's remedial goal of compensation as expressed in § 1-305.

Article 2 provides extremely helpful index provisions: § 2-703 indexes sellers' remedies and § 2-711 indexes buyers' remedies. These provisions must be the starting point for any analysis of a dispute governed by Article 2, because they refer back to earlier provisions that establish the right of a party to obtain a remedy and they also refer forward to the remedies available to that party. As you read the cases and work through the problems in this chapter you should take the opportunity to review previous material by asking yourself continually, "Why is the party entitled to a remedy in the first place, and, based on my answer to that question, to what remedies is the party entitled under these circumstances?" This approach not only will reinforce the material that you already have covered, it will tie those concepts to the remedies available to the party suffering the breach.

A. GENERAL PROVISIONS AND REMEDIES LITIGATION

Before analyzing the remedies provisions specific to sellers and buyers, we will review the general provisions relating to remedies and remedies litigation. Our first topic is the statute of limitations, which provides for a four-year period subject to reduction by agreement of the parties. The complexities arise in determining when the statutory period begins to run. The next topic is the obligation to preserve evidence of the goods in dispute, which enables the other party to inspect them and then (presumably) to resolve the dispute on the basis of the facts. Our third topic is an aggrieved party's general right to receive incidental and consequential damages, although Article 2 prohibits the seller from receiving consequential damages. Finally, we will consider the parties' broad freedom of contract to specify the remedies in the event of a breach. This raises several related but distinct issues: the parties might choose to limit the remedies available in the event of a breach, as is the case when a seller seeks the buyer's agreement that it will be limited to "repair or replacement" of goods that do not conform to warranties; they might choose to exclude recovery of consequential damages in the event that the goods are not conforming, to protect the seller from the potentially limitless damages that a buyer's business might suffer in the event of a breach; or they might choose to liquidate the damages available in the event of a breach, as might be the case if the parties agree to a per diem payment in the event of delay. The four topics in this section provide the general background for the specific remedies provisions covered in the next two sections of this chapter.

1. Statute of Limitations

Every lawyer representing a party engaged in a dispute must be attentive to the applicable statute of limitations. Delay in identifying the problem giving rise to the dispute, protracted negotiations to resolve the dispute, or simple inattention by client or lawyer, raise the possibility that the client will lose its rights by failing to file suit within the statutory limit. At first glance, Article 2 appears to be relatively straightforward: parties must bring suit within four years after the accrual of the cause of action, unless they have agreed to a shorter time that may not be less than one year. Despite appearances, though, numerous complexities lurk in this rule.

Before reading the case and working through the following problems, it is important to understand the structure of § 2-725. First, the parties have the freedom of contract to shorten the applicable time period "to not less than one year," but not to lengthen the time period. § 2-725(1). Second, the section specifies that the cause of action accrues when "the breach occurs," and that "tender of delivery" is the point in time when the seller's breach of warranty occurs. § 2-725(2). There is no "notice" requirement, as the statute provides that the time begins to run "regardless of the aggrieved party's lack of knowledge of the breach." § 2-725(2). Third, the statute makes an exception for the breach of a warranty that "explicitly extends to future performance of the goods," in circumstances where "discovery of the breach must await the time of such performance," by providing that in such circumstances the cause of action accrues only "when the breach is or should have been discovered." § 2-725(2). This exception to the general rule is intuitively sensible, but distinguishing between warranties generally and those warranties that explicitly extend to future performance has proven to be a difficult task for courts. Finally, the statute expressly declines to displace the law regarding the tolling of statute of limitations under general state law. § 2-725(4). In effect, Article 2 leaves the exceptions dealing with situations of injustice or unfairness to law outside the Code. *See, e.g., Evans v. General Motors Corp.*, 314 Ill. App. 3d 609, 615–16, 732 N.E.2d 79 (2000) (reversing dismissal of action brought by minor more than four years after the breach, but brought within two years of the minor reaching the age of majority, pursuant to a state tolling statute).

WASHINGTON FREIGHTLINER v. SHANTYTOWN PIER, INC.
Maryland Court of Appeals
719 A.2d 541 (1998)

RODOWSKY, Judge.

This case involves the application of the four-year statute of limitations under the Sales Article of the Uniform Commercial Code to breaches of implied warranties in the sale of marine engines. The statute is Maryland Code (1975, 1997 Repl. Vol.), § 2-725 of the Commercial Law Article. In relevant part it reads:

> (1) An action for breach of any contract for sale must be commenced within four years after the cause of action has accrued. By the original agreement the parties may reduce the period of limitation to not less than one year but may not extend it.

> (2) A cause of action accrues when the breach occurs, regardless of the aggrieved party's lack of knowledge of the breach. *A breach of warranty occurs when tender of delivery is made*, except that where a warranty explicitly extends to future performance of the goods and discovery of the breach must await the time of such performance, the cause of action accrues when the breach is or should have been discovered.

(Emphasis added).

At issue is whether the statute began to run when the seller caused the engines to be delivered to the boat yard which later installed the engines in a boat that it was constructing for the buyer, or whether the running of the statute was postponed until the engines were "commissioned," that is, when the boat was subjected to a trial run at sea at various speeds.

The plaintiff, Shantytown Pier, Inc. (Shantytown), is a family business based in Ocean City, Maryland, that owns passenger boats. Shantytown sells fishing trips, nature cruises, and other boating excursions to paying passengers. On March 15, 1990, Shantytown contracted with Lydia Yachts of Stuart, Inc. (Lydia), a boatyard in Stuart, Florida, for the construction of a new 77-foot "party/fishing boat," the Ocean City Princess (O.C. Princess). Sometime after June 16, 1990, Shantytown purchased for use in the O.C. Princess three MAN D2840LXE 820-horsepower, 10-cylinder engines from Washington Freightliner, Inc. (WFI), one of the defendants. WFI, based in Capitol Heights, Maryland, is an authorized dealer in engines manufactured by another of the defendants, MAN Roland, Inc. (MAN), a German corporation with offices in the United States. The third defendant in this action is Marine Mechanical Systems, Inc. (MMS), an authorized distributor of MAN engines. MMS is based in Pompano Beach, Florida.

Shantytown purchased the three MAN engines at a total price of $163,000, "FOB Pompano Beach, Florida." The entire purchase price was paid before delivery. MMS caused the engines to be delivered to Lydia no later than September 30, 1990. Lydia completed construction of the O.C. Princess, and it was commissioned on April 20, 1991.

On ten separate occasions during nearly four years of operating the O.C. Princess, Shantytown experienced failures of one or another of each of the three engines. Although some of the failures were due to human error, most were due to complications involving faulty pistons. MAN's agents kept addressing the problems and performing repairs, but the problems, particularly failures related to the pistons, kept recurring. In April 1994, Shantytown, for $30,000, purchased another MAN engine for the O.C. Princess to replace one of the original MAN engines; within months, it too began suffering piston failure.

These failures led Shantytown to file suit on October 6, 1994, against MAN, WFI, and MMS. The complaint alleged breaches of express warranty, of contract, and of the implied warranties of merchantability and of fitness for a particular purpose.

Each defendant moved for summary judgment based, *inter alia*, on limitations grounds. Judge Theodore R. Eschenburg denied these motions. Prior to trial the plaintiff experienced an eleventh piston failure and decided to replace all three MAN engines with engines manufactured by another company. Three days before trial Shantytown, with leave of court, voluntarily dismissed its express warranty and breach of contract claims, leaving only the implied warranty claims against the three defendants.

At a jury trial with Judge Thomas C. Groton, III presiding, the defendants renewed their limitations argument by a motion for judgment at the conclusion of the plaintiff's case and by a motion for judgment at the conclusion of all the evidence, on which the court reserved both rulings. The jury found that the implied warranties had been breached, that there was an agency relationship between all of the defendants, and that the damages were $236,919.21. The court denied the defendants' motion for judgment notwithstanding the verdict.

Judge Eschenburg's order denying the defendants' motion for summary judgment gave no reasons, but Shantytown had argued that tender of delivery had not occurred until the O.C. Princess was commissioned.

. . . .

In denying the motion for judgment notwithstanding the verdict, Judge Groton found that Shantytown was "not given control of the engines until they were placed in the boat and the boat was commissioned, and then when it was first commissioned, the boat wasn't even in their control. It was in the control of . . . more than Lydia. . . . It was some of [the defendants'] representatives that were part of the commissioning that, in essence, were in charge of that process."

The defendants appealed to the Court of Special Appeals, which, in an unreported opinion, affirmed the trial court's ruling on limitations. The Court of Special Appeals, as is this Court, was required to decide whether tender of delivery under § 2-725(2) occurred when the defendants delivered the engines for Shantytown to Lydia or when the O.C. Princess was commissioned. . . .

The Court of Special Appeals held that the defendants had the burden of proving that limitations had run and, because "the trial court had before it evidence from which it reasonably could have decided that the price quotation and testimony at trial constituted sufficient proof of a requirement of commissioning, . . . that [defendants] had thus failed to carry their burden of persuasion."

We granted the defendants' petitions for certiorari, each of which raised the limitations issue.

I

The limitations issue presented here is quite narrow. "A breach of warranty occurs when tender of delivery is made." § 2-725(2). . . . Further, the only statutory exception to accrual on tender of delivery is that, "where a warranty explicitly extends to future performance of the goods and discovery of the breach must await the time of such performance, the cause of action accrues when the breach is or should have been discovered." § 2-725(2). Shantytown does not rely on this statutory exception to accrual, and it denies that a warranty of future performance is necessary to defer accrual of its claim to the commissioning of the engine.

Because the contract of sale is not in evidence, Shantytown cannot argue that the contract has specially defined "tender of delivery." Further, whether the defendants made any affirmations of fact about the engines' performance is immaterial, because the plaintiff has abandoned reliance on any express warranty.

. . . .

II

. . . Section 2-503(1), in relevant part, states:

"Tender of delivery requires that the seller put and hold conforming goods at the buyer's disposition and give the buyer any notification reasonably necessary to enable him to take delivery."

Official Comment 1 to § 2-503 explains that

"[t]he term 'tender' is used in this Title [Two] in two different senses. In one sense it refers to 'due tender' which contemplates an offer coupled with a present ability to fulfill all the conditions resting on the tendering party and must be followed by actual performance if the other party shows himself ready to proceed. Unless the context unmistakably indicates otherwise this is the meaning of 'tender' in this Title and the occasional addition of the word 'due' is only for clarity and emphasis. *At other times it is used to refer to an offer of goods or documents under a contract as if in fulfillment of its conditions even though there is a defect when measured against the contract obligation.* Used in either sense, however, 'tender' connotes such performance by the tendering party as puts the other party in default if he fails to proceed in some manner."

(Emphasis added).

Thus, the Official Comment reveals a narrow and a broad definition of "tender of delivery." The narrow definition is limited to a tender of conforming goods. The broader definition includes the tender of *non* conforming goods. In the context of limitations the narrow meaning of tender of delivery has been rejected by virtually every court that has considered the question. Not the least of the reasons for rejecting the narrow meaning is the logical paradox such an interpretation would create. If "tender of delivery" means "tender of conforming goods," then a seller who never ships conforming goods would never trigger the running of the statute. *See Ontario Hydro v. Zallea Sys., Inc.*, 569 F. Supp. 1261 (D. Del. 1983). That court rejected a "conformity" argument, holding that

> [f]rom a policy standpoint, it is important to note at the outset that the phrase "tender of delivery" can have a broader meaning than the plaintiff contends. . . .
>
> If the Court were to apply the phrase as Hydro suggests, then until the seller tenders conforming goods, the limitation period provided in § 2-725 would never apply. This would circumvent the very purpose of § 2-725, which, as discussed above, is to provide a finite period in time when the seller knows that he is relieved from liability for a possible breach of contract for sale or breach of warranty.

Id. at 1267. . . .

. . . .

Maryland cases which *do* analyze § 2-725 have unambiguously declared that the purpose of the statute is to protect defendants from stale claims. *See Mattos, Inc. v. Hash*, 279 Md. 371, 377, 368 A.2d 993, 996 (1977); *Frericks v. General Motors Corp.*, 278 Md. 304, 309–16, 363 A.2d 460, 462–66 (1976); *see also Mills v. International Harvester Co.*, 554 F. Supp. at 612–13. As one commentator explains, "[t]he result of [§ 2-725(1) and (2)] is a fairly short statute of limitations designed more to permit the parties to destroy their records after four years than to punish them for laches. Thus, for example, a party may be barred from pursuing an action he did not know existed." [W.D.] Hawkland[, Uniform Commercial Code Service] § 2-725:02, at 724.

In *Navistar International Corp. v. Hagie Manufacturing Co.*, 662 F. Supp. 1207, involving the sale of high clearance crop sprayers, the court rejected the argument that "tender of delivery" in § 2-725 ought to be read narrowly. *Id.* at 1210. Quoting the Official Comment to § 2-503, the court emphasized that "*other times [the term 'tender'] is used to refer to an offer of goods or documents under a contract as if in fulfillment of its conditions even though there is a defect when measured against the contract obligation.*" *Id.* The court applied the latter reading. *Id.; see also Ontario Hydro v. Zallea Sys., Inc.*, 569 F. Supp. 1261; *Nelligan v. Tom Chaney Motors, Inc.*, 88 Ill. Dec. 826, 479 N.E.2d 439.

*   *   *

ELDRIDGE, Judge, dissenting:

The majority's analysis begins with the erroneous premise that the determination of when tender of delivery occurred in this case is a question of law. This incorrect premise leads the majority to state that "the defendants had no burden of persuading the trial court factually that accrual of the claim was not postponed until commissioning," despite the fact that the limitations issue was raised on the defendants' motion for judgment. (Majority opinion at 624). From this, then, the majority erroneously concludes, as a matter of law, that tender of delivery occurred in this case when the engines were physically delivered to Lydia.

. . . .

According to Official Comment 1 to § 2-503, the term "tender of delivery" can be used in two senses, what the majority labels "a narrow and a broad" definition. (Majority opinion at 625). The first, "narrow," sense "contemplates an offer coupled with a present ability to fulfill all the conditions resting on the tendering party and must be followed by actual performance if the other party shows himself ready to proceed." Official

Comment 1 to § 2-503, second sentence. The second, "broad," sense "is used to refer to an offer of goods or documents under a contract as if in fulfillment of its conditions even though there is a defect when measured against the contract obligation." *Id.*, fourth sentence.

As stated in Official Comment 1 to § 2-725, the "broad" sense of "tender of delivery" means simply that the seller has offered the goods to the buyer "as if in fulfillment" of the contract. In other words, where a seller offers the goods to the buyer in the good faith belief that they conform to the contract requirements, then the seller has tendered delivery, even if it later becomes apparent that the goods are nonconforming. As Professor Hawkland has stated, in this "broader" sense "the term 'tender' is used in Article 2 of the UCC as an offer by the seller to deliver what he believes incorrectly to be conforming goods." 2 W.D. Hawkland, *Uniform Commercial Code Service*, § 2-503:2 at 931 (1994, 1998). *See also, e.g., Ontario Hydro v. Zallea Systems, Inc.*, 569 F. Supp. 1261, 1267 (D. Del. 1983). It is in this sense that tender of nonconforming goods can trigger the running of the statute of limitations: where the seller offers goods in the belief that his contract obligations have thereby been fulfilled, he has tendered delivery, even if it later turns out that the goods are nonconforming.

The question then in a dispute over whether tender of delivery has occurred, is whether the seller has offered the goods to the buyer "as if in fulfillment" of the contract. Contrary to the majority's assertion that this is a legal determination, it is a factual determination involving inquiry into the terms of the contract and the reasonable beliefs of the seller. For example, it is impossible to know whether the seller believed that its delivery of the goods was in fulfillment of the contract without knowing the terms of the contract. As Professor Hawkland states (Hawkland, *Uniform Commercial Code Service, supra*, § 2-725:2 at 730 n. 2, emphasis added):

> "*It is always a question of fact, however, when tender of delivery has been completed.* This characterization is difficult in situations which the seller agrees not only to deliver component parts but to assemble or install them. Usually, it is held that tender of delivery occurs when the installation or assembly is completed."

See also, e.g., H. Sand & Co., Inc. v. Airtemp Corp., 934 F.2d 450, 456 (2d Cir. 1991) (summary judgment on § 2-725 limitations grounds was improper; a material issue of fact existed as to when tender of delivery occurred); *Huron Tool & Engineering Co. v. Precision Consulting Services, Inc.*, 209 Mich. App. 365, 378, 532 N.W.2d 541, 547 (1995) (same); *Allis-Chalmers Credit Corp. v. Herbolt*, 17 Ohio App. 3d 230, 235, 479 N.E.2d 293, 300 (1984) (grant of summary judgment on statute of limitations grounds was erroneous; question of how delivery was to occur under a sales contract and when it did occur were material questions of fact); *Nation Enterprises, Inc. v. Enersyst, Inc.*, 749 F. Supp. 1506, 1513 (N.D. Ill. 1990) (summary judgment on § 2-725 limitations grounds was improper where a dispute of material fact existed as to whether delivery under the contract required installation of equipment as opposed to mere physical delivery).

In this case, therefore, it was necessary to determine as a matter of fact whether, when they delivered the engines to Lydia for installation in the *O.C. Princess*, the defendants believed that they had fulfilled their contract obligations, despite the fact that the engines later proved to be nonconforming.

. . . .

This is not a case where the seller merely had ongoing responsibilities such as repair and maintenance. Rather, in this case, the parties specifically stated that delivery *included* start up and commissioning. It would be difficult to conclude that the defendants in good faith believed that they had completed their delivery requirements before start up and commissioning had been done. When they delivered the engines to Lydia at Pompano Beach, they did not do so "as if in fulfillment" of the contract, because they knew that fulfillment of the contract required more for delivery-start up and commissioning.

. . . .

Faced with an arsenal of contrary authority, the majority attempts to distinguish the instant case by stating that "[i]n any event, in the case before us, Shantytown [sic] contracted to sell engines-not to sell engines and to install them." (Majority opinion at 631). As noted earlier, however, the majority ignores the fact that Shantytown contracted to buy engines and for their "delivery, . . . including start up and commissioning." This language makes it clear that the defendants in this case undertook start up and commissioning as part of their delivery obligations. . . .

. . . .

PROBLEM 7-1

Surefire Systems agreed to sell an integrated overhead conveyor system to Bluto Manufacturing. Surefire warranted that the conveyor system would be suitable to move Bluto's materials and products around the factory without damaging them. The parties signed a writing that memorialized this warranty, provided that acceptance occurred on delivery to Bluto's factory, and agreed to a one year period for bringing suit. Surefire agreed that it would install and test the integrated system after Bluto accepted the goods and paid 90% of the purchase price, with the balance of 10% due when the system was fully operational.

On April 1, 2004 Surefire delivered all components to Bluto's factory, where they were accepted and payment was made. Surefire began assembling some of the smaller pieces in a vacant part of the warehouse. Bluto requested that Surefire perform the installation and testing during the first two weeks of July, when it had scheduled a factory-wide shutdown. Surefire installed the system, but encountered numerous problems when Bluto's production resumed in mid-July. Surefire continued to work on the system, but it proved to be incapable of transporting certain materials without causing damage to them. On November 1, 2004 Bluto attempted to reject the goods, but Surefire insisted that it could make the system work and refused to remove the system. The parties then engaged in negotiations to resolve the problem, but these negotiations were unsuccessful. Bluto refused to pay Surefire for the installation and brought suit in June 2005 to recover damages due to the fact that the system could not handle all of the materials used by Bluto in its production process.

Surefire defends on the basis that Bluto's suit is barred by the statute of limitations. Analyze this problem under § 2-725 and develop the arguments for both parties. Does it matter whether the breach by Surefire is caused by deficiencies in the components of the conveyor system or by defective installation?

PROBLEM 7-2

On June 1, Samson Industries agreed to manufacture a 175 ton press (known as the "green monster") for Berkwire Manufacturing. Samson made a series of express performance warranties (e.g., the green monster will make 100 widgets per hour) and also agreed to repair or replace defective parts at no cost for one year following acceptance. The parties also agreed to a one year statute of limitations period. On August 1, the green monster was delivered and accepted, and things went smoothly for five weeks. However, on September 5 the green monster began having serious performance problems. On September 14 and 30, October 7, and December 3 and 21, Berkwire notified Samson that the green monster required repairs, and each time Samson sent technicians to repair it. On January 2, Samson sent two technicians to Berkwire's plant for three consecutive months of observation and they made immediate repairs when the machine malfunctioned. On April 1, the technicians left without returning, and Samson claimed no further responsibility for the green monster.

The green monster continued to underperform. Berkwire demanded that Samson refund its money and remove the green monster, but Samson refused. Berkwire eventually sold the machine for scrap and commenced a lawsuit against Samson on September 10. Berkwire was awarded damages by the jury on two theories: that Samson had breached its performance warranties (the green monster was unable to produce 100 widgets per hour), and that Samson had breached its warranty to repair and replace defective parts.

On appeal, Samson argues that Berkwire's suit is barred by the statute of limitations in its entirety. Analyze this problem under § 2-725 and develop the arguments for both parties.

Cases involving personal injury to remote purchasers of goods ordinarily are brought in tort. Nevertheless, parties may also allege a breach of the sales agreement, pursuant to amendments made to Article 2 shortly after its widespread adoption. *See* § 2-318. By extending warranties downstream to remote purchasers, however, the Code presented problems regarding the running of the statute of limitations. Analyze the following case and determine which opinion provides a better interpretation of Article 2.

HELLER v. U.S. SUZUKI MOTOR CORP.
New York Court of Appeals
477 N.E.2d 434 (1985)

SIMONS, J.

On February 15, 1983 plaintiff instituted this action against defendants U.S. Suzuki Motor Corp. and Jim Moroney's Harley-Davidson Sales, Inc., seeking to recover damages for injuries he sustained in a motorcycle accident which occurred July 7, 1979. U.S. Suzuki Motor Corporation is the Japanese manufacturer's distributor of the motorcycle in the United States and Jim Moroney's Harley-Davidson Sales, Inc., is the retailer who sold the motorcycle to plaintiff. The tort causes of action against both defendants were barred by the three-year Statute of Limitations. Accordingly, plaintiff sought to recover on claims that defendants expressly and impliedly warranted the motorcycle safe, merchantable and fit for its intended use. On this appeal he presses only a claim based upon implied warranty pursuant to Uniform Commercial Code § 2-318. The issue before us is the timeliness of plaintiff's action against defendant U.S. Suzuki Motor Corporation, specifically, whether the cause of action accrued on the date of sale to plaintiff by the retailer or on the date of transfer of the motorcycle by the distributor to its immediate purchaser, one Bakers Recreational Equipment, Inc., who then apparently transferred it to the retailer, defendant Jim Moroney's Harley-Davidson Sales, Inc.

Uniform Commercial Code § 2-725 provides that a cause of action for breach of a contract of sale must be commenced within four years after it accrues. The action accrues when the breach occurs and, in the absence of a warranty explicitly extending to future performance, a breach occurs when tender of delivery is made. Construing this language, Special Term denied defendant Suzuki's motion for summary judgment and dismissed its affirmative defense alleging the Statute of Limitations. It held that the cause of action against the distributor accrued when the retailer sold the motorcycle to plaintiff on April 21, 1979. The Appellate Division reversed and dismissed the complaint, holding that plaintiff's cause of action against the distributor accrued when the distributor tendered delivery to its immediate purchaser, March 30, 1978, and therefore that the action was time-barred because it was commenced more than four years later.

* * *

[I]n 1975 the Legislature completely eliminated the requirement of privity for personal injury actions based on implied warranty by adopting a new section 2-318 of the Uniform Commercial Code (L. 1975, ch. 774). In doing so, it adopted the section recommended by the National Conference of Commissioners on Uniform State Laws in 1966 and described as Alternative B to section 2-318 (*see* 1A ULA 53). Its purpose was to make uniform the law in the several jurisdictions desiring to expand the class of beneficiaries entitled to sue in implied warranty but which had not yet adopted the tort theory of strict products liability. Although the Code amendment was proposed to enable consumers to sue remote parties (*see* 1975 N.Y. Legis. Ann., at 110), it was not entirely necessary in New York because we had decided they could do so in 1973 when we decided *Codling v. Paglia*, 32 N.Y.2d 330, 345 N.Y.S.2d 461, 298 N.E.2d 622, and other strict products liability cases following it.

When the Legislature amended section 2-318, it did not amend the limitations period provided in section 2-725 of the Code, however, and notwithstanding the elimination of the requirement of privity, it remains the law that a cause of action against a manufacturer or distributor accrues on the date the party charged tenders delivery of the product, not on the date that some third party sells it to plaintiff (*Doyle v. Happy Tumbler Wash-O-Mat*, 90 A.D.2d 366, 457 N.Y.S.2d 85; *Fazio v. Ford Motor Corp.*, 69 A.D.2d 896, 415 N.Y.S.2d 889; 1 Weinberger, New York Products Liability § 11.04; *cf. Rosenau v. City of New Brunswick*, 93 N.J. Super. 49, 224 A.2d 689). It may be inferred from the amendment of section 2-318, as the dissent does, that the Legislature, by removing the prior requirement of privity, intended the date of retail sale to be the date of accrual, even for causes of action against others in the distributive chain. The short answer to that argument is that the Legislature did not say so and inasmuch as it did not amend section 2-725 to alter the existing rules on the subject we assume it intended no change (McKinney's Cons. Laws of N.Y., Book 1, Statutes § 222).

A major purpose of the uniform acts, and for the Statutes of Limitation they contain, is to eliminate jurisdictional variations so that concerns doing business nationwide will not be governed by different periods of limitation. With that in mind, the Commissioners proposed the four-year limitation period stated in section 2-725 as consistent with modern business record keeping procedure (*see* 1A ULA 525; *Voth v. Chrysler Motor Corp.*, 218 Kan. 644, 545 P.2d 371; *Mysel v. Gross*, 70 Cal. App. 3d Supp. 10, 138 Cal. Rptr. 873). This purpose is frustrated, however, and the period of exposure to liability becomes unpredictable if the cause of action accrues at the date of sale to the plaintiff because the product may have left the hands of remote third parties such as the manufacturer or the distributor years earlier. If the product is resold, as it was here, the limitations period for an action on implied warranty may be extended even longer. Thus, our interpretation is consistent with the purpose for the tender of delivery rule set forth in the uniform laws and by the general rule that the function of Statutes of Limitation is repose (*see* *Schwartz v. Heyden Newport Chem. Corp.*, 12 N.Y.2d 212, 218, 237 N.Y.S.2d 714, 188 N.E.2d 142).

This interpretation does not result in plaintiff's remedy being foreclosed before his cause of action accrued. . . . Plaintiff was injured 15 months after Suzuki sold the motorcycle to Bakers Recreational Equipment, Inc., but he waited almost four more years before instituting this suit. His rights have been lost by his own delay, not by any construction we place on the statute. Furthermore, our interpretation does not limit available remedies generally. A consumer who acts within three years of the date of the accident or four years from the date of sale, as the pertinent statutes provide, may now maintain causes of action in New York to recover against both immediate and remote parties based on express or implied warranty, negligence or strict products liability (*see* *Voss v. Black & Decker Mfg. Co.*, 59 N.Y.2d 102, 106, 463 N.Y.S.2d 398, 450 N.E.2d 204). Thus, there is no need or occasion for us to reinterpret section 2-725 in a manner contrary to its language and past usage. If the limitation period for causes of action based upon warranty is to be extended by fixing a new date of accrual, the Legislature should make that change.

Accordingly, the order of the Appellate Division should be affirmed, with costs.

MEYER, J., dissenting.

* * *

The majority accepts the premise that, despite the absence of privity, a manufacturer is liable to a purchaser from a dealer in the manufacturer's product for a breach of warranty resulting in injury to the purchaser, but nevertheless concludes that the four-year limitations period established by UCC 2-725 begins upon delivery of the product by the manufacturer to the dealer rather than with the dealer's delivery to the purchaser. For a number of reasons, I cannot accept that restrictive reading of the phrase "tender of delivery" used in UCC 2-725 and, therefore, respectfully dissent.

* * *

But although amendment of section 2-318 was necessary to broaden consumer rights, amendment of section 2-725 was not. This follows from the facts that there cannot be a warranty running from manufacturer to consumer until there is a consumer and that in the nature of the transaction there is no consumer until delivery by the dealer-retailer of the product to a particular purchaser. Thus the "tender of delivery" which brings into operation the manufacturer's warranty to the consumer is from the dealer to the purchaser, not from the manufacturer to the dealer.

* * *

The majority's citation of *Doyle v. Happy Tumbler Wash-O-Mat*, 90 A.D.2d 366, 457 N.Y.S.2d 85, suggests that the rationale for its holding is its agreement with *Doyle*'s reasoning that (at p. 370, 457 N.Y.S.2d 85) " 'tender of delivery' . . . is more readily applicable to commercial transactions between a seller and buyer." But *Doyle*'s restrictive reading of "tender of delivery" not only makes it possible that the newly expanded cause of action could be barred by limitations before it came into existence, a result we should not lightly infer was intended by the Legislature, but also wholly overlooks the fact that the amended section 2-318 is a part of the Uniform Commercial Code, which directs that, "The remedies provided by this Act shall be liberally administered to the end that the aggrieved party may be put in as good a position as if the other party had fully performed" (§ 1-106[1]) and that, "This Act shall be liberally construed and applied to promote its underlying purposes and policies" (§ 1-102[1]). The fact that "tender of delivery" may connote a buyer-seller relationship does not exclude interpretation of the phrase as it relates to a buyer's cause of action against the manufacturer to refer to the tender of delivery made by the seller-distributor as the manufacturer's conduit to the buyer, nor in light of the liberal administration and liberal construction provisions of the Code should it be so limited.

No greater support for the majority's conclusion is provided by the suggested relationship between limitations, the record keeping procedures of modern business and the unpredictable period of exposure that results if the action accrues on sale to the plaintiff. While that apparently was the origin of the four-year period established by UCC 2-725(1) when it was adopted in 1964 (*see* Comment to the original section), strict products liability was not then generally recognized. With our acceptance in *Codling v. Paglia* (*supra*), of the strict liability concept, however, and our subsequent holding that the three-year tort limitations period accrued from the date of injury (*Victorson v. Bock Laundry Mach. Co., supra*), the unpredictability of the manufacturer's exposure became for him a way of life and record keeping procedures were no longer sufficiently significant "to dictate the outcome" as to limitations (*Victorson v. Bock Laundry Mach. Co.*, 37 N.Y.2d, at p. 404, 373 N.Y.S.2d 39, 335 N.E.2d 275, *supra*). No more so should those considerations determine when a purchaser's warranty action against a remote manufacturer accrues with respect to the expanded warranty action authorized by the 1975 amendment to UCC 2-318.

The final basis for my disagreement with the majority is that the cases holding that the UCC's four-year limitation period begins to run in favor of a manufacturer only from the date of the retail sale are more numerous (and those that state reasons more closely reasoned) than those on which the majority rely.

*   *   *

2.   Preserving Evidence of Goods in Dispute

Although a seller may breach the contract other than by tendering nonconforming goods, such as by repudiating its obligations or delaying the tender, in many cases the dispute will concern the quality of the goods. Article 2 seeks to facilitate the timely and effective resolution of such disputes by providing that a party may, upon request, inspect and test the goods that are the subject of a dispute. § 2-515. This right to inspect the goods inevitably is in tension with the aggrieved party's right to mitigate its losses by reselling the goods to a third party. Comment 2 explains that this tension is reduced to the extent that the parties must act without delay. For example, the requirement under § 2-607(3)(a) that a buyer must notify the seller of a breach with respect to accepted goods "within a reasonable time" provides the seller with an opportunity to request an inspection of the goods before the buyer disposes of them. *See Atwood v. Southeast Bedding Co.*, 226 Ga. App. 50, 485 S.E.2d 217, 219 (1997) ("Appellants' claims are for defective goods that they had to repair and sell at a discount. Written notice sent only after the relationship has been terminated and all goods either sold or retrieved by the seller does not and cannot serve the purposes of [§ 2-607(3)(a), which informs the seller that it might want to exercise its § 2-515 right of inspection]. . . . The timing of the notice was unreasonable as a matter of law.").

The parties are also subject to discovery rules if the case proceeds to litigation. Generally, discovery rights under the Federal Rules of Evidence are very generous, but this is balanced by discovery orders issued by the judge for the purpose of limiting the time for discovery and keeping the case on track. In *Fenway Cambridge Motor Hotel, Inc. v. American Contract Designers, Inc.*, 1984 U.S. Dist. LEXIS 21556 (D. Mass. Dec. 3, 1984), the court held that the time limits in a discovery order superseded the seller's rights under § 2-515 to inspect the goods under dispute.

Finally, many states provide a variety of remedies for "spoliation of evidence" in civil litigation. This general evidentiary rule places a duty on parties to preserve evidence when litigation concerning the object is pending or reasonably foreseeable. The remedies might include an independent tort action for intentional spoliation of evidence or a claim under general negligence principles, and in rare cases might even trigger criminal sanctions. However, the remedies for spoliation generally are limited to civil and evidentiary sanctions, including raising a presumption that the destroyed items would have supported the other party's case. The following case discusses the interplay of these evidentiary rules with § 2-515.

J.R. COUSIN INDUSTRIES, INC. v. MENARD, INC.
United States Court of Appeals, Seventh Circuit
127 F.3d 580 (1997)

POSNER, Chief Judge.

Section 2-515(a) of the Uniform Commercial Code permits either party to a sale of goods, on reasonable notification to the other, to inspect, test, and sample sold goods that are in the possession of the other party, for the purpose of ascertaining facts and preserving evidence. So it is a little like a pretrial discovery rule; and it is at the center of this diversity breach of contract suit that resulted in a jury's awarding $70,000 in damages to the seller, J.R. Cousin Industries, from which the buyer, Menard, appeals. There are few reported cases dealing with section 2-515(a), and none dealing with the specific issues presented by this appeal; we write largely on a clean slate.

Cousin is an importer of hardware, Menard a retail chain selling home-improvement products. Cousin agreed to sell Menard more than 20,000 low-cost sinks and toilets that had been manufactured by a firm in Mexico. The goods were to be delivered directly by the manufacturer to Menard's stores. Cousin agreed to credit Menard for the price of any of the sinks or toilets that were defective or that Menard's customers returned to Menard for *any* reason, whether or not the returned good was defective. The contract gave Cousin the option, with respect to defective and other returned products, to have them shipped back to it at its expense or to have them destroyed by Menard. Cousin opted for destruction by Menard, presumably because the weight of the goods relative to their value (the price to Menard of the sinks was only $22 and of the toilets only $19) would make it uneconomical to ship them back to Cousin.

The first sinks and toilets were shipped to Menard in December 1994. Menard subtracted from Cousin's invoices what Cousin thought an unusually high amount for customer returns; upon inquiry Cousin was informed by Menard that many of the sinks and toilets were defective. In June of the following year Cousin asked Menard to let it inspect the defective goods at Menard's premises. Menard claims that by this time it had destroyed more than $15,000 worth of the goods because they were defective. After permitting Cousin to inspect a small quantity of undestroyed returned goods, it refused to allow further inspections and destroyed the rest. It subtracted a total of $72,000 from Cousin's invoices, for customer returns, and this is the amount for which Cousin has sued. Cousin claims that Menard broke the contract by violating section 2-215(a) (codified in Wisconsin as Wis. Stat. § 402.515(1)), which if applicable and not waived (issues raised by the appeal) conferred a right of inspection on Cousin. The jury's award of $70,000 gave Cousin slightly less than it was asking, presumably in consideration of the possibility that at least some of the returns either were bona fide or had been destroyed by Menard before it received Cousin's request to inspect the returned goods.

The award of damages may seem very peculiar; as there is no doubt that the contract authorized Menard to destroy any goods bought from Cousin that Menard's customers returned, for whatever reason. Cousin defends the verdict on the ground that section 2-515(a) authorized it by notice to freeze the process of destruction, so that any goods destroyed after it asked Menard to hold them for inspection were destroyed in breach of the contract and Cousin is entitled to their value as damages for the breach. Since some of the goods were destroyed before the June 1995 notice, when the contract clearly authorized such destruction, and since some and perhaps most or even all of the goods destroyed later were defective or returned and hence eligible for destruction under the contract, the jury's decision to award Cousin 97 percent of the full value of the goods that had been returned to Menard may seem an obvious overestimation of the damages. But Menard does not argue (but merely hints) that the jury's award was excessive. It would ill behoove Menard to complain about the size of the award if it violated the Uniform Commercial Code in failing to hold the goods for Cousin's inspection. For by doing this it prevented an accurate estimation of Cousin's damages. Even more important, it also prevented Cousin from attempting to obtain reimbursement for its lost sales from its Mexican supplier, by depriving Cousin of the evidence that the goods were defective, if they were. If most of the returned goods were defective, and if had it not been for Menard's alleged violation of the UCC, Cousin could have recovered the cost of the goods from the manufacturer, the jury's award was not unreasonable — provided the UCC really was violated. Menard argues that section 2-515 is limited to cases in which the buyer either rejects the goods or revokes its acceptance of them, but that in any event Cousin waived by contract any right of inspection that the statute might have conferred on it.

The section does not contain the limitation for which Menard contends; nor is there a reason to interpolate such a limitation by judicial interpretation. Menard cites no cases for its reading because no case addresses the issue (though *General Matters, Inc. v. Paramount Canning Co.*, 382 So. 2d 1262 (Fla. App. 1980), hints at rejection of Menard's position). It cites the unpublished notes by Professor Karl N. Llewellyn, the principal draftsman of the UCC, dated September 18–20, 1945, and filed in Box 4068, Folder 8, in the American Law Institute Archives of the University of Pennsylvania Law School. The section was originally confined to cases of rejection and the notes say it was broadened to take in "one most important case, that of revocation of acceptance when the buyer claims a lien." But the section was not expanded to take in *just* that "one most important case." The section does not refer to rejection and revocation. The wording is perfectly general, perhaps because the draftsmen realized that there might be other "important case[s]" that they hadn't foreseen.

The Official Comment on the section (and only a public comment could be thought to illuminate the thinking of the legislators who state by state voted to adopt the Uniform Commercial Code and thus make it positive law) does not support the gloss that Menard seeks to place on the statutory language. It describes the purpose of the section as being "to afford either party an opportunity for preserving evidence, whether or not agreement has been reached, and thereby to reduce uncertainty in any litigation and, in turn perhaps, to promote agreement." This statement of purpose is as applicable to a dispute over Menard's right to destroy returned goods as it would be if Menard had rejected them.

Were the section limited to rejection and revocation, buyers could sidestep it by accepting defective goods rather than rejecting them, and then, rather than revoking their acceptance, by complaining of a breach of warranty under UCC § 2-714. See Official Comment to section 2-714; *Barry & Sewall Industrial Supply Co. v. Metal-Prep of Houston, Inc.*, 912 F.2d 252, 257 (8th Cir. 1990). Moreover, although section 2-515 functions much like a rule of pretrial discovery, it is operative only before suit is filed. As soon as a suit is filed, the section is superseded by the rules of procedure governing discovery. *Fenway Cambridge Motor Hotel, Inc. v. American Contract Designers, Inc.*, 39 UCC Rep. Serv. 1263 (D. Mass. 1984). This means that when Cousin had to decide whether to invoke its rights under section 2-515, it could not know, under Menard's interpretation of the section, whether it *had* any rights, because it did not know under what legal theory Menard would proceed in the parties' dispute. It is unlikely that the draftsmen wanted the use of the provision to be attended with so much uncertainty or to invite so much gamesmanship.

We conclude that Cousin had a right of inspection under section 2-515 even though Menard was not attempting to reject the goods in dispute or revoke its acceptance of them. We also believe that the jury was entitled to reject the argument that Cousin waived its right of inspection. It is true that the contract entitled Menard to destroy any defective or returned goods. Since the goods in question had little value, especially relative to their weight, the destruction option made a lot more sense than requiring that the goods be returned to Cousin or that Menard document the problem with every returned item. That is all that the parts of the contract on which Menard relies are about. They do not bear on the rights of either party in the event of a dispute. Menard argues that no dispute could arise because Cousin had given it *carte blanche* to destroy its goods. But Cousin did not agree that Menard could dispose of goods that were *not* defective or returned, and since this might happen, Cousin should not be taken to have disarmed itself in advance from being able to investigate whether it might have happened. In fact Menard, very averse to paperwork, based its deductions from Cousin's invoices not on actual returns but on "anticipated" returns. This it had no clear right to do and it certainly had no right to retain these monies if its "anticipations" turned out to be excessive, a matter that Cousin was entitled to investigate with the aid of its statutory right to inspect.

Menard argues rather more practically that given the weight and quantity of the goods, it simply was infeasible for it to segregate and store all the returns. But we take this to mean only that it thinks that Cousin should have paid for the expense of inspection. Cousin *concedes* that Menard was entitled to charge back to it the reasonable expense of storage necessary to permit inspection of the returned goods, subject to reimbursement by Menard should the inspection reveal a breach of the contract. We do not know on what the concession is based. The issue is not addressed in any provision of the Code or in any case. In any event, we cannot attach much significance to the concession, conditioned as it is on there being a right to reimbursement if Cousin wins (as it has done) — for there may not be any such right.

The cost of inspection-related storage is an expense incidental to dispute resolution, and such costs, under the American rule governing litigation expenses other than statutory costs (copying costs, filing fees, and the like), are borne by the party that incurs them rather than being shifted to the winning party. *Autotrol Corp. v. Continental Water Systems Corp.*, 918 F.2d 689, 695 (7th Cir. 1990). They, thus, are not recoverable as incidental or consequential damages under UCC § 2-715. *Bazzini v. Garrant*, 116 Misc. 2d 119, 455 N.Y.S.2d 77, 79 (Dist. Ct. 1982). The American rule is merely a default rule; it is often changed by statute; but so far as we have been able to determine no statute alters the rule for the class of cases to which this litigation belongs. If section 2-515 had a broader domain than dispute resolution, the American rule might not come into play; but it appears not to. It is true, as we noted earlier, that had the returned goods not been destroyed by Menard, Cousin might have been able to use them, if they were indeed defective, to obtain compensation from the manufacturer of the goods, even if Cousin had had no dispute with Menard and even if its claim against the manufacturer was accepted rather than disputed. But whether, in light of the language of section 2-515 and the Official Comment, a party to a contract for the sale of goods can demand inspection of the goods even though there is no dispute between the parties — even though inspection is sought solely because of a potential dispute with a third party — is highly doubtful. We need not pursue the issue, on which we cannot find any authority, just as we need not decide whether Cousin would in fact be liable for the cost of storage, another issue on which there is no law (so prudent parties will allocate the cost in the contract if as in this case it might be substantial). No matter. Menard should have retained the goods and tried to charge the expense of doing so to Cousin. In failing to retain the goods after being notified that Cousin was invoking its rights under section 2-515, Menard violated Cousin's statutory right, and for the reasons explained earlier it cannot complain about the size of the verdict.

QUESTIONS

1. Would Judge Posner respect a clause in a written agreement that permitted the seller to destroy any goods returned by the buyer for credit without further notice, if the clause specifically provided that the buyer waived its rights under § 2-515?

2. Judge Posner notes that the cost of storing goods that are the subject of dispute might be prohibitive, and suggests that parties allocate this cost contractually. Does § 2-515(a) empower a party to prohibit the destruction of goods, or does it just provide for a timely inspection before the party in possession disposes of the goods?

3. Incidental and Consequential Damages

A party suffering a breach is entitled to pursue damages under a variety of provisions. Common to these different calculations of damages are the general provisions that the aggrieved party may recover incidental and consequential damages. Incidental damages are defined broadly for both sellers and buyers. Sellers may recover expenses incurred in dealing with the subject goods "or otherwise resulting from the breach." § 2-710. Comment 1 explains that the "section sets forth the principal normal and necessary additional elements of damage flowing from the breach but intends to allow all commercially reasonable expenditures made by the seller." Similarly, buyers may recover expenses incurred in dealing with the subject goods "and any other reasonable expense incident to the delay or other breach." § 2-715. Comment 1 explains that the "incidental damages listed are not intended to be exhaustive but are merely illustrative of the typical kinds of incidental damage."

Buyers are entitled to recover consequential damages under the modern version of the *Hadley* rule, *Hadley v. Baxendale*, 156 Eng. Rep. 145 (1854), which permits recovery of "any loss resulting from general or particular requirements and needs of which the seller at the time of contracting had reason to know and which could not reasonably be prevented by cover or otherwise. . . ." § 2-715(2)(a). Curiously, Article 2 permits only buyers to recover consequential damages for breach. § 2-715(2). Presumably, the drafters believed that sellers could easily avoid consequential losses by reselling the subject goods. However, cases soon arose in which sellers legitimately claimed that they should recover consequential damages in order to receive the benefit of their bargain, but courts generally held that Article 2 unambiguously provided that only buyers could recover these damages. *See, e.g., Nobs Chemical, U.S.A., Inc. v. Koppers Co., Inc.*, 616 F.2d 212, 216 (5th Cir. 1980) (although the buyer's pre-delivery breach meant that the middleman seller lost its quantity discount with its supplier, court refused to award these consequential losses); *Afram Export Corp. v. Metallurgiki Halyps, S.A.*, 772 F.2d 1358, 1369 (7th Cir. 1985) (Posner, J.) (interest on loan incurred by seller to produce goods for sale to breaching buyer is properly regarded as a consequential loss — an opportunity cost — and therefore not recoverable by a seller).

a. Attorneys' fees as incidental or consequential damages

Given the broad scope of the language permitting parties to recover incidental damages, some parties have attempted to recover their litigation expenses as incidental damages. Alternatively, they have argued that attorney's fees are consequential losses that the breaching party had reason to know would result from the breach. Read the following case and determine if it offers a persuasive reading of the statutory language.

INDIANA GLASS CO. v. INDIANA MICHIGAN POWER CO.
Indiana Court of Appeals
692 N.E.2d 886 (1998)

GARRARD, J.

STATEMENT OF THE CASE

Indiana Glass Company ("Indiana Glass") appeals the trial court's grant of summary judgment in favor of Indiana Michigan Power Company ("I & M") on Indiana Glass's claim for attorney's fees as incidental or consequential damages under the Indiana Uniform Commercial Code (the "UCC"). We affirm.

ISSUE

Whether a buyer may recover attorney's fees as incidental or consequential damages under the UCC for breach of the implied warranties of merchantability and fitness for a particular purpose.

FACTS

Indiana Glass is an Indiana corporation that manufactures glassware at its plant located in Dunkirk. I & M contracted to supply electricity to Indiana Glass pursuant to a written agreement. On several occasions between January 25, 1989, and September 25, 1990, I & M allegedly supplied electricity to Indiana Glass's Dunkirk facility at a diminished or an increased voltage which caused damage to Indiana Glass's manufacturing processes. Accordingly, on January 23, 1991, Indiana Glass filed its complaint against I & M and alleged that I & M was negligent, or in the alternative, that I & M breached the UCC's implied warranties of merchantability and fitness for a particular purpose when it sold and delivered "defective" electricity. Indiana Glass sought damages for lost machine hours, extraordinary maintenance costs, the cost of repairing machinery which was damaged due to voltage fluctuations, and for "all other just and proper relief."

Following a motion for partial summary judgment filed by Indiana Glass, on November 18, 1993, the trial court entered partial summary judgment in favor of Indiana Glass and concluded, as a matter of law, that electricity is a "good" under the UCC and that I & M had not disclaimed the UCC implied warranties of merchantability and fitness for a particular purpose in the parties' agreement. Thus, the trial court determined that Indiana Glass could pursue its UCC claims against I & M.

The parties thereafter entered into a confidential settlement agreement resolving all issues between the parties except Indiana Glass's claim for attorney's fees as incidental or consequential damages under the UCC. The parties filed cross-motions for summary judgment asking for a determination, as a matter of law, on the issue of whether Indiana Glass would be entitled to recover attorney's fees as incidental or consequential damages under the UCC in the event Indiana Glass could establish I & M's breach of the implied warranties. Following a hearing, the trial court granted summary judgment in favor of I & M and concluded that Indiana Glass could not recover attorney's fees as incidental or consequential damages under the UCC. Indiana Glass appeals that determination of law.

DISCUSSION AND DECISION

* * *

In this appeal, we are asked to resolve a pure question of law. Indiana Glass contends that the trial court erred when it concluded, as a matter of law, that a buyer may not recover attorney's fees as incidental or consequential damages under Indiana's UCC. The parties agree that the issue presented is one of first impression in Indiana.

We begin with our well-settled rule that each party to litigation is responsible for his or her own attorney's fees absent statutory authority, agreement, or rule to the contrary. *Crowl v. Berryhill*, 678 N.E.2d 828, 831 (Ind. Ct. App. 1997). The contract between I & M and Indiana Glass makes no provision for the recovery of attorney's fees in the event of breach. Accordingly, we address Indiana Glass's argument that Indiana Code § 26-1-2-715 provides statutory authority for its proposition that a buyer is entitled to recover attorney's fees in the event of the seller's breach of the implied warranties. . . .

Although no Indiana court has had occasion to address this statutory argument under Indiana law, we have encountered this argument under Kentucky law. In *Landmark Motors v. Chrysler Credit Corp.*, 662 N.E.2d 971, 976–77 (Ind. Ct. App. 1996), this Court considered whether attorney's fees were recoverable as incidental or consequential damages pursuant to Kentucky Revised Statutes § 355.2-715, a provision identical to Indiana Code § 26-1-2-715. We held that Kentucky law did not provide for the recovery of attorney's fees as incidental or consequential damages. Specifically, we relied on the Kentucky Court of Appeals decision in *Nick's Auto Sales, Inc. v. Radcliff Auto Sales, Inc.*, 591 S.W.2d 709, 711 (Ky. Ct. App. 1979).

In *Nick's Auto Sales*, the court addressed the question of whether attorney's fees should be included as incidental or consequential damages under the UCC and held that, in accordance with the overwhelming weight of authority from other states, attorney's fees are not recoverable under § 2-715. *Nick's Auto Sales*, 591 S.W.2d at 711. The Kentucky Court of Appeals went on to note that White and Summers, a leading authority on the UCC, has suggested that "[t]he recovery of legal fees is probably available in rare circumstances only." *Id.* (quoting JAMES J. WHITE AND ROBERT S. SUMMERS, HANDBOOK OF THE LAW UNDER THE UNIFORM COMMERCIAL CODE at 302 n.57 (1972)).

Despite the overwhelming weight of authority from other jurisdictions indicating that attorney's fees are not recoverable under § 2-715, Indiana Glass urges us to review the specific language of that section and hold differently. First, Indiana Glass points to § 2-715(1) which provides that incidental damages include "any other reasonable expense incident to the delay or other breach." Indiana Glass argues that this language indicates that the legislature contemplated broad recovery on the part of the buyer in the event of the seller's breach, and that such recovery should include attorney's fees. Contrary to Indiana Glass's position, the commentary to subsection (1) indicates that incidental damages are the reasonable expenses incurred by the buyer in connection with the handling of rightfully rejected goods or goods whose acceptance may be justifiably revoked, or those expenses incurred in connection with effecting cover where goods are non-conforming or have not been delivered. Ind. Code § 26-1-2-715(1), cmt. 1. Attorney's fees were clearly not contemplated as recoverable under this subsection.

Next, Indiana Glass points us to the use of the broad term "any loss" in subsection (2)(a) to describe what is included in a buyer's consequential damages resulting from a seller's breach. Ind. Code § 26-1-2-715(2)(a). Again, there is no indication in the official commentary that the legislature intended for attorney's fees to be recoverable as consequential damages. Moreover, as noted by the Supreme Court of Tennessee, courts consistently have held that, despite the use of the broad language "any loss," the Code makes no change in the general rule that, regardless of the outcome of litigation, each party must bear its own legal expenses. *Kultura, Inc. v. Southern Leasing Corp.*, 923 S.W.2d 536, 540 (Tenn. 1996) (citing 2 ROY RYDEN ANDERSON, DAMAGES UNDER THE UNIFORM COMMERCIAL CODE § 11.34, p. 132 (1992)).

Although we understand Indiana Glass's reliance on the language of Indiana Code § 26-1-1-106(1) which provides that the remedies provided by the UCC "shall be liberally administered to the end that the aggrieved party may be put in as good a position as if the other party had fully performed," we are also cognizant of § 1-103 which specifically states:

> Unless displaced by the particular provisions of IC 26-1, the principles of law and equity, including the law of merchant and the law relative to capacity to contract, principal and agent, estoppel, fraud, misrepresentation, duress, coercion, mistake, bankruptcy, or other validating or invalidating cause, shall supplement the provisions of IC 26-1.

Ind. Code § 26-1-1-103. As noted by the official commentary, this section emphasizes the continued applicability to commercial contracts of all supplemental bodies of law except insofar as they are explicitly displaced by the provisions of the UCC. Ind. Code § 26-1-1-103, cmt. 1. Section 2-715 does not explicitly provide for the recovery of attorney's fees as incidental or consequential damages and, thus, that section was not intended to abrogate the common law in Indiana regarding the recovery of attorney's fees.

We agree with the Kentucky Court of Appeals in *Nick's Auto Sales,* as well as the majority of our sister states, that attorney's fees are not recoverable as incidental or consequential damages under the UCC § 2-715.[1] The trial court properly entered summary judgment in favor of I & M.

---

[1] [3] We note that attorney's fees have been permitted when incurred by the buyer in third-party litigation, a situation not presented here. *See Alterman Foods, Inc. v. G.C.C. Beverages, Inc.*, 168 Ga. App. 921, 310 S.E.2d 755 (1983) (buyer could recover from seller attorney's fees incurred in defense of personal injury action brought by third-party consumer); *Universal C.I.T. Credit Corp. v. State Farm Mut. Auto. Ins. Co.*, 493 S.W.2d 385 (Mo. Ct. App. 1973) (indemnitee in breach of implied warranty action could recover attorney's fees incurred in defense of suit brought by third party).

Affirmed.

QUESTIONS

1. What is the basis for the court distinguishing the cases in the footnote, in which buyers were permitted to recover attorney's fees as an element of damages?

2. The court does not deny the force of Indiana Glass's argument that the definitions of incidental and consequential damages appear broad enough to include attorney's fees incurred by a party as a consequence of another's breach of contract, and that the principle of § 1-106 (now § 1-305) strongly reaffirms the Code policy of making the party that suffers a breach whole. Why isn't this strong enough to meet the "displacement" test of § 1-103(b)?

Consider whether this case reflects an application of the "dog that didn't bark" canon of statutory interpretation. This canon, originating in an opinion by Chief Justice Rehnquist, presumes that a statute does not intend to change a well-settled rule despite the apparent breadth of its language when the drafters were silent about their intent to make such a change. The reference is to Sherlock Holmes' use of a dog's silence to solve a mystery. *See Chisom v. Roemer*, 501 U.S. 380, 396 n. 23, 115 L. Ed. 2d 348, 111 S. Ct. 2354 (1991) ("Congress' silence in this regard can be likened to the dog that did not bark. *See* A. Doyle, *Silver Blaze, in* THE COMPLETE SHERLOCK HOLMES 335 (1927). *Cf. Harrison v. PPG Indus., Inc.*, 446 U.S. 578, 602, 64 L. Ed. 2d 525, 100 S. Ct. 1889 (1980) (Rehnquist, J., dissenting) ("In a case where the construction of legislative language such as this makes so sweeping and so relatively unorthodox a change as that made here, I think judges as well as detectives may take into consideration the fact that a watchdog did not bark in the night.")); *see also Church of Scientology v. I.R.S.*, 484 U.S. 9, 17–18, 98 L. Ed. 2d 228, 108 S. Ct. 271 (1987) (Rehnquist, C.J.) ("All in all, we think this is a case where common sense suggests, by analogy to Sir Arthur Conan Doyle's 'dog that didn't bark,' that an amendment having the effect [of changing the established law] would have been differently described by its sponsor. . . ."). Is the "dog that didn't bark" canon of construction consistent with the interpretive methodology of Article 2?

3. In *Zapata Hermanos Sucesores, S.A. v. Hearthside Baking Co., Inc.*, 313 F.3d 385 (7th Cir. 2002), Judge Posner concluded that the CISG does not displace the "American rule" regarding attorneys fees. Judge Posner reasoned, in part, as follows:

> Zapata brought suit under the Convention for money due under 110 invoices, amounting to some $900,000 (we round liberally), and also sought prejudgment interest plus attorneys' fees, which it contended are "losses" within the meaning of the Convention and are therefore an automatic entitlement of a plaintiff who prevails in a suit under the Convention. [Ed. Note: The judge awarded Zapata all of the attorneys fees that it expended in the litigation.]

> Article 74 of the Convention provides that "damages for breach of contract by one party consist of a sum equal to the loss, including loss of profit, suffered by the other party as a consequence of the breach," provided the consequence was foreseeable at the time the contract was made. Article 7(2) provides that "questions concerning matters governed by this Convention which are not expressly settled in it are to be settled in conformity with the general principles on which it is based or, in the absence of such principles, in conformity with the law applicable by virtue of the rules of private international law [i.e., conflicts of law rules]." There is no suggestion in the background of the Convention or the cases under it that "loss" was intended to include attorneys' fees, but no suggestion to the contrary either. Nevertheless it seems apparent that "loss" does not include attorneys' fees incurred in the litigation of a suit for breach of contract, though certain prelitigation legal expenditures, for example expenditures designed to mitigate the plaintiff's damages, would probably be covered as "incidental" damages. *Sorenson v. Fio Rito*, 90 Ill. App. 3d 368, 45 Ill. Dec. 714,

413 N.E.2d 47, 50–52 (1980); *cf. Tull v. Gundersons, Inc.*, 709 P.2d 940, 946 (Colo. 1985); *Restatement (Second) of Contracts* § 347, comment (1981).

The Convention is about contracts, not about procedure. The principles for determining when a losing party must reimburse the winner for the latter's expense of litigation are usually not a part of a substantive body of law, such as contract law, but a part of procedural law. For example, the "American rule," that the winner must bear his own litigation expenses, and the "English rule" (followed in most other countries as well), that he is entitled to reimbursement, are rules of general applicability. They are not field-specific. There are, it is true, numerous exceptions to the principle that provisions regarding attorneys' fees are part of general procedural law. For example, federal antidiscrimination, antitrust, copyright, pension, and securities laws all contain field-specific provisions modifying the American rule (as do many other field-specific statutes). An international convention on contract law *could* do the same. But not only is the question of attorneys' fees not "expressly settled" in the Convention, it is not even mentioned. And there are no "principles" that can be drawn out of the provisions of the Convention for determining whether "loss" includes attorneys' fees; so by the terms of the Convention itself the matter must be left to domestic law (i.e., the law picked out by "the rules of private international law," which means the rules governing choice of law in international legal disputes).

U.S. contract law is different from, say, French contract law, and the general U.S. rule on attorneys' fee shifting (the "American rule") is different from the French rule (loser pays). But no one would say that French contract law differs from U.S. *because* the winner of a contract suit in France is entitled to be reimbursed by the loser, and in the U.S. not. That's an important difference but not a contract-law difference. It is a difference resulting from differing procedural rules of general applicability.

. . . .

For these reasons, we conclude that "loss" in Article 74 does not include attorneys' fees, and we move on to the question of a district court's inherent authority to punish a litigant or the litigant's lawyers for litigating in bad faith. The district judge made clear that he was basing his award of attorneys' fees to Zapata in part on his indignation at Lenell's having failed to pay money conceded to be owed to Zapata. Although the precise amount was in dispute, Lenell concedes that it owed Zapata at least half of the $1.2 million that Zapata obtained in damages (not counting the attorneys' fees) and prejudgment interest. Lenell had no excuse for not paying that amount, and this upset the judge.

Firms should pay their debts when they have no legal defense to them. *Pacta sunt servanda,* as the saying goes ("contracts are to be obeyed"). In the civil law (that is, the legal regime of Continental Europe), this principle is taken very seriously, as illustrated by the fact that the civil law grants specific performance in breach of contract cases as a matter of course. But under the common law (including the common law of Illinois, which is the law that choice of law principles make applicable to any issues in this case not covered in express terms by the Convention), a breach of contract is not considered wrongful activity in the sense that a tort or a crime is wrongful. When we delve for reasons, we encounter Holmes's argument that practically speaking the duty created by a contract is just to perform or pay damages, for only if damages are inadequate relief in the particular circumstances of the case will specific performance be ordered. In other words, and subject to the qualification just mentioned, the entire practical effect of signing a contract is that by doing so one obtains an option to break it. The damages one must pay for breaking the

contract are simply the price if the option is exercised. *See* Oliver Wendell
Holmes, Jr., *The Common Law* 300–02 (1881); Holmes, "The Path of the Law,"
10 HARV. L. REV. 457, 462 (1897).

Id. at 387–89.

b. Defining and quantifying consequential losses

You may remember from Contracts class that consequential losses are compensable
under the rule of *Hadley v. Baxendale*. Moreover, consequential losses must be
quantified with reasonable certainty and must be proved to be the result of the other
party's breach. Do the following cases reflect a change in the common law analysis of
these factors?

HYDRAFORM PRODUCTS CORP. v. AMERICAN
STEEL & ALUMINUM CORP.
New Hampshire Supreme Court
498 A.2d 339 (1985)

SOUTER, Justice.

The defendant, American Steel & Aluminum Corporation, appeals from the
judgment entered on a jury verdict against it. The plaintiff, Hydraform Products
Corporation, brought this action for direct and consequential damages based on claims
of negligent misrepresentation and breach of a contract to supply steel to be used in
manufacturing woodstoves.

Hydraform was incorporated in 1975 and began manufacturing and selling
woodstoves in 1976. During the sales season of 1977–78 it sold 640 stoves. It purchased
steel from a number of suppliers until July 1978, when it entered into a "trial run"
contract with American for enough steel to manufacture 40 stoves. . . .

When some of the deliveries under this contract were late, Hydraform's president,
J.R. Choate, explained to an agent of American that late deliveries of steel during the
peak season for manufacturing and selling stoves could ruin Hydraform's business for
a year. In response, American's agent stated that if Hydraform placed a further order,
American would sheer and stockpile in advance, at its own plant, enough steel for 400
stoves, and would supply further steel on demand. Thereafter Hydraform did submit a
purchase order for steel sufficient to manufacture 400 stoves, to be delivered in four
equal installments on the first days of September, October, November and December of
1978.

*   *   *

 . . . Deliveries were late, some of the steel delivered was defective, and replacements
of defective steel were tardy. Throughout the fall of 1978 Mr. Choate protested the slow
and defective shipments, while American's agent continually reassured him that the
deficient performance would be corrected. Late in the fall, Mr. Choate finally concluded
that American would never perform as agreed, and attempted to obtain steel from other
suppliers. He found, however, that none could supply the steel he required in time to
manufacture stoves for the 1978–79 sales season. In the meantime, the delays in
manufacturing had led to cancelled orders, and by the end of the season Hydraform had
manufactured and sold only 250 stoves. In September 1979, Hydraform sold its
woodstove manufacturing division for $150,000 plus royalties.

[Ed. Note: The court ruled that the limitation of damages clause included on
American's delivery receipts (and signed by Hydraform's agents) were not effective to
bar Hydraform's claims for consequential damages.]

Since the clause was not enforceable, the trial court allowed the jury to consider
Hydraform's claims for lost profits in the year of the contract, 1978, and for the two

years thereafter, as well as its claim for loss in the value of the stove manufacturing business resulting in a lower sales price for the business in 1979. American argues that the court erred in submitting such claims to the jury, and rests its position on three requirements governing the recovery of consequential damages.

First, under RSA 382-A:2-715(2)(a) consequential damages are limited to compensation for "loss resulting from general or particular requirements and needs of which the seller at the time of contracting had reason to know. . . ." This reflection of *Hadley v. Baxendale*, 156 Eng. Rep. 145 (1854), thus limits damages to those reasonably foreseeable at the time of the contract. *See Gerwin v. Southeastern Cal. Ass'n of Seventh Day Adventists*, 14 Cal. App. 3d 209, 220, 92 Cal. Rptr. 111, 118 (1971); *Petrie-Clemons v. Butterfield*, 122 N.H. 120, 124, 441 A.2d 1167, 1170 (1982). To satisfy the foreseeability requirement, the injury for which damages are sought "must follow the breach in the natural course of events, or the evidence must specifically show that the breaching party had reason to foresee the injury." *Salem Engineering & Constr. Corp. v. Londonderry School Dist.*, 122 N.H. 379, 384, 445 A.2d 1091, 1094 (1982). Thus, peculiar circumstances and particular needs must be made known to the seller if they are to be considered in determining the foreseeability of damages. *Lewis v. Mobil Oil Corporation*, 438 F.2d 500, 510 (8th Cir. 1971).

Second, the damages sought must be limited to recompense for the reasonably ascertainable consequences of the breach. *See* RSA 382-A:2-715, comment 4. While proof of damages to the degree of mathematical certainty is not necessary, *Smith v. State*, 125 N.H. 799, 805, 486 A.2d 289, 294 (1984), a claim for lost profits must rest on evidence demonstrating that the profits claimed were "reasonably certain" in the absence of the breach. *Whitehouse v. Rytman*, 122 N.H. 777, 780, 451 A.2d 370, 372 (1982). Speculative losses are not recoverable.

Third, consequential damages such as lost profits are recoverable only if the loss "could not reasonably be prevented by cover or otherwise." § 2-715(2)(a). *See* § 2-712(1) (*i.e.*, by purchase or contract to purchase goods in substitution for those due from seller). In summary, consequential damages must be reasonably foreseeable, ascertainable and unavoidable.

Applying these standards, we look first at the claim for lost profits for the manufacturing season beginning in September 1978. There is no serious question that loss of profit on sales was foreseeable up to the number of 400 stoves referred to in the contract, and there is a clear evidentiary basis for a finding that Hydraform would have sold at least that number. There was also an evidentiary basis for the trial court's ruling that Hydraform acted reasonably even though it did not attempt to cover until the season was underway and it turned out to be too late. American had led Hydraform on by repeatedly promising to take steps to remedy its failures, and the court could find that Hydraform's reliance on these promises was reasonable up to the time when it finally and unsuccessfully tried to cover.

Lost profits on sales beyond the 400 stoves presents a foreseeability issue, however. Although American's agent had stated that American would supply steel beyond the 400 stove level on demand, there is no evidence that Hydraform indicated that it would be likely to make such a demand to the extent of any reasonably foreseeable amount. Rather, the evidence was that Mr. Choate had told American's agent that the business was seasonal with a busy period of about four months. The contract referred to delivery dates on the first of four separate months and spoke of only 400 stoves. Thus, there appears to be no basis on which American should have foreseen a volume in excess of 400 for the season beginning in 1978. Lost profits for sales beyond that amount therefore were not recoverable, and it was error to allow the jury to consider them.

Nor should the claims for profits lost on sales projected for the two subsequent years have been submitted to the jury. The impediment to recovery of these profits was not total unforeseeability that the breach could have effects in a subsequent year or years, but the inability to calculate any such loss with reasonable certainty. In arguing that a reasonably certain calculation was possible, Hydraform relies heavily on *Van Hooijdonk v. Langley*, 111 N.H. 32, 274 A.2d 798 (1971), a case that arose from a landlord's cancellation of a business lease. The court held that the jury could award damages for profits that a seasonal restaurant anticipated for the three years that lease should have run. It reasoned that the experience of one two-month season provided sufficient data for a reasonably certain opinion about the extent of future profits. The court thus found sufficient certainty where damages were estimated on the basis of one year of operation and profit, as compared with no operation and hence no profit in the later years.

Hydraform's situation, however, presents a variable that distinguishes it from *Van Hooijdonk*. In our case the evidence did not indicate that American's breach had forced Hydraform's stove manufacturing enterprise out of business, and therefore the jury could not assume that there would be no profits in later years. Without that assumption the jury could not come to any reasonably certain conclusion about the anticipated level of sales absent a breach by American. The jury could predict that Hydraform would obtain steel from another source and would be able to manufacture stoves; but it did not have the evidence from which to infer the future volume of manufacturing and sales. Thus, it could not calculate anticipated lost profits with a reasonable degree of certainty.

We consider next the claim for loss in the value of the business as realized at the time of its sale in 1979. As a general rule, loss in the value of a business as a going concern, or loss in the value of its good will, may be recovered as an element of consequential damages. *See Salem Engineering & Const. Corp. v. Londonderry School Dist.*, 122 N.H. at 384, 445 A.2d at 1094; *Salinger v. Salinger*, 69 N.H. 589, 591–92, 45 A. 558, 559–60 (1899); *see also J. Story, Partnership* § 99, at 169–70 (6th ed. 1868).

In this case, however, it was error to submit the claim for diminished value to the jury, for three reasons. First, to the extent that diminished value was thought to reflect anticipated loss of profits in future years, as a capitalization of the loss, it could not be calculated with reasonable certainty for the reasons we have just discussed. Second, even if such profits could have been calculated in this case, allowing the jury to consider both a claim for diminished value resting on lost profits and a claim for the lost profits themselves would have allowed a double recovery. *See Westric Battery Co. v. Standard Electric Co., Inc.*, 522 F.2d 986, 989 (10th Cir. 1975). Third, to the extent that diminished value was thought to rest on any other theory, there was no evidence on which it could have been calculated. There was nothing more than Mr. Choate's testimony that he had sold the business in September of 1979 for $150,000 plus minimum royalties, together with his opinion that the sales price was less than the business was worth. This testimony provided the jury with no basis for determining what the business was worth or for calculating the claimed loss, and any award on this theory rested on sheer speculation.

In summary, we hold that the jury should not have been allowed to consider any contract claim for consequential damages for lost profits beyond those lost on the sale of 150 stoves, the difference between the 400 mentioned in the contract and the 250 actually sold. Nor should the trial court have allowed the jury to consider the claim for loss in the value of the business.

AGF, INC. v. GREAT LAKES HEAT TREATING CO.
Ohio Supreme Court
555 N.E.2d 634 (1990)

RESNICK, Justice.

*　　*　　*

Norman R. Fisher, Jr. gained experience in the field of heat treating by working with his father, who owned a heat treating company. In 1979, Fisher developed a plan to establish his own business — Great Lakes Heat Treating Company, appellant herein. He entered into negotiations with a sales representative from appellee AGF for the purchase of an automated heat treating furnace capable of processing five hundred to five hundred twenty pounds of parts per hour. By letter dated August 3, 1979, Fisher accepted a proposal on behalf of Great Lakes, purchasing a "284 Shaker Hearth Furnace." The furnace was delivered on January 31, 1980. The furnace, however, could not be assembled due to improperly fitting parts. AGF was informed of the problem, and a technician was dispatched to Great Lakes. After additional complaints by Great Lakes and several adjustments, the furnace was finally assembled.

The furnace continued to fail to operate in spite of the assembly by AGF's technician. As the court of appeals succinctly stated, "[t]his failure of operation was only the beginning of a continuous failure of the furnace to operate and/or process 500 pounds of parts per hour. Numerous complaints were lodged by appellant-G.L. [Great Lakes] with regard to the improper operation of the furnace and appellee-A.G.F. attempted to rectify the operating problems on at least six occasions. At one point, appellant-G.L.'s furnace was closed down for a period of two weeks in order to completely rebuild the furnace. Even this attempt at repair, however, failed to allow the furnace to function as originally designed at the rate of 500 pounds of parts per hour."

[Ed. Note: Great Lakes admitted that it had refused to pay the balance due on the furnace, but counterclaimed for damages. The trial court ruled, in part, that Great Lakes could not admit evidence as to lost profits due to the continuing failure of the furnace. The jury returned a verdict in the amount of $9,718.17 on AGF's original complaint, and awarded the amount of $30,000 on Great Lakes' counterclaim. The court of appeals affirmed the trial court's exclusion of evidence concerning lost profits, finding that the evidence was speculative and could not be established with reasonable certainty under Ohio's long-standing "new business" rule regarding proof of lost profits.]

II

The second issue presented for this court's determination concerns the ability to recover lost profits as consequential damages when the party seeking said damages is involved in a new business. Appellant argues that the trial court erred in excluding evidence of lost profits solely because the aggrieved party was a new business. Moreover, appellant contends that the court of appeals erred in the same manner by holding that "the state of Ohio has consistently held that a new business cannot recover lost profits."

The general test in the state of Ohio for the recovery of lost profits is set forth in *Charles R. Combs Trucking, Inc. v. International Harvester Co.* (1984), 12 Ohio St. 3d 241, 12 OBR 322, 466 N.E.2d 883, at paragraph two of the syllabus: "Lost profits may be recovered by the plaintiff in a breach of contract action if: (1) profits were within the contemplation of the parties at the time the contract was made, (2) the loss of profits is the probable result of the breach of contract, and (3) the profits are not remote and speculative and may be shown with reasonable certainty." We further expounded on the third prong of the Combs test, stating that "[i]n order for a plaintiff to recover lost profits in a breach of contract action, the amounts of lost profits, as well as their existence, must be demonstrated with reasonable certainty. . . ." *Gahanna v. Eastgate Properties, Inc.* (1988), 36 Ohio St. 3d 65, 521 N.E.2d 814, syllabus.

Restatement of the Law 2d, Contracts (1981) 146, Section 352, Comment *b*, states as follows:

The difficulty of proving lost profits varies greatly with the nature of the transaction. If, for example, it is the seller who claims lost profit on the ground that the buyer's breach has caused him to lose a sale, proof of lost profit will ordinarily not be difficult. If, however, it is the buyer who claims lost profit on the ground that the seller's breach has caused him loss in other transactions, the task of proof is harder. Furthermore, if the transaction is more complex and extends into the future, as where the seller agrees to furnish all of the buyer's requirements over a period of years, proof of the loss of profits caused by the seller's breach is more difficult. If the breach prevents the injured party from carrying on a well-established business, the resulting loss of profits can often be proved with sufficient certainty. Evidence of past performance will form the basis for a reasonable prediction as to the future. See Illustration 5. *However, if the business is a new one or if it is a speculative one that is subject to great fluctuations in volume, costs or prices, proof will be more difficult. Nevertheless, damages may be established with reasonable certainty with the aid of expert testimony, economic and financial data, market surveys and analyses, business records of similar enterprises, and the like.* See Illustration 6.[2] (Emphasis added.)

As can be seen from the foregoing, the drafters of the Restatement recognized that lost profits may be recovered by a new business provided adequate proof is submitted by the new business. In addition, Official Comment 2 to UCC 2-708 provides support for this proposition, wherein it is stated: " . . . [t]his section permits the recovery of lost profits in all appropriate cases. . . . It is not necessary to a recovery of 'profit' to show a history of earnings, especially if a new venture is involved." While [2-708(2)] relates to a seller's damages for non-acceptance or repudiation of goods, the recognition of recovery for lost profits available to a seller warrants the conclusion that this remedy must also be available to a buyer.

Therefore, we adopt the position taken under the Restatement of Contracts 2d, Section 352, Comment *b*, and expressly recognize that a new business may recover lost profits, so long as the buyer provides a sufficient quantum of proof.[3] Other jurisdictions follow this approach. . . .

In Ohio, therefore, a new business may recover lost profits in a breach of contract action but such lost profits must be established with reasonable certainty. In determining whether a plaintiff has met this burden, we see no reason to depart from the general test for lost profits set forth in *Combs, supra.* Thus, we will apply the tripartite analysis of *Combs* to the facts of this case.

The first prong requires a consideration of whether the parties contemplated profits at the time the contract was made. Appellant was engaged in establishing a new business, and it is appropriate to assume it did so in order to make a profit. Likewise, from the very start of negotiations for the sale of the furnace, both parties demonstrated awareness that the new business would be profit oriented. Thus, appellant satisfies this aspect of the *Combs* test.

The second prong necessitates an inquiry as to whether the lost profits are the probable result of the breach of contract. The record overwhelmingly demonstrates that any lost profits were the direct result of the furnace's constant and continual failure to

---

[2] [1] Illustrations 5 and 6 to Comment *b* state as follows:

> 5. A contracts with B to remodel B's existing outdoor drive-in theatre, work to be completed on June 1. A does not complete the work until September 1. B can use records of the theatre's prior and subsequent operation, along with other evidence, to prove his lost profits with reasonable certainty.

> 6. A contracts with B to construct a new outdoor drive-in theatre, to be completed on June 1. A does not complete the theatre until September 1. Even though the business is a new rather than an established one, B may be able to prove his lost profits with reasonable certainty. B can use records of the theatre's subsequent operation and of similar theatres in the same locality, along with other evidence including market surveys and expert testimony, in attempting to do this.

[3] [2] Recent cases have eroded the once generally accepted rule that lost profits damages for a new business were not recoverable. The development of the law has been to find damages for lost profits of an unestablished business recoverable when they can be adequately proved with reasonable certainty. The earlier cases are either ignored or rationalized as having been based on a finding that on those particular facts the evidence was inadequate as a matter of law to support a judgment for the plaintiff. "What was once a rule of law has been converted into a rule of evidence." DUNN, RECOVERY OF DAMAGES FOR LOST PROFITS 3d (1987) 220, Section 4.2.

operate as was anticipated. In fact, the record discloses that the furnace *never* operated at the capacity as stated in the original proposal between the parties (five hundred pounds of parts per hour). Therefore, appellant satisfies the second prong.

The third factor requires that profits must not be too remote or speculative, and that they be shown with reasonable certainty. As noted previously, both the existence and the amount of lost profits must be demonstrated with "reasonable certainty." *Gahanna, supra.* Further, as discussed previously, Restatement of Contracts 2d, Section 352, Comment *b* provides that " . . . damages [lost profits] may be established with reasonable certainty with the aid of expert testimony, economic and financial data, market surveys and analyses, business records of similar enterprises, and the like."[4] By utilizing these methods a new business may, under the appropriate circumstances, demonstrate lost profits with reasonable certainty. Therefore, we hold that a new business may establish lost profits with reasonable certainty through the use of such evidence as expert testimony, economic and financial data, market surveys and analyses, business records of similar enterprises, and any other relevant facts.

In the case at bar, appellant offered the following evidence as to this issue: (1) testimony of a customer, (2) testimony from a certified public accountant, and (3) testimony of Norman Fisher, president of appellant Great Lakes. The customer, Robert Steinheiser, Vice-President of Sales at Triad Metal Products, testified that "we agreed to give . . . [appellant] everything . . . [appellant] could handle." Additionally, Steinheiser stated that he could "very easily" provide appellant with enough work to run the furnace twenty-four hours a day, seven days a week. However, the witness did not provide any further specificity as to the price or quantity of parts. Charles M. Ciuni, a certified public accountant, testified that he had reviewed financial statements and other documents from a company in a similar type of business, as well as industry statistics from a recognized textbook in this area. Ciuni's opinion testimony was then proffered as to what he believed appellant's lost profits would have been. Lastly, Fisher testified, on proffer, that the average price appellant received per part was twenty cents. Fisher then stated that the loss of profit suffered by appellant was $39,000 per month, using the simple calculation of subtracting expenses from expected revenues based on the average price of a single part.

We conclude that appellant has not demonstrated his lost profits with the required "reasonable certainty." Ciuni cannot be considered an expert witness on the business in question. Moreover, his opinion testimony was without proper foundation and none of the records, documents or sources he used was ever offered as evidence. Additionally, while Ciuni testified that he examined business records of similar companies involved in this line of work, none of these was introduced into evidence. Likewise, Steinheiser provided no specific quantities of either work already performed or work to be performed in the future. Nor did this witness indicate any type of price for the work. Lastly, appellant has not submitted any of its own business records to substantiate its

---

[4] [3] "In one sentence, both the new-business rule and its corollary, that an earnings history is required to project profits (see 4.6), are thrown out the window.

" . . .

" . . . The trend in the cases since 1978 is unmistakable. The modern decisions cited in this section demonstrate an increasing rejection of the traditional new-business rule.

" . . . It is impossible for anyone, including an appellate court, to foresee all the possible situations in which meritorious claims could be asserted for lost profits even though the business to which those profits might accrue had not yet commenced operation. Nor is any worthwhile end to be achieved by permitting one party to breach his contracts with impunity — giving him an option, as it were — because the other party has not yet commenced operation. The trend of the modern cases is plainly toward replacing the old rule of law with a rule of evidence — the unquestionable principle that damages for lost profits must be proven with reasonable certainty and that the evidence must support that finding by the trier of fact."

DUNN, *supra*, at 227–28, Section 4.2.

claims for lost profits. We note that " . . . evidence of lost future profits as an item of compensatory damages need only be reasonable, not specific." *Combs, supra*, 12 Ohio St. 3d at 244, 12 OBR at 325, 466 N.E.2d at 887. In this case, however, appellant has failed to provide adequate evidence to meet this standard.

In conclusion, while new businesses may recover lost profits as damages for breach of contract, such damages must be demonstrated with reasonable certainty. . . .

Judgment accordingly.

DOUGLAS, J., concurring in part and dissenting in part.

. . . I respectfully dissent from the majority's judgment with regard to the loss-of-profits issue. It is my judgment that the loss of profits was properly documented and proven in the trial court.

4. Limiting the Available Remedies by Agreement

As you learned earlier, Article 2 strongly supports the parties' freedom to determine their obligations and rights by agreement. Section 2-719 makes clear that the parties also have substantial freedom to determine the remedies available in the event of a breach. Section 2-719(1)(a) affords great latitude to the parties: they may "limit or alter the measure of damages recoverable" under Article 2; they may add remedies to those provided in Article 2; and they may substitute agreed remedies for those provided in Article 2. Comment 1 reinforces the breadth of this provision in straightforward terms: "parties are left free to shape their remedies to their particular requirements and reasonable agreements limiting or modifying remedies are to be given effect." However, § 2-719(1)(b) provides that agreed remedies are cumulative to those provided in Article 2, "unless the remedy is expressly agreed to be exclusive." Consequently, the parties must *expressly* displace the remedial provisions of Article 2, if that is their intent.

There are typical scenarios in which parties alter the available remedies by agreement. First, they can "limit" the remedies available by providing a damages cap or by providing that the buyer's sole remedy is repair or replacement of the defective goods. A limited remedy provides the seller with an assurance that its liability will not be unlimited in the event of a breach. A collateral goal might be to preclude federal court diversity jurisdiction by capping damages below the statutory "amount in controversy" requirement. *See Valhal Corp. v. Sullivan Assocs.*, 44 F.3d 195 (3d Cir. 1995) (remanding for dismissal because the damages cap of $50,000 precluded diversity jurisdiction). This freedom is limited by § 2-719(2), which withholds enforcement of any such agreement if "circumstances cause an exclusive or limited remedy to fail of its essential purpose," and permits the aggrieved party to pursue all remedies available under the Code. The first subsection below addresses this important limitation.

The parties may also "alter the measure of damages recoverable" by precluding recovery of consequential damages. Although the seller may be willing to accept some uncertainty about its exposure in the event of a breach and therefore not insist on a damages cap, the seller might insist on eliminating consequential damages because these losses may far exceed the buyer's direct losses under the contract and often are difficult to calculate in advance. Section 2-719(3) reiterates that agreements limiting or excluding consequential damages must not be unconscionable, and provides that such agreements for "injury to the person in the case of consumer goods is prima facie unconscionable, but limitation of damages where the loss is commercial is not." The second subsection below explores the special considerations that arise when the parties exclude consequential damages from the available remedies.

In the third subsection below, the first two topics are combined by considering the circumstances in which a buyer might successfully assert that an otherwise valid exclusion of consequential damages should not be enforced because, under the circumstances, the limited remedy has failed of its essential purpose.

The fourth subsection below considers the different issues that arise when the parties agree to liquidate the damages available in case of a breach. Commercial parties are very interested in eliminating uncertain exposure in the event that they cannot perform their obligations, and so Article 2 recognizes a wide scope of freedom of contract to liquidate damages. Nevertheless, Article 2 carries forward the common law concern that the parties not agree to unreasonable or punitive damages in the form of a liquidated damages provision.

The final subsection ties these topics together with a summary problem. You might begin by reading the problem and thinking about it as you read the material and cases.

a. When the limited remedy fails of its "essential purpose"

It is common for parties to substitute exclusive remedies for the remedies provided by Article 2. In particular, many sellers will limit the buyer to "repair and replacement" of defective goods in the event of nonconformity. However, by foreclosing the buyer from suing for damages, these clauses pose the potential for harsh and inequitable results. Consequently, § 2-719(2) permits a party to seek a remedy under Article 2 in the event that circumstances "cause an exclusive or limited remedy to fail of its essential purpose." Comment 2 explains that this is to ensure "that there be at least a fair quantum of remedy for breach," and "that at least minimum adequate remedies be available." The "fail of its essential purpose test" has generated considerable controversy and litigation. Analyze the following early attempt to bring principled decision-making to this area.

Eddy, *On the "Essential" Purposes of Limited Remedies: The Metaphysics of U.C.C. § 2-719(2)*
65 CAL. L. REV. 28, 28–36 (1977)[5]

[Ed. Note: Professor Eddy discusses a typical situation giving rise to litigation in which] the seller employs a restricted "repair-or-replace" warranty and either refuses to repair or is unable to do so. The buyer then urges that the limited remedy has "failed of its essential purpose." Since section 2-719 seeks to encourage a method of law finding, rather than dictate a particular result, proper resolution . . . requires a careful evaluation of the commercial context surrounding the parties' bargain. Only then can the role of the limited remedy within that bargain be understood. Yet courts routinely treat the "essential purpose" of a remedy as a self-evident matter requiring no discussion. This analytic failure has generated at least three pernicious effects. First, the section has been applied to cases that might more properly be analyzed under other Code provisions, notably section 2-302 (unconscionability) or section 2-719(3) (unconscionable limitation or exclusion of consequential damages). Second, cases applying section 2-719(2) to repair-or-replace warranties reflect disagreement about the circumstances that lead that remedy to fail of its essential purpose. Third, again in the warranty cases, courts are divided over whether the failure of purpose of a limited remedy necessarily invalidates an exclusion of consequential damages.

I. UNDISCOVERABLE DEFECTS: UNCONSCIONABILITY VS. FAILURE OF ESSENTIAL PURPOSE

[Ed. Note: Professor Eddy first disputes the traditional reading that unconscionability is determined as of the time of contracting, whereas the test of § 2-719(2) applies at the time of the dispute. He offers an alternative approach.]

Although conceptually a clause's scope of application is established at the time of formation, practically a clause is rarely construed until a given set of circumstances has

---

raised a dispute. At the time of dispute, one then looks backward to the time of formation. To say that a remedy is "initially" fair, or "apparently fair and reasonable" probably means no more than that it is easy to envisage some sets of circumstances in which the remedy operates quite equitably. The actual circumstances which have arisen and now call for the construction of the contract may be either the same or different from those "initially" envisaged. If they are the same circumstances, then, as the remedy operates equitably, the likelihood of dispute is small. When they are different, and the remedy no longer appears to operate equitably, two distinct issues may arise. The first is whether, on a sensible construction, the remedy in fact applies to the circumstances that have arisen. Failure of purpose doctrine addresses this issue; it seeks to guide courts to sensible constructions by directing their attention to the underlying purposes of the remedy in question, and thus dissuades them from mechanical, literal applications having no justification in commercial understanding. If the clause in question has no application to the circumstances now confronted, there is no need for further analysis. But if a court finds that the clause was indeed intended to apply to such circumstances, a second issue may arise: is such a limitation unconscionable? The issue of failure of essential purpose is logically prior to the unconscionability issue — for it is best to decide if the clause applies to the facts in question before deciding if such application would be unconscionable.

Sections 2-719(2) and (3) are best understood as seeking to impose an analytic *process* upon the courts. Section 2-719(2) "does no more than invoke intelligent construction of the contract clause . . . ," the means of assuring such construction is to scrutinize the "purposes" underlying a clause. A three-step analysis may be suggested: 1) determination of the purposes underlying a provision; 2) determination whether application of the remedy in the particular circumstances will further those purposes (or whether there has instead been a "failure of essential purpose"); 3) if the clause does not fail of its essential purpose, determination whether furtherance of the purpose works an unconscionable result.

* * *

II. LIMITED REPAIR WARRANTIES

The analytic process proposed in the previous section may be tested by applying it to the second recurrent situation in which section 2-719(2) is presently utilized: the case of a limited repair warranty provision. Automobiles, many other consumer products, and substantial numbers of commercial and industrial products are typically sold with such a "warranty." These provisions have a number of elements: first, a carefully delineated express warranty is made; second, all other warranties, express or implied, are disclaimed; third, the remedy for breach of the express warranty is limited to a sole remedy of repair or replacement, at the seller's option; and fourth, the provision may additionally state that the seller shall have no liability for consequential damages. When carefully drafted, such a provision accords with the freedom of contract that Article 2 recognizes; indeed, specific Code authority may be cited for each element of the term. Nevertheless, such clauses have been subject to a variety of attacks.

* * *

. . . Such a "repair or replace" provision not only operates equitably but also minimizes senseless economic waste. It assures that in the end the buyer will receive substantially what was bargained for — a functioning item meeting the contract description.

* * *

This rosy picture of the limited repair warranty, however, rests upon at least three assumptions: that the warrantor will diligently make repairs that such repairs will indeed "cure" the defects, and that consequential loss in the interim will be negligible.

So long as these assumptions hold true, the limited remedy appears to operate fairly and, as noted above, will usually withstand contentions of "unconscionability." But when one of these assumptions proves false in a particular case, the purchaser may find that the substantial benefit of the bargain has been lost. The language of the Official Comment to section 2-719 squarely supports this proposition:

> [U]nder subsection (2), where an apparently fair and reasonable clause because of circumstances fails in its purpose or operates to deprive either party of the substantial value of the bargain, it must give way to the general remedy provisions of this Article.

With increasing frequency purchasers are raising section 2-719(2) contentions in such circumstances, and courts have displayed confusion in dealing with the arguments.

Under the analysis previously proposed, the first step is to determine the purposes served by a limited remedy. [H]owever, courts have been slow to recognize the need for such analysis. Instead, while perhaps perceiving implicitly the nature of the transaction and therefore the "essential purpose" of the limited remedy, some courts have chosen to focus on such morally laden issues as the character of defendant's conduct.

*   *   *

In summary, cases applying section 2-719(2) to limited repair warranties demonstrate some of the same weaknesses as the undiscoverable defect cases: too much is being taken for granted. Courts may well be moved by a vague apprehension of the commercial context and the manner in which it bears upon the issues before them, but they do not seek to sharpen their understanding or to explicate it in their opinions. An opportunity for development of the case law upon predictable lines of analogy is therefore lost. At the same time, freed from the requirement of delving into commercial mores, courts are utilizing unfortunate distinctions that appeal more to our sense of moral outrage than our understanding of commercial life. . . . All of these difficulties could be reduced were courts to adhere to the first two steps of the previously suggested analysis: a thoughtful explication of the essential purpose of the limited remedy, as informed by an understanding of the [type of transaction]; and a determination whether that purpose will be furthered by application of the limited remedy in the particular case.

QUESTION

Is Professor Eddy's interpretation of § 2-719 persuasive? Be sure that you understand his suggested approach for applying § 2-719 to "repair or replace" clauses before continuing to the next subsection.

b.   Limiting or excluding consequential damages

Section 2-719(3) signals a greater willingness to permit the parties to limit or exclude consequential damages by providing that they may do so "unless the limitation or exclusion is unconscionable." Since the parties do not have the freedom to agree to unconscionable terms in their contracts for sale, see § 2-302, this provision would appear to impose no new tests or limitations on these clauses. However, the next subsection reveals that the situation is not so straightforward. Before moving to these complexities, read the following case to refresh your understanding of unconscionability analysis as it is applied to a clause that excludes recovery of consequential damages.

NEC TECHNOLOGIES, INC. v. NELSON
Georgia Supreme Court
478 S.E.2d 769 (1996)

HUNSTEIN, Justice.

Arthur and Kathy Nelson brought suit against Curtis Mathes Corporation, C.M. City, Inc. d/b/a Curtis Mathes Home Entertainment Center, and NEC Technologies, Inc. ("NEC"), seeking to recover property damages they sustained in a fire allegedly caused by a defect in the Curtis Mathes television set they had purchased. The Nelsons asserted causes of action sounding in strict liability, negligence, and breach of warranty. Based on language in the express warranty on the television set which provided that the warranty "Excludes All Incidental and Consequential Damages," Curtis Mathes and C.M. City moved for partial summary judgment on the Nelsons' claim for consequential property damages under the breach of warranty claim. Holding as a matter of law that the exclusion was not unconscionable at the time of the sale to the Nelsons, the trial court granted the motion. . . . The Court of Appeals reversed the trial court. . . . We granted certiorari to consider that court's rulings. . . . We reverse.

Georgia law expressly allows manufacturers of products to limit or exclude consequential damages. OCGA § 11-2-719(3). However, manufacturers may not limit or exclude such damages where the result would be unconscionable. *Id.* The Legislature recognized both the distinction between consumer and commercial purchasers of products and the distinction between personal injury and property damages, in that OCGA § 11-2-719(3) expressly states that a limitation on consequential damages for personal injury in the case of consumer goods is prima facie unconscionable. The Legislature could have provided that a limitation on consequential property damages in the case of consumer goods is prima facie unconscionable, as it did with consequential damages for personal injuries, but it chose not to do so. Warranty limitations on the recovery of consequential damages to property in consumer cases have been upheld. *E.g., McCrimmon v. Tandy Corp.*, 202 Ga. App. 233(3), 414 S.E.2d 15 (1991); *Sharpe v. General Motors Corp.*, 198 Ga. App. 313(5), 401 S.E.2d 328 (1991). It follows from a review of OCGA § 11-2-719(3) and case law that only those limitations/exclusions on consequential property damages in consumer cases that are "unconscionable" are barred under Georgia law.

The Uniform Commercial Code and the Georgia UCC, *see* OCGA § 11-1-101 et seq., contain no definition of "unconscionability." This Court has noted that the basic test for determining unconscionability is

> "whether, in the light of the general commercial background and the commercial needs of the particular trade or case, the clauses involved are so one-sided as to be unconscionable under the circumstances existing at the time of the making of the contract." Comment 1 to Uniform Commercial Code § 2-302.

R.L. Kimsey Cotton Co. v. Ferguson, 233 Ga. 962, 965(3), 214 S.E.2d 360 (1975).[6] However, the process by which a court reaches the conclusion that a contract provision is unconscionable has been discussed by our appellate courts only in abbreviated and conclusory fashion. *E.g., Ga. Magnetic Imaging v. Greene County Hosp. Auth.*, 219 Ga. App. 502(5), 466 S.E.2d 41 (1995); *Fiat Auto U.S.A. v. Hollums*, 185 Ga. App. 113(2), 363 S.E.2d 312 (1987). Thus, to assist this Court in resolving this appeal, we have found it helpful to conduct a review of foreign authorities.

---

[6] [2] Other definitions of an unconscionable contract include "such an agreement as no sane man not acting under a delusion would make and that no honest man would take advantage of," *R.L. Kimsey Cotton Co. v. Ferguson, supra*, 233 Ga. at 966, 214 S.E.2d 360, and a contract that is "abhorrent to good morals and conscience. It is one where one of the parties takes a fraudulent advantage of another." *F.N. Roberts Pest Control Co. v. McDonald*, 132 Ga. App. 257, 260, 208 S.E.2d 13 (1974).

It has been recognized that "unconscionability" as set forth in UCC § 2-302 is "not a concept, but a determination to be made in light of a variety of factors not unifiable into a formula." (Footnote and emphasis deleted.) Vol. 1, White & Summers, Uniform Commercial Code (4th Ed.), § 4-3, p. 213. *See also A & M Produce Co. v. FMC Corp.*, 135 Cal. App. 3d 473, 186 Cal. Rptr. 114, 120 (1982) (unconscionability is "a flexible doctrine designed to allow courts to directly consider numerous factors which may adulterate the contractual process"). Foreign courts have generally divided the relevant factors into procedural and substantive elements. *See UCC Unconscionability Warranty Disclaimer*, 38 A.L.R. 4th 25, §§ 2, 3(a)(b). Procedural unconscionability addresses the process of making the contract, while substantive unconscionability looks to the contractual terms themselves. *Id.*; White & Summers, *supra*. A non-inclusive list of some factors courts have considered in determining whether a contract is procedurally unconscionable includes the age, education, intelligence, business acumen and experience of the parties, their relative bargaining power, the conspicuousness and comprehensibility of the contract language, the oppressiveness of the terms, and the presence or absence of a meaningful choice. . . . As to the substantive element of unconscionability, courts have focused on matters such as the commercial reasonableness of the contract terms, the purpose and effect of the terms, the allocation of the risks between the parties, and similar public policy concerns. . . . We find the procedural-substantive analysis of unconscionability helpful and apply it to the case at bar.

For purposes of addressing the motion for partial summary judgment on the consequential property damages issue, the trial court assumed, despite sharply contested evidence adduced by the parties, that the television set was indeed defective.[7] The trial court then considered the evidence before it, consisting of documentary evidence such as the warranty issued by Curtis Mathes[8] as well as the affidavits and depositions of the parties and other witnesses regarding matters such as the manner in which the Nelsons chose a Curtis Mathes television set and how the parties contracted for the purchase of the television set. The trial court expressly pronounced this evidence sufficient to render it unnecessary to hold a hearing as to the warranty's commercial setting, purpose, and effect under OCGA § 11-2-302(2). The trial court granted partial summary judgment to Curtis Mathes and C.M. City on the basis that it was not unconscionable at the time of the sale of the product, *see* OCGA § 11-2-302(1), to exclude recovery of consequential property damages and limit recovery to the replacement of parts, service, labor and like matters.

Our review of the record regarding all of the circumstances surrounding the process

---

[7] [3] The trial court noted that the city fire chief and the fire marshall opined that the fire started from an electrical shortage unassociated with the television set, while the Nelsons' expert opined the fire originated around a defective resistor in the set.

[8] [4] There is some dispute whether the applicable warranty was a six-year or a four-year warranty. Construing the evidence in favor of the Nelsons, as respondents on motions for summary judgment, we will presume the applicability here of the six-year warranty. That warranty was denominated an "Exclusive Six Year Limited Protection Plan." It stated the protection plan was provided by Curtis Mathes Corporation; explained who was covered, how long they were covered and what was covered; and set forth the steps an owner was required to follow to obtain service and possible costs therefor. Under the bold-faced section titled "What Are The Exceptions," there were several brief paragraphs containing various exclusions, such as for damages caused by abuse and acts of nature, shipping and handling charges, and non-coverage of commercial or educational use. The fifth paragraph provides:

> This Exclusive Limited Protection Plan Excludes All Incidental and Consequential Damages. Some states do not allow the exclusion of incidental or consequential damages, so the above exclusion may not apply to you.

This language is followed by a paragraph excluding implied warranties. The warranty concludes with the statement that the protection plan "gives you specific legal rights. You may have other rights which vary from state to state," and then provides that "[f]or further information about this Protection Plan" interested individuals could contact the Curtis Mathes Protection Plan Administrator, setting forth an address and telephone number.

in which these parties entered into the contract for the purchase of the television set reveals no basis for concluding the warranty exclusion should be voided for procedural unconscionability. The language setting forth the warranty exclusion was conspicuous and comprehensible; the warranty apprised consumers that the absolute language in an exclusion may not apply to them; and the warranty itself provided a source to be contacted if further information or clarification was desired (*see* fn.3, *supra*). Ms. Nelson in her deposition detailed the manner in which the television set was purchased.[9] She deposed that she had owned for five years a 40-inch Curtis Mathes television when she decided (during the course of moving furniture to another home) that rather than move the old set, she would exchange it for a new set. She contacted C.M. City and asked a salesperson if the store was interested in an exchange. She was informed that the 40-inch model was no longer available and that the most comparable model had a 46-inch screen. Ms. Nelson arranged during this telephone conversation to have C.M. City pick up the old set and deliver a new 46-inch television to the other home. She received $500 for the trade-in and paid the $1,970.80 balance on the new set in cash. She was aware there was a six-year warranty on the set; the sales receipt also reflects a handwritten notation regarding the six-year warranty. Although employees of C.M. City were deposed, they were unable to provide any further details regarding the transaction.

The record as developed reveals no evidence that the Nelsons looked at other manufacturers' sets, compared warranties between sets available on the market, or made any inquiry of C.M. City or other dealers regarding the extent of warranties available on such sets. The record does reflect that Ms. Nelson was able to bargain over certain matters in the contract, such as the trade-in of the old set and delivery arrangements, and there is some evidence that Ms. Nelson obtained the benefit of a six-year warranty rather than a four-year warranty on the television set. However, there is no evidence that any other aspect of the warranty played any part in the bargaining process or in Ms. Nelson's decision to purchase the television set. Given this evidence, we conclude that Curtis Mathes and C.M. City discharged their burden as movants for summary judgment by demonstrating from the testimony and documents adduced that there is an absence of evidence to support a finding of procedural unconscionability in the warranty limitation in issue. *See generally Lau's Corp. v. Haskins*, 261 Ga. 491, 405 S.E.2d 474 (1991).

We pretermit the issue whether the lack of procedural unconscionability in this case is determinative of the unconscionability issue[10] because we conclude that there is likewise an absence of evidence to support a finding of substantive unconscionability.

Initially, we recognize that the exclusion of consequential property damages in the warranty cannot, in and of itself, be deemed to be against public policy since, as discussed, *supra*, the Legislature has allowed manufacturers to so exclude consequential property damages. What the Legislature allows cannot be contrary to public policy. *Avery v. Aladdin Products Div., etc., Inc.*, 128 Ga. App. 266(2), 196 S.E.2d 357 (1973).[11]

---

[9] [5] It is uncontroverted that Mr. Nelson was not involved in the purchase of the set. The record does not reflect Ms. Nelson's education or age, though it appears that at the time of the purchase she was a mature adult (in that she had recently married Mr. Nelson after the end of a first marriage that had lasted 40 years) and that she possessed some business experience (having worked in a furniture store and as a manager's assistant).

[10] [6] Research supports the statement made in *Fotomat Corp. of Fla. v. Chanda, supra*, 464 So.2d [626] at 629 [(Fla. App. 1985)], that:

> [m]ost courts take a "balancing approach" to the unconscionability question, and to tip the scales in favor of unconscionability, most courts seem to require a certain quantum of procedural plus a certain quantum of substantive unconscionability.

[11] [7] Similarly, because the Legislature also provides a trial court with the authority to refuse to enforce any part of a contract it deems unconscionable or to limit the application of any unconscionable clause as to avoid any unconscionable result, OCGA § 11-2-302(1), we find meritless the Nelson's argument that the entire exclusion clause at issue should be stricken as unconscionable because the exclusion fails to differentiate

OCGA § 11-2-302(1) directs the trial court to determine as a matter of law whether a contract or any clause thereof was unconscionable "at the time it was made": the unconscionability of a contract is not to be judged based on subsequently-acquired knowledge. *See* White & Summer, *supra*, § 4-3, p. 211. There is nothing in the record to indicate that at the time the Nelsons executed the sales contract for their television set, they were not aware of the normal hazards associated with the use of any electrical appliance. A review of the record before the trial court reveals nothing to indicate that Curtis Mathes or C.M. City had any knowledge that the particular design of the television set purchased by the Nelsons posed any greater danger than that presented by other products designed to utilize electricity in their operation. A warranty that limited the consumer's remedy to the replacement of parts, labor, services, and perhaps the value of the television set itself was not unreasonable as a matter of law in light of the remote, albeit dire, possibility that a defect might be present in the television set and that the consequences of the defect might be a fire that could extend beyond the set itself. Thus, while it has been recognized that a contractual term "is substantively suspect if it reallocates the risks of the bargain in [an] objectively unreasonable or unexpected manner, [cits.]" *A & M Produce Co. v. FMC Corp.*, *supra*, 186 Cal. Rptr. at 122, we cannot conclude under the circumstances in this case that the allocation of the risk of property damage to the Nelsons was unconscionable. We recognize that to hold this exclusion of consequential property damages unconscionable could necessitate voiding as unconscionable such exclusions in the warranties of virtually every type of electrical appliance sold to a consumer, a result clearly contrary to the provisions of OCGA § 11-2-719(3).

The Court of Appeals found the exclusion in this case to be unconscionable "given the manufacturer's [Curtis Mathes's] use of its name and reputation as the manufacturer of superior quality products, while failing to disclose that it did not actually manufacture the product." *Nelson v. C.M. City*, *supra*, 218 Ga. App. at 854, 463 S.E.2d 902. The Court of Appeals previously held in the same opinion that Curtis Mathes *was* the manufacturer of the television set, in that "the television was manufactured, prepared, assembled and packaged according to Curtis Mathes's own 'plan, intention, design, specifications, [and] formulation.' [Cit.]" *Id.* at 852(2), 463 S.E.2d 902. Given that the Nelsons themselves assert for purposes of strict liability that Curtis Mathes was the manufacturer of the television set and have sought and obtained such a ruling from the Court of Appeals, *see id.*, we cannot agree with the Court of Appeals that the Nelsons can claim Curtis Mathes is a manufacturer for strict liability but use the fact that Curtis Mathes did not manufacture the product to void a warranty limitation on the basis of unconscionability. Further, given that the unconscionability of contractual provisions is determined as a matter of law, OCGA § 11-2-302(1), we reject the Court of Appeals' holding that as a matter of law a manufacturer commits fraud by selling under its own label and as its own wares a complex product such as a television set which contains components that were not in every aspect designed, formulated, fabricated, constructed, and assembled exclusively by the manufacturer. Such a holding fails to reflect the reality and complexity of today's world-wide marketplace. Because there is an absence of evidence that Curtis Mathes or C.M. City acted fraudulently in the particular manner in which this television set was sold to the Nelsons, *see Lau's Corp. v. Haskins*, *supra*, the trial court correctly held that the exclusion in issue was not unconscionable.

OCGA § 11-2-302 provides Georgia courts with a potent tool for shielding disadvantaged and uneducated consumers from overreaching merchants. However, Georgia law also recognizes and protects the freedom of parties to contract. *See, e.g., National Consultants v. Burt*, 186 Ga. App. 27, 32, 366 S.E.2d 344 (1988).

People should be entitled to contract on their own terms without the

---

between damage to property and personal injury. Because the Nelsons' claim involves only property damages, they cannot show how the exclusion of consequential damages for personal injury was unconscionable as to them.

indulgence of paternalism by courts in the alleviation of one side or another from the effects of a bad bargain. Also, they should be permitted to enter into contracts that actually may be unreasonable or which may lead to hardship on one side. It is only where it turns out that one side or the other is to be penalized by the enforcement of the terms *of a contract so unconscionable that no decent, fairminded person would view the ensuing result without being possessed of a profound sense of injustice,* that equity will deny the use of its good offices in the enforcement of such unconscionability.

Fotomat Corp. of Fla. v. Chanda, supra, 464 So. 2d at 630. Based on a review of the evidence in light of both procedural and substantive elements of unconscionability, we cannot conclude as a matter of law that decent, fairminded persons would possess a profound sense of injustice from the enforcement of this warranty provision excluding the recovery of consequential property damages in the sale of a television set so as to render the exclusion unconscionable under OCGA § 11-2-302. Therefore, the Court of Appeals erred by reversing the trial court when it found that the warranty provision excluding the Nelsons from recovering consequential property damages was not unconscionable and that the Nelsons can recover under their breach of warranty claim only those damages allowed by the warranty. We note that this holding will not leave the Nelsons without recourse for their property damages, as they may seek to recover those losses under their strict liability and negligence causes of action.

Judgment reversed. All the Justices concur.

c. Availability of excluded consequential damages when an exclusive limited remedy fails of its "essential purpose"

The preceding two sections have covered two different rules. Section 2-719(2) permits the parties to limit or exclude remedies unless the limited remedy fails of its essential purpose, in which case "remedy may be had as provided in this Act," and § 2-719(3) permits the parties to exclude consequential damages as long as the exclusion is not unconscionable. A problem arises, however, when a party argues that an exclusive remedy has failed of its essential purpose and then seeks full Article 2 damages, including consequential damages that have been excluded in a separate clause of the contract. For example, if a buyer successfully demonstrates that the "repair" remedy has failed of its essential purpose, should the buyer be permitted to recover all remedies available under Article 2, including consequential damages, even if a separate clause in the contract excludes consequential damages in a manner deemed by the court not to be unconscionable? The following case describes different approaches to synthesizing the provisions of § 2-719.

RAZOR v. HYUNDAI MOTOR AMERICA
Illinois Supreme Court
854 N.E.2d 607 (2006)

FREEMAN, J.

This appeal involves the federal Magnuson-Moss Warranty-Federal Trade Commission Improvement Act (Act) (15 U.S.C. § 2301 *et seq.* (2000)) and the Illinois Uniform Commercial Code (UCC) (810 ILCS 5/ 1-101 et seq. (West 2000)). The only issues raised concern the propriety of the damages awarded to the plaintiff. The primary question is whether the circuit court acted properly in refusing to enforce a contractual clause prohibiting the award of consequential damages. There is also a sufficiency of the evidence challenge to the court's award of warranty damages. We affirm in part, reverse in part, and remand.

BACKGROUND

Plaintiff Shante Razor purchased a new Hyundai Sonata from Gartner Buick, Inc. (Gartner), on August 4, 2001. At the time she purchased the car, plaintiff also bought an optional remote starter and alarm system from an "options" booklet shown to her by the Gartner salesman. Gartner subcontracted the installation of this starter to Professional Sound Installers (ProSound). ProSound did not install it on the date plaintiff purchased her vehicle, but a few weeks later, on August 30, 2001.

The Sonata was the first new car plaintiff had ever purchased. It came with a five-year, 60,000-mile warranty, a copy of which was introduced into evidence. In pertinent part, the warranty provided as follows:

WHAT IS COVERED

Repair or replacement of any component originally manufactured or installed by Hyundai Motor Company or Hyundai Motor America (HMA) that is found to be defective in material or workmanship under normal use and maintenance, except any item specifically referred to in the section 'What is Not Covered.'

* * *

WHAT IS NOT COVERED

Damage or failure resulting from:
– Negligence of proper maintenance as required in the Owner's Manual.
– Misuse, abuse, accident, theft, water/flooding, or fire.

* * *

Any device and/or accessories not supplied by Hyundai.

* * *

INCIDENTAL OR CONSEQUENTIAL DAMAGES, INCLUDING WITHOUT LIMITATION, LOSS OF TIME, INCONVENIENCE, LOSS OF USE OF THE VEHICLE, OR COMMERCIAL LOSS.

The duration of any implied warranties, including those for MERCHANT-ABILITY and FITNESS FOR A PARTICULAR PURPOSE, are limited to the duration of this limited warranty.

Some states do not allow limitations on how long an implied warranty lasts, or the exclusion or limitation of incidental and consequential damages, so the limitations or exclusions set forth regarding this limited warranty may not apply to you. You may also have other rights which vary from state to state.

In late September 2001, plaintiff began experiencing difficulties with the vehicle. On September 26, plaintiff had the vehicle towed to Gartner for service because it failed to start when she turned the key. She experienced the same problem and again had the vehicle towed to Gartner for service on October 6, October 16, and October 25. On the latter occasion, Gartner kept the vehicle for more than two weeks, providing plaintiff with a rental car to use during the time the vehicle was out of her possession. Nevertheless, the problem happened again on November 21, the day before Thanksgiving, when plaintiff had taken the day off from work to go shopping for the holiday. After a technician came to her home and was himself unable to start the car, the vehicle was yet again towed to Gartner for attempted repairs.

Sometimes after being towed to Gartner the vehicle started normally, other times it did not. Gartner technicians attempted various different repairs on the different occasions that the car appeared before them, including replacing the starter, replacing the "ECU power relay," replacing the remote starter with an updated system, and replacing the "trans range switch" and "starter relay." Additionally, after the October 25 no-start, when the vehicle was kept for more than two weeks, ProSound removed the remote starter it had originally installed on plaintiff's vehicle and replaced it with an updated model. Plaintiff was not charged for any of the attempted repairs.

In December 2001, plaintiff filed suit against defendant, Hyundai Motor America (Hyundai). Plaintiff made claims against Hyundai pursuant to the Magnuson-Moss Warranty Act (15 U.S.C. § 2301 et seq. (2000)) for breach of written warranty and breach of implied warranty of merchantability. Plaintiff also alleged that Hyundai had violated the Illinois New Vehicle Buyer Protection Act (815 ILCS 380/1 et seq. (West 2000)).

. . . Plaintiff was the sole witness for her case, and most of the above undisputed facts are drawn from her testimony. In addition, plaintiff testified that she never saw the actual warranty until after she had purchased the car, because the warranty was contained in the owner's manual, which she saw for the first time in the glove box of her vehicle when she drove it off the lot. Plaintiff's purchase contract, a copy of which was introduced into evidence, does not appear to contain or refer to the vehicle warranty. When asked on cross-examination if she had seen the warranty on a placard at Gartner, plaintiff testified that she had not. Plaintiff testified that she had performed all required maintenance on her car, had never been in an accident or been the victim of vandalism, and that no one other than Gartner had ever performed any repairs on the vehicle.

During plaintiff's direct examination, defense counsel objected when plaintiff's counsel inquired regarding her purchase of prior automobiles. During a lengthy sidebar, counsel explained that he was attempting to lay a foundation in order to ask her how much the car's value to her had decreased because of the problems she had with it. The court ruled that plaintiff could not answer such a question. The court indicated that plaintiff could testify "as to what her feelings were, what her frame of mind was and the impact of the slow [sic] start situation on her personal feelings. * * * But as to 'the value of the vehicle would have been such and such because of the no start conditions,' I don't see how you're going to go that far with it." Plaintiff was permitted to testify that the purchase price of her Sonata was $16,522, and that she would eventually have paid a total of $21,249 for the car, including finance charges.

Plaintiff testified that the vehicle did not provide her the type of transportation she expected. She testified, "[I]t's a brand new car. I expected it to be perfect, flawless or minimal problems, certainly not the ones that I encountered here." She testified that she would not purchase the same vehicle today, because it was "proven unreliable," and she would not today pay the price she had originally paid for the vehicle, because "given the problems that this vehicle — that I have had with this vehicle or the problems the vehicle has had, that's like a used car. I would not pay that for a new car with used problems as it were." Plaintiff also testified that the problems she had with the car had caused her considerable inconvenience, including missing days of work. However, on cross-examination, plaintiff admitted she was still driving the car at the time of trial — May 2003 — and had not experienced any difficulties with it since December 2001.

Plaintiff offered her exhibits into evidence and rested. Hyundai moved for a directed verdict, which the court denied in its entirety. During argument on the motion, the court initially ruled that Hyundai's disclaimer of incidental and consequential damages was not unconscionable, but shortly thereafter the court reversed itself and ruled that the disclaimer was unconscionable and would not be enforced. When defense counsel inquired of the court as to the basis for its ruling that the disclaimer was unconscionable, the court responded:

> "THE COURT: The number of attempts that the plaintiff attempted for repairs. The fact that the plaintiff needed, used or intended to use the vehicle for transportation to and from work. The fact that the plaintiff was unable to use

the vehicle for the time period in question for it's [sic] intended use."

After the court denied Hyundai's motion for a directed verdict, the defense called its sole witness, Randy Wood. Wood is treasurer and part owner of ProSound, the company which installed plaintiff's alarm and remote starter system. He testified that ProSound had inspected the system installed on plaintiff's vehicle on more than one occasion, and no problem was ever found. Although ProSound did replace plaintiff's system with the newest model, this was for customer satisfaction purposes only, because ProSound never found anything wrong with plaintiff's system. He did admit on redirect examination that plaintiff's vehicle "may have" had a weak signal coming through its "tack [sic] wire," and if that condition existed it could cause problems for the ProSound system. Wood also testified that the system could itself prevent the car from starting, if one attempted to start it with the key after locking the car with the remote control.

After the defense rested, Hyundai renewed its motion for a directed verdict, including specifically arguing that the court should not have reversed its initial conclusion regarding the enforceability of the consequential damages disclaimer. The court denied Hyundai's motions and submitted the case to the jury.

The jury returned a verdict for plaintiff on the breach of warranty claims, awarding her $5,000 in warranty damages for the diminished value of the Sonata due to the defects, and $3,500 in consequential damages for aggravation and inconvenience and loss of use. The jury also answered "yes" to a special interrogatory which asked, "Did plaintiff prove the aftermarket remote starter-alarm system was not the cause of the no-start condition?" The jury found in defendant's favor, however, on plaintiff's claim under the New Vehicle Buyer Protection Act. The court awarded plaintiff $12,277 in attorney fees and costs.

[Ed. Note: After the appellate court affirmed, this appeal to the Illinois Supreme Court followed.]

ANALYSIS

. . . The arguments now focus exclusively on damages. Hyundai first argues that the circuit court erred in refusing to enforce the contractual exclusion of incidental and consequential damages. Hyundai argues that the mere fact that its warranty failed of its essential purpose does not invalidate the consequential damages disclaimer, and contends that plaintiff introduced no evidence to support the circuit court's ruling that the disclaimer should not be enforced. Second, Hyundai contends that there was insufficient evidence to support the jury's warranty damage award. Finally, Hyundai argues that if this court reverses both damage awards, we must also reverse the circuit court's award of fees and costs. . . .

I. Enforceability of Hyundai's Disclaimer of Incidental/Consequential Damages

The main issue before this court is the enforceability of Hyundai's disclaimer of incidental and consequential damages. Hyundai argues that the disclaimer is independent of the limited remedy, and the disclaimer may stand even if its limited remedy failed of its essential purpose. Hyundai contends that the disclaimer may be overridden only if it is itself unconscionable, a standard which Hyundai argues has not been met in the instant case. Plaintiff responds that the disclaimer should fall with the limited warranty, and contends that even if this court finds them to be severable, the disclaimer in this case was unconscionable.

A. "Independent" vs. "Dependent" Approach to Provisions Limiting Remedy and Excluding Consequential Damages

As previously noted, plaintiff's claim was brought under the Magnuson-Moss Warranty Act (15 U.S.C. § 2301 et seq. (1994)). Under the Act, consumers who have been damaged by any warrantor's failure to comply with its obligations under a written warranty may bring suit "in any court of competent jurisdiction in any State or the District of Columbia." 15 U.S.C. § 2310(d)(1)(A) (1994).

The Act itself does not determine the enforceability of the consequential damages disclaimer, however. . . .

Accordingly, to determine the enforceability of a consequential damages disclaimer in a limited warranty, we look to state law. . . . In Illinois, the sale of goods is governed by article 2 of the Uniform Commercial Code (UCC). 810 ILCS 5/1-101 et seq. (2000). Central to this case is section 2-719 of the UCC, which governs "Contractual modification or limitation of remedy":

"(1) Subject to the provisions of subsections (2) and (3) of this Section and of the preceding section on liquidation and limitation of damages,

(a) the agreement may provide for remedies in addition to or in substitution for those provided in this Article and may limit or alter the measure of damages recoverable under this Article, as by limiting the buyer's remedies to return of the goods and repayment of the price or to repair and replacement of non-conforming goods or parts; and

(b) resort to a remedy as provided is optional unless the remedy is expressly agreed to be exclusive, in which case it is the sole remedy.

(2) Where circumstances cause an exclusive or limited remedy to fail of its essential purpose, remedy may be had as provided in this Act.

(3) Consequential damages may be limited or excluded unless the limitation or exclusion is unconscionable. Limitation of consequential damages for injury to the person in the case of consumer goods is prima facie unconscionable but limitation of damages where the loss is commercial is not." 810 ILCS 5/2-719 (West 2000).

In this case, Hyundai's limited warranty contained both a limitation of remedy and an exclusion of consequential damages. The warranty expressly limited the buyer's remedies to repair and replacement of nonconforming parts, as permitted under section 2-719(1)(a). However, the warranty additionally provided that incidental or consequential damages were "not covered," as permitted under section 2-719(3).

Plaintiff claimed — and the jury found — that the Hyundai limited remedy had failed of its essential purpose because of the persistence of the no-start problem with plaintiff's car. Hyundai does not question this factual determination in this appeal. Thus, according to section 2-719(2) of the UCC, plaintiff was entitled to remedy "as provided in this Act." . . .

This does not end the inquiry insofar as consequential damages are concerned, however. Subsection (3) of section 2-719 is part of "this Act" — i.e., the UCC — and subsection (3) permits a seller to limit or exclude consequential damages unless to do so would be unconscionable. It still must be determined, therefore, whether a limited remedy failing of its essential purpose defeats a disclaimer of consequential damages.

There are two main schools of thought on the issue. Some courts and commentators conclude that a limited remedy failing of its essential purpose operates to destroy any limitation or exclusion of consequential damages in the same contract. This approach is known as the "dependent" approach, because the enforceability of the consequential damages exclusion depends on the survival of the limitation of remedy.

Our appellate court issued one of the seminal cases for the dependent approach, *Adams v. J.I. Case Co.*, 125 Ill. App. 2d 388, 261 N.E.2d 1 (1970). There, the plaintiff purchased a tractor, pursuant to a purchase agreement which limited his remedy to repair and replacement and also disclaimed consequential damages. The tractor had severe mechanical problems and was in a repair shop for over a year. Plaintiff filed suit, seeking consequential damages for the business he claimed to have lost because defendants were "wilfully dilatory or careless and negligent in making good their warranty." The court concluded:

> The limitations of remedy and of liability are not separable from the obligations of the warranty. Repudiation of the obligations of the warranty destroys its benefits. The complaint alleges facts that would constitute a repudiation by the defendants of their obligations under the warranty, that repudiation consisting of their wilful failure or their careless and negligent compliance. It should be obvious that they cannot at once repudiate their obligation under their warranty and assert its provisions beneficial to them.

Adams, 125 Ill. App. 2d at 402–03, 261 N.E.2d 1.

In defense of the dependent approach, the United States District Court for the Northern District of Illinois has reasoned:

> [P]laintiff also was entitled to assume that defendants would not be unreasonable or wilfully dilatory in making good their warranty in the event of defects in the machinery and equipment. It is the specific breach of the warranty to repair that plaintiff alleges caused the bulk of its damages. This Court would be in an untenable position if it allowed the defendant to shelter itself behind one segment of the warranty when it has allegedly repudiated and ignored its very limited obligations under another segment of the same warranty, which alleged repudiation has caused the very need for relief which the defendant is attempting to avoid.

Jones & McKnight Corp. v. Birdsboro Corp., 320 F. Supp. 39, 43–44 (N.D. Ill. 1970) (applying Illinois law). . . .

Plaintiff suggests that the dependent approach is followed by a majority of jurisdictions to consider the issue. While this may have been true 15 to 20 years ago . . . , it is no longer the case. Rather, the majority of jurisdictions now follow the other of the two main approaches, the "independent" approach. 1 E. Farnsworth, Farnsworth on Contracts § 4.28(a), at 605–06 (3d ed. 2004) ("some courts have gone so far as to hold that if UCC 2-719(2) applies, related limitations on remedies should all fall like a house of cards, so that a provision barring recovery of consequential damages would also be invalidated. However, most courts have rejected this view"); *Pierce [v. Catalina Yachts]*, 2 P.3d at 622 ("the majority of jurisdictions view these subsections to be independent") (collecting cases). This school of thought holds that a limitation of consequential damages must be judged on its own merits and enforced unless unconscionable, regardless of whether the contract also contains a limitation of remedy which has failed of its essential purpose.

A representative case adopting the independent approach is *Chatlos Systems v. National Cash Register Corp.*, 635 F.2d 1081 (3d Cir. 1980) (applying New Jersey law). There, the court rejected the dependent approach, holding:

> [T]he better reasoned approach is to treat the consequential damage disclaimer as an independent provision, valid unless unconscionable. This poses no logical difficulties. A contract may well contain no limitation on breach of warranty damages but specifically exclude consequential damages. Conversely, it is quite conceivable that some limitation might be placed on a breach of warranty award, but consequential damages would expressly be permitted.
>
> The limited remedy of repair and a consequential damages exclusion are two discrete ways of attempting to limit recovery for breach of warranty. The Code, moreover, tests each by a different standard. The former survives unless it fails of its essential purpose, while the latter is valid unless it is unconscionable. We therefore see no reason to hold, as a general proposition, that the failure of the limited remedy provided in the contract, without more, invalidates a wholly

distinct term in the agreement excluding consequential damages. The two are not mutually exclusive.

Chatlos Systems, 635 F.2d at 1086. *See also Pierce*, 2 P.3d at 622–23 (adopting independent approach), at 622 n. 16 (collecting cases).

A third approach, "applied relatively infrequently," is the "case by case" approach. D. Hagen, Note, *Sections 2-719(2) & 2-719(3) of the Uniform Commercial Code: The Limited Warranty Package & Consequential Damages*, 31 VAL. U. L. REV. 111, 131 (1996). Under this approach, "[a]n analysis to determine whether consequential damages are warranted must carefully examine the individual factual situation including the type of goods involved, the parties and the precise nature and purpose of the contract." *AES Technology Systems, Inc. v. Coherent Radiation*, 583 F.2d 933, 941 (7th Cir. 1978).

Neither of the parties to this appeal argues in favor of the case-by-case approach, which has been criticized as "not supported by the [UCC] or its official comments." 31 VAL. U. L. REV. at 132. . . .

We find the case-by-case approach injects uncertainty into the UCC, an area of the law in which uniformity and certainty are highly valued. . . . We decline to adopt it.

Rather, we agree with the reasoning in *Chatlos Systems*, and adopt the independent approach. The independent approach is more in line with the UCC and with contract law in general. Nothing in the text or the official comments to section 2-719 indicates that where a contract contains both a limitation of remedy and an exclusion of consequential damages, the latter shares the fate of the former. See J. Eddy, *On the "Essential" Purposes of Limited Remedies: The Metaphysics of UCC 2-719(2)*, 65 CAL. L. REV. 28, 92 (1977) (failure of essential purpose is separate and independent from validity of consequential damage disclaimer); E. Eissenstat, Note, *Commercial Transactions: UCC § 2-719: Remedy Limitations and Consequential Damage Exclusions*, 36 OKLA. L. REV. 669, 677 (1983) ("a consequential damages disclaimer should be governed by its own [UCC] standard of unconscionability, independent of whether a limited remedy has failed"). To the contrary, as noted in *Chatlos Systems*, the different standards for evaluating the two provisions — "failure of essential purpose" versus "unconscionability" — strongly suggest their independence. See also 1 White and Summers' Uniform Commercial Code § 12-10(c), at 668 (4th ed. 1995) (endorsing the independent approach as most in accord with considerations of freedom of contract).

When a contract contains a limitation of remedy but that remedy fails of its essential purpose, it is as if that limitation of remedy does not exist for purposes of the damages to which a plaintiff is entitled for breach of warranty. See 810 ILCS 5/2-719(2) (West 2000) ("remedy may be had as provided in this Act"). When a contract contains a consequential damages exclusion but no limitation of remedy, it is incontrovertible that the exclusion is to be enforced unless unconscionable. 810 ILCS 5/2-719(3) (West 2000). Why, then, would a limitation of remedy failing of its essential purpose destroy a consequential damages exclusion in the same contract? We see no valid reason to so hold.

Indeed, the dependent approach operates to nullify all consequential damage exclusions in contracts which also contain limitations of remedy. For if the limited remedy fails of its essential purpose, the consequential damages exclusion would also automatically fall — regardless of whether it is unconscionable — and if the limitation of remedy does not fail of its essential purpose, the buyer would not be entitled to consequential damages in any event; he would be entitled only to the specified limited remedy.

The two provisions — limitation of remedy and exclusion of consequential damages — can be visualized as two concentric layers of protection for a seller. What a seller would most prefer, if something goes wrong with a product, is simply to repair or replace it, nothing more. This "repair or replacement" remedy is an outer wall, a first defense. If that wall is breached, because the limited remedy has failed of its essential purpose, the seller still would prefer at least not to be liable for potentially unlimited consequential damages, and so he builds a second inner rampart as a fallback position. That inner wall is higher, and more difficult to scale — it falls only if unconscionable.

The independent approach has not been immune to criticism, of course. The Eighth Circuit has rejected the independent approach under Minnesota law, based on the concern that "a buyer when entering into a contract does not anticipate that the sole remedy available will be rendered a nullity, thus causing additional damages." *Soo Line R.R. Co. v. Fruehauf Corp.*, 547 F.2d 1365, 1373 (8th Cir. 1977) (applying Minnesota law). Additionally, one commentator has chastised the independent approach for "rel[ying] on imprecise assumptions about the parties' intent and an unpersuasive interpretation of section 2-719." K. Murtagh, Note, *UCC Section 2-719: Limited Remedies and Consequential Damage Exclusions*, 74 CORNELL L. REV. 359, 362 (1989) (concluding that independent approach is "inherently weak"). This article suggests that by engaging in "literal construction of the parties' contract," the independent approach "encourages overly formalistic drafting," which "unfairly favors the party who can afford sophisticated bargaining techniques to ensure the use of his contract terms." 74 CORNELL L. REV. at 363. The article also contends that it is erroneous to conclude that the parties intend to shift the risk of consequential loss to the buyer, because "[t]he language structure itself does not indicate that the parties even considered the possibility of the ineffective limited remedy." 74 CORNELL L. REV. at 364. *Adams* and *Jones & McKnight*, two of the earliest cases adopting the dependent approach, implicitly concluded that the independent approach was simply unfair to the buyer. See *Adams*, 125 Ill. App. 2d at 402–03, 261 N.E.2d 1; *Jones & McKnight*, 320 F. Supp. at 43–44.

We recognize these objections to the independent approach, but do not find them compelling. The reasoning in *Adams* and *Jones & McKnight*, for example, is based on the seller's failure to perform being willful. This incorporates considerations of bad faith on the part of the seller. As we discuss below, the seller's bad faith is a possible basis for finding enforcement of a limitation of consequential damages to be unconscionable. However, the dependent approach strips away limitations of consequential damages whenever a limited remedy fails of its essential purpose, without regard to the good or bad faith of the seller, which we believe goes too far.

The objections to the independent approach in *Soo Line* and the law review article noted above are similarly unpersuasive. Both argue that the independent approach is unfair because the buyer may not intend to renounce consequential damages when the limited remedy has failed of its essential purpose. *Soo Line*, 547 F.2d at 1373; 74 CORNELL L. REV. at 364. But this seems to ignore the plain language of the contract in a fundamental way — for if the buyer does not intend to renounce consequential damages when the limited remedy has failed, in what context could the disclaimer of consequential damages operate? As noted above, we believe this is a fundamental defect in the dependent approach, that it renders the disclaimer of consequential damages an utter nullity. If a limited remedy has not failed of its essential purpose, that is of course the buyer's only remedy, by definition — this is what it means to have a limited remedy. So in this circumstance a disclaimer of limited damages would be of no effect because it would be redundant. If, as the above critics argue, the disclaimer of limited damages ought not to be enforced when the limited remedy has failed of its essential purpose, the language would never have any effect. Moreover, to the extent that the independent approach encourages parties to pay attention in the drafting process (see 74 CORNELL L. REV. at 363), we see this as a point in favor of the independent approach, rather than the contrary. . . .

We conclude that the independent approach is the better-reasoned and more in accordance with the plain language of the UCC. This conclusion is buttressed by the fact that a majority of jurisdictions to consider the issue have adopted the independent approach. Illinois generally follows the majority interpretation of UCC provisions, in order to serve the underlying UCC policy of "mak[ing] uniform the law among the various jurisdictions." *Connick v. Suzuki Motor Co.*, 174 Ill. 2d 482, 491, 221 Ill. Dec. 389, 675 N.E.2d 584 (1996), quoting 810 ILCS 5/1-102(2)(c) (West 1994). Contractual limitations or exclusions of consequential damages will be upheld unless to do so would be unconscionable, regardless of whether the contract also contains a limited remedy which fails of its essential purpose.

B. Unconscionability

Accordingly, the mere fact that the jury found the limited remedy to have failed of its essential purpose does not destroy the provision in the warranty excluding consequential damages. However, this does not mean that the exclusion of consequential damages will necessarily be upheld. Rather, that provision must be judged on its own merits to determine whether its enforcement would be unconscionable. 810 ILCS 5/2-719(3) (West 2000).

A determination of whether a contractual clause is unconscionable is a matter of law, to be decided by the court. 810 ILCS 5/2-302(1) (West 2000). Unconscionability can be either "procedural" or "substantive" or a combination of both. Procedural unconscionability refers to a situation where a term is so difficult to find, read, or understand that the plaintiff cannot fairly be said to have been aware he was agreeing to it, and also takes into account a lack of bargaining power. Substantive unconscionability refers to those terms which are inordinately one-sided in one party's favor.

Hyundai argues that plaintiff introduced no evidence to support the trial court's determination that the consequential damages exclusion was unconscionable. We disagree. The record reveals a number of facts which tend to support a finding of unconscionability. The warranty was entirely preprinted. Plaintiff — a consumer — had no hand in its drafting, and no bargaining power at all with respect to its terms. Moreover, the clause in question is intended to limit the drafter's liability. Each of these facts leads this court to disfavor the clause. However, we need not — and we do not — hold that these general circumstances alone or in combination render the clause unconscionable.

An additional fact particular to this case tips the balance in plaintiff's favor. That is the lack of evidence that the warranty, which contained the disclaimer of consequential damages, had been made available to the plaintiff at or before the time she signed the sale contract. The warranty and its consequential damages exclusion were contained in the owner's manual, which was placed in the glove compartment of the car, where it was unavailable to the consumer until after she took delivery. No portion of the sale contract contained in the record before us even mentions the warranty. Moreover, plaintiff testified without contradiction that she never saw any part of the written warranty, much less the disclaimer of consequential damages, until she looked in her owner's manual after she had signed the contract and driven the car off the lot. Thus, on this record, we must conclude that the warranty information, including the disclaimer of consequential damages, was not made available to the plaintiff at or before the time she signed the purchase contract.

* * *

To enforce the clause in these circumstances, we conclude, would indeed be unconscionable. See *Frank's Maintenance & Engineering, Inc. v. C.A. Roberts Co.*, 86 Ill. App. 3d 980, 991 n. 2 (1980) ("a limitation of liability given to the buyer after he makes the contract is ineffective"). Accordingly, we affirm the circuit court's order to that effect, as well as the $3,500 which represents that portion of the jury verdict intended to recompense plaintiff for the consequential damages she incurred.

[Ed. Note: The court went on to remand the case to the trial court for a new determination of the plaintiff's damages under her warranty claims.]

QUESTIONS

1. Assess the *Razor* case on the initial question of whether the limited remedy has failed of its essential purpose. Does the court do a better job of explaining its analysis than the early court decisions discussed by Professor Eddy?

2. Consider a different approach to synthesizing the provisions of § 2-719. Rather than beginning with the premise that subsection (2) governs clauses that create exclusive remedies and that subsection (3) governs clauses that exclude consequential damages, would it be more accurate to read (2) as providing the test for all clauses that exclude or limit remedies, including a provision that excludes consequential damages? Under this reading, (3) does not provide the exclusive test for enforcing an exclusion of consequential damages. Because (3) appears just to be a reminder of the general unconscionability rule of § 2-302, it may be most accurate to read (3) as establishing that an exclusion of consequential damages is not *in itself* unconscionable, except when the clause limits "damages for injury to the person in the case of consumer goods." In other words, (3) does not "protect" an exclusion of consequential damages from the "fails its essential purpose test" of (2); rather, an exclusion of consequential damages is prima facie conscionable and therefore enforceable, unless the exclusion fails its essential purpose in the agreement. This suggested approach to reading § 2-719 would not do away with the complexity of the required analysis, but it would focus the analysis on (2) rather than creating a phantom conflict between (2) and (3). Would Professor Eddy find this reading of § 2-719 persuasive?

3. Another possible reading of § 2-719 is to regard subsection (3) as an independent test for the enforceability of clauses excluding consequential damages, since (3) can be interpreted as more than just a reminder of the general unconscionability rule of § 2-302. Does (3) go beyond the requirement in § 2-302 that a clause of a contract may not be "unconscionable at the time that it was made"? Does this necessarily mean that the enforceability of an exclusion of consequential damages should be assessed only under (3)?

d. Liquidated damages as an agreed remedy

The parties to a contract may choose to "liquidate" the damages in the event of a breach by agreeing in advance to the amount of damages. Both parties can benefit by liquidating an otherwise uncertain damages remedy: the plaintiff may avoid under-compensation in cases where its losses are difficult to quantify with reasonable certainty, and the defendant may be more willing to contract if it knows the risk of non-performance in a situation that otherwise presents the potential for unlimited liability.

The common law viewed liquidated damages clauses with suspicion, refusing to enforce clauses that had the effect of a "penalty" that deterred efficient breaches. Some courts refused to enforce liquidated damages clauses if the defendant could show that the plaintiff in fact suffered no loss due to the breach. Other courts require the liquidated sum to be reasonable in light of both the losses anticipated at the time of contracting and the losses actually incurred. Most important, courts enforced such clauses only if the plaintiff could demonstrate that its probable losses, considered at the time of contracting, were uncertain or difficult to prove, although the courts differed as to whether this was a condition of enforceability or merely a consideration to be weighed.

Article 2 adopts a liberalizing attitude that treats these traditional common law considerations as factors to be weighed under a general condition of reasonableness. Article 2A places even less constraint on the parties' freedom of contract, making no mention of the common law "penalty" concept. *See* § 2A-504.

RODRIGUEZ v. LEARJET, INC.
Kansas Court of Appeals
946 P.2d 1010 (1997)

MARQUARDT, Presiding Judge.

Miguel A. Diaz Rodriguez (Diaz) appeals from the district court's decision that a liquidated damages clause in his contract with Learjet, Inc., (Learjet) was reasonable and enforceable.

On August 21, 1992, Diaz executed a contract with Learjet to purchase a model 60 jet aircraft. The contract called for a $250,000 deposit to be made upon execution of the contract; a $750,000 payment to be made on September 18, 1992; a $1,000,000 payment to be made 180 days before the delivery date of July 30, 1993; and the balance of the purchase price to be paid upon delivery.

Diaz paid Learjet $250,000 on the day that he executed the contract, but made no other payment.

At the time of the purchase, Diaz worked for Televisa. Diaz was purchasing the aircraft at the request of Alejandro Burillo, his supervisor at Televisa. Near the end of September 1992, Burillo told Diaz that he no longer wanted the aircraft. Diaz testified that he called Alberto Castaneda at Learjet and told him that he was not going to buy the aircraft and that he wanted Learjet to return his $250,000 deposit.

On September 30, 1992, Castaneda sent Diaz a fax, requesting payment. On October 6, 1992, Castaneda wrote Diaz a letter, which stated, in part: "Unless we receive payment from you or your company by October 9, 1992, [Learjet, Inc.,] will consider this agreement terminated and will retain all payments as liquidation damages in accordance with Paragraph — . . . of Section VII . . . of said agreement." By letter dated October 20, 1992, Learjet informed Diaz that it considered their contract terminated and that the $250,000 deposit was being retained as liquidated damages.

The contract provides, in part:

> Learjet may terminate this Agreement as a result of the Buyer's . . . failure to make any progress payment when due. . . . If this Agreement is terminated by Learjet for any reason stipulated in the previous sentence Learjet shall retain all payments theretofore made by the Buyer as liquidated damages and not as a penalty and the parties shall thenceforth be released from all further obligations hereunder. Such damages include, but are not limited to, loss of profit on this sale, direct and indirect costs incurred as a result of disruption in production, training expense advance and selling expenses in effecting resale of the Airplane.

After Diaz had breached the parties' contract, Circus Circus Enterprises, Inc., (Circus) contracted with Learjet to buy the aircraft. Circus requested that changes be made to the aircraft, which cost $1,326. Learjet realized a $1,887,464 profit on the sale of the aircraft to Circus, which was a larger profit than Learjet had originally budgeted.

Diaz filed suit against Learjet, seeking to recover the $250,000 deposit. Diaz' petition alleged, in part, that the actual amount of Learjet's liquidated damages was not $250,000 and that Learjet's retention of the $250,000 deposit was unreasonable and an unenforceable penalty.

The district court initially granted Learjet's motion for summary judgment, holding that the liquidated damages provision of the contract was reasonable. Diaz appealed that decision. On appeal, this court held that the district court had erred in using the wrong standard to evaluate the liquidated damages clause and in not examining all of the necessary factors and remanded the case to the district court for further consideration of the reasonableness of the liquidated damages clause.

On remand, a bench trial was held. Following the presentation of evidence, the district court found that Learjet was a lost volume seller and that its actual damages included lost profits. The district court held that $250,000 in liquidated damages was reasonable and upheld the liquidated damages clause.

Diaz argues that the district court erred in holding that the liquidated damages clause was reasonable and enforceable. Diaz reasons that the liquidated damages clause was unreasonably large and, therefore, void as a penalty.

A determination concerning the reasonableness and enforceability of a liquidated damages clause is a question of law subject to unlimited review by this court. *Kvassay v. Murray*, 15 Kan. App. 2d 426, 429, 808 P.2d 896, *rev. denied*, 248 Kan. 996 (1991).

K.S.A. 84-2-718 governs liquidated damages in contracts for the sale of goods and provides, in part:

> (1) Damages for breach by either party may be liquidated in the agreement but only at an amount which is reasonable in the light of the anticipated or actual harm caused by the breach, the difficulties of proof of loss, and the inconvenience or nonfeasibility of otherwise obtaining an adequate remedy. A term fixing unreasonably large liquidated damages is void as a penalty.

In *Kvassay*, 15 Kan.App.2d at 430, 808 P.2d 896, this court noted that "reasonableness is the only test" for liquidated damages under the Uniform Commercial Code. This court paraphrased the three criteria for measuring the reasonableness of a liquidated damages clause provided in K.S.A. 84-2-718: "(1) anticipated or actual harm caused by breach; (2) difficulty of proving loss; and (3) difficulty of obtaining an adequate remedy." 15 Kan.App.2d at 430, 808 P.2d 896.

A liquidated damages clause that "fixes damages in an amount grossly disproportionate to the harm actually sustained or likely to be sustained" is considered a penalty and will not be enforced by the courts. *Luminous Neon, Inc. v. Parscale*, 17 Kan.App.2d 241, 243, 836 P.2d 1201 (1992) (quoting 22 AM.JUR.2D, *Damages* § 701, p. 758). If a liquidated damages clause is invalidated as a penalty, then the nonbreaching party may recover actual damages instead. *White Lakes Shopping Center, Inc. v. Jefferson Standard Life Ins. Co.*, 208 Kan. 121, 125, 490 P.2d 609 (1971). The burden of proving that a liquidated damages clause is unenforceable rests with the party challenging its enforcement. *TMG Life Ins. Co. v. Ashner*, 21 Kan.App.2d 234, 250, 898 P.2d 1145 (1995).

Diaz' challenge to the reasonableness of the liquidated damages clause focuses on the first factor of K.S.A. 84-2-718 — the anticipated or actual harm caused by the breach. The question of whether a seller qualifies as a lost volume seller is relevant when evaluating whether a liquidated damages clause is reasonable in light of the anticipated or actual harm caused by the breach.

Diaz argues that the district court erred in concluding that Learjet qualifies as a lost volume seller. As a lost volume seller, Learjet's actual damages would include lost profits, notwithstanding that Circus purchased the aircraft which Diaz had contracted to buy and that Learjet made a profit on the Circus sale. The two contracts contained identical base prices, and both contracts had escalation clauses. The evidence indicates that the lost profit from the Diaz contract would have been approximately $1.8 million.

* * *

Courts have "unanimously" held that a lost volume seller can recover lost profits under § 2-708(2) of the Uniform Commercial Code. *R.E. Davis Chemical Corp. v. Diasonics, Inc.*, 826 F.2d 678, 681 & n. 2 (7th Cir. 1987); *see* 1 WHITE & SUMMERS, UNIFORM COMMERCIAL CODE § 7-9, p. 385 n. 4 (4th ed.1995) (listing cases that have applied § 2-708[2] to lost volume sellers). The Kansas Legislature has enacted this statute as K.S.A. 84-2-708(2).

In *Jetz* [*Serv. Co. v. Salina Properties*], 19 Kan.App.2d [144] at 148, 865 P.2d 1051 [(1993)], this court explained:

> The "lost volume seller" measure of damages "refers to the lost volume of

business the non-breaching seller incurs on buyer's breach. When the seller resells the entity he expected to sell to the original buyer, he usually deprives himself of something of value — the sale to a new buyer of another similar entity." [*Snyder v. Herbert Greenbaum & Assoc.*, 38 Md.App. 144, 154 n. 3, 380 A.2d 618 (1977)].

* * *

Awarding lost profits to a lost volume seller serves the general principle that the purpose of awarding damages is to make a party whole by restoring the nonbreaching party to the position that that party occupied prior to the breach — to place a seller in as good a position as if a buyer had performed. K.S.A. 84-1-106; *Cerretti v. Flint Hills Rural Electric Co-op. Ass'n*, 251 Kan. 347, 360, 837 P.2d 330 (1992); *see Jetz*, 19 Kan.App.2d at 146–48, 865 P.2d 1051.

The issue in *Jetz* was whether the plaintiff qualified as a lost volume lessor, and this court did not expressly state the specific requirements for qualifying as a lost volume seller. The *Jetz* court held that lost volume status is available to businesses providing services and identified the following evidence as sufficient to affirm the trial court's finding that the plaintiff was a lost volume lessor:

> [J]etz Service is in the business of supplying coin-operated laundry equip-ment; it has several warehouses in which it has available for lease about 1,500 used washers and dryers; it continually looks for new locations in which to install laundry equipment; it would have been able to fulfill the Kansas City lease without using the machines from Salina Properties; and it is uncontro-verted Jetz Service would have been able to enter into both transactions irrespective of the breach by Salina Properties.

19 Kan.App.2d at 152, 865 P.2d 1051.

In *Diasonics*, 826 F.2d at 685, the court held that in order to qualify as a lost volume seller and recover for lost profits, a seller must establish three factors: (1) that it possessed the capacity to make an additional sale, (2) that it would have been profitable for it to make an additional sale, and (3) that it probably would have made an additional sale absent the buyer's breach. *See also R.E. Davis Chemical Corp. v. Diasonics*, 924 F.2d 709, 711 (7th Cir. 1991) (restating rule formulated in prior appeal of case); Kansas Comment 2 to 84-2-708 (citing first *Diasonics* case).

Here, in finding that Learjet qualified as a lost volume seller, the district court referred to *Jetz*, 19 Kan.App.2d 144, Syl. P 2, 865 P.2d 1051.

Applying the more specific criteria established in *Diasonics*, 826 F.2d at 684–85, there is adequate evidence to support the district court's finding. The master scheduler for Learjet testified that Learjet was operating at 60 percent capacity during the relevant time period and that Learjet was able to accelerate its production schedule to produce more of the model 60 planes in any given year. Learjet also presented testimony about its accounting system which indicated that an additional sale would have been profitable to Learjet. Learjet's profit from the Circus transaction and the similarity between the Diaz contract price and the Circus contract price also indicate that the additional sale would have been profitable.

We agree with the district court that Learjet qualifies as a lost volume seller and that the $250,000 in liquidated damages was reasonable in light of the anticipated or actual harm caused by the breach. *See* K.S.A. 84-2-718(2).

Even if we were to conclude that Learjet was not a lost volume seller, there is authority to support the holding that the liquidated damages clause was reasonable. In *Aero Consulting Corp. v. Cessna Aircraft Co.*, 867 F.Supp. 1480, 1493–94 (D.Kan. 1994), the court held that a liquidated damages clause in an aircraft purchase agreement was reasonable under Kansas law. The *Aero* court did not consider the lost volume theory. The base price of the aircraft was $3,995,000. The liquidated damages, which were in the form of a deposit that was retained by Cessna after Aero breached, equaled $425,000. The court found that the liquidated damages clause "was reasonable in light of the damages that Cessna could reasonably anticipate would flow from such a cancellation of the contract." 867 F.Supp. at 1494. The court also noted that "in light of the nature of the production of aircraft and the costs associated with maintaining production, it would not be feasible for Cessna to otherwise obtain an adequate remedy for breach." 867 F.Supp. at 1494. Under both analyses, the liquidated damages claimed by Learjet were reasonable.

Affirmed.

QUESTIONS

1. The *Rodriguez* court found that the plaintiff suffered actual loss due to the breach because it was a lost volume seller. Would the liquidated damages clause be enforceable if Learjet was operating at full capacity at the time of the breach?

2. If Learjet is a lost volume seller entitled to its lost profits in the event of a breach under § 2-708(2), why would it agree to a liquidated damages clause rather than suing for lost profits in the event of a breach? If Learjet could prove lost profits of $1.8 million on this sale, why would it be content to accept the $250,000 as liquidated damages?

COASTAL LEASING CORP. v. T-BAR S CORP.
North Carolina Court of Appeals
496 S.E.2d 795 (1998)

WALKER, Judge.

Plaintiff entered into a lease agreement (lease) with defendant T-Bar S Corporation (T-Bar) in May of 1992, whereby plaintiff agreed to lease certain cash register equipment (equipment) to T-Bar. Under the lease, T-Bar agreed to monthly rental payments of $289.13 each for a total of 48 months. Defendants George and Sharon Talbott (appellants) were the officers of T-Bar and personally guaranteed payment of all amounts due under the lease.

After making 18 of the monthly payments, appellants and T-Bar defaulted on the lease in December of 1993. On 28 February 1994, plaintiff mailed a certified letter to appellants and T-Bar, return receipt requested, advising them that the lease was in default and, pursuant to the terms of the lease, plaintiff was accelerating the remaining payments due under the lease. They further advised appellants and T-Bar that if the entire amount due of $8,841.06 was not received within 7 days, plaintiff would seek to recover the balance due plus interest and reasonable attorneys' fees, as well as possession of the equipment. The record shows that appellants and T-Bar each received this letter on 1 March 1994.

On 10 March 1994, plaintiff mailed a certified letter and "Notice of Public Sale of Repossessed Leased Equipment" (notice of sale) to appellants and T-Bar at the same address, again return receipt requested. This letter advised appellants and T-Bar that plaintiff had taken possession of the equipment and was conducting a public sale pursuant to the terms of the lease. Although the date on the notice of sale stated that the sale was to be held on 23 March 1994, the sale was actually scheduled to be held on 25 March 1994. This letter and notice of sale were returned to plaintiffs "unclaimed" on 29 March 1994.

Plaintiffs conducted a public sale of the equipment on 25 March 1994, and no one appeared on behalf of appellants or T-Bar. There being no other bidders, plaintiff purchased the equipment at the sale for $2,000.00.

On 4 October 1994, plaintiff leased some of the same equipment to another company at a rate calculated to be $212.67 for 36 months. Plaintiff then filed this action on 6 October 1994, seeking to recover the balance due under the lease, minus the net proceeds from the 25 March 1994 public sale, plus interest and reasonable attorneys' fees. Appellants filed an answer and counterclaim on 27 July 1995. Plaintiff then filed a motion for summary judgment against appellants on 8 July 1996. When T-Bar failed to answer, a default judgment was entered against it on 30 December 1996.

After a hearing, the trial court entered summary judgment on 15 January 1997, in favor of plaintiff on its complaint and appellants' counterclaims and entered judgment against appellants for the sum of $7,223.56 plus interest and attorneys' fees of $1,083.54.

At the outset, we first note that summary judgment is appropriate only "if the pleadings, depositions, answers to interrogatories, and admissions on file, together with the affidavits, if any, show that there is no genuine issue as to any material fact and that any party is entitled to a judgment as a matter of law." N.C. Gen.Stat. § 1A-1, Rule 56(c) (1990); *Pressman v. UNC-Charlotte*, 78 N.C.App. 296, 300, 337 S.E.2d 644, 647 (1985), *disc. review allowed*, 315 N.C. 589, 341 S.E.2d 28 (1986).

Equipment leasing transactions are an ever increasing segment of commercial activity in North Carolina as well as in the rest of the United States. According to recent U.S. Department of Commerce statistics, "leasing transactions accounted for approximately $168.9 billion of new equipment installed in 1996, an expansion of 11.6% over 1995." Stephen T. Whelan et al., *Leases*, 52 Bus. Law. 4, at 1517 (1997).

A threshold issue in this case is whether the transaction involved is a lease or a security interest disguised as a lease. If it is a security interest disguised as a lease, it will be governed by N.C. Gen.Stat. § 25-9 (Article 9). However, if it is a lease, it will be governed by N.C. Gen.Stat. § 25-2A (Article 2A). *See* N.C. Gen.Stat. § 25-2A-103 cmt. j (1995).

By its terms, Article 2A "applies to any transaction, regardless of form, that creates a lease." N.C. Gen.Stat. § 25-2A-102 (1995). Further, a "lease" is defined as "a transfer of the right to possession and use of goods for a term in return for consideration, but a sale . . . is not a lease." N.C. Gen.Stat. § 25-2A-103(1)(j) (1995). In contrast, a transaction involves a security interest if it meets the general definition set forth in part 2 of Article 1. *See* N.C. Gen.Stat. § 25-1-201(37)(a) (1995). Since both parties agree that the transaction at issue in this case is not a security interest, but rather is a lease, Article 2A controls.

Before addressing appellants' assignments of error, we should note that Article 2A did not become effective in this State until 1 October 1993. Therefore, there is an absence of case law interpreting this Article.

In their appeal, appellants contend that the trial court erred by granting summary judgment in favor of plaintiff because there exists a genuine issue of material fact as to whether: (1) the liquidated damages clause contained in Paragraph 13 of the lease is reasonable in light of the then-anticipated harm caused by default; and (2) plaintiff conducted the sale of the equipment in a commercially reasonable manner.

As to appellants' first contention, the official commentary to Article 2A states that "in recognition of the diversity of the transactions to be governed [and] the sophistication of many of the parties to these transactions . . . , freedom of contract has been preserved." N.C. Gen.Stat. § 25-2A-102 Official Comment (1995). Also, under general contract principles, when the parties to a transaction deal with each other at arms length and without the exercise by one of the parties of superior bargaining power, the parties will be bound by their agreement. *See Suits v. Old Equity Life Insurance Co.*, 249 N.C. 383, 386, 106 S.E.2d 579, 582 (1959).

Article 2A recognizes that "[m]any leasing transactions are predicated on the parties' ability to agree to an appropriate amount of damages or formula for damages in the event of default or other act or omission." N.C. Gen.Stat. § 25-2A-504 Official Comment (1995). N.C. Gen.Stat. § 25-2A-504 states, in pertinent part:

(1) Damages payable by either party for default, or any other act or omission . . . may be liquidated in the lease agreement but only at an amount or by a

formula that is reasonable in light of the then-anticipated harm caused by the default or other act or omission.

N.C. Gen.Stat. § 25-2A-504(1) (1995). This liquidated damages provision is more flexible than that provided by its statutory analogue under Article 2, N.C. Gen.Stat. § 25-2-718. The Article 2 liquidated damages section provides, in pertinent part:

(1) Damages for breach by either party may be liquidated in the agreement but only at an amount which is reasonable in the light of the anticipated or actual harm caused by the breach, *the difficulties of proof of loss, and the inconvenience or nonfeasibility of otherwise obtaining an adequate remedy. A term fixing unreasonably large liquidated damages is void as a penalty.*

N.C. Gen.Stat. § 25-2-718(1) (1995) (emphasis added). A review of these statutes reveals two major differences.

First, the drafters of Article 2A chose not to incorporate the two tests which are required by Article 2, i.e., the difficulties of proof of loss and the inconvenience or nonfeasibility of otherwise obtaining an adequate remedy. In fact, the official commentary to N.C. Gen.Stat. § 25-2A-504 states that since "[t]he ability to liquidate damages is critical to modern leasing practice . . . [and] given the parties' freedom to contract at common law, the policy behind retaining these two additional requirements here was thought to be outweighed." N.C. Gen.Stat. § 25-2A-504 Official Comment (1995).

Secondly, the drafters of Article 2A recognized that in order to further promote freedom of contract, it was necessary to delete the last sentence of N.C. Gen.Stat. § 25-2-718(1), which provided that unreasonably large liquidated damages provisions were void as a penalty. As such, the parties to a lease transaction are free to negotiate the amount of liquidated damages, restrained only by the rule of reasonableness.

"The basic test of the reasonableness of an agreement liquidating damages is whether the stipulated amount or amount produced by the stipulated formula represents a reasonable forecast of the probable loss." 3A Hawkland and Miller, *Uniform Commercial Code Series* § 2A-504:02 (1993). However, "no court should strike down a reasonable liquidated damage agreement based on foresight that has proved on hindsight to have contained an inaccurate estimation of the probable loss. . . ." *Id.* And, "the fact that there is a difference between the actual loss, as determined at or about the time of the default, and the anticipated loss or stipulated amount or formula, as stipulated at the time the lease contract was entered into . . . ," does not necessarily mean that the liquidated damage agreement is unreasonable. Id. This is so because "[t]he value of a lessor's interest in leased equipment depends upon 'the physical condition of the equipment and the market conditions at that time.'" *Pacificorp Capital, Inc. v. Tano, Inc.*, 877 F.Supp. 180, 184 (S.D.N.Y. 1995) (citation omitted). Further, in determining whether a liquidated damages clause is reasonable:

[A] court should keep in mind that the clause was negotiated by the parties, who are familiar with the circumstances and practices with respect to the type of transaction involved, and the clause carries with it a consensual apportionment of the risks of the agreement that a court should be slow to overturn.

Hawkland and Miller, *supra*, at § 2A-504:02.

In this case, Paragraph 13 of the lease (the liquidated damages clause) reads as follows:

13. REMEDIES. If an event of default shall occur, Lessor may, at its option, at any time (a) declare the entire amount of unpaid rental for the balance of the term of this lease immediately due and payable, whereupon Lessee shall become obligated to pay to Lessor forthwith the total amount of the said rental for the balance of the said term, and (b) without demand or legal process, enter into the premises where the equipment may be found and take possession of and

remove the Equipment, without liability for suit, action or other proceeding, and all rights of Lessee in the Equipment so removed shall terminate absolutely. Lessee hereby waives notice of, or hearing with respect to, such retaking. Lessor may at its option, use, ship, store, repair or lease all Equipment so removed and sell or otherwise dispose of any such Equipment at a private or public sale. In the event Lessor takes possession of the Equipment, Lessor shall give Lessee credit for any sums received by Lessor from the sale or rental of the Equipment after deduction of the expenses of sale or rental and Lessor's residual interest in the Equipment. . . . Lessor and Lessee acknowledge the difficulty in establishing a value for the unexpired lease term and owing to such difficulty agree that the provisions of this paragraph represent an agreed measure of damages and are not to be deemed a forfeiture or penalty. . . .

All remedies of Lessor hereunder are cumulative, are in addition to any other remedies provided for by law, and may, to the extent permitted by law, be exercised concurrently or separately. The exercise of any one remedy shall not be deemed to be an election of such remedy or to preclude the exercise of any other remedy. No failure on the part of the Lessor to exercise and no delay in exercising any right or remedy shall operate as a waiver thereof or modify the terms of this lease.

After a careful review, we conclude the liquidated damages clause is a reasonable estimation of the then-anticipated damages in the event of default because it protects plaintiff's expectation interest. The liquidated damages clause places plaintiff in the position it would have occupied had the lease been fully performed by allowing it to accelerate the balance of the lease payments and repossess the equipment. Therefore, since there is no evidence that plaintiff exercised a superior bargaining position in the negotiation of the liquidated damages clause, no genuine issue of material fact exists as to its reasonableness, and the trial court did not err by enforcing its provisions.

Appellants next contend that the trial court erred by granting summary judgment for plaintiff because a genuine issue of material fact existed as to whether plaintiff conducted the sale of the equipment in an appropriate manner. Although they concede that plaintiff had the authority under N.C. Gen. Stat. § 25-2A-527(1) (1995), as well as under the lease, to dispose of the equipment by resale, appellants argue that plaintiff did not conduct the sale in a "commercially reasonable manner."

However, for the reasons discussed below, we find that the 25 March 1994 sale of the equipment was not a "sale" within the meaning of the lease, and we therefore decline to address the issue of commercial reasonableness.

Article 2 defines a "sale" as consisting of "the passing of title from the seller to the buyer for a price." N.C. Gen.Stat. § 25-2-106(1) (1995). In this case, we note that since the transaction involves a lease, and not a security interest, title to the equipment was never transferred to appellants or T-Bar, but remained with plaintiff at all times. *See* N.C. Gen.Stat. § 25-2A-302 (1995). The lease specifically provides that plaintiff retained title to the equipment. Section 6 of the lease states, in pertinent part, "[n]o title or right in said equipment shall pass to Lessee except the rights herein expressly granted." Further, Section 18 of the lease provides that "the title to the equipment subject to this Lease is retained by the Lessor and the Lessee covenants that it will not pledge or encumber the equipment in any manner whatsoever. . . ."

Therefore, since plaintiff retained title to the equipment at all relevant times, the portion of the liquidated damages clause which allowed plaintiff, upon default, to repossess the equipment and then "sell or otherwise dispose of any such equipment at a public or private sale" must reasonably be interpreted as providing plaintiff with the right to sell or release the equipment to the appellants or another third party, not to itself. A contrary conclusion would permit a lessor to "purchase" repossessed equipment, even though it never relinquished title, at a price not necessarily related to its market value. The lessor could then release the equipment to another party, crediting the defaulting lessee only for the amount realized from the purported sale. Accordingly, the trial court erred by treating the 25 March 1994 sale as a "sale" under the terms of the liquidated damages clause and calculating the amount of appellants' credit based on such purported sale.

In conclusion, we affirm the trial court's determination that the liquidated damages clause in the lease is enforceable against the appellants. However, we reverse and remand the case for a determination of how much credit, if any, the appellants are entitled to receive under the terms of the liquidated damages clause.

Affirmed in part, reversed in part and remanded.

LEWIS AND TIMMONS-GOODSON, JJ., concur.

e.　Putting it all together: limiting remedies and liquidating damages

In the following Problem, focus on how the interrelated, yet distinct, tests concerning limited remedies and liquidated damages would be applied.

PROBLEM 7-3

Bob is an avid baker and a part-time law student. Bob is hoping to earn some additional money by supplying all of the specialty baked goods for the weekly Sunday Brunch at the nearby Luxury Hotel currently under construction. On May 11, Bob contracts with Sam's Restaurant Supplies, Inc. to have two commercial ovens and related kitchen equipment installed in his house, enabling Bob to produce the quantity of baked goods required by Luxury. Bob agrees to pay $60,000 for the equipment. Bob informs Sam's that time is of the essence, because the contract with Luxury hinges on Bob's ability to meet its needs as soon as it opens. Although Luxury was very impressed with Bob's sample tortes and pastries, it is uneasy about contracting with a nonprofessional. Bob explains to Sam's that Luxury has reserved the right to secure another baked goods supplier if Bob is unable to meet Luxury's needs when it opens on June 1.

Bob and Sam's negotiate an addendum to their written contract to deal with the possibility of delay in delivery of the oven. Although Luxury is not yet open for business, it has provided Bob with forecasts of its Sunday Brunch attendance and its anticipated bakery requirements. Although Bob has never operated a bakery business, he has compiled a forecast of anticipated profits based on his operating costs, capital expenditures, and projected sales to Luxury. On the basis of all this information, Bob reasonably expects to earn between $500 and $1,500 profits weekly. Bob and Sam's include the following in their agreement to protect both parties.

> LIQUIDATION AND LIMITATION OF DAMAGES. Sam's acknowledges that Bob will suffer lost profits in the event of non-excused delay by Sam's as a direct result of the loss of use of the equipment being sold pursuant to this Agreement. Sam's agrees that Bob will be entitled to payment of the liquidated sum of $100 for each calendar day of non-excused delay.

> Bob acknowledges that the price of the equipment being sold pursuant to this Agreement would be substantially higher if Sam's was exposed to unlimited liability for breach of contract. Therefore, Bob also agrees that Sam's will not be liable for damages if the equipment fails to conform to the contract. Instead, Bob's exclusive remedy for nonconformity is Sam's obligation to repair or replace any part of the equipment that does not conform to the contract.

> THIS CLAUSE PROVIDES THE EXCLUSIVE REMEDY FOR BREACH OF CONTRACT BY SAM'S, AND UNDER NO CIRCUMSTANCES WILL SAM'S BE LIABLE FOR CONSEQUENTIAL DAMAGES.

First Scenario: Sam's delivers the equipment 60 days late, without excuse. Fortunately for Bob, construction of the Luxury Hotel was not completed until 60 days after the expected completion date. Bob was able to supply the baked goods for the first Sunday Brunch, and so Luxury remains satisfied with Bob's performance and does not terminate their contract. Sam's can prove that Bob would not have sold any baked goods to Luxury during the 60-day period of delay, and that Bob had no other customers during this time. When Bob receives Sam's invoice for the purchase price of $60,000, Bob responds by mailing a check in the amount of $54,000. Bob informs Sam's that the remaining $6,000 is being withheld as liquidated damages pursuant to their contract.

1. Is Bob breaching the contract by refusing to pay the full purchase price for accepted goods? *See* §§ 2-607(1) and 2-717.
2. Is Bob entitled to recover the liquidated damage amount of $100 for each of the 60 days of non-excused delay?
3. Would the analysis change if Bob was leasing the equipment? *See* § 2A-504 and *Coastal Leasing Corp.*

Second Scenario: Sam's delivers the equipment on the specified delivery date. Unfortunately, the equipment does not work properly and Bob is unable to make baked goods. Bob called Sam's to his house on four consecutive days to fix the equipment, but he still was unable to bake the goods. Bob demanded that Sam's immediately supply him with replacement equipment, but Sam's continued to insist that the equipment could be repaired quickly. Unfortunately for Bob, the equipment was not repaired in enough time for the first Sunday Brunch, and Luxury exercised its right to terminate its contract with Bob. Bob is unable to find other customers. Bob resells the used kitchen equipment and again concentrates on law school studies. Bob brings suit against Sam's, alleging that Sam's breach of contract caused him to lose the contract with Luxury, resulting in lost profits for the foreseeable future. Sam's responds by admitting that the equipment was nonconforming, but asserting that Bob's exclusive remedy was repair of the equipment, and that Sam's properly repaired the equipment within one week.

1. Can Bob challenge the clause limiting his remedies to repair or replacement by arguing that it fails its essential purpose under the contract?
2. Assume that Bob is successful in arguing that the limited remedy of repair or replacement fails its essential purpose. Can Bob recover consequential damages in his suit for damages?

B.   SELLER'S REMEDIES

We begin by considering the remedies available to an aggrieved seller. We proceed chronologically by considering the remedies available to a seller depending on when the breach occurs. First, we consider the seller's rights when the buyer breaches the contract before the seller has tendered the goods to the buyer. In particular, we assess the seller's right to complete manufacture and resell the goods, to scrap goods not yet completely manufactured, and to obtain the price of the goods if they cannot reasonably be resold to another party. In the second subsection, we analyze the special rules relating to the seller's ability to stop delivery of goods in transit to the buyer, or, in special circumstances, to reclaim goods already received by the buyer. In the third subsection, we consider the general damages formula for pre-acceptance breaches by the buyer. In the final subsection, we cover the seller's right to obtain the contract price of the goods when the buyer has accepted them.

1.   Preshipment Breach: Seller's Rights with Respect to Goods in Its Possession

If the buyer breaches a contract for sale, the seller has a general right to cancel the contract. § 2-703(f). One obvious application of this right to cancel is the seller's right to refuse to deliver the goods to the breaching buyer. § 2-703(a). If the seller has not completed manufacturing the goods when the buyer breaches, Article 2 recognizes that the seller might reasonably want to mitigate its losses by completing the manufacturing process and selling the finished goods to another party. If the requirements of § 2-704 are met, the seller may identify existing goods to the contract and then choose to complete their manufacture and resell them, or sell the incomplete goods as scrap. § 2-703(c). In the event the seller decides to resell finished goods identified to the contract, § 2-706 provides the requirements of the resale and the measure of damages. In the event the seller decides to sell as scrap, § 2-708(2) would control. As an alternative to reselling the goods and suing for damages, § 2-709(1)(b) and (2) specify the circumstances in which the seller may recover the price of goods in its possession. § 2-703(e).

a.   Seller's rights with respect to unfinished goods

Section 2-704 establishes the seller's rights with respect to goods in its possession when the buyer breaches. The seller may identify conforming goods in its possession or control to the contract for sale, which allows the seller to fix its damages by reselling the goods to a third party. § 2-704(1)(a). If the goods are unfinished at the time of breach, the provision provides the seller with four options. First, it may sell the unfinished goods if they "have demonstrably been intended for the particular contract." § 2-704(1)(b). Second, it may "complete the manufacture and wholly identify the goods to the contract," in order to resell them to a third party. § 2-704(2). Third, it may "cease manufacture and resell for scrap or salvage value." § 2-704(2). Finally, in typical Article 2 fashion, the seller is authorized to "proceed in any other reasonable manner." § 2-704(2).

These choices are not completely within the seller's discretion, however. Read the following case, carefully analyze the criteria established by § 2-704 for judging the seller's decision about whether to complete the manufacturing process, and then answer Problem 7-4.

YOUNG v. FRANK'S NURSERY & CRAFTS, INC.
Ohio Supreme Court
569 N.E.2d 1034 (1991)

[Syllabus of the Court]

Plaintiff-appellant, William G. Young, had been cutting evergreen boughs on Michigan farms and selling them in the Toledo area since 1971. In 1975, after he had built up a customer base of twenty-five to thirty, Young began selling boughs to defendant-appellee, Frank's Nursery & Crafts, Inc. From 1976 through 1987, Young dealt exclusively with Frank's. Young's sales to Frank's had grown from $10,224 that first year to an order for $238,332.85 issued in early 1987 that is the subject of this case.

After receiving the order, Young began preparations to carry it out, even though the boughs were not to be cut until the following fall. Young obtained cutting rights from Michigan farmers for all the boughs to fill the three-hundred-sixty-ton order from Frank's. He also repaired his machinery and made seventy-five new hand tyers with which to tie the evergreen bundles. On June 30, 1987, Frank's mailed a new purchase order to Young, reducing its requirements to about seventy tons. At trial, Young estimated that the reduction had the effect of cutting the contract price from the original $238,332.85 to under $60,000. Young subsequently called three other evergreen bough buyers and two brokers about purchasing some of the material that Frank's no longer wanted. Those attempts to find other buyers were fruitless, Young testified, because other potential buyers already had their fall orders set by the time Young inquired in July. He did cut enough material to fill Frank's reduced order.

[Ed. Note: Young sued for breach of contract, seeking its lost profits on the sale of the boughs. Frank's admitted the breach of contract, but contested damages. Frank's argued that Young could have cut and sold the boughs to a third party, thereby mitigating its losses. Frank's argued that Young should receive damages under § 2-708(1), which awards a seller the difference between the market price and the contract price. This measure would be appropriate if Young should have sold the boughs to another party, as it would give him the difference, if any, between this hypothetical resale and the contract price. Young sued for lost profits under § 2-708(2). The jury awarded Young $132,902 as lost profits. The court of appeals reversed, holding that the trial judge erred in instructing the jury that the defendant had the burden of proving that Young's decision not to cut all the boughs originally ordered was commercially unreasonable.]

WRIGHT, Justice.

This is a case of first impression in Ohio, but the law under the Uniform Commercial Code is clear on the issue of a seller's remedies where the buyer commits an anticipatory breach.

The court of appeals correctly stated that the primary issue was which party had the burden of proving that the seller's decision to stop manufacture was commercially reasonable. The court erred, however, in its reliance upon *Detroit Power Screwdriver v. Ladney* (1970), 25 Mich.App. 478, 181 N.W.2d 828, as authority for the proposition that the plaintiff had to prove that his decision to cease manufacturing was commercially reasonable.

The better position is that where a buyer commits an anticipatory breach of a contract and the seller proceeds under UCC 2-704(2) and 2-708 for his remedy, the burden of proving that the seller acted in a commercially unreasonable fashion in deciding to cease manufacturing is on the buyer. UCC 2-704, Official Comment 2; 1 WHITE & SUMMERS, UNIFORM COMMERCIAL CODE (3rd ed.1988) 377, Section 7-15. The appellate court appears to have overlooked [2-704] when it analyzed the argument of Frank's. That section deals with seller's rights and obligations regarding unidentified and incomplete goods, which is precisely the situation here.

At the time of the breach, in July 1987, Young had not begun to assemble the goods that he had contracted to sell to Frank's. [Section 2-703], "Buyer's wrongful rejection, revocation of acceptance, or nonpayment: remedies of seller," lists the seller's principal remedies under the code. Because the goods in this instance were unidentified to the contract, [2-703(c)] directs the seller to the next section, [2-704], for his remedy. In turn, [2-704(2)], provides:

> Where the goods are unfinished an aggrieved seller may in the exercise of reasonable commercial judgment for the purposes of avoiding loss and of effective realization either complete the manufacture and wholly identify the goods to the contract or *cease manufacture and* resell for scrap or salvage value or *proceed in any other reasonable manner.* (Emphasis added.)

The theme of this section is mitigation. WHITE & SUMMERS, *supra,* at 377, in analyzing the import of this section, contends that the official comments to the UCC " . . . make clear that the burden is on the buyer to prove that the seller failed to use reasonable commercial judgment."

These respected commentators view the entire section as placing the burden on the breaching buyer:

> To read 2-704 as consistent with the general rules of mitigation, we would interpret it to mean that the seller must exercise commercially reasonable judgment not only when he decides to complete, but also when he decides not to.

> . . . Of course to preserve the usefulness of 2-704, the courts will have to be careful to place the burden on the buyer and to insist that he come forward with persuasive evidence that the seller acted in a commercially unreasonable way

     before they foreclose [the] seller from the right to complete or not complete.

Id. at 379–380.

Mitigation is an affirmative defense in Ohio. . . . Thus, we must rule that the trial judge was correct in placing the burden on Frank's to show that Young's decision not to complete cutting all the evergreen boughs originally ordered was commercially unreasonable.

* * *

Next, Young would look to [2-708], "Nonacceptance or repudiation; seller's damages," to determine the nature of his damages. The trial judge succinctly and clearly spelled out for the jury its responsibilities in this area, apportioning the burden of proof between Young and Frank's as required by the UCC.

* * *

[Section 2-708(2)] was offered by the trial judge as an alternate measure if the jury found that Young's decision not to cut the boughs was appropriate. In that case, the jury would have had to conclude that there was no market, as Young contended, and therefore, according to the statute, he should receive the profits that he would have made had there been full performance by the buyer.

Logic and equity, as well as the law, sustain the jury's verdict [for lost profits pursuant to 2-708(2)]. Therefore, we reverse the judgment of the court of appeals and reinstate the judgment of the trial court.

PROBLEM 7-4

    Sundries, Inc. manufactures coffee bean grinders and has contracted to sell 5,000 units to Beanbucks. The written terms of the contract include: "$100,000 F.O.B. Beanbuck's warehouse, Atlanta; delivery prior to June 1." On May 1, Sundries has fabricated the units at a cost of $70,000 but has not yet installed the electrical wiring, which is an additional $15,000 expense. That afternoon, Beanbucks e-mailed Sundries as follows: "Due to the shift in demand to hot tea, we will be unable to accept delivery of the coffee bean grinders. Please cancel our contract immediately."

    The 5,000 unfinished grinders have a scrap value of $10,000, but they are worthless as consumer goods without the wiring. Sundries believes that it might be able to sell the 5,000 finished grinders for as much as $60,000, but that there was at least a 50% chance that it will be able to sell them for only $40,000. The cost to transport the goods to Atlanta would be $5,000.

    1. Is Sundries acting within its rights if it decides to complete the manufacturing process, but ultimately is able to resell the goods for only $40,000?

    2. Is Sundries acting within its rights if it decides to sell the units for scrap?

    3. Who bears the burden of proving whether Sundries is acting within its rights?

b.   Seller's right to resell identified goods and the measure of damages

    An aggrieved seller may choose to resell the goods to a third party and recover damages. § 2-703(d). Section 2-706 governs the seller's right to resell goods and the seller's obligations when reselling. Section 2-706(2) provides that the "resale must be reasonably identified as referring to the broken contract, but it is not necessary that the goods be in existence or that any or all of them have been identified to the contract before the breach." This provision recognizes the seller's rights under § 2-704 to identify conforming goods to the contract following a breach, to resell unfinished goods demonstrably intended for the contract, or to finish incomplete goods for resale.

Section 2-706(1) specifies the measure of damages if the resale is "made in good faith and in a commercially reasonable manner." Subsection (2) provides additional details about the requirement of commercial reasonableness, and subsections (3) and (4) provide specific requirements depending on whether the seller resells "at private sale" (by contract) or "at public sale" (by auction). Subsection (6) makes clear that the seller is acting on its own behalf in reselling the goods: consequently, it "is not accountable to the buyer for any profit made on any resale." In contrast, when a buyer is authorized to resell non-conforming goods in its possession to recover its loss, the buyer must return to the seller any sums that exceed its "security interest" in the goods. § 2-711(3).

We turn first to the question of whether the seller has resold the goods in good faith, and in a commercially reasonable manner. Read the following two cases, address the questions that follow, and then work through the problems.

AFRAM EXPORT CORPORATION v. METALLURGIKI HALYPS, S.A.
United States Court of Appeals, Seventh Circuit
772 F.2d 1358 (1985)

Posner, Circuit Judge.

The appeal and cross-appeal in this diversity breach of contract suit raise a variety of interesting issues, in particular of personal jurisdiction and contract damages.

Afram Export Corporation, the plaintiff, is a Wisconsin corporation that exports scrap metal. Metallurgiki Halyps, S.A., the defendant, is a Greek corporation that makes steel. In 1979, after a series of trans-Atlantic telephone and telex communications, the parties made a contract through an exchange of telex messages for the purchase by Metallurgiki of 15,000 tons of clean shredded scrap, at $135 per ton, F.O.B. Milwaukee, delivery to be made by the end of April. Metallurgiki apparently intended to use the scrap to make steel for shipment to Egypt, pursuant to a contract with an Egyptian buyer. Afram agreed to pay the expenses of an agent of Metallurgiki — Shields — to inspect the scrap for cleanliness before it was shipped.

The scrap for the contract was prepared, in Milwaukee, by Afram Metal Processing Company. Both Afram Metal Processing and the plaintiff Afram Export are wholly owned subsidiaries of Afram Brothers. All three are Wisconsin corporations, and have the same officers and directors. Unless otherwise indicated, when we say "Afram" we mean "Afram Export."

Shields arrived to inspect the scrap on April 12. He told Afram that the scrap was clean but that Metallurgiki would not accept it, because the price of scrap had fallen. Sure enough, Metallurgiki refused to accept it. Afram brought this suit after selling the scrap to other buyers. Metallurgiki unsuccessfully challenged the court's jurisdiction over it, then filed a counterclaim alleging that Afram had broken the contract and had thereby made it impossible for Metallurgiki to fulfill its contract with the Egyptian purchaser.

After a bench trial, the district judge gave judgment, for Afram for $425,149 and dismissed the counterclaim.

[Ed. Note: Afram cross-appealed, contending that the judge should have awarded damages in the amount of $483,750, which was the difference between the contract price and the prices that Afram claimed it received when it resold the goods.]

*　　*　　*

. . . Afram claims that it sold all of the scrap rejected by Metallurgiki at a public sale on June 15, 1979, and that its damages should therefore be based on the price of that sale, which was $102.75 per ton. The district judge disagreed. He found that two-thirds of the scrap had been sold at a substantially higher price to Luria Brothers on June 4 ($118 — actually somewhat less, because Afram defrayed some freight costs) and the other third to International Traders on September 15 at a price of $103. Afram points out that the sale on June 4 actually was made by its affiliate, Afram Metal Processing Company, and further argues that since all Afram scrap is sold from the same pile in Milwaukee it is arbitrary to treat the first sale after the breach of contract as the cover transaction, rather than the sale that Afram designated as that transaction.

We agree with the district judge that the sale on June 4 was a cover transaction, even though the nominal seller was a different corporation from the plaintiff. Not only are both corporations wholly owned subsidiaries of another corporation, not only do all three corporations have the same officers and directors, but the record indicates substantial commingling of assets and operation of the three corporations as a single entity. Shortly after Metallurgiki's rejection, Zeke Afram, an officer of both Afram Export (the party to the contract with Metallurgiki) and Afram Metal Processing (the nominal owner of the scrap sold on June 4), called Luria Brothers and explained that he had extra scrap for sale because of a buyer's breach; apparently he did not bother to indicate which Afram corporation he was calling on behalf of. The June 4 sale followed shortly. The conversation and the timing of the sale are powerful evidence that the breach enabled the sale — that it would not have occurred but for the breach — and hence that the revenue from the sale must be subtracted from the contract price to determine Afram's loss. *Cf. Servbest Foods, Inc. v. Emessee Industries, Inc.*, 82 Ill.App.3d 662, 668–72, 37 Ill.Dec. 945, 951–53, 403 N.E.2d 1, 7–9 (1980).

But this does not dispose completely of the issue of the cover price. If the sale on June 15 was "made in good faith and in a commercially reasonable manner," it fixed Afram's damages on the remaining one-third of the scrap. UCC § 2-706(1), Wis.Stat. § 402.706(1). The question may seem less than earthshaking since the June 15 sale price and the September sale price which the district court used as the cover price for the remaining third were only 25 cents per ton apart. But the bona fides of the June 15 sale casts additional light on the intercorporate relations of the Afram group and hence on the proper interpretation of the sale to Luria Brothers. In any event, the district judge was entitled to find that neither condition in section 2-706(1) was satisfied. *Cf. Coast Trading Co. v. Cudahy Co.*, 592 F.2d 1074, 1080–81 (9th Cir. 1979). The June 15 "sale" was about as pure a bookkeeping transaction — as empty of economic significance — as can be imagined. *Cf. Milbrew v. Commissioner of Internal Revenue*, 710 F.2d 1302, 1305 (7th Cir. 1983). It consisted of a transfer of the scrap on the books of one affiliated corporation to the books of another. The transferor and transferee were not only under common ownership but were operated as if they were limbs of a single organism. The scrap itself was not moved; it remained on the scrap heap till sold later on. No invoice or check for the sale was produced at trial. The inference that the sale was designed simply to maximize the enterprise's damages, leaving it free to resell the scrap at higher prices later on, is overpowering. The sale of the scrap three months later to International Traders at a (slightly) higher price provided better evidence of what the enterprise actually lost, so far as the scrap not sold to Luria Brothers is concerned, by Metallurgiki's breach of contract.

[Ed. Note: The district court was affirmed with respect to the calculation of Afram's damages under § 2-706.]

QUESTIONS

1. Would the result in *Afram Export* change if Afram sent a written notification to the buyer that it intended to sell the goods to a related entity, specified the date of the sale, price, and other relevant terms, and invited the buyer to purchase the goods or to find another buyer if it believed that the sale price was inadequate?

2. Should all resales to a related business entity be deemed commercially unreasonable due to the opportunity for the seller to inflate damages? Read the next case after thinking about the benefits and problems with a bright-line rule. *See also* § 9-615(f).

ALLIED GRAPE GROWERS v. BRONCO WINE COMPANY
California Court of Appeal
203 Cal. App. 3d 432 (1988)

BALLANTYNE, Associate Justice.

Bronco Wine Company crushes grapes for use as wine. Allied Grape Growers is a cooperative corporation consisting of many grape growers in the business of supplying grapes to wineries. In 1981, Bronco and Allied entered into a contract for the supply and purchase of approximately 30,000 tons of red and white grapes per year for use in bulk wines.

A major dispute arose in 1982 when Bronco allegedly breached the contract by not accepting grapes or for downgrading grapes and paying lower prices for them. Allied eventually won its lawsuit with a jury award of approximately $3.4 million for its breach of contract claims.

*   *   *

Allied contended at trial that Bronco's three-tiered quality program, initiated by Bronco in 1982, and Bronco's practice of downgrading its grapes breached the general contract standards agreed to by the parties. Allied contended that the practices were totally arbitrary, that its grapes met contract standards including sugar content, and that Bronco's purpose in engaging in these practices was that it had purchased more grapes to crush than it had contracts to sell to other wineries.

Allied succeeded in delivering approximately 17,500 tons of Thompson grapes under the contract. Bronco paid an average price of $103 per ton. Allied contended that its grapes met contract standards and that it was entitled to $150 per ton. . . .

On March 16, 1983, Bronco repudiated its contract with Allied. Because there was no other market for its grapes, other than the Bronco contract, Allied formed a subsidiary corporation called ISC to purchase the grapes. Allied contended that the market value of its grapes in 1983 was $100 per ton and that ISC could only purchase the grapes for $85 per ton, for a loss of $15 per ton.

The jury awarded $2.65 million for Bronco's breach of contract in 1982. It awarded another $744,658 for Bronco's breach of contract in 1983.

*   *   *

DAMAGES FOR 1983 CROP

Bronco repudiated its contract with Allied in March of 1983. Allied, unable to find any purchaser for its grapes, created a subsidiary corporation called ISC to purchase the 1983 grape crop. The prevailing price for grapes in 1983 was $100 per ton. The value of the grapes to ISC was only $70 per ton. To minimize damage to growers and to ISC, the loss of $30 per ton was split between ISC and the growers. ISC bought the grapes for $85 per ton. Its loss was the same as the growers' loss, or $15 per ton.

Bronco makes three contentions on appeal. It claims that Allied and ISC operated as a single entity, making a resale to itself legally impossible under California Uniform Commercial Code section 2706. Bronco also claims that the resale of the 1983 Thompsons to ISC was not commercially reasonable. Finally, Bronco contends that Allied failed to comply with the notification requirements of section 2706.

A. *Commercial reasonableness of resale to an affiliated entity.*

Prominent commentators note that California Uniform Commercial Code section 2706 basically requires that all resales be conducted in a commercially reasonable manner and that sellers act in good faith. (WHITE & SUMMERS, UNIFORM COM. CODE (2d ed. 1980) § 7-6, pp. 265–266.) The express provisions of the code section and the official comments to the section do *not* prohibit resales of goods to affiliated entities and they do *not* state that such sales are per se commercially unreasonable.

Bronco relies on only two authorities interpreting section 2706 for the proposition that all resales to affiliated entities are commercially unreasonable. In *Afram Export Corp. v. Metallurgiki Halyps, S.A.* (7th Cir. 1985) 772 F.2d 1358, a seller of scrap metal sold scrap to its affiliate after the buyer backed out of the transaction. The resale turned out to be nothing more than a bookkeeping transaction. The evidence at trial showed that the scrap was sold at a higher price several months later than the sale price to the affiliate. The court found that the sale price on the open market was a better indicator of the true market value and the seller's actual loss than the seller's resale to its own affiliate. (*Id.* at pp. 1367–1368.)

In *Coast Trading Co. v. Cudahy Co.* (9th Cir. 1979) 592 F.2d 1074, a grain seller resold approximately one-half of a 10,000-ton grain contract rejected by the buyer to a Montana merchandiser. The evidence showed that although the market price was $105 per ton, the resale was for only $100 per ton to the Montana merchandiser. Nine days later the Montana company resold the grain back to the original seller for a profit of only 25 cents per ton. The plaintiff seller eventually sold the grain for a $133,566 profit. The seller's transaction with the Montana company was held to be commercially unreasonable and in bad faith. (*Id.* at pp. 1080–1081.)

Neither case holds that the resale of goods to an affiliate is commercially unreasonable. Both cases find that the resale to an affiliate or closely related company was a sham because the transactions were purely paper transactions and because the sellers eventually sold their goods at higher prices on the open market than they received from the initial resale. The sellers in the *Afram* and *Coast Trading* cases were not acting in good faith during resale. Rather than mitigating their damages, they were inflating their damages with the phony transfer of goods to obtain a dual recovery of damages. The sellers were first receiving extra funds from the more profitable resale of goods after sham transfers, and then by way of judgment from the defaulting buyer based on the price obtained from the sham resale.

The substantial evidence tendered by Allied at trial showed that the prevailing market price for Allied's 1983 crop was $100 per ton. The grapes were sold to ISC, which was the only buyer Allied could find, for $85 per ton. Although the grapes only had a value to ISC of $70 per ton, Allied did not seek damages calculated at the total loss, which was $30 per ton. It limited its damage claim to the growers' loss based on the difference between what its contract would have been with Bronco ($100 per ton) and what it actually received from ISC ($85 per ton).

The sale to ISC was consummated only as a last resort. Allied tried a number of times to sell its grapes to other wineries. It searched extensively for other buyers but there was no market for grapes not already under contract. Allied tried several times to get Bronco to honor its contract. In mid-August of 1983 Bronco adamantly refused to accept any Allied grapes. Because of the glut of grapes from 1982, there was no market for unsold grapes. Without the ISC transaction, Allied's only options were to let its grapes rot in the field, causing a loss of $100 per ton, or to sell its grapes to an alcohol distiller which would not even cover picking and harvesting costs.

Without any other outlet, Allied's only other option was to create ISC and to attempt to market its own wines. ISC had no marketing plan for bulkwines when it was created. It was originally conceived as a producer of finer bottle wines.

This transaction is not even remotely comparable to those found in *Afram* and *Coast Trading*. In those cases, there was an actual market for the goods being sold. Here, in sharp contrast, there was no market for Allied's product outside its contract with Bronco unless it could sell its product to an affiliate.

Although ISC was an affiliated entity, its sole purpose was to attempt to mitigate the growers' losses. Without ISC's purchase of Allied's 1983 grape crop, growers would have lost $100 per ton (less their saved harvesting and transportation costs) rather than a loss of $15 per ton. If the ISC resale was truly a sham, one is left to wonder why Allied did not bring suit to recover $30 per ton for the grapes since the actual value of the grapes to ISC was only $70 per ton.

Unlike the transactions in *Afram* and *Coast Trading,* Allied's resale to ISC actually worked to mitigate Bronco's damages. The sale, under the depressed conditions existing for grapes in 1983 was commercially reasonable and executed in good faith.

B. *Notice of Resale.*

To receive damages pursuant to section 2706 based on the difference between the contract price and the actual resale price, the seller must notify the buyer of its intent to resell if the sale is a private sale.[12] Bronco argues that even though it repudiated the contract, Allied was still obligated to notify Bronco of a private resale pursuant to subdivision (3) of section 2706.

We need not resolve here the issue of whether a defaulting buyer repudiating a contract is entitled to notice of resale by the seller under section 2706. One vital fact remains absolutely undisputed. Allied sent Bronco notice in a legal pleading related to this litigation that it intended to resell the 1983 crop. Bronco received notice before the crop was resold. Bronco does not dispute that it received sufficient notice that satisfied the requirements of section 2706, subdivision (3). Instead, it argues that it is entitled to a retrial because the jury did not hear evidence that Bronco received actual notice and that Allied failed to plead and prove compliance with subdivision (3) of section 2706.

This argument must unequivocally fail under California law. No purpose would be served in retrying this case so that Allied's counsel could submit evidence to the jury that Bronco received actual notice of Allied's intent to resell the 1983 crop. Because Bronco received the notice, it was not prejudiced by Allied's failure to actually prove the point at trial.

[Ed. Note: The judgment against Bronco was affirmed.]

* * *

PROBLEM 7-5

Star Petroleum agreed to sell 300,000 barrels of No. 2 heating oil to Baskins Oil Co., "FOB Boston Harbor" for a price of ".90 cents per gallon," with delivery "no later than August 1." On July 16, Star advised Baskins that it should be prepared to accept delivery from the vessel *Bordeaux* on July 28. The parties agreed that an undivided part of the oil on board the *Bordeaux* was identified to the contract. On July 27, Baskins repudiated its obligation under the contract due to falling prices. Star, wishing to lift the oil from the *Bordeaux* without delay so as not to incur substantial harbor charges, convinced Liberty Oil to take early delivery of 300,000 barrels of No. 2 heating oil pursuant to a preexisting contract under which Liberty had agreed to purchase 600,000 barrels on or before October 1 for 90 cents per gallon. On July 28, the market price for No. 2 heating oil had dropped to 82 cents per gallon.

On September 15, Star notified Baskins that it would be reselling the 300,000 barrels of oil to a third party for the current market price of 78 cents per gallon. Star planned to resell oil from the shipment originally intended to satisfy its contract with Liberty. In the time following Baskins' breach, Star had found a new buyer for the oil. In response, Baskins asserts that Star already had resold the goods identified to its contract for the same price as its contract price, and so it refused to be accountable for any damages.

---

[12] [11] California Uniform Commercial Code section 2706, subdivision (3), states that: "(3) Where the resale is at private sale the seller must give the buyer reasonable notification of his intention to resell."

Is Star entitled to receive damages based on the resale price of 78 cents per gallon?

PROBLEM 7-6

Byzantine Art Gallery agreed to purchase five paintings from Smith's Museum for $100,000. Subsequently, during a market decline in art prices, Byzantine repudiated its contractual obligation by claiming wrongly that the agreement had not been finalized. At this time the fair market value of the paintings was $90,000. Smith's curator was upset by this rather boorish attitude and immediately called Byzantine's curator. Byzantine's curator expressed concern and requested a letter from Smith's curator detailing Smith's claim, promising to investigate the matter. Four weeks later, Byzantine's lawyer disclaimed her client's obligation to purchase the paintings in a letter to Smith's. On this date the fair market value of the paintings was $80,000. Four weeks after receiving this letter Smith's sold the paintings to another museum after giving Byzantine reasonable notification that it intended to resell the paintings. The resale price was $70,000, which was also the fair market value of the goods on the date of the sale.

Smith's claims damages of $30,000 under § 2-706. How should Byzantine argue against this claim?

PROBLEM 7-7

Return to the facts of Problem 7-4 in which Sundries, Inc. resold goods. For this problem only, assume that Sundries acted in a commercially reasonable manner under § 2-704 and that it was entitled to resell the goods after completing their manufacture and also entitled to resell the goods as scrap. Calculate the damages available to Sundries, Inc. under § 2-706 for both scenarios.

c. Seller's right to obtain the contract price from the buyer for goods in its possession

Section 2-703(e) provides that "in a proper case" the seller may obtain the contract price of the goods from the buyer. Section 2-709 governs the seller's right to sue the buyer for the price, and is best understood as the seller's "specific performance" remedy. However, unlike a true judgment for specific performance, the court's contempt power will not be available to enforce the buyer's obligation. Work through the following problem to determine the conditions under which the seller is entitled to sue for the contract price before the buyer has accepted the goods.

PROBLEM 7-8

Banana Computers, Inc. develops sophisticated computer software. Banana is interested in building morale among its workers and obtaining a little free advertising at the same time. Banana agrees to purchase 100 mountain bikes and 25 jogging strollers from Southern Motivational Supplies for distribution to top employees. Southern agrees to purchase the products from manufacturers in an unfinished condition, and then paint the bikes and strollers with Banana's corporate design. Banana packages its software in distinctive neon pink boxes emblazoned with a neon yellow banana in the shape of a lightning bolt. The parties agreed that Banana would pick up the bikes and strollers on June 1. On May 25, Banana suffered a severe financial setback when the Air Force unexpectedly canceled plans to purchase software.

On June 1, Banana went to Southern's warehouse, inspected the bikes and strollers, and stated that it would not accept them because "the colors just weren't right." Southern believes that Banana is attempting to escape the contract, and wants to know what it should do. It would be impractical to strip the products down to bare metal and repaint them, and painting over the design would produce only a marginal quality product. Southern is unsure if anyone would purchase the bikes and strollers as is, given their somewhat obnoxious look, and it assumes that Banana would assert its trademark rights and refuse to permit Southern to sell the products to the public with Banana's corporate colors and design.

1. Can Southern sue Banana for the contract price? What additional facts would you need to develop?

2. Assume that Southern sues for the price, and that during the litigation Frankie's Salvage Emporium offers to buy the bikes and strollers for ten percent of the contract price. Frankie's intends to sell the products at a sharply discounted price after painting over the design. Can Southern sell the goods to Frankie's (after all, the proceeds will help to fund the litigation)?

2.   Seller's Right to Withhold Delivery of Goods to Buyer

If the buyer breaches while the goods are in transit, the seller may stop delivery if the requirements of § 2-705 are met. § 2-703(b). This right is derivative of the seller's general right to cancel the contract in the event of buyer's breach. § 2-703(f). The underlying principle of protecting the seller from additional harm after a breach is intuitive and uncontroversial. Surely it would be strange to require the seller to tender the goods to the buyer after the buyer has breached the contract. Similarly, Article 2 affords special protections to the seller if the buyer becomes insolvent, even if the buyer has not yet breached the contract. In the case of insolvency, the seller may refuse to deliver the goods to the insolvent buyer unless it receives cash, § 2-702(1), and may stop delivery of goods in transit under § 2-705. If the buyer already has received the goods while insolvent, the seller may reclaim the goods from the buyer on demand within ten days of their delivery, § 2-702(2), but this remedy of reclamation is the seller's exclusive remedy, § 2-702(3). Once again, the underlying purpose of these provisions is obvious. The buyer's principal obligation under the agreement is to pay the price, and so the buyer's insolvency has much the same effect as an anticipatory repudiation. Of course, if the insolvent buyer reaffirms its intention to conclude the transaction and is in a position to pay cash for the goods, then the seller has no basis for refusing to proceed.

a.   Seller's pre-delivery rights when buyer is insolvent

The seller's remedies under § 2-702 are triggered by the buyer's insolvency. The remedies available to the seller are clear: if the seller has not yet shipped the goods, it can refuse to do so unless the buyer agrees to pay cash upon delivery, and if the goods already are in transit, the seller may stop delivery of the goods to effectuate its right to demand payment in cash. Less clear are the circumstances that permit the seller to invoke these remedies. What does "insolvency" mean in this context, and how can the seller be confident that the buyer is insolvent? *See* § 1-201(23). Consider the following problem regarding the seller's right under § 2-702(1) to withhold delivery unless the insolvent buyer agrees to pay cash upon delivery.

PROBLEM 7-9

Seras Electrical Supply, Inc. sells electrical materials and supplies to contractors. Bolous Electrical Contracting, Inc. is an electrical contractor that maintains an "open account" with Seras. The "open account" is renewable every year, and provides that Bolous may purchase materials from Seras on credit, with payment due 30 days after delivery of the materials. Bolous solicited prices from Seras for the purposes of bidding on what would be the largest subcontract in Bolous's history. Bolous incorporated Seras's quotation of $88,000 into its bid, and was the lowest bidder. Bolous then mailed a purchase order to Seras for the materials. When Seras received the purchase order it investigated Bolous and determined that it did not meet its criteria for credit purchases for an order this size. Consequently, Seras refused to deliver the goods unless Bolous agreed to pay cash on delivery. Bolous decided to purchase the goods from another supplier for $98,000. Bolous then withheld $10,000 that it owed Seras under separate credit purchases from earlier in the month.

Seras sues Bolous for the $10,000, and Bolous defends by arguing that Seras breached their "open account" agreement by refusing to tender goods on credit. How will the parties' lawyers argue the case under the following alternative scenarios.

1. Seras proves that its investigation after receiving the purchase order from Bolous revealed that Bolous's account with Seras was past due.

2. Seras proves that its investigation after receiving the purchase order from Bolous revealed that Bolous's account with Seras was past due, a credit report from Dun & Bradstreet listed several past-due accounts, a credit report from the National Association of Credit Management showed that nearly two-thirds of Bolous' obligations were past due, and three other electrical suppliers reported that Bolous was past due on their accounts.

3. Seras proves everything in question 2. above, but Bolous proves that its agreement with Seras entitled Bolous to receive the goods on credit, and Bolous argues that Seras can't "rewrite" the contract just because it later regrets having extended credit to Bolous.

b.   Seller's right to stop delivery of goods in transit to the buyer

The seller may stop delivery of goods in the possession of a "carrier or bailee" in certain circumstances even if the buyer is not insolvent. Section 2-705(1) provides that the seller may "stop delivery of carload, truckload, planeload, or larger shipments . . . when the buyer repudiates or fails to make a payment due before delivery." Comment 1 explains that the seller is entitled to stop delivery only of large shipments in cases not involving the buyer's insolvency because of the burden placed on carriers and other bailees to identify the goods in question. This remedy is an important one, since the seller who has suffered a breach by the buyer does not want to increase its loss by surrendering the goods to the buyer.

Section 2-705(2) specifies various points in time after which the seller loses its right to stop delivery. Obviously, if the buyer has received the goods, the seller may no longer stop delivery, § 2-705(2)(a), but instead is limited to any right of reclamation that it might have under § 2-702. Less obvious are situations when the buyer has gained title and control over goods that remain in the possession of a third party. *See* § 2-705(2)(b)-(d). The following case illustrates one of these limits on the seller's right to stop delivery.

SIDERPALI, S.P.A. v. JUDAL IND., INC.
United States District Court, Southern District of New York
833 F. Supp. 1023 (1993)

KRAM, District Judge.

*   *   *

BACKGROUND

Conipost is a manufacturer of metal products, including steel shafts for use as posts in street and highway lighting. Plaintiff Siderpali, S.P.A. ("Siderpali") is an Italian corporation that owns Conipost and served as Conipost's financier during the relevant time period. Judal is a manufacturer, vendor and distributor of street lighting equipment and accessories. Judal Sales Corp. ("Judal Sales") is a New York corporation that functions as the sales and negotiator of contracts for Judal. Defendant Schreer is president and part owner of Judal. Defendant Netumar is an ocean common carrier that transports cargo between ports in Brazil and the United States.

In May, 1989, Judal and Conipost entered into a contract whereby Conipost agreed to produce and sell to Judal steel shafts for use as light poles. Judal, in turn, entered into a contract to supply the light poles to the City of New York. Pursuant to the contract between Conipost and Judal, the purchase price of the poles was $169,504.00. Of that amount, Judal paid $70,000.00 in cash to a New York bank prior to delivery. The balance, $99,504.00, was to be paid by letter of credit obtained at Sunkyong Bank by Judal ("Letter of Credit") for the benefit of Conipost. In addition, as security for Judal's cash payment, plaintiff Siderpali agreed to post a standby letter of credit ("Standby Letter"), issued by Banca Commerciale in Bologna, Italy, in the amount of $80,000.00. The Standby Letter stated that the sum of $80,000.00 would be available to Judal upon presentation of "[a] statement duly signed by an authorized officer of your company . . . certifying that Conipost Ltd. . . . has failed to deliver to yourselves within September 15, 1989" the light poles.

On September 7, 1989, Schreer made a demand on the Standby Letter. In his demand letter, Schreer stated:

> The terms of the credit call for a statement from an authorized officer of Judal to certify that Conipost . . . has failed to deliver the goods, encompassed within the credit, within the September 15, 1989 final date. I therefore state that the goods . . . have not been delivered.

In reliance upon Schreer's letter, Banca Commerciale made a payment on the Standby Letter to Judal in the amount of $80,000.00.

On September 13, 1989, Conipost placed the goods in the possession of Netumar in Santos, Brazil. Soon thereafter, Netumar issued a negotiable order bill of lading ("Bill of Lading") to Judal, which on its face entitled Judal to take possession of the six containers of light poles. Conipost was subsequently paid on the Letter of Credit in the amount of $99,500.00. The goods arrived at the New York port in and around October 27, 1989.

On October 30, 1989, Judal claims that its agent engaged trucks and drivers to pick up the containers, and hired cranes and operators to unload the cargo at its warehouse. Affidavit of Alan Schreer, sworn to on June 27, 1990 ("Schreer Aff."), ¶ 3. Despite Judal's presentation of the Bill of Lading, however, Netumar refused to release the cargo, claiming that it had been notified by Conipost that a fraud had been committed by Judal, and that the cargo should therefore be delivered to Conipost instead. Judal contends that, thereafter, on November 1, 1989, Netumar allowed Judal to pick up only one container. Affidavit of Karen M. Kim, sworn to on June 27, 1990 ("Kim Aff."), ¶ 4.

This action commenced in and around November 1, 1989, when plaintiffs brought an order to show cause seeking a temporary restraining order preventing Netumar from delivering the containers of cargo to Judal. The Court denied plaintiffs' motion for a temporary restraining order, and thereafter, on November 8 and 9, 1989, Netumar released the remaining containers to Judal.

In its Amended Complaint, plaintiffs allege four causes of action against the Judal Defendants. The first and fourth causes of action allege fraud against Judal and Schreer respectively, in calling upon the Standby Letter. The second and third causes of action allege conversion and breach of contract against Judal. By Order dated September 4, 1992 (the "September Order"), this Court accepted Magistrate Judge Gershon's Reports and Recommendations granting summary judgment to plaintiffs on their breach of contract and conversion claims (counts two and three of the Amended Complaint). The Court also adopted that portion of the Magistrate Judge's report (1) dismissing the complaint against Judal Sales Corp.; (2) denying Schreer's motion to dismiss the fourth cause of action on the ground that he was protected by the corporate shield doctrine; and (3) denying Judal's motion to dismiss the fraud claim against it.

The Judal Defendants answered the amended complaint on January 4, 1990, and

Judal asserted three counterclaims against plaintiffs. . . .

In its answer, Judal also asserts one cross-claim against defendant Netumar. This cross-claim alleges that Netumar's refusal to release the goods to Judal on October 30, 1989 was improper and illegal, causing Judal damages in the sum of $10,324.00 for the payments Judal was required to make for trucks, cranes, operators and demurrage charges.

*   *   *

DISCUSSION

*   *   *

II. Plaintiffs' Motion for Summary Judgment Dismissing the Judal Defendants' Counterclaims.

Plaintiffs move, pursuant to Federal Rule of Civil Procedure 56(c), for summary judgment dismissing Judal's first and third counterclaims on the grounds that there are sufficient undisputed facts to overcome Judal's allegations of breach of contract, and that Judal has failed to present sufficient evidence to justify allowing these claims to survive. Judal contends that the existence of genuine issues of fact warrant a trial on the counterclaims. For the reasons that follow, plaintiffs' motion is denied.

*   *   *

C. Judal's Third Counterclaim

Judal's third counterclaim alleges that Conipost improperly instructed defendant Netumar to refrain from releasing the containers to Judal, thereby causing Judal damages in the sum of $10,324.00 for trucking, cranes, operators and demurrage charges. Conipost argues . . . that, by improperly calling on the Standby Letter, Judal, in effect, took back almost half of the purchase price of the light poles. Thus, Conipost contends that it was justified in notifying Netumar to stop delivery. Judal asserts, however, that even if it improperly called upon the Standby Letter, plaintiffs had no legal right to advise Netumar not to deliver the poles as Judal was in possession of the Bill of Lading.

As the Court finds that Conipost initially had the right to withhold the goods under section 2-705(1), the pertinent issue is whether Conipost had "negotiated" to Judal "any negotiable document of title covering the goods," *see* N.Y.U.C.C. § 2-705(2)(d), thereby precluding Conipost from stopping delivery. Negotiation is defined as the "transfer of an instrument in such form that the transferee becomes a holder." N.Y.U.C.C. § 3-202(1).

It is undisputed that, soon after Conipost placed the light poles in the possession of the carrier, Netumar issued the Bill of Lading to Judal, which on its face entitled Judal to take possession of the six containers of light poles. Thus, as the Bill of Lading had already been negotiated to Judal, Conipost was not entitled to stop delivery of the goods. Accordingly, Conipost's motion to dismiss Judal's third counterclaim on the grounds that it was entitled to instruct the carrier not to deliver the light poles to Judal is denied.

*   *   *

IV. Defendant Netumar's Motion for Summary Judgment and Judal's Cross-Motion for Summary Judgment

*   *   *

B. Judal's Cross-Motion

Judal cross-moves for summary judgment and for sanctions against Netumar. Judal argues that, since title to the goods passed to it when Judal was provided with the Bill of Lading, Netumar was not justified in refusing to release the containers. This contention was addressed by Judge Gershon in [his Report and Recommendation to the District Judge, referenced as "RRIII"]. The Magistrate Judge held that Judal possessed title to the goods once it was issued the Bill of Lading. RRIII at 9. According to the Magistrate Judge:

> Section 7-104(1)(a) of the Uniform Commercial Code provides that a bill of lading is negotiable "if by its terms the goods are to be delivered to bearer or to the order of a named person." It is not in dispute between Judal and Netumar that what was issued to Judal was a negotiable order bill of lading. Under U.C.C. 7-303(2), the holder of a negotiable bill of lading "can hold the bailee according to the original terms." Unless there are instructions on the negotiable bill of lading that indicate otherwise (and it is undisputed that there are none here), the holder of the bill of lading retains title. Thus, the U.C.C., like prior New York law, "permits a change of instructions to be made only by the holder and requires notation of such changes on the bill. . . ."

RRIII at 9.

The Magistrate Judge further held that Netumar had not established that it was presented with conflicting claims entitling it to delay delivery pursuant to U.C.C. § 7-603. RRIII at 9. According to the Magistrate Judge, the mere fact that Netumar had received a telex from Conipost demanding that Netumar refrain from delivering the containers could not be considered an adverse claim justifying delay in the face of Judal's presentation of the Bill of Lading. RRIII at 10. Additionally, the Magistrate Judge stated that

> the law, as set forth above, is clear and unequivocal that Netumar had no right to interfere with delivery to Judal on a mere phone call or telex from plaintiffs or their attorneys to the effect that plaintiffs were now claiming delivery for themselves. U.C.C. § 7-303(2) (allowing the holder of a negotiable bill of lading to "hold the bailee according to the original terms"; permitting a change of instructions to be made only by the holder; and requiring any such change to be noted on the bill) would be significantly deprived of its intended power to protect holders of negotiable bills of lading if the shipper's communication in this case could be used to defeat for several days the holder's right to delivery.

RRIII at 10–11. Netumar has not refuted this recitation of the law, and has brought forth no genuine issues of material fact precluding summary judgment in Judal's favor. Accordingly, Judal's cross-motion for summary judgment is granted.

Judal also moves for sanctions against Netumar for bringing a "frivolous motion which is baseless in fact and in law." As set forth in Part I.B., *supra*, sanctions are imposed where an attorney "multiplies the proceedings in any case unreasonably and vexatiously." 28 U.S.C. § 1927. Netumar and its counsel clearly misrepresented the Court's September Order, in which the Court found plaintiffs liable for converting the proceeds of the Standby Letter. In fact, contrary to Netumar's assertion, the Court has never found that Judal was not entitled to the cargo. Moreover, Netumar clearly ignored the effect of this Court's prior holding that the Pomerene Bills of Lading Act, 49 U.S.C. § 90(a), is not applicable to this case. In sum, Netumar's motion was neither "well-grounded in fact" nor "warranted by existing law or a good faith argument for the extension, modification or reversal of existing law." *Eastway Constr. Corp. v. City of New York*, 762 F.2d at 254. Accordingly, Netumar and its counsel are hereby required to pay to Judal all reasonable costs, expenses and attorneys' fees incurred by Judal in opposing Netumar's motion for summary judgment.

NOTES AND QUESTIONS

1. The carrier or bailee may face conflicting claims for the goods when it receives a direction from the seller to stop delivery but the buyer continues to insist on delivery. Section 2-705(3) provides some protection for the carrier or bailee in this situation. Under the facts of *Siderpali*, should the common carrier, Netumar, be able to secure reimbursement from Conipost for the damages that it must pay to Judal?

2. Does *Siderpali* make any practical sense? Why would the court conclude that Conipost could not stop delivery of the goods to Judal, even after it is discovered that Judal has cheated Conipost by fraudulently drawing on the letter of credit guaranteeing shipment?

3. It is important to understand that the standby letter of credit was paid according to its terms. Under Article 5 of the Uniform Commercial Code pertaining to Letters of Credit, the bank issuing the letter of credit "shall honor a presentation that, as determined by the standard practice . . . appears on its face strictly to comply with the terms and conditions of the letter of credit." § 5-108(a). This is known as the "independence principle," because the issuer's obligation on the letter of credit is independent of any breach of contract in the underlying sales transaction. In light of the independence principle, for future transactions Conipost might want to add to the requirements specified in the letter of credit that must be satisfied by its buyer before it may draw on the letter of credit.

Even if Conipost had been advised by the bank of Judal's demand for payment under the letter of credit and Conipost could persuasively demonstrate to its bank that the draw was completely fraudulent, the bank is under no obligation to dishonor the presentation. *See* § 5-109(a)(2) (in certain cases of material fraud the issuer is *permitted*, but not required, to dishonor). In such a situation, Conipost might best be advised to seek a temporary injunction from a court that orders the issuer not to honor Judal's presentation until the merits of the allegations of fraud can be reached. *See* § 5-109(b).

3. Seller's Damages for Pre-Acceptance Breach

If the buyer breaches the contract when the goods are in the seller's possession, the seller often will resell the goods to another buyer and then look to the breaching buyer for damages under § 2-706. In the event that the seller is unable to resell the goods for a reasonable price, the seller may be entitled to recover the purchase price under § 2-709. However, there will be cases where the seller has not resold the goods to another buyer, and is not entitled to recover the price of the goods from the buyer. In such cases, § 2-708 provides a general damages provision to effectuate the general objective of providing the seller with the benefit of its bargain.

The damages formula in § 2-708(1) generally provides for a recovery of any difference between the contract price that the seller was entitled to receive from the buyer and the market value of the goods in the seller's possession. In effect, this formula constructs a "hypothetical resale" of the subject goods by assuming that the seller has sold the goods for the market price and therefore is injured to the extent that this hypothetical resale is less than the contract price, plus any incidental losses caused by the breach and less any expenses of performance saved by the breach. However, this general formula will not adequately compensate the seller in every case. In the event that the measure of damages determined under this general formula is "inadequate," § 2-708(2) provides an alternative "lost profits" measure of recovery for the seller.

The following materials begin by working through the details of the general market price damages formula of § 2-708(1). In the next subsection, the materials cover those situations in which the general formula is "inadequate," and then work through the details of the alternative lost profits formula of § 2-708(2). In the final subsection, the materials address the seller's ability to choose a remedy from among the options that we have considered.

a. The contract-market damages formula

Work through the damages formula in § 2-708(1) by solving the following problem.

PROBLEM 7-10

Synchronous Machines, Inc. manufactures computerized cash registers at a facility located in Palo Alto, California. BudgetMart is a large nationwide discount retailer based in Little Rock, Arkansas. BudgetMart decided to purchase state of the art machines from Synchronous to upgrade its accounting and inventory functions at the point of sale in its stores. The agreement was reached on August 1, prior to Synchronous commencing large-scale production of the machines. Until that date, Synchronous had not filled a single order for more than 1,000 machines. BudgetMart agreed to purchase a total of 20,000 machines and related support equipment. To permit Synchronous to meet its obligations, and to permit BudgetMart to phase in the use of these machines across the country, the parties agreed that Synchronous would ship 5,000 units every three months, beginning January 1. BudgetMart agreed to pay $1,000 for each machine, F.O.B. Palo Alto ($5 million for each installment; $20 million for the entire contract).

On October 1, owing to the soaring popularity of its machines, Synchronous was offered $20 million to supply 10,000 machines to be delivered within six months. Because Synchronous was operating at full capacity, it asked BudgetMart to modify their agreement to delay shipments so that Synchronous could accept the additional order. However, BudgetMart was interested in converting its stores as quickly as possible and refused to modify the contract.

On December 1, Synchronous's competitor unveiled a new generation computerized cash register that immediately rendered Synchronous's model obsolete. BudgetMart immediately repudiated its contract with Synchronous under the mistaken belief that it was not yet a final agreement, and that even if there was a final agreement it would be unenforceable under § 2-201. BudgetMart then signed a purchase agreement with Synchronous's competitor on December 31. As a result of the sudden obsolescence of its computerized cash register, Synchronous watched the market price of its machine fall rather dramatically during the year. Because its competitor is a small California-based company with a more limited production capacity, Synchronous's machine depreciated in value more rapidly in the California market that was fully serviced by its competitor. The market value of Synchronous's machine is represented in the following table.

Date	Market Value (Little Rock)	Market Value (Palo Alto)
1/1	$2,000	$900
4/1	$1,500	$750
7/1	$1,000	$500
10/1	$750	$500

Synchronous paid its lawyer $5,000 to write several demand letters and to attempt to negotiate a resolution of the dispute with BudgetMart. Additionally, because Synchronous was unable to sell its inventory in the dwindling market, it paid $5,000 to a warehouse for storing the machines intended for the BudgetMart contract.

A. Calculate Synchronous's damages under § 2-708(1). Pay particular attention to when the market price is determined for purposes of the formula.

B. Why aren't Synchronous's damages measured at the time of Buyer's repudiation?

C. Can Synchronous recover based on the price of $2,000 per machine offered in October rather than the $1,000 contract price? *See* § 1-305.

D. Assume that Synchronous's lawsuit is uncontested and comes to verdict in June, after only two of the installment dates have passed. How would Seller's damages under § 2-708(1) be calculated?

b. The lost profits damages formula

If the measure of damages under § 2-708(1) is "inadequate," § 2-708(2) provides an alternative "lost profits" approach to measuring the seller's damages. The following case provides an overview of situations in which the market-contract measure proves to be inadequate.

KENCO HOMES, INC. v. WILLIAMS
Washington Court of Appeals
972 P.2d 125 (1999)

MORGAN, J.

Kenco Homes, Inc., sued Dale E. Williams . . . for breaching a contract to purchase a mobile home. After a bench trial, the trial court ruled primarily for Williams. Kenco appealed, claiming the trial court used an incorrect measure of damages. We reverse.

Kenco buys mobile homes from the factory and sells them to the public. Sometimes, it contracts to sell a home that the factory has not yet built. It has "a virtually unlimited supply of product," according to the trial court's finding of fact.

On September 27, 1994, Kenco and Williams signed a written contract whereby Kenco agreed to sell, and Williams agreed to buy, a mobile home that Kenco had not yet ordered from the factory. The contract called for a price of $39,400, with $500 down.

The contract contained two conditions pertinent here. According to the first, the contract would be enforceable only if Williams could obtain financing. According to the second, the contract would be enforceable only if Williams later approved a bid for site improvements. Financing was to cover the cost of the mobile home and the cost of the land on which the mobile home would be placed.

The contract provided for damages. It stated, "I [Williams] understand that you [Kenco] shall have all the rights of a seller upon breach of contract under the Uniform Commercial Code, except the right to seek and collect 'liquidated damages' under Section 2-718."

The contract provided for reasonable attorney's fees. It stated, "If you prevail in any legal action which you bring against me, or which I bring against you, concerning this contract, I agree to reimburse you for reasonable attorneys' fees, court costs and expenses."

In early October, Williams accepted Kenco's bid for site improvements. As a result, the parties (a) formed a second contract and (b) fulfilled the first contract's site-improvement-approval condition. Also in early October, Williams received preliminary approval on the needed financing.

On or about October 12, Williams gave Kenco a $600 check so Kenco could order an appraisal of the land on which the mobile home would be located. Before Kenco could act, however, Williams stopped payment on the check and repudiated the entire transaction. His reason, according to the trial court's finding of fact, was that he "had found a better deal elsewhere."

When Williams repudiated, Kenco had not yet ordered the mobile home from the factory. After Williams repudiated, Kenco simply did not place the order. As a result, Kenco's only out-of-pocket expense was a minor amount of office overhead.

On November 1, 1994, Kenco sued Williams for lost profits. After a bench trial, the superior court found that Williams had breached the contract; that Kenco was entitled to damages; and that Kenco had lost profits in the amount of $11,133 ($6,720 on the mobile home, and $4,413 on the site improvements). The court further found, however, that Kenco would be adequately compensated by retaining Williams' $500 down payment;[13] that Williams was the prevailing party; and that Williams should receive reasonable attorney's fees in the amount of $1,800. Because Kenco had already received its $500, the court entered an $1,800 judgment for Williams, and Kenco filed this appeal.

In this court, Williams does not contest the trial court's finding that he breached the contract. Thus, the only issues are (1) whether the superior court used the correct measure of damages, and (2) whether the superior court properly awarded attorneys' fees to Williams.

I.

Under the Uniform Commercial Code (UCC), a nonbreaching seller may recover "damages for non-acceptance" from a breaching buyer.[14] The measure of such damages is as follows:

> (1) Subject to subsection (2) and to the provisions of this Article with respect to proof of market price (RCW 62A.2-723), the measure of damages for non-acceptance or repudiation by the buyer is the difference between the market price at the time and place for tender and the unpaid contract price together with any incidental damages provided in this Article (RCW 62A.2-710), but less expenses saved in consequence of the buyer's breach.

> (2) *If the measure of damages provided in subsection (1) is inadequate to put the seller in as good a position as performance would have done* then the measure of damages is the profit (including reasonable overhead) which the seller would have made from full performance by the buyer, together with any incidental damages provided in this Article (RCW 62A.2-710), due allowance for costs reasonably incurred and due credit for payments or proceeds of resale.[15]

As the italicized words demonstrate, the statute's purpose is to put the nonbreaching seller in the position that he or she would have occupied if the breaching buyer had fully performed (or, in alternative terms, to give the nonbreaching seller the benefit of his or her bargain). A party claiming damages under subsection (2) bears the burden of showing that an award of damages under subsection (1) would be inadequate.[16]

In general, the adequacy of damages under subsection (1) depends on whether the nonbreaching seller has a readily available market on which he or she can resell the goods that the breaching buyer should have taken. When a buyer breaches before either side has begun to perform, the amount needed to give the seller the benefit of his or her bargain is the difference between the contract price and the seller's expected cost of performance. Using market price, this difference can, in turn, be subdivided into two smaller differences: (a) the difference between the contract price and the market price, and (b) the difference between the market price and the seller's expected cost of performance. So long as a nonbreaching seller can reasonably resell the breached goods on the open market, he or she can recover the difference between contract price and

---

[13] [7] Kenco argues at length that the trial court viewed this $500 as "liquidated damages," and awarded it to the exclusion of other, compensatory damages. The trial court's written and oral manifestations show, however, that the court intended the $500 to be compensatory damages, not liquidated damages, notwithstanding an apparent misstatement in the second sentence of Finding of Fact 16. It follows that liquidated damages are not an issue in this case.

[14] [9] [UCC 2-703(e)].

[15] [10] [UCC 2-708] (emphasis added).

[16] [11] *See also* [UCC 1-106].

market price by invoking subsection (1), and the difference between market price and his or her expected cost of performance by reselling the breached goods on the open market. Thus, he or she is made whole by subsection (1), and subsection (1) damages should be deemed "adequate." But if a nonbreaching seller cannot reasonably resell the breached goods on the open market, he or she cannot recover, merely by invoking subsection (1), the difference between market price and his or her expected cost of performance. Hence, he or she is not made whole by subsection (1); subsection (1) damages are "inadequate to put the seller in as good a position as performance would have done"; and subsection (2) comes into play.

The cases illustrate at least three specific situations in which a nonbreaching seller cannot reasonably resell on the open market. In the first, the seller never comes into possession of the breached goods; although he or she plans to acquire such goods before the buyer's breach, he or she rightfully elects not to acquire them after the buyer's breach. In the second, the seller possesses some or all of the breached goods, but they are of such an odd or peculiar nature that the seller lacks a post-breach market on which to sell them; they are, for example, unfinished, obsolete, or highly specialized. In the third situation, the seller again possesses some or all of the breached goods, but because the market is already oversupplied with such goods (i.e., the available supply exceeds demand), he or she cannot resell the breached goods without displacing another sale.[17] Frequently, these sellers are labeled "jobber," "components seller," and "lost volume seller," respectively; in our view, however, such labels confuse more than clarify.

To illustrate the first situation, we examine *Copymate Marketing v. Modern Merchandising*,[18] a case cited and discussed by both parties. In that case, Copymate had an option to purchase three thousand copiers from Dowling for $51,750. Before Copymate had exercised its option, it contracted to sell the copiers to Modern for $165,000. It also promised Modern that it would spend $47,350 for advertising that would benefit Modern. It told Dowling it was exercising its option, but before it could finish its purchase from Dowling, Modern repudiated. Acting with commercial reasonableness, Copymate responded by cancelling its deal with Dowling and never acquiring the copiers. It then sued Modern for its lost profits and prevailed in the trial court. Modern appealed, but this court affirmed. Because Copymate had rightfully elected not to acquire the copiers, it had no way to resell them on the open market; subsection (1) was inadequate; and subsection (2) applied. Thus, Copymate recovered its contract price with Modern ($165,000), minus the expected cost of performing its contract with Modern ($51,750 for Dowling, $47,350 for advertising, and $180 for a miscellaneous import fee), for a total of $65,720.

To illustrate the second situation, we again examine *Copymate*. Based on substantial evidence, the *Copymate* trial court found that after Modern's repudiation, Copymate had "no active or reasonably available market for the resale of the . . . copiers."[19] One reason was that the copiers had been in storage in Canada for nine years; thus, they seem to have been obsolete. Again, then, Copymate could not resell the copiers on the open market; subsection (1) was inadequate; and subsection (2) provided for an award of "lost profits."

To illustrate the third situation, we examine *R.E. Davis Chemical Corp. v. Diason-*

---

[17] [16] . . . In passing, we observe that this lost volume situation can be described in several ways. Focusing on the breached unit, one can say that due to a market in which supply exceeds demand, the lost volume seller cannot resell the breached unit without sacrificing an additional sale. Focusing on the additional unit, one can say that but for the buyer's breach, the lost volume seller would have made an additional sale. Focusing on both units, one can say that but for the buyer's breach, the lost volume seller would have sold both units. Each statement is equivalent to the others.

[18] [18] 34 Wash. App. 300, 660 P.2d 332 (1983).

[19] [19] 34 Wash. App. at 302, 660 P.2d at 332.

ics.[20] In that case, Davis breached his contract to buy medical equipment from Diasonics. Diasonics was in possession of the equipment, which it soon resold on the open market. Diasonics then sued Davis for "lost profits" under subsection (2), arguing that "it was a 'lost volume seller,' and, as such, it lost the profit from one sale when Davis breached its contract."[21] The trial court granted summary judgment to Davis, but the appellate court reversed and remanded for trial. Other courts, the appellate court noted, "have defined a lost volume seller as one that has a predictable and finite number of customers and that has the capacity either to sell to all new buyers or to make the one additional sale represented by the resale after the breach."[22] This definition, the appellate court ruled, lacks an essential element: whether the seller *would* have sold an additional unit but for the buyer's breach. On remand, then, Diasonics would have to prove (a) that it *could* have produced and sold the breached unit in addition to its actual volume, and (b) that it *would* have produced and sold the breached unit in addition to its actual volume.

In this case, Kenco did not order the breached goods before Williams repudiated. After Williams repudiated, Kenco was not required to order the breached goods from the factory; it rightfully elected not to do so; and it could not resell the breached goods on the open market. Here, then, "the measure of damages provided in subsection (1) is inadequate to put [Kenco] in as good a position as [Williams'] performance would have done"; subsection (2) states the applicable measure of damages; and Kenco is entitled to its lost profit of $11,133.

II.

The second issue is whether Kenco is entitled to reasonable attorneys' fees. The parties' contract provided that the prevailing party would be entitled to such fees. Kenco is the prevailing party. On remand, the trial court shall award Kenco reasonable attorneys' fees incurred at trial and on appeal.

Reversed with directions to enter an amended judgment awarding Kenco its lost profit of $11,133; reasonable attorneys' fees incurred at trial and on appeal; and any ancillary amounts required by law.

SEINFELD, J., AND BRIDGEWATER, C.J., concur.

QUESTIONS

1. A seller may recover "lost profit" damages under § 2-708(2) only on a showing of "inadequacy." What must the seller prove to be inadequate, and what is the standard of adequacy?

2. The *Kenco* court described three situations where the market-contract formula of § 2-708(1) proves to be inadequate. Before proceeding to the problems, it is important that you understand these different scenarios.

(A) The first situation involves "jobbers," colloquially known as "middle-men," who suffer a breach. Why is § 2-708(1) inadequate to compensate jobbers? If a jobber has purchased the goods for resale to the breaching buyer and is in possession of the goods when the buyer breaches, would § 2-708(1) still be inadequate?

(B) The second situation involves "components" sellers. The *Kenco* court defines this group to include a seller that suffers a breach when it has only unfinished goods in its possession (which includes situations in which it has only a "component" of the final goods). Why is § 2-708(1) inadequate for such "component" sellers? The court also

---

[20] 826 F.2d 678 (7th Cir. 1987).

[21] 826 F.2d at 680.

[22] 826 F.2d at 683. In essence, then, these courts hold that a lost volume seller is one who proves at trial that his or her supply of product exceeds the demand for such product on the relevant market.

includes within this group those sellers who are in possession of goods that are "obsolete" or "highly specialized," such that the seller has no potential resale market. If the market-contract measure is inadequate for such sellers, would there be remedy available to them other than the lost profits measure of § 2-708(2)?

(C) Finally, the court describes "lost volume sellers" as the third group of sellers who should be entitled to lost profits under § 2-708(2). Why is the market-contract measure inadequate for sellers in this position? What is the significance of the *Diasonics* court's emphasis that a "lost volume seller" must prove not only that it *could* have produced or acquired an additional unit if the buyer had not breached, but also that it *would* have done so if not for the buyer's breach making another unit available? Under what situation would a seller be capable of supplying a good to a new buyer, but choose not to do so?

Use the following problem to determine if the remedy provided by § 2-708(1) is "inadequate," and if so to determine how damages should be calculated under § 2-708(2).

PROBLEM 7-11

Bexon Petroleum contracted with Santo Chemical to purchase 1,000 metric tons of cumene, an additive for high-octane motor fuel, for the price of $540 per ton. Bexon repudiated the agreement and refused to accept delivery after the market price of cumene plunged to $240 per ton. Santo had arranged to purchase the cumene in Brazil for $400 per ton, and had arranged for delivery to the defendant in accordance with the contract for the cost of $45 per ton. Santo immediately advised its Brazilian supplier that it no longer required 1,000 tons of its current order for 4,000 tons. Consequently, Santo lost a quantity discount offered by its Brazilian supplier and was forced to pay $425 per ton (an additional $25 per ton) for the 3,000 tons that it had agreed to purchase for other buyers.

Santo sued Bexon for breach of contract. Santo argued that it was entitled to damages under § 2-708(1), calculated as follows:

$$\begin{array}{r} \$540,000 \text{ (K price)} \\ -\ \$240,000 \text{ (Market Price)} \\ +\ \underline{\$75,000 \text{ (Consequentials)}} \\ =\ \$375,000 \end{array}$$

Bexon countered by arguing that Santo should be limited to its lost profits under § 2-708(2), which was far less than $375,000. Santo responded by saying that it should be forced to accept damages under § 2-708(2) only if the damages under § 2-708(1) are "inadequate," and that its alleged excess recovery clearly precludes a finding of inadequacy.

What damages should Santo receive in this case?

c.   Seller's election of remedies

The index provision of § 2-703 lists the remedies available to a seller in the alternative, suggesting that the seller might have the right to choose which remedy to pursue. Comment 1 reinforces this interpretation by providing: "This Article rejects any doctrine of election of remedy as a fundamental policy and thus the remedies are essentially cumulative in nature and include all of the available remedies for breach." In addition, you should recall that the parties have the freedom to contract for limited remedies or liquidated damages, *see* §§ 2-718 and 2-719, and that remedies provided by law other than Article 2 may be available to a plaintiff, *see* § 1-103(b). Of course, some remedies are explicitly limited only to certain circumstances, such as the action for the price under § 2-709, which is "exhaustive in its enumeration of cases" where the seller is entitled to recover the price. § 2-709, Comment 6.

At first glance, it would appear that the seller is free to choose from all of the available remedies regardless of how it responds to the breach, since there is no "fundamental policy" that any particular course of action operate as an "election" of the available remedies. Thus, even if a seller resells the subject goods to another buyer, it might seek to recover general damages under § 2-708(1) if that measure provided a greater recovery than § 2-706. This interpretation is brought into question, however, by reading the next sentence of § 2-703, Comment 1: "Whether the pursuit of one remedy bars another depends entirely on the facts of the individual case." It is unclear whether this language refers only to the obvious point that a seller may not seek contradictory or duplicative remedies, or whether it suggests that sellers may not always have a choice of available remedies. Does the following case provide a satisfactory answer?

TESORO PETROLEUM CORP. v. HOLBORN OIL CO. LTD.
New York Supreme Court
547 N.Y.S.2d 1012 (1989)

LEHNER, J.

The sole issue presented on the motion and cross motion for partial summary judgment is whether, in the event plaintiff establishes a contract between the parties and a breach thereof, the measure of damages should be governed by UCC 2-706 (difference between contract price and resale price) or UCC 2-708 (difference between contract price and market price at time of tender).

FACTS

Plaintiff asserts that it contracted to sell approximately 10 million gallons of gasoline to defendant at a price of $1.30 per gallon, having purchased it a few days earlier at $1.26 per gallon. After plaintiff sent notice of the name of the vessel to deliver the product, it was informed by defendant that the gasoline would not be accepted in view of the absence of a binding agreement resulting from the untimely acceptance of its offer. While the loaded vessel was proceeding to New York, plaintiff negotiated the sale of the cargo on board to Esso Sapa in Argentina for $1.10 per gallon.

CONTENTIONS OF THE PARTIES

Plaintiff claims that because of a sudden sharp drop in price, the value of the gasoline at the time of defendant's breach was between 75 cents to 80 cents per gallon and that, although it resold the product for $1.10 per gallon, its recovery should not be limited to its actual loss resulting from the breach (20 cents per gallon plus incidentals), but rather it is entitled to recover the difference between market price and contract price. If plaintiff were to prevail on this claim, it could recover at least $3,000,000 in excess of its actual contractual loss (10,000,000 gallons times difference of 30 cents per gallon between the resale price of $1.10 and highest market price discussed of approximately 80 cents per gallon).

Plaintiff justifies this recovery by asserting that it, rather than the defaulting buyer, is entitled to the benefit of its ability to resell the gasoline at above market price. Although the price for which one actually sells merchandise is evidence as to its market value, and there is no explanation as to why Esso Sapa was willing to pay a premium of about 40% above market to obtain this cargo, the question as to the actual market value is not raised for determination on this motion.

Plaintiff maintains that since gasoline is fungible, it, as a dealer in that commodity, could have made a profit not only on the sale to defendant, but also could have purchased gasoline on the open market and made a second profit on the resale to Esso Sapa. Hence it asserts (putting aside incidental damages) that by recovering damages of 50 cents per gallon (assuming a market price of 80 cents per gallon at the time) from defendant, it will be in the same position as if defendant had complied with its alleged contract and accepted the gasoline and paid $1.30 per gallon. This is calculated by deducting from such 50 cents per gallon damages, the loss of 16 cents per gallon (difference between purchase price of $1.26 and sales price to Esso Sapa of $1.10) with a resulting 34 cents per gallon net profit. This equals the total of the 4 cents per gallon profit it would earn on the alleged contract if performed (difference between purchase price of $1.26 and contract price of $1.30) and the 30 cents profit that allegedly could be earned if it purchased gasoline on the open market at 80 cents per gallon and resold it to Esso Sapa at $1.10. To support its position, plaintiff relies on UCC 2-703 as giving it the option to proceed against a defaulting buyer under either UCC 2-706 or 2-708.

Defendant, on the other hand, asserts that if plaintiff establishes a breach, its damages should be limited to its actual loss resulting therefrom, which would be 20 cents per gallon plus incidental damages. In this regard defendant points to UCC 1-106, which it asserts sets forth the policy of the Code to place an aggrieved party in as good a position as if the other party had fully performed, and contends that granting plaintiff the profit it seeks would result in a windfall which would be inconsistent with such policy. Further, defendant maintains that permitting plaintiff to choose its remedy to maximize its damages would be inconsistent with the requirement that a party mitigate damages.

* * *

DISCUSSION

Although the Official Comment to section 2-703 states that the "Article rejects any doctrine of election of remedy as a fundamental policy and thus the remedies are essentially cumulative in nature," it concludes that "[w]hether the pursuit of one remedy bars another depends entirely on the facts of the individual case."

In 1 WHITE AND SUMMERS, UNIFORM COMMERCIAL CODE (at 354 [Practitioner's 3d ed. 1988]), the distinguished authors indicate that the Code and Comments in this area are "equivocal," and that "[w]hether the drafters intended a seller who has resold to recover more in damages under 2-708 . . . is not clear." (*Op. cit.*, at 352.)

On this question, White and Summers conclude that: "a seller who resells goods reasonably identified to the broken contract for a price above the 2-708(1) market price should be limited to the difference between the contract price and his actual resale price. We believe that this is an exact measure of his expectation and that he should not recover more than that. As indicated above, the buyer bears the burden of showing that the seller was not a lost volume seller, and that the goods which in fact were resold were those that would have been delivered to him, the breaching buyer." (*Op. cit.*, at 356.) In so concluding the authors expressed the following caveat: "All of the foregoing discussion assumes that the buyer who wishes to limit the seller to the difference between the contract and the resale price can show that the goods resold were in fact the goods contracted for. If the seller could have fulfilled the buyer's contract by buying on the market or by a choice among a variety of fungible goods, the buyer will be unable to limit the seller to 2-706 damages. The buyer will not be able to prove that the resale is 'reasonably identified as referring to the broken contract.' Put another way, the difference between the contract and a specific resale price is not the proper measure of the seller's expectation damages unless that resale is a substitute for the one actually conducted." (*Op. cit.*, at 355.)

The foregoing position has generally been that enunciated by the courts that have considered the issue. In *Nobs Chem. v. Koppers Co.* (616 F.2d 212, 215 [5th Cir. 1980]), the court (after observing the lack of "any law directly on point") limited damages on a breach of contract for the sale of chemicals to that provided in UCC 2-706. It heavily relied on the policy provision set forth in UCC 1-106(1) that "[t]he remedies provided by this Act shall be liberally administered to the end that the aggrieved party may be put in as good a position as if the other party had fully performed," concluding that: "No one insists, and we do not think they could, that the difference between the fallen market price and the contract price is necessary to compensate the plaintiffs for the breach. Had the transaction been completed, their 'benefit of the bargain' would not have been affected by the fall in market price, and they would not have experienced the windfall they otherwise would receive if the market price-contract price rule contained in § 2.708(a) is followed." (Supra, at 215; accord, H-W-H Cattle Co. v. Schroeder, 767 F.2d 437, 440 [8th Cir. 1985] [where the admonition of UCC 1-106 carried the day, the court finding that the section suggested that it "should look through the form of a transaction to its substance when necessary to fulfill the parties' expectations expressed in the contract"]; Coast Trading Co. v. Cudahy Co., 592 F2d 1074 [9th Cir. 1979]; Union Carbide Corp. v. Consumers Power Co., 636 F. Supp. 1498, 1501 [ED Mich. 1986] [where it was stated that UCC 2-708 did "not authorize awards of damages which put the seller in a better position than performance would have put them"].)

*   *   *

Plaintiff asserts that the foregoing cases are inapposite because New York legislative history calls for a different result. This argument is based on the 1956 New York Law Revision Commission (Appendix IV, at 396) recommendation to delete language in the draft of UCC 2-703(e) that would have limited UCC 2-708 to situations where the "goods have not been resold." This recommendation was apparently accepted by the Commissioners on Uniform State Laws, and hence the Code in New York, and elsewhere does not contain such language. This is hardly reason to call for an interpretation of the Code in New York different from that in other States.

In explaining this deletion, White and Summers state: "It is possible that the New York Law Revision Commission had in mind the seller who would not receive a windfall by suing under 2-708(1) and simply wanted to make it clear that a seller who makes a good faith attempt to comply with 2-706 but fails may then resort to 2-708(1). Nothing in their report suggests that they considered the case in which 2-706 recovery would be small because the seller sold at a price very near to the contract price yet the contract-market differential under 2-708 would be large." (Op. cit., at 354.) In B & R Textile Corp. v. Rothman Indus. (101 Misc. 2d 98 [Civ. Ct., NY County 1979]), UCC 2-708 was used in the type of situation contemplated by the authors. There damages were measured by that section because a UCC 2-706 recovery was not permissible due to the seller's failure to give the required notice of intention to resell. In that case, however, damages were the same under either measure as the market price was found to be the same as the resale price.

Further, Official Comment 2 under UCC 2-706 states that "[f]ailure to act properly under this section deprives the seller of the measure of damages here provided and relegates him to that provided in Section 2-708" (emphasis supplied), thus implying that it was contemplated that UCC 2-708 recoveries would be less than the contract-resale price differential authorized in UCC 2-706. Moreover, if UCC 2-708 could not be employed if the goods had been sold, a merchant who sells from inventory would lose his profit if required to reduce damages recoverable from a defaulting buyer by the amount of the sale price of the item when sold to another customer. Thus, in Neri v. Retail Mar. Corp. (30 NY2d 393, 400 [1972]), the Court of Appeals, in allowing a UCC 2-708(2) recovery of lost profits by a retailer of boats, quoted the following from an illustration contained in HAWKLAND, SALES AND BULK SALES (1958 ed): "Thus, if an automobile dealer agrees to sell a car to a buyer at the standard price of $2000, a breach by the buyer injures the dealer, even though he is able to sell the automobile to another for $2000. If the dealer has an inexhaustable supply of cars, the resale to replace the breaching buyer costs the dealer a sale, because, had the breaching buyer performed, the dealer would have made two sales instead of one. The buyer's breach, in such a case, depletes the dealer's sales to the extent of one, and the measure of damages should be the dealer's profit on one sale."

Thus, it is clear that the deletion of the proposed condition for the use of UCC 2-708 does not mean that the drafters of the Code contemplated the type of recovery sought by plaintiff herein.

Plaintiff, in essence, wishes to be accorded the same treatment as the car dealer in Professor Hawkland's illustration. However, there are significant differences that warrant the court declining such application. Here plaintiff was selling to Esso Sapa a specific cargo aboard a specific vessel, and thus the gasoline aboard that ship may be considered as goods identified (*see,* UCC 2-501[1][a]) to a broken contract.

On page two of plaintiff's initial memorandum of law it is stated: "After unsuccessfully attempting to convince [defendant] to honor its contract, [plaintiff] scrambled to find a new buyer and, on July 17, after feverish, lengthy and deliberate negotiations, concluded a sale to Esso Sapa." On page 348 of the deposition of plaintiff's witness he testified that, in seeking to sell the gasoline to a representative of Esso Sapa, "I asked him to buy the cargo."

These statements are illustrative of the fact that although gasoline of the type involved in the action is fungible, and thus may be purchased in the marketplace by anyone (including traders such as plaintiff) in a position to finance the transaction, the sale here to Esso Sapa was clearly a substitute for the one plaintiff claims it actually contracted for with defendant.

If plaintiff's damages are measured in accordance with UCC 2-706, it would be receiving the benefit reasonably to be expected when it entered into the alleged contract with defendant. Granting it the approximately $3,000,000 additional recovery that it seeks would result in a windfall which cannot be said to have been in the contemplation of the parties at the time of their negotiations, and would be inconsistent with the policy of the Code as expressed in UCC 1-106.

Accordingly, the court concludes that the proper interrelationship of sections 2-706 and 2-708 is that summarized by White and Summers above and followed in the cases cited. Thus, in the event plaintiff prevails and establishes a breach of contract at trial, its damages will be measured in accordance with section 2-706.

The situation would be different if plaintiff's sale were from its inventory (in which case it would be treated as the car dealer mentioned above), or if it had already contracted to sell the product to Esso Sapa, or perhaps even if it was then actually engaged in negotiations for trades in this type of gasoline. However, no such claim is made. The statement in plaintiff's reply memorandum of law that "in all likelihood, [plaintiff] would have negotiated such a sale [to Esso Sapa] even in the absence of [defendant's] breach" is not supported by any facts in the record, as there are no allegations that plaintiff had any negotiations then pending for the sale of this type of gasoline with Esso Sapa or any other party. This is simply a case where plaintiff, in an effort to mitigate its damages, went out and made a sale of a specific identified cargo of gasoline aboard a vessel then proceeding to New York.

The motions for partial summary judgment are decided in accordance with the foregoing.

QUESTIONS

1. The *Tesoro* court relies principally on § 1-106 [now § 1-305], and previous cases that have relied on this provision, to justify its determination that the plaintiff is limited to resale damages under § 2-706. Does this provide a definitive rule, or will future courts be required to balance the individual facts of cases before them?

2. The *Tesoro* court distinguishes Tesoro from Professor Hawkland's hypothetical car dealer that has an inventory of goods, suggesting that Tesoro might have been able to recover under § 2-708 if it was selling oil out of inventory that can be replenished.

What is the basis for making this distinction? How would you characterize a seller such as the car dealer? Is there a statutory basis for concluding that a seller in the car dealer's position should not be compensated under § 2-706 on the basis of a resale?

3. There clearly are at least some situations recognized in the current law where a seller "elects" a remedy by its actions. If the seller does not meet the requirements of a particular remedies section because of its actions, it will be precluded from pursuing that remedy. The *Tesoro* court discussed the *B&R Textile Corp.* case, which held that a seller that resells goods but fails to comply with the procedural requirements of § 2-706 will not be entitled to damages under § 2-706. This result follows the direction of § 2-706, Comment 2, that a seller's failure "to act properly under this section deprives the seller of the measure of damages here provided and relegates him to that provided in Section 2-708."

d.   Limiting seller's damages to losses that could not have been avoided by reasonable resale

You will recall from Contracts class that there is a general principle of "mitigation of damages," which provides that a party suffering a breach may not recover damages for loss "that the injured party could have avoided without undue risk, burden or humiliation." RESTATEMENT (SECOND) CONTRACTS § 350(1). If a breaching buyer is able to prove that the seller could have resold the goods to another buyer for the contract price, but chose not to do so, should the seller be precluded from recovering full contract-market damages? Consider the following case.

SCHIAVI MOBILE HOMES, INC. v. GIRONDA
Maine Supreme Judicial Court
463 A.2d 722 (1983)

NICHOLS, JUSTICE.

The principal issue in this appeal involves a retailer's duty to mitigate damages following a customer's breach of a contract for the purchase from the retailer of a mobile home.

On January 23, 1979, the Defendants, Frank Gironda, Jr., and Patricia Gironda, signed a contract with the Plaintiff, Schiavi Mobile Homes, Inc., for the purchase from that corporation of a yellow, two-bedroom mobile home for a total purchase price of $23,028.69. The Defendants paid a $1,000 deposit.

After undergoing difficulties — medical, financial, and marital — the Defendants breached the purchase contract. In September 1979, Howard Palmer, an agent of Schiavi, contacted Frank Gironda, Sr., the father of Frank, Jr. Palmer asked if Frank, Jr., was still planning to purchase the mobile home. Frank Gironda, Sr., responded that because of his son's problems and his son's relocation to the West Coast, he did not know what he planned to do. Frank, Sr., then asked Palmer if he could purchase the home so his son would not lose his deposit. He expressed a willingness to mortgage his own home for this purpose. Palmer responded that this would not be necessary.

On November 7, 1979, the Plaintiff sold this mobile home to a third party for $22,000, and then commenced this action in Superior Court, Oxford County, seeking from the Defendants $4,800 in lost profits and interest expense allegedly incurred as a result of the Defendants' breach. Following a jury-waived trial, the Superior Court awarded the Plaintiff judgment in the amount of $759.45.[23] Thereupon the Plaintiff appealed,

---

[23] [1] This judgment reflected the retention by the Plaintiff of the $1,000 deposit. The Superior Court calculated damages by subtracting the resale price of the home ($22,000) from the contract price ($23,028.69) and then adding in incidental damages for floor-plan interest accruing from the breach ($731.45). We note that these figures yield a damage amount of $1,760.14, which after subtracting the deposit, should have resulted in

asserting that it was entitled to recover lost profits and greater incidental damages. The Defendants cross-appealed, contending first, that the sale contract was unconscionable and invalid, and second, that the Superior Court erred in awarding any damages in light of the Plaintiff's failure to mitigate. We deny the appeal and sustain the cross-appeal.

The determinative issue in this case concerns the retailer's alleged failure to mitigate damages. At trial only one witness, Frank Gironda, Sr., was called. The father testified as to his conversation with Palmer, in which he expressed his willingness to purchase the mobile home. Although admitting that he did not at that time have ready cash sufficient to cover the cost of the home, he testified that he owned a $30,000 house free and clear and had been ready to mortgage it for that purpose. Questioned by the court as to his willingness to purchase the mobile home in place of his son, the witness testified that he told Palmer that he was willing to buy the mobile home if his son could not be found. He said, "That's the way we operate in our family, Your Honor."

The Plaintiff presented no evidence on the issue of mitigation. After argument by counsel, the Superior Court ruled from the bench that the Plaintiff had not failed to properly mitigate damages, because the offer by the Defendant's father was conditional and vague.[24] In so ruling, the court misapplied the doctrine of mitigation.

It has long been the rule in this state that when a contract is breached, the nonbreaching party has an affirmative duty to take reasonable steps to mitigate his damages. As early as 1830 this Court declared that if a party "has it in his power to take measures, by which his loss may be less aggravated, this will be expected of him." *Miller v. Mariner's Church*, 7 Me. 51, 55 (1830). Similarly, in *Grindle v. Eastern Express Company* we stated that:

> [T]he law makes it incumbent upon a person for whose injury another is responsible, to use ordinary care and take all reasonable measures within his knowledge and power to avoid the loss and render the consequences as light as may be; and it will not permit him to recover for such losses as by such care and means might have been prevented.

67 Me. 317, 325 (1877).

The common law duty to mitigate damages survives Maine's enactment of the Uniform Commercial Code in 1963. While the U.C.C. does not explicitly require the mitigation of damages, it does provide that "principles of law and equity" not displaced shall supplement the Code's provisions. 11 M.R.S.A. § 1-103 (1964). The duty to mitigate is also implicit in the Code's broad requirements of good faith, commercial reasonableness and fair dealing. *See American National Bank and Trust Company of Chicago v. Weyerhaeuser Company*, 692 F.2d 455, 468 (7th Cir. 1982); 11 M.R.S.A. §§ 1-203, 2-103 (1964); *see also* 11 M.R.S.A. § 1-106, Comment 1 (1964) ("damages must be minimized").

The touchstone of the duty to mitigate is reasonableness. The nonbreaching party need only take reasonable steps to minimize his losses; he is not required to unreasonably expose himself to risk, humiliation or expense.

In the instant case the Superior Court never focused directly on the reasonableness of the Plaintiff's failure to pursue the offer of Frank Gironda, Sr., to purchase the mobile home in the place of his son. Instead the court solely concerned itself with the legal sufficiency of the father's offer. This approach was fraught with error.

First, the father's announced willingness to purchase the mobile home was conditioned only on his son not being found; that is, upon there being a breach of the son's contractual obligation. That was the same contingency from which arose the Plaintiff's

---

a judgment of $760.14. The court also awarded the Plaintiff $500 in interest, costs and attorney's fees.

[24] [2] The court ruled: "I'm going to find for Schiavi on this issue. It is conditional. Even if it weren't, I think this is similar to purchase and sale where you have an actual intent before suing to recover damages. You can't do business on this kind of vague promises and understanding otherwise nobody would know where he stands."

duty to mitigate. As soon as that duty to mitigate arose, the Plaintiff had available to it a then unconditional willingness on the father's part to buy the mobile home.

Second, the father asked the Plaintiff if he could purchase the mobile home in place of his son, and at the time he was ready, willing and able to make the purchase. We cannot agree with the Superior Court's conclusion that the father's offer was too vague to have constituted the foundation for a binding contract when accepted by the Plaintiff.

In any event, the duty to mitigate is more than just a duty to accept legally enforceable offers. Upon learning of the Defendants' breach, the Plaintiff was obligated to take reasonable affirmative measures to keep its losses to a minimum. Palmer's conversation with Frank Gironda, Sr., in September, 1979, revealed that he had a party willing to pay the full price of the mobile home. Regardless of whether the father actually made a valid "offer," the retailer had a duty to pursue this opportunity to minimize the effects of the breach. Instead, the Plaintiff waited another two months and then sold the home for $1,028.69 less than Frank Gironda, Sr., was willing to pay.

There is no evidence in the record that the Plaintiff's failure to sell to its customer's father rested on any legitimate ground. Because the Plaintiff did not take reasonable measures to mitigate its damages, we conclude that the Superior Court erred in awarding it damages based on the ultimate reduction in the selling price of the mobile home.

This case must be returned to that court for a recomputation of damages.

Our conclusion that the Plaintiff did not properly mitigate its damages disposes of the Plaintiff's primary argument on appeal, that the Superior Court erred in not awarding it lost profits under 11 M.R.S.A. § 2-708(2) as a "lost-volume seller."[25] In order to minimize its damages, the Plaintiff should have sold the mobile home to Frank Gironda, Sr. Had it done so there would have been no lost-volume potential inasmuch as it is clear from the record that the father was interested in purchasing the home only because his son was unable to do so. A sale to Frank Gironda, Sr., would not have occasioned any lost profits. *See* Sebert, Remedies Under Article Two of the Uniform Commercial Code: An Agenda for Review, 130 U. Pa. L. Rev. 360, 387–88 (1981).

Accordingly, because the Plaintiff failed to sell the home to Frank Gironda, Sr., it cannot now be heard to complain that its sale to a third party resulted in lost profits. We leave for another day the question of the validity of lost-volume recovery.

The Plaintiff also contends that the Superior Court erred in not awarding it "floor-plan interest"[26] for the entire period between the date of breach (April 20, 1979) and the date of resale (November 7, 1979). The court did award the Plaintiff floor-plan interest from April 20 to August 17, 1979, the date on which the Plaintiff paid off a loan which it had taken out to purchase the mobile home in question. The Plaintiff claims that it was entitled to floor-plan interest on the use of its own money tied up in the mobile home after the loan had been repaid; that is, from August 17 to November 7, 1979.

We note initially that the Plaintiff's failure to sell the home to Frank Gironda, Sr., in September bars recovery of any interest expense incurred after that point in time. Thus, the only relevant period is from the date the loan was repaid, August 17, to the date in September when the Plaintiff turned down the father's offer.

Several of the seller's remedies provided under the Uniform Commercial Code for

---

[25] [6] Stated generally, the concept of lost-volume posits that a seller of goods who conducts a resale following a breach will not be "made whole" if only allowed to recover the difference between the contract price and resale price when the resale is made to a second customer, at the expense of a second sale. The concept presupposes a situation in which supply outstrips demand and in which the second customer would have been successfully solicited by the seller had the original breach not occurred. Assuming these conditions, the seller is awarded lost profits as compensation for his "loss" of a sale to one customer. [Citations omitted.]

[26] [7] "Floor-plan interest" is the interest a retailer pays in borrowing money to purchase an item it plans to sell, the loan being secured by the item on the retailer's "floor."

breach of contract permit the recovery of incidental damages. *See* 11 M.R.S.A. §§ 2-706, 2-708, 2-709 (1964). The Code defines "seller's incidental damages" as follows:

> Incidental damages to an aggrieved seller include any commercially reasonable charges, expenses or commissions incurred in stopping delivery, in the transportation, care and custody of goods after the buyer's breach, in connection with return or resale of the goods or otherwise resulting from the breach.

11 M.R.S.A. § 2-710.

While we would agree that floor-plan interest actually paid by a seller after a breach may constitute recoverable incidental damages . . . we cannot read the phrase "commercially reasonable charges, expenses or commissions" as including wholly hypothetical charges that a seller would assert as arising out of the use of his own funds to pay off a loan. The Official Comment to section 2-710 states that the section "intends to allow all commercially reasonable *expenditures* made by the seller." (Emphasis added). Interest a seller would purport to pay itself is not an expenditure.[27] Accordingly, in denying the Plaintiff floor-plan interest extending beyond the actual payment of such interest, the Superior Court committed no error.

* * *

Remanded for further proceedings consistent with the opinion herein. All concurring.

QUESTIONS

1. Is the court correct that the common law "duty" to mitigate losses supplements Article 2 by operation of § 1-103(b)? If this specific point was litigated, how would you argue in favor of the court's result, and how would you argue against the result?

2. Assume that a court finds that the common law "duty" of mitigation has been displaced by Article 2. How would you argue on behalf of the defendant that Article 2 directly provides that a seller's damages should be reduced to the extent that the seller could have minimized its losses by reasonable actions and without undue burden?

PROBLEM 7-12

Simply Luxurious is a retail furniture store. Retail price markups on furniture average 40–60%, and so each retailer has a fair amount of flexibility in pricing its merchandise. Bernard agreed to purchase a leather chaise lounge from Simply for $10,000. The chaise lounge was signed and numbered (1,264/5,000) by its postmodern designer, Dewey Cheetum, and was considered a collector's item. Subsequently, Bernard discovered on the Internet that other retailers were selling chaise lounges from the same limited series for $8,000, including shipping to his home. The wholesale price of the chaise lounges to all dealers in the United States is $5,750. Bernard promptly repudiated his agreement with Simply and purchased another chaise lounge in the series (3,248/5,000) from a different retailer.

First Scenario. Simply had three chaise lounges in its inventory when Bernard repudiated. Over the next few months, Simply sold all three chaise lounges for $10,000 to three different buyers. Simply then ordered three more chaise lounges but was informed that the last of the 5,000 units had been sold. Assuming that Bernard breached his agreement to purchase the chaise lounge, what damages should Simply recover?

Second Scenario. Simply decides that the value of the chaise lounges will increase in the future, and that displaying the chaise lounge in its front window is a good way to

---

[27] [8] Taken to its logical limits, the Plaintiff's theory would allow a seller to recover as incidental damages interest on the value of any goods later resold whether or not prior financing was involved. Section 2-710 does not go this far.

encourage potential customers to come into its store. Consequently, Simply decides not to sell the chaise lounge numbered 1,264, although several customers offer to pay $10,000 to purchase it from Simply. Assuming that Bernard breached his agreement to purchase the chaise lounge, and that at the time of trial Simply still has possession of the chaise lounge, what damages should Simply recover?

4. Seller's Action for the Price Following Acceptance

We have seen that, prior to the buyer's acceptance of the goods, the seller has the right to "specific performance" in the form of an action for the contract price only under certain limited conditions. Once the buyer accepts the goods, however, an action for the price is the only appropriate remedy. Under § 2-607(3), the buyer is obligated "to pay at the contract rate for any goods accepted." The price is payable even if the seller has breached the agreement, although by complying with the requirements of § 2-717, the buyer may properly deduct from the price any damages that it claims from the seller for an alleged breach of the same contract. Consequently, once the seller has delivered goods and they have been accepted by the buyer, the seller's only possible loss is the buyer's failure to pay the price of the goods.

Section 2-709(1)(a) simply states that the seller "may recover" the price of "goods accepted," and so it is not immediately clear that this is an exclusive remedy for cases involving accepted goods. However, the fundamental principle of § 1-305 that the party suffering a breach should "be put in as good a position as if the other party had fully performed" compels the conclusion that the seller is entitled to no more and no less than a judgment for the unpaid contract price, along with any incidental losses arising from the failure of payment. There is no basis for an award of damages calculated with regard to market prices or expected profit under the contract in these circumstances.

In response to an attempt by a seller to obtain greater advantage under the lost profit formula of § 2-708(2) by recovering the full value of (then) worthless coal deposits while also retaining ownership of the deposits, a trial court properly limited the seller's recovery to the contract price and recognized the buyer's right to the coal deposits:

> On reflection, this court thinks the flaw lies with Decker's assumption that as a wronged seller it can freely choose whichever remedy offers the largest possible recovery. Rather the UCC's remedial scheme for sellers establishes something of a hierarchy of remedies tied to particular frequently recurring fact patterns. In a given case, one is ordinarily obligated to use the remedy which best fits the facts of that case and which produces a result which is in line with the broad remedial goals of the UCC: that the aggrieved party be put in as good a position as if the other party had fully performed, but no better. [citing the *Nobs Chemical* case] . . . In the instant case, those considerations mean that Decker is limited to the recovery available under § 2-709, the action for the price.

Commonwealth Edison Co. v. Decker Coal Co., 653 F. Supp. 841, 843 (N.D. Ill. 1987). This case presents yet another example of the limitations on the scope of the seller's right to "elect remedies."

The seller's right to obtain the price of accepted goods leaves the buyer with the burden of dealing with the goods. This is true even if the buyer no longer has any use for the goods, which may very well be the case if the goods are nonconforming. In response to a buyer arguing that the seller has an obligation to mitigate damages by accepting a return of the goods for credit to the buyer's account, one court held that "there is no obligation under § 2-709 on the part of the seller to accept a return of previously accepted goods." *Siemens Energy & Automation, Inc. v. Coleman Elec. Supply Co.*, 46 F. Supp. 2d 217, 219 (E.D.N.Y. 1999) (quoting *Unlaub Co. v. Sexton*, 568 F.2d 72, 76 n.3 (8th Cir. 1977) and other cases). Another case offered two rationales for this result. The majority opinion found that the general common law duty of mitigation has been displaced and superceded by § 2-709(a)(1) which does not require mitigation, while the concurring justice found that there would be no common law duty to mitigate anyway when a party is suing only for the agreed return under a contract. *See F & P Builders v. Lowe's of Texas, Inc.*, 786 S.W.2d 502, 502–03 (Tex. App. 1990).

One might assume that this rule is largely academic, since a seller presumably would be very interested in receiving the goods in question to offset its loss rather than relying exclusively on a lawsuit for damages against a buyer that may be experiencing financial distress. However, the *Siemens* case illustrates two important reasons why the seller may not be interested in the goods and why an apparently inefficient rule that forces the buyer to deal with the goods may make sense. First, the seller may feel confident that sufficient assets exist to pay the contract price if it has secured payment of the contract price with personal guaranties by principals in the buyer's business. *See id.* at 218 (describing personal guaranties for the benefit of the seller, albeit only in an amount equal to half of the outstanding debt). More importantly, the accepted goods become part of the buyer's inventory and are likely to be subject to an after-acquired inventory clause in a security agreement between the buyer and its lender. This would give the lender priority over the goods in the event that it seeks to assert its rights over collateral to secure its loan. As the court explained,

> Here, had Siemens accepted the return of goods which were subject to a perfected security interest, Siemens would have opened itself up to liability for conversion, clearly an undue risk [that eliminates any generalized argument for a duty to mitigate]. Case law is full of suits by secured creditors against manufacturers and suppliers for wrongly converting the creditors' collateral. In those cases, the manufacturers accepted returned goods upon which the secured creditors had obtained liens.

Id. at 219. We will see in the next section that floating lien creditors can trump the right of a seller to reclaim the goods. Sellers, then, should exercise caution before agreeing to a return of accepted goods in satisfaction of some or all of the outstanding price owed by the buyer.

One final issue has proved somewhat more problematic for courts. In addition to the contract price, § 2-709(1) provides that a seller is entitled to recover "any incidental damages under" § 2-710. When a buyer refuses to pay the price, the seller justifiably will demand damages to compensate for the loss caused by the delay in payment. This loss generally is quantified as interest on the unpaid price. However, courts differ as to whether interest on a liquidated sum owed under a contract is compensable as incidental damages, or whether interest is better classified as consequential damages, to which sellers are not entitled. The definition of incidental damages is broadly phrased, including any damages "otherwise resulting from the breach," but the Comment suggests that the purpose is to compensate the seller for out of pocket expenditures relating to the breach. Regardless, even if the court deems market rate interest on the unpaid price to be consequential damages and therefore unavailable to sellers, courts generally will still award statutory prejudgment and post-judgment interest as a matter of right. *See Firwood Mfg. Co. v. General Tire, Inc.*, 96 F.3d 163, 172–73 (6th Cir. 1996) ("Firwood was entitled to claim statutory interest from the date on which suit was filed . . . even if, as a seller, it was not entitled to interest as a measure of damages under the U.C.C.").

PROBLEM 7-13

Brilliant Photoshop purchases supplies from Sureshot Photographic Wholesalers on 30-day credit. Brilliant's business has been declining steadily, and near the end of July it becomes apparent that it will not be able to make the coming month's payroll. On July 28 Brilliant receives a quarterly shipment of supplies from Sureshot worth $10,000. Brilliant's owner calls Sureshot that same day, states that he has inspected the goods and discovered that they are nonconforming, advises Sureshot that he is rejecting the shipment, and states that he will hold the goods for Sureshot to come and pick them up.

Sureshot picks up the goods and discovers that they are conforming. Sureshot brings suit against Brilliant for the $10,000 unpaid contract price and offers to return the goods to Brilliant upon payment of the price.

Argue on behalf of Brilliant that Sureshot should not prevail in an action for the price.

You should note that some courts have held that Article 2 distinguishes between whether the buyer has "effectively" rejected the goods, and whether the buyer has "rightfully" rejected the goods.

5. Seller's Right to Reclaim Goods from Buyer

If the buyer defaults on its obligation to pay for goods that it has accepted, the seller may not be comforted by the knowledge that it can bring a lawsuit for damages. After all, the buyer's default most likely stems from the buyer's financial difficulties, and therefore the prospect of recovering damages is uncertain. Similarly, if the buyer has accepted goods on credit and the seller then learns that the buyer was insolvent when it received the goods, the seller will not want to wait for the insolvent buyer to default on its payment obligation before seeking relief. In both of these situations, Article 2 incorporates the seller's common law right to "reclaim" the goods from the buyer. This right of reclamation has the potential to be a valuable remedy for the seller, since the seller is in the best position to convert the goods into cash by reselling them to another customer. Unfortunately, Article 2 is uncharacteristically clumsy and opaque in setting forth the seller's right to reclaim goods from the buyer. The rights of a credit seller to reclaim goods from an insolvent buyer are set forth in § 2-702, and the rights of a cash seller to reclaim goods from a buyer that has failed to pay for them are set forth in § 2-507(2). After first reviewing these two different statutory bases for reclamation, we compare the reclamation rights of credit-sellers and cash-sellers with respect to several important issues that arise in the typical case. You might want to begin by looking at the summary problem at the end of these materials, and work through the problem as you read the materials.

a. Distinguishing credit-sellers and cash-sellers

If a seller has tendered goods to a buyer on credit and then discovers that the buyer was insolvent when it received the goods, the seller faces a substantial risk that it will not receive payment. Consequently, even though payment is not yet due under the contract, § 2-702(2) permits the credit-seller to reclaim the goods, subject to a number of restrictions. In the words of one court, reclamation "is a narrow and unique remedy" that imposes a "stringent" burden of proof on the credit-seller. *Scotts Co. v. Hechinger Co.* (*In re* Hechinger Inv. Co. of Del., Inc.), 274 B.R. 402, 405 (Bankr. D. Del. 2001).

A seller that tenders goods in exchange for immediate payment would appear to have no worries about the buyer's performance. However, some payment mechanisms do not result in an immediate transfer of cash to the seller. For example, the buyer is entitled to deliver a check upon delivery of the goods, "unless the seller demands payment in legal tender and gives any extension of time reasonably necessary to procure it." § 2-511(2). Payment by check is only conditional, however, until the check clears the bank collection process. § 2-511(3). Thus, if a seller tenders goods in exchange for a check, only to find several days later that the buyer has insufficient funds in its account to cover the check, the seller has not been "paid" for the goods. Section 2-507(2) provides that the buyer's "right as against the seller to retain or dispose of" the goods tendered by the seller "is conditional upon his making the payment due." Thus, if the buyer's check fails to clear after it is deposited by the seller, the buyer loses its right to retain possession of the goods. This is a rather cumbersome way of saying that the cash-seller has a right to reclaim the goods from a buyer that fails to pay upon tender of the goods as required by the contract. *See* Comment 3 ("This subsection (2) codifies the cash seller's right of reclamation which is in the nature of a lien."); *Citizens Bank of Roseville v. Taggart*, 143 Cal. App. 3d 318, 191 Cal. Rptr. 729, 730–31 (1983) ("The right of a cash seller to reclaim goods sold in a 'bad check' transaction is not specifically treated in the code. However, a reclamation right in a cash seller situation, has been held to be inherent in sections 2-507(2) and 2-511(3). . . . These provisions, construed together, evidence a legislative intent that a buyer cannot retain and, conversely, a seller has the right to reclaim goods sold in a cash transaction if the buyer's check is dishonored.").

b.   Limitations on the seller's right to reclaim goods

i.   Time limit on the seller's right to reclaim

Under § 2-702(2), the credit-seller must exercise its right of reclamation by making a demand[28] within ten days after the buyer receives the goods on credit, unless the seller can prove that a "misrepresentation of solvency has been made to the particular seller in writing within three months before delivery," in which case the ten-day limitation does not apply. The courts have interpreted the ten-day limit strictly, and so the seller's right of reclamation is significantly limited to unusual situations in which it learns of the buyer's insolvency soon after delivery and then acts immediately. *See, e.g., Eastman Cutting Room Sales Corp. v. Ottenheimer & Co.*, 221 Ga. App. 659, 472 S.E.2d 494, 494 (1996) (because "receipt" is defined in § 2-103(1)(c) as taking physical possession of the goods, the court held that the seller could not reclaim goods that were completely delivered on May 26, but not installed until June 28, despite seller's demand for reclamation within ten days of the installation); *In re Samuels & Co., Inc. v. Mahon*, 526 F.2d 1238 (5th Cir. 1976) ("[A]lthough the code expressly grants a credit seller the right and power to reclaim goods from a breaching buyer, the right is triggered only by specific and limited circumstances; it can be asserted only if an exacting procedure is followed. . . . The code's ten-day provision is an absolute requirement. There is no exception in the Code Sections or Comments, express or implied, to the statutory period.")

In contrast, § 2-507(2) does not expressly place any time limit on the cash-seller's right to reclaim the goods. Unfortunately, this clear difference in the statutory language was obscured by the original Comment 3, which stated that the ten-day limitation of § 2-702 should also be applied to cash sellers under § 2-507(2). Many courts followed the direction in the original Comment and applied the ten-day limit to cash-sellers, *see Holiday Rambler Corp. v. First Nat'l Bank & Trust Co.*, 723 F.2d 1449, 1452 (10th Cir. 1983), but several courts read the statutory language as written and recognized that cash-sellers were treated differently under common law rules. *See Burk v. Emmick*, 637 F.2d 1172, 1176 (8th Cir. 1980) ("where a cash seller reclaims goods sold to a breaching buyer, the only limitation imposed upon the seller's right is a reasonableness requirement"). In 1990, the Permanent Editorial Board revised Comment 3 to make clear that § 2-507(2) imposes no fixed time limit within which cash sellers must reclaim the goods. The Comment currently reads:

> Should the seller after making such a conditional delivery fail to follow up his rights, the condition is waived. This subsection (2) codifies the cash seller's right of reclamation which is in the nature of a lien. There is no specific time limit for a cash seller to exercise the right of reclamation. However, the right will be defeated by delay causing prejudice to the buyer, waiver, estoppel, or ratification of the buyer's right to retain possession. Common law rules and precedents

---

[28] If the buyer is in bankruptcy, then the credit-seller must satisfy the requirements of § 546(c) of the Bankruptcy Code, which requires that the demand be in writing. There are other differences between § 2-702(2) and § 546(c). One question, as yet undecided, is whether § 546(c) established a right of reclamation which is not dependent upon the seller's compliance with § 2-702(2).

governing such principles are applicable (Section 1-103).

§ 2-507, comment 3. This clarification recognizes that when a cash-seller discovers that payment has not been made (because the buyer's check bounces), it is entitled to greater protection than a credit seller that has become insecure about receiving payment. However, even the cash-seller remains subject to the common law "reasonable time" limitation.

ii. The seller may only reclaim the goods tendered under the contract

Reclaiming credit-sellers face an additional time constraint since they are entitled to reclaim only the precise goods sold to the buyer. This rule is reflected in the statutory language of § 2-702(2), stating that the credit-seller may reclaim "the goods" in question. Thus, one court found "that where a supplier has sold and delivered raw materials on credit to an insolvent buyer, and on the date written demand is made for reclamation the raw materials have been manufactured into a finished product, UCC § 2-702 does not grant the supplier the right to reclaim the finished product." *In re Wheeling-Pittsburgh Steel Corp.*, 74 B.R. 656, 658 (Bankr. W.D. Pa. 1987) (refusing seller's right to reclaim 1,964 tons of coal that had been manufactured into coke, but recognizing seller's right to reclaim 286 tons of unprocessed coal that remained on top of an undifferentiated pile of coal in buyer's yard).

The seller's rights under § 2-507(2) are phrased as a limitation on the buyer's right to retain or dispose of the goods, rather than as a right of the seller to reclaim the goods. Although not expressly stated, it seems clear from the context that the cash-seller's rights similarly are limited to the goods tendered under the contract, and do not extend to any goods manufactured with the contract goods. Thus, it appears that all sellers must act quickly, because they will have no reclamation rights as to goods delivered under the contract that have been processed or manufactured into finished goods.

iii. Reclamation as an exclusive remedy

Under § 2-702(3), a "successful reclamation of goods [by credit-sellers] excludes all other remedies with respect to them." Comment 3 explains that the "preferential treatment" accorded to the seller by this section, which permits the seller to obtain a remedy prior to the price coming due, justifies making the remedy exclusive. In reality, this limitation is not likely to prejudice the credit-seller. Most credit-sellers are unsecured, and so, if the insolvent buyer proceeds to bankruptcy, they are likely to receive very little payment, if any, on their claim for damages.

In contrast, § 2-507(2) is silent as to whether reclamation by cash-sellers is an exclusive remedy. Consider whether the following case is persuasive in holding that cash-sellers who successfully reclaim goods under the contract are not precluded from pursuing other available remedies.

BURK v. EMMICK
United States Court of Appeals, Eighth Circuit
637 F.2d 1172 (1980)

HEANEY, Circuit J.

I

This appeal arises out of a transaction in which plaintiff Willard Burk contracted to sell approximately 950 head of yearling steers to defendant Bob Emmick, d/b/a Emmick Cattle Company. The terms of the sales contract provided that the buyer would make a $15,000 down payment and tender the balance upon delivery.

The contract was amended, postponing the delivery date and modifying the manner in which payment would be made. The amended agreement called for payment of a major portion of the purchase price at delivery by sight draft drawn upon the co-defendant, Northwestern National Bank of Sioux City. The balance of the purchase price was to be covered by the buyer's personal note. Just prior to delivery, the defendant Bank orally guaranteed to the seller that funds were available to cover the sight draft so that delivery could be made. The seller made delivery, but the sight draft was not accepted by the Bank and the buyer's personal note was never honored.

Subsequent to these transactions, the seller reclaimed the cattle and resold them for less than the original contract price. Thereafter, the seller sued the buyer in the United States District Court for the Northern District of Iowa, alleging breach of contract and fraud. The seller also sued the Bank on a promissory estoppel theory, reasoning that he detrimentally relied upon the Bank's oral assurance that funds were available to cover the sight draft, thus inducing the seller to make delivery and suffer pecuniary injury. The case was tried to a jury and a verdict was returned on the seller's breach of contract claim against the buyer in the amount of $19,300. The jury also returned a verdict in the seller's favor against the Bank on the promissory estoppel claim in the amount of $24,700.

All parties filed post trial motions. The seller moved to amend the judgment by increasing the amount of the award. The buyer and the Bank moved for judgment notwithstanding the verdict, for a new trial, and to amend the judgment. All motions were denied, and all parties appealed. We affirm.

II

The buyer and the Bank argue that Iowa Code § 554.2702 controls this case. The buyer contends this section bars a seller who successfully reclaims goods from further recovering a deficiency judgment. The Bank agrees that section 2-702 applies, but asserts that because the seller failed to demand return of the goods within ten days of delivery, the reclamation was improper. The Bank asserts that it has an interest in the cattle superior to the unpaid seller based upon a preexisting security interest covering after-acquired property of the defendant buyer.

In resolving the questions posed by this appeal, we first determine the relative rights of the parties involved in this sales transaction.

[Ed. Note: The court first held that the bank was not a third-party purchaser for value in good faith, in light of the jury finding that the bank misled the seller. We will discuss the rights of good faith purchasers for value in the next section.]

*   *   *

B. The rights of the cash seller under the UCC.

Section 2-703 indexes the remedies available to a seller upon the buyer's breach. The right of reclamation is not specifically mentioned there. The cash seller's right to reclaim has been drawn from the language of sections 2-507 and 2-511.

Section 2-507(2) gave the seller in this case the right to reclaim the cattle which were sold and not paid for. The buyer's main contention is that once the seller had successfully reclaimed the goods, he could not also seek a deficiency judgment. The buyer asserts the election of remedies provision in section 2-702(3) is applicable to a cash seller's section 2-507 right of reclamation. We do not agree. There is nothing in the language of the Code or the Comments to suggest that the election of remedies provision applies to a cash seller's reclamation under section 2-507. In fact, the concept of election of remedies is foreign to the liberal remedial provisions intended by the drafters of the UCC. *See* § 2-703 Comment 1. *See also* 2 R. Anderson, Uniform Commercial Code, § 2-703:5 at 337 (1971).

The buyer also asserts that the seller failed to demand reclamation within ten days of delivery of the cattle. Some courts have decided that a cash seller's reclamation right is subject to the ten-day limitation provision covering credit sale transactions involving insolvent buyers under section 2-702, but those decisions are factually dissimilar. The courts that have imposed the ten-day limitation have concerned the respective rights of a good faith purchaser or trustee in bankruptcy and an unpaid seller. But here, a good faith purchaser is not involved. Nor are we faced with the conflicting interests of an unpaid seller and a trustee in bankruptcy representing the interests of a bankrupt's creditors. Rather, the conflict is between the unpaid cash seller and the breaching buyer, and the question is whether the seller may reclaim and recover a deficiency judgment from that buyer.

It is instructive to note that the buyer in the case at bar has never forcefully opposed the seller's right to reclaim; rather, it has focused its primary attention upon the seller's right to a deficiency. This is understandable in light of the fact that the buyer was not prejudiced by the seller's reclamation, improper or not. Had the seller not reclaimed the goods, he could have sued for the full contract price. *See* UCC §§ 2-703, 2-709.

Our holding is quite limited. We determine that as between the seller and the buyer, where a cash seller reclaims goods sold to a breaching buyer, the only limitation imposed upon the seller's right is a reasonableness requirement. Since we determine that the buyer was not prejudiced by the seller's delay in reclaiming the cattle, we find the seller's reclamation was not unreasonable.

Furthermore, the district court was correct in determining that section 2-702 did not properly apply to the instant case. By its very terms, that section applies when the seller discovers the buyer to be insolvent and when the underlying transaction is a credit sale. The transaction that gave rise to this lawsuit was a cash sale. As the district court reasoned, the fact that payment was made by a draft that was subsequently dishonored does not alter the nature of the underlying transaction. *See In re Helms Veneer Corp.*, 287 F. Supp. 840, 844 (W.D. Va. 1968).

The district court properly determined that section 2-703 controls this case. This section declares the right of the aggrieved seller to: (1) withhold delivery; (2) stop delivery by any bailee; (3) proceed under section 2-704; (4) resell and recover damages as provided in section 2-706; (5) recover damages for nonacceptance or the price; or (6) cancel. In this case, the seller properly chose the fourth alternative. This section's applicability to this case is highlighted by Official Comment 3, which provides: "In addition to the typical case of refusal to pay or default in payment, the language in the preamble, 'fails to make a payment due,' is intended to cover the dishonor of a check on due presentment, or the non-acceptance of a draft. . . ." UCC § 2-703 Official Comment 3.

In this case, when the draft was not accepted by the Bank, the seller chose to reclaim the cattle pursuant to section 2-507 and resell them. Section 2-703(d) allows the seller to recover a deficiency judgment upon a reasonable resale.

III

Finally, section 2-706 provides that the recoverable deficiency is the difference between the original contract price and the amount realized upon a commercially reasonable resale. The jury was properly instructed on the section 2-706 damage formula. The district court further instructed the jury that:

> in the event you find for the plaintiff Burk and against the defendant Emmick in Count I of the Complaint but find that the plaintiff Burk's resale of the cattle was not effected in good faith and in a commercially reasonable manner, the actual and compensatory damages to which the plaintiff Burk is entitled is the difference between the market price at the time and place for delivery and the unpaid contract price agreed upon by Burk and Emmick, together with any

incidental damages, but less expenses saved in consequence of buyer's breach.

If the measure of damages provided in the above paragraph is inadequate to put the seller in as good a position as full performance of the contract by the defendant Emmick would have done, then the measure of damages is the profit (including reasonable overhead) which the plaintiff Burk would have made from full performance by the defendant Emmick, together with any incidental damages and giving due allowance for costs reasonably incurred and due credit for payments or proceeds of resale.

This was a proper instruction and the jury could rationally have used this damage formula in arriving at its damage award. The award is supported in the record as a whole. A jury award may not be set aside unless it is flagrantly inadequate or not supported by the record. . . . Since we determine that such is not the case here, the jury's verdict stands as rendered.

QUESTIONS

1. The court concluded that the statutory language did not make reclamation an exclusive remedy for a cash seller, but what reasoning supports distinguishing a cash-seller from a credit-seller?

2. Why does the court calculate damages under § 2-706? Does the text of § 2-706 cover this situation? How would the court calculate damages if the reclaiming seller had retained the goods and not resold them?

iv. Third-party rights that supersede the seller's right of reclamation

Another significant limitation on the credit-seller's right of reclamation is found in § 2-702(3), which provides that the seller's right is "subject to the rights of a buyer in ordinary course or other good faith purchaser under this Article (Section 2-403)." Even if the credit-seller moves quickly to reclaim goods from an insolvent buyer, it might find that its interest has been rendered worthless due to a good faith purchase of the goods by a third party. Even if the goods have not been resold, they may be subject to the interests of the buyer's secured creditors.[29] The majority of courts have held that the buyer's floating lien creditors[30] meet the statutory definition of a good faith purchaser for value, and therefore, they conclude that the unsecured interests of a reclaiming seller are subordinated to creditors that have a valid security interest in the after-acquired inventory[31] of the buyer. *See United States Trust Co. v. Raritan River Steel Co. (In re American Spring Bed Mfg. Co.)*, 153 B.R. 365, 372 (Bankr. D. Mass. 1993) ("A prior perfected lien creditor is regarded as a good faith purchaser [the definition of which includes taking by lien], whose rights are superior to those of a reclaiming seller."). The rights of secured creditors are conditioned on good faith: recall that in *Burk v. Emmick, supra*, the Court held that the lender lost its status as a purchaser for

---

[29] The buyer's secured creditors would have rights in the buyer's assets to secure debts owed by the buyer to the secured party, as recognized in Article 9 of the UCC.

[30] A "floating lien creditor" acquires a security interest in the assets of the buyer-debtor as these assets change over time, without need to constantly update the list of assets. Any raw materials on hand, or inventory in stock, would likely be subject to a "floating lien," even though the raw materials and inventory are constantly being turned over and cannot be specifically identified as collateral at the time of the loan agreement.

[31] Section 9-204 makes clear that a floating lien creditor may acquire a security interest in assets that are acquired by the debtor after the creation of the security agreement. As explained in Official Comment 2: "This section adopts the principle of a 'continuing general lien' or 'floating lien.' It validates a security interest in the debtor's existing and (upon acquisition) future assets, even though the debtor has the liberty to use or dispose of collateral without being required to account for proceeds or substitute new collateral."

value because it acted in bad faith by misleading the seller. The priority of the buyer's secured creditors over the reclaiming seller is now made explicit, in the case of the buyer's bankruptcy, by § 546(c).

A credit-seller can obtain status as a secured creditor of the buyer under Article 9. A seller who creates a security interest in goods for the purpose of securing all or part of the sales price holds what is known as a "purchase-money security interest." *See* § 9-103(a), (b). A seller must "perfect" this interest by filing a written financing statement that provides notice to the world of the seller's purchase-money security interest in these goods. § 9-310(a).[32] The seller's purchase-money security interest in the goods generally trumps other security interests, § 9-324(a), but in certain cases the seller must provide notice to parties that have a floating lien against the buyer's inventory if the seller is to be accorded priority, § 9-324(b), (c). Comment 2 explains that this additional burden is imposed on the seller to prevent the buyer-debtor from defrauding a floating lien creditor who might be making advances against the buyer-debtor's acquired inventory. These details from Article 9 mean, simply stated, that a seller can obtain a priority security interest in goods sold on credit, but only at the cost of complying with the filing and notification requirements under Article 9.

The situation for cash-sellers is the same. Although the text of § 2-507(2) only speaks to the competing rights of the buyer and seller, Comment 3 states that if "third parties are involved, Section § 2-403(1) protects good faith purchasers." Following this Comment, courts have held that cash-sellers are subordinated to secured creditors that have valid liens on the buyer's inventory. *See Cooperative Fin. Ass'n v. B & J Cattle Co.*, 937 P.2d 915, 920 (Colo. Ct. App. 1997) ("a perfected security interest resulting from an after-acquired property clause prevails over the retained interest of an unpaid cash-seller" (citations omitted)). This interpretation changes the common law rule, which vested the reclaiming cash-seller with rights superior not only to secured creditors, but also to subsequent purchasers.

> At common law, a cash seller had greater rights than a credit seller by virtue of the cash seller's retention of title until the price of the goods was paid for. A cash purchaser who was somehow able to snatch the goods from the seller without paying or who more likely paid for the goods with a bad check, was treated no better than a thief. . . . The cash seller had the power to reclaim goods even though they had been resold by the buyer to a good faith purchaser because the buyer could receive no greater rights than his seller. A credit seller, however, gave his buyer voidable title to the goods in the buyer's possession, and a credit seller could not reclaim the goods from a bona fide purchaser. . . . The Uniform Commercial Code abolished this common law distinction between cash and credit sales, providing that a purchaser gains voidable title even though the transaction is a cash sale [citing § 2-403].

First Nat'l Bank of Ariz. v. Carbajal, 132 Ariz. 263, 645 P.2d 778, 781 (1982) (en banc). This interpretation has the effect of subordinating all reclaiming sellers to the interests of subsequent purchasers and also to the interests of secured creditors who hold floating liens on the buyer's inventory. Unlike credit-sellers who have the opportunity to comply with the formalities of Article 9 in order to protect their interests in the goods against claims by secured parties in the event of the buyer's default, cash-sellers who are surprised to find that the buyer's check doesn't clear will not even contemplate this possibility.

The following case reveals that not every lien creditor will have rights superior to competing claims by a reclaiming seller.

---

[32] When the seller has sold "consumer goods," it need not file a UCC financing statement in order to perfect its purchase-money security interest in these goods. *See* §§ 9-309(1), 9-310(b)(2). Sellers of non-consumer goods, however, must file to perfect their interests under the general rule of § 9-310(a).

CITIZENS BANK OF ROSEVILLE v. TAGGART
California Court of Appeal
191 Cal. Rptr. 729 (1983)

CARR, Associate J.

At issue in this appeal are the conflicting claims of a cash seller, Braxton Motor Company (hereafter Braxton) and a lien creditor, Citizens Bank of Roseville (hereafter Bank), to an automobile purchased by Richard Taggart (Taggart) by a check returned for insufficient funds. The trial court ruled in favor of Braxton. We affirm.

In 1980 and 1981, Bank extended credit to Taggart by way of two unsecured promissory notes in the face amounts of $15,000.00 and $5,000.00. Taggart defaulted on the notes and Bank brought suit in the Placer Superior Court, and secured a judgment against Taggart in excess of $30,000.00.

A writ of execution was issued and in September 1982 the Placer County sheriff levied on a 1982 brown four-door Cadillac, registered in Texas, with Taggart listed as the registered owner. No legal owner was identified on the registration.

On September 10, 1982, a third-party claim was filed by Braxton pursuant to Code of Civil Procedure section 689. Braxton is an automobile dealer in the State of Oklahoma. On May 20, 1982, Braxton sold the Cadillac to Taggart for a cash price of $15,864.30, paid by Taggart by check. Before the check cleared, Taggart received the boon of the vehicle and a certificate of ownership. The check was subsequently returned for lack of sufficient funds.

In the third-party claim proceeding, after hearing, a judgment was entered that Braxton had title to the Cadillac when the writ of execution was levied. Bank appeals.

We perceive the California Uniform Commercial Code is controlling herein, and consider initially Braxton's right, if any, to reclaim the vehicle by reason of Taggart's failure to pay the purchase price.

[Ed. Note: The court first held that the seller's right of reclamation under § 2-507(2) was not subject to the 10-day limitation found in § 2-702(2).]

[W]e must now determine Braxton's rights as against the Bank. Neither section 2-507(2), the general cash sale provision, nor section 2-511(3), the "bad check" provision, describe the rights of the cash seller in relation to the rights of third parties; both sections by their terms apply only to the relationship between buyer and seller.

The pertinent code section for resolution of this question is section 2-403. . . . This section gives a transferor power to pass good title to bona fide purchasers for value even though the transferor does not possess good title. (*Burk v. Emmick, supra*, 637 F.2d at p. 1174.) As noted in *Matter of Samuels & Co.*, [526 F.2d 1238 (5th Cir. 1976)] at p. 1242:

> Section [2-403(1)] gives good faith purchasers of even fraudulent buyers-transferors greater rights than a defrauded seller can assert.
>
> The provision anticipates a situation where (1) a cash seller has delivered goods to a buyer who has been paid by a check which is subsequently dishonored, [§ 2-403(1)(b), (c)] and where (2) the defaulting buyer transfers title to a Code-defined "good faith purchaser." The interest of the good faith purchaser is protected *pro tanto* against the claims of the aggrieved seller. . . .
> The Code expressly recognizes the power of the defaulting buyer to transfer good title to such a purchaser even though the transfer is wrongful as against the seller. The buyer is granted the *power* to transfer good title despite the fact that under [§ 2-507] he lacks the *right* to do so.[33]

---

[33] [8] As noted in Mann & Phillips, [*The Cash Seller Under the Uniform Commercial Code*, 20 B.C. L. REV. 370 (1979),] prior to the code, "[w]here a good faith purchaser for value bought the seller's goods from the

Bank, however, does not have the status of a good faith purchaser, a fact which Bank conceded in the trial court.

Bank is a lien creditor.[34] Section 2-403(4), states: "The rights of . . . lien creditors are governed by the divisions on secured transactions [Article 9], bulk transfers [Article 6], and documents of title [Article 7]." [Articles] 6 and 7, however, say nothing about the rights of lien creditors. (*See* Mann & Phillips, *supra*, p. 394.) Bank directs us to no provision in [Article] 9 which sets forth the rights of a lien creditor vis-a-vis a cash seller. (*See* Sixth Progress Report to the Legislature, Part 1: The Uniform Commercial Code, p. 466 (hereafter *Sixth Progress Report*).)[35] The code does not solve the priority problem as between a lien creditor and cash seller. (*Ibid.*)

Section 1-103 empowers courts to look to the common law if the code has not displaced prior law. (*Ibid.*) Under the common law, *the unpaid cash seller prevails over an attaching lien creditor.* (*See* Mann & Phillips, *supra*, at pp. 373–374, fn. 27 and authorities cited therein; pp. 393–394.) The California rule is in accord: "It is generally true that an attaching creditor in California takes subject to all secret liens and latent equities, unless protected by some specific statute, *and takes only the interest which his debtor has with all its infirmities.*" (*Sixth Progress Report*, at p. 466; emphasis added.) In *Henry v. General Forming, Ltd.* (1948) 33 Cal. 2d 223, 225–226, 200 P.2d 785, the Court stated: "[T]he well-settled rule [is] that an attaching creditor, seeking to subject the property of a debtor to the payment of his debt, obtains a lien only upon the title or interest which the debtor has, and where no actual interest is shown the attaching creditor gets nothing by virtue of his levy. The lien attaches to the real and not the apparent interest of the debtor." (*See also Barron v. Tattenham* (1962) 199 Cal. App. 2d 128, 131, 18 Cal. Rptr. 676; "The rule is well established that an attaching creditor who gives no new value has none of the characteristics of a bona fide purchaser. He stands in the shoes of the debtor, and his lien attaches only to the debtor's interest at the time of the levy.")

We are persuaded the common law rule is sound and particularly appropriate under the facts here presented. Bank, unlike the typical good faith purchaser for value, did not give value *for the automobile*, nor did Bank in making the loans rely on the ostensible ownership or voidable title of Taggart to the automobile.[36] There is no policy reason for granting Bank status equivalent to a good faith purchaser and allowing it priority over Braxton. (*See* Mann & Phillips, *supra*, at p. 389, fn. 98.)

We conclude the trial court correctly determined the rights of Bank subordinate to those of Braxton.

The judgment is affirmed.

REGAN, Acting P.J., and EVANS, J., concur.

QUESTIONS

1. Does the court rule in favor of the seller because it is a cash-seller, despite the interpretation of § 2-507(2) in accordance with Comment 3 to subordinate the interests of reclaiming cash-sellers to good faith purchasers?

---

buyer, courts were divided over which party prevailed, although twentieth century courts generally held that the seller lost his right to reclaim." (At p. 373; footnotes omitted.)

[34] [9] Section 9-310(3) provides: "A 'lien creditor' means a creditor who has acquired a lien on the property involved by attachment, levy, or the like. . . . ."

[35] [10] Indeed, section 9-104 states in relevant part: "This division does not apply . . . (h) [t]o a right represented by a judgment; . . . ." Thus, [Article] 9 seemingly does not apply to judicial liens such as "[t]he lien of an unsecured creditor who arms himself with judgment and levies. . . ." (WHITE & SUMMERS, UNIFORM COMMERCIAL CODE (2d ed. 1980) § 22-2, p. 875, & fn. 15.)

[36] [11] As noted previously, the notes were unsecured and were executed prior to Taggart's acquisition of the automobile.

2. In the excerpt that follows, Professor Tabac challenges the judicial rule that floating lien creditors with perfected security interests in the buyer's after-acquired inventory are "good faith purchasers" who deserve priority over reclaiming sellers. Is his argument persuasive?

Tabac, *Battle for the Bulge: The Reclaiming Seller vs. The Floating Lien Creditor*
2001 Colum. Bus. L. Rev. 509, 509–14, 520–31, 535–38[37]

Trade credit is a very big business and an important source of financing.[38] Its low costs make it attractive to small businesses with limited resources. Unlike secured creditors, who insist on cushions to support their longer-term debts, trade creditors who sell goods, like the small businesses they support, are risk-takers. They deliver their goods on cheap, short-term, unsecured credit, trusting their debtors to pay up.

A trade creditor is more likely to lend, and to lend more than a secured creditor. The service they perform for the economy is so valuable that these entrepreneurs are subsidized under federal and state law. Bankruptcy-bound debtors can prefer them[39] and the Uniform Commercial Code gives them a lien even when they have not asked for one.

*   *   *

Secured creditors also feed off of a buyer's ownership. The priority contest with the secured creditor, however, may have a different ending than it does with the lessee. The floating lien creditor, for example, prevails even though his debtor would be forced to yield to the seller. This, even though no advances were made against the sold good and no foreclosure occurred. Because of a failure to file, the seller may have been unaware that the floating lienor existed, and the floating lien creditor may have been equally ignorant about the existence of the sold goods.

Under the prevailing view, the secured creditor's lack of reliance on the sold goods is of no consequence: the unpaid seller still loses. However, the Code does not provide for this outcome. It exists because of a misreading of the Code's text. This view is also at odds with the other Code articles that regulate goods. It clashes, for example, with the rule that explicitly provides that only subsequent lessees can defeat the reclaiming seller.[40] Finally, it contradicts what the Code drafters foresaw for reclamation; namely, that it "constitutes preferential treatment as against the buyer's other creditors."[41]

How did this happen? This construction was lobbied for by some venerable commercial law scholars who concluded that certain market principles were more powerful than the language penned by the Code's drafters. Respectfully, I submit that this view repudiates Code language and policy, commercial history, and basic restitution principles, not to mention good sense.

*   *   *

Is it unfair to allow the floating lienor, who gave up nothing in reliance on the sold

---

[37] Copyright 2001. All rights reserved. Reprinted by permission. This work originally appeared at 2001 Colum. Bus. L. Rev. 509 (2001).

[38] [2] Professor Garvin estimates that $6 trillion in trade credit is extended each year and that $30 billion in goods is subject to reclamation. Larry T. Garvin, *Credit, Information and Trust in the Law of Sales: The Credit Seller's Right of Reclamation*, 44 UCLA L. Rev. 247, 251 (1996).

[39] [8] 11 U.S.C. § 547(c)(2) (1994). The provision is "a means of encouraging normal credit transactions and the continuation of short-term credit dealings with troubled debtors so as to stall rather than hasten bankruptcy." *In re Fred Hawes Org., Inc.*, 957 F.2d 239, 243 (6th Cir. 1992).

[40] [18] UCC § 2A-503 (1990).

[41] [14] UCC § 2-702, cmt. 3. "Creditor" includes "secured creditors." UCC § 1-201(12) (1999).

goods, to trump the unpaid seller? I believe that it is. I hope to illustrate that, as the Code stands, only buyers, lessees and secured creditors who rely to their detriment on the sold goods should win this priority contest.

[Ed Note: Professor Tabac's thesis is that the Amended Code should not bring this misreading of Article 2 into the amended statutory language.]

I. Code Buyers: Purchasers of Title

[Ed. Note: Professor Tabac discusses the history of the reclamation remedy at common law as revolving around the concept of "title" to the goods.]

A. Rights and Powers to Transfer Title Under Articles 2 and 2A

* * *

Whatever limitations exist on Article 2 reclamation are imposed by Article 2, specifically, subsection (3) of Section 2-702. Only two kinds of "purchasers" can defeat the reclaiming seller under Article 2 as it is written. One is the buyer in the ordinary course of business. The other is a good faith purchaser who takes title for value. Both are Article 2 "buyers" who must rely on their seller's apparent ownership by giving fresh value and taking delivery.

This is the Article 2 negotiability policy. It protects buyers who rely on the apparent ownership of goods that Article 2 constructs. The Article 2A policy, which protects lessees who rely on the apparent ownership of their lessors, is identical.

B. Power to Sell Under Articles 3 and 8

[Ed. Note: Professor Tabac notes that Articles 3 and 8 create a much broader right of apparent ownership, owing to the interest in ensuring greater negotiability for commercial paper.] Under these articles, apparent ownership of property, which carries with it the power to create good title to property, can arise in a finder or even a thief. If a person takes lost or stolen Article 3 or 8 paper, he may be able to cut off prior ownership claims to this kind of Code property in the same way that a person who acquires money can cut off such claims. Whether or not the owner consents or participates in the transfer of title is irrelevant.

* * *

Unlike goods, the fact that Code paper (or money) was lost or stolen has no bearing on the validity of those rights. Even a thief or a finder of Code paper can enforce it. By creating the rights that Code paper contains, the obligor has in fact consented to bind himself to whomever comes into possession of the paper, including the finder or thief. Mere possession of goods does not necessarily carry such consent. This is what makes Code paper so much more negotiable than goods.

But the thief or finder cannot enforce Code paper against its rightful owner. Only an innocent purchaser of the paper can cut off ownership claims. . . . Apparent ownership, and with it, the power to cut off ownership claims, therefore arises more easily with Code intangibles than it does with goods.

Why should different market forces rule goods and Code paper? It has to do both with the kind of property they are and the kind of expectations they create in people who would purchase them. Goods have a limited negotiability compared with Code paper because of what still survives of the doctrine of caveat emptor. The rule that a finder or a thief cannot create ownership of goods is so fundamental, and understood, that a buyer of goods or of the title document that serves as their proxy, knows that he will have to give the goods up if they are stolen. Secured lenders who advance funds against goods know that too, which is why they routinely check the debtor's source of title. But the purchaser of Code paper validly held or controlled by him expects to be able to enforce the rights that appear in it unless he knows that someone else is asserting an ownership claim to it.

II. Much Less Than Title: Code Lessees and Secured Parties

*   *   *

A "security interest" is much less than "ownership" or even "possession" and "use" for that matter. A security interest can be created either by agreement or can arise by operation of law. It is a lien that attaches to property rights. It may, therefore, attach to "title," "possession," "use," or all of these rights at once. The secured party does not acquire title to the goods or their use as the case may be. Rather, he thrives off of his debtor's title to or lesser rights to exploit the collateral.

The lien of a secured creditor is, therefore, wholly derivative; it depends upon whether and to what extent his debtor can assert "rights" to Code property. If a secured creditor attempts to attach his claim to property in which his debtor cannot assert rights, he, like his debtor, is subject to being ousted by someone who can.

Thus, in a reclamation contest between a secured creditor and a seller of goods, the questions will be, does the buyer-debtor have "rights" to the property to which a security interest can attach, and, if he does, may those rights be asserted against a reclaiming seller?

*   *   *

The Uniform Commercial Code, as written and enacted, allows relying "buyers" of goods and "lessees" to be protected from reclaiming sellers. It may even allow, although it does not expressly provide, relying secured creditors to prevail over reclaiming sellers. But what it does not do is permit secured creditors who do not rely on the sold goods to triumph over reclaiming sellers.

III. How the Code Has Been Misread

Given the plain meaning of the Code language, how did the floating lien creditor come to occupy his favored position? It had nothing to do with any superior equity he might have against the reclaiming seller. An existing creditor's claim to sold goods for which his debtor has not paid is not, in itself, a superior equity. It was through the advocacy of a few prominent commentators who believed that market principles were much more important than property rights.

These commentators pressed for a negotiability of goods that rivaled that of commercial paper. Among them were Samuel Williston, who drafted the Uniform Sales Act, and Lawrence Vold, who published a respected treatise on sales. The policy to be served was security in commercial transactions. If unrelying secured creditors are permitted to triumph over reclaiming sellers, they contended, commerce will be conducted more efficiently and more expectations will be fulfilled, which will serve the greater good.

To make their case for the floating lien creditor, they stopped just short of theft, and began with the settled one: the innocent buyer from a seller with voidable title. If left undisturbed, they pointed out that the defective exchange generates further commitments from still more buyers and other kinds of purchasers. Multiplied expectations are, after all, no more than the desired consequences of classical consideration, which justifies enforcement of bargained-for exchanges. One of these enhanced expectations, they contended, may be held by the floating lien creditor. Unlike the resale buyer, he does not give new value in reliance on the sold good, but he may contribute something just as valuable to the market. By learning that the debtor has acquired the goods, but not knowing of their seller's right to reclaim them, the floating lien creditor might forego foreclosing on his debtor and, thus, keep him in business. For that reason, they asserted, the floating lienor should prevail over the reclaiming seller.

The courts, however, were less introspective. The Revisionist position was adopted by them through a misreading of the Code language rather than by sorting out the interdependent property interests within their Code barriers. Leading the cases that hold that the floating lien creditor takes prior to the Article 2 reclaiming seller is *In re Samuels & Co*,[42] where the Fifth Circuit concluded that a floating lien creditor, who acts in good faith, takes free of the seller's right to reclaim, even if the creditor did not rely on the sold goods. The result is fair, the court reasoned, because the reclaiming seller can always protect itself by entering into a secured transaction with his buyer and achieve the superpriority that Article 9 gives to the purchase money lender.

The statutory path to the Fifth Circuit's holding proceeded as follows: a reclaiming seller, under Article 2, must rely on either cash or credit theories of reclamation. These Article 2 theories provide that the buyer has title to the goods, but that it is voidable, and that the seller can rescind the transaction and recover it.

Both Article 2 sellers are, therefore, subject, the court recognized, to the claims of certain good faith purchasers. But the protected purchasers must find their shelter under Article 2, specifically Section 2-403, not under Article 9. The Code so provides by explicit language,[43] and the court agreed. Upon reaching Section 2-403, however, the court lost its way. The Fifth Circuit concluded that, as a good faith purchaser for value under the Code, an Article 9 floating lien creditor can take priority over the reclaiming seller.

An examination of Section 2-403 shows, however, that it does not apply to secured creditors. With "title" as its centerpiece, Section 2-403 controls Article 2 ownership rights, not "leasehold" or "security" interests.[44] Consequently, the Section applies only to "sales," the subject of the article in which it is found. What Section 2-403 does is empower a buyer with voidable title to create good title in an innocent, value-giving buyer. The protected Section 2-403 "purchaser" will, therefore, take "title" to the goods, not a "leasehold interest" or a "security interest" in them. These interests are created and governed, respectively, by Articles 2A and 9. In fact, Section 2-403 expressly diverts secured creditors to Article 9 to determine what rights they might have as purchasers from a buyer with voidable title.[45]

As I have used "title" interchangeably with "ownership," the Revisionists have used "security interest" interchangeably with "title." In so doing, they have destroyed the boundary between Articles 2 and 9. As seen through the kaleidoscope employed by the Fifth Circuit, "the Code is an integrated statute whose Articles and Sections overlap and flow into one another."[46] Under Section 2-403, as drafted, however, it is clear that the only good faith purchasers who can defeat the reclaiming seller are both buyers.[47] One

---

[42] [135] Samuels was the subject of considerable litigation. *See* No. BK 3-1314 (N.D. Tex. 1972) (findings of fact of Bankruptcy Ref. Whitehurst), *rev'd* No. 73-1185 (N.D. Tex.), *rev'd and remanded*, 483 F.2d 557 (5th Cir. 1973), *rev'd and remanded sub nom. Mahon v. Stowers*, 416 U.S. 100, 40 L. Ed. 2d 79, 94 S. Ct. 1626 (1974) (per curiam), *rev'd sub nom. In re Samuels & Co.*, 510 F.2d 139 (5th Cir. 1975), *rev'd on reh'g*, 526 F.2d 1238 (5th Cir. 1976) (en banc), *cert. den. sub nom. Stowers v. Mahon*, 429 U.S. 834, 50 L. Ed. 2d 99, 97 S. Ct. 98 (1976).

[43] [144] "The seller's right to reclaim . . . is subject to the rights of a buyer in ordinary course or other good faith purchaser *under this Article* (Section 2-403)." § 2-702(3) (emphasis added).

[44] [148] If a security interest arises under Article 2, the Code directs that Article 9 governs it, not Article 2. UCC § 9-110 (2000).

[45] [153] UCC § 2-403(4) (2000).

[46] [155] *Samuels*, 526 F.2d at 1241.

[47] [156] Referring to its subsection (1), UCC 2-403, cmt. 1 says that "the provisions of the section are applicable to a person taking by any form of 'purchase' as defined by this Act." Relying on the "official"

is the buyer in the ordinary course of business, the other is a buyer in a resale from a buyer with voidable title. The concept, hence, the boundary between a "sale" and a "secured transaction" governed respectively by Articles 2 and 9 of the Code, is indisputable.

*   *   *

IV. Resolving the Conflict

The trade creditor knows what his risks are. His security is limited. If he has misjudged his debtor, he must act promptly to avoid the transaction, before a resale buyer is misled by his buyer's apparent ownership of the goods. The Article 9 secured creditor's expectations are clear: he knows that he can only assert claims to collateral in which his debtor has "rights."

Through a misreading of the Code, however, the expectations of both kinds of Code creditors have been undermined. There is something inherently wrong with a rule that allows a lender, who never counted on exploiting certain property as collateral, to take it from a person who was never paid for it. Yet this is the effect of the Code's misreading. The stream of commerce becomes a torrent sweeping the unpaid seller away in it.

Unhappy with what Article 9 gave them, secured creditors lobbied for the greater status enjoyed by Article 2 buyers. Treating floating lien creditors like buyers of goods has undermined the Code's operation by distorting its property interests. The Article 2 negotiability principles in place produce a principled outcome for every interest. The reclaiming seller, his buyer, his buyer's transferees, along with the greater good are all treated fairly under the Code as it is presently drafted.

Consider, first, the competing equities just after the seller delivers the goods, before they are negotiated away under Article 2. Delivery was made on Seller's expectation that Buyer would pay for the goods, but Buyer cannot pay because Buyer is insolvent. Buyer has possession of goods that, in good conscience, he should not keep and no one has changed his position in reliance on these goods. If seller makes his timely reclamation demand and recovers the goods, no one will have been prejudiced.[48]

Consider now what happens if Seller does not make a timely demand or if Buyer negotiates the goods to a buyer in the ordinary course or other good faith buyer. The floating lienor is entitled, without worry from the reclaiming seller, to all proceeds of the sale. Unlike the floating lien creditor, who relies on proceeds even more than on the goods that will generate them, seller did not bargain for proceeds. Hence, seller is not entitled to proceeds, either by expectation or by Code rule. The Article 2 sales contract gives the trade creditor only a limited lien against the sold goods. Beyond that, he stands no higher than the other general creditors of his buyer.

The Code affords the reclaiming seller a very narrow window within which to enforce his property claim. He must make a timely demand for the goods. Timely demand or not, if the goods are promptly resold to qualifying buyers, leased to a subsequent lessee or taken by a secured creditor for fresh value, the seller's reclamation right will be damaged or destroyed.

---

comments to interpret Code sections is generally not approved. *E.g., Simmons v. Clemco Indus.*, 368 So. 2d 509, 514 (Ala. 1979). In any event, when the comment was appended to the section, the section required that its good faith purchasers take delivery of the goods, which, of course, would rule out the floating lien creditor but not all secured creditors. *See* Julian B. McDonnell, *The Floating Lienor as Good Faith Purchaser*, 50 S. Cal. L. Rev. 429, 450–51 (1977).

48 [181] Allowing the seller to recover equipment from the floating lienor will produce only "marginal harm" because equipment is often leased and secured creditors do not rely on it. Larry T. Garvin, *Credit, nformation, and Trust in the Law of Sales: The Credit Seller's Right of Reclamation*, 44 UCLA L. Rev. 247, 315 (1996). As for inventory flow, upon which the floating lien creditor does rely, the seller can deal with it more efficiently by reselling it — it has expertise here that a lender does not have — and thus avoid depreciation. *Id.* at 316.

Does this outcome fairly balance the equities of the competing parties? Yes, I submit. Like Code paper acquired by an innocent purchaser, the goods will have been negotiated away under the more limited Article 2 negotiability policy that respects the historic nature of goods and the expectations that people have about exploiting them. The security interest will then attach to their proceeds, property to which the debtor has "rights" and the reclaiming seller has none. The trade creditor's bargain was either for a solvent debtor or the limited reclamation rights that Article 2 gives him.

[Ed. Note: Professor Tabac concludes that, as currently written, Article 2 respects the reasonable expectations of all parties involved, and he urges the Drafting Committee not to write the misinterpretations by the courts into the language of the Amended Code.]

QUESTION

Are credit-sellers really left without protection, since they are free to create a security interest in the goods and to perfect that interest and gain priority over other security interests in the goods by complying with the requirements of Article 9? Does Professor Tabac's argument lose force in light of this self-protection option?

PROBLEM 7-14

Seras Electrical Supply, Inc. sells electrical materials and supplies to contractors. Bolous Electrical Contracting, Inc. is an electrical contractor that maintains an "open account" with Seras. The "open account" is renewable every year, and provides that Bolous may purchase materials from Seras on credit, with payment due 30 days after delivery of the materials. On March 1, Bolous ordered $10,000 in supplies, and Seras delivered the goods to Bolous on March 7. Subsequently, Seras learned that Bolous was not paying any of its suppliers and was facing the prospect of imminent bankruptcy. On March 11, Seras called Bolous and demanded a return of the goods.

First Scenario: Reclaiming the Goods. It is now March 12 and you are advising Seras in your office. Has Seras preserved its right to reclaim the goods? Is there anything else that Seras should do to protect its interests?

How would your answer be different if Bolous was not a credit purchaser, but instead had purchased the goods by writing a "bad check"?

Second Scenario: Exclusivity. Assume that Seras believes that it will only receive 80% of the original price by reselling to a third party, because many of the boxes have been opened. Can Seras sue Bolous for the deficiency in the resale value?

How would your answer be different if Bolous was not a credit purchaser, but instead had purchased the goods by writing a "bad check"?

Third Scenario: Third-Party Rights. Can Seras successfully reclaim the goods if Bolous has already sold them to one of its customers, if the goods are still in the original packaging and have not been resold? Can Seras successfully reclaim the goods if Bolous is subject to bankruptcy proceedings and its undersecured creditors are asserting rights in Bolous's inventory pursuant to their security agreements? Does Professor Tabac make a persuasive argument that courts have misinterpreted the competing rights of floating lien creditors and reclaiming sellers?

How would your answer be different if Bolous was not a credit purchaser, but instead had purchased the goods by writing a "bad check"?

C. BUYER'S REMEDIES

We now turn to consider the remedies available to an aggrieved buyer. As we did with seller's remedies, we will proceed chronologically by considering the remedies available to a buyer depending on when the breach occurs. First, we consider the buyer's rights in the goods prior to delivery by the seller, with a particular focus on the competing rights of buyers and third-party secured creditors. Next, we consider the buyer's ability to secure an order of specific performance. In the third subsection, we consider the buyer's remedial options prior to acceptance of the goods, with the primary focus on the buyer's choice between "covering" by making a substitute purchase from a third party, or instead suing for damages based on the market price of the goods. In the final subsection we will consider the damages available to a buyer who has accepted goods despite the seller's breach.

1.   Buyer's Rights in the Goods Prior to Delivery

As Karl Llewellyn famously observed, a buyer is interested in obtaining goods, not in acquiring the right to prevail in a lawsuit for damages.[49] Non-consumer buyers generally resell the goods in the course of their business, or use the goods as part of their own manufacturing process (either as equipment or materials). Consequently, failure to obtain goods in a timely manner is likely to disrupt their business relationships with third parties and can lead to substantial losses that may be difficult to measure. Consumer buyers, on the other hand, generally are purchasing goods for enjoyment rather than economic gain, and therefore are predominantly interested in the goods themselves rather than damages for breach of contract to provide the goods. In the following section, we consider the buyer's remedy of specific performance, which might include court orders for the seller to manufacture goods and then deliver them to the buyer. In this section, our focus is the buyer's more specific remedy of compelling the seller to deliver goods that have been identified to the contract but that have not yet been tendered to the buyer.

The buyer has the right to gain possession of identified goods under two different Code provisions. First, under § 2-716(3), the buyer may "replevy" goods in the seller's possession if the buyer cannot reasonably "cover" by obtaining the goods from other sources. Second, under § 2-502, the buyer may recover goods for which it has paid all or part of the purchase price under certain circumstances. As we saw with the seller's right to reclaim goods from a defaulting buyer, the rights of third-party creditors and the overlay of bankruptcy law complicates the analysis.

a.   Buyer's right to replevy goods

The buyer may "replevy" goods in the seller's possession pursuant to § 2-716(3). Replevin is an old common law cause of action that permits a person with the right to possess goods to obtain them from a person who wrongfully holds them. Read § 2-716(3) carefully and determine what the buyer must prove to replevy goods from a seller. We will later see that effecting "cover" is defined by Article 2 and means "to purchase goods in substitution for those due from the seller." § 2-712(1). For present purposes, you may consider the buyer's ability to "effect cover" to mean the buyer's ability to purchase goods from another party that will fulfill the buyer's needs for the goods that the seller is under contract to deliver.

PROBLEM 7-15

Synchronicity Electronics agreed to sell 10,000 newly-developed video cards to BIM Computers. BIM paid a 10% deposit on March 15. BIM then entered into contracts to sell 10,000 computers that it planned to assemble using Synchronicity's video cards. Because Synchronicity's video cards are the state of the art for the industry, BIM prominently advertised to its purchasers that the computers would include these video

---

[49] You may recall that this insight forms the basis of the innovation of § 2-609, as reflected in Comment 1: "This section [conferring a right to demand adequate assurance of due performance] rests on the recognition of the fact that the essential purpose of a contract between commercial men is actually performance and they do not bargain merely for a promise or for a promise plus the right to win a lawsuit."

cards. Shortly after Synchronicity commenced manufacturing the video cards, it received a better offer from another customer. One week prior to the shipment date, on May 1, Synchronicity called BIM and repudiated their agreement. During this conversation, BIM learned that Synchronicity has manufactured the 10,000 video cards and has packaged them for delivery to BIM. Synchronicity stated that it would ship the boxes to BIM to arrive on time, but only if BIM agreed to pay the additional amount offered by the other customer. Otherwise, Synchronicity has expressed its intention to re-label the boxes and to ship them to its other customer.

You are in-house counsel at BIM. The Director of Purchasing comes to your office within minutes of the phone conversation and demands that you take immediate action. The Director tells you that the Vice-President for Sales believes that the injury to BIM's customer relations will be substantial but difficult to quantify if BIM cannot supply computers with Synchronicity cards. Therefore, the ability to sue Synchronicity for damages for breach of contract in this case provides no real consolation. BIM wants to obtain the 10,000 completed units immediately.

Can BIM replevy the video cards under § 2-716(3)?

In the next section we will analyze BIM's option of seeking specific performance of its contract with Synchronicity. Does the right of replevin give BIM any greater rights than the general remedy of specific performance set forth in § 2-716(1)? Compare the language of § 2-716(1) and § 2-716(3) carefully.

b. Buyer's right to recover goods from seller

The buyer may also recover the goods from the seller under § 2-502, which recognizes that the buyer has a "special property" interest in goods for which it has paid all or part of the purchase price, and which have been identified to the contract. However, the buyer may enforce its "special property" only in certain circumstances specified in the statute. Identify the elements of § 2-502 and then work through the following cases and problems.

IN RE CSY YACHT CORPORATION
United States Bankruptcy Court, Middle District of Florida
42 B.R. 619 (1984)

PASKAY, C.J.

This is a Chapter 11 case and the matter under consideration is an objection by the Debtor, CSY Yacht Corporation (CSY) to claim number 72 filed by Alan R. Jaegar and Katherine Jaegar (Jaegars). The claim under challenge was filed as a priority claim in the amount of $900 and as secured in the amount of $39,100. CSY does not object to the priority claim asserted under § 507(a)(5) of the Bankruptcy Code nor to the allowance of an unsecured claim for $37,000, but does object to the claim as secured. The Jaegars claim secured status of this claim on the basis that they have a special property interest in CSY's materials, supplies and parts inventory pursuant to Fla. Stat. § 672.502 (1981).

The matter came on for hearing and the parties, by stipulation, created the record through submission of depositions. The facts as adduced from the record as created and pertinent to resolution of the matter may be summarized as follows:

At the time pertinent to the transaction under consideration, CSY was engaged in the business of manufacturing and selling sailing yachts. The Jaegars became interested in purchasing a yacht from CSY after attending a sailing school conducted by one of CSY's affiliates. Before executing the sales contract, the Jaegars paid an initial deposit of $1,000 to CSY in August of 1980 and a second deposit of $4,000 on February 5, 1981 toward the purchase of a 44-foot cutter to be constructed by CSY for a total purchase price of $176,111. On February 24, 1981, the Jaegars executed the sales purchase agreement with CSY and pursuant to the agreement paid an additional $35,000 towards the purchase price of the yacht.

CSY was in poor financial condition and by the spring of 1981 following the receipt of the Jaegars $35,000, CSY ceased constructing any new yachts. The Jaegers' yacht was one of several yachts which were never started.

On August 28, 1981, CSY filed its petition for relief pursuant to Chapter 11 of the Bankruptcy Code. While operating as a debtor in possession, CSY completed the yachts which were already under construction at the time of the commencement of the case and then proceeded to sell its unneeded inventory. Notice of Sale was sent to all interested parties and creditors of CSY. The Notice provided that the items would be sold free and clear of all liens and any liens or claims against the items sold would attach to the proceeds of the sale. In February, 1982 the sale was concluded.

The Jaegars did not file their claim contending a secured position until March 29, 1982. It is without dispute that the Jaegars do not have a security agreement nor did they file a financing statement pursuant to § 679.302 in order to perfect a security interest under Article 9 of the UCC as adopted in this State by Florida Statute § 679.101. The basis for the Jaegars' asserted secured claim is based on paragraph 14 of the sales and purchase agreement which provides as follows:

> The boat and all materials, engines, and equipment attached to the boat or any material in the possession of the builder and designated for use on the boat shall become the property of the purchaser upon the payment of the first installment. The boat and all the materials, engines, and equipment in the possession of the builder shall be subject to a lien in favor of the builder as against the purchaser. In the event of any rejection of any materials or equipment by the purchaser, title to such goods will revest in the builder.

It is the Jaegars' position that they have a right to recover goods from CSY as an insolvent seller under Fla. Stat. § 672.502 and that this right was transferred to the proceeds of the sale under the notice of the sale. . . .

In order for a buyer to recover goods in the seller's possession after the seller has become insolvent, several elements must be present. The buyer must: (1) have a special property interest in the goods under Fla. Stat. § 672.501; (2) have paid part or all of the purchase price; and (3) keep good a tender of any unpaid portion of the purchase price. Additionally, the seller must become insolvent within ten days following the receipt of the first installment of the purchase price. 3A BENDER's UNIFORM COMM. CODE SERV., § 14.03[2] (1983).

There is no dispute that the Jaegars paid part of the purchase price or that they were willing to keep good a tender for the remaining balance. The only issues to be resolved are whether the Jaegars have a special property interest in the goods and whether CSY became insolvent within ten days of receiving the $35,000 installment.

* * *

According to Fla. Stat. § 672.501, the buyer obtains a special property interest when the goods are identified. In the present case, the Jaegars contracted to purchase a yacht to be built in the future. Pursuant to paragraph 14 of that contract, the boat and all materials, engines, and equipment attached to the boat would become property of the Jaegars upon payment of the first installment. Since construction of the boat never commenced, there were obviously no materials, engines, or equipment attached to the boat.

As noted earlier, Paragraph 14 of the contract further provides that any materials designated for use on the boat shall become property of the Jaegars upon payment of the first installment. The Jaegars contend that this provision is inconsistent with Paragraph 3(b) which requires the installment to be paid at least 30 days prior to construction of the hull, unless CSY designated the materials to be incorporated into the boat from its inventory when it received the first installment.

Paragraph 3(b) merely requires that 30% of the purchase price be paid before construction will begin. Identification is governed by paragraph 14 which occurs when the materials were "designated" by CSY. Nothing in the record indicates that the materials were set aside or ever designated for the Jaegars' yacht.

In the alternative, the Jaegars take the position that the materials and inventory of CSY constitute a tangible bulk and that reference to the materials in the contract is for an undivided share of the fungible bulk which is sufficient to establish identification for purposes of UCC 2-501. In support of their position, the Jaegars rely on Comment 5 of UCC 2-501 which provides as follows:

> 5. Undivided shares in an identified fungible bulk, such as grain in an elevator or oil in a storage tank, can be sold. The mere making of the contract with reference to an undivided share in an identified fungible bulk is enough under subsection (a) to effect an identification if there is no explicit agreement otherwise.

The Jaegars' reliance on Comment 5 is misplaced. The contract did not refer to an identified fungible bulk such as 35,000 pounds of fiberglass and resin. Rather, the contract explicitly referred to those materials "designated" for use on the Jaegars' yacht. As a result, this Court is satisfied that the Jaegars' contention is without merit.

In light of the foregoing, the Court is satisfied that the materials were never identified so as to create a special property interest pursuant to UCC 2-501. As a result, the Jaegars cannot recover any property from CSY under UCC 2-502.

This being the case, it is unnecessary to address the question of whether CSY became insolvent within ten days after it received the $35,000 installment from the Jaegars.

A separate final judgment will be entered in accordance with the foregoing.

QUESTION

The version of § 2-502 in effect at the time the previous case was decided would have required that the buyer prove that the seller became insolvent within 10 days of the initial payment. Would that be a required element of the buyer's proof under the current version of the section?

PROBLEM 7-16

Security Solutions designs and manufactures security computer systems. Security agreed to build and install a system at the world headquarters of Billoti Manufacturing. Billoti agreed to pay $286,000 for the system. Billoti paid $50,000 upon signing the agreement on February 3, as provided in the contract. On March 8, Billoti paid $150,000 as specified in the contract, upon Security's representation that it had manufactured all of the components and was preparing to install the system. Security had followed its standard policy of assigning a contract control number to all material and equipment utilized in the performance of a specific contract or job. In this case, all the material and equipment for Billoti's contract had been assigned the accountability control number AO3017 and had been segregated into a "staging area" at Security's warehouse. This procedure allowed Security to maintain internal accountability and control over the materials and equipment which it utilized in the performance of specific contracts. On March 10, Security informed Billoti that it was considering filing for bankruptcy, and that its financial condition would not permit it to finalize its contract obligations. Security admitted that its finances had been deteriorating rapidly ever since the end of January, and that it had not been paying any of its suppliers since mid-February.

Can Billoti obtain the goods that have been assigned the accountability control number AO3017? Will Billoti's rights in the goods be affected if Security files for bankruptcy?

PROBLEM 7-17

Sullivan's Auto Sales has arranged to acquire four automobiles that have been designed and outfitted to look like the ceremonial pace car for this year's NASCAR race at Daytona. The cars have been manufactured, but have not yet been shipped to dealers. Brendan Beers is an avid NASCAR fan. Brendan agreed to purchase one of the commemorative cars for $36,500. Sullivan's drew up a contract that specified a delivery date of March 1, described the car by make, model, and its unique Vehicle Identification Number, acknowledged that Brendan had paid a $500 deposit toward the purchase price, and provided that Brendan would be responsible for paying the balance of the purchase price upon tender of delivery. Subsequently, Sullivan's decided to cancel its contracts to sell the cars in the belief that they will appreciate in value dramatically in the next few years. Sullivan's sent a letter to Brendan, enclosed a check for $500, and advised Brendan that he would likely be able to find one of the commemorative cars for sale from another dealer, but that Sullivan's was limited by the manufacturer to purchasing only four of the cars.

If Brendan refuses to accept the $500 refund and tenders the $36,000 balance of the purchase price to Sullivan's, can he secure a judicial order directing Sullivan's to tender the car for which he contracted?

c. Third-party rights that supersede the buyer's right to recover goods from seller

A significant question is raised when third parties assert rights in the goods that the buyer is trying to recover from the seller. Section § 2-402(1) provides that the rights of unsecured creditors of the seller are trumped by the buyer's rights to recover goods or to obtain specific performance, subject only to other law such as Article 9 and state law regarding fraudulent transfers. *See* § 2-402(2), (3). However, secured creditors have a substantial claim to the goods as against a buyer seeking to recover goods from the debtor, and thus more difficult questions arise. For example, if the seller's inventory financier forecloses its interest and seeks to liquidate the inventory on hand to satisfy the seller's indebtedness, should the secured creditor prevail over the buyer that has paid all or part of the purchase price of goods that are still in the seller's inventory? Moreover, conflicts with third parties will not be limited to the insolvency situation. Buyers seeking to recover goods from the seller might find that the seller has sold the goods outright to another party.

PROBLEM 7-18

Return to the facts of Problem 7-17. If Sullivan's bank foreclosed on Sullivan's assets pursuant to its rights under a Security Agreement, seizing the car identified in Brendan's contract prior to delivery to Brendan, can Brendan assert his rights as a reclaiming buyer against the bank? Carefully read §§ 1-201(9) and 9-320(a), and determine how these sections relate to Brendan's potential rights under § 2-502.

What if Sullivan's sold the car identified in Brendan's contract to another customer, who paid $38,500 and was unaware of Brendan's claim to the car? Would Brendan be able to recover the car from the third-party buyer?

2. Buyer's Right to Specific Performance

The common law courts traditionally disfavored the remedy of specific performance for a variety of historical and practical reasons. Historically, the equity courts had jurisdiction to order specific performance, and the law courts asserted their dominance in part by limiting recourse to equitable remedies to situations in which an award of damages at law would be inadequate. An award of damages was deemed inadequate in situations where the performance owed was "unique," as in the case of real estate, since the party suffering a breach would not be able to purchase a substitute performance with the damages that could be awarded at law. Practical problems also counseled against ordering specific performance, since it might be difficult for the court to articulate precisely what the breaching party must do and also difficult for the court to supervise the performance to ensure compliance. The classic example is the difficulty courts might face in ordering an opera singer to perform according to his contract, even if his performance might be regarded as unique, since there may be disputes about whether the performance was sufficient.

a. Proper circumstances for an award of specific performance

Section 2-716 represents a break from the traditional common law rule disfavoring an award of specific performance. Comment 1 acknowledges that this remedy remains within the discretion of the judge, continuing the "equitable" approach to the remedy, but also indicates an intent "to further a more liberal attitude than some courts have shown in connection with the specific performance of contracts of sale." As a modern commercial statute, Article 2 is freed of the historical curiosities of the common law. Additionally, because Article 2 only governs transactions in goods, the practical difficulties in awarding specific performance are less relevant. Typically, the court will only need to order the breaching seller to deliver goods to the buyer as required by the contract, although some long-term sales agreements may require a more complex order and subsequent oversight.

If the goods in question are "unique" in the common law understanding, courts should readily order specific performance. *See, e.g., Software Customizer v. Bullet Jet Charter (In re Bullet Jet Charter)*, 177 Bankr. Rep. 593 (Bankr. N.D. Ill. 1995) (because there were no planes on the market similar to the plane in question — which had long range fuel tanks, low airframe time, and had been refurbished according to the contract specifications — specific performance was appropriate). However, the liberal approach of Article 2 authorizes an award of specific performance not only "where the goods are unique" but also "in other proper circumstances."

LACLEDE GAS CO. v. AMOCO OIL CO.
United States Court of Appeals, Eighth Circuit
522 F.2d 33 (1975)

Ross, Circuit J.

The Laclede Gas Company (Laclede), a Missouri corporation, brought this diversity action alleging breach of contract against the Amoco Oil Company (Amoco), a Delaware corporation. It sought relief in the form of a mandatory injunction prohibiting the continuing breach or, in the alternative, damages.

I.

[Ed. Note: The court first held that Laclede had agreed to purchase its requirements of propane from Amoco, for the purpose of supplying new residential developments with gas in anticipation of extending its natural gas lines to these developments at some time in the future.]

II.

*   *   *

. . . Generally, the determination of whether or not to order specific performance of a contract lies within the sound discretion of the trial court. *Landau v. St. Louis Public Service Co.*, 364 Mo. 1134, 273 S.W.2d 255, 259 (1954). However, this discretion is, in fact, quite limited; and it is said that when certain equitable rules have been met and the contract is fair and plain "specific performance goes as a matter of right." *Miller v. Coffeen*, 365 Mo. 204, 280 S.W.2d 100, 102 (1955), quoting *Berberet v. Myers*, 240 Mo. 58, 77, 144 S.W. 824, 830 (1912). (Emphasis omitted.)

With this in mind, we have carefully reviewed the very complete record on appeal and conclude that the trial court should grant the injunctive relief prayed. We are satisfied that this case falls within that category in which specific performance should be ordered as a matter of right. *See Miller v. Coffeen, supra*, 280 S.W.2d at 102.

Amoco contends that four of the requirements for specific performance have not been met. Its claims are: (1) there is no mutuality of remedy in the contract; (2) the remedy of specific performance would be difficult for the court to administer without constant and long-continued supervision; (3) the contract is indefinite and uncertain; and (4) the remedy at law available to Laclede is adequate. The first three contentions have little or no merit and do not detain us for long.

There is simply no requirement in the law that both parties be mutually entitled to the remedy of specific performance in order that one of them be given that remedy by the court. *Beets v. Tyler*, 365 Mo. 895, 290 S.W.2d 76, 80 (1956); *Rice v. Griffith*, 349 Mo. 373, 161 S.W.2d 220, 225 (1942).

While a court may refuse to grant specific performance where such a decree would require constant and long-continued court supervision, this is merely a discretionary rule of decision which is frequently ignored when the public interest is involved. *See, e.g., Joy v. St. Louis*, 138 U.S. 1, 47 (1891); *Western Union Telegraph Co. v. Pennsylvania Co.*, 129 F. 849, 869 (3d Cir. 1904); *Municipal Gas Co. v. Lone Star Gas Co.*, 259 S.W. 684, 690–691 (Tex. Civ. App. 1924), *aff'd*, 117 Tex. 331, 3 S.W.2d 790 (1928).

Here the public interest in providing propane to the retail customers is manifest, while any supervision required will be far from onerous.

Section 370 of the Restatement of Contracts (1932) provides:

> Specific enforcement will not be decreed unless the terms of the contract are so expressed that the court can determine with reasonable certainty what is the duty of each party and the conditions under which performance is due.

We believe these criteria have been satisfied here. As discussed in part I of this opinion, as to all developments for which a supplemental agreement has been signed, Amoco is to supply all the propane which is reasonably foreseeably required, while Laclede is to purchase the required propane from Amoco and pay the contract price therefor. The parties have disagreed over what is meant by "Wood River Area Posted Price" in the agreement, but the district court can and should determine with reasonable certainty what the parties intended by this term and should mold its decree, if necessary accordingly.[50] Likewise, the fact that the agreement does not have a definite time of duration is not fatal since the evidence established that the last subdivision should be converted to natural gas in 10 to 15 years. This sets a reasonable time limit on performance and the district court can and should mold the final decree to reflect this testimony.

It is axiomatic that specific performance will not be ordered when the party claiming breach of contract has an adequate remedy at law. *Jamison Coal & Coke Co. v. Goltra*, 143 F.2d 889, 894 (8th Cir.), *cert. denied*, 323 U.S. 769 (1944). This is especially true when the contract involves personal property as distinguished from real estate.

However, in Missouri, as elsewhere, specific performance may be ordered even

---

[50] [3] The record indicates that Laclede has now accepted Amoco's interpretation and has agreed that "Wood River Area Posted Price" means Amoco's posted price for propane at its Wood River Refinery.

though personalty is involved in the "proper circumstances." Mo. Rev. Stat. § 400.2-716(1); Restatement of Contracts, *supra*, § 361. And a remedy at law adequate to defeat the grant of specific performance "must be as certain, prompt, complete, and efficient to attain the ends of justice as a decree of specific performance." *National Marking Mach. Co. v. Triumph Mfg. Co.*, 13 F.2d 6, 9 (8th Cir. 1926). *Accord, Snip v. City of Lamar*, 239 Mo. App. 824, 201 S.W.2d 790, 798 (1947).

One of the leading Missouri cases allowing specific performance of a contract relating to personalty because the remedy at law was inadequate is *Boeving v. Vandover*, 240 Mo. App. 117, 218 S.W.2d 175, 178 (1949). In that case, the plaintiff sought specific performance of a contract in which the defendant had promised to sell him an automobile. At that time (near the end of and shortly after World War II), new cars were hard to come by, and the court held that specific performance was a proper remedy since a new car "could not be obtained elsewhere except at considerable expense, trouble or loss, which cannot be estimated in advance."

We are satisfied that Laclede has brought itself within this practical approach taken by the Missouri courts. As Amoco points out, Laclede has propane immediately available to it under other contracts with other suppliers. And the evidence indicates that at the present time propane is readily available on the open market. However, this analysis ignores the fact that the contract involved in this lawsuit is for a long-term supply of propane to these subdivisions. The other two contracts under which Laclede obtains the gas will remain in force only until March 31, 1977, and April 1, 1981, respectively; and there is no assurance that Laclede will be able to receive any propane under them after that time. Also it is unclear as to whether or not Laclede can use the propane obtained under these contracts to supply the Jefferson County subdivisions, since they were originally entered into to provide Laclede with propane with which to "shave" its natural gas supply during peak demand periods.[51] Additionally, there was uncontradicted expert testimony that Laclede probably could not find another supplier of propane willing to enter into a long-term contract such as the Amoco agreement, given the uncertain future of worldwide energy supplies. And, even if Laclede could obtain supplies of propane for the affected developments through its present contracts or newly-negotiated ones, it would still face considerable expense and trouble which cannot be estimated in advance in making arrangements for its distribution to the subdivisions.

Specific performance is the proper remedy in this situation, and it should be granted by the district court.[52]

CONCLUSION

For the foregoing reasons the judgment of the district court is reversed and the cause is remanded for the fashioning of appropriate injunctive relief in the form of a decree of specific performance as to those developments for which a supplemental agreement form has been signed by the parties.

QUESTIONS

1. The court spends a great deal of time discussing the common law of contracts in *Laclede*. Is Article 2 the governing law? Why didn't the court limit its analysis to Article 2?

2. Compare Laclede with the following case that applies Article 2 in some detail to

---

[51] [4] During periods of cold weather, when demand is high, Laclede does not receive enough natural gas to meet all this demand. It therefore adds propane to the natural gas it places in its distribution system. This practice is called "peak shaving."

[52] [5] In fashioning its decree, the district court must take into account any relevant rules and regulation promulgated under the Federal Mandatory Allocation Program.

determine whether specific performance is an appropriate remedy for the aggrieved buyer.

COPYLEASE CORP. OF AMERICA v. MEMOREX CORP.
United States District Court, Southern District of New York
408 F. Supp. 758 (1976)

LASKER, District Judge.

By Memorandum Opinion dated November 12, 1975, 403 F. Supp. 625, we determined that Memorex Corporation (Memorex) breached its contract with Copylease Corporation of America (Copylease) for the sale of toner and developer and directed the parties to submit proposed judgments with supporting documentation relating to the availability of injunctive relief, or, more precisely, specific performance. We have studied the submissions and conclude that further testimony is necessary to determine the propriety of such relief.

Memorex takes the position that under California law Copylease is not entitled to specific performance of this contract. Copylease argues that the remedy is available — if not under California law, then under our general federal equitable powers.

. . . [W]e are inclined to agree with Memorex that the law of California controls the issuance of the equitable relief sought here by Copylease.

We also agree with Memorex that the provision in the contract granting Copylease an exclusive territory, on which Copylease places primary reliance in its request for specific performance, is not in itself an adequate basis under California law for an award of such relief. *Long Beach Drug Co. v. United Drug Co.*, 13 Cal. 2d 158, 88 P.2d 698, 89 P.2d 386 (1939). California law does not consider a remedy at law inadequate merely because difficulties may exist as to precise calculation of damages. *Hunt Foods, Inc. v. Phillips*, 248 F.2d 23, 33 (N.D. Cal. 1957) (applying California law); *Thayer Plymouth Center, Inc. v. Chrysler Motors Corp.*, 255 Cal. App. 2d 300, 63 Cal. Rptr. 148, 152 (4th Dist. Ct. App. 1967), and cases cited there. *Long Beach Drug* and *Thayer Plymouth* also demonstrate the more fundamental refusal of California courts to order specific performance of contracts which are not capable of immediate enforcement, but which require a "continuing series of acts" and "cooperation between the parties for the successful performance of those acts."

. . . Absent some exception to this general rule, therefore, Copylease will be limited to recovery of damages for the contract breach.

An exception which may prove applicable to this case is found in Cal. UCC § 2-716(1). That statute provides that in an action for breach of contract a buyer may be entitled to specific performance "where the goods are unique or in other proper circumstances." Cal. UCC § 2716(1) (1964). In connection with its claim for interim damages for lost profits from the time of the breach, Copylease argues strongly that it could not reasonably have covered by obtaining an alternative source of toner because the other brands of toner are distinctly inferior to the Memorex product. If the evidence at the hearing supports this claim, it may well be that Copylease faces the same difficulty in finding a permanent alternative supplier. If so, the Official Comment to § 2716 suggests that a grant of specific performance may be in order:

> Specific performance is no longer limited to goods which are already specific or ascertained at the time of contracting. The test of uniqueness under this section must be made in terms of the total situation which characterizes the contract. Output and requirements contracts involving a particular or peculiarly available source or market present today the typical commercial specific performance situation. . . . However, uniqueness is not the sole basis of the remedy under this section for the relief may also be granted "in other proper circumstances" and *inability to cover is strong evidence of "other proper circumstances."*

Cal. UCC § 716, Comment 2 (1964) (emphasis added).

If Copylease has no adequate alternative source of toner the Memorex product might be considered "unique" for purposes of § 2716, or the situation might present an example of "other proper circumstances" in which specific performance would be appropriate.

If such a showing is made, it will be necessary to reconcile California's policy against ordering specific performance of contracts which provide for continuing acts or an ongoing relationship with § 2716 of the Code. Although we recognize that the statute does not require specific performance, the quoted portion of the Official Comment seems clearly to suggest that where a contract calls for continuing sale of unique or "noncoverable" goods this provision should be considered an exception to the general proscription. Output and requirements contracts, explicitly cited as examples of situations in which specific performance may be appropriate, by their nature call for a series of continuing acts and an ongoing relationship. Thus, the drafters seem to have contemplated that at least in some circumstances specific performance will issue contrary to the historical reluctance to grant such relief in these situations. If, at the hearing, Copylease makes a showing that it meets the requirements of § 2716, the sensible approach would be to measure, with the particulars of this contract in mind, the uniqueness or degree of difficulty in covering against the difficulties of enforcement which have caused courts to refrain from granting specific performance. It would be premature to speculate on the outcome of such analysis in this case.

QUESTIONS

1. What arguments will the lawyers make on remand regarding the appropriateness of an order of specific performance on these facts?

2. A number of courts require the plaintiff to demonstrate that it has no adequate remedy at law in order to obtain an order of specific performance. *See, e.g., Weathersby v. Gore*, 556 F.2d 1247, 1258 (5th Cir. 1977). ("The adoption of the Uniform Commercial Code by Mississippi does not suggest that [the the requirement of "no adequate remedy at law" is] now to be rejected.") The *Weathersby* court found the Official Comments to be of "little guidance," and concluded that "the Mississippi Supreme Court would apply a restrictive reading of [§ 2-716]," "considering the reluctance" in older common law cases for the court to award this remedy. It is not irrelevant that *Weathersby* involved a buyer seeking specific performance of a contract for the sale of cotton, despite a ready market for cotton that could easily fix its damages.

Can you ground the traditional common law inquiries (inadequate remedy at law; difficulty of formulating and supervising an order) in the language of Article 2? Is this an example of what Professor Frisch has argued is the "inertia of habit" that leads courts to decide cases under established principles even in the face of statutory innovations? *See* David Frisch, *Commercial Common Law, the United Nations Convention on the International Sale of Goods, and the Inertia of Habit*, 74 TUL. L. REV. 495 (1999).

3. Can the parties agree that the goods are "unique" or that the contract for sale involves "other proper circumstances" and provide that specific performance is the exclusive remedy for a breach of contract? *See* §§ 1-302 and 2-719(1).

4. Would the result in the case be different under the CISG if Copylease, with its place of business in the United States, filed suit in United States District Court against a toner manufacturer that had a place of business in another Contracting State? *See* CISG Art. 7, Art. 28, and Art. 46.

PROBLEM 7-19

Boise Electric is an electricity generation and transmission cooperative that owns a coal burning plant. Boise contracted with Simplicity Engineering to design and manufacture a pollution control device to bring Boise's plant into conformity with clean air laws. The device is large, complex, and technically intricate. Shortly after installation, it became apparent that the device was not operating in accordance with the Simplicity's warranties, both express and implied. Simplicity's technicians worked on the device for six months, and they were only able to achieve the warranted results for short periods of time. However, Simplicity ceased efforts to correct the problems after six months and wrongfully claimed that Boise was responsible for the malfunctions.

Boise sued Simplicity and demanded specific performance of Simplicity's warranty obligations. Boise argued as follows:

1. Because the device is not bringing the plant into compliance with air quality regulations, it is of little or no value to Boise.

2. Monetary damages would suffice as a remedy only to the extent that they would cover the cost of bringing the performance of the device up to the level of warranted performance.

3. Temporary mitigation measures undertaken by Boise, including spraying anhydrous ammonia into the device during its operation, might be banned in the future by state regulators. Additionally, future costs of anhydrous ammonia for the useful life of the device are speculative due to deregulation and a widely fluctuating market.

Is Boise's reasoning persuasive? Is this case within the rationales offered by the *Laclede* and *Copylease* courts?

b.   The problem of third-party purchasers

In addition to the practical difficulties of ordering a breaching seller to perform, the buyer faces difficulties obtaining specific performance if the goods that are the subject of the contract are in the hands of a third party at the time of litigation. An astute buyer will immediately seek a temporary restraining order and preliminary injunction to prevent the seller from transferring the goods during the litigation. The following case discusses the buyer's strategy if the goods have been transferred to a third party prior to commencement of the litigation.

RUDDOCK v. FIRST NATIONAL BANK OF LAKE FOREST
Illinois Appellate Court, Second District
559 N.E.2d 483, 201 Ill. App. 3d 907 (1990)

REINHARD, J.

[Ed. Note: Martin Ruddock contracted with the Bank, as guardian of the estate of Rowland Stevens, to purchase a rare astronomical clock for $7,000 at a public sale. Elmer and Pauline Crum claimed that the Bank had earlier agreed to grant them a right of first refusal. When the Bank's officer, Ronald Kilgus, informed the Crums that the clock had been sold, they threatened litigation. Subsequently, the Bank refused Ruddock's tender of $7,000 and sold the clock to the Crums.]

Plaintiff testified that for the past 10 years he had been conducting an in-depth study of astronomical clocks. Plaintiff testified that the subject clock represented the pinnacle of the development of the precision pendulum clock in the United States. The clock was a master clock for the Western Union Time Service. Ernest Martt, a horologist, testified that the clock was 1 of possibly 12 of its type manufactured. He testified that at the time of trial the clock was worth $40,000. Plaintiff testified that the clock was worth $30,000 to $35,000 at the time of trial.

Plaintiff filed his complaint in this action on May 5, 1986. Originally, plaintiff sought relief against the Bank only, seeking an award of damages sufficient to enable him to purchase the clock from the Crums. Subsequently, on May 15, 1987, plaintiff amended his complaint, seeking specific performance against the Crums. Plaintiff's amended complaint also advanced a claim for intentional interference with contractual relations against the Crums, seeking recovery for attorney fees allegedly incurred as a result of the Bank's breach of its contract with him. The Crums raised the affirmative defense of *laches* to the claim for specific performance. With respect to the intentional interference with contract claim, the Crums raised the one-year statute of limitations for intentional torts as an affirmative defense.

On January 24, 1989, the trial court entered judgment in favor of plaintiff against the Bank in the amount of $28,000, but denied plaintiff's section 2-611 motion for attorney fees. The trial court found, *inter alia*, that plaintiff had a valid contract with the Bank; that the Crums had no valid right of first refusal but were *bona fide* purchasers for value; that the action was filed within the statute of limitations and was not barred by *laches*; and that the value of the clock at the time of judgment was $35,000. The trial court found in favor of the Crums on plaintiff's claims for specific performance and intentional interference with contract. Following the filing of a post-trial motion by the Bank, the trial court reduced the damages award to $7,000.

Plaintiff initially contends that the trial court erred in failing to award him specific performance of the contract for the sale of the clock despite the fact that it had subsequently been sold and delivered to the Crums. Plaintiff maintains that, because the Crums purchased the clock with notice of the prior sale, an order of specific performance may be entered against them. The Bank responds that, under the circumstances here, denial of the equitable remedy of specific performance was proper. The Crums contend that the principle allowing a buyer under certain circumstances to obtain specific performance despite a sale to a third party is applicable only to contracts for the sale of real property. The Crums additionally maintain that plaintiff had no contract with the Stevens estate both because the evidence of negotiations between plaintiff and Ronald Kilgus does not show the formation of a contract and because at the time of these negotiations the Bank did not have court approval to dispose of the clock by private sale. Alternatively, the Crums contend that the remedy of specific performance is unavailable to plaintiff because he has an adequate remedy at law. Moreover, the Crums contend that the action against them for specific performance was barred by *laches* and the statute of limitations. The Crums further argue that plaintiff abandoned his contract. Finally, the Crums argue that plaintiff was not entitled to equitable relief because he was guilty of unclean hands.

Section 2-716(1) of the Uniform Commercial Code provides that "[s]pecific performance may be ordered where the goods are unique or in other proper circumstances." The determination of whether to grant specific performance lies within the discretion of the trial court. (*Dawdy v. Sample* (1989), 178 Ill. App. 3d 118, 127, 532 N.E.2d 1128; Ill. Ann. Stat., ch. 26, par. 2-716, Uniform Commercial Code Comment, at 594 (Smith-Hurd 1963).) Article 2 of the Code seeks to further a more liberal attitude than some courts have shown in connection with the specific performance of contracts of sale. Ill. Ann. Stat., ch. 26, par. 2-716, Uniform Commercial Code Comment, at 594 (Smith-Hurd 1963).

The requirement of uniqueness has clearly been satisfied in the present case as the evidence establishes that the clock is one of a very few of its type manufactured, may be the only one in existence, and is of historical significance. Furthermore, the Crums' attorney stipulated the clock was unique.

The question remains whether specific performance is available in view of the fact that subsequent to plaintiff's negotiations with the Stevens estate the clock was sold and delivered to the Crums. Plaintiff argues that because the Crums had notice of the sale to him, their purchase of the clock is no impediment to an order of specific performance. In support of this proposition, plaintiff cites, *inter alia*, *Stein v. Green* (1955), 6 Ill. 2d 234, 128 N.E.2d 743, which involved the question of a lessee's right to possession of real property as against a subsequent purchaser of the property. The court stated, "it has long been held that every subsequent purchaser, with notice, becomes subject to the same equities as the party from whom he purchased and, although not personally liable, may be compelled to perform any contract of his vendors." 6 Ill. 2d at 241, 128 N.E.2d at 747.

The Crums respond that the principle stated above is inapplicable to contracts for the sale of personal property. There appears to be no case law in Illinois addressing the right of a purchaser of personal property to specific performance against a subsequent purchaser with notice of the prior sale. However, cases from other jurisdictions suggest that specific performance is available in such circumstances. *Myhre v. Myhre* (Mont. 1976), 554 P.2d 276, involved a contract for the sale of stock. The court observed: "[t]he rule seems to be that one who acquires or purchases property, knowing that the property is subject to a contract to be sold to another, may be compelled to perform the contract in the same manner and to the same extent as his grantor would have been liable to do had the grantor not made the transfer to him." 554 P.2d at 281; *see also Chandler Trailer Convoy, Inc. v. Rocky Mountain Mobile Home Towing Services, Inc.* (1976), 37 Colo. App. 520, 552 P.2d 522.

The only reason the Crums suggest for distinguishing between real and personal property in this context is that ownership interests in personal property are not subject to recordation and, therefore, cannot be easily discovered by potential purchasers. We are not persuaded. The rule proposed allowing specific performance would work no hardship on such unwary purchasers since notice of the prior sale is necessary.

The trial court apparently denied specific performance based on its finding that the sale to the Crums was a valid sale to a *bona fide* purchaser. The record clearly establishes, however, that that sale only occurred after the Crums were notified that the clock had been sold to plaintiff. Thus, this finding is in error, and, as we discuss below, the denial of specific performance was an abuse of discretion.

*   *   *

The Crums additionally maintain that an award of damages was an adequate remedy at law and, accordingly, plaintiff was not entitled to specific performance. This position is without merit. The fact that a value can be assigned to an item of personalty does not necessarily make damages an adequate remedy. The Code's principal requirement for an order of specific performance is that the goods be unique. (Ill. Rev. Stat. 1987, ch. 26, par. 2-716.) Here, the record clearly demonstrates that the clock is unique.

The Crums argue that the trial court erred in not invoking the doctrine of *laches* to bar this action because although plaintiff's cause of action, if any, arose in December 1982, he did not file suit against the Crums until May 15, 1987. The Crums contend that a letter sent to them by plaintiff, stating that he understood their position, was calculated to lull them into believing he would not bring suit against them. The Crums also note that during the period following the alleged breach and prior to the commencement of the action against them for specific performance, the value of the clock increased dramatically. The Crums maintain that under these circumstances the equitable defense of *laches* is applicable.

Laches is an equitable principle which bars recovery by a litigant whose unreasonable delay in bringing an action for relief prejudices the rights of the other party. (*People ex rel. Daley v. Strayhorn* (1988), 121 Ill. 2d 470, 482, 521 N.E.2d 864.) Whether the defense of laches is available is to be determined based upon the facts and circumstances of each case. (*Nancy's Home of the Stuffed Pizza, Inc. v. Cirrincione* (1986), 144 Ill. App. 3d 934, 941, 494 N.E.2d 795.) Mere delay in asserting a right does not constitute laches. (*Cirrincione*, 144 Ill. App. 3d at 941, 494 N.E.2d at 800.) A defendant must show prejudice or hardship rather than mere passage of time. *Cirrincione*, 144 Ill. App. 3d at 941, 494 N.E.2d at 800.

The Crums note that it has been stated that "a marked appreciation or depreciation in the value of the property which is the object of controversy, such that the granting of relief would itself work an inequity, is evidence of injury or prejudice justifying the invocation of laches. . . . In regard to the right at equity to have specific performance of a contract of sale, unreasonable delay coupled with a material advance in value is fatal, for equity will not allow a purchaser to remain in the wings gambling on the future rise in price." (*Schroeder v. Schlueter* (1980), 85 Ill. App. 3d 574, 576–77, 407 N.E.2d 204.) As the Crums note, the highest appraisal of the clock at the time of sale was $7,000. At the time of trial, testimony placed the value between $30,000 and $40,000. Even so, under the circumstances here, we do not view the increase in value as requiring application of the doctrine of *laches*, particularly in view of the fact that plaintiff's delay in asserting his claim against the Crums may have been, in part, attributable to the fact that he was initially attempting to negotiate a purchase of the clock from them. Nor is there any indication that plaintiff waited to file suit to take advantage of any expected increase in value.

The Crums also point out that they expended a fairly substantial sum of money, $2,500, restoring the clock. Nonetheless, as an equitable remedy can be fashioned to compensate the Crums for benefits conferred by restoration work, we do not view their expenditure of money as necessarily foreclosing an award of specific performance. It is well established that application of the doctrine of *laches* is within the sound discretion of the trial court and a finding by that court will not be disturbed on review unless the determination is so clearly wrong as to constitute an abuse of discretion. (*In re Marriage of Yakubec* (1987), 154 Ill. App. 3d 540, 544, 507 N.E.2d 117.) We find no abuse of discretion in the trial court's finding with respect to *laches*.

With respect to plaintiff's right to specific performance, the Bank contends that the trial court properly relied on plaintiff's delay in filing the action for specific performance and the increase in the clock's value in denying specific performance. It is apparent, however, from the trial court's rejection of the defense of *laches* that the trial court did not rely on these factors, but, rather, denied specific performance based upon its conclusion that the Crums were *bona fide* purchasers against whom specific performance would not lie. That finding was erroneous as we have previously determined.

For all the foregoing reasons, we conclude that the trial court abused its discretion in refusing to order specific performance. In view of our resolution of this issue, it is unnecessary to consider issues pertaining to the proper measure of damages raised in plaintiff's appeal and the Bank's cross-appeal.

In view of the fact that the Crums purchased from the Stevens estate the clock for the same amount as plaintiff contracted to pay the estate, an appropriate order of specific performance requires payment of the purchase price of $7,000 by plaintiff to the Crums. Moreover, the Crums are entitled to compensation for the benefit of the restoration work performed on the clock. We note that during the proceedings below and in his appellate brief, plaintiff indicated his willingness to compensate the Crums for the cost of repairs. The record shows that the Crums expended $2,500 in repairing the clock. Accordingly, we reverse the portion of the judgment of the circuit court denying plaintiff specific performance and awarding plaintiff damages, and, pursuant to Supreme Court Rule 366(a)(5) (107 Ill. 2d R. 366(a)(5)), the Crums are ordered to deliver the clock to plaintiff upon payment of $9,500. In other respects, the judgment of the circuit court is affirmed.

Affirmed in part; reversed in part. INGLIS and DUNN, JJ., concur.

QUESTIONS

1. The Crums apparently did not counterclaim in this case, but only raised defenses. What is the basis, then, for the court's judgment that Ruddock must pay $2,500 to the Crums?

2. Does the court identify which factors are most important to its decision in the case? Does § 2-716 provide any guidance about weighing these factors?

c.   The payment of money as a form of specific performance

Specific performance generally is considered an alternative to money damages, but in some instances courts have held that the seller must specifically perform by paying money damages to the buyer. Consider the following case and problem.

KING AIRCRAFT SALES, INC. v. LANE
Washington Court of Appeals
68 Wash. App. 706, 846 P.2d 550 (1993)

PEKELIS, Acting C.J.

Joe Lane, Jr., d/b/a The Lane Company, and Lane Aviation, Inc. (Lane) appeal the judgment of the trial court awarding King Aircraft Sales, Inc., d/b/a King Aviation Services (King) $338,280.60 in damages, prejudgment interest, attorney fees, and statutory costs for its breach of a contract to sell two airplanes to King. The principal issue presented in this appeal, one of first impression in Washington, is whether the trial court may award money damages as a remedy in a claim for specific performance under the Uniform Commercial Code (UCC), RCW 62A.2-716. The trial court found King was entitled to specific performance and, because the planes were no longer available, awarded relief in the form of "value." The trial court determined value by using a lost expectation of profit approach resulting in an award of $157,010 plus return of the $10,000 deposit. In addition, the trial court awarded prejudgment interest of $35,688.60 and attorney fees in the amount of $135,454 and statutory costs of $128.

Lane appeals the award of these amounts. King cross-appeals from the trial court's determination of value using the expectation of lost profit approach instead of the wholesale "blue book" value. We affirm all of the trial court's rulings except for the award of attorney fees and the amount of the prejudgment interest, which we reverse.

FACTS

The trial court found that in October 1988, King made a written offer to purchase two "quality, no damage" aircraft from Lane for $870,000. The offer was accompanied by a $10,000 deposit. Lane accepted the King offer both in writing and by depositing the $10,000 deposit. The acceptance created a contract of sale between the parties. King was to perform certain requirements but prior to the expiration of the time to perform, Lane advised King it was backing out of the agreement and that it had reached agreement with another party, Western Aircraft (Western), for the sale of the planes. Because at the time Lane backed out of the contract the time for King's performance had not yet expired, the trial court concluded that Lane's action was a breach of the contract.

King made it clear to both Lane and Western that it intended to enforce its contract with Lane and filed suit in Texas state court, seeking a temporary restraining order (TRO) to prohibit the sale of the aircraft to anyone other than King. The Texas state court issued the TRO. However, the case was later removed to a federal court in Texas, which denied King's motion to extend the TRO.

Lane then rescinded the Western contract and returned Western's deposit. Although Lane refused to honor the original contract with King, in settlement attempts pending litigation, it offered to sell the planes to King for the same price, but "as is," rather than "quality, no damage" airplanes as required in the original contract. King refused to purchase the planes under the terms of Lane's proposal and insisted on compliance with the original contract. At this time, King had tentatively arranged to resell the planes for a profit of approximately $165,000.

After the federal court in Texas refused to extend the TRO, King brought this action in Washington and sought a TRO to prohibit the sale of the planes. In addition, King's complaint sought specific performance of the contract and other appropriate relief.

After the King County Superior Court granted the TRO, King dismissed its federal court action. Subsequently, in December 1988, the King County Superior Court dissolved the previously granted TRO and sanctioned King for having misled the court and for failing to give proper notice of hearing to the other parties.

In January of 1989, long before trial, Lane sold both planes "as is" to Priester Aviation (Priester) for $870,000. Priester put the planes on the market and resold them separately in a series of transactions.

After the Washington TRO was quashed, King moved for leave to reinstate and amend its complaint in Texas federal court to add a claim for legal remedies and once again add Lane as a defendant. The federal court granted the motion and an amended complaint was filed. However, Lane moved to dismiss the federal action for lack of personal jurisdiction. Lane's motion was granted and the action was dismissed without prejudice.

In early June 1990, King retained its third Washington counsel to proceed with the instant action in Washington. Previously, former counsel, and/or King acting pro se, had agreed to set the case for trial on August 6, 1990. The case schedule specified a discovery cutoff date of June 18, 1990, and July 2, 1990 was the last day to file dispositive motions. As of June 8, 1990, no depositions had been taken and Lane, through counsel, had not responded to discovery requests served by previous counsel. King's new counsel filed motions to continue the action and to amend the "Washington" complaint to add a claim for damages for the breach of contract. The motions were denied. King also attempted to interject a damages claim into the suit in the context of a response to a cross claim by Lane for intentional interference. The trial court granted Lane's motion to strike the damages claim and also dismissed Lane's cross claim. No appeal was taken from these rulings.

King's claim for specific performance and "other appropriate relief" was tried before the court without a jury. After trial, the court in its oral opinion ruled that Lane had breached the contract between the parties and that King should recover the "value" of the planes, as measured by the profit made by Priester, on its resale of the planes. Neither party had introduced evidence on this point, so the court ordered the parties to conduct post-trial discovery on the sale of the planes by Priester. Both parties objected to reopening the case for additional discovery.

Ultimately, the trial court did not hold an additional hearing on the issue of value. Instead, the trial court considered correspondence of counsel and affidavits as well as briefing on the issue of value. Priester was deposed and the parties learned that one of the planes had been sold in a complicated 3-plane transaction and that the other plane had been altered and "cannibalized," thus, making comparisons and a determination of value from these sales virtually impossible. Lane contended that Priester lost money on the resale of the planes, and alternatively suggested the trial court consider the blue book measure of *wholesale* value for the planes. King countered that a blue book measure of value could be correct as long as the court used retail value, adjusted upwards by 25 percent because of the exceptional condition of the planes.

The trial court entered findings of fact that a contract was formed and that Lane breached the contract before the time for King's performance expired. In addition, the trial court found the planes were fairly characterized as "one of a kind" or "possibly the best" in the U.S.; however, it was not proven that the planes were "unique" because there were others of the same make and model available. However, the planes were so rare in terms of their exceptional condition that King had no prospect to cover its anticipated re-sales by purchasing alternative planes, because there was no possibility of finding similar or better planes.

Therefore, the trial court concluded that under the total surrounding circumstances, this case appropriately fell within the "other proper circumstances" clause of the specific performance statute of RCW 62A.2-716(1) and, therefore, King was entitled to specific performance. Relying on the Official Comments to RCW 62A.2-716, the trial court noted that the inability to cover was strong evidence of "other proper circumstances" for an action/award of specific performance. Because the planes were no longer available, the trial court concluded that specific performance should take the form of the value of the aircraft at the time of the breach. The trial court concluded this value could be measured either by the blue book value, including increased price adjustments for the prime condition of the planes, or by King's expectation of profit. The trial court chose the latter and awarded judgment to King as set forth above.

I.

Lane's principal claim on appeal is that because this was solely an action for specific performance under the UCC, and because the goods had been sold and thus inaccessible, no remedy was available to King. Lane contends the trial court had no authority to make a dollar value award. Its argument is as follows: Because King failed to plead a claim for monetary damages in its original complaint and had twice been denied permission by the court to add such a claim, no right to a damages remedy existed. However, because an adequate remedy at law existed, albeit not one available to King, specific performance was not proper here, either.

We disagree and find that the remedy fashioned by the trial court was proper under the UCC and Washington common law.

The UCC, § 2-716, codified in Washington as RCW 62A.2-716 provides:

62A.2-716 Buyer's right to specific performance or replevin.

(1) *Specific performance may be decreed where the goods are unique or in other proper circumstances.*

(2) The decree for specific performance may include such terms and conditions as to payment of the price, *damages,* or other relief as the court may deem just.

(3) The buyer has a right of replevin for goods identified to the contract if after reasonable effort he is unable to effect cover for such goods or the circumstances reasonably indicate that such effort will be unavailing or if the goods have been shipped under reservation and satisfaction of the security interest in them has been made or tendered.

(Emphasis added.)

The UCC, like its predecessor, the Uniform Sales Act, does not expressly require that the remedy at law be inadequate in order to invoke specific performance. However, the stated intent of the drafters of the UCC was to continue "in general prior policy as to specific performance and injunction against breach," and also "to further a *more liberal attitude* than some courts have shown" toward specific performance. (Emphasis added.) Official Comment 1, RCW 62A.2-716.

Nevertheless, there is a split of authority among those jurisdictions which have considered whether a buyer's remedy at law must be inadequate before specific performance can be granted.

* * *

[However, we] find the liberal interpretation urged by the UCC drafters to be entirely consistent with the common law of our state. Prior to adoption of the UCC, our cases did not always require the absence of a legal remedy before awarding specific performance nor did these cases require the goods to be absolutely "unique." Hence, the liberal approach to "other proper circumstances" suggested in Official Comment 2, RCW 62A.2-716 is not a departure from our law.[53]

---

[53] [3] This distinguishes our situation from the case relied upon by Lane, *Klein v. PepsiCo, Inc.*, 845 F.2d

The trial court here expressly relied on *Welts v. Paddock*, 139 Wash. 668, 247 P. 953 (1926). In *Welts*, a car was bargained for but was no longer available, and thus specific performance in the form of the car itself was impossible. Nevertheless, the court held that the trial court correctly awarded specific performance in the form of a judgment for the value of the particular car. *Welts*, 139 Wash. at 669–70, 247 P. 953.

The decision of the trial court is also supported by the case of *Zastrow v. W.G. Platts, Inc.*, 57 Wash. 2d 347, 350, 357 P.2d 162, 360 P.2d 354 (1960), in which the court held that "once a court of equity has properly acquired jurisdiction over a controversy, such a court can and will grant whatever relief the facts warrant, including the granting of legal remedies." In *Zastrow* the prayer for relief not only requested specific performance, but also "'such other and further relief as to the court seems meet and proper.'" The *Zastrow* court also found significant the fact that it was because of the appellant's own acts in relation to the property that the awarding of specific performance became impractical.

This holding was consistent with the earlier case of *Morgan v. Bell*, 3 Wash. 554, 28 P. 925 (1892). The rule stated by the *Morgan* court was: "[I]f the defendant has by his own act incapacitated himself from performance, the court of equity may, instead of dismissing the plaintiff's suit [for specific performance], award him the legal remedy of damages. POMEROY ON CONTRACTS, § 294." *Morgan*, 3 Wash. at 564.

Nevertheless, Lane claims that King has not met the requirements of § 2-716 because it has not shown an inability to cover. . . . Lane contends that King should have "covered" with the "as is" offer of November 4 and if there were additional repair costs or other expenses, it could have sued for the difference. Furthermore, Lane argues that even if the trial court was correct in finding that King did not have to cover by accepting its November 4 proposal, RCW 62A.2-713 sets forth the measure of damages for a buyer who does not cover — the difference between the market price when the buyer learned of the breach and the contract price. . . .

Here, the trial court held in conclusion 4 that King was under no obligation to purchase the planes on terms other than as contained in the contract. Specifically, the trial court found that King was under no obligation to accept the new November 4 proposal, which the trial court deemed to be considerably different from the original contract agreement. Lane neither assigns error to this conclusion nor to finding 29 which supports it. Lane has also failed to assign error to that part of conclusion 5 stating that plaintiff was unable to "cover" with alternate aircraft, but has only assigned error to the apparent contradiction between finding 39 (airplanes not unique) and conclusion 5 (both aircraft are unique).[54] An unchallenged conclusion of law becomes the law of the case. *State v. Slanaker*, 58 Wash. App. 161, 791 P.2d 575, *review denied*, 115 Wash. 2d 1031, 803 P.2d 324 (1990); *Millican of Wash., Inc. v. Wienker Carpet Serv., Inc.*, 44 Wash. App. 409, 413, 722 P.2d 861 (1986).

Therefore, the findings and conclusions listed above will not be disturbed on appeal.

We conclude the trial court properly determined that specific performance was an appropriate remedy here. At the time King commenced its action for specific performance, Lane was still in possession of the planes; thus, the court properly acquired equity jurisdiction. The airplanes, although not necessarily "unique," were rare enough

---

76 (4th Cir. 1988). There, the Fourth Circuit reversed a trial court decision awarding specific performance in the form of damages in the sale of a corporate jet which, as in the instant case, was no longer available. Despite the trial court's finding that the plane was unique, or in the alternative, that the plaintiff's inability to cover with another plane was strong evidence of "other circumstances" for purposes of awarding specific performance under § 2-716, the Fourth Circuit held that Virginia's adoption of the UCC did not abrogate the common law rule that specific performance is inappropriate where damages are recoverable and adequate. *Klein*, 845 F.2d at 80.

[54] [5] Considering the "other proper circumstances" standard, it is immaterial that the goods may not have been precisely "unique."

so as to make the ability to cover virtually impossible. Furthermore, Lane, by its own act of selling the planes, incapacitated itself from performance. Under these circumstances, the court of equity did not err in finding that "other proper circumstances" were present for issuance of relief under a claim of specific performance under the UCC. The trial court had the discretion to award the legal remedy of damages or other relief deemed just by the trial court. *See Morgan*, 3 Wash. at 564; RCW 62A.2-716(2). For the reasons above, we conclude that under RCW 62A.2-716 and Washington common law, the trial court's determination that "other proper circumstances" existed is correct and permitted it to fashion the relief it did.

*   *   *

III.

Lane also appeals from what it claims was the trial court's denial of its right to a jury trial. Lane contends that because the trial court ultimately based its theory of recovery on a legal theory of damages, its denial of an earlier request for a jury for the reason that the claim was grounded in equity was erroneous. Lane demanded a jury trial early in the history of this action. After pre-trial rulings precluded King from seeking monetary damages, Lane acknowledged that trial by jury was no longer available because the action was one solely in equity. However, at no time during the trial did Lane formally renew its demand for a jury.

Lane now alleges it was denied its his right to a jury trial under Const. art. 1, § 21. That section of the Washington State Constitution provides that "[t]he right of trial by jury shall remain inviolate." In a civil action, a right to a jury trial exists where the action is purely legal in nature. *Brown v. Safeway Stores, Inc.*, 94 Wash. 2d 359, 365, 617 P.2d 704 (1980); *see also Allard v. Pacific Nat'l Bank*, 99 Wash. 2d 394, 399, 663 P.2d 104 (1983). Where the action is purely equitable in nature, however, there is no right to a trial by jury. *Brown*, 94 Wash. 2d at 365.

The overall nature of a civil action is determined by considering all the issues raised by all the pleadings. *Brown*, 94 Wash. 2d at 365. In determining whether a case is primarily equitable or legal in nature, the trial court is accorded wide discretion, the exercise of which will not be disturbed except for a clear abuse. *Brown*, 94 Wash. 2d at 368. Here, the pleadings were all in equity. Although the court's remedy is akin to "damages," the jurisdiction and the underlying action were, and continued to be, equitable in nature.

Here, because Lane still had possession of the planes at the time the action was brought, specific performance was possible. Lane acknowledged that the action was in equity and did not press its jury demand. Nevertheless, by the time trial began, it was known that specific performance, in the sense of recovery of the planes, was not going to be possible. Even though in the course of arguing against awarding King a monetary recovery, Lane's counsel reminded the trial court that he had made a jury demand, he did not actually renew his demand and ask the trial court to rule on it. We hold Lane has waived the right to now argue that it had a right to a jury.

AGID and GROSSE, JJ., concur.

PROBLEM 7-20

George Bander agreed to purchase a rare Astin-Martin sportscar from Sportster Motors for $40,000. Subsequently, Sportster refused to tender the car, and Bander declared Sportster to be in breach of contract. At this time, the market value of the car had risen to $60,000. Bander consistently demanded performance, but did not proceed with legal action. During this time period, he was busy purchasing other rare cars for his collection, including a Ferrari and a Lamborghini. Bander ultimately filed suit against Sportster two years later, immediately after Sportster sold the car to a third party for $225,000 in a dramatically rising market. The third party had no notice of Bander's contract to purchase the car. At the time that the case came to trial, the market had fallen and the car now was valued at $80,000. Bander never purchased a similar Astin-Martin during this time, so he did not "cover" in response to the breach.

The jury determined that the car was "unique," but awarded damages to Bander under the formula of § 2-713 in the amount of $20,000 (representing the difference between the $60,000 value of the car at the time that Bander learned of the breach and the contract price of $40,000). Following trial, Bander moved for judgment on his alternative request for an award of specific performance in the form of damages by imposing a constructive trust on the proceeds of the sale by Sportster to the third party.

What arguments should Bander make to the trial judge, and how should Sportster respond to these arguments? Who bears the burden of proof, and what are the criteria for judgment?

3.   Buyer's Rights Prior to Acceptance of the Goods

Section 2-711 provides a buyer suffering a breach with several options and corresponding remedies. Generally, in response to a breach the buyer may either purchase conforming goods from another seller and use that transaction as the basis for measuring its damages, § 2-711(1)(a), or it may recover damages based on the difference between the market value of conforming goods and the contract price, § 2-711(1)(b). Additionally, if the buyer has rightfully rejected goods tendered by the seller or rightfully revoked its acceptance, § 2-711(3) recognizes that the buyer has a security interest in those goods with regard to certain expenses and payments.

a.   Buyer's security interest in rejected goods

If the buyer has a right to reject the goods or to revoke its acceptance, and the buyer effectively rejects or revokes, § 2-711(3) provides that the buyer has a security interest in the goods and may sell them to satisfy this interest. Work through the details of the buyer's rights in the goods in the following problem.

PROBLEM 7-21

Sharden Kitchen Equipment, Inc. is a wholesaler of kitchen equipment designed for restaurant use. Bistro is a restaurant. Bistro ordered three new stoves from Sharden. Pursuant to the agreement, Bistro paid a $10,000 deposit against the $20,000 purchase price when the agreement was signed, agreeing to pay the $10,000 balance within 30 days of delivery. Sharden delivered the goods on May 1. Unfortunately, the stoves were unmerchantable, and Bistro rightfully rejected the goods by immediately notifying Sharden on May 2.

1. Assume that Sharden agrees to pick up the stoves, investigate whether they are non-conforming, and (if they are non-conforming) attempt to repair them. Bistro refuses to permit Sharden to remove the stoves unless it returns the $10,000 deposit to Bistro. Is Bistro acting within its rights, or is it interfering with Sharden's right to cure its tender?

2. Assume that on May 5, Bistro contacted a supplier of second-hand kitchen equipment to remove the three stoves and purchase them for $8,000. Bistro then purchased new kitchen stoves from another supplier. Bistro did not notify Sharden that it was selling the goods. Has Bistro acted within its rights? Is Bistro also entitled to recover damages from Sharden?

3. Assume that on May 5, Bistro was able to sell the three stoves for $12,000. Bistro argues that it should be permitted to retain the $12,000 as liquidated damages. Is Bistro acting within its rights?

4. Assume that on May 5, Bistro was able to sell the three stoves for $12,000. Bistro argues that it should be compensated $10,000 for the return of its deposit, $100 interest on that sum from the time the deposit was paid, a $1,000 commission for arranging the sale, $600 as compensation for the cost to rent three temporary stoves until the stoves could be replaced, and $400 in attorney's fees for costs incurred in seeking the advice of its lawyer. Is Bistro acting within its rights?

b. Buyer's right to purchase substitute goods and recover damages

In many cases, an aggrieved buyer will want to secure the goods as quickly as possible to minimize the harm caused by the breach. Although an order of specific performance serves this purpose, the buyer may find that this is an impractical remedy in many cases. For example, the buyer may not meet the requirements of § 2-716, the seller's breach may be caused by its inability to obtain or manufacture the goods for the contract, or the buyer may not be in a position to wait until the order of specific performance is issued and enforced. As a result, many buyers will respond to a seller's breach by obtaining substitute goods from a third party. Section 2-712 recognizes the buyer's right to make a substitute purchase, known as "covering," and provides for an award of damages for any loss sustained. The cover remedy is designed to permit the buyer to obtain substitute goods immediately, and to provide the damages necessary to place the buyer in the position it would have been in if the seller had performed under the contract. Under § 2-712(1), the buyer has the right to cover if: it is making "any reasonable purchase of or contract to purchase goods in substitution for those due from the seller," if it does so "without unreasonable delay," and if it does so in "good faith." As with the provision governing the seller's right to resell goods, the obligation of good faith plays an important role in balancing Article 2's recognition that commercial reality requires that the buyer have some flexibility in securing substitute goods, with the recognition that buyers may be tempted during litigation to characterize their actions strategically in order to maximize their recovery of damages.

i. Purchasing goods in substitution

Section 2-712(1) makes clear that the buyer need not purchase goods identical to the goods due under the contract, but instead is entitled to purchase "goods in substitution." Comment 2 explains that this may be accomplished with a series of contracts rather than a single contract, and that it pertains to goods that are "commercially usable as reasonable substitutes under the circumstances." It should come as no surprise that the flexibility of this standard has resulted in litigation. A less obvious problem for courts arises when buyers "cover" by manufacturing the goods themselves, or by drawing from their inventory, since the statute refers to a substitute "purchase."

HUGHES COMMUNICATIONS GALAXY, INC. v. UNITED STATES
United States Court of Appeals, Federal Circuit
271 F.3d 1060 (2001)

RADER, Circuit J.

Following a trial on damages for breach of contract, the United States Court of Federal Claims awarded Hughes Communications Galaxy, Inc. $102,680,625. *Hughes Communications Galaxy, Inc. v. United States*, 47 Fed. Cl. 236 (2000) (*Hughes V*). Because the Court of Federal Claims did not abuse its discretion in calculating damages, this court affirms.

I.

* * *

In December 1985, NASA and Hughes entered into a Launch Services Agreement (LSA), which required NASA to use its "best efforts" to launch ten of Hughes' HS-393 satellites on space shuttles. The LSA required NASA to continue using its best efforts to launch Hughes' HS-393s until it launched all ten HS-393s or until September 30, 1994, whichever was earlier.

NASA compiled "manifests" of all shuttle payloads scheduled for launch on shuttles. NASA reissued these manifests periodically to account for changed circumstances. The manifests listed commercial payloads in order of their planned or firm launch dates and scheduled a shuttle for each launch. After NASA and Hughes entered the LSA, NASA assigned Hughes' satellites specific slots on a manifest.

In January 1986, the space shuttle Challenger exploded. Following the Challenger explosion, NASA suspended operation of the shuttles until September 1988. Further, in August 1986, President Reagan announced that NASA would no longer launch commercial satellites on shuttles. On July 10, 1986, NASA completed the last manifest before President Reagan's announcement. It projected that NASA would launch eight Hughes satellites on shuttles by September 1994. Thereafter, NASA compiled a new manifest that only included "shuttle unique" and "national security and foreign policy" payloads. That manifest did not list any Hughes satellites. Later NASA informed Hughes that it would almost certainly not launch any Hughes satellites on shuttles.

After 1986, Hughes launched three of its HS-393s on expendable launch vehicles (ELVs), one of which was the JCSAT-1. Hughes also launched several similar satellites on ELVs, including six HS-601 satellites. The HS-601s are similar to the HS-393s, except they are more powerful and better suited for ELV launches. While the ELV launches provided an alternative to shuttle launch services under the LSA, Hughes incurred more costs by launching satellites on ELVs rather than on shuttles.

Hughes sued the United States Government for breach of contract and for taking its property without providing just compensation. The Court of Federal Claims granted summary judgment to the Government on both claims based on the sovereign act defense. This court reversed that summary judgment and remanded. On remand, the Court of Federal Claims granted summary judgment for Hughes for breach of contract. Before holding a trial on damages, the Court of Federal Claims ruled that the Government could not produce evidence to reduce its damages by the amount Hughes had passed on to its customers in increased prices.

At the damages trial, Hughes sought to prove damages by showing its increased costs in launching satellites on ELVs, rather than on shuttles. Hughes presented two main methods for calculating the increased costs. The first method, the Ten HS-393 Satellites Method, compared the costs of launching ten HS-393s on shuttles under the LSA with the costs of launching ten HS-393s on ELVs. Because Hughes had actually launched only three HS-393s on ELVs, the method based the ELV launch costs on the actual costs of launching the three HS-393s. The second method, the Primary Method, compared Hughes' actual costs of launching ten satellites on ELVs with the costs that Hughes would have incurred by launching ten satellites on shuttles under the LSA. The ten satellites included the three HS-393s, the six HS-601s, and one HS-376. [Ed. Note: As explained below, Hughes developed the HS-601 to replace the HS-393 specifically because of the need to launch the satellites on ELVs.]

The Court of Federal Claims used the Ten HS-393 Satellites Method to calculate Hughes' increased costs of "cover." [Ed. Note: NASA challenged a number of features of the court's calculation, but these challenges were rejected.]

Based on its modified HS-393 method, the court awarded Hughes $102,680,625 in damages for its increased launch costs. Hughes and the Government both appeal. This court has jurisdiction under 28 U.S.C. § 1295(a)(3) (1994).

II.

* * *

The Court of Federal Claims awarded Hughes its increased costs of "cover." If a seller breaches a contract for goods, the buyer may "cover" or, in other words, obtain substitute goods from another seller. UCC § 2-712 (1997); E. Allan Farnsworth, Farnsworth on Contracts, § 12.11 (2d ed. 1998). Additionally, courts often award an analogous remedy for breach of service contracts such as the LSA. Farnsworth, *supra*, § 12.11. While the cover remedy of the Uniform Commercial Code does not govern this analogous remedy under the LSA, the Uniform Commercial Code provides useful guidance in applying general contract principles. Because both parties and the Court of Federal Claims have referred to this remedy as a "cover" remedy, this court will also use this term to refer to the remedy for Hughes' increased costs of obtaining substitute launch services.

The substitute goods or services involved in cover need not be identical to those involved in the contract, but they must be "commercially usable as reasonable substitutes under the circumstances." UCC § 2-712 cmt. 2. Whether cover provides a reasonable substitute under the circumstances is a question of fact. *Bigelow-Sanford, Inc. v. Gunny Corp.*, 649 F.2d 1060, 1065 (5th Cir. 1981) (stating that whether cover is reasonable is a "classic jury issue" (quoting *Transammonia Export Corp. v. Conserv., Inc.*, 554 F.2d 719, 724 (5th Cir. 1977))).

When a buyer of goods covers, the buyer's remedy for the seller's breach as to those goods equals the difference between the cost of the replacement goods and the contract price plus other losses. UCC § 2-712; Farnsworth, *supra*, § 12.11. Similarly, if the seller breaches a contract for services, the buyer's remedy for cover equals the difference between the cost of the substitute services and the contract price plus other losses. Farnsworth, *supra*, § 12.11 (where a building contractor breaches a first contract and the owner obtains substitute performance under a second contract, the owner can recover "any additional amount required by the second contract beyond what the owner would have had to pay under the first").

The Government cross appeals, arguing that Hughes should only be able to recover damages for the three HS-393s that it actually launched. While Hughes did not actually launch the fourth and fifth HS-393s that the Court of Federal Claims used to calculate damages, Hughes did incur costs in launching the HS-601s. The Court of Federal Claims found that Hughes developed the HS-601s to replace the HS-393s because the HS-601s were better suited for ELV launches, and that Hughes would have launched ten HS-393s on shuttles, given the opportunity. The Government disputes these findings, asserting that Hughes developed the HS-601s for independent business reasons, specifically, the more powerful HS-601s were more marketable. On this point, however, the Court of Federal Claims specifically credited testimony of Hughes' witnesses that Hughes would not have developed the HS-601 if the Government had not breached the LSA and that Hughes could have designed the HS-393 to accommodate the additional power of the HS-601. This testimony directly supports the Court of Federal Claims' finding that "the HS-393 could have been used in place of the HS-601" for HS-601 launches during the contract period. Thus, the trial court found that the HS-601 launches were reasonable substitutes under the circumstances of this breach.

Additionally, the Court of Federal Claims specifically found that no credible evidence supported the Government's attack on the HS-601 as a reasonable substitute. Specifically, the Government argues that at the time of contracting, the Government could not have foreseen "the demise of the HS-393" as a result of its breach. However, the Court of Federal Claims' damages method does not compensate Hughes for the "demise of the HS-393." Rather it compensates Hughes for increased launch costs. Had Hughes kept using the HS-393s, it would likely have incurred the same damages that the Court of Federal Claims awarded.

In sum, the Court of Federal Claims hinged its determination of this issue on credibility. Such determinations are virtually never clear error. *First Interstate Bank v. United States*, 61 F.3d 876, 882 (Cir. 1995). Furthermore, while the damages calculation might have been easier if Hughes had kept launching HS-393s on ELVs, ease of proof in potential future litigation is not sufficient justification to require Hughes to continue launching satellites that were ill-suited for ELV launches. As the victim of the breach, Hughes was within its rights to obtain commercially reasonable substitute launch services even if the substitute services were not identical to those covered by the LSA. The Court of Federal Claims thus did not clearly err in holding that Hughes successfully covered by launching HS-601s on ELVs. Accordingly, this court rejects the Government's cross appeal.

The Court of Federal Claims' use of increased HS-393 launch costs provided reasonable certainty in calculating damages. The trial court compared the costs of launching HS-393s on ELVs with the costs of launching the same HS-393s on shuttles. That comparison provided a basis for assessing Hughes' increased costs in launching the HS-601s. Under this method, the Court of Federal Claims accounted for any measurable difference in value to Hughes between the HS-393 launches and the HS-601 launches. *See* Farnsworth, *supra*, § 12.11 ("[A]ny measurable difference in quality [of a substitute] can be compensated for by a money allowance."). Accordingly, the Court of Federal Claims used the increased costs for HS-393s as a reasonable approximation of the increased costs incurred by Hughes in launching the substitute HS-601s. Under this method, the trial court did not abuse its discretion. *See S.W. Elecs. & Mfg. Corp. v. United States*, 228 Ct. Cl. 333, 655 F.2d 1078, 1088 (1981) (the trial court need only "make a fair and reasonable approximation").

The LSA states that damages "shall be limited to direct damages only and shall not include any loss of revenue, profits or other indirect or consequential damages." As discussed above, the increased costs represent direct damages incurred by Hughes in obtaining substitute launch services. Additionally, the damages do not include any lost revenues or profits, only increased costs. Finally, the damages are not consequential. The Uniform Commercial Code is instructive on this point. It allows recovery of the difference between the cost of cover and the contract price "together with any incidental and consequential damages," UCC § 2-712 (emphasis added), thereby distinguishing between consequential damages and the direct cost of cover. In sum, the Court of Federal Claims did not abuse its discretion by awarding Hughes damages for its increased costs incurred by obtaining substitute launch services for two HS-601s in addition to the three HS-393s.

Hughes decided to launch the JCSAT-1 satellite, a particular HS-393, on an ELV several months before President Reagan's announcement in 1986 that NASA would no longer launch commercial satellites on shuttles. NASA only breached its best efforts obligation after President Reagan's announcement. However, the LSA is not limited to launching particular satellites, such as the JCSAT-1. Rather, the LSA specifies a particular type of satellite (HS-393) in its preamble, and refers to the ten satellites as "HC-9 through HC-18." Thus, Hughes could have substituted another HS-393 for JCSAT-1, and Hughes still would have launched ten HS-393s on shuttles if NASA had provided those services under the LSA. Accordingly, the Court of Federal Claims did not abuse its discretion by awarding Hughes damages for the increased costs of launching the JCSAT-1.

* * *

IX.

The Government sought to reduce Hughes' damages by the amount Hughes recouped by increasing prices to customers, in other words, by the amount Hughes "passed through" to its customers. The Court of Federal Claims did not allow the Government to assert this defense at the damages trial. According to the Court of Federal Claims, this type of mitigation is too remote to consider.

Although not in the breach of contract context, the Supreme Court has addressed this issue. In *Southern Pacific Co. v. Darnell-Taenzer Lumber Co.*, 245 U.S. 531 (1918), a railroad overcharge case, the Court addressed the reduction of damages because the damaged party allegedly passed the unreasonable charge on to its customers. The Court stated: "The answer is not difficult. The general tendency of the law, in regard to damages at least, is not to go beyond the first step. As it does not attribute remote consequences to a defendant so it holds him liable if proximately the plaintiff has suffered a loss." *Id.* at 533–34. In an antitrust case, the Court noted that calculating pass-through damages reductions would present "the nearly insuperable difficulty of demonstrating that the particular plaintiff could not or would not have raised his prices absent the overcharge or maintained the higher price had the overcharge been discontinued." *Hanover Shoe, Inc. v. United Shoe Mach. Corp.*, 392 U.S. 481, 493 (1968). Similarly, allowing a pass-through damages reduction in a breach of contract action would destroy symmetry between reduction and escalation of damages. Moreover a standard for pass-through reductions would entail extremely difficult burdens for the trial court. Thus, the Supreme Court's reasoning also applies to this breach of contract action. The Court of Federal Claims did not abuse its discretion by disallowing pass-through damages reductions.

CONCLUSION

Because the Court of Federal Claims did not abuse its discretion in determining Hughes' damages for the Government's breach of the LSA, this court affirms.

QUESTIONS

1. Why doesn't Article 2 apply to this dispute? Why does the court apply the rule of § 2-712 even though the case does not come within the scope of Article 2?

2. The court briefly discusses why it affirms the decision of the Court of Federal Claims to prevent the Government from proving that Hughes was able to mitigate part of the increased cost of cover by raising the prices it charged its customers. What is the rationale offered by the court? Can you develop additional arguments for both sides on this issue?

ii. Without unreasonable delay and in good faith

The key test for any cover transaction is whether the buyer acted expeditiously and in good faith. Ordinary commercial incentives should cause the buyer to act efficiently in order to minimize its out-of-pocket costs. However, years later during litigation, the buyer may attempt to designate the "cover" transactions strategically, so as to maximize its recovery. Read the following cases and determine whether Professors White and Summers are correct that the good faith test might boil down to assessing the buyer's behavior under the "golden rule":

> A lawyer might test a client's good faith under 2-712 by asking: "How, where, and when would you have procured these goods if you had not been covering and had no prospect of a court recovery from another?" If the client can answer truthfully that it would have spent its own money in the same way, the court should demand no more.

WHITE & SUMMERS, UNIFORM COMMERCIAL CODE § 6-3, p. 190 (4th ed. 1998) (an earlier version of this treatise is quoted and applied in *Dangerfield v. Markel*, below).

OLOFFSON v. COOMER
Illinois Appellate Court
296 N.E.2d 871 (1973)

ALLOY, P.J.

Richard Oloffson, d/b/a Rich's Ag Service appeals from a judgment of the circuit court of Bureau County in favor of appellant against Clarence Coomer in the amount of $1,500 plus costs. The case was tried by the court without a jury.

Oloffson was a grain dealer. Coomer was a farmer. Oloffson was in the business of merchandising grain. Consequently, he was a "merchant" within the meaning of section 2-104 of the Uniform Commercial Code. (Ill. Rev. Stat. 1969, ch. 26, § 2-104). Coomer, however, was simply in the business of growing rather than merchandising grain. He, therefore, was not a "merchant" with respect to the merchandising of grain.

On April 16, 1970, Coomer agreed to sell to Oloffson, for delivery in October and December of 1970, 40,000 bushels of corn. Oloffson testified at the trial that the entire agreement was embodied in two separate contracts, each covering 20,000 bushels and that the first 20,000 bushels were to be delivered on or before October 30 at a price of $1.12 3/4 per bushel and the second 20,000 bushels were to be delivered on or before December 15, at a price of $1.12 1/4 per bushel. Coomer, in his testimony, agreed that the 40,000 bushels were to be delivered but stated that he was to deliver all he could by October 30 and the balance by December 15.

On June 3, 1970, Coomer informed Oloffson that he was not going to plant corn because the season had been too wet. He told Oloffson to arrange elsewhere to obtain the corn if Oloffson had obligated himself to deliver to any third party. The price for a bushel of corn on June 3, 1970, for future delivery, was $1.16. In September of 1970, Oloffson asked Coomer about delivery of the corn and Coomer repeated that he would not be able to deliver. Oloffson, however, persisted. He mailed Coomer confirmations of the April 16 agreement. Coomer ignored these. Oloffson's attorney then requested that Coomer perform. Coomer ignored this request likewise. The scheduled delivery dates referred to passed with no corn delivered. Oloffson then covered his obligation to his own vendee by purchasing 20,000 bushels at $1.35 per bushel and 20,000 bushels at $1.49 per bushel. The judgment from which Oloffson appeals awarded Oloffson as damages, the difference between the contract and the market prices on June 3, 1970, the day upon which Coomer first advised Oloffson he would not deliver.

Oloffson argues on this appeal that the proper measure of his damages was the difference between the contract price and the market price on the dates the corn should have been delivered in accordance with the April 16 agreement. Plaintiff does not seek any other damages. The trial court prior to entry of judgment, in an opinion finding the facts and reviewing the law, found that plaintiff was entitled to recover judgment only for the sum of $1,500 plus costs as we have indicated which is equal to the amount of the difference between the minimum contract price and the price on June 3, 1970, of $1.16 per bushel (taking the greatest differential from $1.12 1/4 per bushel multiplied by 40,000 bushels). We believe the findings and the judgment of the trial court were proper and should be affirmed.

It is clear that on June 3, 1970, Coomer repudiated the contract "with respect to performance not yet due." Under the terms of the Uniform Commercial Code the loss would impair the value of the contract to the remaining party in the amount as indicated. (Ill. Rev. Stat. 1969, ch. 26, § 2-610.) As a consequence, on June 3, 1970, Oloffson, as the "aggrieved party," could then:

(a) for a commercially reasonable time await performance by the repudiating party; or

(b) resort to any remedy for breach (Section 2-703 or Section 2-711), even though he has notified the repudiating party that he would await the latter's performance and has urged retraction; . . . .

If Oloffson chose to proceed under subparagraph (a) referred to, he could have awaited Coomer's performance for a "commercially reasonable time." As we indicate in the course of this opinion, that "commercially reasonable time" expired on June 3, 1970. The Uniform Commercial Code made a change in existing Illinois law in this respect, in that, prior to the adoption of the Code, a buyer in a position as Oloffson was privileged to await a seller's performance until the date that, according to the agreement, such performance was scheduled. To the extent that a "commercially reasonable time" is less than such date of performance, the Code now conditions the buyer's right to await performance. (*See* Ill. Rev. Stat. Ann. 1969, ch. 26, § 2-610, Illinois Code Comment, Paragraph (a).)

If, alternatively, Oloffson had proceeded under subparagraph (b) by treating the repudiation as a breach, the remedies to which he would have been entitled were set forth in section 2-711 (Ill. Rev. Stat. 1969, ch. 26, § 2-711), which is the only applicable section to which section 2-610(b) refers, according to the relevant portion of 2-711:

> (1) Where the seller fails to make delivery or repudiates or the buyer rightfully rejects or justifiably revokes acceptance then with respect to any goods involved, and with respect to the whole if the breach goes to the whole contract (Section 2-612), the buyer may cancel and whether or not he has done so may in addition to recovering so much of the price as has been paid:

> > (a) "cover" and have damages under the next section as to all the goods affected whether or not they have been identified to the contract; or

> > (b) recover damages for non-delivery as provided in this Article (Section 2-713). . . .

Plaintiff, therefore, was privileged under Section 2-610 of the Uniform Commercial Code to proceed either under subparagraph (a) or under subparagraph (b). At the expiration of the "commercially reasonable time" specified in subparagraph (a), he in effect would have a duty to proceed under subparagraph (b) since subparagraph (b) directs reference to remedies generally available to a buyer upon a seller's breach.

Oloffson's right to await Coomer's performance under section 2-610(a) was conditioned upon his:

(i)   waiting no longer than a "commercially reasonable time"; and
(ii) dealing with Coomer in good faith.

Since Coomer's statement to Oloffson on June 3, 1970, was unequivocal and since "cover" easily and immediately was available to Oloffson in the well-organized and easily accessible market for purchases of grain to be delivered in the future, it would be unreasonable for Oloffson on June 3, 1970, to have awaited Coomer's performance rather than to have proceeded under Section 2-610(b) and, thereunder, to elect then to treat the repudiation as a breach. Therefore, if Oloffson were relying on his right to effect cover under section 2-711(1)(a), June 3, 1970, might for the foregoing reason alone have been the day on which he acquired cover.

Additionally, however, the record and the finding of the trial court indicates that Oloffson adhered to a usage of trade that permitted his customers to cancel the contract for a future delivery of grain by making known to him a desire to cancel and paying to him the difference between the contract and market price on the day of cancellation. There is no indication whatever that Coomer was aware of this usage of trade. The trial court specifically found, as a fact, that, in the context in which Oloffson's failure to disclose this information occurred, Oloffson failed to act in good faith. According to Oloffson, he didn't ask for this information:

> I'm no information sender. If he had asked I would have told him exactly

what to do. . . . I didn't feel my responsibility. I thought it his to ask, in which case I would tell him exactly what to do.

We feel that the words "for a commercially reasonable time" as set forth in Section 2-610(a) must be read relatively to the obligation of good faith that is defined in Section 2-103(1)(b) and imposed expressly in Section 1-203. (Ill. Rev. Stat. 1969, ch. 26, § 2-103(1)(b) and § 1-203.)

The Uniform Commercial Code imposes upon the parties the obligation to deal with each other in good faith regardless of whether they are merchants. The Sales Article of the Code specifically defines good faith, "in the case of a merchant . . . [as] honesty in fact and the observance of reasonable commercial standards of fair dealing in the trade." For the foregoing reasons and likewise because Oloffson's failure to disclose in good faith might itself have been responsible for Coomer's failure to comply with the usage of trade which we must assume was known only to Oloffson, we conclude that a commercially reasonable time under the facts before us expired on June 3, 1970.

Imputing to Oloffson the consequences of Coomer's having acted upon the information that Oloffson in good faith should have transmitted to him, Oloffson knew or should have known on June 3, 1970, the limit of damages he probably could recover. If he were obligated to deliver grain to a third party, he knew or should have known that unless he covered on June 3, 1970, his own capital would be at risk with respect to his obligation to his own vendee. Therefore, on June 3, 1970, Oloffson, in effect, had a duty to proceed under subparagraph (b) of Section 2-610 and under subparagraphs (a) and (b) of subparagraph 1 of Section 2-711. If Oloffson had so proceeded under subparagraph (a) of Section 2-711, he should have effected cover and would have been entitled to recover damages all as provided in section 2-712, which requires that he would have had to cover in good faith without unreasonable delay. Since he would have had to effect cover on June 3, 1970, according to section 2-712(2), he would have been entitled to exactly the damages which the trial court awarded him in this cause.

Assuming that Oloffson had proceeded under subparagraph (b) of Section 2-711, he would have been entitled to recover from Coomer under Section 2-713 and Section 2-723 of the Commercial Code, the difference between the contract price and the market price on June 3, 1970, which is the date upon which he learned of the breach. This would produce precisely the same amount of damages which the trial court awarded him. (*See* Ill. Rev. Stat. 1969, ch. 26, § 2-723(1).)

Since the trial court properly awarded the damages to which plaintiff was entitled in this cause, the judgment of the circuit court of Bureau County is, therefore, affirmed.

Affirmed.

STOUDER and SCOTT, JJ., concur.

QUESTIONS

1. The facts indicate that Oloffson "covered" by purchasing substitute fungible goods when the date for Coomer's performance had passed. Why isn't Oloffson awarded cover damages under § 2-712?

2. You will soon learn that the market-price measure of damages measures the market price "at the time the buyer learned of the breach." This is not necessarily the time when a buyer will cover, since it may take the buyer some time to line up a substitute transaction. In *Oloffson*, the court measured the market-price damages as of the day that Coomer repudiated. Assume that Oloffson had covered two weeks after Coomer's repudiation, at an increased cost of $0.15 per bushel. Would this be a cover transaction that would serve as the measure of damages under § 2-712? Why or why not?

DANGERFIELD v. MARKEL
North Dakota Supreme Court
278 N.W.2d 364 (1979)

ERICKSTAD, C.J.

This appeal arises as a result of our decision in *Dangerfield v. Markel*, 252 N.W.2d 184 (N.D. 1977), in which we held that Markel, a potato grower, breached a contract with Dangerfield, a potato broker, to deliver potatoes, thus giving rise to damages under the Uniform Commercial Code. On remand the district court awarded Dangerfield $47,510.16 in damages plus interest and costs less an award to Markel of $3,840.68 plus interest. Markel appeals contending, among other things, that the district court made an erroneous award of damages to Dangerfield, and Dangerfield cross-appeals for an additional $101,675 in incidental and consequential damages. We affirm the district court judgment.

The facts in this case are stated in detail in two previous appeals to this court.[55] By contract dated June 13, 1972, Markel (seller) contracted to sell Dangerfield (buyer) 25,000 cwt. of chipping potatoes during the 1972–1973 shipping season. The seller allegedly breached the contract by refusing to deliver 15,055 cwt. of potatoes during the contract period and the buyer was allegedly forced to purchase potatoes on the open market to fulfill a contract with potato processors. As a result of this alleged breach, the buyer claimed to have suffered severe financial hardship, shortage of capital, damaged business reputation, loss of business and lessened business growth. He prayed for general damages of $56,310 and consequential damages of $101,745, less a set-off of $3,840.68 withheld by the buyer from payments due the seller for potatoes delivered. The seller counterclaimed for the $3,840.68 withheld by the buyer and for additional damages allegedly suffered as a result of the buyer's alleged breach of contract. The trial court found for the seller and the buyer appealed to this court.

In *Dangerfield, supra*, we determined that the seller had breached the contract; consequently, we reversed and remanded the case to the trial court for a determination of damages under the Uniform Commercial Code. . . . [The trial court] awarded the buyer general damages of $35,197.08 plus incidental damages of $19.50, less the seller's counterclaim of $3,840.68. On December 23, 1977, the buyer moved to amend this award pursuant to Rule 52(b), N.D.R. Civ. P., and on June 14, 1978, the trial court awarded the buyer $47,510.16 plus interest and costs less an award to the seller of $3,840.68 plus interest.

*   *   *

The primary issue on this appeal is whether or not the trial court made an erroneous award of damages to the buyer under the Uniform Commercial Code. The trial court in essence found that the buyer was entitled to damages pursuant to Section 41-02-91, N.D.C.C. (§ 2-712, UCC) for the amount expended by the buyer to purchase the 15,055 cwt. of potatoes still due under the contract:

> It appears to the Court that the Defendant [seller] . . . should be liable for the difference in price including freight, if any, between the quantity of the potatoes remaining to be delivered under the . . . contract after February 10, 1973 [date of breach], and the price including freight, if any, that the plaintiff [buyer] actually paid for potatoes to "cover" the supply that the plaintiff, Dangerfield, had a right to expect to be delivered . . . under . . . [the] contract during the remainder of the 1972–1973 potato shipping season.

---

[55] [1] This case completes the *Dangerfield v. Markel* hat trick. In *Dangerfield v. Markel*, 222 N.W.2d 373 (N.D.1974), we considered the application of the Statute of Frauds and a number of other procedural matters. In *Dangerfield v. Markel*, 252 N.W.2d 184 (N.D.1977), we held that Markel breached the agreement between the parties, thus entitling Dangerfield to damages. In this case, we are asked to review the computation of damages.

The court determined that the buyer completed "covering" the contract on March 21, 1973, which was 38 days after the date of breach. During the first 18 days of this cover period, the buyer's purchases averaged $4.41 per cwt. During the remaining twenty days, the buyer's purchases averaged over $5.41 per cwt., with many purchases made at $6.00 per cwt.

* * *

Seller argues in substance that 38 days for the buyer to cover in a rapidly rising market is improper under Sections 41-02-90 and 41-02-91, N.D.C.C. (§§ 2-711 and 2-712, UCC); therefore, he submits that Section 41-02-92, N.D.C.C. (§ 2-713, UCC) should have been used to compute damages.

The seller submits that the market price at the time of the breach was between $3.75 and $4.25 per cwt. He argues that a proper measure of damages pursuant to Section 41-02-92, N.D.C.C., would be an average of $4.00 per cwt. minus the contract price at the time of the breach ($1.90), or damages of $31,615.50 as opposed to the present award of $47,510.16, a reduction of $15,894.66.

The buyer responds that due to the perishable nature of the product involved in this case and the installment nature of the contract, the cover period was not unreasonable pursuant to Section 41-02-91, N.D.C.C.; therefore, the damages are correct.

The pre-code measure of damages for a breach of contract for the sale of goods was to allow the aggrieved party the difference between his bargain (contract price) and the market price. Although this worked reasonably well in the majority of cases, practical problems arose in determining the market price as well as the related questions of "as of when" and "where." After the seller's breach, the buyer faced a dilemma, i.e., to ensure that he would be fully compensated for the seller's breach, the buyer had to make a substitute purchase that the finder of fact would later determine to be at the "market value." This "20-20 hindsight approach" by the factfinder produced questionable results. Therefore, Section 2-712, UCC, (Section 41-02-91, N.D.C.C.) was added to the buyer's arsenal of remedies. This section allows the buyer to make a substitute purchase to replace the goods that were not delivered by the seller and the damages are measured by the difference between the cost of the substitute goods and the contract price. *See* J. WHITE & R. SUMMERS, HANDBOOK OF THE LAW UNDER THE UNIFORM COMMERCIAL CODE 175–180 (1972); R. NORDSTROM, HANDBOOK OF THE LAW OF SALES 439–44 (1970); T. QUINN, UNIFORM COMMERCIAL CODE COMMENTARY AND LAW DIGEST, 2-445–2-448 (1978).

The official comment to Section 2-712, UCC, states that "the test of proper cover is whether at the time and place the buyer acted in good faith and in a reasonable manner, and it is immaterial that hindsight may later prove that the method of cover used was not the cheapest or most effective."

In order for Section 2-712, UCC, to apply, the buyer must make a reasonable purchase in good faith without unreasonable delay. If a buyer fails to cover or covers improperly, e.g., waits an unreasonable length of time or buys in bad faith, he may still be entitled to some relief.

The seller argues that the buyer's purchases did not satisfy the criteria of Section 2-712, UCC; therefore, he is limited to the traditional measure of damages. Specifically, the seller argues that the buyer was obligated to purchase the entire cover on the date of the breach or shortly thereafter in order to mitigate his damages.

Although we have not dealt directly with the question of proper cover pursuant to Section 2-712, UCC, we stated in *Jamestown Terminal Elevator, Inc. v. Hieb*, 246 N.W.2d 736, 738 (N.D. 1976), at Syl. 10 that the "determination of a reasonable time to 'cover' following a breach of contract rests in the discretion of the jury and generally will not be interfered with on appeal where there is substantial evidence to sustain the verdict." Although there was no jury present in this case, the question of reasonable time to cover following a breach of contract is still a question of fact and we are governed by the "clearly erroneous" standard of Rule 52(a), N.D.R. Civ. P.

Similarly, the criteria of good faith and reasonable purchase are also questions of fact and will not be set aside unless clearly erroneous. *See Transammonia Export Corp. v. Conserv., Inc.*, 554 F.2d 719 (5th Cir. 1977); *Kiser v. Lemco Industries, Inc.*, 536 S.W.2d 585 (Tex. Civ. App. 1976).

The record indicates that the buyer could not cover the balance of the contract on the date of the breach:

Q: Once you learned you were not going to receive any more potatoes from Mr. Markel in February of 1973, did you attempt to buy potatoes to cover the shortage on the contract?

A: I did.

Q: Were you able to go out right at that time on February 12th or 13th, and buy quantity to cover the remaining balance on the contract?

A: No, I was not able to.

Q: Why was this?

A: Well, we were continuing on rising market, no one wanted to commit more than one or two loads at any one time, so would load on basis whatever day they got car, they would accept whatever market was at that day.

Q: If I understand what you are saying correctly, is that potatoes that were available at that time had to be bought and you would have to take delivery and ship them, that what you mean?

A: That's correct.

Q: That's correct?

A: Right.

Q: You were not able to buy potatoes in February for delivery in May?

A: No.

Q: Were you able to buy potatoes in middle of February for delivery say a month or two later?

A: No.

Q: Did you try to do this?

A: Yes.

Furthermore, the trial court was obviously of the opinion that the buyer acted in good faith under the circumstances:

Based upon the foregoing facts and the Uniform Commercial Code as quoted above, the Court is of the opinion that the plaintiff having elected to "cover" the defendant's breach was not obliged to purchase the entire cover as of the date of the breach since this contract called for installment deliveries over a period of months during the 1972, 1973 potato shipping season. In the absence of a showing of plaintiff so as to increase his damages against the defendant, the Court will view as reasonable a course of purchases of cover stocks from time to time. This ruling is particularly called for in this case where the subject of the contract is a bulky perishable commodity and the quantities must be warehoused at carefully controlled temperatures to avoid freezing or undue deterioration in holding. It would be unreasonable under these circumstances to hold the covering buyer to a February 10, 1973, market price date for immediate delivery of the entire amount of cover necessary to complete the contract of sale. This is particularly true where, as here, the quantity and bulk of goods in question is large and where the goods normally would flow into commerce upon delivery rather than into storage.

It is generally accepted that if the buyer complies with the requirements of Section 2-712, UCC, his purchase is presumed proper and the burden of proof is on the seller to show that cover was not properly obtained. *Kiser v. Lemco Industries, Inc., supra* at 589; *Laredo Hides Co., Inc. v. H & H Meat Products Co., Inc.*, 513 S.W.2d 210, 221 (Tex. Civ. App. 1974).

In *Laredo*, a Texas Court of Appeals was presented with a similar question. The buyer sued the seller to recover damages for breach of contract for the sale of cattle hides. The buyer agreed, pursuant to the contract, to purchase the seller's entire cattle hide production from March through December 1972. The contract provided no specific quantity but provided that deliveries be made at least twice a month. On March 3, 1972, the first delivery of hides was made under the contract. On March 21, 1972, the seller refused to sell any more hides to the buyer because of a payment dispute. The Texas court found that the seller had waived any objection and therefore breached the contract. The buyer was forced to purchase hides on the open market in substitution for the hides that were to have been delivered under the contract. The court awarded damages to the buyer for the substitute purchase minus the contract price, even though the cover "purchases had to be made periodically throughout 1972 since Laredo Hides [buyer] had no storage facilities, and the hides would decompose if allowed to age," and even though "the market price for hides steadily increased following the execution of the contract in question."

. . . We are mindful of the Code's basic remedial message in Section 41-01-06, N.D.C.C., (§ 1-106 UCC) to put the aggrieved party in the position performance would have. White and Summers, in their Hornbook series on the Uniform Commercial Code, comment on Sections 1-106 and 2-712:

> If 2-712 is to be the remedy used by more aggrieved buyers than any other remedy, then the courts must be chary of finding a good faith buyer's acts unreasonable. The courts should not hedge the remedy about with restrictions in the name of "reasonableness" that render it useless or uncertain for the good faith buyer. Indeed, one may argue that the courts should read very little substance into the reasonableness requirement and insist only that the buyer proceed in good faith. A question a lawyer might put to test his client's good faith under 2-712 is this: "How, where, and when would you have procured these goods if you had not been covering and had no prospect of a court recovery from another?" If the client can answer truthfully that he would have spent his own money in the same way, the court should not demand more.

J. White & R. Summers, Handbook of the Law Under the Uniform Commercial Code, at p.178.

We do not feel that the seller met his burden of showing that cover was improperly obtained in this case or that the district court's findings were clearly erroneous. Consequently, we affirm the district court judgment on this issue.

* * *

The district court's judgment is affirmed in all respects.

Sand, Paulson, Pederson, and Vande Walle, JJ., concur.

PROBLEM 7-22

Sleepeasy is a North Carolina manufacturer, and Bargain City Furniture is a New York wholesaler. Bargain purchased 1,000 sleeper sofas with Grade B fabric, agreeing to pay $400 for each sofa. The sofas were to be shipped in four equal installments, F.O.B. North Carolina, on March 1, April 1, May 1, and June 1. Shipping costs totaled $15,000. On February 15, Sleepeasy repudiated its obligations under the contract. On

June 1, Bargain purchased 1,000 sleeper sofas with Grade A fabric from an alternate supplier, agreeing to pay $450 for each sofa, F.O.B. New York, immediate delivery. Bargain tried unsuccessfully to find sleeper sofas with Grade B fabric, and it decided not to charge its customers extra for Grade A fabric in order to compensate for the delay in getting sofas to its customers.

How should Sleepeasy's lawyer respond when Bargain claims that it is entitled to $50,000 damages ($50 for each of the 1,000 sofas)? Can Bargain justify its claim?

PROBLEM 7-23

Billingsworth Historical Society, Inc. is a corporation established to preserve a famous American homestead, the Billingsworth Estate, and to provide tours and historical information about the Estate. Billingsworth runs a small gift shop in the basement of the mansion at the point where the tours end. Generally, the gift shop generates profits that cover thirty percent of Billingsworth's total operating expenses. Billingsworth sells a collection of T-shirts, magnets, picture books, coffee mugs, and reproductions of the mansion. Due to limited shelf space and limited storage space for inventory, Billingsworth is constantly trying new items and discontinuing items that do not sell.

On July 15, Billingsworth agreed to purchase 5,000 bronze reproductions of the mansion from Signature Novelties, for delivery on November 1. Billingsworth agreed to pay $15 for each reproduction, and intended to sell them for $25 each in the gift shop. This item was intended to be the "high end" item in the shop. Due to problems with its overseas manufacturer, Signature advised Billingsworth on September 1 that it would be unable to provide the reproductions. Billingsworth decided to use the shelf space that was to be dedicated to the Signature reproductions to purchase 5,000 crystal Christmas tree ornaments with the estate logo. These ornaments also were intended to be "high end" items. Billingsworth paid $22 for each ornament and sold them for $30. Later, in March, Billingsworth agreed to purchase 5,000 bronze reproductions of the mansion from a different supplier for the price of $16 each.

Billingsworth later sued Signature for breach, arguing that it "covered" by purchasing the crystal ornaments. Billingsworth demanded the difference between the cover price ($22) and the contract price ($15), or $7 per unit. Is Billingsworth entitled to receive $35,000 damages? Is there an alternative way to measure the damages that Billingsworth should receive?

c.   Buyer's market price damages for pre-acceptance breach

If the buyer suffers a breach and decides not to cover by purchasing substitute goods, Article 2 provides a market price measure of damages. By awarding the "difference between the market price at the time the buyer learned of the breach and the contract price," § 2-713 operates as a "hypothetical cover" by awarding as damages the loss that the buyer would have sustained *if* the buyer had immediately covered at the market price. After working through the calculations of damages under § 2-713, the balance of this section considers some of the subtle problems that arise in the interplay of the cover remedy and market price damages.

i.   Calculating damages; the consequences of failing to cover

Article 2 makes clear that a buyer suffering a breach is not required to purchase goods in substitution. The statute provides that a buyer "may" cover, § 2-712(1), and more specifically provides that the failure "of the buyer to effect cover within this section does not bar him from any other remedy," § 2-712(3). Comment 3 emphasizes the underlying policy "that cover is not a mandatory remedy for the buyer. The buyer is always free to choose between cover and damages for non-delivery under the next section."

Section § 2-713 mirrors the seller's market-price formula in § 2-708(1). The aggrieved buyer is entitled to recover the market price less the contract price, plus incidentals and consequentials, but less any expenses saved as a result of the breach. Significantly, § 2-715 defines consequential damages to include only "loss . . . which could not reasonably be prevented by cover or otherwise . . . " § 2-715(2)(a). This limitation operates as a general mitigation rule: a buyer that could have reasonably avoided consequential loss will be barred from recovering those avoidable losses. Therefore, if a buyer chooses not to cover and sues for damages under § 2-713, the buyer will not recover consequential losses under the market-price formula if these losses could have been avoided by cover.

Although simple to state, the rule invites complexities in its application. Recall that the cover remedy is flexible, permitting the buyer to purchase "substitute goods." When a buyer chooses not to cover, should courts employ the same broad definition of what counts as a cover transaction when determining the availability of consequential damages?

GLENN DISTRIBUTORS CORP. v. CARLISLE PLASTICS, INC.
United States District Court, Eastern District of Pennsylvania
2000 U.S. Dist. LEXIS 12350 (2000)

GILES, J.

Glenn Distributors Corp. ("Glenn") brought this diversity action against Carlisle Plastics, Inc. ("Carlisle"), seeking damages for breach of a sales contract. A jury returned a verdict in favor of Glenn. It answered Special Interrogatories finding that the parties had formed a contract, that Carlisle had breached it, that Glenn had lost profits in the amount of $230,003 for goods ordered but not delivered, and that Glenn was owed $14,000, plus interest, for goods paid for but not delivered. Carlisle now moves, pursuant to Fed.R.Civ.P. 50(b), for Judgment as a Matter of Law. For the reasons that follow, the motion is granted as to Glenn's claim of lost profits. Therefore, this court rules that Glenn's entitlement for breach of contract is limited to the $14,000 paid to Carlisle, plus interest, for a total judgment of $16,139.40.

Background

Factual Background

Glenn is in the business of purchasing and reselling close out items. These are items or products originally intended for sale to retailers but which remain unsold for various reasons: the particular item was discontinued; the item was seasonal; the expiration dates were drawing to a close; or the retail size or packaging had changed and a decision was made to dispose of the old packages. Glenn does not limit its business to the purchase and sale of particular types of goods, but rather trades in a wide range of food, plastics, and other items. Glenn purchases products from, among others, Hershey, Nestle, Carnation, and Johnson & Johnson, as well as Carlisle. Glenn finds and purchases close-out products through contacts with manufacturer sales representatives and at trade shows; it resells the items to various customers, mainly by bringing them to warehouses located in Philadelphia, New York, and Chicago. Glenn Segal ("Segal") is the founder and president of Glenn.

Carlisle is in the business of manufacturing plastic items, particularly trash bags, and selling to both wholesale and retail customers. Carlisle sells close-outs to numerous close-out purchasers, such as Glenn. Glenn purchases two broad categories of trash bags from Carlisle, one sold under the brand name "Ruffies," the other being "private label," items sold under various generic or supermarket store names. Glenn and

Carlisle have a business relationship dating back at least to 1995.

The material facts surrounding this particular business transaction are not in dispute; in dispute are the meaning and consequences of the transaction at issue.

* * *

Procedural History

[Ed. Note: The case was tried to a jury. Glenn offered evidence that a contract for sale existed and was breached by Carlisle. Glenn submitted a 104-page Damages Report containing Segal's calculation of the average gross and net profits made by Glenn on the sale of the trash bags purchased from Carlisle under the contract prior Carlisle's refusal to sell additional bags.]

Segal also testified as to Glenn's efforts at cover, that is, to find replacement goods to sell and recoup its lost profits. According to Segal, he went to trade shows, looked in the marketplace, and spoke to salesmen, attempting to find both Ruffies and other supermarket brands, without success. He did not identify anyone to whom he spoke at trade shows. He testified that Ruffies brand only was available from Carlisle and that he was not able to find supermarket brands at the close-out prices. Segal acknowledged that Glenn did not have contracts or oral or written agreements with any particular purchasers for any particular goods and no customer had a legal obligation to purchase any additional goods that Glenn might have received from Carlisle. However, Segal also testified that, based on his experience in running the business, he would have been able to sell additional Carlisle trash bags had they been delivered. He testified that he had received and sold almost 75% of the goods received under P.O. No. 10354 within a few months of receiving the goods, and therefore he believed that he could have sold the other 25% with no problem. He also testified that Glenn had completed four or five orders with Carlisle previously and never had any difficulty selling Carlisle trash bags. Moreover, he testified that several customers who previously had purchased Carlisle products from Glenn were happy with the product, were looking for more, and were waiting for additional goods to be shipped to Glenn. There was no testimony as to any other efforts to find and sell products to recoup profits and no testimony as to what Glenn did or attempted to do with the $250,000 that it did not send to Carlisle under this contract.

On cross-examination, Segal stated that the only two options he could see for obtaining identical or substitute goods were to purchase goods from Carlisle or to buy the same goods from a supermarket at retail, a higher price. He further testified that he thought about who else might make private label trash bags, but could not think of anyone. He further stated that he spoke to someone at Carlisle and to a former Carlisle salesman named David Rose, but did not speak to anyone else about trying to replace the trash bags that were not delivered.

On May 15, 2000, the jury returned answers to Special Interrogatories as follows:

1. Has the Plaintiff proven that there was an agreement between the parties that contained the terms of *quantity, price, delivery,* and *payment* that the Plaintiff contends were understood and agreed upon? YES

2. Considering the agreement as you have found it, has the Plaintiff proven that the Defendant breached it? YES

3. In what dollar amount, if any, has the Plaintiff proven, to a reasonable degree of certainty, its lost profits for goods ordered but not delivered? $230,003.00.

4. In what dollar amount has the Plaintiff proven that it is entitled to the return of money paid for goods which were not delivered? $14,000.

If the verdict as molded were to stand, Glenn also would be entitled to prejudgment interest on the overpayment amount (although not on lost profits) at the statutory rate of 6%, from November 1, 1997 to May 18, 2000, for an additional award of $2,139.40 bringing the total award for overpayment to $16,139.40 and the total damages award to $246,142.40.

* * *

Discussion

* * *

Liability

[Ed. Note: The court found that the jury finding of liability in favor of Glenn was supported by the evidence.]

Damages

* * *

Damages Report and Proof of Amount of Lost Profits

[Ed. Note: The Court held that the jury determinations that Glen had overpaid $14,000 for goods accepted, and that Glenn had lost $230,000 in profits on the goods not delivered were supported by sufficient evidence.]

Proof of Efforts at Cover

This cannot end this court's inquiry as to lost profits, however. Glenn also must present sufficient evidence of its reasonable efforts to "cover," that is, to purchase and resell replacement goods in an effort to offset its anticipatory losses. Because the evidence does not support a jury finding that Glenn made reasonable efforts under the circumstances to cover, Glenn is precluded as a matter of law from recovering lost profits. Thus, the jury award of lost profits cannot stand.

A buyer's failure to cover when cover reasonably is available precludes recovery of consequential damages, such as lost profits. *See* 13 Pa. C.S. § 2715(b)(1) (providing for the recovery of such consequential damages "which could not reasonably be prevented by cover or otherwise"); *see also National Controls [Corp. v. National Semiconductor Corp.]*, 833 F.2d [491] at 495 [(3d Cir. 1987)] (stating that, under Pennsylvania law, lost profits are recoverable as consequential damages in proper cases). A buyer covers by "making in good faith and without unreasonable delay any reasonable purchase of or contract to purchase goods in substitution for those due from the seller." 13 Pa. C.S. § 2712(a). The Pennsylvania Uniform Commercial Code envisions goods qualifying for cover to be "goods not identical with those involved but commercially usable as reasonable substitutes under the circumstances of the particular case." 13 Pa. C.S. § 2712 cmt. 2. The test of proper cover is "whether at the time and place the buyer acted in good faith and in a reasonable manner." *Id.* The plaintiff bears the burden of proof of establishing that it made good faith and reasonable efforts to cover. *Cf. Big Knob Volunteer Fire Co. v. Lowe & Moyer Garage, Inc.*, 487 A.2d 953, 959 (Pa. Super. Ct. 1985) (discussing plaintiff's burden of proof of establishing cover).

On direct examination, Segal testified about his cover efforts, stating that, in general, he went to trade shows and spoke to trash bag salesmen in efforts to find replacement items and that he was unable to find replacement bags at close-out prices. More specifically, he testified on cross-examination that he talked only to two people — someone at Carlisle and David Rose, a former Carlisle salesman. He also stated that he tried to think of where else he might find replacement trash bags at close-out prices, but was unable to think of anyplace or anyone. He stated that he felt that his only other option was to go to a supermarket and purchase the items he wanted at retail prices. There are two problems with this evidence.

First, it is not detailed or specific enough to establish that Glenn took reasonable efforts under the circumstances. Even drawing the most favorable inferences from his testimony, it establishes only that Segal talked to several people in the industry but could not find the identical Carlisle products (Ruffies or similar private-label trash bags) from any other manufacturer at the same prices. However, the cover obligation is a general duty to mitigate or reduce damages. *Cf. Big Knob Volunteer Fire Co.*, 487 A.2d at 961. A cover opportunity need not enable Glenn to recoup all its losses, only some portion of them. A cover good need not be identical, but only a good that is a reasonable commercial substitute. Therefore, if Glenn could find substantially similar, even if not identical goods, at similar, even if slightly higher prices, it was obligated to purchase and attempt to sell those goods. Only if the profits earned on such cover sales were less than the profits that would have been earned under the Carlisle contract, would the difference be recoverable as lost profits damage.

What is noteworthy about the evidence of cover is what is missing. Segal does not identify any competing manufacturers or other sources to whom he actually spoke about purchasing replacement goods. He does not identify anyone, other than Carlisle itself and a former contact at Carlisle, to whom he spoke at trade shows. He provides no details about what he learned about the price and availability of reasonable substitutes from any conversations that he had. He provides no details about whether there were goods available in the market or from other manufacturers that were substantially similar and why any such goods were not reasonably suitable substitutes. Nothing was presented to show that Segal took efforts that, based on his twenty years of experience in the business, reasonably might have enabled Glenn to find and sell replacement goods under the circumstances.

Second, Glenn's efforts at cover were not reasonable as a matter of law, given the nature of its business. As discussed *supra,* cover is not limited to purchasing identical goods; rather, the goods must be "commercially usable as reasonable substitutes under the circumstances of the particular case." 13 Pa. C.S. § 2712 cmt. 2. In other words, it must be an item that the plaintiff, in the course of its business, could sell for a similar profit. Glenn is not in the business of selling trash bags; Glenn is in the business of selling a myriad of close-out items from a myriad of manufacturers, including Hershey, Nestle, Carnation, and Johnson & Johnson, to a myriad of purchasers. Moreover, Glenn did not have specific contracts, agreements, or written or oral orders to sell trash bags to specific customers. Glenn was not obligated to sell trash bags to any particular customer. At best, several customers expressed an interest in purchasing additional Carlisle items in the future.

Under the circumstances, Glenn's cover duty required it not only to look for replacement trash bags to sell to the same customers as had bought previous Carlisle products, but to look for any replacement close-out items from any of its suppliers that Glenn could re-sell to any customers to recover some or all of its profit. For example, Glenn could have recouped some of its lost profits by purchasing and reselling Hershey product to some customer, although perhaps not to the same customers which would have purchased the trash bags. However, there is no evidence that Glenn took any steps to look for, purchase, or sell items other than trash bags. There also is no evidence that Glenn did anything with the $250,000 that it held and controlled and could have used to purchase cover goods. Glenn's legal obligation was to make reasonable efforts and to present evidence of those efforts or to present evidence of why some cover approach would have been unreasonable. Absent more substantial evidence that it met or attempted to meet its reasonable cover obligations, Glenn cannot recover lost profits.

Glenn points to the fact that the jury had re-read to it Segal's testimony on cover, which Glenn argues shows that the jury carefully weighed and considered the evidence and Segal's credibility. While that might be true, it does not change the fact that the evidence of cover presented to the jury was, as a matter of law, insufficient to support that verdict. Glenn's obligation was to present "the minimum quantum of evidence from which a jury might reasonably afford relief." *Parkway Garage, [Inc. v. City of Philadelphia*,] 5 F.3d [685] at 691 [(3d Cir. 1993)] (citation omitted). Glenn failed to present the minimum quantum of evidence on the question of cover that is required as a matter of law.

Conclusion

For the foregoing reasons, Carlisle's motion for judgment as a matter of law is granted. Accordingly, the jury verdict and judgment in favor of Glenn in the amount of $244,003 is vacated. Judgment shall be modified and entered in favor Glenn and against Carlisle in the sum of $16,139.40, plus legal interest from May 18, 2000 to the date of this Judgment.

[Ed. Note: The district court's decision in *Glenn Distributors* was ultimately reversed on other grounds by the Court of Appeals.]

PROBLEM 7-24

"Because You Deserve It, Inc.," is a mail-order retailer based in Dallas, Texas that targets young, affluent customers by offering unique leisure products. Sedgewick, Inc., is a manufacturer based in Duluth, Minnesota. Because ordered 1,000 deluxe dog houses from Sedgewick, to be shipped in two equal installments on February 1 and April 1. Both installments were to be shipped F.O.B. Duluth. The dog houses were constructed of cedar clapboard, had a miniature ceiling fan, and included the plumbing fit-up to connect a "drinking fountain" that provided cold water to the dog on demand. The contract price was $500 per dog house. Because expected to offer the dog houses in its spring catalog for $750.

The first installment arrived at Because's warehouse on February 3. Because paid $10 per dog house to the carrier, and incurred expenses of $1 per dog house to inspect the goods. Because immediately inspected them, discovered that they were unmerchantable, and rightfully rejected the shipment on February 4. Sedgewick did not respond to Because's complaints, and it informed Because on April 1 that it was not shipping the second installment since Because had not paid for the first installment.

Because decided to drop the deluxe dog house from its spring catalog rather than attempting to negotiate a substitute contract with another supplier on such short notice. The market prices for the dog houses offered at trial were reconstructed by identifying the prices charged by manufacturers of similar dog houses. These manufacturers served smaller markets and the prices reflected the varying demand in the different markets. Two important factors affecting the market price are the number of hot days in the area and the number of potential purchasers with significant disposable income. The market prices established by expert testimony were as follows:

Date	Market Value (Dallas)	Market Value (Duluth)
Feb. 4	$480	$450
April 1	$650	$550

1. What damages will Because recover under § 2-713 for Sedgewick's breach of the first installment?

2. What damages will Because recover under § 2-713 for Sedgewick's breach of the second installment?

3. What if Because had the opportunity on April 1 to purchase 1,000 dog houses for

$500 each, but chose not to do so? Is Because's right to damages under § 2-713 affected by its refusal to "cover"? *See* § 2-712. Does Because's failure to effect cover affect Because's right to obtain consequential damages for lost profits? *See* § 2-715.

PROBLEM 7-25

Assume the facts in the *Glenn Distributors* case, but with the following additions. Glenn has ample warehouse space to store the products it purchases, and these products are moved to its customers (retail businesses) within a matter of days. How should District Judge Giles rule on a Motion for Reconsideration if Glenn argues that the evidence of record demonstrates that Glenn had the capacity to purchase and resell more goods than were available at the time of the breach. In other words, Glenn argues that it has proved that all of its actual or potential (reasonable) purchases following the breach by Carlisle Plastics would not have exhausted its capacity to purchase the plastic bags and resell them to its customers. Should Glenn prevail in its claim for consequential damages despite a failure to make every possible "cover" purchase of close-out items? Is there a helpful analogy to seller's remedies that Glenn could draw in support of its argument?

ii. The problem of "internal cover" and the proper measure of damages

In some cases the buyer is also a producer of the good that it is purchasing from the seller. If the seller breaches, can the buyer "cover" by producing the goods in its own facilities or drawing from its own inventory? Several courts have found that § 2-712 should be read in a flexible manner to award damages on the basis of an "internal cover," despite the clear reference in the statute to a "purchase" of substitute goods. *See, e.g., Dura-Wood Treating Co. v. Century Forest Industries, Inc.*, 675 F.2d 745, 753–54 (5th Cir. 1982). In the following case, Judge Posner holds that an "internal cover" does not trigger the damages formula of § 2-712, and that the buyer is relegated to the general damages formula of § 2-713. Is Judge Posner's analysis convincing?

CHRONISTER OIL CO. v. UNOCAL REFINING AND MARKETING
United States Court of Appeals, Seventh Circuit
34 F.3d 462 (1994)

POSNER, C.J.

Chronister Oil Company brought this diversity suit for breach of contract against Union Oil Company (Unocal), to which Chronister had agreed to sell 25,000 barrels of gasoline. Unocal counterclaimed, charging that it was Chronister, not Unocal, that had broken their contract. The case is governed by the Uniform Commercial Code as interpreted by the Illinois courts; and the magistrate judge, to whom the case was assigned for trial by consent of the parties, held after a bench trial that Chronister had broken the contract, and he awarded damages of $26,000 to Unocal, precipitating this appeal.

The contract, made February 9, 1990, provided that Chronister, an oil trader, would deliver the 25,000 barrels to Colonial Pipeline (for shipment to Unocal) on the "front seventh cycle," and fixed a price of 60.4 cents a gallon. The term "front cycle" is pipelinese for the first half of what is normally a ten-day period for shipping a particular grade of product in a petroleum pipeline. The cycles begin on January 1, so the "front seventh cycle" would be approximately the first five days of March — apparently no effort is made to pin down the dates of the cycles and half cycles more precisely. To fulfill the contract, Chronister on March 1, 1990, made a contract with another oil trader, Enron, which in turn made a contract with a supplier, Crown Petroleum, to deliver the 25,000 barrels to Colonial Pipeline's pipeline at Pasadena, Texas for shipment east and north to terminals from which Unocal would deliver the gasoline to its dealers. Enron decided to have the gasoline delivered to Colonial's pipeline on March 5. But when the day arrived and Colonial tested the gasoline preparatory to taking it into its pipeline, it found that the gasoline contained too much water, and refused to take it. Unocal was informed on the morning of March 6 (which apparently was still within the front seventh cycle) and immediately called Chronister, demanding (at least implicitly, as we'll explain) assurances that Chronister would comply with the contract. Chronister got in touch with Enron, which agreed to supply another 25,000 barrels, but for shipment on the back seventh cycle, that is, later in March, or on the eighth cycle, later still. Unocal wasn't interested, and within hours, while Chronister was trying to solve the problem, Unocal took the precaution of diverting 25,000 barrels of gasoline that it already owned and that were in the pipeline in transit to a storage facility to Baton Rouge to its distribution terminals farther up the line — a measure Unocal describes as "provisional cover" — in effect supplying the 25,000 barrel deficit from inventory, but giving Chronister until the following day (March 7) to come up with conforming product.

Yet later the same day (March 6), Chronister, despite Unocal's adamant refusal to accept anything but front seventh cycle gasoline, accepted Enron's offer of substitute performance on the back seventh cycle and again offered this to Unocal. Again, Unocal insisted that it would take only front seventh cycle product — either the Crown Petroleum gasoline drained of its water or other product that could be injected into the pipeline in time. With Unocal unwilling to accept the 25,000 barrels on the back seventh cycle that Chronister had perhaps precipitately agreed to take from Enron, Chronister sold this gasoline to another company, Aectra Refining, at 55.3 cents a gallon. Claiming that by refusing to accept the substitute performance Unocal had broken the contract, Chronister filed this suit for damages based on the difference between the contract price and the lower price at which it sold the 25,000 barrels to Aectra. Unocal counterclaimed, contending that it was Chronister that had broken the contract and seeking damages equal to the difference between the contract price and the average cost of its inventory (63.14 cents), from which it had made up the loss of the 25,000 barrels promised by Chronister. The district court agreed with Unocal that Chronister, not Unocal, had broken the contract, and it awarded damages to Unocal on its counterclaim.

Chronister's appeal makes no reference to Unocal's alleged breach or to any damages sustained by Chronister as a result of that breach; we may assume that this claim has been abandoned and that all Chronister wants us to decide is that it did not break the contract or that if it did, Unocal sustained no damages. We agree with the second point, but not the first. The contract specified delivery on the front seventh cycle and Chronister could not deliver then because of the water in the gasoline. It argues that if Unocal hadn't pulled the plug on it at 10:30 a.m. on March 6, it would have found a way to meet its contractual obligations, whether by draining the excess water from Crown's gasoline, or by delivering gasoline to entry points to the pipeline closer to Unocal's terminals, or even by buying gasoline from Unocal! But Unocal informed Chronister that Unocal's action in "covering" (as Unocal calls it, erroneously as we shall see) its loss out of inventory was provisional until March 7 and would be rescinded if Chronister could deliver 25,000 barrels of gasoline to the pipeline by then; and thus forced to put up or shut up, Chronister shut up. Because oil companies that market their product through retail dealers, like Unocal, try to minimize the amount of inventory that they must hold against possible supply interruptions yet dare not find themselves unable to supply their dealers, a failure to deliver gasoline to such companies in timely fashion cannot be thought an immaterial breach. The fact that Chronister was not responsible for the water in the gasoline is of no significance. Liability for breach of contract is normally and here strict liability.

* * *

We move to the issue of damages. The point of an award of damages, whether it is for a breach of contract or for a tort, is, so far as possible, to put the victim where he would have been had the breach or tort not taken place. *Nicolet Instrument Corp. v. Lindquist & Vennum*, 34 F.3d 453, 457 (7th Cir. 1994). Unocal had, back in February, promised to pay Chronister 60.4 cents a gallon. By the first week of March, the price of gasoline for delivery to the Colonial Pipeline had fallen. On March 6, Chronister sold 25,000 barrels to Aectra at 55.3 cents a gallon, and it is not argued that Chronister could have gotten a higher price. Uncontradicted evidence revealed that there had been a similar sale at a similar price on March 2. Had Unocal gone out in the market and covered by buying 25,000 barrels on March 6 or 7 it would have paid somewhere in the neighborhood of 55 cents a gallon, and thus, would have *saved* 5 cents a gallon as a result of Chronister's breach. It makes no difference that instead of buying the gasoline on the open market it took it from inventory. As a matter of fact, because of an impending change in pressure by Colonial Pipeline that would make Unocal's inventory, stored mainly in a 300,000 barrel storage facility in Baton Rouge, shortly unshippable, Unocal had a strong interest in drawing down its inventory. The breach was a godsend. At argument, Unocal's counsel candidly acknowledged that Unocal was made better off as a result of the breach and that this was evident not only by the time of trial, and hence early enough to figure in the calculation of damages, *Rea v. Ford Motor Co.*, 560 F.2d 554, 557 (3d Cir. 1977), but within fifteen days after Chronister's breach.

Nevertheless, argues Unocal, it was entitled by UCC § 2-712 to cover by obtaining a substitute for the lost 25,000 barrels, even from itself, and to obtain as damages the difference between the cover price, which it deems to be 63.14 cents a gallon, the average cost of the inventory from which it obtained the substitute supply of gasoline, and the contract price of 60.4 cents. This is a misreading of section 2-712, as the only two Illinois-law cases pertinent to the issue hold. *Draper v. Minneapolis-Moline, Inc.*, 100 Ill. App. 2d 324, 241 N.E.2d 342, 345 (1968); *Rash Ranco Corp. v. B.L.B. Inc.*, 762 F. Supp. 1339, 1341 (N.D. Ill. 1991). Section 2-712 defines cover as purchasing or making a contract to purchase a substitute good. Unocal did not purchase any gasoline to take the place of the lost 25,000 barrels. It decided *not* to purchase a substitute good but instead to use a good that it already owned. You can't "purchase," whether in ordinary language or UCC speak (*see* § 1-201(32)), what you already own. The purpose of the cover provision is not to allow buyers to obtain damages when they have not been hurt, but to provide a market measure of the hurt. Taking a good out of your inventory and selling it is not a purchase in a market. There is no purchase price to use as a ready index of the harm that the buyer incurred by the seller's breach.

Two cases from other jurisdictions have shoehorned this kind of "self-cover" into section 2-712. *Cives Corp. v. Callier Steel Pipe & Tube, Inc.*, 482 A.2d 852, 858 (Me. 1984); *Dura-Wood Treating Co. v. Century Forest Industries, Inc.*, 675 F.2d 745, 753–54 (5th Cir. 1982). They had no need to do this violence to the text. Section 2-712 is not the only buyer's remedy that the UCC authorizes. The very next section allows the buyer to obtain damages measured by the difference between market price and contract price. If a reasonable response for the buyer to the breach would be to make the product itself, then the difference between the market price of that product and the contract price would be an appropriate measure of the harm from the breach. *Neibert v. Schwenn Agri-Production Corp.*, 219 Ill. App. 3d 188, 161 Ill. Dec. 841, 845, 579 N.E.2d 389, 393 (1991); *URSA Farmers Cooperative Co. v. Trent*, 58 Ill. App. 3d 930, 16 Ill. Dec. 348, 350–51, 374 N.E.2d 1123, 1125–26 (1978). That is what *Cives* and *Dura-Wood* hold; they merely cite the wrong section.

Unocal's response in diverting gasoline in transit to storage was reasonable; the only question, upon which its damages if any turn, is what that cost it. What it had paid for the gasoline — even less, the *average* price that it had paid for *all* the gasoline that it had not yet sold (the average cost of its inventory, in other words) — was not the cost of diverting the gasoline from storage to sale. At least it was not cost in a sense relative to damages. The object of an award of damages, as we have already noted, is to put the victim in the same place that he would have been in had the breach or other wrong of which he complains not occurred. It is to compensate him for a loss *that he would have avoided* had the violation not occurred. The concept of loss that underlies the computation of legal damages thus resembles the economist's concept of "opportunity cost": the opportunity one gives up by engaging in some activity is the cost of that activity, *Afram Export Corp. v. Metallurgiki Halyps, S.A.*, 772 F.2d 1358, 1369–70 (7th Cir.1985). We must ask what Unocal gave up as a consequence of the breach, and whether it was something of value.

By diverting the gasoline in order to protect itself against Chronister's breach of contract, Unocal gave up the opportunity either to sell the gasoline on the market (in order to lighten its inventory), which we know would have yielded it substantially less than the average cost of its inventory because the market price was much lower than that cost, or to have a larger — an unnecessarily and, it would soon prove, unusably larger — inventory. Neither course of action would have yielded value equal to Unocal's average cost of inventory or equal to the contract price. The first point shows that the average cost of inventory was the wrong figure to use in estimating Unocal's damages, and the second point shows that it had no damages. The 25,000 barrels it diverted to its dealers cost it less — was worth less — than the 25,000 barrels that Chronister failed to deliver to it as promised. Sellers usually break their contracts in a rising market, where they can get more for the product by selling to someone other than the buyer with whom they signed the contract. Here a seller in a declining market broke a contract that he desperately wanted to perform, conferring a windfall gain on the buyer — which the latter would like as it were to double with the help of the courts.

The judgment of the district court is affirmed insofar as it determined that Chronister broke its contract with Unocal. But it is reversed with respect to damages and remanded with directions to enter judgment for Unocal for nominal damages (to which for reasons we do not understand every victim of a breach of contract, unlike a tort victim, is entitled, *Stromberger v. 3M Co.*, 990 F.2d 974, 976 (7th Cir.1993)) only.

QUESTIONS

1. Would Judge Posner's analysis fit the situation where the buyer manufactures the substitute goods? Shouldn't the buyer be entitled to receive the difference between its manufacturing costs and the contract price for the goods because this situation, which was the situation in the *Dura-Wood* case cited in *Chronister Oil*, is more like a "purchase" of "substitute goods"? The *Dura-Wood* court based its holding in the purpose of § 2-712 to relieve the buyer of having to prove the market price for the goods when it purchases substitute goods in good faith and without unreasonable delay. In other words, the "cover" price is a proxy for the market price, which would be represented by the buyer's own production costs.

2. Why would a buyer ever sue for recovery under § 2-712 after manufacturing its own substitute goods? The buyer in *Dura-Wood* sought an award of consequential damages for the lost profits caused by tying up its production facilities, but this claim was met by a stiff rebuke from the court:

> The record demonstrates good faith on the part of Dura-Wood in choosing to cover by manufacturing the cross-ties internally. Dura-Wood took price quotations and ultimately determined it could produce the ties at a lower price. The district court's finding that Dura-Wood acted in good faith — which is implicit in its determination regarding actual damages — is not clearly erroneous.

*   *   *

> The district court awarded Dura-Wood $42,000 as "potential profits" that it lost "by using its own facilities to produce cross-ties to replace those which the defendant refused to provide." In other words, the district court found that, when Dura-Wood covered by internally manufacturing the cross-ties, it could have been producing cross-ties and selling them to new or different customers

instead of producing them in substitution for goods due from Century Forest.

*   *   *

However, the district court's damage award for "potential profits" does not fall within the contemplation of section 2-715. It is true Dura-Wood, by manufacturing its own cross-ties, covered for less money than if it had purchased ties from some other source. It is also true that, while Dura-Wood was producing its cross-ties, its facilities were tied up and Dura-Wood was unable to manufacture goods for new or different contracts. However, Dura-Wood could have minimized its overall losses. The cost of producing the ties plus the cost of lost profits resulting from Dura-Wood's inability to enter into new or different contracts was greater than the cost of simply purchasing the cover goods from another source. If Dura-Wood had purchased ties from someone else, its facilities would not have been tied up and Dura-Wood would have been able to enter new or different contracts. As a result, Dura-Wood would have had lower overall costs. Century Forest should not be obligated to pay for Dura-Wood's poor choice.

Dura-Wood Treating Co. v. Century Forest Ind., Inc., 675 F.2d 745, 754–55 (5th Cir. 1982). Does this mean that a buyer can never win by claiming an internal cover by manufacturing substitute goods because its true "cost," including the "opportunity costs" of lost sales will always be the market price, and a manufacturing cost that exceeds the market price is likely to be regarded as evidence that the buyer "covered" in bad faith?

d. Election of remedies and related problems

i. Is the buyer deemed to have elected a remedy by deciding to cover?

You will recall that we discussed the extent to which a seller suffering a breach may choose to resell the goods and recover under § 2-706 or to recover market-price damages under § 2-708. As a general matter, the seller is free to choose its course of action following breach, but in the *Tesoro* case, the court held that the seller is not free to resell the goods and then sue for market-price damages. An actual resale by the seller was deemed to operate as an election for resale damages.

A parallel situation exists under the provisions regarding buyer's remedies, where the buyer is free to elect between purchasing substitute goods and recovering damages under § 2-712 or suing for market-price damages under § 2-713. One difference, as we have seen, is that the buyer does pay a price for choosing not to cover: the buyer is precluded from recovering consequential damages that could have been avoided by a cover transaction. But this one difference does not answer the broader question: Should a buyer who covers after a breach be deemed to have made a "factual election" that limits the buyer to recovering damages only under § 2-712?

Ellen Peters, a commercial law professor at Yale Law School who served as an Associate Reporter for the Restatement (Second) Contracts and later was appointed to be Chief Justice of the Connecticut Supreme Court, wrote a widely influential article at the time that Article 2 was being adopted by the states. She argued that a buyer who covers should nevertheless be entitled to obtain market based damages under § 2-713. After carefully reading her argument, apply it to the problem and try to develop the counter-arguments that would limit a covering buyer to the damages available under § 2-712.

Ellen Peters, *Remedies for Breach of Contracts Relating to the Sale of Goods Under the Uniform Commercial Code: A Roadmap for Article Two*
73 YALE L.J. 199, 259–61 (1963)[56]

Proper interpretation of the market-contract formula is confusing enough when the aggrieved party premises recovery on that basis alone, having foregone the opportunity to enter into substitute transactions. What happens, however, if the seller has in fact resold, or the buyer covered? Does the existence of the substitute preclude reliance on the market-contract standard, or does the complainant have a free option to choose whichever measure turns out to be the more favorable? To permit the option is to allow speculation at the expense of the party in breach; forbidding it allows the party in breach to profit from a substitute transaction which he can neither compel nor control. On this conflict of policy, the Code speaks expressly only in Comment 5 to 2-713, the buyer's market-contract formula:

> The present section provides a remedy which is completely alternative to cover under the preceding section and applies only when and to the extent that the buyer has not covered.

Comment 5 is clear enough; but nothing supporting this position can be found in the text of 2-713. However, 2-711, which lists the buyer's rights upon rightful rejection, states its alternatives in a sequence consistent with Comment 5: "the buyer may . . . 'cover' and have damages under the next section [which contains the cover-contract formula] . . . , or . . . recover damages for non-delivery [the market-contract formula]." Section 2-711 is clear that a buyer need not cover, unless he so chooses, but seemingly requires damages to be measured by cover if cover has been effectuated. In the case of a seller suing for non-acceptance, there is no parallel limitation, either in comment or text. The only possible explanation for such a difference in the treatment of buyers and sellers would have to be derived from inequalities in the statements of the other half of the option, the market-contract formulae. Perhaps the seller needs a freer hand when he resells than the buyer who covers because the seller's market-contract formula is so erratic a measure of damages.

But the history of the development of these remedies over the various drafts of the Uniform Commercial Code suggests a quite different explanation. Until the 1957 version, 2-703 on seller's remedies prefaced his right to recover damages for non-acceptance with "so far as any goods have not been resold." At that point then, the market-contract formula was equally conditional for both buyers and sellers, the buyer's rights then being identical in text and comment to their present 1962 statement. The 1957 amendment, deleting this language, was promulgated, according to the Report of the 1956 Recommendations of the Editorial Board, at the suggestion of the New York Law Revision Commission "to make it clear that the aggrieved seller was not required to elect between damages under Section 2-706 and damages under Section 2-708." This comment is instructive on two counts: it indicates a purpose to safeguard alternative remedies, and, more important, it characterizes the amendment as a clarification rather than as a change. The latter point might be dismissed as mere face-saving on the part of the revision committee but for the fact that changes are called changes in other comments. If the committee's characterization is correct, the references to resale, even in the old 2-703 on seller's remedies, was addressed not to the existence of a resale but to whether the resale was being relied upon to measure damages. But if this is an accurate reading of the old 2-703, it is equally appropriate to a free choice among the buyer's remedies under 2-711.

A non-restrictive reading of the various remedies sections to preserve full options to

---

use or to ignore substitute transactions as a measure of damages makes more sense than Comment 5 for a number of reasons. It preserves a parity of remedy for buyers and sellers. It is consistent with a number of other Code sections which frown on premature election of remedies. It is a good deal easier to administer, since it would be most difficult to ferret out from a reluctant complainant information about transactions sufficiently related to the contract in breach to qualify as cover or resale. Finally, preservation of the option encourages recourse to actual market substitutes, since it guarantees to the injured party that he will not lose all remedy in the event of an unusually favorable substitute contract. It is thus consistent with the Code's overall interest in keeping goods moving in commerce as rapidly as possible.

PROBLEM 7-26

Starbuzz contracted to deliver 10,000 bushels of coffee beans to Beanery, Inc., on June 1, at the price of $5 per bushel. Beanery learned that Starbuzz was delivering his beans late, and so it demanded adequate assurances of due performance in writing. Starbuzz was unable to provide such assurances and so Beanery rightfully canceled the contract on April 1. At that time, the cost of coffee beans had risen to $7 per bushel due to interruptions in supply. During the ensuing months the supply problems abated. On June 10, Beanery purchased 10,000 bushels of coffee beans from another supplier at a cost of $5.50 per bushel.

Beanery argues that it is entitled to $20,000 in damages under § 2-713 (based on the market price differential at the time Beanery learned of the breach). Starbuzz responds that Beanery is entitled only to $5,000 in damages under § 2-712 (based on the difference between the "cover" price and the contract price).

Who should prevail? Is Beanery entitled to receive market-price damages in light of the arguments made by Justice Peters, or is Beanery properly limited to cover damages in light of the statement in Comment 5 that the market-price formula "applies only when and to the extent that the buyer has not covered"? How would you respond to Justice Peters' arguments?

ii. Limiting market-contract damages to actual damages

Even if it makes some sense as a general matter to limit covering buyers to the damages provided by § 2-712, it is not necessarily the case that a buyer that chooses not to cover should automatically receive market-contract damages. We saw that § 2-708(1) provides a contract-market measure of damages for sellers suffering a breach, but that § 2-708(2) provides an alternative lost profits measure when the contract-market measure is "inadequate" to compensate the seller for its lost expectation. In contrast, § 2-713 provides only a market-contract measure, and does not provide an alternative in the event that the market-contract does not adequately determine the buyer's lost expectation. How should a court respond if the buyer has elected not to cover, but the general market-price measure of damages of § 2-713 appears to overcompensate the buyer?

ALLIED CANNERS & PACKERS, INC. v. VICTOR PACKING CO.
California Court of Appeal, First Appellate District
162 Cal. App. 3d 905 (1984)

ROUSE, J.

Allied Canners & Packers, Inc. (Allied) appeals from a judgment entered in its favor, following a trial to the court, in an action for damages for breach of two sales contracts. It contends that the trial court erroneously determined that it was a broker rather than a buyer under the contracts and therefore failed to apply the proper measure of damages specified in the California Uniform Commercial Code (Commercial Code). We determine that Allied was a buyer within the meaning of the Commercial Code, but conclude that under the facts and circumstances of this case, the trial court awarded the proper amount of damages.

The facts initially giving rise to the controversy are essentially undisputed. Allied is a corporation engaged in the business of exporting dry, canned and frozen food products. Its principal place of business is San Francisco. Respondent, Victor Packing Company (Victor), is engaged in the business of packing and processing fruits and is located in Fresno. On September 3, 1976, Allied entered into a contract with Victor whereby Victor was to sell and deliver five containers (each holding 37,500 pounds) of select Natural Thompson Seedless (NTS) raisins, to be delivered FOB at the Port of Oakland during the month of October, 1976, at a time and to a vessel later to be designated by Allied. On September 8, 1976, the parties entered into a second contract whereby Victor agreed to sell and deliver an additional five containers of NTS raisins on the same terms.

The Raisin Administrative Committee (RAC), established pursuant to a federal marketing order, determines the amount of raisins which may be sold as "free" raisins (those which may be sold anywhere but are usually sold in the United States or Canada due to the prices available), and the amount which must be sold as "reserve" raisins (those which may be sold only outside the Western Hemisphere or to certain government-sponsored programs). Packer members of RAC may purchase reserve raisins from RAC. Victor was a member of RAC at the time of the transactions involved here. Allied, as an exporter, was not eligible for membership in RAC and could not buy raisins from RAC. From September 1, 1976, until 8:30 a.m. on September 10, 1976, the price at which packer members could purchase reserve NTS raisins from RAC was 22 cents per pound, substantially below the prevailing market price.

A packer seeking to buy "reserve" raisins must file an application with RAC and make a deposit of 95 percent of the purchase price. When the application is approved, the packer can obtain release of the raisins by paying the remaining 5 percent of the price. If the packer is selling directly to a foreign buyer, it must provide RAC with the name of that buyer. If it is selling to an exporter, the packer must provide RAC with the name of the exporter, and the exporter must provide RAC with the name and address of the foreign importer to whom it will sell the raisins. RAC keeps the name of the foreign importer confidential, as frequently the exporter, in order to protect his business sources, does not want the packer to have that information.

In this case, Allied had contracts to sell the raisins to Japanese firms. It provided the names of those firms to RAC, which did not disclose the names to Victor. Allied's contracts with Victor provided for Victor to sell the raisins at 29.75 cents per pound with a discount of 4 percent.

Allied characterizes the 4 percent as "the standard trade discount" while Victor characterizes it as a "commission." Regardless of the characterization, the parties agree that Allied was to realize a gain of $4,462.50 in the transaction.[57] Although the record is not entirely clear as to the terms of Allied's contracts with the Japanese firms, it appears that Allied was to net 29.75 cents per pound on the raisins, since its total gain was to be $4,462.50.

Heavy rains during the night of September 9, 1976, severely damaged the raisin crop which was drying on the ground, adversely affecting the supply of raisins in the Fresno area. On September 10, 1976, RAC withdrew its offer to release reserve raisins to members who had not mailed or brought checks for application deposits prior to 8:30 a.m. on that date. Victor had not, prior to that time, made application for purchase of reserve raisins in order to fulfill the contracts with Allied. Both Victor and Allied attempted to persuade RAC to sell 375,000 pounds of NTS raisins to Victor, but such

---

[57] [1] Ten containers of raisins, each holding 37,500 pounds of raisins, would hold a total of 375,000 pounds. At 29.75 cents per pound, the total price would be $111,562.50. Four percent of that sum equals $4,462.50.

efforts were unsuccessful. The raisins which had been in the reserve pool were later released into free tonnage. On September 15, 1976, Victor notified Allied that it would not deliver the raisins as required by the contracts. Victor conceded that it thereby breached those contracts.

Allied did not cover by purchasing raisins on the open market. The earliest that either party could have bought raisins was October 1976, when the price of raisins was in the vicinity of 80 to 87 cents per pound.[58] One of Allied's buyers agreed to rescind its contract to purchase three containers of raisins, but another buyer, Shoei Foods Industrial Co., Ltd. (Shoei), demanded delivery of the remaining seven containers. Allied's contract with Shoei, however, contained a provision holding it harmless from liability caused by strikes, fires, accidents and other developments beyond its control. At trial, Allied conceded that it had not been sued by Shoei for any damages resulting from its failure to deliver raisins to Shoei, but suggested that Shoei would hold off suing it until this action against Victor was concluded. Judgment was entered in this case in July 1981, nearly five years after the transaction occurred. Although the statute of limitations for a breach of contract action had expired (Code Civ. Proc., § 337, subd. 1), Shoei had never brought suit against Allied, and there is no indication that Allied voluntarily paid damages to Shoei.

Allied argued at trial, and contends on appeal, that it was the buyer under its contracts with Victor and therefore entitled to damages pursuant to Commercial Code section 2713, subdivision (1) . . . .

Allied contends that pursuant to section 2713, subdivision (1), it is entitled to damages in the amount of $150,281.25, representing the difference between the contract price of 29.75 cents per pound and a market price of 87 cents per pound for 262,500 pounds (seven containers) of NTS raisins. The trial court, however, refused to apply section 2713 because it determined, purportedly as a matter of fact, that Allied was a broker, not a buyer, and therefore not subject to the provisions of the Commercial Code governing a buyer's remedies for breach of contract by a seller. The court concluded that Allied was damaged only to the extent of its lost "commission" as a broker in the sum of $4,462.50. Judgment for that amount was entered in Allied's favor.

While we perceive that the trial court was attempting to limit Allied's damages to those actually suffered, and felt that application of the formula set forth in section 2713, subdivision (1), would result in a windfall to Allied, it could not properly do so on the basis that Allied was not a "buyer" within the meaning of the Commercial Code. Although Victor urges that this case turns upon whether there is substantial evidence to support the trial court's "finding" that Allied was a broker not a buyer, we believe that whether Allied was a broker or a buyer is a conclusion of law to be drawn from the pertinent facts in this case, which are basically undisputed. (*See* 6 WITKIN, CAL. PROCEDURE (1971 ed.) *Appeal*, § 210, pp. 4200, 4201 ["Existence of the legal relationship of agency or independent contract, and the scope of employment, are questions of law"], and cases there cited.)

Section 2103, subdivision (1)(a), defines buyer as follows: "'Buyer' means a person who buys or contracts to buy goods." The contracts between Allied and Victor mention only those two parties and provide that Victor was to ship the raisins to Allied at the dock in Oakland. Victor did not even know the name of Shoei. Certainly, had Victor shipped the raisins but Allied not paid for them, logic dictates that Victor would have sued Allied for payment as the buyer.

Victor argues that Allied was not buying for its own account because Shoei was sending it a letter of credit to pay for Shoei's purchase of the raisins. Nevertheless, the evidence is uncontroverted that Allied would be sent an invoice from Victor in such

---

[58] [2] The trial court found that the price at the time was 80 cents per pound. The parties, however, stipulated that the price was 87 cents per pound on October 18, 1976, when the market reopened. Due to the conclusion we reach in this opinion, it is unnecessary to resolve this discrepancy.

transactions, and Allied would pay Victor with a check drawn on its general company account.

In essence, Victor is arguing that, because Allied had already contracted to sell the raisins to another, it was not a buyer in its transaction with Victor. As the manager of RAC testified at trial, "An exporter is a person [who] buys raisins and sells them to somebody else." Certainly, it is not uncommon for an exporter to have "back-to-back" contracts, one to buy and the other to sell. Such entities are often referred to as "middlemen" or persons having "forward contracts" in discussions of buyer and seller remedies under the Uniform Code. (*See, e.g.*, WHITE & SUMMERS, UNIFORM COMMERCIAL CODE (2d ed. 1980) § 6-4, p. 224; Simon & Novack, *Limiting the Buyer's Market Damages to Lost Profits: A Challenge to the Enforceability of Market Contracts* (1979) 92 HARV. L. REV. 1395, 1404 (hereafter cited as *Market Damages*).)

We conclude that Allied was a buyer in its contract with Victor and that it had a "forward contract" to sell the raisins to Shoei. As such, the remedies provided to a buyer by the Commercial Code are applicable to it. Thus, we turn to a consideration of the correct application of such remedies in this case.

A buyer's primary remedies for nondelivery of goods by a seller are provided by sections 2712 ("cover" damages), 2713 (damages when buyer has not covered), 2715 (incidental and consequential damages), and sections 2502 and 2716 (replevin or specific performance under certain circumstances). Of these sections, only the provisions of sections 2712, 2713, and 2715 are pertinent to our discussion here.

Sections 2-712 and 2-713 of the Uniform Code are sometimes referred to as "cover" and "hypothetical cover," since the former involves an actual entry into the market by the buyer while the latter does not. (*See* Childres, *Buyer's Remedies: The Danger of Section 2-713* (1978) 72 Nw. U. L. REV. 837, 841 [applying those terms] (hereafter cited as *Buyer's Remedies*); Peters, *Remedies for Breach of Contracts Relating to the Sale of Goods Under the Uniform Commercial Code: A Roadmap For Article Two* (1963) 73 YALE L.J. 199, 259 [market under section 2-713 is "purely theoretical"] (hereafter cited as *Remedies for Breach of Contracts*).) It has been recognized that the use of the market-price contract-price formula under section 2-713 does not, absent pure accident, result in a damage award reflecting the buyer's actual loss. (*Buyer's Remedies, supra,* at pp. 841–842; *Remedies for Breach of Contracts, supra,* at p. 259; *Market Damages, supra,* 92 HARV. L. REV. 1395 et seq.; WHITE & SUMMERS, UNIFORM COMMERCIAL CODE, *supra,* at p. 224.)

For example, in this case it is agreed that Allied's actual lost profit on the transaction was $4,462.50, while application of the market-contract price formula would yield damages of approximately $150,000. In *Market Damages, supra,* Simon and Novack describe the courts as divided on the issue of whether market damages, even though in excess of the plaintiff's loss, are appropriate for a supplier's breach of his delivery obligations and observe: "Strangely enough, each view has generally tended to disregard the arguments, and even the existence, of the opposing view. These two rival bodies of law, imposing in appearance, have passed each other like silent ships in the night." (92 HARV. L. REV. 1395, 1397.) In *Buyer's Remedies, supra,* Professor Childres similarly points out that the courts have generally not undertaken any real analysis of the competing considerations involved in determining the correct measure of damages in such circumstances. (72 Nw. U.L. REV. 837, 844 et seq.) We shall undertake such an analysis.

Professors White and Summers, after noting their belief that "the Code drafters did not by [section 2-713] intend to put the buyer in the same position as performance would have" (WHITE & SUMMERS, UNIFORM COMMERCIAL CODE, *supra,* at p. 224), advance two possible explanations for the section. First, they suggest that it is simply a historical anomaly: "Since cover was not a recognized remedy under pre-Code law, it made sense under that law to say that the contract-market formula put buyer in the same position as performance would have *on the assumption that the buyer would purchase substitute goods.* If things worked right, the market price would approximate the cost of the substitute goods and buyer would be put 'in the same position. . . .' But under the Code, 2-712 does this job with greater precision, and 2-713 reigns over only those cases in which the buyer does not purchase a substitute. Perhaps the drafters retained 2-713 not out of a belief in its appropriateness, but out of fear that they would be dismissed as iconoclasts had they proposed that the court in noncover cases simply award the buyer any economic loss proximately caused by seller's breach." (*Ibid.*)

They conclude, however, that probably the best explanation for section 2-713 "is that it is a statutory liquidated damage clause, a breach inhibitor the payout of which need bear no close relation to plaintiff's actual loss." (WHITE & SUMMERS, UNIFORM COMMERCIAL CODE, *supra*, at p. 225.) They then observe that this explanation conflicts with the policy set forth in section 1-106, which provides in subdivision (1): "The remedies provided by this code shall be liberally administered *to the end that the aggrieved party may be put in as good a position as if the other party had fully performed*, but neither consequential or special nor penal damages may be had except as specifically provided in this code or by other rule of law." (Italics added.) They find section 2-713 consistent, however, with a belief that plaintiffs recover too little and too infrequently for the law of contracts to be effective, and offer no suggestion for resolution of the conflict. (*Ibid.*)

In her article *Remedies for Breach of Contracts, supra*, then-Professor Peters states:

> Perhaps it is misleading to think of the market-contract formula as a device for the measurement of damages. . . . An alternative way of looking at market-contract is to view this differential as a statutory liquidated damages clause, rather than as an effort to calculate actual losses. If it is useful in every case to hold the party in breach to some baseline liability, in order to encourage faithful adherence to contractual obligations, perhaps market fluctuations furnish as good a standard as any.

(73 YALE L.J. 199, 259.) She does not discuss the conflict between the market-contract formula and the "only as good a position as performance" policy embodied in section 1-106.

Simon and Novack state: "While it is generally recognized that the automatic invocation of market damages may sometimes over-compensate the plaintiff, a variety of arguments have been employed by commentators and courts to justify this result: the desirability of maintaining a uniform rule and of facilitating settlements; the public interest in encouraging contract performance and the proper functioning of the market; the prevention of defendant's unjust enrichment; the restoration of the very 'value' promised to plaintiff; and the inherent difficulty and complexity of proving actual economic losses not encompassed within the contract terms." (Fns. omitted; *Market Damages, supra*, 92 HARV. L. REV. 1395, 1403.) That a defendant not be unjustly enriched by a bad faith breach is a concern widely shared by commentators and courts. (*Id.*, at p. 1406, fn. 51, and cases there cited.)

Viewing section 2-713 as, in effect, a statutory provision for liquidated damages, it is necessary for us to determine whether a damage award to a buyer who has not covered is ever appropriately limited to the buyer's actual economic loss which is below the damages produced by the market-contract formula, and, if so, whether the present case presents a situation in which the damages should be so limited.

One view is that section 2-713 of the Uniform Code, or a substantively similar statutory provision, establishes the principle that a buyer's resale contract and damage claims made thereunder are irrelevant to an award of damages, and that damages therefore cannot be limited to a plaintiff's actual economic loss. (*See* 11 WILLISTON, CONTRACTS (3d ed. 1968) § 1388 [Uniform Code]; *Coombs and Company of Ogden v. Reed* (1956) 5 Utah 2d 419 [303 P.2d 1097] [Uniform Sales Act]; *Brightwater Paper Co. v.*

Monadnock Paper Mills (1st Cir. 1947) 161 F.2d 869 [Massachusetts Sales Act then in effect]; *Goldfarb v. Campe Corporation* (1917) 99 Misc. 475 [164 N.Y.S. 583] [New York Sales Act then in effect].) Simon and Novack, while favoring that view, concede that it can be argued that the provision of section 1-106 that an aggrieved party be put " 'in as good a position as if the other party had fully performed' " calls for an opposite conclusion. (*Market Damages, supra*, 92 Harv. L. Rev. 1395, 1412–1413, fn. 71.)

Although we find no cases discussing the interaction of section 1-106 and section 2-713, we note that some pre-Uniform Code cases held that a limitation to actual losses should be placed upon the market price-contract price measure of damages under general contract principles. (*See, e.g., Foss v. Heineman* (1910) 144 Wis. 146 [128 N.W. 881]; *Isaacson v. Crean* (1917) 165 N.Y.S. 218; *Texas Co. v. Pensacola Maritime Corporation* (5th Cir. 1922) 279 Fed. 19.) One author on the subject has apparently concluded that such a limitation is appropriate under the Uniform Code when the plaintiff-buyer has a resale contract and the existence of the resale contract is known to the defendant-seller: "It may be supposed . . . that the buyer was bound by a contract made before the breach to deliver to a third person the very goods which the buyer expected to obtain from the seller, and the price under the resale contract may be less than the market price at the time of the breach. If the reason generally given for the rule permitting the recovery of additional damage because of an advantageous resale contract existing and known to the defendant when he contracted be applied, namely, that such consequential damages are allowed because the parties supposedly contract for them, it would follow that in every case the damage that the defendant might normally expect to follow from breach of his contract should be recovered even though the plaintiff actually suffered less damage than the difference between the contract price and the market price." (4 Anderson, Uniform Commercial Code (3d ed. 1983) § 2-711:15, pp. 430–431.)

*   *   *

We conclude that in the circumstances of this case — in which the seller knew that the buyer had a resale contract (necessarily so because raisins would not be released by RAC, unless Allied provided it with the name of the buyer in its forward contract), the buyer has not been able to show that it will be liable in damages to the buyer on its forward contract, and there has been no finding of bad faith on the part of the seller — the policy of section 1106, subdivision (1), that the aggrieved party be put in as good a position as if the other party had performed, requires that the award of damages to the buyer be limited to its actual loss, the amount it expected to make on the transaction. We note that in the context of a cover case under section 2712, a Court of Appeal has recently approved the use of section 1106 to limit damages to the amount that would put the plaintiff in as good a position as if the defendant had performed. (*Sun Maid Raisin Growers v. Victor Packing Co.* (1983) 146 Cal. App. 3d 787, 792 [194 Cal. Rptr. 612].)

We need not determine in this case what degree of bad faith on the part of a breaching seller might warrant the award of market-contract price damages without limitation, in circumstances otherwise similar to those involved here, in order to prevent unjust enrichment to a seller who deliberately breaches in order to take advantage of a rising market. Although Allied implies that Victor was guilty of bad faith here because after its breach it allowed another packer to acquire reserve raisins to which it was entitled at 36.25 cents per pound, rather than acquiring the raisins and delivering them to Allied, the record is simply not clear on Victor's situation following the rains. It does appear clear, however, that, as the trial court found, the rains caused a severe problem, and Victor made substantial efforts to persuade RAC to release reserve raisins to it in spite of its failure to get its check to RAC before 8:30 a.m. on September 10, 1976. We do not deem this record one to support an inference that windfall damages must be awarded the buyer to prevent unjust enrichment to a deliberately breaching seller. (*Compare Sun Maid Raisin Growers v. Victor Packing Co., supra*, 146 Cal. App. 3d 787 [where, in a case coincidentally involving Victor, Victor was expressly found by the trial court to have engaged in bad faith by gambling on the market price of raisins in deciding whether to perform its contracts to sell raisins to Sun Maid].)

The judgment is affirmed. Each party is to bear its own costs on appeal.

KLINE, P.J., and SMITH, J., concurred.

QUESTIONS

1. Assume that Victor repudiated its agreement with Allied because it could sell raisins from its inventory to other buyers at the much higher market rate following the heavy rains. The court suggests that Allied might be entitled to full market-price damages in these circumstances. Does this make sense in light of the reasoning in the case?

2. What if Allied submitted evidence that Shoei terminated its business relationship with Allied after Allied was unable to supply raisins under their contract. Could Allied recover its anticipated profits from future dealings with Shoei (discounted to present value)? If not, how could Allied avoid this loss?

3. Not all courts have followed the Allied Canners approach to this problem. Does the following case provide a more convincing analysis? Can you critique the following case using the Allied Canners analysis?

TEXPAR ENERGY, INC. v. MURPHY OIL USA, INC.
United States Court of Appeals, Seventh Circuit
45 F.3d 1111 (1995)

REAVLEY, Circuit J.

In this contract dispute, appellant Murphy Oil USA, Inc. complains of the jury charge and the damages awarded to appellee TexPar Energy, Inc. Finding no reversible error, we affirm.

BACKGROUND

On May 29, 1992, TexPar contracted to purchase 15,000 tons of asphalt from Murphy at an average price of $53 per ton. On the same day, TexPar contracted to sell the 15,000 tons to Starry Construction Company at an average price of $56 per ton. Hence, TexPar stood to profit by $45,000 if both contracts were performed.

During the first half of 1992, the price of asphalt varied widely. Evidence was presented of prices ranging from $40 to $100 per ton. The wide range of prices reflected volatile market forces. From the supply standpoint, asphalt is one of the end products of petroleum refining, and must be sold or stockpiled to accommodate the production of more valuable petroleum products. Demand depends in large measure on the availability of government funding for highway construction. Weather also affects asphalt supply and demand. The price rose rapidly in June of 1992, and consequently, the sale price of $53 per ton lost its attractiveness to Murphy.

In May and early June, TexPar took delivery of 690 tons of asphalt; but, on June 5, Murphy stopped its deliveries and notified TexPar that its sales manager lacked authority to make the contract. By then, the price of asphalt had risen to $80 per ton. Starry insisted that TexPar deliver the full 15,000 tons at $56 per ton as TexPar and Starry had agreed. Ultimately, with TexPar's approval, Starry and Murphy negotiated directly and agreed on a price of $68.50 per ton. This arrangement was reached several weeks after the repudiation by Murphy. By this time the market price had dropped, according to TexPar. TexPar agreed to pay Starry the $12.50 difference between the new price of $68.50 per ton and the original $56 per ton price. TexPar therefore paid Starry approximately $191,000 to cover the price difference.

The jury found that the difference between the market price ($80) and the contract price ($53) of the undelivered asphalt (14,310 tons) on the date of repudiation (June 5), amounted to $386,370. The court entered judgment for this amount.

DISCUSSION

*   *   *

The district court applied UCC § 2-713, Wis. Stat. Ann. § 402.713 (West 1994), which provides a measure of the buyer's damages for nondelivery or repudiation. . . . Murphy does not dispute that if this provision is applied, the damages awarded are proper, since Murphy does not dispute the quantity of goods, the market price or the date of notice of repudiation used by the jury to calculate damages. Instead, Murphy argues that the general measure of damages in a breach of contract case is the amount needed to place the plaintiff in as good a position as he would have been if the contract had been performed. Murphy argues that since TexPar's award — $386,370 — far exceeds its out-of-pocket expenses ($191,000) and lost profits ($45,000) occasioned by the repudiation, the court erred in instructing the jury merely to find the difference in market price and entering judgment in that amount.

We cannot quarrel with Murphy that the general measure of damages in contract cases is the expectancy or "benefit of the bargain" measure. The UCC itself embraces such a measure in § 1-106, providing that the UCC remedies "shall be liberally administered to the end that the aggrieved party may be put in as good a position as if the other party had fully performed. . . ." Wis. Stat. Ann. § 401.106 (1994).

Nevertheless, we do not believe that the district court erred in awarding damages based on a straightforward application of § 402.713. That provision is found in the article on the sale of goods, and specifies a remedy for the circumstances presented here — the seller's nondelivery of goods for which there is a market price at the time of repudiation.

We can see no sound reason for looking to an alternative measure of damages. Murphy argues that TexPar shouldn't be awarded a "windfall" amount in excess of its out-of-pocket damages. Since it depends on the market price on a date after the making of the contract, the remedy under § 402.713 necessarily does not correspond to the buyer's actual losses, barring a coincidence. Our problem with Murphy's suggested measure of damages is that limiting the buyer's damages in cases such as this one to the buyer's out-of-pocket losses could, depending on the market, create a windfall for the seller. If the price of asphalt had fallen back to $56 per ton by the time Starry and Murphy had arranged for replacement asphalt, TexPar's damages would have been zero by this measure, and Murphy could have reaped a windfall by selling at the market price of $80 in early June instead of the $53 price negotiated with TexPar.

Murphy argues that it did not in fact realize a windfall, since its cost of production was $70 per ton and it eventually agreed to sell to Starry for $68.50. We find this argument unpersuasive. Applying the market value measure of damages under UCC § 2-713, as the district court did, is expressly allowed under the Code. Since § 2-713 addresses the circumstances of a seller's nondelivery of goods with a market price, we see no error in applying this specific provision over the more general remedies provision found at § 1-106. *See Tongish v. Thomas*, 251 Kan. 728, 840 P.2d 471, 474 (1992) ("[B]ecause it appears impractical to make [§ 1-106] and [§ 2-713] harmonize in this factual situation, [§ 2-713] should prevail as the more specific statute according to statutory rules of construction."). The UCC § 2-713 remedy serves the purpose of discouraging sellers from repudiating their contracts as the market rises, if the buyer should resell as did TexPar, or gambling that the buyer's damages will be small should the market drop. It also has the advantage of promoting uniformity and predictability in commercial transactions, by fixing damages on the date of the breach, rather than allowing the vicissitudes of the market in the future to determine damages. *Id.* 840 P.2d at 476 ("Damages computed under [§ 2-713] encourage the honoring of contracts and market stability.").

*   *   *

iii.   Limiting cover damages to actual damages

If the buyer does cover, it would seem that § 2-712 always would provide the buyer with its lost expectation. Work through the following problem and determine whether Article 2 supports the claim that in some circumstances a covering buyer should not recover damages under the formula in § 2-712.

PROBLEM 7-27

Shuregrow is a California lettuce grower and distributor. Shuregrow agreed to deliver 14 loads of lettuce each week to Boddington Supplies, an Ohio lettuce broker, for a price of $50,000 per weekly delivery. The agreement commenced on January 1 and expired the following December 31. From January 1 through June 30, Shuregrow tendered the loads in a timely fashion and was paid by Boddington in accordance with their agreement. After the price of lettuce rose dramatically during May and June, however, Shuregrow told Boddington that it would refuse to deliver any more lettuce, unless Boddington agreed to pay market prices. Boddington refused. Shuregrow failed to make the first delivery in July, and missed all subsequent weekly deliveries for the six months remaining under its contract. Shuregrow purported to cancel the contract immediately, and then arranged to make spot sales to other buyers of the 14 loads per week at prevailing market prices. Shuregrow received $100,000 for the first week's shipment to its new buyer, but as the prices in the industry moderated, it was receiving only $70,000 by the end of the six month period.

Boddington sells all of the lettuce that it purchases from Shuregrow to Restaurant Supplies, a company that chops and shreds lettuce and then sells it to fast food restaurants. Boddington's contract with Restaurant Supplies provides that Boddington will be paid on a "cost-plus" basis. Specifically, Restaurant Supplies agreed to pay Boddington its actual cost in purchasing the lettuce, plus a 5% ($2,500 per week) commission. Restaurant Supplies has a similar "cost-plus" arrangement with its buyers.

After Shuregrow refused to perform, Boddington went on the spot market and obtained a six-month contract for twenty-six consecutive weekly deliveries of 14 loads of lettuce per week, at a cost of $100,000 per weekly delivery. Under its contract with Restaurant Supplies, Boddington was paid $105,000 for each weekly delivery during the six-month period ($100,000 cost, plus 5% commission).

What damages should Boddington receive?

4.   Buyer's Damages for Breach with Respect to Accepted Goods

After the buyer accepts the goods and loses its right to revoke acceptance (whether by choice or inadvertence), the buyer's right to obtain damages is governed by § 2-714. This measure of damages is phrased as a straightforward principle: the buyer may recover "the loss resulting in the ordinary course of events from the seller's breach as determined in any manner which is reasonable." However, the statute makes clear that the notice required under § 2-607(3) is a prerequisite to recovery. We begin with the notice prerequisite and then examine the measure of damages for breach following acceptance.

a.   Notifying the seller of the breach

Section 2-607(3) provides that once a buyer has accepted a tender it must, "within a reasonable time after he discovers or should have discovered any breach, notify the seller of breach." The consequence for failing to notify the seller of the breach within a reasonable time is that the buyer is "barred from any remedy." This harsh rule provides a breaching seller with a complete defense to Article 2 claims; consequently, lawyers representing sellers are well advised to raise this defense whenever possible. One hotly contested issue has been whether the buyer provides the requisite notice by filing the lawsuit. In answering this question, courts have looked to the underlying purposes and policies of the notice requirement.

BROOKINGS MUNICIPAL UTILITIES, INC. v. AMOCO CHEMICAL CO.
United States District Court, District of South Dakota
103 F. Supp. 2d 1169 (2000)

PIERSOL, C.J.

The defendants, Amoco Chemical Company and Amoco Reinforced Plastics Company (ARPCO), have filed a Motion for Summary Judgment on the Merits of the Complaint filed against them by the plaintiffs, Brookings Municipal Utilities, Inc. and the City of Brookings, South Dakota.

BACKGROUND

[Ed. Note: Brookings oversaw the construction of a sewer line known as the "Southwest Interceptor" by a private company ("NCU"). Brookings approved several types of pipe based on the manufacturer's warranties, including ARPCO's "Techite" pipe. Brookings intended the sewer line to have a useful life of fifty years, and therefore only approved sewer pipes that would resist corrosion and meet the ASTM sewer pipe specifications. The contractor subsequently purchased and installed Techite pipe between 1975 and 1980. The pipe allegedly did not conform to the warranties, leading to problems.]

After installation, the Southwest Interceptor suffered three corrosion-related incidents. On April 25, 1983, a twenty-foot section of pipe broke, necessitating repair of the pipe and prompting Rittershaus [the design engineer] to advise NCU and Amoco of the problem. Almost thirteen years later, on April 14, 1996, a motorist named Heidi Aylward drove her car into what she thought was a mud puddle, but which turned out to be a fifteen-foot deep sinkhole caused by a break in the sewer line. Another break was discovered in June of 1996. After this third break, plaintiffs determined that a majority of the pipeline was damaged, and decided to replace all of the Techite pipe in the Southwest Interceptor at a cost of $1,056,788. Plaintiffs did not discuss the problems with the pipeline with representatives from the defendants or NCU before replacing the pipeline, or before filing this lawsuit.

[Ed. Note: The plaintiff's complaint included causes of action for breach of warranty and breach of implied warranty.]

DISCUSSION

*   *   *

B. Breach of Warranty Claims

Under § 2-607(3) of the UCC, where a tender of goods has been accepted, "[t]he buyer must within a reasonable time after he discovers or should have discovered any breach notify the seller of breach or be barred from any remedy." SDCL 57A-2-607(3). The purpose [of] the notice requirement is to: (1) give the seller sufficient time to investigate the breach of warranty claim while the facts are still fresh; (2) foster settlement through negotiation; (3) allow the seller to avoid future defects; (4) allow the seller to minimize damages; and (5) protect the seller from stale claims. *Hepper v. Triple U Enterprises, Inc.*, 388 N.W.2d 525, 527 (S.D. 1986). Plaintiffs have conceded that they failed to give notice of breach to NCU or defendants before filing this lawsuit. Instead, plaintiffs argue that the notice requirement does not apply to them because they are not "buyers" of the Techite pipe and that, under the circumstances of this case, their failure to provide notice under § 2-607(3) should be excused.[59] Neither of these arguments is persuasive.

Plaintiffs were required to provide notice of breach to "the seller" under § 2-607(3). The notice requirement "is a fundamental prerequisite of a buyer's recovery for breach of warranty." *Ehlers v. Chrysler Motor Corp.*, 88 S.D. 612, 226 N.W.2d 157, 159 (1975). Plaintiffs contend that they are exempt from the notice requirement, arguing that they are not "buyers" under § 2-607(3) because they did not buy the Techite pipe from defendants. As defendants point out, the cases which plaintiffs cite for this proposition involved allegations of personal injury by a plaintiff who did not purchase the product by which he was injured. *See Cole v. Keller Indus., Inc.*, 132 F.3d 1044 (4th Cir. 1998) (employee injured while using ladder purchased by his employer); *Yates v. Pitman Mfg., Inc.*, 257 Va. 601, 514 S.E.2d 605 (1999) (workman injured by crane being used to deliver coal to his employer). In contrast, plaintiffs bought the Techite pipe from NCU, and are therefore "buyers" required to provide notice under the statute.

That does not mean that plaintiffs were required to provide notice directly to defendants. A majority of courts addressing the issue have interpreted the language of § 2-607(3) as contemplating only "a transaction between the buyer and the immediate seller," and thus as requiring notice only to "the party that tendered the goods to the buyer, i.e. the immediate seller." *See Church of Nativity v. WatPro, Inc.*, 474 N.W.2d 605, 609–10 (Minn. App. 1991) (listing cases), *aff'd on other grounds*, 491 N.W.2d 1 (Minn. 1992); *Cooley v. Big Horn Harvestore Systems, Inc.*, 813 P.2d 736, 741–42 (Colo. 1991) (en banc) (listing additional cases).[60] One court has recognized an exception to the immediate seller rule, requiring notice to a remote manufacturer by an end-buyer who dealt directly with the manufacturer in consummating the sale of the product. *See Carson v. Chevron Chem. Co.*, 6 Kan. App. 2d 776, 635 P.2d 1248, 1256 (1981). In this case, the immediate seller was NCU, the defendants were the remote manufacturers, and plaintiffs, through Banner, worked closely with both NCU and the defendants. There is no reason, however, to decide whether the South Dakota Supreme Court would adopt the immediate seller rule and deem notice to NCU sufficient under § 2-607(3), or whether it would require notice to defendants under the exception articulated in Carson, because plaintiffs did not notify NCU of the breach. *See In re Air Bag Prod. Liab. Litig.*, 7 F. Supp. 2d 792, 804 n.18 (even though the Texas Supreme Court had expressly reserved judgment on whether notice to an immediate seller satisfies the requirements of § 2-607(3), recovery was barred where plaintiffs made no attempt to notify either the manufacturer or the immediate seller).

Plaintiffs have not pointed to any circumstances which could excuse their failure to provide notice prior to filing this lawsuit. While plaintiffs claim that defendants knew about defects in Techite pipe from problems with other buyers, a seller's actual knowledge of defects does not excuse a buyer from providing notice of breach:

> The notice "of the breach" required is not of the facts, which the seller presumably knows quite as well as, if not better than, the buyer, but of buyer's

---

[59] [6] Plaintiffs' argument might also be phrased as claiming that, in the context of this case, notice by lawsuit is sufficient under § 2-607(3). While the adequacy of notice of breach is generally a question of fact, "where the circumstances are such as to lead to only one reasonable conclusion, the question is one of law." *Vander Eyk v. Bones*, 77 S.D. 345, 91 N.W.2d 897, 901 (1958). As discussed in the text below, notice by lawsuit is inadequate under § 2-607(3) as a matter of South Dakota law.

[60] [7] This interpretation is based primarily on the plain language [of] the words "tender," "the buyer," and "the seller" in § 2-607(3). *See* Ronald A. Anderson, *Uniform Commercial Code*, § 2-607:128 (1997) ("the Code does not speak of 'a' buyer or 'any' buyer, as being required to give notice, but rather of 'the' buyer, who, of course, should be 'the buyer' to whom the seller allegedly liable for breach of warranty has sold the goods"). It has also been based on the presumption that the immediate seller will in turn inform the manufacturer, thus satisfying the policy goals of § 2-607(3). *See Church of the Nativity*, 474 N.W.2d at 610 ("The immediate seller can be expected to notify the manufacturer and the parties further up the chain of distribution. . . .").

claim that they constitute a breach. The purpose of the notice is to advise the seller that he must meet a claim for damages, as to which, rightly or wrongly, the law requires that he shall have early warning.

American Mfg. Co. v. United States Shipping Bd. Emergency Fleet Corp., 7 F.2d 565, 566 (2d Cir. 1925) (Learned Hand, J.).

[Ed. Note: Judge Hand was discussing a similar requirement under the Uniform Sales Act, the predecessor to the UCC]; *see also Aqualon Co. v. Mac Equip., Inc.*, 149 F.3d 262, 266–67 (4th Cir. 1998) (describing the continuing widespread adherence to Judge Hand's description of the notice requirement). Plaintiffs' argument that notification would have "delayed replacement" and "continued to expose the public to an unreasonable risk of harm" is unpersuasive, because plaintiffs fail to explain how defendants could have delayed replacement of the pipe.[61] Finally, the argument that defendants had an opportunity to negotiate with plaintiffs and investigate plaintiffs' claims shortly after the lawsuit was filed also fails to excuse plaintiffs' failure to provide notice. *Hepper*, 388 N.W.2d at 529 ("Notice of breach by summons and complaint is obviously insufficient since it clearly frustrates the purposes of timely notice."). Because there was no adequate notice, plaintiffs are barred from a remedy for breach of warranty under § 2-607(3).

MICROSOFT CORPORATION v. LOGICAL CHOICE COMPUTERS, INC.
United States District Court, Northern District of Illinois
42 U.C.C. Rep. Serv. 2d 727 (2000)

PALLMEYER, J.

Plaintiff Microsoft, Inc. ("Microsoft") initiated this litigation, charging Defendants Logical Choice Computers, Inc. and its president, Dennis Dayson (collectively "LCC") with distributing counterfeit Microsoft software products. After Microsoft asserted federal infringement and common law unfair trade practices claims against LCC, LCC brought third-party claims against its own suppliers, Third-Party Defendants Acecom, Inc. ("Acecom"), and Software & More, Inc. ("Software & More"). LCC charges Acecom and Software & More with breach of contract, common law fraud, and violation of the Illinois Consumer Fraud and Deceptive Trade Practices Act, 815 ILCS 505/1 *et seq.* LCC claims that it purchased the allegedly counterfeit software from Acecom and Software & More, who are now liable to LCC for breaching contracts for the sale of software products and for fraudulently representing that the software at issue in the original action was genuine Microsoft product. Both Acecom and Software & More move to dismiss the third-party complaint pursuant to Federal Rules of Civil Procedure 12(b)(1) and 12(b)(6). For the reasons discussed here, the court grants Acecom's motion to dismiss Count I with prejudice, and Counts II and III without prejudice. Further, the court grants Software's motion to dismiss Counts IV through VI without prejudice.

FACTUAL BACKGROUND

LCC is in the business of assembling computer systems for sale from components and software purchased from dealers. The original complaint arose from LCC's April 17, 1997 sale of alleged counterfeit copies of Microsoft Windows 95 and LCC's February 17, 1999 sale of alleged counterfeit copies of Microsoft Office Pro 97 to undercover investigators. By letter dated June 20, 1997, Microsoft notified LCC that the software purchased by its investigators in April was counterfeit, and demanded that LCC discontinue its distribution of such counterfeit software. After the second sale of

---

[61] [9] Plaintiffs do argue that "any type of notice to Amoco to provide them a chance to replace the Southwest Sewer Interceptor Project" would have had this effect, but do not cite any authority indicating that they would have been obligated to permit defendants to replace the pipe, which plaintiffs had already accepted. *Compare* SDCL 57A-2-508 (seller's right to cure prior to acceptance).

allegedly counterfeit software, Microsoft brought a federal infringement and common law unfair competition action against LCC on March 1, 1999.

On August 17, 1999, LCC filed the third-party claims against two of its software suppliers, Acecom and Software & More. LCC claims that it purchased the allegedly counterfeit version of Microsoft 95 from Acecom, and the allegedly counterfeit version of Microsoft Office Pro 97 from Software & More. Based on these allegations, LCC seeks recovery against Acecom and Software & More for breach of contract (Counts I and IV), common law fraud (Counts II and V), and for violations of the Illinois Consumer Fraud and Deceptive Trade Practices Act, 815 ILCS 505/1 *et seq.* (Counts III and VI) (the "Consumer Fraud Act"). Both Acecom and Software & More move to dismiss the third-party complaint for lack of subject matter jurisdiction pursuant to Federal Rule Civil Procedure 12(b)(1) and for failure to state a claim pursuant to Federal Rule Civil Procedure 12(b)(6). For the reasons set forth below, the court concludes that it has jurisdiction over the action, but grants both motions and dismisses with prejudice the breach of contract claim against Acecom and without prejudice all remaining claims.

DISCUSSION

*   *   *

C. Breach of Contract

LCC alleges that Acecom's and Software & More's sale and delivery of alleged counterfeit software constitutes a breach of contract and a "complete failure . . . [to] perform[ ] thereunder." Acecom argues that despite having notice of the counterfeit nature of the software in June of 1997, LCC does not allege, as required by Section 2-607(3)(a) of the Uniform Commercial Code ("UCC"), 810 ILCS 5/2-607(3)(a), that it ever notified Acecom of the alleged problem before filing the third-party complaint.

Because the transactions at issue constitute contracts for the sale of goods, they are governed by the UCC. *See Ryan v. Wersi Elec. GmbH & Co.*, 3 F.3d 174, 181 (7th Cir. 1993). Pursuant to Section 2-607(3)(a) of the UCC, a buyer must notify the seller of its claim for breach or "be barred from any remedy." *See* 810 ILCS 5/2-607(3)(a). Further, if the claim is one for infringement, "and the buyer is sued as a result of such a breach he must so notify the seller within a reasonable time after he receives notice of the litigation or be barred from any remedy over for liability established by the litigation." *See* 810 ILCS 5/2-607(3)(b). Notice is required in order to provide the seller with the opportunity to cure a defect and thereby minimize damages, protect its ability to investigate a breach and gather evidence, and to encourage negotiation and settlement thereby avoiding protracted litigation. *See Maldonado v. Creative Woodworking Concepts, Inc.*, 296 Ill. App. 3d 935, 939, 694 N.E.2d 1021, 1025 (3d Dist. 1998).

LCC charges Acecom and Software & More with breaching the UCC's warranty against infringement. *See* 810 ILCS 5/2-312 ("[A] seller who is a merchant regularly dealing in goods of the kind warrants that the goods shall be delivered free of the rightful claim of any third person by way of infringement[.]"). As such, LCC is required to "directly notify the seller of the troublesome nature of the transaction or be barred from recovering for a breach of warranty." *See Connick v. Suzuki Motor Co., Ltd.*, 174 Ill.2d 482, 492, 675 N.E.2d 584, 589 (1996). Indeed, notice is particularly important in infringement actions because the UCC allows the seller to exercise its option to demand that the buyer turn control of the litigation, including settlement, to him. *See* 810 ILCS 5/2-607(5)(b).

Here, LCC had knowledge of the defective nature of the products in the Acecom transaction in June 1997, and had knowledge of the defective nature of the products in the Software & More transaction in March 1999. Nowhere in its third-party complaint does LCC allege that it provided any notification to either Acecom or Software & More.

Failure to allege sufficient notice can be fatal to a complaint alleging breach of warranty under the UCC. *See Connick*, 174 Ill. 2d at 495, 675 N.E.2d at 591. Direct notice is not required, however, in the following situations: (1) when the seller has actual knowledge of the problem with the particular product at issue; or (2) when the seller is deemed to have been notified by the buyer's complaint alleging a breach of warranty. *See id.*, 174 Ill. 2d at 492, 675 N.E.2d at 589. LCC did not allege actual knowledge on the part of Acecom or Software & More. In response to Acecom's lack of notice argument, however, LCC now argues that Acecom was reasonably notified by the filing of the third-party complaint in August 1999. Through its submission of the complaint-notice argument, LCC effectively concedes that it did not provide direct notice of the breach to Acecom before filing the complaint.

LCC's complaint-notice argument does not save its breach of contract claim against Acecom. The Illinois Supreme Court has expressly held that notice provided solely by the filing of a complaint alleging a breach against the seller satisfies the Section 2-607(3) notice requirement only when the buyer is a consumer who has suffered personal injuries. *See Connick*, 174 Ill. 2d at 495, 675 N.E.2d at 590–91. This distinction is premised upon the UCC's preference that a breach, in the absence of resulting personal injuries, be cured without a lawsuit. *See id.* LCC is not a typical consumer, but rather a merchant buyer, and furthermore has not alleged any personal injuries resulting from the transactions at issue.[62] Accordingly, the court grants with prejudice Acecom's motion to dismiss Count I.

Software & More does not rely on the UCC notice requirement in support of its motion to dismiss Count IV. As such, the matter has not been briefed, and LCC has not formally conceded that it failed to provide pre-litigation notification of a breach to Software & More. Accordingly, the court grants without prejudice Software & More's motion to dismiss Count IV. Because complaint-notice will likewise not save LCC's claim against Software & More, however, the court cautions LCC that it should not replead this claim, unless it actually did provide pre-litigation notice to Software & More, or can show actual notice on the part of Software & More.

QUESTIONS

1. Both *Brookings* and *Microsoft* emphasize the underlying purposes and policies of the notice requirement, but they refer to case precedent rather than the statutory language and the official comments. What are the underlying purposes and polices, and how would you establish them in a case of first impression?

2. Note that the buyer in *Microsoft* was sued for "infringement," and in turn was suing the seller for liability over. Under § 2-607(3)(b), does it make more sense to regard the buyer's action of suing the seller as a third-party defendant to be sufficient notice?

3. Section 2-607(3)(a) requires the buyer not only to provide notice, but to provide notice within a reasonable time after the buyer "discovers or should have discovered" the breach. This is generally a question of fact for the jury, unless the jury could not reasonably find the delay to be reasonable. *See, e.g., Hays v. General Electric Co.*, 151 F. Supp. 2d 1001, 1012–13 (N.D. Ill. 2001) (reviewing case law and determining that the jury could reasonably find that an eight to nine month lapse of time was reasonable).

4. In *Brookings*, the court interpreted South Dakota law to provide that the seller's knowledge of defects in its Techite pipe did not excuse the buyer's failure to provide notice of the breach. In *Microsoft*, the court interpreted Illinois law to provide that the seller's actual knowledge of the problem with the particular product at issue operated to relieve the buyer of providing direct notice of the breach. Develop the arguments

---

[62] [3] In any event, in this court's view, notice to Acecom more than two years after LCC learned from Microsoft about the alleged breach of warranty would be untimely as a matter of law.

about the significance of the seller's knowledge in the following problem.

PROBLEM 7-28

On June 1, Samson Industries agreed to manufacture a 175 ton press (known as the "green monster") for Berkwire Manufacturing. Samson expressly warranted that the green monster would process 100 units per hour, and agreed that it would repair or replace any defective parts for one year. On August 1, the machine was delivered and accepted, and things went smoothly for five weeks. However, on September 5, the green monster began having serious performance problems. On September 14 and 30, October 7, and December 3 and 21, Berkwire notified Samson that the green monster required repairs, and each time Samson sent technicians to repair it. On January 2, Samson sent two technicians to Berkwire's plant for two consecutive months of repair work. On March 1, the technicians left without returning. When the technicians left Berkwire's facility they knew that the green monster would not process 100 units per hour, but they could not think of any additional repairs that could be performed.

The green monster continued to perform poorly. Berkwire had no further communications with Samson. Berkwire commenced a lawsuit against Samson on July 1. Samson argued that the case should be dismissed because Berkwire did not provide the required notice under § 2-607(3) before bringing the lawsuit. Outline the arguments for both parties on the question whether Berkwire should be barred from any remedy under Article 2.

b.   Buyer's burden of proving nonconformity

One of the most significant consequences of the buyer's acceptance is a shift of the burden of proof concerning a breach with regard to the goods. If the buyer rejects a seller's tender of goods, the seller, in his action against the buyer for the price or similar damages, has the burden of proving that the rejection was wrongful. Once the buyer has accepted the goods, however, § 2-607 provides that the buyer must establish the seller's breach of the sales contract. Comment 6 to the section makes clear that the rule regarding the burden of proof "becomes one purely of procedure when the tender accepted was non-conforming and the buyer has given the seller notice of breach under [2-607](3)."

To understand the practical ramifications of the burden of proof of damages after acceptance issues, consider the following case. In your reading of the opinion, keep in mind how your analysis of the court's conclusions would bear upon the advice you would give a client buyer or seller.

FLOWERS BAKING CO. v. R-P PACKAGING, INC.
Virginia Supreme Court
329 S.E.2d 462 (1985)

Russell, J.

This appeal turns on questions concerning the formation of contracts under the Uniform Commercial Code (Code §§ 8.2-204 and 8.2-305) and subsidiary questions concerning the Statute of Frauds (Code § 8.2-201(3)(a)) and the burden of proving nonconformity of goods to a contract (Code § 8.2-607(4)).

Kern's Bakery of Virginia, Inc. (Kern's) operated a bakery in Lynchburg in 1977. R-P Packaging, Incorporated (R-P), of Columbus, Ga., was a manufacturer of cellophane wrapping material which was used by Kern's in packaging its product. In later 1977, Kern's decided to change its system for the packaging of cookies produced in the Lynchburg plant from a tied bread bag to a tray covered with printed cellophane wrapping. Kern's plant manager discussed the proposed change with R-P's representative and furnished R-P with several trays filled with cookies to enable R-P to take measurements to determine the appropriate size for the cellophane covering. In addition, R-P was requested to design appropriate "artwork" to be printed on the cellophane wrapping.

On December 28, 1977, Kern's plant manager gave R-P's representative a verbal "order" for cellophane wrap, which was transmitted to R-P's home office. On January 4, 1978, R-P prepared and mailed to Kern's a written acknowledgment of the "order," which contained specifications, delivery instructions, order date, and quantity. The word "Later" was typed in the space provided for the contract price. The sale price, $13,375.11, was filled in subsequently, on a date not shown by the evidence. The symbol "W/A" was written in the space titled "Acknowledgment Date." At the bottom of the acknowledgment form was typed: "Produce printing plates per artwork sent to Frank Tarpley, but first send photostats with color stripe to customers for approval before etching."

R-P's representative testified that "W/A" stood for "will advise," which, in company parlance, meant that R-P did not have approval from the customer to proceed. He also testified that the etchings were "new artwork being done from scratch" and that the acknowledgment "indicates that we are not to proceed with the etching until we've had approval from the customer." He added, "We had the orders, but the customer had not either approved the final design or size, or something, so the order was simply entered and nothing was happening to it until such time as they gave us approval." R-P's president testified, "Until we got an approval from the customer, we could not print it; they would not do anything until they were notified by the Sales Department that the customer had approved it."

On January 3, 1978, the day before R-P's acknowledgment form was issued, without notice to R-P, Kern's sold all its assets in Lynchburg to Flowers Baking Company of Lynchburg, Inc. (Flowers). The written agreement between the two baking companies, dated January 3, 1978, provided that Flowers would not assume all of the liabilities of Kern's, but Kern's represented that all pending contracts involving more than $5,000, to which it was a party, were listed in the agreement, and that Kern's would indemnify Flowers from all liability arising from any misrepresentation or breach of warranty. The order for cellophane from R-P was not listed. R-P's acknowledgment, of course, arrived at the Lynchburg plant after Flowers had assumed control and was never received by Kern's.

R-P sent a sample unprinted roll of the cellophane wrapping to the Lynchburg plant to be run on the plant's packaging equipment as a test for size. Although no such test was performed, the plant manager, who had worked under Kern's but was still operating the plant for Flowers, advised R-P's representative in mid-February that the material was satisfactory, and said, "Proceed with the order." On the following day, R-P's representatives met with Flowers' manager at the Lynchburg plant to discuss the proposed "artwork." Flowers' manager approved it, except for an agreed change of name from Kern's to Flowers, and requested that the material be produced and shipped as soon as possible.

Flowers received the printed wrapping material about March 27, 1978. Flowers' manager testified that he telephoned R-P's representative about ten days later, stating that the material was too short to fit the trays and that the printing was not centered. R-P's representative testified that he was unaware of any complaint about the material until mid-June. He also testified that the material conformed exactly to the order as placed by Flowers. Flowers returned the material to R-P by overnight express on July 27, 1978, without obtaining R-P's consent. The acknowledgment form contained a provision stating: "Buyer waives all claims relating to goods unless received in writing by Seller within thirty (30) days of receipt of the goods. No goods shall be returned by Buyer for any reason without Seller's written approval."

R-P brought this action against Kern's and Flowers for $13,375.11, as the purchase price of the packaging material. Flowers also cross-claimed against Kern's for indemnity under the terms of the January 3, 1978 agreement. At a pretrial conference, the court ruled as a matter of law that there was no contract between R-P and Kern's. Kern's was accordingly dismissed as to R-P's claim and as to Flowers' cross-claim. R-P's claim against Flowers went to jury trial. Flowers conceded that it was indebted to R-P for a $3,933 reorder of the packaging material. The jury returned a verdict in R-P's favor against Flowers for the remaining balance of $9,642.11.

*   *   *

Flowers finally contends that in the jury trial on R-P's claim against Flowers, the court erred in granting Instruction 1, which told the jury that Flowers had the burden of proving that the goods failed to conform to the contract. Flowers argues that R-P's action for the purchase price was brought under Code § 8.2-709(1)(a), which expressly conditions the seller's right of recovery upon the buyer's acceptance of the goods. Rather than making an acceptance under Code § 8.2-606, Flowers says that it rightfully rejected the goods under Code § 8.2-602. In those circumstances, the argument runs, the burden is on the seller to prove that the goods conformed to the contract.

"Acceptance" is a term of art under the Uniform Commercial Code. Code § 8.2-606(1)(b) provides that acceptance occurs when the buyer, having had a reasonable opportunity to inspect the goods, fails to make an *effective* rejection. In order to be effective, notice of the rejection must be given to the seller within a reasonable time. Code § 8.2-602(1), official comment 1. The issue whether notice of rejection was given within a reasonable time under the circumstances is ordinarily one of fact for the jury and was properly submitted to the jury in this case. If notice of rejection was given unreasonably late, the rejection is not "effective," acceptance is implied by Code § 8.2-606(1)(b), and the burden of proof is on the buyer, pursuant to Code § 8.2-607(4), to establish any nonconformity of the goods to the contract. The foregoing rules are provided by the U.C.C. to cover cases in which the goods are alleged to be nonconforming. If the goods in fact conform to the contract, the buyer has a positive duty to accept them, and his failure to do so constitutes a "wrongful rejection" which gives the seller immediate remedies for breach. Code § 8.2-602(3), official comment 3.

Here, both issues of fact were properly submitted for the jury's determination: whether reasonable notice of rejection was given by Flowers to R-P, and whether the cellophane wrap in fact failed to conform to the specifications agreed upon by the parties. Upon principles too familiar to require citation, the jury's resolution of the conflicting evidence upon these subjects, embodied in a final judgment on the verdict, is conclusive on appeal.

As an abstract principle, if the goods failed to conform, and if timely notice of rejection had been given to the seller, the rejection would have been both "rightful" and "effective." There would, therefore, have been no acceptance; Code § 8.2-607(4) would have been inapplicable; and the burden would have remained upon the plaintiff seller, as at common law, to prove that it had performed the contract by producing and delivering conforming goods. In those circumstances, Instruction 1 would be erroneous. *Miron v. Yonkers Raceway, Inc.*, 400 F.2d 112, 119 (2d Cir. 1968).

Flowers has waived its right to complain of error in Instruction 1 by submitting Instruction 1B, which was granted by the court. 1B told the jury that it should find for Flowers if it found from a preponderance of the evidence, (1) that the goods were nonconforming, and (2) that the goods were "rightfully rejected" by Flowers. 1B was the mirror image of 1, and was entirely consistent with it. It relied on the same theory. Obviously, someone must carry the burden of proving rightful rejection if the jury is to find it by a preponderance of the evidence. Yet, it is a proposition advanced only by Flowers. The implication is clear that Flowers' tendered instruction contemplates that Flowers must carry the burden of showing rightful rejection. To show that its rejection was rightful, it must show the goods failed to conform.

Further, the error in Instruction 1 was harmless under the facts of the case. One of the principal factual issues at trial was whether the prospective buyer, either Kern's or

Flowers, had arbitrarily changed the size of the trays without notice to R-P, after giving R-P trays of the original dimensions as a basis for calculating the size of the cellophane wrap. R-P's representative testified that such a change had been made; a witness for Flowers said that Flowers had not done so. The jury resolved this dispute, if it was one, in R-P's favor. R-P's evidence that it had produced the wrap in strict conformity to the agreed specifications was unrefuted. If the tray size were changed, it would affect both the fit of the wrap and the centering of the "artwork." The jury also necessarily accepted R-P's evidence that it had submitted a plain roll of the wrap for Flowers to run on its machinery as a test for size, that such a test would have revealed any nonconformity as to size, that Flowers had failed to make any such test, but had approved both the sample and the "artwork"; and had directed R-P to produce the goods and deliver them as soon as possible. In this factual context, there was no evidence to support Flowers' theory that it had rightfully rejected the goods, the only circumstance which would have cast the burden of proof of conformity upon R-P.

For the foregoing reasons, the judgment will be affirmed.

QUESTION

Flowers demonstrates the interrelation among the acceptance, rejection, and burden of proof issues. As a practical matter, what difference will it make who bears the burden of proof?

c.   Calculating damages for breach following acceptance

The general rule of § 2-714(1) provides simply that the buyer should be awarded "the loss resulting in the ordinary course of events from the seller's breach," but § 2-714(2) suggests a formula that should measure the proximate damages in a breach of warranty case, barring special circumstances. Calculate the damages to which the buyer is entitled in the problem that follows.

PROBLEM 7-29

On December 1, Bacchus Liquors agreed to purchase 500 bottles of premium Chardonnay from Serenity Winery for $15 per bottle, with delivery to be in September. On September 1, Serenity mistakenly tendered 500 bottles of premium Cabernet Sauvignon. Due to crop damage during the Spring, the market price of Chardonnay had shot up to $20 per bottle on September 1. The market price of Cabernet Sauvignon was $17 on September 1. If Bacchus accepts the tendered wine, how much must it pay? Is Bacchus entitled to recover damages?

Now, assume that prices in the wine industry have dropped generally since the time of contracting. The market value of Cabernet Sauvignon on September 1 is $13 per bottle, and the market value of Chardonnay on September 1 is $10 per bottle. Bacchus decides to accept the Cabernet when it is wrongfully tendered, given that it is more valuable than Chardonnay. How much must Bacchus pay for the wine? Is Bacchus entitled to damages?

CHATLOS SYSTEMS, INC. v. NATIONAL CASH REGISTER CORP.

United States Court of Appeals, Third Circuit
670 F.2d 1304 (1982)

PER CURIAM

This appeal from a district court's award of damages for breach of warranty in a diversity case tried under New Jersey law presents two questions: whether the district court's computation of damages under N.J. Stat. Ann. § 12A:2-714(2) was clearly erroneous, and whether the district court abused its discretion in supplementing the damage award with pre-judgment interest. We answer both questions in the negative and, therefore, we will affirm.

Plaintiff-appellee Chatlos Systems, Inc., initiated this action in the Superior Court of New Jersey, alleging, inter alia, breach of warranty regarding an NCR 399/656 computer system it had acquired from defendant National Cash Register Corp. The case was removed under 28 U.S.C. § 1441(a) to the United States District Court for the District of New Jersey. Following a non-jury trial, the district court determined that defendant was liable for breach of warranty and awarded $57,152.76 damages for breach of warranty and consequential damages in the amount of $63,558.16. *Chatlos Systems, Inc. v. National Cash Register Corp.*, 479 F. Supp. 738 (D.N.J. 1979), *aff'd in part, remanded in part*, 635 F.2d 1081 (3d Cir. 1980). Defendant appealed and this court affirmed the district court's findings of liability, set aside the award of consequential damages, and remanded for a recalculation of damages for breach of warranty. *Chatlos Systems, Inc. v. National Cash Register Corp.*, 635 F.2d 1081 (3d Cir. 1980). On remand, applying the "benefit of the bargain" formula of N.J. Stat. Ann. § 12A:2-714(2) (Uniform Commercial Code § 2-714(2)), the district court determined the damages to be $201,826.50,[63] to which it added an award of prejudgment interest. Defendant now appeals from these damage determinations, contending that the district court erred in failing to recognize the $46,020 contract price of the delivered NCR computer system as the fair market value of the goods as warranted, and that the award of damages is without support in the evidence presented. Appellant also contests the award of prejudgment interest.

Waiving the opportunity to submit additional evidence as to value on the remand which we directed, appellant chose to rely on the record of the original trial and submitted no expert testimony on the market value of a computer which would have performed the functions NCR had warranted. Notwithstanding our previous holding that contract price was not necessarily the same as market value, 635 F.2d at 1088, appellant faults the district judge for rejecting its contention that the contract price for the NCR 399/656 was the only competent record evidence of the value of the system as warranted. The district court relied instead on the testimony of plaintiff-appellee's expert, Dick Brandon, who, without estimating the value of an NCR model 399/656, presented his estimate of the value of a computer system that would perform all of the functions that the NCR 399/656 had been warranted to perform. Brandon did not limit his estimate to equipment of any one manufacturer; he testified regarding manufacturers who could have made systems that would perform the functions that appellant had warranted the NCR 399/656 could perform. He acknowledged that the systems about which he testified were not in the same price range as the NCR 399/656. Appellant likens this testimony to substituting a Rolls Royce for a Ford, and concludes that the district court's recomputed damage award was therefore clearly contrary to the evidence of fair market value — which in NCR's view is the contract price itself.

Appellee did not order, nor was it promised, merely a specific NCR computer model, but an NCR computer system with specified capabilities. The correct measure of damages, under N.J. Stat. Ann. § 12A:2-714(2), is the difference between the fair market value of the goods accepted and the value they would have had if they had been as warranted. Award of that sum is not confined to instances where there has been an increase in value between date of ordering and date of delivery. It may also include the benefit of a contract price which, for whatever reason quoted, was particularly favorable for the customer. Evidence of the contract price may be relevant to the issue of fair market value, but it is not controlling. *Mulvaney v. Tri State Truck & Auto Body, Inc.*, 70 Wis. 2d 760, 767, 235 N.W.2d 460, 465 (1975). Appellant limited its fair market value analysis to the contract price of the computer model it actually delivered. Appellee

---

[63] [2] The district court found the fair market value of the system as warranted to be $207,826.50; from this it subtracted its determination of the value of the goods delivered, $6,000.

developed evidence of the worth of a computer with the capabilities promised by NCR, and the trial court properly credited the evidence.[64]

Appellee was aided, moreover, by the testimony of Frank Hicks, NCR's programmer, who said that he told his company's officials that the "current software was not sufficient in order to deliver the program that the customer [Chatlos] required. They would have to be rewritten or a different system would have to be given to the customer." Appendix to Brief for Appellee at 2.68. Hicks recommended that Chatlos be given an NCR 8200 but was told, "that will not be done." *Id.* at 2.69. Gerald Greenstein, another NCR witness, admitted that the 8200 series was two levels above the 399 in sophistication and price. *Id.* at 14.30. This testimony supported Brandon's statement that the price of the hardware needed to perform Chatlos' requirements would be in the $100,000 to $150,000 range.

Essentially, then, the trial judge was confronted with the conflicting value estimates submitted by the parties. Chatlos' expert's estimates were corroborated to some extent by NCR's supporters. NCR, on the other hand, chose to rely on contract price. Credibility determinations had to be made by the district judge. Although we might have come to a different conclusion on the value of the equipment as warranted had we been sitting as trial judges, we are not free to make our own credibility and factual findings. We may reverse the district court only if its factual determinations were clearly erroneous. *Krasnov v. Dinan*, 465 F.2d 1298 (3d Cir. 1972).[65]

Upon reviewing the evidence of record, therefore, we conclude that the computation of damages for breach of warranty was not clearly erroneous. We hold also that the district court acted within its discretion in awarding pre-judgment interest, *Chatlos Systems, Inc. v. National Cash Register Corp.*, 635 F.2d at 1088.

The judgment of the district court will be affirmed.

ROSENN, CIRCUIT J., dissenting.

The primary question in this appeal involves the application of Article 2 of the Uniform Commercial Code as adopted by New Jersey in N.J.S.A. 12A:2-101 et seq. (1962) to the measure of damages for breach of warranty in the sale of a computer system. I respectfully dissent because I believe there is no probative evidence to support the district court's award of damages for the breach of warranty in a sum amounting to almost five times the purchase price of the goods. The measure of damages also has been misapplied and this could have a significant effect in the marketplace, especially for the unique and burgeoning computer industry.[66]

In July 1974, National Cash Register Corporation (NCR) sold Chatlos Systems, Inc. (Chatlos), a NCR 399/656 disc computer system (NCR 399) for $46,020 (exclusive of 5 percent sales tax of $1,987.50). The price and system included:

The computer (hardware)	$40,165.00

---

[64] [4] We find the following analogy, rather than the Rolls Royce-Ford analogy submitted by appellant, to be on point:

> Judge Weis: If you start thinking about a piece of equipment that is warranted to lift a thousand pounds and it will only lift 500 pounds, then the cost of something that will lift a thousand pounds gives you more of an idea and that may be —
>
> Counsel for Appellee: That may be a better analogy, yes.
>
> Judge Weis: Yes.

[65] [5] The dissent essentially is based on disagreement with the estimates provided by Chatlos' expert, Brandon. The record reveals that he was well qualified; the weight to be given his testimony is the responsibility of the factfinder, not an appellate court.

[66] [1] Plaintiff's expert, Brandon, testified that generally 40 percent of all computer installation result in failures. He further testified that successful installations of computer systems require not only the computer companies' attention, but also the attention of the customers' top management.

Software (consisting of 6 computer programs)	$ 5,855.00
	$46,020.00

NCR delivered the disc computer to Chatlos in December 1974 and in March 1975 the payroll program became operational. By March of the following year, however, NCR was still unsuccessful in installing an operational order entry program and inventory deletion program. Moreover, on August 31, 1976, Chatlos experienced problems with the payroll program. On that same day and the day following NCR installed an operational state income tax program, but on September 1, 1976, Chatlos demanded termination of the lease[67] and removal of the computer.

When this case was previously before us, we upheld the district court's liability decision but remanded for a reassessment of damages, instructing the court that under the purchase contract and the law consequential damages could not be awarded. Consequential damages, therefore, are no longer an issue here.[68]

On remand, the district court, on the basis of the previous record made in the case, fixed the fair market value of the NCR 399 as warranted at the time of its acceptance in August 1975 at $207,826.50. It reached that figure by valuing the hardware at $131,250.00 and the software at $76,575.50, for a total of $207,826.50. The court then determined that the present value of the computer hardware, which Chatlos retained, was $6,000. Putting no value on the accepted payroll program, the court deducted the $6,000 and arrived at an award of $201,826.50 plus pre-judgment interest at the rate of 8 percent per annum from August 1975.

*   *   *

II.

A.

I believe that the district court committed legal error. The majority conclude that the standard of review of the district court's determination of the fair market value of the goods for the purpose of awarding damages is whether the trial judge's determination of market value is clearly erroneous. I disagree. Had the court merely miscalculated the amount of damages, I might agree with the majority's standard, for then our concern would be with basic facts. Here, however, no evidence was introduced as to the market value of the specific goods purchased and accepted had the system conformed to the warranty. Thus, the matter before us is one of legal error, and our standard of review is plenary. But even under the standard applied by the majority, the district court should be reversed because its determination of market value is not supported by probative evidence.

There are a number of major flaws in the plaintiff's attempt to prove damages in excess of the contract price. I commence with an analysis of plaintiff's basic theory. Chatlos presented its case under a theory that although, as a sophisticated purchaser,

---

[67] [3] Chatlos decided to lease the system rather than purchase it outright. To permit this arrangement, NCR sold the system to Mid Atlantic National Bank in July 1975 for $46,020, which leased the system to Chatlos. Chatlos made monthly payments to Mid Atlantic in amounts which would have totaled $70,162.09 over the period of the lease.

[68] [4] Besides rejecting the district court's award of consequential damages, this court on the previous appeal disagreed with the district court's starting point of $70,162.22, the amount Chatlos obligated itself to pay to the bank, for two reasons: (1) the price Chatlos paid the bank included the bank's finance charges which should have been excluded; and (2) the district court erred in refusing to consider Chatlos' evidence of fair market value, which is the starting point for determining damages under section 2-714(2).

it bargained for several months before arriving at a decision on the computer system it required and the price of $46,020, it is entitled, because of the breach of warranty, to damages predicated on a considerably more expensive system. Stated another way, even if it bargained for a cheap system, i.e., one whose low cost reflects its inferior quality, because that system did not perform as bargained for, it is now entitled to damages measured by the value of a system which, although capable of performing the identical functions as the NCR 399, is of far superior quality and accordingly more expensive.

The statutory measure of damages for breach of warranty specifically provides that the measure is the difference at the time and place of acceptance between the value "of the goods accepted" and the "value they would have had if they had been as warranted." The focus of the statute is upon "the goods accepted" — not other hypothetical goods which may perform equivalent functions. "Moreover, the value to be considered is the reasonable market value of the *goods delivered*, not the value of the goods to a particular purchaser or for a particular purpose." *KLPR-TV, Inc. v. Visual Electronics Corp.*, 465 F.2d 1382, 1387 (8th Cir. 1972) (emphasis added). The court, however, arrived at value on the basis of a hypothetical construction of a system as of December 1978 by the plaintiff's expert, Brandon. The court reached its value by working backward from Brandon's figures, adjusting for inflation.

Although NCR warranted performance, the failure of its equipment to perform, absent any evidence of the value of any NCR 399 system on which to base fair market value, does not permit a market value based on systems wholly unrelated to the goods sold. Yet, instead of addressing the fair market value of the NCR 399 had it been as warranted, Brandon addressed the fair market value of another system that he concocted by drawing on elements from other major computer systems manufactured by companies such as IBM, Burroughs, and Honeywell, which he considered would perform "functions identical to those contracted for" by Chatlos. He conceded that the systems were "[p]erhaps not within the same range of dollars that the bargain was involved with" and he did not identify specific packages of software. Brandon had no difficulty in arriving at the fair market value of the inoperable NCR equipment but instead of fixing a value on the system had it been operable attempted to fashion a hypothetical system on which he placed a value. The district court, in turn, erroneously adopted that value as the fair market value for an operable NCR 399 system. NCR rightly contends that the "comparable" systems on which Brandon drew were substitute goods of greater technological power and capability and not acceptable in determining damages for breach of warranty under section 2-714. Furthermore, Brandon's hypothetical system did not exist and its valuation was largely speculation.

B.

A review of Brandon's testimony reveals its legal inadequacy for establishing the market value of the system Chatlos purchased from NCR. Brandon never testified to the fair market value which the NCR 399 system would have had had it met the warranty at the time of acceptance. He was not even asked the question.

* * *

Not only did Brandon not testify in terms of the value of the NCR 399, but he spoke vaguely of "a general estimate . . . as to what the cost might be of, let's say, developing a payroll or purchasing a payroll package today and installing it at Chatlos." He explained that what he would do, without identifying specific packages, would be to obtain price lists "from the foremost organizations selling packages in our field, in that area," organizations such as Management Science of America in Atlanta, and take their prices for specific packages. When asked what packages he would use for this system, he replied, "I would shop around, frankly." Speculating, he testified, "I think that I would go to two or three alternatives in terms of obtaining packages." When asked to address himself to the packages that he would provide for this system, he acknowledged that the programs he had in mind were only available "[for] certain types of machines." For example, he conceded that these programs would not be available for the Series 1 IBM mini-computer, "with the possible exception of payroll."

Thus, the shortcomings in Brandon's testimony defy common sense and the realities of the marketplace. First, ordinarily, the best evidence of fair market value is what a willing purchaser would pay in cash to a willing seller. . . . The price they agreed upon for an operable system would ordinarily be the best evidence of its value. The testimony does not present us with the situation referred to in our previous decision, where "the value of the goods rises between the time that the contract is executed and the time of acceptance," in which event the buyer is entitled to the benefit of his bargain. *Chatlos, supra*, 635 F.2d at 1088. On the contrary, Chatlos here relies on an expert who has indulged in the widest kind of speculation. Based on this testimony, Chatlos asserts in effect that a multi-national sophisticated vendor of computer equipment, despite months of negotiation, incredibly agreed to sell an operable computer system for $46,020 when, in fact, it had a fair market value of $207,000.

Second, expert opinion may, of course, be utilized to prove market value but it must be reasonably grounded. Brandon did not testify to the fair market value "of the goods accepted" had they met the warranty. Instead, he testified about a hypothetical system that he mentally fashioned. He ignored the realistic cost advantage in purchasing a unified system as contrasted with the "cost of acquiring seven separate application components" from various vendors.

Third, in arriving at his figure of $102,000 for the software, Brandon improperly included the time and cost of training the customer's personnel associated with the installation of the system. In a deposition prior to trial, Brandon testified that his valuation of the software included the time necessary to train Chatlos' personnel in the use of the system. On direct examination at trial, he testified that the $102,000 value fixed for software and programming did not include the time and cost necessary to train Chatlos' personnel in the use of the system, indicating that the cost of training a customer and his personnel is "definitely" not included in the price of programming and software. When confronted with his prior inconsistent deposition, he conceded that in his estimate of $102,000 "we included the Chatlos time."

Fourth, the record contains testimony which appears undisputed that computer equipment falls into one of several tiers, depending upon the degree of sophistication. The more sophisticated equipment has the capability of performing the functions of the least sophisticated equipment, but the less sophisticated equipment cannot perform all of the functions of those in higher levels. The price of the more technologically advanced equipment is obviously greater.

It is undisputed that in September 1976 there were vendors of computer equipment of the same general size as the NCR 399/656 with disc in the price range of $35,000 to $40,000 capable of providing the same programs as those required by Chatlos, including IBM, Phillips, and Burroughs. They were the very companies who competed for the sale of the computer in 1974 in the same price range. On the other hand, Chatlos' requirements could also be satisfied by computers available at "three levels higher in price and sophistication than the 399 disc." Each level higher would mean more sophistication, greater capabilities, and more memory. Greenstein, NCR's expert, testified without contradiction that equipment of Burroughs, IBM, and other vendors in the price range of $100,000 to $150,000, capable of performing Chatlos' requirements, was not comparable to the 399 because it was three levels higher. Such equipment was more comparable to the NCR 8400 series.

Fifth, when it came to the valuation of the hardware, Brandon did not offer an opinion as to the market value of the hypothetical system he was proposing. Instead, he offered a wide ranging estimate of $100,000 to $150,000 for a hypothetical computer that would meet Chatlos' programming requirements. The range in itself suggests the speculation in which he indulged.

III.

The purpose of the N.J.S.A. 12A:2-714 is to put the buyer in the same position he would have been in if there had been no breach. *See* Uniform Commercial Code 1-106(1). The remedies for a breach of warranty were intended to compensate the buyer for his loss; they were not intended to give the purchaser a windfall or treasure trove. The buyer may not receive more than it bargained for; it may not obtain the value of a superior computer system which it did not purchase even though such a system can perform all of the functions the inferior system was designed to serve. Thus, in *Meyers v. Antone*, 227 A.2d 56 (D.C. App. 1967), the court held that where the buyers contracted for a properly functioning used oil heating system which proved defective, they were free to substitute a gas system (which they did), change over to forced air heating, or even experiment with a solar heating plant. "They could not, however, recover the cost of such systems. They contracted for a used oil system that would function properly, and can neither receive more than they bargained for nor be put in a better position than they would have been had the contract been fully performed." *Id.* at 59 (citations omitted).

Because Brandon's testimony does not support Chatlos' grossly extravagant claim of the fair market value of the NCR 399 at the time of its acceptance, the only evidence of the market value at the time is the price negotiated by the parties for the NCR computer system as warranted.

> There are many cases in which the goods will be irreparable or not replaceable and therefore the costs of repair or replacement can not serve as a yardstick of the buyer's damages. . . . When fair market value cannot be easily determined . . . the purchase price may turn out to be strong evidence of the value of the goods as warranted.

J. WHITE & R. SUMMERS, UNIFORM COMMERCIAL CODE § 10-2, at 380 (2d ed. 1980) (footnotes omitted).

Thus, where there is no proof that market value of the goods differs from the contract price, the contract price will govern, . . . and in this case that amounts to $46,020. Chatlos has retained the system hardware and the district court fixed its present value in the open market at $6,000. The court properly deducted this sum from the damages awarded.

IV.

Chatlos purchased the NCR payroll program and acknowledged at trial that the program operated fully and satisfactorily beginning February or March 1975 until October 1978 when it discontinued its use. The district court assigned no value to it because there was no evidence of fair market value. However, the law is clear that without evidence of a value other than contract price, that price should be accepted as the fair market value of the payroll program. The parties agreed on a contract price of $1,000 and that sum should be deducted from the measure of damages.

*   *   *

VI.

On this record, therefore, the damages to which plaintiff is entitled are $46,020 less $6,000, the fair market value at time of trial of the retained hardware, and less $1,000, the fair market value of the payroll program, or the net sum of $39,020.

Accordingly, I would reverse the judgment of the district court and direct it to enter judgment for the plaintiff in the sum of $39,020 with interest from the date of entry of the initial judgment at the rate allowed by state law.

QUESTIONS

1. The court explains that Chatlos leased the computer and the software. Why didn't the court apply Article 2A? Would the result in the case change under Article 2A?

2. Would Judge Rosenn permit an award of damages based on the fair market value of the least expensive computer system that could perform as warranted, even if that system was not an NCR system and was more expensive than the 399/656? Does Judge Rosenn disagree with the majority's characterization of the law, or the application of the law to the facts in the record?

d.   The buyer's right of recoupment under § 2-717

When the buyer accepts the goods, it becomes obligated to pay the purchase price in accordance with the contract. § 2-607(1). The measure of damages under § 2-714 assumes that the buyer is obligated to pay the purchase price and has the goods in its possession. Consequently, the measure is the amount of money necessary to bring the value of the non-conforming goods in the buyer's possession up to the value that the buyer is entitled to receive under the contract. However, the seller's claim for the price will not necessarily be offset immediately by the buyer's claim for damages, since the buyer has no defense to its obligation to pay the price and the seller's liability for breach may be unclear, until after years of litigation.

Section 2-717 provides the buyer with a right of recoupment to deal with this situation. The buyer is entitled, upon notice to the seller, to deduct from the price owed to the seller the amount of damages that the buyer has suffered. Consequently, even if the buyer's claims present questions of fact that cannot be resolved by summary judgment, the seller is not entitled to summary judgment for the full purchase price. Instead, the seller's action for the price must await resolution of the buyer's claims. *See Rotorex Co., Inc. v. Kingsbury Corp.*, 42 F. Supp. 2d 563, 577–78 (D. Md. 1999). This common sense rule means that the buyer will not be ordered to pay the full purchase price immediately, and then await an award of damages in the same transaction years later when the litigation concludes.

TABLE OF CASES

[References are to pages. Principal cases appear in all capital letters.]

[References are to pages. Principal cases appear in all capital letters.]

[References are to pages. Principal cases appear in all capital letters.]

[References are to pages. Principal cases appear in all capital letters.]

[References are to pages. Principal cases appear in all capital letters.]

[References are to pages. Principal cases appear in all capital letters.]

[References are to pages. Principal cases appear in all capital letters.]

O

P

R

[References are to pages. Principal cases appear in all capital letters.]

[References are to pages. Principal cases appear in all capital letters.]

[References are to pages. Principal cases appear in all capital letters.]

TABLE OF STATUTES

[References are to page numbers.]

INDIANA CODE

IOWA CODE

KANSAS STATUTES ANNOTATED

KENTUCKY REVISED STATUTES

MAINE REVISED STATUTES ANNOTATED

MARYLAND CODE

MASSACHUSSETTS GENERAL LAW ANNOTATED

NORTH DAKOTA CENTURY CODE

NORTH DAKOTA RULES OF CIVIL PROCEDURE

OFFICIAL CODE OF GEORGIA

OREGON REVISED STATUTES

PENNSYLVANIA COMMERCIAL CODE

PENNSYLVANIA CONSOLIDATED STATUTES

RESTATEMENT OF CONTRACTS

RESTATEMENT (SECOND) OF CONTRACTS

UNIFORM COMMERCIAL CODE (REVISED)

UNIFORM COMPUTER INFORMATION TRANSACTIONS ACT (UCITA)

UNIFORM MOTOR VEHICLE CERTIFICATE OF TITLE AND ANTI-THEFT ACT (UMVCTA)

UNIFORM VEHICLE CODE (UVC)

UNITED STATES CODE (USC)

UNITED STATES CONSTITUTION

VERMONT RULES OF CIVIL PROCEDURE

VERMONT STATUTES

VERNON'S ANNOTATED MISSOURI STATUTES

VIRGINIA CODE

WASHINGTON STATE CONSTITUTION

WEST VIRGINIA CODE

WISCONSIN STATUTES

WYOMING STATUTES

INDEX

[References are to pages.]

[References are to pages.]

[References are to pages.]